THE MINISTRY OF ILLUSION

The Ministry of Illusion

Nazi Cinema and Its Afterlife

Eric Rentschler

Harvard University Press

Cambridge, Massachusetts
London, England

Printed in the United States of America

Second printing, 1998

LIBRARY OF CONGRESS CATALOGING-IN-PUBLICATION DATA

Rentschler, Eric.
The ministry of illusion : Nazi cinema and its afterlife / Eric Rentschler.
p. cm.
Includes bibliographical references and index.
ISBN 0-674-57639-X (acid-free paper) (cloth)
ISBN 0-674-57640-3 (paper)
1. National socialism and motion pictures. 2. Motion pictures—Germany—History. 3. Motion pictures in propaganda—Germany. I. Title.
PN1995.9.N36R46 1996 96-11731
791.43′75′0943—dc20 CIP

In memory of Karsten Witte

CONTENTS

Preface ix

Abbreviations and Special Terms xv

Introduction: The Power of Illusions 1

Part I. Fatal Attractions 25

1. A Legend for Modern Times: *The Blue Light* (1932) 27
2. Emotional Engineering: *Hitler Youth Quex* (1933) 53

Part II. Foreign Affairs 71

3. Home Sweet *Heimat: The Prodigal Son* (1934) 73
4. Hollywood Made in Germany: *Lucky Kids* (1936) 99
5. Astray in the New World: *La Habanera* (1937) 125

Part III. Specters and Shadows 147

6. The Elective Other: *Jew Süss* (1940) 149
7. The Führer's Phantom: *Paracelsus* (1943) 171
8. Self-Reflexive Self-Destruction: *Münchhausen* (1943) 193

Epilogue: The Testament of Dr. Goebbels 215

Appendix A. Films and Events, 1933–1945 225

Appendix B. Directorial Filmographies 272

Appendix C. American Film and Videotape Sources 293

Notes 299

Bibliography 389

Index 445

PREFACE

I first encountered the cinema of the Third Reich as a twenty-year-old foreign student sitting in the large auditorium of a German university. Over many evenings during the summer semester of 1969, I watched features and documentaries by Veit Harlan, Leni Riefenstahl, and Fritz Hippler along with war newsreels and short subjects. At the time my relationship to this body of work was clear-cut and unambiguous: Nazi cinema meant fascist propaganda; as bad objects went, you could not find a worse one. A national film production in the service of an authoritarian state, it gave shape to malevolent dreams and murderous designs. I got to know the Third Reich's sights and sounds through the prism of the German student movement and Young German Film. This postwar generation had commandeered the speeding express train of history, clutching at the emergency brake and insisting on a change of course.

The project of what subsequently became known as the New German Cinema was exhilarating. I followed its development avidly during the 1970s, at times up close, at others from a distance. This gathering of filmmakers sought to challenge the Nazi past and to contest its impact on the present, to create more credible German images that might become part of a better German history. After much work on these unreconciled and unruly directors, I was eager to know more about the negative legacy, the arsenal of impressions and feelings which had ignited and fueled so much of this generational revolt. Siegfried Kracauer's *From Caligari to Hitler* had acquainted me with the films of the Weimar Republic, with the celluloid fantasies that presaged and previewed National Socialism. About Nazi features, however, Kracauer had very little to say. If German films prefigured Hitler, I wondered, how did they figure once Hitler rose to power?

I wished to grasp what made the films administered by Goebbels at once so reviled and yet so resonant. I did not initiate this project in search of undiscovered cinematic hallmarks or underappreciated *auteurs*. Nor did I set out to reclaim (much less vindicate) film history's most problematic epoch.

I reviewed the substantial secondary literature on the subject. Over a decade I watched more than 300 of the era's features as well as many short subjects and documentaries. I sifted through daily newspapers and popular periodicals, contemporary trade papers, film journals, and fan magazines. Working mainly in Berlin, I combed archival holdings, scrutinizing scripts, letters, press kits, and sundry other artifacts. Comparing my findings with the dominant scholarship, I could not escape the conclusion that the film culture of this era had at best been only partially surveyed and in many ways vastly misapprehended. Looking at the books and articles on Nazi cinema, I found that scholars tended to be either too dismissive or too indulgent, inclined to sweeping panoramas rather than close-up perspectives, more smitten by thematic structures than by formal shapes. And I could not understand why commentators concentrated solely on the making and partaking of films during the Third Reich, why they acted as if these works had ceased to exist. This cinema's continuing presence and different function in the public sphere after 1945 surely warranted closer attention.

My initial exposure to films of the Third Reich remained a decisive formative experience, both guiding and limiting my subsequent explorations. In my student days, I had thought of cinema in the Third Reich as a function more of a 1984 than of a Brave New World. This was particularly easy to do as long as I equated Goebbels' Ministry of Propaganda with a Ministry of Fear. It relied on "doublethink" and institutionalized cynical reason, manipulating the flow of information, dominating all sectors of the public sphere, and infiltrating the private realm. Nazi Germany, I firmly believed, was like Orwell's dystopia: a society in which there was no free space, a world in which even one's dreams were monitored, an order that allowed no alterity. Big Brother represented a collective projection, the political construction of a party that demanded total and unquestioned allegiance.

As I examined the era's mass culture more carefully, however, I encountered more than the duty-bound, no-nonsense, and angst-ridden society of lore. Photographs from the period (both official images and private snapshots) so often displayed the cheerful faces and animated physiques of an invigorated German populace. This condition was, to be sure, not enjoyed by everyone. Contingencies of birth, political conviction, or sexual preference resulted in many people's being denied membership in the privileged Aryan nation. For those marginalized by National Socialism, life and being were an altogether different experience. These individuals were ostracized and persecuted, forced to leave Germany or to lead a shadow existence;

many of them were incarcerated, tortured, and executed. This racial state disciplined bodies in a variety of ways; under its auspices, euthanasia, sterilization, and genocide coexisted with an array of creature comforts and material compensations. Fear and loathing were crucial parts of the system, but National Socialism could not—and did not—rule by terror alone.

Hitler's Germany, similar to Huxley's Brave New World, was also an exercise in emotional engineering, a political order that openly proffered tourism, consumerism, and recreation as dialectical complements to law, order, and restriction. Fascism had at once a sinister and a pleasing countenance—and cinema embodied the agreeable facade in its most scintillating incarnation. Looking at the alternately gripping and cheerful appeal of Nazi feature films, I realized I would have to refine my analytical tools. These were not movies that simply ranted and raved; most of them seemed to have nothing to do with politics. The distinction between political and unpolitical films, I came to understand, was in fact one that the Nazis had implemented and that postwar commentators continued to employ. The Nazi film industry wanted its cinema to appear both national and international, open and regulated, modern and eternal. Film under Goebbels was to become a *Volkskunst* that would foster an imagined community, a *Volksgemeinschaft*. A popular medium and a vehicle of mass culture, film preserved old forms of identity while offering a new (and powerful) instrument of consensus-building.

This project, initiated in 1985, took a dramatic turn after 1990. Closure had seemed near; but in the wake of reunification and renewed debates about the German past and national identity, I could not shake off the unpleasant feeling that as one born in the United States I had all along been claiming the victor's moral high ground as if it were a birthright. Increasingly my exchanges with colleagues and acquaintances about German history and German film history became strained and testy. Why, one of my best friends in Berlin asked me, was it necessarily wrong to conceptualize German film history in decades rather than along lines of political epochs? Were the Allies to dictate for all time the terms of German collective memory? A debate about film criticism at the Free University during the summer of 1989, a fierce showdown between ideological and formalist critics, repeatedly invoked the cinema of the Third Reich. These discussions disturbed and irritated me, especially when I sensed a rising tendency to gloss over the political subtexts of Nazi films for the sake of spurious aesthetic appreciations.

These confrontations also prompted me to take pause and to interrogate my own assumptions. Was not my own position toward these films and the

German past in a crucial—and problematic—way detached? Did I not seek to combat the popular postwar fascination with fascism by overcompensating, resolutely distancing myself from this corpus of films and body of experience? My ideological objections and analytical reservations came too easily and seemed too pat. I had watched many of these films dozens of times; I would be lying if I said that these screenings had been only tedious and unpleasant. Living with this body of work for almost ten years, I came to recognize how much of this cinema's fatal appeal derived from a modern society's not altogether illegitimate desires for a better life. The utopian energies tapped by the feature films of the Third Reich in a crucial manner resembled, indeed at times consciously emulated, American dreams. These late encounters prompted me to take a necessary final step, to probe what Nazi Germany's society of spectacle might have to do with the media-driven culture in which I grew up and the world of mass-produced images in which I live.

Professor Gladney, the fictional director of a Center for Hitler Studies at a Midwestern college in Don DeLillo's novel *White Noise*, develops an entire subdiscipline around the infamous Nazi personality. Gladney handles Hitler like a hot commodity, using the charismatic figure to raise his own stock, hosting an international conference at his home institution with discourse about the Führer as its main attraction. (A colleague, inspired by Gladney's example, seeks to do the same thing with Elvis.) The novel lays out the ways in which academic endeavors follow the laws of the market. These examples, anything but farfetched in our age of cultural studies, also intimate how Nazi cinema could easily become a trendy item, a locus for further confirmations of fashionable agendas. The kind of cultural studies I have in mind, though, is less playful in its approach to these films and their multiple determinants. I would like to comprehend how National Socialists used the mass media to create illusions, and to demonstrate how Goebbels' Ministry of Propaganda constituted an ongoing project as well as an often makeshift and occasionally precarious endeavor. And, of course, I want to fathom why these audiovisual illusions have proved to be so durable for more than half a century.

■ ■ ■

This study was conceived from the start as a book. Over the years I always first presented films in university lectures and seminars, testing my ideas and learning from students before going on to articulate preliminary conclusions in the form of conference papers and public lectures. I am very thankful for the interest and energy of various student groups; spirited graduates and undergraduates at Stanford University and the University of California at Irvine provided me with numerous new perspectives and helped me to clarify my own readings. I also profited from the responses of colleagues at German Film Institutes held at Clark University and the University of Chicago. Audiences at many universities, conferences, cinémathèques, museums, and Goethe-Institutes in North America and Europe listened to my reflections and provided comments that helped me to refine my arguments.

In several cases I transformed work-in-progress into articles. My earliest deliberations on *The Blue Light* appeared in the spring 1989 issue of *October*, and a preliminary reading of *Münchhausen* in the spring 1990 number of *Film Quarterly*. A much different German-language anticipation of Chapter 7 came out in the winter 1991 issue of *Germanic Review*. Parts of two sections from Chapter 4 were published in *German Politics and Society* (Fall 1992). Much of Chapter 3 was included in a recent special issue of *New German Critique* on German film history (Fall 1993) and the first issue of *Film-Exil* (1992). An earlier version of Chapter 1 was published in the September 1995 issue of *Modernism/Modernity*; I thank Johns Hopkins University Press for permission to use it.

My work on the book necessitated numerous extended stays in Germany. I would like to express thanks to the Alexander von Humboldt-Stiftung, the German Academic Exchange Service, the John Simon Guggenheim Foundation, and the Research and Travel Committee and Office of the Dean of the UCI School of Humanities, which provided the material support for research sojourns and leaves of absence. The Stiftung Deutsche Kinemathek in Berlin was my main base of operations. Its director, my friend and colleague Hans Helmut Prinzler, graciously opened the institution's vast holdings to me and offered me opportunities to watch many rare films in 35mm copies. Werner Sudendorf and Wolfgang Jacobsen provided important leads to rare materials. Helga Belach shared her files on the *Revuefilm*. Peter Latta helped me ferret out the stills for this volume, all of which appear with the permission of the Stiftung Deutsche Kinemathek. The librarians at the Deutsche Film- und Filmsehakademie Berlin were likewise generous with their time and resources. Gerd Gemünden and Jan-Christopher Horak also drew my attention to crucial resources.

Patricia Williams' enthusiastic response to an early outline helped convince me that my in-progress endeavors might well warrant a lengthier undertaking. Lindsay Waters of Harvard University Press was a congenial and an indulgent editor who continued to show patience and good faith even at those moments when I myself was wondering if the promised book would ever emerge from its perpetual state of becoming. Alison Kent graciously guided the manuscript through its preliminary production stages and promptly answered my many queries. Ann Hawthorne proved to be a reliable and meticulous copy editor whose vigilance spared me many potential embarrassments.

Numerous individuals provided important comments and responded to drafts of various chapters. Anne Friedberg, Martin Jay, Gertrud Koch, Deborah Little, Heide Schlüpmann, Giovanni Spagnoletti, and Katie Trumpener all made observations and suggestions that were incorporated in the final manuscript. My UCI Film Studies colleagues Rhona Berenstein and Linda Williams gave me tough, constructive, and useful line-by-line feedback on a preliminary manuscript. David Bathrick and Anton Kaes also read the entire first draft; their detailed commentary and incisive criticism were crucial in bringing central points into focus.

To Lisa Fluor I owe an immense personal debt. She shared her life and offered encouragement while I grappled with this book for the best part of a decade, keeping me company even on weekend evenings while I watched yet another film with Hans Albers or Kristina Söderbaum, wondering every so often if there was one with Willy Birgel (her favorite) I had not yet shown her. Her careful eyes went over every word of the manuscript in its multiple versions, catching gaps of logic and infelicitous formulations as well as pointing out garbled phrases. More than anyone, she helped me figure out what I wanted to say and how I should say it.

Finally, I want to acknowledge the impetus and inspiration of my late friend, Karsten Witte. We first met over lunch in 1979 on a snowy winter day at the "Dippegucker" in Frankfurt. In our many exchanges over the years until his tragic death in October 1995, I frequently enjoyed his personal generosity and acute intellect, learning immensely from his keen ability to comprehend the political meaning of aesthetic shapes, admiring greatly his capacity for articulating insights in language that was at once elegant, incisive, and nuanced. Without his decades of work on Nazi cinema this book would be unthinkable. I dedicate this volume to his memory.

Irvine/Berlin
December 1995

ABBREVIATIONS AND SPECIAL TERMS

Bewegungsfilme	Movement films; propaganda features released in 1933 after Hitler's rise to power
Blubo	Short for *Blut und Boden*, "blood and soil," a distinctly premodern attachment to rural landscapes and peasant culture
FRG	Federal Republic of Germany
HJ	Hitlerjugend; Hitler Youth
KPD	German Communist Party, banned by the Nazis after the Reichstag fire in 1933
NSDAP	National Socialist Workers Party of Germany
ProMi	Propagandaministerium, short for Ministry of Public Enlightenment and Propaganda
RFK	Reichsfilmkammmer; Reich Film Chamber
RM	Reichsmark; monetary unit in Germany, 1924–1948
SA	Sturmabteilungen; Storm Troops, the Nazi party's paramilitary force, crucial in Hitler's rise to power but effectively neutralized after the June 1934 "Night of the Long Knives" purge
SPIO	Spitzenorganisation der Deutschen Filmindustrie; the main professional representative group for the German film industry
SS	Schutzstaffeln; protective troops, a quasi-military unit of the NSDAP, employed as special police
Systemzeit	"System era," a Nazi epithet for the Weimar Republic
völkisch	Literally, "belonging to the people," a term used by the Nazis with particularly strong nationalistic and racist connotations
Volksgemeinschaft	"National community," an imagined classless German collectivity with a dramatic historical destiny and a dis-

	tinct racial identity, which was to become above all a creation of the modern mass media
Ufa	Universum-Film Aktiengesellschaft, the most venerable and internationally renowned German film studio

THE MINISTRY OF ILLUSION

The Nazi warrior of popular imagination: armored body, marital pose (Emil Lohkamp in *Hans Westmar*).

Introduction: The Power of Illusions

> One of the principal tasks of film is to transmit to posterity a true picture of the past and, seen in this light, all the films that we are making today one day will be truly "historical."
>
> *Wolfgang Liebeneiner, 1943*

> Spectators sat and were stunned by *Triumph of the Will.* They suddenly recognized that what thirty-two camera eyes see is worth a thousand times more than what the two eyes of an individual are capable of perceiving. Now it became clear to millions why the camera must be placed in the service of the community—even, if necessary, by force. An apparatus that intensifies the human capacity for seeing a thousandfold can be used only in the service of pure and noble mass guidance. In the hands of a criminal it can become an instrument for mass murder.
>
> *Otto Kriegk, 1943*

Out of the Past

"Those Nazis," claims a character in Don DeLillo's novel *Running Dog,* "had a thing for movies. They put everything on film . . . Film was essential to the Nazi era. Myth, dreams, memory."[1] Audiovisual machinery played a crucial role in National Socialist designs for living, in radical attempts to control human activity and dominate the physical world.[2] Adolf Hitler and his minister of propaganda, Joseph Goebbels, were keenly aware of film's ability to mobilize emotions and immobilize minds, to create overpowering illusions and captive audiences. Calculating *metteurs-en-scène,* they employed state-of-the-art technology in a profusion of celebrations, light shows, and mass extravaganzas. Hitler's regime can be seen as a sustained cinematic event, in Hans Jürgen Syberberg's famous phrase, "a film from Germany."[3] If the Nazis were movie mad, then the Third Reich was movie made. And those movies are still very much with us today.

German cinema of the Third Reich, even a half-century after Hitler's demise, prompts extreme reactions and hyperbolic formulations. Given the atrocities of National Socialism, the movies, newsreels, and documentaries made under its aegis represent for many commentators film history's darkest hour. The prospect of having to watch the 1,094 German features premiered from 1933 to the end of the war in 1945 might well seem like a cinephile's purgatory. Imagine being strapped to a seat, like Alex in *A Clockwork Orange,* forced to partake of an unceasing stream of ideological intemperance and kitschy hyper-*gemütlichkeit.* Nazi cinema has the reputation of a monstrosity concocted by a Ministry of Fear, the sinister creation of a propaganda machine whose workings resemble Dr. Mabuse's 1,000 eyes and *1984*'s panoptic state apparatus. "Never before and in no other country," Wim Wenders once wrote, "have images and language been abused so unscrupulously as here, never before and nowhere else have they been debased so deeply as vehicles to transmit lies."[4] In many minds, Nazi cinema is an infamous and abject entity: its most memorable achievement is the systematic abuse of film's formative powers in the name of mass manipulation, state terror, and world-wide destruction.

Despite its adversaries, however, Nazi cinema has had and continues to have many apologists and admirers. Outraged voices may have demonized this corpus of film in the hopes of exorcising Goebbels' legacy, but their interventions have in decisive ways gone unheeded.[5] Nazi features are anything but universally proscribed or detested; they are still shown today in many places. Most of the era's films exist and—with a precious few exceptions—remain in circulation. They have become an integral part of everyday entertainment fare throughout Germany. Take, for instance, the various retrospectives over the last two decades at the Berlin Film Festival. During the late 1970s there were intriguing programs devoted to "Love, Death, and Technology: The Cinema of the Fantastic, 1933–1945" (1977); "Censorship: Forbidden German Films, 1933–1945" (1978); and "We're Dancing around the World: German Revue Films, 1933–1945" (1979), all of them accompanied by well-researched critical brochures.[6] Recent festivals have given rise to series on the film years 1939 and 1945, as well as a comprehensive portrait of productions made in Babelsberg.[7] Elsewhere in Berlin, Nazi-era films have shown up regularly in special screenings, such as the elaborate selection of films which accompanied the city's 750th anniversary celebration in 1987.

Later in 1992, the seventy-fifth birthday of the Ufa studio occasioned a massive display in Berlin's Historical Museum. A 2.4-million-mark enterprise, "Die Ufa 1917–1945. Das deutsche Bildimperium" (Ufa, 1917–1945: The German Empire of Images) constituted the largest film exhibit in the history of the Federal Republic, occupying 2,400 square meters and twenty-one large rooms, featuring a retrospective with 70 of Ufa's 600 features. A twenty-foot-tall Blue Angel, made of styrofoam, lounged on a barrel with her legs crossed and lorded over the proceedings, an awkward concession to public taste. The curators took pains to insist that Ufa was not just Metropolis, Mabuse, and Marlene, carefully recalling the darker aspects of the studio's history and documenting the political realities that coexisted with Ufa fantasies, offering historical commentaries and critical perspectives both in the exhibit and in the accompanying literature. Great effort was expended to avoid nostalgic rhetoric and to be politically responsible. The exhibit received frequent praise for its feats of design, presentation, and research.[8]

For many visitors, the Ufa exhibit seemed to be a sentimental journey guided by a celebratory rather than a critical itinerary. "That existed only once and will never happen again! Ufa-film—the best of all time," effused one visitor in the Historical Museum's guest book, joining appreciative respondents in a host of languages. For other observers, the tribute to "The German Empire of Images" caused dismay and irritation; the exhibition seemed to lack analytical reserve and historical distance. "Isn't it just typical of the restoration period in which we live that people worship Ufa in such a grand German manner?" opined one viewer. "Why don't you just go ahead and put a gold frame around the swastika?" asked another.[9] The Ufa exhibit, several commentators alleged, was an act of reclamation, an attempt to rekindle dreams of a greater Germany, a quite timely endeavor in a reconstituted nation casting about for viable legacies and overarching commonalities.[10] Such suspicions ascribed to the event an ideological agenda that reflected an environment of intense revisionism and rekindled German nationalism. The desire for a native dream factory echoed Wim Wenders' complaints that the Federal Republic has been overrun by foreign images *(fremdbebildert)* and desperately needs to resurrect its own narrative traditions.[11] Ufa has reemerged as the answer to many wishes, as the memory of a potent national dream machinery, as the force that once challenged Hollywood's occupation of German hearts and minds.

Matinee screenings in big cities throughout Germany provide weekly opportunities to take in old movies. The "Eva Lichtspiele" in Wilmersdorf, a suburb of Berlin, shows "films people want to see again" on Wednesday afternoons at 3:30.[12] In June 1991 its selections were *Ich vertraue Dir meine*

Frau an (*I Entrust My Wife to You,* 1943), *Der Unwiderstehliche* (*Mr. Irresistible,* 1937), *Spuk im Schloß* (*Spook in the Castle,* 1945), and *Preußische Liebesgeschichte* (*Prussian Love Story,* 1938). Across town, in the St.-Michaels-Heim, the "Berliner Filmclub," an "institution for the preservation of German film," in existence since 1949, also presents evergreens and classics on Monday evenings. In that same month its choices included *Dr. Crippen an Bord* (*Dr. Crippen on Board,* 1942), *Die Reiter von Deutsch-Ostafrika* (*The Horsemen from German East Africa,* 1934), and *Kora Terry* (1940). Similar programs, attended mainly by senior citizens, have unreeled throughout the postwar decades at the "Astor" on Kurfürstendamm, in East Berlin's "Camera" and "Babylon," in Munich's "Gloria," "Rex," and "Arena," in Frankfurt's "Turmpalast," to name only a small sampling of such venues.

More prominently, films of the Third Reich have played an integral role on German television, for example, on the Second Channel (ZDF) and particularly on the Bavarian regional station (BR). In 1980 Nazi films accounted for 8.7 percent of all features aired on West German stations, a total of 113 titles. By 1989 the number had risen to 169.[13] Invariably these selections are cheerfully introduced as fond memories or old standards; announcers rarely say anything about these films' political provenance. For decades the popular Monday primetime offerings of the East German First Channel (DDR I) provided a veritable cross-section of Nazi productions. (Here too local program listings typically left out any reference to the year of production.)[14] Several hundred films from the Third Reich are now being marketed by video retailers. The well-stocked media department of Berlin's Kaufhaus des Westens (KadeWe) contains Ufa musicals, melodramas with Paula Wessely and Pola Negri, Heinz Rühmann vehicles, militaristic Fridericus films (Veit Harlan's *Der große König/The Great King*), *Heim ins Reich* titles such as *Menschen ohne Vaterland (People without a Fatherland)* and *Flüchtlinge (Fugitives),* colonial epics such as *Germanin* and *Quax in Afrika,* even anti-Semitic comedies such as *Robert und Bertram.* Popular tunes from Ufa films and hit songs from the epoch by Hans Albers, Willi Forst, and Zarah Leander (to name but a few) likewise can be frequently heard on the radio and purchased widely. The few living stars appear on talk shows to reminisce about the "golden age of German cinema." The alternately breezy and melodramatic memoirs of filmmakers and actors who worked during the period abound in bookstores or public libraries.

Nazi cinema is also no stranger to the catalogues of American commercial distributors. The German Language Video Center offers "50 years of assorted German cinema" in a brochure in which *Ohm Krüger, Opfergang (The Great Sacrifice)*, and *Patrioten (Patriots)* appear on the same page with *Nachtschwester Ingeborg* (*Night Nurse Ingeborg*, 1958) and *Otto ist auf Frauen scharf* (*Otto Has the Hots for Women*, 1972). The advertising copy bills Harlan's *Kolberg* as "a powerful epic of a Prussian town's rebellion against Napoleon's occupation forces. Based on true story. A CLASSIC! Produced during the final three years of World War II, using Germany's top talents, artists, and scores of extras. Directed by Veit [Harlan]." International Historic Films presents a comparable selection of films, but does so with at least a modicum of discretion. Its comprehensive catalogue bears a caveat about these productions: "Besides often being enjoyable as entertainment, they offer valuable insights into the world view of the Nazi Government and Nazi Germany as a whole." Facets Video in Chicago offers the complete works of Leni Riefenstahl and Luis Trenker. Unlicensed English-language versions of *Jud Süß (Jew Süss)* and *Der ewige Jude (The Eternal Jew)* can be bought from a number of U.S. sources. Increasingly, Nazi films have been analyzed in American university classrooms and become a topic of scholarly debates and discussions.[15]

Neither lost in time nor forgotten, Nazi productions have in fact had a durable and dynamic postwar career throughout Europe and America. In the early 1980s Luis Trenker traveled with his films through the United States on a Goethe-Institut tour. Transvestites continue to dress up as Zarah Leander; her films and songs represent nostalgia vehicles for older audiences as well as camp objects fetishized by urban hipsters. Four and a half decades after its premiere, *Münchhausen* unreels before thousands of viewers in summertime open-air screenings at the Berlin Waldbühne. Sold-out houses applaud *Die Feuerzangenbowle (The Punch Bowl)* in holiday showings throughout the FRG. In June 1992 the Consulate General of Germany in Los Angeles held an evening reception whose *pièce de résistance* was a reprise of *Der zerbrochene Krug* (*The Broken Jug*, 1937), a film beloved by Hitler.[16] For over two decades, British cineastes have seen Douglas Sirk's Ufa films as masterpieces of subversion. Impassioned auteurists have extolled "the humanity, sensitivity, and integrity of Leni Riefenstahl."[17] Veit Harlan has become a *cause célèbre;* for a time during the 1980s, the prominent German television station WDR contemplated a production that would reconsider the director of *Jew Süss* and *Kolberg* as a consummate stylist and master of the melodrama.

Far from simply being banished to the dustbin of history as aberrations and atrocities, the spectacles and paraphernalia of National Socialism have assumed a privileged place in American mass culture.[18] SS uniforms and party regalia provide props for both alternative fads and mainstream trends in fashion. Nazi phantasms have engendered television series, movies of the week, and Hollywood features, from *Hogan's Heroes, Indiana Jones,* and *Holocaust* to *Swing Kids, Shining Through,* and *Schindler's List.* As celebrities go, Hitler's posthumous renown rivals that of Elvis Presley. Consider this exchange from Don DeLillo's *White Noise:*

> "In the middle of it all is Hitler, of course."
> "He was on again last night."
> "He's always on. We couldn't have television without him."[19]

Ritualized tableaus with leather-clad taskmasters and supine victims reenact a kinky Nazism in arthouse rétro chic such as Luchino Visconti's *The Damned* and Liliana Cavani's *The Night Porter.*[20] Large-circulation magazines have carried photographs of Mick Jagger and Andy Warhol hobnobbing with Leni Riefenstahl. The media followed Madonna as she took a guided tour of the recent "Degenerate Art" exhibit at the Los Angeles County Museum of Art. Jodie Foster has announced plans for a Riefenstahl biopic. Set designers for *Batman Returns* drew generously on the work of Albert Speer and Arno Breker.[21] George Lucas restaged the closing scene from *Triumph of the Will* in the finale of *Star Wars;* a recent rock video by Michael Jackson likewise unabashedly recycles Riefenstahl's images of soldier males paying deference to their master. American artists pilfer the Nazi legacy with relish. The beautiful divers, dancers, and discus-throwers of *Olympia* serve as prototypes for television commercials, magazine ads, and photo spreads. The mass ornaments of Nuremberg are reconfigured in the contemporary shape of Super Bowl halftimes, human flags, and hands across America.[22] If Nazi horrors continue to repulse, the shapes of fascism continue to fascinate.

To scrutinize Nazi films, then, involves more than indulging antiquarian interests and revisiting a faraway past. "Our continuing fascination with the Nazis," observes J. Hoberman, "is not only that they represent an absolute evil, but that they pioneered spectacular politics—mass rallies, orchestrated media campaigns, and pseudo-documentaries meant to glorify a star-leader."[23] Seen in this way, contemporary American media culture has more than a superficial or vicarious relationship with the Third Reich's society of spectacle. Indeed, the incessant recycling of Nazi sights and sounds surely represents a crucial measure of today's postmodernism.[24] A direct line leads from the Nazis' vanguard deployment of pyrotechnic histrionics and audiovisual excesses to the profuse present-day investment in constant simulations and hyperreal events.[25] In many respects, these images from the past are very close to us, closer than we might imagine, closer than some people might like. How, then, am I, as an American film historian writing in the mid-1990s, to talk about them? What tone should I use, what approach should I take? One thing is certain: this discussion must account for a legacy that extends from the Third Reich into our own lives today.

Adversaries and Apologists

Popular mythology typically represents the Nazi era as a site of terror, violence, and destruction, as a protracted horror movie in which the devil and his minions set out to conquer the world. In a similar fashion, commentators often render films from the Third Reich as the cinema from Hell. This image, however, seems ill chosen when one actually sits down with what turns out to be occasionally intriguing, but generally unspectacular and rarely exceptional, fare. The customary tropes of the uncanny and horrendous hardly apply to the vast majority of the epoch's productions, to its generic entertainments, innocuous comedies, frothy melodramas, and historical period pieces, films that unfold in settings far removed from the Third Reich, in places where one rarely sees a swastika or hears a "Sieg Heil."[26] (If one is looking for sinister heavies garbed in SS black or crowds of fanatics saluting their Führer, one does best to turn to Hollywood films of the 1940s.) *Hitlerjunge Quex (Hitler Youth Quex), Triumph of the Will, Jew Süss, Kolberg,* and other infamous state-sponsored productions may have commanded most of the attention in previous studies of Nazi cinema. Nonetheless, such works were the exception, not the rule; they constituted a very small portion of the era's features. Films in the Third Reich emanated from a Ministry of Illusion, not a Ministry of Fear.

Film sociologist Gerd Albrecht's positivistic compendium, *Nationalsozialistische Politik,* documents just how prominently generic productions figured in the Third Reich; they constituted 941 of its 1,094 feature films, including 295 melodramas and biopics, 123 detective films and adventure epics.[27] Almost half of all features—to be precise, 523—were comedies and musicals (what the Nazis termed *heitere,* "cheerful" films), light fare directed by ever-active industry pros such as Erich Waschneck, E. W. Emo, Carl Boese, Hans Deppe, Georg Jacoby, and Hans H. Zerlett, peopled with widely revered stars such as Hans Albers, Marika Rökk, Heinz Rühmann, and Ilse Werner, as well as character actors such as Paul Kemp, Fita Benkhoff, Theo Lingen, Grete Weiser, Paul Hörbiger, and Hans Moser. Such works seem to demonstrate that the Nazi regime created space for innocent diversions; they reflect, claim revisionist historians, a public sphere not completely subjugated by state institutions. Many of these films, as we shall see, have received recognition as noteworthy achievements, as grand hallmarks of German cinema, in some cases even as bearers of oppositional energies. Were these illusions indeed harmless, or were they malevolent, or maybe both at the same time? Were they sometimes subversive or, as ideological critics insist, always affirmative? In these matters there exists a dramatic variance of opinion.

How one presents Nazi cinema remains above all a question of where one places this problematic and controversial corpus. Am I to view these films *en masse* as abominations and cast them into oblivion? Or should I seek to integrate them—or at least some of them—into film history and the German past and, in so doing, to reclaim them as legitimate objects for the present and the future? Even the term "Nazi cinema" would seem to deserve caution: do all German films made during the Third Reich warrant this appellation? I stand before a contested and only partially explored territory, choosing between guides with violently opposed agendas and quite dissimilar itineraries. Let me, at the outset, consider two typical tours through this embattled sector of film history.

The first tour takes me to a Teutonic Horror Picture Show. Film played a central role in the operations of the Ministry of Propaganda, serving as a mass mobilizer and an ideological weapon. The NSDAP sought to permeate all sectors of daily life. It "coordinated" institutions and organizations, purging the film world of Jews, socialists, Communists, and anyone else it deemed objectionable or untrustworthy. The Ministry of Propaganda evaluated film scripts, oversaw activities in the various studios, checking each finished production carefully, determining how films were to be advertised and reviewed, deciding which works warranted official recognition. Almost every feature made during the period must therefore be understood as the reflection of party structures and strategic priorities.[28] Under Hitler, argues Erwin Leiser, there was no such thing as a " 'non-political' film." Entertainment films functioned "to distract the audience from reality and lull them to sleep, generally by means of the battery of clichés manufactured in the arsenal of Nazi propaganda."[29] German films of the Third Reich thus represent the creations of a totalitarian government, modern fantasy wares implemented in the wider frameworks of public persuasion, state terror, and world war.

The second tour offers a much less disturbing view. In no other art form, argues social historian Richard Grunberger, did 1933 "constitute as little of a break as in filmmaking. Had a cinema-going Rip van Winkel [*sic*] dozed off in the Depression and woken in the Third Reich he would have found the screen filled with the self-same images."[30] Even after Hitler came to power and "coordinated" the film industry, studios were in crucial ways able to operate like private enterprises. "Unpolitical" films thrived, and longstanding popular legacies endured, allowing for a continuity of scripts and genres which would persist in postwar comedies, musicals, homeland films, and adaptations of novels and dramas. Studios were dream factories, not propaganda machines. Goebbels quickly "grasped the fact that conveyor-belt brownshirt epics were box-office poison—not because of the public's political antipathies, but because of its craving for experiences in the cinema which were different from those within it."[31] According to Klaus Kreimeier, film under Goebbels was hardly an agent of heavy-handed demagoguery, but rather the innocuous provider of small pleasures. The Ministry of Propaganda was not a smoothly running political apparatus; the network of competing instances was in fact so complex that no one really could fully keep track of its workings. Even when the system functioned effectively, it still demonstrated much irrationalism and inconsistency.[32]

The Ministry of Propaganda monitored much of Germany's film production during the Third Reich. Nonetheless, Goebbels and his chain of command were neither omniscient nor omnipotent. "Not everything, but much was possible," argues Kreimeier. "The possible often seemed too risky, while the 'impossible' occasionally was overlooked, silently tolerated or in fact praised."[33] Dissidents and nonconformists found refuge in the Nazi film world; in David Stewart Hull's assessment, it became a gathering point of resistant energies.[34] Prominent personalities such as Hans Albers made no secret of their antigovernment sentiments. They enjoyed such large followings, though, that the party was forced to tolerate them. The film world, it is further asserted, dared on frequent occasion to challenge the government.[35] There may have been, say sympathetic critics, a few flagrantly political "state" productions; by and large, though, German film of the Third Reich was a popular cinema (especially during the war) of formula fare and escapist diversion replete with well-known stars, upbeat scores, and alluring production values. Contemporary audiences were hardly just an amorphous public manipulated by an ideological apparatus;

they also included viewers who saw through tendentious agitprop and had a keen awareness of oppositional nuances. In this view, most German films made during the Third Reich were *not* Nazi films; some of them endure today as classics; many of them still grace television, matinee, and festival programs; and only a limited few warrant caution or political sensitivity.[36]

While ideological critics revile Nazi films, cineastes savor their aesthetic delights. Take, for instance, the proprietor of the "Werkstattkino" in Munich, referred to by an interviewer as "Anatol." He openly admires Nazi productions, insisting that many of them deserve cult-film status. He screens them just as he would any other film, without a special introduction or a critical discussion. "We show Nazi films," maintains Anatol, "because they're grandiose. They were perfectly crafted, they made an optimal use of form. The Nazi era was simply the golden age of German film, there's no getting around it." Pressed by his interviewer, the exhibitor becomes a bit testy. He knows his words pose a provocation. Fascism fascinates him, but let it be clear: "I hate totalitarian regimes."[37] The frank response is typical of both critical and popular spectators, in and outside of Germany, who would argue that the films of the Third Reich, regardless of their provenance, have an undeservedly negative status, both politically and aesthetically. International apologists laud the artistry of Leni Riefenstahl's documentaries, Anglo-American enthusiasts claim that Nazi film produced some important *auteurs,* German cineastes insist that we grant the melodramas of Veit Harlan and Wolfgang Liebeneiner more careful attention. Other commentators argue that we should reevaluate films of the Third Reich altogether. "Film in the Nazi state," insists one, "had to a great extent nothing to do with Nazi cinema!"[38]

The first tour presents a monolithic dynamics in which all becomes conspiracy, other-direction, and overdetermination. This approach does not allow much room for differentiation; clearly, not every film operated in a similar way; surely there must be shades of meaning, variations in form, appeal, and function. How are we to distinguish between state-initiated productions such as *Jew Süss* and *Wunschkonzert (Request Concert)* and light comedies with Hans Moser and Heinz Rühmann without necessarily denying that all contain ideological determinations? The approach likewise reduces contemporary audiences to volitionless Cesares and Janes mesmerized by Caligariesque master showmen. "Between 1933 and 1945," one postwar critic writes, "every trick of publicity was used to persuade the spectators that their rulers wanted and offered them what was best."[39] The era's viewers, claims Leiser, "were to be manipulated without being shown the direction in which they were being led."[40] Films become a form of audiovisual coercion and moviegoers the helpless and innocent objects of political machinations, their minds pounded into mush by a mighty apparatus.[41] This rhetoric at best describes official designs; it does not fully acknowledge Goebbels' constant anxiety and uncertainty about viewer response. Until 1939 the ProMi frequently found itself troubled by German film's lack of resonance and its modest public profile. The prospect of an all-encompassing ideological control, of films that overwhelmed audiences and enjoyed unconditional success, was at best a Nazi dream—and a postwar myth.[42] Recent film historians have granted Goebbels the all-encompassing popular dominion that in actual fact the Ministry of Propaganda achieved only on occasion.

Critics such as Leiser and David Welch speak of films as if they were written scripts rather than complex audiovisual artifacts. (For Albrecht and for Bogusław Drewniak films represent less objects of critical analysis than raw material for charts, inventories, and statistics.) Welch examines "Nazi film production as a reflection of National Socialist ideology" and shows how party priorities and policies became transferred into cinematic documents.[43] His analyses typically concentrate on extended quotations from screenplays. The author limits his sampling to overtly political films, broaching entertainment films only in passing, confining their status to that of innocuous escapist vehicles.[44] He and Leiser stress dominant themes, overt messages, and intended meanings, paying little attention to formal emphases and visual surfaces, to things such as body language, the use of frame space, and movement between images. Viewed in this manner, Nazi films bear little ambiguity or contradiction, much less unintended or unconscious meanings. Propaganda does not show or suggest; it speaks. Sometimes it whispers; usually it shrieks. What about the concerted use of sound and music, I find myself wondering, much less the visual innuendoes and the associations created by dissolves, fades, and cuts? Why do flashbacks figure so rarely in prewar films and show up so frequently after 1941? How am I to account for the conspicuous use of back projection in wartime productions? To concentrate exclusively on themes, trends, and manifest contents is to ignore these films' semiotic complexity. Such an approach assumes meanings as given rather than produced in—and inextricably bound to—audiovisual presentations and public performances.

The second itinerary, on the other hand, privileges aesthetics over politics, stressing the artistic autonomy and resistant energy at work in the productions of the Third Reich. Everyone seems to have been making subversive films, not just Helmut Käutner, Reinhold Schünzel, and Wolfgang Staudte, but also Luis Trenker, Leni Riefenstahl, maybe even Veit Harlan. And regardless of Hans Steinhoff's and Karl Ritter's party allegiances, cineastes such as Francis Courtade and Pierre Cadars still praise these directors' work for its formal power and narrative interest.[45] Such analyses isolate films, examining them in the context of cinema art and outside of a larger social history. Aesthetic redemptions, however, also have political consequences. Seen together with the anecdotal memoirs of stars and directors, revisionist interpretations such as those of Hull, Rabenalt, and Wendtland create the impression that the German film industry amounted to a secret nation of resisters and freedom fighters.[46] Entertainment films become at worst harmless and innocuous diversions; at best they represent classics of German cinema, viable artifacts in a national legacy. If a crucial part of the public sphere during the Third Reich becomes less politically impacted and even in some cases artistically legitimated, then one is well on the way to normalizing and neutralizing significant sectors of the everyday under the Nazi dictatorship. And if this is the case, perhaps Germans might look at the years 1933–1945 with a different regard. Such discourse, be it conscious or unwitting, fits into a larger strategy of exorcism and disavowal; it promotes a rewriting of German history, a latterday de-Nazification of the Third Reich.

How am I to mediate these extremes, without on the one hand simply condemning 1,094 features or, on the other, seeking to reactivate problematic entities by obscuring their social and historical functions? I face an impasse. To repress or to redeem—and at what costs? If the one approach is resolutely dismissive, the other is unabashedly permissive. As I review the era's films, I want to consider how lighthearted shapes and innocuous forms contained political meanings and served ideological purposes, to examine more carefully the cinemas and public spheres in which these fantasies once circulated as well as the venues in which they still unreel today, to remember that these films were—and are!—being watched by real people, not ideal spectators, by diverse audiences, not just gatherings of critics and scholars. Nazi cinema is not 1984; neither is it a nest of resistant potential.

Preliminary Answers, Unasked Questions

Previous books on cinema in the Third Reich have little to say about Nazi film aesthetics, about the look and texture of these features, about the properties that made some of them so resonant and well-regarded.[47] Crucial questions receive only partial answers or go unasked altogether. In what ways did the German dream factory of the 1930s and 1940s appropriate and consciously recycle Hollywood fantasies? What is the place of Nazi cinema in German film history as well as film history at large? What lessons does film under Goebbels impart regarding the use and abuse of the mass media, and are those lessons perhaps timely? Clearly, the spectrum of possibility in Nazi cinema is hardly exhausted by *Triumph of the Will, Jew Süss, Ich klage an (I Accuse),* and *Kolberg.* Neither does it suffice to claim, for instance, that the films of Leni Riefenstahl pose a contradiction between dazzling art and vicious ideology, as if one might separate form and function or aesthetics and politics.[48] It is equally shortsighted to label everything made during the period as either crude propaganda or unbearable kitsch; film flourished during the Third Reich, at times enjoying acclaim and popularity that postwar German producers would never come close to regaining (see Table 1).

The past decade may well have witnessed many calls for detailed investigations of Nazi film aesthetics, but there have been few conclusive responses. Susan Sontag's 1975 essay, "Fascinating Fascism," remains the classic statement on the subject.[49] It analyzes the emotional and artistic appeal of Leni Riefenstahl's spectacles, their brute symmetry and overwhelming choreography, their stunning gatherings of human material in mass celebrations. Clearly, Sontag's acute comments about how monumen-

Table 1 Cinemas and admissions in the Third Reich

Year	Number of cinemas	Number of admissions (millions)
1933	5,071	245
1934	4,889	259
1935	4,782	303
1936	5,259	362
1937	5,302	396
1938	5,446	442
1939	6,923	624
1940	7,018	834
1941	7,043	892
1942	7,042	1,062
1943	6,561	1,116
1944	6,484	1,101

Source: Hans Helmut Prinzler, *Chronik des deutschen Films 1895–1994* (Stuttgart/Weimar: Metzler, 1995).

tality and ornamentality interact in ritual displays and how political relations reappear in aesthetic patterns suggest the similar concerns of Siegfried Kracauer's exemplary article "The Mass Ornament," as well as Walter Benjamin's subsequent evocation of how fascism introduces aesthetics into political life.[50]

Karsten Witte's contributions allow an even more differentiated and historically informed sense of how a state apparatus colonized fantasy production and occupied generic patterns (especially romantic comedies, revue films, and literary adaptations). Fascist aesthetics for Witte represent a function of formal surfaces and channeled fascination, structures of experience encoded in visual and aural signs. The films of the Third Reich, according to Witte, recycle and transform in a peculiar fashion, converting the concrete into the abstract, movement into static pattern, open space into bound compositions, overwhelming viewers with "extreme perspectives of extreme uniformity."[51] Revue films such as *Wir tanzen um die Welt* (*We're Dancing around the World,* 1939) feature female dancers whose moves are stylized and choreographed, exhibitions of regimentation and discipline every bit as uncompromising as those in *Triumph of the Will.*[52] The Nazi counterpart to the Hollywood musical puts civilians on parade and translates Riefenstahl's ritualized tableaus of marching troops and singing soldiers into a popular film genre, permitting "the masses of viewers assembling in the cinema to renew the celebration of their inner Reich party convention."[53] Witte's body of work provides the most significant systematic and theoretical attempt to account for the visual and aural specificity of Nazi film texts as well as their sociohistorical function.

Following Witte's cue in a quest for other routes of access to Nazi cinema, I encounter a host of historical and theoretical challenges as I traverse uncharted or at best sketchily mapped terrain. If I am to speak more conclusively about the special character of German films of the Third Reich, I need to consider the relation of Nazi cinema to films made during the Weimar Republic and the postwar era, to focus on continuities of careers and genres. I also need to be mindful of the conscious way in which German feature films of the era look to Hollywood and emulate classical cinema.[54] If I characterize Nazi cinema as a contested entity, I surely must take into account the numerous debates and ongoing controversy it has generated during the postwar period, both in and outside of Germany. And if I write as a child of the Allies and not, like Witte, as a German coming to grips with and critically confronting a collective legacy, clearly I operate from a different situation and speak in a different voice, with other emphases and inflections.

Beyond Witte, only a small number of commentators (Julian Petley, Mihal Friedmann, and Stephen Lowry) have combined history, theory, and analysis in their discussions of the Third Reich's films.[55] No one, however, has addressed in detail the relationship between the ways in which Nazi film presented itself to contemporaries and how it presents itself to us today.[56] The Third Reich occasioned extensive discussion about the theory and praxis of film in trade papers such as *Lichtbild-Bühne* and *Film-Kurier* and in journals such as *Der Deutsche Film,* periodicals featuring lengthy deliberations on literary adaptation, authorship, spectatorship, sexual difference, mimesis, and the political role of cinema. Previous work has all but ignored the period's vast theoretical and technical discourse about the media. I encounter a few case studies of important directors, but no in-depth understanding of the relations between ideology and style, political function and artistic resolve, accommodation and resistance. Nor do I find any sustained and nuanced discussions of Nazi film's audiences, counterparts to Patrice Petro's and Miriam Hansen's accounts of female spectators and the early German cinema.[57] The so-called standard works on Nazi cinema likewise tell me very little about questions of sexuality and gender; in general, they provide decidedly disembodied portraits of the era's fantasy production. At best there exist several recent analytical discussions of women's central function in the films of the Third Reich.[58]

Wanting to move beyond previous approaches, I seek a more precise awareness of the form, address, and appeal of Nazi films. Rather than reducing them to ideological containers in which the Ministry of Propaganda packaged affirmation and falsehood, I aim to read them as ambiguous and complex entities, as still resonant portrayals of an age's different inclinations and disparate wishes, works that have given rise to divergent official and popular responses since the Third Reich.[59] I want to extend Susan Sontag's term and consider these films as "fantasizing fascism," that is, as films that lie and confess, affirm and disavow, obfuscate and enlighten, as films that in seeking to stylize everyday reality also revealed much about the psychopathology of the Third Reich. In other words, I will consider not only what Nazi films wanted to show the viewer but also what they actually disclose about National Socialism. "It's not enough to call a Nazi film a Nazi film," Enno Patalas noted. "Its structures must be opened for inspection—and that means revealing its unconscious workings as well."[60] I want to measure carefully formal and temporal parameters, to treat these films as historical entities *and* living presences, artifacts whose effective existence also affects many people today.

Points of Departure

As I begin my own tour of Nazi cinema, let me make my emphases known and my premises apparent:

Premise 1: The cinema of the Third Reich is to be seen in the context of a totalitarian state's concerted attempt to create a culture industry in the service of mass deception. The Ministry of Propaganda endeavored to discipline distraction, to instrumentalize sights and sounds in the hopes of engineering and orchestrating emotion, to remake German film culture in the service of remaking German culture and the nation's political body. Film theorists have often speculated about the ideological effects of the "dominant cinema," proposing that classical narratives seek to mesmerize and mystify viewers by means of imaginary seductions.[61] Film production in the Third Reich offers a strikingly concrete example of such a theoretical construct put into practice; it demonstrates how a state apparatus consciously set out to administer the making and partaking of cinematic sights and sounds. "From the script to the final print—every single filmmaking process must be disciplined," claimed ProMi administrator Fritz Hippler.[62] The Nazis dictated how films were to be publicized and discussed, painstakingly watching over audience response, monitoring applause and laughter in the cinema, listening to and worrying about word of mouth on the street.[63]

Film was to map the universe in accordance with party designs, to provide a comprehensive lexical guide to the past and present, to account for all signs of life from the smallest atom to the mightiest being.[64] Using different modalities (features, shorts, and documentaries that blended rabble-rousing agitprop, high drama, and escapist recreation), films charted physical reality and occupied psychic space. Screen narratives often provided the illusion of room to move while remaining organized and administered by the state. And films did not exist in isolation, but indeed circulated and resonated in a state-regulated public sphere.[65] National Socialism was a totalitarian government that employed film as the most important vehicle in its media dictatorship, as a psychotechnology[66] designed to channel the flow of impressions and information.

Premise 2: Entertainment played a crucial political role in Nazi culture. The era's many genre films maintained the appearance of escapist vehicles and innocent recreations while functioning within a larger program. Goebbels eschewed overt agitation; he wanted films with formal assurance and

Film stars as idealized Aryan physiognomies: Hans Albers and Käthe von Nagy in *Flüchtlinge/ Fugitives.*

Performers with classical features: Willy Fritsch and Käthe Gold in *Amphitryon*.

popular appeal,[67] fantasy productions that would expand German market shares and alleviate the need for foreign imports.[68] He sought to create a star system; he cultivated scriptwriters and directors. Like any Hollywood entrepreneur, he checked box-office returns and stressed the crucial role of advertising and publicity in generating product recognition. From the start Goebbels articulated a desire to create a cinema that could both satisfy the domestic market and function as a foreign emissary. Film was redesigned as a mechanized means to animate primal emotion, a modern technology to stir the soul's inner speech. It was to move the hearts and minds of masses while seeming to have little in common with politics or party agendas.[69]

Narrative films of the Third Reich granted few direct glimpses of everyday life in the new Germany. Nazi features were more a showplace for strong feelings and cheerful diversions than they were a forum for realistic tableaus or topical thematics. Reflecting about the medium's most essential calling, a German critic observed in October 1937: "In one regard both word- and image-fanatics will agree, namely that the task of film art can only be to bring about the strongest experience possible by means of film—that is, sound film, with all the optical and acoustic possibilities which this art form, like no other, possesses."[70] Party loyalist Hans Spielhofer noted that most German films avoided present-day settings.[71] They did not show Nazi emblems and Hitler salutes or proclaim party slogans; to do so would have threatened foreign box-office potential. Nonetheless, he sought a way "to make today's Germany the dominant setting for our contemporary cinema and not taint contemporary films with the scent of 'Nazi' films."[72] The decision to eradicate signs of the times and to take flight from present was not made by subversive forces or oppositional artists. The order came from the top.

If Nazi culture often put on a happy face or feigned an innocuous countenance, its cinema provided the definitive embodiment of this agreeable semblance. Images, maintained Nazi film theorists, should enthrall and enchant audiences just as music should liberate people from the bounds of time and space.[73] "One has to look a long time," argued the leading organ of Nazi youth, *Wille und Macht,* early in 1938,

> before one finds a cinema program announcing a film with an obvious political slant. Even the most suspicious filmgoers cannot claim that German films seek to hit them over the head with politics or to impose a world view. Except for portions of the newsreels, cinema in a newly politicized Germany amounts to an unpolitical oasis. A really clever person might claim that even if there are no propaganda films, there still is propaganda tucked away beneath film's surface details. This person, though, will have a hard time finding examples to prove his point . . . The more we go to the

movies, the more inescapable is the feeling that the world we see on the screen by and large has nothing to do with the National Socialist world we live in.[74]

As the passage makes clear, even party members realized the variance between the Third Reich's film features and Nazi realities. Leisure pursuits and mass cultural offerings appeared to have little in common with political priorities—and this illusion was carefully cultivated by the party apparatus.

Premise 3: Nazi film culture—and Nazi propaganda in general—must be understood in terms of what Goebbels called an "orchestra principle." "We do not expect everyone to play the same instrument," he argued; "we only expect that people play according to a plan." Not every instrument plays the same tune when we hear a concert; still, the result is a symphony.[75] Hardly monolithic or monotone, the features, documentaries, and newsreels made in Nazi Germany, together with an array of orchestrated diversions (radio programs, mass rallies, gigantic spectacles, holidays and commemorations—a world, in short, of festivals, pageants, flags, uniforms, and emblems), imbued the everyday with an aura of drama and excitement, organizing work and leisure time, occupying physical and psychic space, and thus militating against alternative experience and independent thought.

Cinema in the Third Reich involved a division of labor between heavy hands and light touches. Propaganda films and entertainment offerings were equally represented in the annual lists of hits. For the 1933–1934 season the back-to-the-fatherland opus *Flüchtlinge (Fugitives)* shared the spotlight with the peasant farce *Krach um Jolanthe (The Trouble with Iolanthe)*. A year later the Willi Forst fin-de-siècle drama *Maskerade (Masquerade)* topped the charts, followed closely by the nationalistic homecoming epic *Ein Mann will nach Deutschland (A German Wants to Go Home)*.[76] Trade papers likewise demonstrated a shared emphasis. A *Film-Kurier* headline of January 1936, for instance, is literally split: on one side of the page we read "Ufa signs Lilian Harvey," on the other, "The Riefenstahl School."[77]

On a typical outing to the movies, viewers witnessed a colorful evening (the prototype for the Adenauer era's *bunter Abend*), a veritable audiovisual variety show: advertisements (both slides and filmed commercials); a newsreel (generally more overtly ideological, although even here one finds a variety of offerings from the silly to the solemn); in fancier cinemas, a live stage show; a documentary short subject *(Kulturfilm);* and, finally, the main feature.[78] "What the entertainment films might have lacked in primary Nazi ideology was more than made up for by *Kulturfilme,*" remarks Hartmut Bitomsky. "The features may well have shown revues and romances, but culture films assumed the political burden."[79] In any case, the mix made for an affective smorgasbord. The premiere screening of *Jew Süss* in 1940, for instance, was preceded by a short subject titled *Unsere Kinder—Unsere Zukunft (Our Children—Our Future),* the weekly newsreel, and a live performance of Franz Liszt's "Les Préludes."[80] Goebbels stressed the importance of variation, of "repeating the same thing in different forms."[81] If the Nazi state became a grand aesthetic construction in which "the political itself is instituted and constituted (and regularly re-grounds itself) in and as work of art,"[82] then it is clear that this *Gesamtkunstwerk* involved a pastiche in which politics and entertainment were inextricably bound.

The Third Reich fostered the modern era's first full-blown media culture, strategically instrumentalizing state-of-the-art technology, introducing radios into almost every household, developing television, staging political events as grand photo opportunities, replaying military conquests in the form of weekly newsreels. *Request Concert,* whose inspiration came from Goebbels, provides an idealized self-portrait of National Socialism's society of spectacle. It starts with Hitler's arrival at the 1936 Olympics and takes us on a tour of Berlin. Its subsequent points of interest include the battlefield of war, an affair of the heart, and above all a popular radio broadcast that binds private destinies to an imaginary collective fate. *Request Concert* depicts a world in which the media dictate people's feelings, in which everyday experience is above all a function of simulated stimuli and other-directed desires. Nazi films' political effect, then, is not just the simple function of explicit propaganda transmitted by dialogue, what critics often refer to as the "message" or "manifest meaning." What is far more crucial is the polyphonic way in which Nazi films channel perception and render reality, how images and sounds work in a variety of modalities to account for the entire spectrum of human experience, presenting a world view that literally seeks to encompass—and control—everything.

Premise 4: It is by now a truism that we cannot speak of National Socialism without speaking about aesthetics. I think we must also speak about mass culture. When critics talk about a so-called Nazi film aesthetics, they usually have in mind Leni Riefenstahl's party documentaries, linking her films' auratic allure to the impact of Arno Breker's monstrous sculptures and Albert Speer's monumental designs. These structures are overwhelming constructions that dwarf human perspectives and shatter pedestrian conceptual frameworks. Riefenstahl's *Olympia* treats athletes as raw material and transforms their bodies into abstract shapes and mass ornaments. This formalizing process climaxes in the famous diving sequence in which well-known figures become faceless and nameless entities who perform in an unreal space. We see the sublime forms of divers in mesmerizing slow motion as they descend through the heavens and drop like bombs. These apparitions of life are ideal and definitely not of this earth. Fascist artworks exercise a powerful and persuasive effect: they present seductive intimations of oblivion with visual beauty and operatic glory. Well-proportioned bodies, divorced from physical reality and raised to ethereal heights, provide aesthetic pleasure of the first order. "Fascist art," in Sontag's often-quoted formulation, "glorifies surrender, it exalts mindlessness, it glamorizes death."[83] Nazi aesthetics amount to emotional violence, stunning and captivating beholders so strongly that they literally become captive audiences. In this understanding, fascist art is of a piece with state terror.

National Socialism, however, did not rule by external force alone. It also effected means to monitor its citizens from within.[84] It hit people over the head, but it also soothed egos and massaged the masses, blending fustian and soma. National Socialism aestheticized the political and—in a hyperbolic extension of expressionism's world-as-will dynamics—organized brute demonstrations of physical strength in geometrical patterns under the eye of the artist/leader/Führer. Still, even the most persuasive commentaries (such as Sontag's) have underestimated the primary role of mass culture and the popular in the Third Reich's hyperstylization of collective will. Nazi aesthetics were not just "official art" and politically correct endeavor; they involved a much wider range of possibility. Critics have by and large bracketed the popular in their estimations of the era's culture, or simply written it off as kitschy, derivative, and trivial. Yet the popular clearly played a prominent and ubiquitous role in everyday life, in cinemas, radio programs, dance halls, advertisements, tourist offerings, and the latest consumer items. In its cynical belief that it offered people what they wanted, Nazi mass culture emulated and replicated American patterns of recognition. It produced an entertainment industry with secondhand popular fare: hit tunes, request concerts, fashion trends, fan magazines, glossy commercials, household appliances, mass audiences, and film fanatics who eagerly awaited each week's new movies.

Premise 5: When critics decry Nazi cinema as an abomination, they protest too much. Commentators today speak of Nazi aesthetics in general as parasitic, distorted, and inhuman,[85] invoking (in a curious act of retrospective projection) those very propensities Hitler and Goebbels ascribed to a maligned "degenerate" art. They concentrate on the hyperformed and the grotesque proportions of Arno Breker's and Josef Thorak's superhuman bronzes, the excesses of Albert Speer's architectural designs and his spectacular light shows. Officially sanctioned painting of the Third Reich is seen as a motley patchwork of neoclassical, romantic, and Biedermeier impulses. Art historians denounce the era's epigonality and provincialism, stressing a lack of formal sophistication and emphasizing trivial content and subject matter.[86] It is common to reduce all Nazi films to hate pamphlets, party hagiography, or mindless escapism, films with too much substance or none at all, either execrable or frivolous. In the process, the reliance of the era's cinema on classical Hollywood conventions goes unnoticed, as does the recourse of so many productions and so much of Nazi film culture to American techniques and popular genres.[87]

Though in many respects idiosyncratic, films of the Third Reich are hardly unfamiliar. As Thomas Elsaesser observes, they "appear readable in terms of classical narrative in much the same way as do Hollywood films of the 1930s."[88] This phenomenon may well explain why Nazi cinema equally fascinates and disturbs postwar American audiences. There remains much to learn about its different aesthetic shapes and its various historical functions. Nazi cinema did not suddenly come out of the dark when Hitler rose to power; after his demise it would not simply disappear from view. As a film historian, I cannot isolate these films as hideous anomalies: Nazi film was traditional through and through. Drawing on recent discussions about Nazi culture and the public sphere during the Third Reich, I want to be more nuanced in addressing the relationship between politics and entertainment and be less hasty about casting artifacts from the period aside as harmless pieces of fluff or, alternatively, celebrating them as subversive exceptions. Neither a dumping ground of propaganda nor a moronic cult of distraction and surely not a locus of resistance, Nazi feature production warrants more careful scrutiny.

My exploration of these films at this moment brings me into a minefield of explosive issues, ranging from the "historians' debate" about the status of Nazi war crimes to recent disputes about the proper place of Nazi art and architecture within contemporary culture.[89] With the dismantling of the Berlin Wall and the end of the Cold War, much less reunification, renegotiations of German national identity likewise bear heavily on the discussion. As time passes, the legacy of the Third Reich looms ever larger. In addition, I remain mindful of the problematic postmodern relationship to the images and imaginary products of the Third Reich, a fascination that so often has tended to be, in the words of Alvin Rosenfeld, "relentlessly unhistorical and hence an easy trigger for fantasies of the most extreme kind."[90] Previous surveys have afforded at best partial views and in various respects led to aporias and dead ends. The following chapters seek to open up other routes of access and along the way to suggest sites for new explorations and future interventions.

PART I

Fatal Attractions

“I wanted to form my own image” (Leni Riefenstahl).

ONE

A Legend for Modern Times: *The Blue Light* (1932)

Go laughing down the way of your great calling. Here you have found your heaven and in it you will be eternal.

Julius Streicher to Leni Riefenstahl, 1937

The evil eye is the *fascinum,* it is that which has the effect of arresting movement and, literally, of killing life.

Jacques Lacan

A Master Text

No career illustrates Nazi cinema's complex and extensive history as dramatically as that of Leni Riefenstahl. Debuting as a dancer, she went on to acclaim as a screen star during the Weimar Republic. In the mid-1930s she became the Third Reich's most famous director and, after 1945, film history's most controversial filmmaker. She is still very much with us today; indeed, she is more present than ever, some six decades after she commandeered the cameras that recorded the 1934 Nuremberg rally. Stars and dignitaries from all over the world flocked to her ninetieth birthday party in 1992; in fashionable Munich circles the event was the talk of the town. Stephen Schiff's portrait and Helmut Newton's photographs of the remarkably vital senior citizen graced the pages of *Vanity Fair.*[1] John Simon's rave notice about her memoirs appeared on the cover of the *New York Times Book Review.*[2] *Time* extolled "Riefenstahl's Last Triumph" and touted her autobiography as one of 1993's five best nonfiction books.[3] Ray Müller's three-hour documentary homage, *Die Macht der Bilder* (*The Wonderful Horrible Life of Leni Riefenstahl,* 1993), played at the New York Film Festival and found wide release and enthusiastic press coverage. Early in 1994, rumors circulated in Hollywood that Madonna wanted to option Riefenstahl's memoirs; later that year, shortly before

Thanksgiving, CNN let it be known that Jodie Foster intended to produce a Leni biopic.

The Führer's protégée and confidante, the woman who directed the definitive Nazi self-portrait, *Triumph des Willens* (*Triumph of the Will*, 1935), Riefenstahl remains the Third Reich's most visible living celebrity and a constant object of lurid speculation, be it as "Hitler's girlfriend,"[4] a "Nazi pin-up girl,"[5] or a "fallen goddess."[6] The spectacle of Riefenstahl has always made for good press. Championed in the 1930s by Avery Brundage, Josef von Sternberg, Walt Disney, Douglas Fairbanks, and Charlie Chaplin, her subsequent admirers have included Jean Cocteau, Dusan Makavejev, Mick and Bianca Jagger,[7] Andy Warhol, Siegfried and Roy, and George Lucas. Even Rainer Werner Fassbinder once courted Riefenstahl, asking her in a letter to be his cinematographer for *Querelle:* "I think you might be able to develop a strong feeling for my work. And besides, this would make me very proud."[8] Riefenstahl has a large throng of enthusiasts, especially in America, partisans who disregard her embattled past and celebrate her cinematic genius. For the British film historian Kevin Brownlow, her cause has become a crusade: "Art transcends the artist . . . politics and art must never be confused . . . these old adages are forgotten instantly the name of Riefenstahl is raised. And it is our fault. We have ourselves been the victims of insidious propaganda."[9] Her apologists support the filmmaker's claim that she never was anything more than an artist compelled by an aesthetic calling.

Detractors, on the other hand, assert that Riefenstahl's unquestionable artistic powers were put to nefarious purposes, that her pact with Hitler was tantamount to sympathy for the devil, that her hagiographical portraits legitimated the Nazi leadership and helped consolidate the new order.[10] Susan Sontag, in her influential 1975 essay, coined the term "fascinating fascism" in a larger discussion of Riefenstahl's continuing appeal. Nazism's substance has become neutralized in formalistic appreciations; its theatrical spectacles and ritualistic scenarios reappear in fetishized and sexualized appropriations. Aesthetes and camp followers applaud the beauty of Riefenstahl's images and divest them of political meaning. "Without a historical perspective, such connoisseurship prepares the way for a curiously absent-minded acceptance of propaganda for all sorts of destructive feelings—feelings whose implications people are refusing to take seriously."[11] Riefenstahl's documentaries of the 1930s demonstrate, in Sontag's assessment, a brute symmetry and an overwhelming choreography, "the massing of groups of people; the turning of people into things; and the grouping of people/things around an all-powerful, hypnotic leader-figure or force."[12]

The fluid traveling shots in *Triumph of the Will,* elaborates Karsten Witte, "work with induced movement intended to set inanimate matter into waving motion and make human masses freeze into stone blocks. The masses are allowed to enter the picture, but only their leaders are allowed to speak. Hitler himself is the main actor, here celebrating his wedding fantasies with the masses."[13]

Riefenstahl considers such assertions outrageous. She insists her work was no party to Hitler. Asked by Ray Müller what fascist aesthetics might be, she says that for her the phrase has no meaning.[14] "What do I have to regret, where does my guilt lie?" inquires the unreconciled filmmaker in the closing moments of the documentary. The past plagues her like an albatross. Her life assumes a tragic dimension, according to a recent assessment, "for she seems to have borne the brunt of public shame more openly and more frequently than the real culprits of the regime."[15] The director sees herself as a person unfairly maligned, the object of witch hunts and never-ending persecution.

In response to her assailants, Riefenstahl has regularly called on *Das blaue Licht (The Blue Light),* her directorial debut of 1932, as a character witness.[16] *Sieg des Glaubens* (*Victory of Faith,* 1933) and *Triumph of the Will* may glorify the Führer. *Olympia* (1938), financed by the government and overseen by the ProMi, renders Hitler as a modern Zeus with an omnipotent gaze, an *Übermensch* with an *Überblick.*[17] *Tag der Freiheit!—Unsere Wehrmacht* (*Day of Freedom,* 1935) celebrates a reconstructed army and a soon-to-be-remilitarized nation. *The Blue Light* does not lend itself so readily to political objections. Its young and inexperienced director had not met Hitler and knew nothing of *Mein Kampf.* The film's scriptwriter, Béla Balázs, was a Jewish intellectual and a prominent leftist.[18] Unlike the later documentaries, the mountain film appears to be the work of a naive artist.[19]

The Blue Light tells the legend of Junta, a strange woman living in the Alpine heights above a Tyrolean village, who has privileged access to a cave of crystals. On full-moon nights a blue light emanates from this secret grotto, luring young men from the valley to seek out the source of the radiant beam.[20] Their quest invariably ends in death and causes the townspeople to vilify Junta. A painter from Vienna, Vigo, befriends the outcast woman. He becomes her protector and falls in love with her. Following her one blue-lit night, he discovers the way to the cave. He draws a map, thinking that the safe passage to the grotto will serve the best interests of both Junta and the villagers. The townspeople arm themselves with tools and climb to the cave, plundering the valuable crystals and celebrating their newfound fortune. Finding her private sanctuary ravaged, Junta despairs and plunges to her death.

The impetus for *The Blue Light,* Riefenstahl recalls, came from personal reveries: "I began to dream and my dreams turned into images of a young girl who lived in the mountains, a creature of nature. I saw her climbing, saw her in the moonlight."[21] Gripped by this vision, Riefenstahl set out to make her own film, assuming the part of Junta and taking on the role of director and coproducer. In forming her own images, Riefenstahl created her life's fantasy. Speaking to *Cahiers du cinéma* in 1965, she explained how *The Blue Light* forecast her future: "Well, when her dream is destroyed Junta dies. I spoke of that as my destiny. For that is what was accomplished, much later, in me, after the war when everything collapsed on us, when I was deprived of all possibility of creating. For art, creation—this is my life, and I was deprived of it. My life became a tissue of rumors and accusations through which I had to beat a path."[22]

Riefenstahl's film sanctifies elemental nature and its enchanting powers. And the director identifies herself as an artist whose true homeland resides in this sublime and special space. Most commentators view Junta as an embodiment of her creator, an artist who, in the words of an American enthusiast, "had her own intuitive feelings about nature and was destroyed by her naive disregard of the real world around her, the world she set out to avoid."[23] Riefenstahl becomes a romantic poet-priestess whose vision transcends reality and history, someone whose films reflect a fascination with beauty, strength, and harmony.[24] In this view, *The Blue Light* allows us to read her more controversial output in the correct light.

Justifiably or not, Riefenstahl has come to embody a haunting past that refuses to go away. Postwar controversies about the filmmaker have led to an impasse between moral castigation and aesthetic vindication. She becomes either an unrepentant Nazi propagandist or a misunderstood artistic genius. Seeing herself as a victim, Riefenstahl aligns herself with a Jew, borrowing Albert Einstein's soothing words as the epigraph to her *Memoir:* "So many things have been written about me, masses of insolent lies and inventions, that I would have perished long ago, had I paid any attention. One must take comfort in the fact that time has a sieve, through which most trivia run off into the sea of oblivion." The filmmaker is central to any consideration of Nazi aesthetics and its disputed place in history. And central to any discussion of Leni Riefenstahl and Nazi cinema is the relationship of film art to a larger general history, of romantic fantasies to

German dreams, of aesthetic reveries to political realities. Riefenstahl's debut feature and founding myth, *The Blue Light,* is, without question, a master text.

A Vampire Film

Like Riefenstahl's career, her debut film spans three epochs of German political history, from the Weimar era and the reign of Hitler to the Bonn republic. Shot on location in Switzerland and South Tyrol during the summer of 1931, *The Blue Light* premiered in Berlin at the Ufa-Palast am Zoo on 24 March 1932.[25] In the wake of *Olympia*'s great success, it was reprised on 27 September 1938. After the war it was reedited and newly scored for what Riefenstahl described as "a dazzling gala screening" in Rome on 21 November 1951.[26] The film reappeared a few months later in Austria (where it bore the title *Die Hexe von Santa Maria/The Witch of Santa Maria*) as well as in the Federal Republic. *The Blue Light* has assumed different countenances in its various incarnations. The National-Verleih press booklet for the postwar version bills it as "a standard work in German film history," "a film of lasting quality . . . that must be numbered among the most unforgettable titles."

Similarly reverent critical discussions convey the impression that the film, an example of canonical greatness, has remained unaffected by tradition or time's passage. Typically, commentators praise the director's immediacy and intuition, her atmospheric images and breathtaking panoramas. Her genius, so it would seem, flourished freely, breaking new ground while remaining unfettered by models or conventions.[27] Apart from the film's "romantic mysticism" and the title's deference to Novalis' "blue flower,"[28] Riefenstahl's originality and sole authorship seem beyond question—until we start to look at the shifting casts of players. The 1932 opening sequence announces "*The Blue Light,* a mountain legend from the Dolomites, rendered in images by Leni Riefenstahl, Bela Balacz [*sic*], Hans Schneeberger." Although the director subsequently acknowledged Carl Mayer's important assistance with the script and Arnold Fanck's editorial counsel, neither name shows up in the credits. Six years later, the titles now proclaim "*The Blue Light,* a mountain legend told and shaped into images by Leni Riefenstahl." The first version of the film lists the Jewish scriptwriter Balázs as a coauthor; the second does not. Nor do we find any mention of coproducer Harry Sokal. In its postwar incarnation *The Blue Light* becomes simply "a mountain legend by Leni Riefenstahl."

From its very first signs, *Blue Light* appears as the product of unacknowledged forces. "I wanted to make a film without the film industry, without a producer, and without a director," Riefenstahl would later declare.[29] None of the three versions discloses the book from which she gained her initial impetus, the well-known Swiss writer Gustav Renker's 1930 novel, *Bergkristall (Mountain Crystal)*.[30] In early accounts she would aver that she had adapted a peasant legend of the Alps; later (as in her *Memoir*) she would insist that the narrative was derived from her own dream images. The filmmaker claims a direct access to her story ("everything that happened came from my head"),[31] which in fact had come to her in a much more mediated fashion. Renker's *Bergkristall* is a tale about an artist who flees the big city to an Alpine retreat. There he becomes enchanted by a huge mountain from which emanates a "blue light." "It really exists," swears one of the villagers. One can see it "around midnight when the moon is full."[32] In Renker's novel a rock formation and its mysterious quarry become a painter's obsession. Here, too, an artist from the city becomes enamored of a woman who herds sheep and lives with a young boy in the wild.

The film's title also recalls the blue flower from Novalis' *Heinrich von Ofterdingen,* the quintessential symbol of the romantic quest. One of Riefenstahl's early dance routines bore the name "Die blaue Blume." Before becoming a dancer, she attended the State Academy of Arts and Crafts in Berlin, where she studied painting and drawing. Riefenstahl demonstrates considerable familiarity with nineteenth-century art history and especially the work of Caspar David Friedrich.[33] *The Blue Light* abounds with images reminiscent of Friedrich, with sweeping unpeopled mountainscapes. Certain compositions explicitly evoke him, for instance the shot in which Vigo peers from a panoramic height like the "Wanderer above the Sea of Fog" or the one in which Junta stands before a precipice in the manner of "Woman on the Abyss."[34] *The Blue Light* infuses nature with an arousing power; like Friedrich, Riefenstahl transforms exterior landscapes into emotional spaces.[35] The physical world becomes irreal and fantastic, molded by an imagination whose highest goal is to represent the invisible and the ineffable. Friedrich's use of landscape, as Alice Kuzniar has argued, "turns the medium of perception into its object of depiction." His idealized topographies provide "the epitome of romantic self-reflexive art or the art that, instead of referring to the natural world outside it, calls attention to the means, conditions, and operations of its being."[36] Riefenstahl imparts a self-reflexive dimension to her own art by introducing a romantic landscape

A solitary and silhouetted figure dwarfed by Alpine elements: mountain film compositions reflect Caspar David Friedrich's dramatic contrasts between foreground and background.

painter into her narrative, an artist, though, whose ultimate creation will be the map that brings modernity to the village and perdition to Junta.[37]

If the images and the artistic impetus go back to Friedrich's evocative landscape painting, the narrative proper comes equally as a legacy of the nineteenth century. The earliest versions of the film, the 1932 and 1938 releases, contain a frame story redolent of many German *Novellen,* a village tale offered up to visitors.[38] Confronted with trinkets bearing Junta's picture when they drive into Santa Maria, a dapper honeymooning couple from the city enter a hotel room to find a religious painting with the same votive image.[39] "Who really is this Junta?" asks the young woman. The proprietor, as if awaiting the question, sends for a leather-bound volume that bears Junta's countenance and legend. The film then dissolves from her image on the book to a shot of a mist-covered crystal, opening to a view of Junta clasping the mineral and yielding to an extended flashback. We move from the contemporary setting to 1866 and learn who Junta is and what her image has to do with the crystals proffered to the tourists. The inscribed narrative serves a function similar to the story's point of orientation, the image- and mapmaker Vigo: both resolve seeming enigmas, offering routes of access to terrains deemed mysterious and demonic.

The film's images may recall the highflown language of nature worship and the "noble awe" of the sublime,[40] but the narrative as a whole stems from an intelligence able to fathom nature's mysteries and to transform superstition into knowledge. This undeniably modern impetus, as we know from German literary history, inheres in the *Novelle,* a genre often featuring frame stories whose apparent supernatural foundations give way to the more tangible loci of human agency, causality, and rationality, shifting from a naive world view to a sentimental one.[41] This legacy found its way into the complex and self-conscious frame structures of many Weimar films.[42] The nested narrative of *The Blue Light* resolves the mystery of Junta. During the tale, Junta evolves from an agent of the uncanny, a witch and a curse, into a public martyr and a popular icon. The film's romantic images hallow nature's mystery and impart to the elemental a stirring resonance; the narrative, on the other hand, casts seemingly inexplicable phenomena in terms both pragmatic and transparent. Romantic images that accentuate nature's irrational potential take their place in a story logic governed by enlightened reason.

Another crucial (and more widely acknowledged) generic legacy for Riefenstahl was the Weimar mountain film *(Bergfilm),* a popular vein in which she received her start as an actress.[43] The Alpine dramas, filmed on location amidst majestic peaks, feature vigorous athletes confronting untamed elements. Bound by a hardy code, these feckless males stand above the pedestrian world of restriction and cultivation, viewing themselves as souls in touch with a mightier destiny, the call of the mountains. Sporting visual effects caught in glaciers, rocky peaks, and snowscapes, Arnold Fanck, the

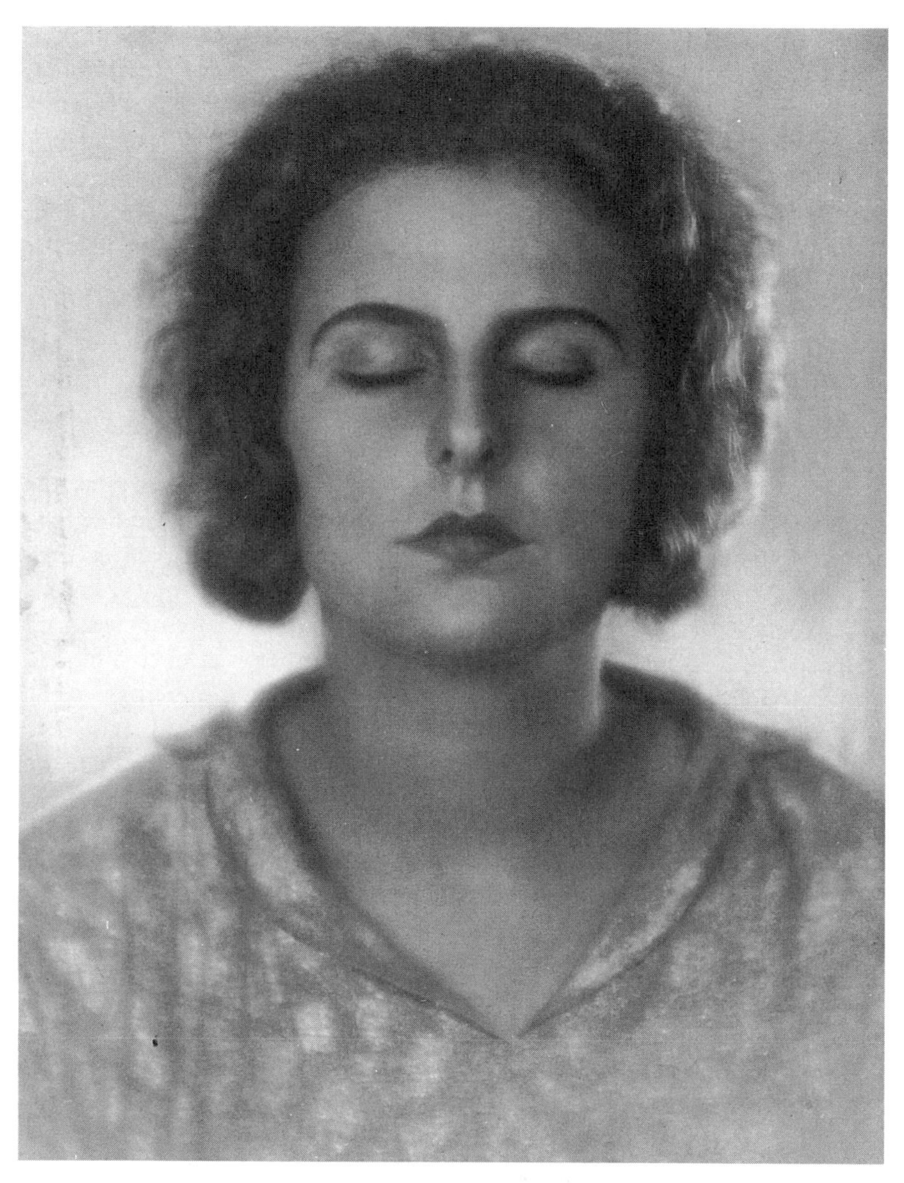

A female Cesare from the Cabinet of Dr. Fanck (Riefenstahl as Diotima in *The Holy Mountain*).

master of this form, built his *Bergfilme* around romantic melodramas, triangles involving two climbers, usually close companions, and a mutually shared love interest who causes disturbance. Siegfried Kracauer appropriately dubbed the films "a mixture of sparkling ice-axes and inflated sentiments," indicting the *Bergfilme* for their immature male protagonists, without commenting on the conspicuous role played by women in these scenarios.[44]

Riefenstahl's feature film debut came in *Der heilige Berg* (*The Holy Mountain,* 1926). We first see the actress in a close-up portrait; her face is pale, her eyes are shut. Anticipating Junta's ultimate incarnation, this initial view appears to be a death mask. The face is that of Diotima who comes to life in a dance by the sea. The editing renders the fluid choreography of her gestures and leaps at one with the natural forces that cause the waves to break. The dancer's image reappears on a poster announcing her evening performance in a resort hotel. Robert, the mountain climber, finds himself perplexed after Diotima's show. He flees into the Alpine peaks, as the intertitles put it, "to master the overwhelming impression." In the *Bergfilm,* men seek to master mountains and women—with mixed success. Catastrophe ensues when Robert and his younger companion learn they are rivals for Diotima's affection. They perish in a climbing accident. Remorseful and guilt-ridden, Diotima returns to the sea. The mourner is at once inhibited and inhabited, a woman whose sole obsession remains her memories of the dead admirers. In conceptualizing *The Blue Light,* Riefenstahl wanted to create a *Bergfilm* in which a woman figured more prominently than the mountains.[45] In so doing, she clearly recognized their paradigmatic equivalence in the generic economy.

Like many nineteenth-century *Novellen,* mountain films probe the mysteries of nature with the tools of modernity. Besides snowscapes, billowing clouds, and unpeopled expanses, Fanck's films show us tourists, resort hotels, automobiles, airplanes, observatories, and weather stations. Contemporaries in the 1920s frequently hailed the ability of Fanck's camera both to venerate and to penetrate nature, to sanctify its secrets and still disclose its uncanny properties.[46] Critics recognized the genre's synthesis of mountains and machines, of natural force and technological power, of bodily energy and spiritual endeavor, its impressive merger between the physical world and the sophisticated scientific devices that measure and elaborate it. For Fanck nature remained mute and unexpressive unless captured by a camera, a modern restatement of Schelling's romantic transcendentalism, the belief that human awareness of oneself and the world around one brings "the unconscious life in nature to conscious expression."[47] In this way, mediated effects become natural presence, formal will imparts to raw material its true identity, man-made machines render the real authentic.[48] Riefenstahl, in a similar fashion, combined the callings of a romantic artist and a technical engineer. "With light you can turn the camera into a magic instrument," she reportedly boasted to Fanck, "and if you also use colour filters to change the tonal values you can succeed in altering the outdoors and stylizing nature."[49]

Many critics have observed that Riefenstahl, like F. W. Murnau, sought to grant natural settings an eerie and ethereal aspect, something she accomplished through special effects, technical ploys involving time-lapse photography, filters, smoke machines, and modulated lighting.[50] Both directors recasted the still lifes of romantic painting in moving images. Neither wanted to reflect physical reality, but instead to probe its hidden secrets and its subterranean reaches. "Too often," complained Murnau, "pictures have made the world banal instead of revealing new heights and depths in life."[51] He wanted to photograph thought, to make images that spoke more strongly than words. *The Blue Light* exudes at times what Balázs termed the "chilly draft from doomsday" atmosphere of Murnau's silent classic, *Nosferatu* (1922).[52] Balázs was of course a great admirer of Murnau and one of his most eloquent supporters, so these similarities are hardly coincidental. Frieda Grafe has likewise pointed out the resemblance between Vigo's approach to the mountain village and Hutter's entry into the realm of the vampire.[53] *The Blue Light*'s reliance on *Nosferatu,* however, transcends the atmospherics of single scenes and technical touches. Both films dramatize a disparity between images attuned to primal emotions and unconscious desires and an intelligence that seeks to render the inexplicable and unsettling in terms of human generality. In *Nosferatu* the visual track often conflicts with written signs, producing a profoundly ironic tension. Murnau's tableaus show us things that the narrator, a city scribe, only partially understands and in some cases simply fails to comprehend.[54]

Like *Nosferatu, The Blue Light* uses the stylized image of a woman as a point of departure and a focus of attention. We first encounter both heroines enclosed by frames: the close-up of Ellen Hutter at the window, the picture of Junta on the cover of the village chronicle. Both women sleepwalk at night and commune with nature's primordial powers. The two films cast a woman in the role of martyr, whose sacrificed body saves lives, indeed ensures a community's well-being. Ellen becomes the agent of civilization in its battle against the demonic side of nature it wishes to disavow, the repressed energies vested in Nosferatu.[55] She takes on this responsibility after reading *The*

Book of the Vampires and making a conscious decision. Junta also becomes a martyr, but this role is not of her choice. She does not understand Vigo as he explains the advantages of mining the grotto and thus has no voice in the destruction of her most intimate space. In both films a community fortifies itself against outside threats. In *Nosferatu* this involves the sublimation of nature's underworld and the exorcism of its darker side. The price of civilization in *The Blue Light* similarly entails a processing of elemental forces and the exorcism of a dangerous sensuality. Both films culminate in scenes in which a heroine lies supine and has all vitality sucked out of her. Ellen holds Nosferatu by her bedside until the creature dissolves in the rising sun; Vigo stands over Junta's corpse in the early morning light.[56]

Itself the product of considerable recourse to tradition, of recasting and recycling, *The Blue Light* offers a legend that reflects—and embodies—a distinctly modern process of appropriation. The narrative dramatizes the plundering of nature and the undoing of a woman, stylizing the double violation in the form of a village chronicle, the "Historia della Junta" offered for the amusement and edification of tourists. Riefenstahl's film sanctifies premodern landscapes and documents a village's entry into modernity. In so doing, it enacts a tension between the romantic worship of nature and an enlightened instrumental reason. Riefenstahl's sympathies and those of her film seem unquestionably aligned with Junta and the mountain girl's pristine world. Or at least so it would seem.

Histories of Horror

Junta's victimization at the hands of mercenary contemporaries, claims Riefenstahl, presages the filmmaker's own subsequent suffering. Her autobiographical reading has set the tone for many discussions and continues to inform appraisals, most recently in the *New York Times. The Blue Light,* for Vincent Canby, is a "very significant film," "the fable-like story of a woman whose search for the ideal, not unlike Ms. Riefenstahl's search in a very different world, leads to disaster." The reviewer applauds the film and goes on to position the director as beyond good and evil: "She's too complex, too particular and too arrogant to be seen as either sympathetic or unsympathetic."[57] The special status of Riefenstahl's debut film has remained undiminished despite the interventions of strident detractors. Siegfried Kracauer and Susan Sontag have offered compelling and controversial assessments of German mountain films. They see *The Blue Light* as escapist fare with regressive implications, a work whose high altitudes and lofty attitudes celebrate protofascist dispositions: fulsome antirationalism, blind enthusiasm, and overwrought pathos. For Kracauer, Junta "conforms to a political regime which relies on intuition, worships nature and cultivates myths."[58] Sontag likewise connects the cult of the mountains with the sanctification of the Führer, "the ultimate affirmation of and escape from the self into the brotherhood of courage and into death."[59]

Both Kracauer and Sontag have come under frequent attack and been called ax-grinding ideologues or moralistic zealots. Resolute auteurists defend Riefenstahl's visual power, blithely dismissing these interventions: "And anyway," wisecracks Andrew Sarris, "she never claimed to be working for British intelligence while she was making *Triumph of the Will.*" Sontag, argues Sarris,

> quotes from the very few film historians who support her position, and ignores or insults the rest. Siegfried Kracauer's very questionable *From Caligari to Hitler* is trotted out as if it were holy writ, its mandate for 20-20 hindsight renewed. Still, the problem with either a prosecution or a defense of Riefenstahl is that so much of the evidence has disappeared in the rubble of the Third Reich that we can never be quite sure whether Leni was Little Eva (as she claims) or Lucretia Borgia (as Sontag suggests) or (more likely) an opportunistic artist who has been both immortalized and imprisoned by the horror of history.[60]

Why Kracauer's book is "very questionable" does not receive further comment. Which missing evidence Sarris has in mind is equally open to speculation. And precisely what the critic means by "the horror of history" remains anyone's guess. Is it simply fate, one wonders, or does it involve human agency? Within broader and far-reaching arguments, Kracauer and Sontag link *The Blue Light* to National Socialist sensibility, indeed, to its history of horror. For them the film is less a romantic tale than a political allegory. Their comments about the film are brief and provocative, suggestive, but either too terse (Sontag) or schematic (Kracauer) to be conclusive. If one follows their lead, one can indeed go further.

In her discussion of *The Blue Light,* Sontag provides a noteworthy postmortem. The cause of Junta's death lies in "the materialist, prosaic spirit of envious villagers and the blind rationalism of her lover, a well-meaning visitor from the city."[61] Sontag goes on to make important general observations regarding Nazi art's celebration of death, its desire to contain physical desire—and to stifle female volition. "The fascist ideal," she claims, "is to transform sexual energy into a 'spiritual' force, for the benefit of the community. The erotic (that is, woman) is always present as a temptation, with the most admirable response being a heroic repression of the sexual impulse."[62] *The Blue Light* recodes Christian symbols in its secular religion of abandon and death. Early in the film, Vigo stumbles across figures etched onto a rocky mountainside, a martyr surrounded by mourners, a creation merging elemental nature and human sacrifice in an artistic construction. As he passes the faces carved in stone, Vigo asks, "What are those figures?" The question echoes the tourist's initial query about the mountain girl. The connection is not fortuitous, for after her demise, Junta will reappear as a religious martyr and an aesthetic countenance.

As in *The Holy Mountain,* sexual energy becomes a spiritual force. The outsider is the object of lascivious stares, her body linked by the editing with wild animals. Her attraction and that of the blue light cause suicidal frenzy among the village's young males. She becomes the target of the imperiled community's anger and aggression, for the boys dying on the rocks are its future fathers. Junta's primal vitality and erotic magnetism are a public menace. These disturbing forces will become harnessed and transformed, bringing collective relief and welcome prosperity. Junta's face transmutes into a crystal-studded image as the frame dissolves into the portrait adorning a book with her story.[63] The same image will serve as a kitsch object offered by children to newly arrived visitors, the picture of someone whose afterlife as a legend, fetish, and commodity, has a crucial bearing on the Alpine community's spiritual—and material—welfare.[64] Without a doubt, the citizens of Santa Maria act as consummate recyclers of native tradition, hawking crystal images of the local hero and attracting tourists with their gripping village tale.

The mountain hamlet we see in the film's prologue lives in an age of automobiles and tourism, yet abides as a hardy *Gemeinschaft* at one with elementary nature. On the whole the residents of Santa Maria do not seem avaricious or enterprising. Their stark and noble features, captured in affectionate close-ups, recall Dürer woodcuts. The intertitles of the original framing passage introduce the townspeople of the present as a healthy folk unsullied by modern malaise:

> We, the people of the Dolomites, far from the strife and turmoil of the outside world, dwell primarily in the rugged wilderness and magnificence of the Italian Tyrol. We are a simple peasant folk, and strange legends have come down to us through the centuries casting shadows on the peace of

> our lives. Above all do we cherish the legend of Junta, the mountain girl, whose story we have reverently engraved for future generations.[65]

Oskar Kalbus, an eminent film publicist in the Third Reich, praised the Alpine community's racial vitality, admiring physiognomies that extended back to the Visigoths.[66] The village, effused a British commentator in the mid-1960s, appeared "to blend with all aspects of the past and present; time itself seemed petrified as the mute figures carved from rock; the faces of peasants appeared out of archaic time, touched by a stoic dignity."[67] Recent critics have lauded the film's ethnographic intensity and linked Riefenstahl's sympathetic handling of the Sarn Valley peasants with her affectionate treatment of the Nuba tribespeople.

The film may well convey blood-and-soil sentiment, but it also shows a thriving nascent culture industry. The village works over reality and reproduces itself, recycling signs from the past as a form of pseudoeternity, making mountains and mountain girls into powerful images and spellbind-

Faces with the sharp features of woodcuts: the physiognomies of the mountain villagers, effused Nazi commentators, possessed an undeniable racial hardiness.

ing tales. The film puts these dynamics on display and positions the legend as an expression of collective regret and sorrow. An acute formulation by Kracauer recognizes, though, how profoundly the village profits from the tragedy: "To be sure, at the end the village rejoices in its fortune and the myth seems defeated, but this rational solution is treated in such a summary way that it enhances rather than reduces Junta's significance."[68] The film pictures the celebration after the cavern's exploitation as an ecstatic moment with disquieting overtones, especially in the close-up of spilled wine glasses, whose traces on the table suggest the flow of blood. Greedy villagers, the shot intimates, have opportunistically plundered the mountain cavern, despoiling nature and robbing Junta. The scene as a whole, however, also amounts to a structural reversal of an earlier tableau that showed subdued townspeople living under the threat of the blue light.

The prologue acknowledges a village's injustice, but the act seems to bear no trace of human agency: "strange legends" have come down to this peasant folk and "cast shadows" on the peace of their lives. The "horror of history" once again seems to be up to its old tricks. The community continues to circulate the story, marketing a legend purchased at a bloody price. The chronicle both acknowledges and yet glosses over the fact of violence and expropriation, rendering the mercenary act as a necessary evil—in Kracauer's words, a "rational solution." The solution intimates another history of horror, a "final solution" that also involved a reckoning with people branded as outsiders and a communal act of violence.

The initial version of *The Blue Light* ends with a coda, a return to the framing episode. A honeymooning couple from the city have driven into Santa Maria, garbed in aviator glasses and long trenchcoats that obscure their gender. This would appear to be an indication of a modern world in which traditional orientations no longer hold sway, in which patriarchy has lost its grip. The telling of the tale makes a strong impression on the urban pair; for when we segue back to the contemporary setting, the united and more conventionally attired couple walk to their hotel room window, looking out onto a waterfall and a mist-shrouded mountain. The site of the blue light, despite the incursion of the villagers, retains its evocative beauty. The legend of the blue light also has an undiminished power: in relating how domestic order was restored in the past, it serves to set things right in the present.

At face value, *The Blue Light* seems marked by romantic sentimentality and an antimodern persuasion. When we look more closely, we find the undeniable awareness of a sophisticated modern rationality, an elaborate ideological construction in the form of a legend that accompanies the exploitation of nature, a woman, the past. The final page of the story proclaims: "This was the sad end of poor Junta from Santa Maria. Her memory however continues to live on in the village which has inflicted such terrible injustice on her. For without her such great riches would never have come to it from the wonderful 'hell' of Mount Cristallo." The text relates a village's wonderful horrible life. It pays lip service to the mistreatment of Junta but establishes a causality between a "terrible injustice" and the "great riches" that came from it. During the film the only images of mourning are Vigo's tear and the aggrieved countenances of parents and relatives whose sons have tumbled to their deaths in their quest for Junta and the blue light. The townspeople of Santa Maria mine the elemental and a woman, place them in lucrative ornamental shapes, and create a captivating story that glosses over their instrumental designs.

The elemental, the ornamental, and the instrumental come together in Santa Maria's cottage culture industry. Its offerings unite premodern sentiment and modern rationale in a manner that anticipates National Socialism's synthesis of romanticism and technology. The Nazis claimed to worship a world of nature and innocence. They devoted much effort, however, to recycling that nature and to molding it into new structures. The reshaping process accorded with larger agendas and reflected the workings of an instrumental rationality. It is precisely this third dimension, though, that often became mystified and disavowed. National Socialism, as we know from Ernst Bloch, recognized the mighty appeal of nonsynchronous sensibilities, thoughts out of keeping with modern realities, especially a romantic anticapitalism fueled by a discontent with contemporary civilization. One turned to an evocative past of simple peasants, open countrysides, and idyllic communities, utilizing "gothic dreams against proletarian realities," "needs and elements from past ages" of decisive value in the state's coordinated effort to capture the imaginations of its citizenry and to offer sustenance for their fantasy life.[69]

For all its idealized landscape painting and blood-and-soil rhetoric, German fascism pursued the domination over nature through a vast technology that extended from the rationalized way in which an entire country was organized to an elaborate bureaucratic mechanism to a military machine, a world war, and ultimately the death camps, vast factories that recycled bodies, pressing out of human material every possible commercial gain. The Third Reich practiced a reactionary mode of modernism, an instrumentalism blending the cultural system of the romantic past with the rationality of modern technology.[70] Riefenstahl's debut remains both instructive and provocative for us today as a film made during the Weimar era which prefigures Nazi fantasy production, as a film shrouded in the jargon of authenticity which, as a fictional text and a material object, enacts the dialectic of enlightenment.

Junta's metamorphosis destroys and recasts a female image; it reassembles her dead body and person in new structures. As Vigo leans over her limp shape in a translucent morning light, in a subjective shot that aligns the camera's perspective with that of the onscreen artist, Junta's physiognomy takes on a different appearance. The dead woman becomes a living legend, a popular memory and a popular story as well as a popular icon. The transformation divests her of independent life and forms what once was a continual disturbance and a constant source of anxiety into less disruptive shapes.[71] Vigo is a stand-in for the camera, an evil eye with a friendly face, an anti-Pygmalion who transforms the object of his erotic desire into an auratic image. If Riefenstahl resembles anyone in the film, it is the artist from Vienna who paints and pursues Junta, expropriating landscapes and

Vigo (Mathias Wieman) leans over the sleeping body of Junta like a vampire ready to strike; later he will assume the same pose as he beholds the mountain girl's corpse.

physiognomies with a marked regard for the aesthetic worth and commercial value of these raw materials.

Emanations of the Blue Light

In a crucial way, *The Blue Light* is a horror film, a film about a community's confrontation with the uncanny and a collective act of exorcism. Both the narrative and the reception history of Riefenstahl's debut feature reveal much about the dynamics behind the making and marketing of legends. *The Blue Light* was surely not made by Nazis. It was certainly seen by Nazis and applauded by Nazis. Indeed, Hitler was one of the film's earliest admirers. It has come to play a seminal role in the Third Reich's most famous director's dealings with her Nazi past. Riefenstahl's reclamation of the film as a lifescript falls into place with her concerted attempts over time to recast the film, from its production to its reception, in her own image. What began as the rendering of a local legend by a team, involving a director, scriptwriter, and cameraman, has become the product of a single formative influence, of an artist who provided the vision, the story, the dialogue, the images—in short, the entire production.[72] Revision and erasure have gone hand in hand with this *auteur*'s willful triumph, fostering a director's myth and the myth of a director while making for changing shades of meaning in the different emanations of *The Blue Light*.[73]

The reception history of *The Blue Light* follows twists and turns that boggle the mind. The film met with mixed reviews and lackluster box-office returns upon its initial German run in 1932. The *Film-Kurier* notice bore the headline "Zwei Legenden" and compared the film about Junta's legend unfavorably to a reprise of Chaplin's legendary feature, *The Gold Rush*. In Chaplin's silent masterpiece "everything speaks despite the lack of sound." In Riefenstahl's debut one "misses an ordering hand and a visual word. This work's world is not seen filmically, but rather photographically." For all its impressive images, the film lacked substance; it was "sick at the core" and "misbegotten."[74] Riefenstahl reputedly blamed Jewish critics for the film's devastating failure and railed against their inability to understand German culture.[75] She felt vindicated by foreign responses to the film, especially by the silver medal awarded her at the Venice Biennale in 1932. The film would also receive a gold medal at the Paris World Fair in 1937 and one in Venice in 1959 as a film classic.

In an effort to capitalize on *Olympia*'s massive success, *The Blue Light* was revived in September 1938. An interviewer in *Film-Kurier* attributed the film's initial German failure to "non-Aryan sectors," seconding the director's wish that her work might now enjoy the enthusiastic response "denied it earlier because of bad will and incomprehension."[76] The Degeto Kulturfilm version purged the names of Jewish coworkers, including the producer Harry Sokal and the coauthor Béla Balázs. Riefenstahl in fact had denied the latter any payment for his considerable work on the film, responding to Balázs' urgent inquiry with a note on Kaiserhof stationery: "I grant to Herr Gauleiter Julius Streicher of Nuremberg—publisher of *Der Stürmer*—power of attorney in matters of the claims of the Jew Béla Balázs on me."[77] The document signed in her hand belies the account in her *Memoir,* in which Riefenstahl describes how her "friend" Balázs wrote about his flight to Moscow after Hitler's rise to power, how she wept as she held his letter in her hand. "An ardent Communist, he wanted to remain in Russia for the time being."[78]

In 1951 Riefenstahl reassembled outtakes of the film, added a new score, redubbed the voices, and later rereleased *The Blue Light,* now shorn of its framing passages.[79] This reshaping of the narrative changes Riefenstahl's story. For without the prologue and coda, there remains no temporal distance between the premodern and the contemporary world. Instead, we now have a melancholy tale addressed to a timeless present. We see no tourists, no tourist industry. If any flashback now determines how we see *The Blue Light,* it is the filmmaker's retrospective reading of the film as a personal paradise lost: "As if it were a premonition, *The Blue Light* told of my ultimate fate: Junta, the strange mountain girl, living in a dream world, persecuted and driven out of society, dies because her ideals are destroyed."[80] Riefenstahl would seek to return to paradise and remine *The Blue Light* in projected (but unrealized) recastings of the source as a ballet and a remake with Pier Angeli as Junta and Laurence Harvey as Vigo.[81]

In October 1963, the director's first feature played in the Nuremberg Meistersingerhallen to resounding applause. Carl Müller, prominent owner of the Studio für Filmkunst in Bremen, described the event: "Hundreds couldn't get in . . . Rarely have I seen such an enthused audience . . . How often I heard people say, 'What a film!'—Why don't they make films like this anymore?"[82] *The Blue Light* endures as a masterpiece, a hallmark of Weimar—and German—cinema, an important title in a celebrated career, consequences of Riefenstahl's reevaluation by auteurists in the 1960s and 1970s, first in America, Great Britain, and France, then later in Germany.[83] The "Hitler-wave" in the Federal Republic of the mid- and late 1970s also led to renewed public fascination with Riefenstahl, on television, radio, and

An advertisement for *The Blue Light* from the 1930s blends the lure of the mountains, the countenance of a woman, and blood-and-soil iconography.

in the print media. With the appearance of her memoirs and Ray Müller's directorial portrait, the filmmaker and her myth yet again enthrall international audiences. *Time* deems *The Wonderful Horrible Life* perhaps "the last great Riefenstahl film."[84]

The first feature and the director's recollections relate the myth of a "wonderful horrible life," but let us not forget Leni Riefenstahl's considerable hand in the creation of these narratives that render her a victim of history, suggesting an equivalence between her fate and that of the Jews. The mountain girl's tragic destiny is both the product of a script and a director's *mise en scène,* for Riefenstahl stood both in front of *and* behind the camera. She conceived Junta as an embodiment of purity, "a young girl, intact and innocent, whom fear made retract at any contact with reality, with matter, with sex."[85] Junta's cavern has a vaginal opening and its interior is a womblike space. The grotto will be violated, and so too will be Junta. The story, relates the filmmaker, came to her in a violent dream: "I watched her being chased and pelted with stones, and finally I dreamed of this girl as she fell away from a wall of rock and slowly plunged into the depths."[86] The child of nature becomes the film's quarry. The camera constantly stalks Junta, exposing her figure, caressing her face, fetishizing her body with filters, soft-focus lighting, and striking compositions: it literally loves her to death. Riefenstahl assumes a double role, actress in a punitive fantasy in which she acts upon herself, at once victim and victimizer, masochist and sadist, both the object and the agent of violence.

In her only other feature film, *Tiefland* (*Lowlands,* 1954), Riefenstahl also assumes the female lead role, focusing on the itinerant dancer Marta as the hapless object of erotic desire and repeated rape. Here too the director commingles voyeurism and exhibitionism, capturing the fascinated and lusty reactions of male audiences to Riefenstahl's onscreen presence and replicating their lecherous gaze with a camera that feasts on her own body's movements. Helma Sanders-Brahms has recently urged that *Lowlands* be read as Riefenstahl's attempt at self-rehabilitation. Don Sebastian is "the wolf," an obvious Hitler-surrogate; the film shows how a woman makes herself available to the tyrant and comes to recognize the error of her ways and to resist her tormentor.[87] Even if this interpretation sounds plausible, one should bear in mind that the film, though shot during the war, was not completed until 1954. For all its putative resistant energy, *Lowlands* still relishes yet another Riefenstahl persona who is patently helpless, indeed subservient to male power. Marta submits to the Marquis "as though in a trance"[88] and can free herself from the malevolent lord only through the intervention of her nature-boy lover. Riefenstahl's work, both onscreen and in writing, abounds in moments in which she makes a spectacle of her own suffering.[89]

A film about the sacrifice of a woman for the sake of a community, *The Blue Light* endeared Riefenstahl to the man who would become Führer. "Once we come to power," Hitler reputedly said to Riefenstahl when they first met in 1932, "you must make my films."[90] Her mountain girl was made to measure for soldier males; for here, as Gisela von Wysocki observes, one found "the beautiful soul, purity of desire, a self-effacing, purpose-free essence. Her body is yearning and image. In the connotations of the age it becomes a monstrous surface for fascist propaganda, erected against the equality of the sexes, against prostitution in the big cities, against the 'degeneration' of the modern woman."[91] Riefenstahl would put her person and her image at the disposal of the state leadership and the Nazi party.[92] She focused on the new man marching in front of the camera while disavowing her own person behind the camera. Repeatedly she has claimed that she staged nothing and just let events speak for themselves.[93]

The Führer's "perfect woman"[94] was also Nazi Germany's most celebrated filmmaker. (Only two other women, Thea von Harbou and Else Wegener, directed features in the Third Reich.) To describe Riefenstahl as the "most powerful woman in German fascism," however, is both accurate and misleading, for that status came at the price of servitude to a male order and a denigration of female volition.[95] Riefenstahl had little to do with other women; she resolutely steered clear of Nazi Germany's female organizations. Belonging to a woman's world, according to Margarete Mitscherlich, "would not have brought her sufficient glory or fame." Together with the *Herrenmenschen* of the Thousand-Year Reich, she both despised and deprecated women: "Femininity in its real physical materiality held no attraction for her."[96] Riefenstahl's fixation on masculine might, then, is of a piece with her documentary images of women who stand on the sidelines cheering the men who make history, as well as her feature film enactments of female suffering. It stands to reason that the director's most important work celebrates the triumph of male will.

The same film that provided Riefenstahl a ticket of admission to the new order would be used, after the war, as an identity card to clear her from charges of Nazi collaboration. Riefenstahl maintains she only served the cause of beauty, an artistry and an authorship outside of time and beyond any political or religious persuasion. Of course, strength and beauty are anything but immutable categories. Béla Balázs, Riefenstahl's erstwhile

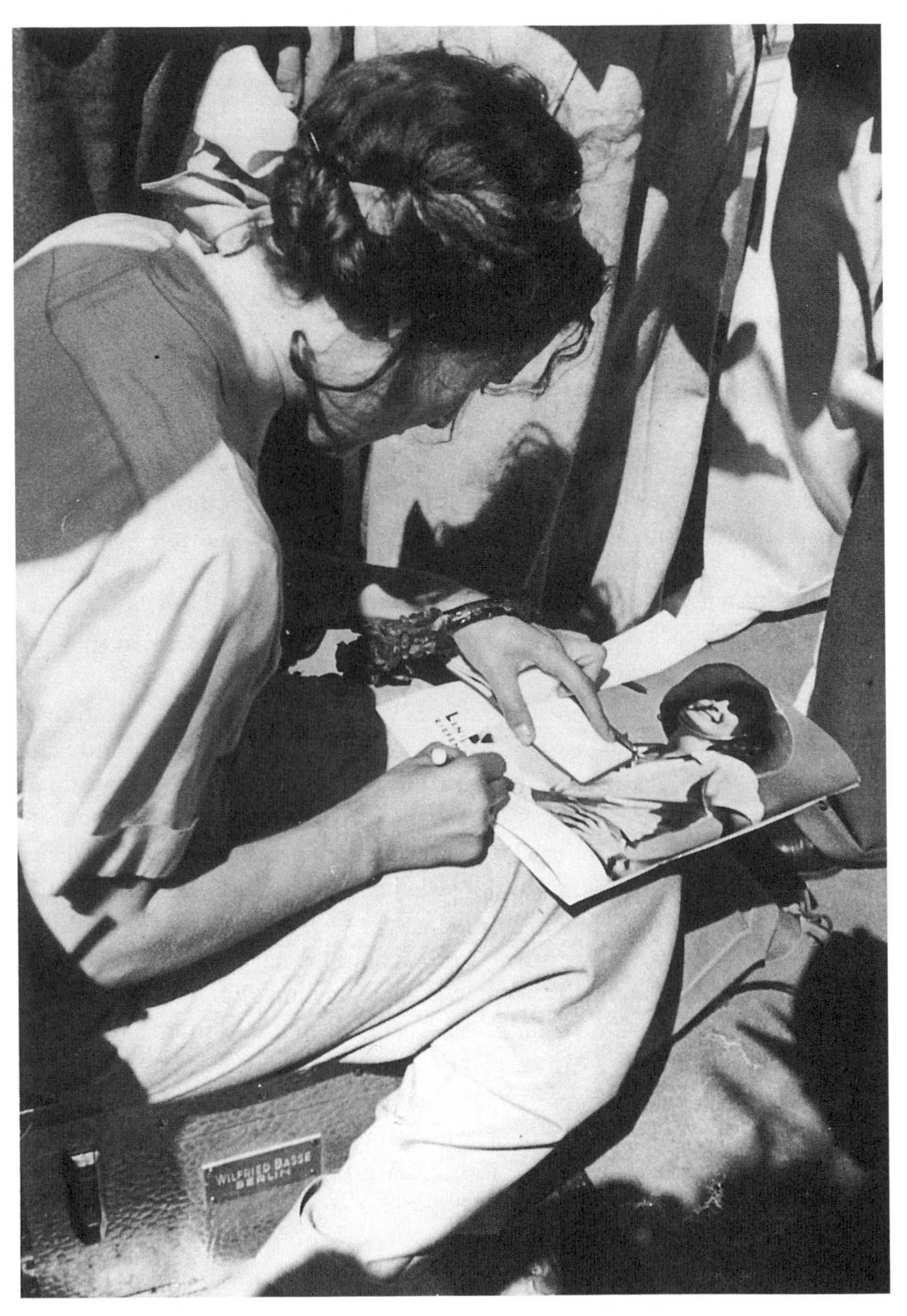

"Leni Riefenstahl does not care about ideas. She reacts to life as though it were a pageant in which we are all engaged to play particular and inevitable roles" (Robert Gardner).

collaborator, knew this well. Beauty for him was not an absolute, an unchanging, ahistorical, "objective reality." Rather, it represented "a subjective experience of human consciousness" and was a function of different "races, epochs and cultures."[97] The Nazis knew this as well. During the Third Reich, beauty played a central role in the party's aesthetics as well as in its racial politics and medical policies. While Riefenstahl sat at an editing table reworking the sublime physiques from the Berlin games, the afflicted physiognomies of the sick and mentally ill from *Opfer der Vergangenheit* (*Victims of the Past,* 1937) confronted viewers in German cinemas. Nazism's ideals of physical strength and beauty were inextricably bound to its disdain for degenerate, diseased, and disabled bodies.[98]

Nazi Germany's most prominent filmmaker remains its preeminent survivor. Like many other artists who worked during the Hitler era, the director denies her role in history and declares that her endeavors stand outside of time. International cineastes likewise claim that her rightful place is in the pantheon of cinema's immortals.[99] National Socialist leaders often spoke of art's eternal power and of film's timeless aesthetics while enlisting artists and filmmakers in political campaigns and historical missions. The task of the artist, Goebbels said in 1937, lay in capturing life, in shaping, concentrating, and compressing it in expressive forms: "Art is nothing other than the shaper of emotion. It comes from emotion and not from the intellect; the artist is nothing other than the person who grants meaning to this emotion. He differs from normal human beings not because he has emotion, but because he has the power to impart form to feelings."[100] Leni Riefenstahl's art fulfilled a timely service by imparting form to *völkisch* feelings. It created beautiful images that fueled Nazi fantasies, images of heroic men and subservient women.

As a work of art and an artifact, *The Blue Light* anticipates and embodies the operations of the cinematic machine under National Socialism. It illustrates the continuing attraction of that machine and its central movers to this very day. The feature film has been enlisted as the key document in Riefenstahl's revisionist fiction; the personal myth of an unknowing and innocent artist has reappeared as a multimedia event and a mass-market recollection. In this melodramatic spectacle, shaped by Riefenstahl, endorsed by influential critics, followed by audiences throughout the world, the famous Nazi insider has reemerged as the Third Reich's most celebrated outcast.

"Never had a song sounded like this song. Never had a path led into the distance like this one. The head knew nothing more of the legs. There was no burden. The eye was everything. Everything was image. The march was sound, a noise, a joyous stream" (Karl Aloys Schenzinger).

TWO

Emotional Engineering: *Hitler Youth Quex* (1933)

Action does not mean "deciding in favor of" . . . for that presupposes that one knows in favor of what one is deciding; rather, action means "setting off in a direction," "taking sides," by virtue of a mandate of destiny, by virtue of "one's own right" . . . It is really secondary to decide in favor of something that I have come to know.

Alfred Bäumler

There in the bleak, gray twilight, yellowed, tortured eyes stare into the emptiness. His tender head has been trampled into a bloody pulp. Long, deep wounds extend down the slender body, and a deadly laceration tears through his lungs and heart . . . Yet it is as if life stirs anew out of pale death. Look now, the slender, elegant body begins to move. Slowly, slowly he rises as if conjured up by magic, until he stands tall in all his youthful glory right before my trembling eyes. And without moving his lips, a frail child's voice is heard as if speaking from all eternity . . . "What is mortal in me will perish. But my spirit, which is immortal, will remain with you. And it . . . will show you the way."

Joseph Goebbels

Mediating the New Order

Hitlerjunge Quex (Hitler Youth Quex), like *The Blue Light,* is a legend for modern times, a film with a fatal attraction.[1] It sanctifies an adolescent's heroic deed, reshaping a young boy's dead body into an icon. It demonstrates a cinema of clear lines and straightforward answers, a medium charged with a mission: it aims to *show* the way. The film illustrates a political process and intimates a master narrative wherein human subjects become state objects and living beings give way to abstract patterns. *Hitler*

Youth Quex both heralds a new order and prefigures its subsequent self-destruction.[2]

The first feature film substantially supported by the new government and produced under the protectorate of the youth leader of the German Reich, Baldur von Schirach, *Hitler Youth Quex* offers a stirring example of how the National Socialists employed a modern medium for state purposes, occupying a vast technology to craft gripping narratives and promote popular legends. Goebbels well recognized film's potential value as a political instrument when he became minister of popular enlightenment and propaganda in March 1933.[3] Nonetheless, a comprehensive policy did not immediately manifest itself in the declarations of the self-avowed "passionate lover of filmic art."[4] Being in power did not mean controlling culture; swift legislation could not ensure overnight legitimation; any campaign of coordination *(Gleichschaltung)* would demand different strategies on different fronts.

The National Socialists had become the masters of public life. Whether they would also become the masters of popular imagination remained to be seen.[5] The minister entered the scene with a mixture of swagger and circumspection, proclaiming a desire to combat a spiritual crisis and "reform German film from the ground up." In his early programmatic declarations, Goebbels blended natural and martial metaphors, speaking of film as a body and a territorial surface, declaring himself the physician whose surgery would purge an afflicted organism of harmful alien elements.[6] He scorned wishy-washy entertainments without national character, clear contours, and a sense of the historical moment. A new cinema for a new Germany must rediscover the innate laws of the medium and realize its mission as a mover of masses. "It takes imagination," he proclaimed, "to grant life to the innermost purpose and innermost constitution of a new world."[7]

Repeatedly, Goebbels stressed that film should exercise a discernible effect, that it must act on hearts and minds. Its calling should be that of a popular art *(Volkskunst),* an art that simultaneously served state purposes and fulfilled personal needs. The new film must free itself from *l'art pour l'art* dalliance, intellectual liberalism, and wanton commercialism. However makeshift and ambiguous his first proclamations might have seemed (they apparently made for some confusion), Goebbels pointed the way to a popular, contemporary, and distinctly national cinema.[8] Film, he proclaimed, should emanate from political life and find its way to the deepest recesses of German soul and soil. Such a reform would take time and would demand energy and sensitivity. It made no sense to enforce an authoritarian dogmatism, to "proselytize from morning till night."[9] Political ideas must assume aesthetic forms. That did not mean reenacting parades and spectacles, photographing marching storm troopers, and fetishizing flags and emblems. "Arousing the masses, that's something we know a thing or two about," Goebbels boasted, and in so doing set aside a special place for film apart from mass rallies and overt agitation. Mere loyalty to the party would not guarantee success. Authentic film art must transcend the everyday and "intensify life."[10]

Hitler Youth Quex did precisely that, intensifying life to the point of devivification. It focused on a human subject and transformed him into a political property. The film remade and ultimately overcame a boy's mind and body, rendering the material spiritual, transmuting being into form. This process involved the occupation of a real-life destiny and its orchestrated functionalization by the mass media. Herbert Norkus, a Hitler Youth in the Berlin working-class district Beuselkietz, had died at the hands of Communist assailants while distributing leaflets during the election of January 1932. Quickly enlisted as a Nazi martyr, Norkus became the subject of impassioned editorials and inspirational public addresses. Memorial services for the boy occasioned elaborate marches and demonstrations throughout Germany. His death received annual consecration on 24 January, a date of ritual observance during the Third Reich for all fallen Hitler Youths.[11]

These recognitions accompanied a wide range of popular renderings: novels, plays, poems, and songs.[12] Karl Aloys Schenzinger immortalized Norkus in *Der Hitlerjunge Quex,* a novel written between May and September 1932 and prepublished in installments in the Nazi party organ, the *Völkischer Beobachter,* before the book's release in December. The volume would become obligatory reading for Germany's youth, undergoing innumerable editions, registering sales of more than half a million copies by 1945.[13] Soon after Schenzinger's novel appeared, Ufa announced plans for a film version directed by Hans Steinhoff and produced by Karl Ritter, a project actively supported by the NSDAP leadership.

The premiere took place in the Munich Ufa-Phoebus-Palast on 11 September 1933, a festive event attended by party dignitaries (including Hitler, Göring, and Hess) and accompanied by a gala performance of Anton Bruckner's Fourth Symphony by the eighty members of the Reich Symphony Orchestra.[14] The film received the rating "artistically especially worthwhile," prompting words of praise from Goebbels, who wrote the prominent Ufa executive Ernst Hugo Correll: "If *Hitler Youth Quex* represents the first large-scale attempt to depict the ideas and world of National Socialism with the art of cinema, then one must say that this attempt, given the possibilities of modern technology, is a full-fledged success."[15] Germany's greatest film company, proclaimed the *Lichtbild-Bühne* on 12 September, had mobilized "its extraordinary technical, material, and artistic means" to create "a lasting document of human and social circumstances, of the spiritual and emotional impulses that brought about the turn in Germany's history."[16] The film likewise met with a degree of commercial success, even if it did not match that of the more popular contemporaneous Ufa productions directed by Gustav Ucicky, *Morgenrot (Dawn)* and *Flüchtlinge (Fugitives)*. Having cost a modest 320,000 RM (an amount slightly above average for the time), it ran for fifteen days in the massive Ufa-Palast am Zoo, and by the end of January 1934 had attracted over a million viewers.[17]

Like the two other feature films screened in 1933 which portrayed party martyrs, *SA-Mann Brand* and *Hans Westmar, Hitler Youth Quex* unfolds as a family drama against the political and economic crisis of the late Weimar years.[18] Heini Völker, a printer's apprentice, joins a Communist youth group at the prompting of his father, an unemployed worker and war veteran, a choleric drinker who torments his mournful wife. Heini quickly becomes disenchanted with the unruly comrades during a weekend outing and flees their alcoholic and sexual revelry. Retreating into the woods, he spies a group of Hitler Youths and looks on their nighttime ceremony with fascination, an interest undiminished even after the Nazis discover him and send him away. He returns to Berlin effusing about their discipline and order, singing their anthem to his mother and causing his father to scold and beat him. Despite this outburst and the encouragement of the Communist leader, Stoppel, Heini seeks out the young Nazis Fritz and Ulla. He refuses to participate in a Communist raid on the new Hitler Youth dormitory, but cannot fully convince the Nazis of his good faith until he warns them that Stoppel and his group plan to bomb the new hostel. Mother Völker, confronted by an enraged Stoppel after the Communist plot backfires, fears for her son but does not know how to protect him. In desperation, she turns on the gas to put an end to both herself and the sleeping boy.

After awakening in a hospital, Heini finds himself surrounded by a group of Hitler Youths who express their gratitude and present him with a uniform and a mirror. As a result of his mother's death and his father's submission to the special plea of the HJ Group Leader Cass, Heini moves into a Nazi dormitory. Active and energetic (so much so that his alacrity gains the nickname "Quex" (quicksilver), Heini works all night to print leaflets for the upcoming election and insists on distributing them in his old neighborhood, Beuselkitz. Members of Stoppel's group, headed by the vicious Wilde, learn of Heini's presence and chase him through the streets, cornering him in a fairground, where Wilde stabs him with the knife once coveted by Heini. When his Nazi cohorts reach him, it is too late. With his last breath Heini gestures upward and utters the words, "Our flag flutters before us, it leads . . ." as the image segues into a close-up of a party banner over which marching figures parade in geometric configurations.

"Make Way, You Old Men!"

Herbert Norkus was resurrected in the form of a boy who overcomes his own past and the internationalism inherent in the name of his father. Heini "Völker" is a servant of the German *Volk,* a hero who responds to a *völkisch* calling and a historical mission.[19] He resembles spirited comrades in arms who, possessed by patriotic fervor, fell in droves during the first months of World War I, a shared martyrdom made explicit in a contemporary press booklet: "Hunted down by the commune and caught, he [Heini] dies the sacrificial death of German youth, just as an earlier generation died before him at Langemarck, death for the sake of the new fatherland."[20] The film narrative depicts how Heini becomes a Hitler Youth, how human material *(Völker)* becomes expediency incarnate ("Quex"), a vehicle of transport and tempo, a political medium.[21] Quex's last words strike up a triumphant song and give way to a rousing march, a symphonic conclusion and an invitation to a dance of death.[22]

Nazi cinema originated as a site of transformation, an art and technology implemented to engineer emotion, to create a new man—and to recreate woman in the service of the new order and the new man. The different being envisioned here was an amalgam of vitalism and irrationality, a creature longing for spiritual rebirth, for ecstatic life undaunted by cerebration. In some respects, *Hitler Youth Quex* reached back to expressionist scenarios, the *Wandlungsdramen* of Ernst Toller, Georg Kaiser, and Ernst Barlach, plays in which angry sons rebel against tradition, confronting and even murdering their fathers, forsaking the bourgeois family in a search for more fulfilling communal ties. In both instances we find essentialized emotions, the pathos of what Gottfried Benn called a "constructive mind."[23] "Facts, things, feelings, and persons do not exist for it in their own right, but only as parts in a working relationship to other parts. Even as content gives way to form, the concept of 'being' yields to the concept of 'functioning.' "[24] Similarly, the influential right-wing author Ernst Jünger valorized objectified human bodies. His new man relinquishes existence as an individual, steeling blood and brains into the reified technical potential of the "type" *(Typus)*.[25] *Hitler Youth Quex* puts a hero into motion by inhabiting his person, dissolving his family, and arresting his life. Heini becomes a part of a larger whole and thereby whole in his existence as a part.[26] He functions as a role model, for his comrades in the film, for the many young Germans who watched this film.

Cinema assumed a key place within state institutions of discipline, figuring as a mode of education, military training, and recreation. Film, claimed Nazi Minister of Education Bernhard Rust in 1934,

> is particularly important for our youngest citizens—the schoolchildren. Film must not only help them grasp contemporary political problems; it must also provide children knowledge about Germany's great past, and profound understanding regarding the future development of the Third Reich. The National Socialist State definitely and deliberately makes film the transmitter of its ideology.[27]

National Socialism sought to organize the will of youth, to enlist it in a historical mission. In challenging established authority, the party meant to usurp the place held by ineffective leaders of a moribund generation, in effect to proclaim, as Gregor Strasser did in 1933, "Make way, you old men!"[28] The NSDAP institutionalized Oedipal revolt, directing the young against "the parental home, church, school, and other outdated forms and role models. In its youth organizations it assumed the central role in the rebellion of sons against their fathers."[29]

Forgoing the Oedipal triangulation characteristic of the classical narrative, *Hitler Youth Quex* begins only as a family drama; by its end both parents have disappeared, the dead mother briefly mourned,[30] the father having surrendered his son to the brigade leader.[31] The party supersedes the family and bridges classes. Fritz and Ulla live in a decidedly bourgeois household, but their parents are nowhere to be seen, and their upper-middle-class background in no way conflicts with their newfound political identity. Hitler's order redefines family and social configurations to become the dominant source of allegiance. (Elsewhere, the Nazi government may have paid lip service to the role of the family. Nonetheless, it "simultaneously deprived parents of the qualities on which a child's respect might have been founded.")[32] The film's project, in short, was to fabricate a new political subject by redirecting identification.[33] It provided a cinematic

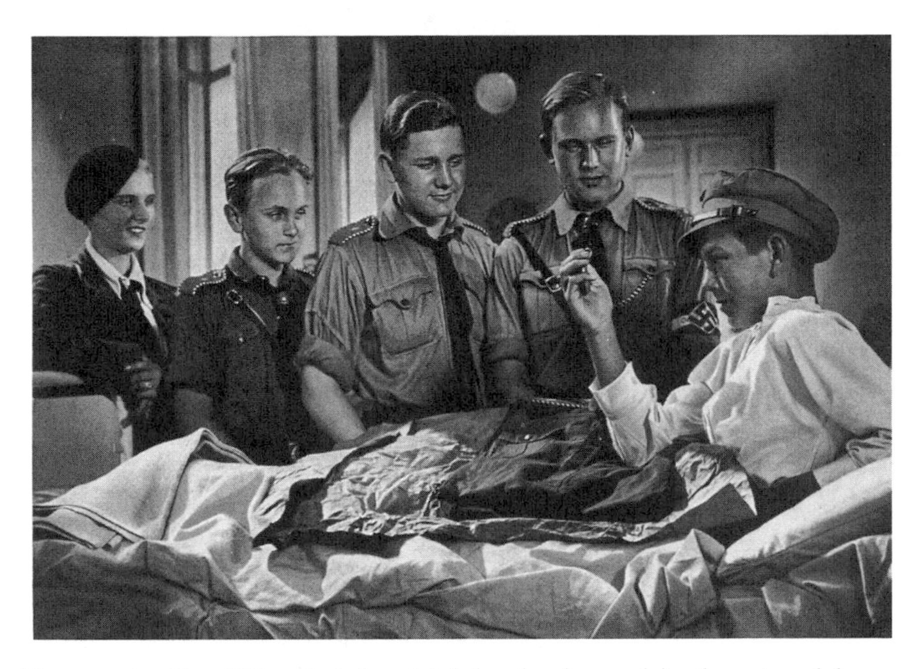

No sooner has Frau Völker died of gas inhalation than her son joins the party and dons a Hitler Youth uniform. The *Mütze* (cap) replaces the *Mutter*.

Bildungsroman that aimed to rebuild the youth of a nation.[34] A movement occupied an individual in the hope of overcoming masses, fashioning images of self-alienation so compelling that an entire generation could, as Walter Benjamin put it, "experience its own destruction as an aesthetic pleasure of the first order."[35]

Crucial to Heini's evolution is the acquisition of an ersatz ego, a sense of self derived not from parents but from a party. Quex's new vocation also demands he forsake sensual pleasure and sexual desire. Grundler, his roommate in the Nazi hostel, puffs on a cigarette and makes suggestive comments about Ulla. "You're one fine comrade," retorts Heini, setting himself apart from such intemperance, aligning himself with the otherwise unsullied ranks of Hitler Youth. Grundler plays a song from an escapist film about bawdy sailors which was composed by a Jewish artist.[36] Heini sings of a flag and a party. One will betray his comrades; the other will die for a cause. Aesthetic preferences, the film intimates, mark one's person and define one's very being.

The Communists constitute, as Gregory Bateson has noted, a structured and systematic counterpart to the Nazis. Communist dissolution and lack of discipline stand in direct opposition to Nazi containment and resolve.[37] While Stoppel and his cohorts drink, gamble, and carry on, the Hitler Youths stand solemnly before a campfire and honor the summer solstice. Heini denies the sexual innuendoes of Gerda and rejects her advances. Grundler submits to physical temptation, shirking his duty and betraying the cause. Heini, at his most self-indulgent, enjoys a comradely kiss from Ulla and sips a mug of beer with Cass. Coming into his own, though, means steeling the body and hardening the will, suppressing physical attachments and all-too-human desires.

Heini is first drawn to the party when he witnesses a nocturnal spectacle and experiences an immediate and intense fascination. Similarly, youngsters who partook of this film found themselves overcome by its audiovisual enticements. Bernhard K., ten years old when he first saw *Hitler Youth Quex* in 1933, could vividly recall the film many decades later:

> Communist youths were shown. All of them dressed like ruffians. Unsavory figures. Then they set up camp and even girls were with them. Everything was really disgusting. The Hitler Youth on the other hand: all dressed the same, clean, nice, with leaders who had everything under control. I still remember today that after the film we all agreed: the Nazis made an altogether great impression, there was discipline, we wanted to join in. The Communists, on the other hand, no, our parents would never have let us be part of a bunch like that.[38]

Just as Heini is overcome by the sights and sounds of a new order, so too did this filmic dramatization seek to overwhelm its young viewers, to shape them into captive audiences.[39]

The Fairground and the Forest

The opening sequence of *Hitler Youth Quex* fixes on a street, a space governed by crime, chaos, and mass contagion, offering images well known to audiences of 1933. The shots portray an askew world in which a youth's attempt to steal an apple and a shopkeeper's angry reaction ignite a political spectacle: debates among bystanders and expressions of outrage, the quick opportunism of Communist rabble-rousers, whose agitation causes a riot necessitating police intervention. The iconography here consciously evokes memories of Zille films by Gerhard Lamprecht such as *Die Verrufenen* (*Slums of Berlin,* 1925) and *Die Unehelichen* (*Children of No Importance,*

1926), as well as proletarian dramas derived from Soviet models such as *Mutter Krausens Fahrt ins Glück* (*Mother Krause's Trip to Happiness,* 1929) and *Kuhle Wampe* (1932).[40] Steinhoff's direction seems quite insistent about its reliance on Weimar's cinematic legacy, borrowing as well from *Berlin-Alexanderplatz* (1931), *M* (1931), and *Die 3-Groschen-Oper* (*The Threepenny Opera,* 1931).

Hans Steinhoff's career as a filmmaker stretched back to the early 1920s; he had worked in numerous generic veins, gaining respect (if not inordinate admiration) for his technical precision, skillful handling of players, and careful crafting of dramatic materials.[41] Cameraman Konstantin Irmin-Tschet likewise had worked on famous Ufa films directed by, among others, Fritz Lang, Robert Siodmak, and Wilhelm Thiele. How are we to understand the film's recourse to Weimar cinema, given the National Socialists' dim view of most *Systemzeit* features[42] and Goebbels' firm desire to replace them with a new German film—as well as the unequivocal party allegiance of both Steinhoff and production head Karl Ritter?[43]

Previous accounts of *Hitler Youth Quex* stress how it brings together conservative images and left-wing impulses, blending Hugenberg and Münzenberg. The Ufa film evokes the atmospheric urban venues of Weimar and revisits working-class spaces: narrow apartments, smoky pubs, joyless streets.[44] Carryovers also inhere at the levels of theme, motif, and dramaturgy, be it an obsession with knives and a pursuit scene straight out of *M*, or the fairground barker and his gruesome ballad, which recall *The Threepenny Opera.* Heini's family seems lifted from films made by Phil Jutzi, who directed both *Mother Krause's Trip to Happiness* and *Berlin-Alexanderplatz.* His father is a latterday Franz Biberkopf, a disabled individual for whom class consciousness offers little succor;[45] his mother, like Mutter Krause, turns on the gas to take leave of her misery.[46] These familiar elements allowed audiences convenient points of reference. Critics typically speak of an artistic continuity with Weimar film, coming to conclusions like that of Courtade and Cadars: "If one puts all ideology aside, which surely is not easy, then one must say that from a technical and aesthetic perspective *Hitler Youth Quex* is an outstanding film."[47]

What people have tended to obscure in their catalogues of intertexts, however, is that most of Steinhoff's borrowings are negatively charged. *Hitler Youth Quex* retreads memories in order to clear the way. It overcomes a past of inflation and despair and points to a hopeful future; in reckoning with Weimar film, it presages a new cinema. It recycles proletarian films by Jutzi, Brecht, and Dudow, remaking Herta Thiele's confident and sensual

Anni of *Kuhle Wampe* into the de-eroticized Hitler *Mädel* Ulla. It also draws on Lang and Pabst, at the same time pursuing a strategy meant to transcend Weimar cinema in the name of a higher film art.[48]

Central to the structure of *Hitler Youth Quex* are two spaces and the fascination they contain for Heini, namely the fairground and the forest. Going back as far as *Das Cabinet des Dr. Caligari* (*The Cabinet of Dr. Caligari,* 1920), the fairground recurs throughout Weimar film as a privileged site of agitation, spectacle, and desire, a realm of motion and excitement, a proto-cinematic cult of distraction.[49] The carnival ground—described in Schenzinger's novel as "a truly fantastic world"[50]—initially lures Heini with its attractions and games of chance. It is here where he glimpses a knife with eight blades, an object that will repeatedly appear during the film. It is here where the Communist Stoppel seeks to win over the boy and where the vampish Gerda makes her rounds, whirling on the carousel and later seducing Grundler. It is here where Heini will die. The fairground becomes a realm of sex, peril, and dissolution, a province of impermanence and intoxication. The film presents the fairground as a locus of illicit sights and sounds, leaving no doubt that the Communists are quite at home in this world of uncertainty.

The Communists do not, however, control the fairground. They lack a distinctive formal will and a spectacle of their own making. Whether partaking of carnival attractions or mimicking Nazi gestures, the group attests to an absence of substance and identity.[51] Stoppel and his cohorts recreate the fairground in the forest, transforming nature into a site of cardplaying, sexual dalliance, and rampant consumption. Heini flees into the woods to abandon amorphous masses and cluttered images, seeking fresh air and open space. Gradually the commune's accordion gives way to brass fanfares and a song, a strident tempo and spirited lyrics. Curious, Heini follows the sound, stopping behind a bush to look down on neat rows of boys and girls standing about a fire, listening to their leader hallow rising flames and celebrate a better Germany. The natural setting and human ornament merge; this is a spectacle that rivets Heini's gaze, a ceremony with an impressive composition, a striking choreography, a binding power.[52] If the Communists contaminate nature, the Nazis contain it. The forest no longer appears as an extended fairground, but rather takes on the countenance of a training camp.[53] It is not nature, but an extremely domesticated nature that overwhelms Heini, a mass shaped as a larger body, compact columns of human potential, energy, and purpose fueled by a mysterious force.[54] When he later seeks to recount his experience, the boy can only describe physical

"The forest (the 'German' forest) seems to have provided a model for the formation of the ornamented fascist mass. The forest was the shaped desire of German men, teeming woman/nature brought to order. In the forest, the *sons* were united as 'members' of the rank-and-file" (Klaus Theweleit).

activity and recite the words of a song about a flag and a movement. Sights and sounds, not argument and rhetoric, have won him over.

The Personal Touch

In 1938 the Museum of Modern Art acquired a copy of *Hitler Youth Quex* from the Reichsfilmarchiv. During World War II the prominent ethnographer Gregory Bateson undertook a close thematic reading of the film as part of an endeavor to comprehend National Socialism through its cinematic self-depictions. Bateson recognized that the lies of propaganda also contain distinct truths, that "this film, insofar as it is an integrated work of art . . . must tell us about the psychology of its makers, and tell us perhaps more than they intended to tell."[55] Approaching the film with "the sort of analysis that the anthropologist applies to the mythology of a primitive or modern people," Bateson pointed out how the film, in its systematic structuring of oppositions between the NSDAP and KPD, illustrates the projective workings of Nazi subjectivity. Communists appear as unbearable self-images, what Nazis think they "would be like without their discipline or—psychologically speaking—what they *are* like under the veneer of that discipline."[56] Sensitive to how the film carries out its ideological agenda within a narrative setting, Bateson recognized its rhetorical power. Aside from a few brief comments about lighting contrasts and visual motifs, however, his thematic analysis had little to say about matters of form.[57]

Most subsequent discussions of *Hitler Youth Quex* speak of the film as overt propaganda, as a dramatization of "the struggle for the German soul between National Socialism and Communism."[58] Similar to the contemporaneous *SA-Mann Brand* and *Hans Westmar,* claims David Welch, *Hitler Youth Quex* embodies the "lie direct," that is, "film is exploited entirely for propaganda purposes; there are no subtle pretensions of mixing art with politics."[59] Given what he considers a lack of refinement, Welch finds no need to address questions of representation or to distinguish between propaganda and ideology.[60] Nor is visual acumen necessary. The message is clear; we need only to listen: "From start to finish, the National Socialist ideology is loudly and unashamedly proclaimed."[61]

Welch's procedure resembles Anglo-American wartime responses to Nazi propaganda. Commentators spoke of it as primitive and unrefined, readily transparent to anyone endowed with common sense. As Thomas Doherty demonstrates, American wartime audiences "were educated to the ideological power of mass communications, flattered over their superior powers of apprehension, and assured of their democratic immunity to the falsehoods of Axis enticements." Nazi ideologues were seen as clumsy and obvious, incapable of duping a more sophisticated American public. Hollywood productions of the 1940s represented German ploys as risible and flat-footed, assuming "a condescending and professorial tone when addressing its poor relations in mass communications. Look, the screen seemed to say, see how amateurish are the tricks, how easily exposed are the secrets, of these lesser media, so prone to manipulation and cheap effects."[62] *Divide and Conquer,* a Warner Brothers short of 1943, asserted that a Nazi media con-man was no match for a movie-conscious American: "You are up to his tricks. You can see through his technique."[63] This brash strategy, meant to build public confidence, surely had its justification in the context of a world war. In our present setting, however, such smugness becomes an interpretive disability that blinds the viewer to textual subtleties.

Commentators repeatedly dwell on the confrontation between Brigade

Leader Cass and Herr Völker as the film's "key scene," a showdown in which former class enemies "fight for the young hero's mind."[64] These analyses concentrate on the dialogue, dealing with the film as if it were a written script. We read nothing about composition, blocking, gesture, about the visual surface of the text in question.[65] This "key scene" likewise seems to stand in isolation. We gain no precise sense of its place in a larger narrative structure. Here Nazi propaganda would seem to speak forthrightly and apodictically. As Klaus Theweleit reminds us, though, we dare not dwell solely on what fascist language "says"; we need to comprehend how it functions.[66] If anything, the scene in question and the narrative as a whole rely more strongly on tactile rather than verbal persuasion. The film appeals to a feeling rather than a thinking spectator. If the party member prevails, it is not because of what he says, but because of how he speaks. And what convinces is the personal touch.

A closer look at the famous confrontation bears this out, a scene of nine shots lasting a little more than three minutes.[67] The convalescing Heini, dressed in pajamas and bearing a cane, sits on a park bench (shot #322). We cut to Herr Völker and Cass walking toward him (#323), moving to a closer view of them as they approach the boy (#324). The two enter the frame to greet Heini in a complex shot that lasts almost seventy-five seconds (#325). Initially, Heini stands to the right of his father and Cass; Völker then moves aside as Heini shakes hands with the *Bannführer*. The youth's question, "Where am I to go?" in essence reiterates the compositional dilemma. The father, who has turned his back, spins around, insisting the boy belongs with him. "*That* is the question," retorts Cass as the camera changes its position to exclude the father from the frame, thereby anticipating the scene's final outcome.

Cass and Heini sit down on a bench. "Where does the boy belong today?" the brigade leader asks, going on to effuse about the wanderlust of youth. "Boys are something wonderful!" he rejoices, his homoerotic enthusiasm undeniable.[68] The camera lingers for a long while in a close-up of Cass's animated face, panning to capture Heini's transfixed response. "Where does the boy belong?" repeats Cass. We pan right from Heini to his father, who peers at his now offscreen son; the camera then dollies back to give us a two-shot of Herr Völker and his son. Heini, though, is elsewhere, contemplating a faraway world, coming to himself only when his father elbows him and bids him speak.

After his initial question, Heini remains silent for the duration of the scene, positioned between the two adults as they square off in a physical confrontation. While Herr Völker hunches down, his hands tightly gripping a hat between his legs, he articulates the body language of someone diminished and depleted, paralyzed by the past (#327–328). The camera cuts to a two-shot of father and progeny (#329), displaying wounded sons of Germany in need of help. The scene's climactic take (#330) lasts forty-five seconds. Reversing angles, the camera cuts to a vantage point behind the bench, realigning itself so that the offscreen viewer experiences the showdown from Heini's perspective. Both men stand up during the face-off: Cass confident, hands in pocket, his voice controlled; Völker huffy, limbs taut, expression grim. Cass belittles Völker's Communist allegiances, his comrades, the International. The *Bannführer* asserts his superiority, commanding the frame, casting a shadow and looking down on Völker, physically and verbally harassing his opponent, asking him where he was born, in what city, in what country. His face brightly contoured by the light, Cass repeats the ultimate answer as an irrevocable truth ("In Germany, that's right!"), his fingers moving back and forth between himself and his interlocutor: "In *our* Germany!" His hand reaches out and repeatedly taps Völker on the chest: "Think about that, why don't you!"[69]

A hand reaches out and touches a listener. A compelling presence provides a role model for Heini, a better self-image for Herr Völker, a point of orientation for the offscreen viewer. A subsequent scene, another prolonged take, bears out just how strong an impression Cass has made (#335). Speaking over beer with Stoppel, Völker repeats the *Bannführer*'s catechism, but also, more importantly, assumes Cass's compositional place and reenacts his persuasive performance. Völker's gaze is now firm, his manner confident. He confronts an interlocutor with a challenge whose impact goes beyond words and logic, whose ultimate effect is that of a physical demonstration. He, like his son, is won over and transformed, recast in the image of a new Germany.[70] Stoppel also takes pause. Later we see him with a copy of the Social Democratic *Vorwärts,* suggesting at least a partial shift of political allegiance. In the end, likewise, he warns Heini and sidetracks the boy's pursuers.

We dare not underestimate the formal surfaces and visual strategies of Nazi films, even in the case of one of its most undeniably propagandistic productions. Goebbels and directors such as Steinhoff understood well the power of images, how they could stir imaginations and activate emotions. "The camera is the star among the film studio's equipment," cinematographer Konstantin Irmin-Tschet would later write; "it stands at that pinnacle of perfection which supports the art of great performers . . . Being beautiful

Father Völker (Heinrich George) demonstrates to Stoppel (Hermann Speelmans) how well the former Communist has learned his Nazi catechism.

is not the thing; the point is being clear! Whoever sees clearly, sees most artistically!"[71] Karl Aloys Schenzinger likewise recognized that visual impressions could offer clear points of orientation. In the novel *Der Hitlerjunge Quex,* Heini thumbs through the pages of the Nazi magazine *Illustrierter Beobachter,* coming across a photograph of a proud young boy standing at attention, underneath which stands the caption "Germany's future." Immediately Heini makes the portrait a part of his own person, embracing "the boy deeply in his heart."[72] Later Heini comes across an account of the Tyrolean war of liberation (the backdrop used by Luis Trenker in his 1932 film, *Der Rebell/The Rebel*), lying in bed and dreaming about what he has read: "There had been a moving story about a boy who had dragged munitions and water to the Tyrolean troops, until a French bullet laid him to rest. Like that boy in the story, he too saw the flag with the red eagle rising out of the darkness, he heard the noise of the rifles and the cries of the victors."[73]

What does *Hitler Youth Quex* disclose about early Nazi film aesthetics? Goebbels sought to transform the film apparatus into a tool of the state, a medium of myth, legend, and fantasy which would relieve reality of its dialectical complexity. The primary task as the NSDAP came into power was that of reshaping public imagination in accordance with its own persuasions, of presenting an appealing and compelling *Weltanschauung*. At issue here was nothing less than the control over perceptual possibility.[74] Among all the media, film would from the start assume a primary, indeed seminal role in the Third Reich. *Hitler Youth Quex* fulfilled essential aspirations of Nazi fantasy production. First of all, film was enlisted to simplify the world rather than to complicate it—in essence, to dedialecticize reality. In the early 1930s, this meant winning over cynical and weary minds to a cause by presenting a world of clear fronts and unimpeachable certainties. "Reason as such," claimed a contemporary editorial titled "National Socialist Film?" "has been divested of its cold power and has become what it should be: the technique of thinking with the heart."

Second, the medium's proper calling was to heighten experience, to provide an emotional frisson. "We demand of art," continued the editorial,

> that it genuinely move us and not just stupefy us with sensations; we demand of art that it probe the foundations of humanity and plumb its ultimate depths; it must show us the breathing of the soul and not, as has been the case for so long, just the pounding of the brain. We want to partake of the rhythmics of the soul, not just the monotonous uniform march of international intellectuals.[75]

Goebbels' rhetoric and that of productions such as *Hitler Youth Quex* stressed immediate and authentic existence. The new German cinema strived for a visceral appeal. In the process, film was to become an industrialized means of behavior modification.

National Socialism, despite its ideological pretensions to a coherent world view, was to a great degree the function of stirring spectacles and pyrotechnic demonstrations. Film provided the special effects with which the Third Reich created itself. The flow of images, like the movement of a party, afforded nonstop excitement and ever-shifting perspectives. Each employed elaborate choreographies and dramatic displays of emotion in the name of making fictional worlds become real. Both reached out to beholders, aiming to control their undivided attention.

In *Hitler Youth Quex*, we witness the fabrication of a new man. This new man is no material being. The film tells the story of how a young boy becomes a political property. Inscribing an appeal to spectacle within a medium of spectacle, *Hitler Youth Quex* sought to bind a nation's youth to a party's cause. While claiming youth, the NSDAP also sought to reclaim cinema, realizing the power of both entities in its campaign to transform the German nation. *Hitler Youth Quex* puts a party design into motion; its *mise en scène* reshapes a scene and reforms a country, leaving behind Weimar tableaus of loitering and crime, progressing toward final images of personal sacrifice and collective abandon. We open on a site of hunger and confusion; we end with the ecstatic vision of a future order. With a trajectory that leads from a mob of agitated onlookers to a configuration of spirited participants, the film forsakes the agitprop of proletarian realism in the name of a classless society's transcendent power. It disdains the illicit voyeurism and sensual abandon of a decadent regime and privileges the fixed gaze and erect body of a new order, asking spectators to take the discursive leap from Caligari to Hitler, to transform the fairground into the parade ground.[76] This involves a shift of specular allegiance as well, an exchange of the distraction of flowing skirts and whirling carousels for the intoxication of billowing banners and parallel lines.

Hitler Youth Quex mediates the myth of a martyr in order to mobilize emotions. The dead Herbert Norkus becomes the raw material for the fictional Heini Völker, who, brought back to life by a nameless amateur actor,[77] metamorphoses into Hitler Youth Quex, whose dying body in turn segues into a waving flag that becomes a screen for the sights and sounds of a party. Human substance evaporates into disembodied function; a corpse evanesces into a medium for a movement. The climactic moments of *Hitler Youth Quex* impress upon viewers a consonance between a waving flag and filmic flux.[78] Both provide attractions that bind spectators and subjects: to a movement, to a medium. The final sequence involves a celebration of death in which human sacrifice is experienced as aesthetic reverie.

"The flag means more than death" ("Die Fahne ist mehr als der Tod") are the film's closing words. This film, likewise, is more than just a film, as its last shot of storm troopers marching offscreen into the battles of the future intimates. *Hitler Youth Quex* is not only an early Nazi feature, but a remarkable preview of coming attractions, a *Bewegungsfilm* that shows the way to war and a nation's collective self-destruction.[79] As Max Picard later observed, this new order would not lead to a new world. It "is a rupture rather than the real thing; this beginning is in fact the end."[80] Surrendering one's person, participating in a great spectacle, and acting in a celluloid fantasy will become of a piece for Germany's marching minions. *Hitler Youth Quex* emanates from a cinematic apparatus that is to be in equal measure a dream machine and a death factory.

PART II

Foreign Affairs

"If you don't ever go away, you can't ever come home."

THREE

Home Sweet *Heimat*: *The Prodigal Son* (1934)

The world-city means cosmopolitanism in place of "home" . . . To the world-city belongs not a folk but a mob. Its uncomprehending hostility to all the traditions representative of the Culture (nobility, church, privileges, dynasties, convention in art, and limits of knowledge in science), the keen and cold intelligence that confounds the wisdom of the peasant, the new-fashioned naturalism that in relation to all matters of sex and society goes far back to quite primitive instincts and conditions, the reappearance of the *panem et circenses* in the form of wage disputes and sports stadia—all these things betoken the definite closing down of the Culture and the opening of a quite new phase of human existence—antiprovincial, late, futureless, but quite inevitable.

Oswald Spengler

Essential to our feeling and thinking and in accordance with our own demographic insights is precisely a provincialization of thought and a strengthening of existing bonds to what we call blood and soil.

Peter von Werder

Heimat for me is not a political concept, but rather an object of love granted to man by God. I approach it with humility. To love one's *Heimat* is to love other people, to experience religion, and to understand human fears and joys . . . Loyalty to one's *Heimat* seen in this light is a spiritual reaction against Nazi materialism and blood-and-soil drivel and against Marxist atheism and class hatred as well.

Luis Trenker, 1978

Heim ins Reich

Heimat: such a simple word for such a difficult, complex, in a sense impossible entity. *Heimat,* homeland: a place, a feeling; a physical space, a province of the psyche; at once something inordinately rich and something irretrievably lost. Its ultimate extension might be characterized, as Ernst Bloch once suggested, as a utopian terrain where no one has ever been, the enchanted world that we intuit as children in a sweet glimmering of a truly hopeful human condition.[1] To contemplate *Heimat* means to imagine an uncontaminated space, a realm of innocence and immediacy. Musing about *Heimat* can provoke fits of giddiness; the thought spirits one to pleasant places. Its lack in real lives also makes people sad and bitter. *Heimat* intoxicates and transports, possessing "the apparently plastic powers" ascribed by French myth to wine. A function with variable terms, "it can serve as an alibi to dream as well as reality, it depends on the users of the myth."[2]

In October 1992 the media celebrated Luis Trenker's hundredth birthday and commemorated his long career in the service of the *Heimat.* Several months later, in January 1993, the world remembered the sixtieth anniversary of Hitler's rise to power, an event that, among other consequences, compelled numerous film artists to flee Germany. Trenker, driven less by political concerns than by professional prospects, repeatedly contemplated a move to America during the 1930s. After 1945 he would dispute claims that he had associated with party luminaries, maintaining he had been blacklisted by Goebbels, hunted by the Gestapo, and made to run for his life. In the end Luis Trenker would arise as the German *Heimat*'s most prominent public defender. Tracking Trenker's career, following his various moves throughout the 1930s and 1940s, studying his postwar return to the limelight, we encounter a figure whose relation to the *Heimat* involved repeated shifts of field and changes of course. The homeland may stand for a locus of timeless sanctity; in the hands of its most vigorous twentieth-century proponent, it also served as a quite resilient and very lucrative force.

Luis Trenker's *Der verlorene Sohn* (*The Prodigal Son,* 1934),[3] like *Hitler Youth Quex,* puts a champion of the homeland on parade. Brothers in arms fighting on different fronts, Heini Völker combats Communist internationalism while Trenker's protagonist confronts urban modernity. In the end, both warriors return from the street to the soil, Heini to a resting place as a popular hero, Tonio to his station as a dutiful son and future patriarch. *Hitler Youth Quex* created a political subject, a boy who renounces his family and person and becomes a function of a party design. A subsequent film by

Hans Steinhoff, the Prussian costume drama *Der alte und der junge König* (*The Old and the Young King,* 1935), likewise portrayed the making of a state servant, depicting how rebellious Young Fritz becomes Frederick the Great. Introduced quite literally as a missing person, in shots of an empty bed and a vacant chair, the prince denies his preordained role as a member of the royal family and heir to the throne, as a soldier and leader of the Prussian folk. Aided by his mother and disguised as a Frenchman, Fritz attempts an escape to England. Apprehended by his father, the malingerer and traitor must undergo harsh reeducation in order to constitute himself as a commanding presence.[4] He forsakes his own desire for the sake of a higher calling and takes his place in a larger pattern.[5] The king-to-be forswears ornate circles and aimless motions, salons teeming with gamblers, coquettes, and dandies. He resituates himself in a world of straight lines, uniformed masses, and unquestioned allegiances, joining the masculine space of the parade ground and the state, assuming its language and order. A once errant prince reenters the Prussian court to become the great king.

It was striking, Ernst Bloch observed in 1934, how often fugitives cropped up in contemporary features. Threatened and persecuted by the new order, numerous citizens in the Reich were packing their bags and making haste to cross borders. German films, however, showed images of emigrants *returning* to the fatherland. Enacting a collective ritual, new releases displayed ecstatic characters on the march, Germans fleeing back "to the land of Göring."[6] Johannes Meyer's *Der Flüchtling aus Chicago* (*The Fugitive from Chicago,* 1934) focuses on an enterprising German engineer, Michael Nissen, out to make his fortune in the American Midwest. His companion, imprisoned as a felon, inherits an automobile factory, the Munich "Dux-Werke," and convinces the virtuous friend to take his place. Back in Germany, Nissen confronts the malaise of the Weimar Republic: economic uncertainty, mass unemployment, incompetent leadership. Surmounting a host of difficulties, he quickly has the business back on its feet and the workers on his side. Were he not so young and dashing, quips Bloch, one might call the new master "a father of the fatherland—or at least of the factory."[7] A charismatic leader returns to clean house and restore order; clearly, this fugitive is a man of the hour.

Paul Wegener's *Ein Mann will nach Deutschland (A German Wants to Go Home),* an Ufa production that premiered on 26 July 1934, portrays a German engineer living in South America who hears in 1914 of war across the ocean. Realizing his obligation, he sets out for Europe, joined by a German comrade. The road back involves physical hardships, treacherous terrains, and hostile seas, obstacles faced by patriots who have, as the Nazi publicist Oskar Kalbus put it, "only one thought: home to Germany, to help protect a fatherland under attack."[8]

Another Ufa film, honored as the best German feature for the 1933–34 season, Gustav Ucicky's *Flüchtlinge (Fugitives),* unfolds on the Sino-Soviet frontier in 1928, against a backdrop of mass confusion and political upheaval.[9] Cluttered initial images of chaotic streets lead us to a group of Volga Germans on the run from Bolshevik oppressors. While seeking sanctuary in an international zone across the Chinese border, they bicker as an ineffective high commission deliberates about their fate. The narrative unites the motley gathering in a common cause under Arneth (Hans Albers), a bitter ex-officer who has deserted the Weimar Republic. (In the words of the original program brochure: "They had imprisoned and persecuted him because he loved the fatherland.") Arneth is a man of action. "No more words!" he screams. "It reeks here already of too many words." He organizes the group, commandeering a train and clearing a path of escape. The final images show the unified group pulling out of Harbin as the jubilant hero announces their destination: "Deutschland. Heim . . . nach Hause."

"Out of the flaming inferno, home to a German heaven":[10] films such as *Fugitives* assured exiled citizens of the Reich a safe return passage. These Nazi retrospectives stressed how the Weimar democracy had undermined national well-being, surrendering Germany to irresponsible and illegitimate interests who had transformed native soil into a foreign state. The Harbin of *Fugitives* represents a displaced Weimar Republic, an extraterritorial zone of multiple languages, nationalities, and races, where red commissars run amok through streets of turmoil and frenzy, where politicians talk much and do nothing to relieve German suffering.[11] With the new order, Germans could reclaim and reinhabit a country that many (like Arneth) had given up for lost. Nazi films of various sorts showed refugees returning after years in abeyance, their long hibernation over as the nation reawakened from a nightmare.[12] Seemingly innocuous comedies released in 1935 such as *Punks kommt aus Amerika (Punks Comes from America)*[13] and *Frischer Wind aus Kanada (Fresh Breeze from Canada)* echoed the "Heim ins Reich" sentiments of Detlef Sierck's Ibsen adaptation, *Stützen der Gesellschaft (Pillars of Society),* as well as the political melodrama *Friesennot (Frisians in Peril),* a tale about German destinies on Russian soil. Trenker's 1934 release, *The Prodigal Son,* reflected the larger cultural scenario and stood out as the most expressive enactment of this national homecoming.

Patriots on dangerous ground: above, Willi Schur, Karl Ludwig Diehl, and Hermann Speelmans in *A German Wants to Go Home;* below, captive Volga Germans in *Fugitives.*

The opening images of *The Prodigal Son* present sweeping panoramas, shots blending Alpine majesty, Christian iconography, and a romantic idyll, gentle dissolves and cuts between clouds, landscapes, animals, and mountain dwellers.[14] Trenker's hero will leave this bucolic paradise of his own volition.[15] *The Prodigal Son* illustrates a moral lesson, the schoolteacher's homily, "If you don't ever go away, you can't ever come home" ("Wer nie fortkommt, kommt nie heim").[16] The vigorous and self-confident Tonio Feuersinger (played by Trenker) occupies the center of attention in St. Laurein, a premodern sanctuary. He enjoys the affections of the attractive Barbl, commands a group of woodchoppers, plows his father's fields, and leads his team to triumph in the annual ski competition sponsored by the wealthy American, Mr. Williams. His boyish curiosity about exotic places is encouraged by an invitation from Lilian, Williams' fetching daughter. A climbing accident in which a friend perishes finally prompts Tonio to curse the mountains and take the leap.

Tonio crosses the ocean and quickly finds himself down-and-out in a depression-ridden America. He attempts to call on Mr. Williams, but he and his daughter are away. Dejected and penniless, he moves from one job to another. Employed as a ring attendant in Madison Square Garden, he intervenes when a boxer brutally pummels an incapacitated opponent and catches the attention of Lilian and her father. Lilian seeks to win Tonio for herself and the New World. On the verge of relenting, Tonio glimpses a *Rauhnacht* mask Mr. Williams has brought back from St. Laurein. The imported icon unleashes powerful memories. The prodigal son feels the call of the homeland and returns for the winter solstice celebration. His father embraces him, and Tonio assumes his place as Sun King, the *Rauhnacht* master of ceremonies. Amidst ecstatic revelry, Tonio finds Barbl and, in the film's choral conclusion, worships with her at a midnight mass.

America figures in this scenario as a site of seduction and a dangerous object of desire. Neither malaise nor discontent prompts Tonio to contemplate unfamiliar climes. He does not flee oppression or poverty, nor does he seek to regain something lost. Hunger for experience spurs Tonio's wanderlust. He wants to partake of different sights and sounds, to visit exotic places he has seen only on a map. The result is a nightmarish thrashing by a soulless modernity. Exposure to America changes the confident mountain climber and consummate skier into a distraught vagrant, a transient hounded by the police. The emigrant gains a heightened respect for his native soil and homeland community. Tonio renounces the New World and purges his fascination for a life beyond his native horizon. It is a rite of passage; before he can truly come home, he has to have his foreign affair: "Wer nie fortkommt, kommt nie heim."[17] Like many features in the Third Reich, *The Prodigal Son* grants a wish in order to vanquish wishful thinking, indulging a fantasy to counter affective energies out of keeping with collective interests.[18] True to its biblical title, the film presents a moral parable. For its contemporary audiences, it also provided a political catechism. For us today it offers a history lesson as well.

There's No Place like Home

"I've always been a faithful and loving son of the homeland," boasted Trenker on his ninetieth birthday in 1982,[19] an event observed throughout the German media and later captured in Hans-Jürgen Panitz's documentary film homage, *Fast ein Jahrhundert* (*Almost a Century,* 1986). "An uncrowned king" and "a living legend," Trenker inspired sympathy, admiration, and enthusiasm. Proud of his South Tyrolean roots and his Ladin background, he treasured the landscape of his youth, the village in the Dolomites, St. Ulrich.[20] Stubborn and firm, he spoke with animation of his refusal to betray his homeland, either to the Italian fascists or to Nazi ideologues. His secret of success lay in an unwavering loyalty—to himself, his *Heimat,* his religious faith. Repeatedly during the documentary, both celebrant and commentator speak of Trenker as "the prodigal son." Trenker, like Tonio, could have made his fortune in America, but preferred to stay at home.

Nazi observers in 1934 also hailed *The Prodigal Son* as a tribute to local patriotism, despite ongoing concern about Trenker's negotiations with Hollywood.[21] Radio reports about the work-in-progress—it first bore the title *Sonnwend (Solstice),* later *Die große Sonnwend (The Great Solstice)*—extolled stunning visual contrasts between mountain ranges and cityscapes, praising Trenker's allegiance to "God's free nature" and affirming his skepticism about a foreign nation where plutocrats and Social Darwinism held sway. The production received considerable advance notice and raised great expectations: "Every German wishes and hopes that Trenker's vision of divine creation and its liberating grandeur will be shared by all German filmmakers and that out of the film of the past will arise the art work of the future, a film shaped by a world view rooted in nature, an authentic German folk."[22] *Die große Sonnwend,* commentators predicted, might well mark a decisive turning point, *eine große Wende,* for German film.[23]

The Deutsche Universal film, a German-American enterprise, premiered on 6 September in Stuttgart and a month later in Berlin to rousing ovations.

The film's Jewish producer, Paul Kohner, was not in attendance, having left Europe and taken up permanent residence in southern California, from where he would wage a concerted effort to bring his friend Trenker to Hollywood.[24] After the first screening, Trenker went onto the stage for repeated curtain calls. As he and his guest Max Schmeling departed from the Universum der Schwäbischen Urania, throngs of admirers swarmed around them, and the two required a police escort.[25] In emotional phrases, critics commended the film's optical brilliance, symphonic structure, and epic power, lauding Trenker's script, direction, and acting as well as the performance of Maria Anderngast, the camera work of Albert Benitz and Reimar Kuntze, and the music of Giuseppe Becce. "The best film of the year," proclaimed the *Lichtbild-Bühne.*

Above all, contemporary commentators were awestruck by the America sequence. Trenker, said the *Film-Kurier* reviewer, used neither stock footage nor postcard panoramas. His location shooting showed Manhattan from a different perspective and with a singular intensity. From the distance, as Trenker described it, it seemed so immense and overpowering, this "city of seven million, the world metropolis, the city of skyscrapers, millionaires, and starving masses, the world capital of all races and languages, the metropolis of all light and shadow."[26] Experienced up close, the melting pot turns into a caldron; the journey to America becomes "a trip to Hell."[27] The film's great impact lay in the confrontation between the tranquility of the homeland and the horror of the big city, an urban space, maintained Trenker, "whose ultimate meaning can only be chaos and destruction."[28]

The film also found strong official endorsement. A premiere screening took place in Dresden later in September, a festivity supporting the National Socialist Public Welfare *(Volkswohlfahrt)* attended by members of the party, SA, SS, and Wehrmacht as well as other state and civic luminaries.[29] It garnered a prize in 1935 at the Venice festival, where it represented Germany together with, among other titles, Steinhoff's *The Old and the Young King* and Riefenstahl's *Triumph des Willens (Triumph of the Will).*[30] It also served party blood-and-soil campaigns, sanctifying, as the *Film-Kurier* reported, an intact community that since pagan times has maintained its racial purity and German heritage.[31] *The Prodigal Son* championed folk traditions and transfigured national realities, yielding a rare blend of political conviction and artistic excellence: "Leadership, about which there has been so much recent discussion, is an exemplary achievement, a deed that elevates and transports. In art as well! You who are always talking about culture, stop making speeches and follow Trenker's example and people will take you seriously!"[32] *The Prodigal Son* provided a prototype for a popular German film that might move the hearts and stir the minds of masses.[33]

Rejecting the agitprop of *Bewegungsfilme* such as *SA-Mann Brand* and *Hans Westmar* as well-intended but heavy-handed political pamphlets, Goebbels pleaded for lighter touches and finer approaches.[34] Precisely the energy and élan of Trenker's *Der Rebell* (*The Rebel,* 1932) had excited Hitler and the propaganda minister, prompting the latter to praise it as a film so powerful that it "could even bowl over non–National Socialists."[35] *The Prodigal Son,* remarked a critic in the SA newspaper, *Der Angriff,* displayed virtues rarely encountered in domestic productions: clarity and intuition, color and spontaneity. National Socialist ideas permeated the director's images, wordlessly yet undeniably. Trenker was not explicit; still, the viewer felt the difference. To reach the hearts of mass audiences, Trenker took a detour rather than the direct route, appealing to people with "grandiose, skillful imagery."[36] What power came from the merging of political persuasion and aesthetic acumen: "Here, without experiments and without routine, we have an active avant-garde; here is a National Socialist film art driven by immediacy and instinct."[37] Goebbels envisioned a film that edified as it entertained, that diverted attention while directing desire, incorporating political values in well-crafted popular packages. *The Prodigal Son* fit well into this program, indulging the wish for another life so that audiences might recognize the danger abiding in non-German spaces, be they geographic or psychic. It is no surprise that despite its Hollywood coproducer, *The Prodigal Son* did not gain a U.S. distributor and after the war was banned by Allied censors as "anti-American."

The Prodigal Son was not on the list of proscribed films for long, however. It would go on to enjoy attention in the 1950s, as would Trenker, who even beyond his death in 1990 at ninety-seven remained a lustrous public personality. Far more venerated and much less embattled than Leni Riefenstahl, Trenker engendered sympathies never fully accorded his female counterpart and competitor, even if the two had much in common. Both got their screen starts as actors in Arnold Fanck's Alpine melodramas, becoming directors who starred in and directed their own mountain films,[38] harvesting initial accolades with images of premodern landscapes and pastoral communities. The two were outspoken advocates of visual immediacy, champions of a film art free from artifice and verbal ballast.[39] Both gained Hitler's favor and played an important (albeit contested) role after 1933, despite apparently strained relations with Goebbels, tensions emphasized repeatedly by the two directors in their career recollections.[40] In the postwar years, they remained vigorous and fit, individuals frequently pictured in outdoor settings, exuberant senior citizens constantly on the go. With an indefatigable vitality, the two demonstrated—in their physical appearances, in their personal utterances—an apparent obliviousness to the passage of time.

Up to his death Trenker was quite at home in his homeland. His was an unmistakable countenance: a hardy voice, an infectious smile, sterling white teeth, a broad forehead, granitelike chin, and an ever-tan face. He hammed it up in front of cameras, an avuncular figure garbed in a corduroy suit and a spiffy hat, a rope around his chest, a pipe in his mouth.[41] He signed his name to more than forty books (novels, travel guides, and memoirs), which have sold more than 8 million copies. He acted in, directed, and produced a host of films (features, shorts, documentaries, and travelogues), maintaining a high profile on German and Austrian television, becoming an influential lobbyist for the tourist, clothing, and sporting-goods industries as well as an ecological activist. His was an upbeat existence, one without Riefenstahl's defensiveness and self-pity, free of regret or resentment. Very rarely did he maunder about unfriendly critics such as Siegfried Kracauer who deemed him a proto-Nazi. "Alles gut gegangen," reads the title of Trenker's memoirs: "Everything went well."[42]

Only briefly under scrutiny as a Nazi sympathizer, Trenker made a swift postwar comeback, although features such as *Von der Liebe besiegt* (*Overcome by Love,* 1956), *Wetterleuchten um Maria* (*Lightning around Maria,* 1957), and *Sein bester Freund* (*His Best Friend,* 1962) did not begin to match his artistic and popular successes of the 1930s. He regained notoriety primarily as a television celebrity, a "Münchhausen of the mountains."[43] He withstood occasional debacles, accusations that he willingly collaborated with both Hitler and Mussolini, complaints that he had not authored all the books written under his name,[44] charges (which proved to be valid) that he had sold forged copies of Eva Braun's diaries to the boulevard press,[45] gossip about the ninety-year-old's liaison with his much younger secretary.[46] No matter how ugly the scandal, Trenker remained unflappable under pressure and sovereign in matters of damage control.

In his postwar declarations Trenker resumed his well-known role as a champion of the homeland—with a few alterations. He positioned himself as a nationalist, but in no way as a supporter of National Socialism. "I never paid much mind to politics," he insisted. The Nazis "were glad to have me. My films could be sold abroad with ease, and that meant big money."[47] His local pride and religious faith knew nothing of party allegiances.[48] As a defender of Jews and a devout Catholic, Trenker claimed in a letter to

Kohner on 3 November 1945, he had been burdened by constant troubles and worries. His last Nazi feature, *Der Feuerteufel* (*The Fire Devil,* 1940), he maintained, openly indicted the Hitler order. No other German filmmaker had dared at the time to be so outspoken.[49] Lamenting that he had been censured by Goebbels and at loose ends since 1940, Trenker characterized himself as a victim of political oppression.

Wartime documents relate a different story. After the Axis treaty of October 1939 between Germany and Italy, German-speaking residents of South Tyrol had the option of resettling in the Reich or remaining residents of Italy. (By 1943, 70,000 people would relocate, above all in Bavaria and Austria.)[50] Trenker's loyalties were put to the test. He took his time in making a decision, and his hesitation caused outrage among party officials.

In an impassioned letter of 21 February 1940, Trenker wrote Nazi sculptor Josef Thorak that his loyalties to the Third Reich did not conflict with his Alpine origins, and, in the process, reannexed his South Tyrolean homeland for a greater Germany:

> You know that I set up my main residence in Berlin twelve years ago and that I have represented the German cause in my speeches and writings over the last twenty years. How strongly I feel about my homeland, which fills both my soul and my art, is clear to anyone who knows my work. But no one can claim that I am a bad German because I am unwilling to forsake my native German soil [South Tyrol, which had been part of Italy since 1919] now and forever. The mountain valleys down there are my primordial homeland, the big city can never replace them. You will understand me when I say that I can accomplish more for the German cause here at home and in the world with the precious treasure of my mountain homeland in my heart than I could if I were to give it up and to lose it completely.[51]

A few days later, on 27 February, he sent a two-page communiqué to Hitler and pledged his undying allegiance: "You, my Führer, have followed my work from *The Rebel* to *The Fire Devil,* and you can rest assured that when the moment of truth comes I will know exactly where I belong and where I shall take my stand."[52] A short note from Trenker to the head of the Reich Film Division on 11 June 1940 stated unequivocally where Trenker stood vis-à-vis his *Heimat.* He requested formally that he be listed in the professional organization of German filmmakers as a "reichsdeutsches" member, "because as a South Tyrolean resident I opted for the German Reich on 28 March 1940."[53] That summer he also became a member of the NSDAP.

Many postwar critics have presented Trenker as a nonconformist who, against imposing odds, made oppositional films during the Third Reich. The Nazis actively antagonized Trenker and denied him their support, submits William K. Everson, the director's most ardent North American admirer. Had *The Prodigal Son* and *The Emperor of California* not won festival prizes in Venice, Goebbels would have suppressed them.[54] This image of Trenker as a dissenter, of course, was not universally shared, especially not by exiled German filmmakers in the Anti-Nazi League. Even Paul Kohner, Trenker's unabashed admirer and persevering spokesman, could not deny the hostile sentiment toward Trenker in Hollywood's emigrant community.[55]

Following a lengthy wartime silence, Trenker reestablished contact with Kohner in 1945, denying that he had ever cozied up to the Nazis. Kohner responded with coolness but seemed at least willing to consider Trenker's new ideas for films. One of them was to be based on the supposedly authentic diaries of Eva Braun. Realizing how problematic a film with Hitler's lover as an identification figure might be for postwar audiences, Kohner declined and in a letter of 20 July 1946 even scolded Trenker:

> Does it in any way worry you that people might feel—if a woman who was so close to Hitler like Eva Braun—was on sufficiently friendly terms with you to come to you and bring such important papers, that this might not entirely coincide with your previous declarations that you had to flee from the Gestapo to Italy and the Alps and hide in mountain villages, etc. You also mentioned you met her in the winter of 1943 in Berlin when, according to some previous statements, you said you never got back to Berlin.

If these allegations were published, Kohner concluded, they might cause Trenker severe political damage.

Later Trenker requested Kohner's help in clearing his name. On this occasion, too, Kohner's reply was guarded. There remained, he wrote, "considerable differences of opinion" about the filmmaker's political status. Had Trenker received the clearance of the Allied Control Commissions or gone through de-Nazification proceedings? asked Kohner on 19 December 1947. "I'm an Italian citizen," Trenker replied on 31 December; as such, he was not subject to de-Nazification. Unable to comprehend the negative sentiments toward him and casting about for employment, a desperate

Trenker pleaded to Kohner in a letter on 23 April 1949: "If you see [Erich] Pommer, pass on my greetings to him and put in a good word for me. Pommer [as Allied film commissioner] is now the all-powerful man in Germany." Kohner interceded, and Pommer's intervention worked wonders.[56] Trenker was now in the clear. His reputation rose quickly once again, both within and beyond German-language borders.

International cineastes came to celebrate Trenker's films of the 1930s as precursors of Neorealism. The director, with customary immodesty, boasted that Vittorio De Sica's *The Bicycle Thief* (1948) derived its formal impetus from the Manhattan sequence of *The Prodigal Son.*[57] In 1982 the government of the Federal Republic honored Trenker for his lifelong contributions to German cinema with a Film Ribbon in Gold. Even a pop star of a younger generation, Fr. Nudel, eulogized him as an inspiration in her hit of the early 1980s, "Hohe Berge" ("Tall Mountains"). "When I think of Trenker," the Hamburg singer effused, "I get all worked up." In 1983 the Goethe-Institut sent the still vigorous filmmaker on tour with *The Prodigal Son* and *The Emperor of California.* Bill Pence, director of the Telluride Film Festival, recalled Trenker's visit in glowing terms: "For the 10th year we had the first tribute ever given to Luis Trenker. He was tremendously popular."[58] In a lengthy homage, William Everson hailed him as "one of the major European film-makers of the 30s," "Germany's John Wayne and John Ford rolled into one."[59]

Tonio Does Manhattan

Without a doubt, *The Prodigal Son* and its director have fared well over the years. The feature resurfaced during the Adenauer era in the heyday of the homeland film. The Alpine community may look the same in the 1953 rerelease, but when asked where he comes from, Tonio, former local patriot of South Tyrol, now can be heard to say, "from Bavaria!"[60] Exhibitors, recommended the Unitas-Film advertising materials, should play up the film's international success and exploit it as "Luis Trenker's masterpiece" in which "love of the homeland triumphs over foreign glamor and wealth." The marketing rhetoric glossed over the film's anti-Americanism and emphasized its universal appeal: "This film excited the whole world. Trenker at the peak of his talent! And once again we are moved by the stirring force of these images, charmed by the beauty of the mountain world."[61]

The film touted by Nazi critics in 1934 as a "standard work" circulates today in a collection of films financed and administered by the Foreign

Office of the Federal Republic. What strange sequence of events has recast an agent of blood-and-soil sentiment and anti-American agitation as a post-war ambassador and a hallmark of world cinema? How could a filmmaker who had prided himself on—and profited from—Hitler's patronage establish himself after 1945 as the exemplary embodiment of a "better" Germany's homeland? One factor is constant in this success story, namely Trenker's public persona as a loyal native son. *The Prodigal Son* is his founding myth, the cornerstone of a long career based in the homeland. *Heimat,* it would seem, is a mutable force, both durable and flexible, reaffirming one's place no matter where one goes, no matter when (or with whom) one travels. Luis Trenker trafficked in the homeland for almost a century.[62]

In the Third Reich, *völkisch* mythologists mobilized German blood and soil (*Blut und Boden, Blubo* for short) as a counterforce to reason and modernity, deploying its suggestive power to arrest minds and stir emotions. Take, for instance, Lulu von Strauss und Torney's poem of 1936, "Väterheimat" ("Homeland of the Fathers"):

> Wanderers, unrested souls,
> We move about like fugitives,
> A dream of roots and soil
> Lingers darkly in our senses,—
> And in the pulsating stream
> Deep from the holy source
> Swells to our heart and burns,
> Fathers, before your threshold:
> Blood that knows the earth![63]

Heimat conjured up idealized images of sanctity and immediacy while undergoing elaborate political instrumentation, arising as *pastorale militans.*[64]

Nature, race, and folk served as transhistorical categories for the "irrationalistic naturalism" that Herbert Marcuse analyzed in an essay of 1934:

> In the train of this naturalism follows a glorification of the peasantry as the only estate still "bound to nature." It is celebrated as the "creative, original source," as the eternal pillar of society. The mythical glorification of the renewal of agriculture has its counterpart in the fight against the metropolis and its "unnatural" spirit. This fight expands into an attack on the rule of reason in general and sets loose all irrational powers.[65]

The homeland at once provides meaning and forecloses thought. A space rooted in cyclical nature and therefore timeless, it is the site of the true and the genuine as well as an imposing obstacle to what Marcuse terms "responsible, autonomous, rational practice."[66]

Trenker's mountaintop homeland, immortalized on the screen, possesses an immutable countenance. The first lines of *The Prodigal Son* articulate a wish for a space beyond time. "I'd like to sit here like this forever," Barbl says to Tonio as the two luxuriate in a pastoral setting.[67] The closing *Rauhnacht* sequence likewise celebrates the eternal power of elements and seasons, displaying a locus where, as Leo Löwenthal remarked of Knut Hamsun's novels, "nature's timetable replaces the timetable of history."[68] Löwenthal and Marcuse (who reflected on *Blubo* discourse at the same time as Trenker crafted his paean to German blood and soil) recognized the dire consequences of this temporal denial: "The social counterpart to the law of natural rhythm is blind discipline."[69] Organic "fact" as a primal given defies mind and reason. To submit to nature means bowing to its inexorable might. For Trenker, obedience to a timeless homeland went hand in hand with a deference to a shifting cast of political powers.

The Prodigal Son contrasts the glory of the homeland with the malaise of modern Manhattan. Tonio's sojourn abroad becomes an experience of loss. Divorced from his native soil, the traveler degenerates into a nonentity. In St. Laurein, Tonio lords over every spectacle and captures the fancy of attractive women.[70] Upon first arriving in New York, he stands out briefly among the crowds in a dapper trench coat; camera movements and cuts likewise defer initially to the gaze of the curious tourist. Subsequent shots from above the Empire State Building, however, register a shrunken Tonio overwhelmed by the urban mass. One cut after another dwarfs the visitor, and the scene ultimately reduces him to a speck on the horizon.[71] The German's regress above all involves a change of appearance: shabbier clothing, a hunched posture, a less vigorous gait. More and more he blends into street crowds. No longer is he the master of his own movements. He lingers in front of a labor exchange, one face among the unemployed masses. A landlady evicts him, and the newly homeless person huddles under neon lights in Times Square. His face shrouded in shadows, he looks into the camera and disappears in a cut to the impersonal, almost abstract nocturnal city.

The camera records the undoing of the man who was to be Sun King. No longer does it track energetically; it limps behind the emigrant and stares down at his wornout shoes. The editing loses the fluidity of the mountain scenes, the exuberant motions of woodcutters, the smooth rhythms of trees tumbling down and sliding into the water,[72] the breathtaking cutting between silhouetted downhill skiers. Cuts now shuffle Tonio about, displacing him from shot to shot. The camera tilts down to the distraught protagonist sitting below the Statue of Liberty, moving to a medium close-up. He looks back and forth, head in hand, rising to walk along the water, looking out to sea, and exiting the frame. The next image, a low-angle medium close-up of Tonio, would seem to maintain continuity—except that in the distance we see a boat on the water and, indeed, the Statue of Liberty. Between shots Tonio has been transferred across the water from Liberty Island to the Battery; succeeding shots convey him to Brooklyn. The transient treads uncertainly and wanders aimlessly, inhabiting a world that denies him sanctuary and sustenance.[73] Trenker's modernistic montage dramatizes the shock experience of modernity: disjunctive and mismatched cuts lend formal expression to the negative force of the big city.[74]

The escape from Manhattan restores Tonio to an unchanged Alpine setting. The homeland affords the antidote for all the ills of America: an organic community rather than lonely crowds, seasonal rhythms instead of the march of time, a vital local culture in place of vulgar mass spectacle. *The Prodigal Son* takes leave of a previous era's fascination with America and modernity, replacing Weimar's foreign enthusiasms with homegrown diversions.[75] Trenker's film contrasts the natural plenitude of the mountains with the spiritual poverty of the metropolis, imparting to *Heimat* such emotional power that it might break America's hold on the collective imagination. The United States becomes a realm of inhuman tempo and brutal competition, a country whose embrace of the new undermines all that is valuable and abiding.[76]

National Socialist film policy aimed to restore Germany to its own sights and sounds. "The best international film," claimed the *Film-Kurier* at the start of 1934, "is the national film." Filmmakers used to fancy themselves cosmopolitans and eschew German culture, emulating Hollywood's latest fad or what tastemakers in Paris deemed *au courant.* "The national rejuvenation in Germany has done away with this nonsense of imitating foreign styles and customs. Today the German film is what it should and must be: German."[77] One declared, at least for the moment, a *Kulturkampf* against the vestiges of a previous era's Americanism and internationalist pretensions. It was one of many wars to be waged against a shifting cast of enemies, both imaginary and real, skirmishes that would occupy numerous fronts, including the Reich's cinemas.[78]

Battle lines were drawn which separated national domain and foreign territory. Making these divisions appear self-evident and indisputable demanded intense ideological effort; such labor could not always conceal profound uncertainty and ambivalence. Inherent similarities between seeming opposites pose themselves in *The Prodigal Son,* affinities between the premodern community and the modern metropolis. For all of Trenker's vaunted realism, it is a vagrant imagination rather than a veristic impetus which determines the shape of American spaces.[79] Tonio's first mental images of the New World come into being as a function of what he lacks at home. And the United States in fact seems quite near. The passage from Tyrol to New York does not require an excruciating journey; it happens in a flash. *The Prodigal Son* leaps from a mountaintop to an urban setting, segueing via a matched dissolve from the peaks of the Dolomites to the skyscrapers of Manhattan. Beyond its overt Manichaeism, the film (no doubt unwittingly) displays how two different worlds condense in the German psyche, suggesting that inland and abroad are in some ways not far apart. The other becomes something of a double. Indeed, one might even say: the other is a soul brother.

Blurred Borders

At once a panegyric and a panacea, *The Prodigal Son* extols the homeland and exorcises a foreign body. It is not enough simply to glorify Germany; one must fully divest America of its imaginary allure. Trenker's film rescues its hero from the threat of modernity and massification, restoring Tonio to his origins, reclaiming him for the eternal present of a premodern past.[80] The final sequence captures the stirring *Rauhnacht,* a raucous event celebrated over several days before Christmas in various southern German and Austrian mountaintop venues. On this occasion, villagers worship nature and sanctify tradition.[81] Going back to a pagan spectacle, a Germanic homage to Wotan and the hunt, the festival also doubles as the tamer winter solstice *(Wintersonnenwende)* of the Nazi calendar.[82]

Another prodigal son had appeared in Richard Billinger's highly successful play of 1931, *Rauhnacht,* a drama Trenker knew well.[83] Simon, an ex-monk, also returns from a sojourn abroad to experience the *Rauhnacht.* In his case, though, the event brings catastrophe. Years in Africa as a missionary have warped his mind and tainted his being. A village girl asks Simon what things were like among the natives, and, overcome by the winter solstice revelry, he becomes a savage. A contemporary reviewer described Werner Krauss's rendering of Simon in Jürgen Fehling's powerful Berlin production:

> He tells the girl, whom just a few minutes later he will slaughter, about Africa, he pulls a devil's mask over his face, takes a Negro drum in hand, its noise meant to drown out the screams of the tormented, and suddenly this person becomes uncanny, spooky, he beats the drum, he dances, he screams, and in his screaming resounds the eternal song of eternal suffering, and the stomping of his body in fantastic rhythms leaves one breathless and shivering as one witnesses this transformation of a human being.[84]

Irrational nature and the unbridled life force take on sinister contours. More disturbing yet, Billinger's drama reveals an unsettling psychic landscape in which homeland and outland merge, for Simon's heart of darkness remains calm until the Germanic *Blubo* festival activates memories of African blood ritual. Clearly, this primitivist topography is every bit as imaginary as Trenker's journey into the New York night.

Images of blacks had served as key points of reference in Weimar debates about Americanism and German national identity. Depending on the speaker's cultural politics, "Negroes" *(Neger)* represented either a source of renewal for a moribund civilization or the mindless primitivism of alien hordes. By and large, discussants recognized how Americanism reflected German concerns and conditions, that it posed "a new orientation to being, grown out of and formed in our European destiny."[85] Responding with enthusiasm to Josephine Baker and the "Revue Nègre," Yvan Goll described how black dancers took the continent by storm. Garbing themselves in European trappings, they frolicked with instinct and abandon. Their lithe movements and uninhibited performances made a travesty of a paralyzed and comatose Occident.[86] These denizens of New York ghettos "dance with their blood, with their life, with all the memories in their short history: memories of transport in stinking ships, of early slave labor in America, of much misfortune."[87] The black entertainers from abroad, claimed Theodor Lessing, cut through all the neuroses and complexes of a decadent white culture. Lessing's description of Josephine Baker, like Goll's, cannot help but take us aback: "Healthy, unassuming, and with a clear conscience, an innocent natural naked baby ape walks among long since housebroken and cultivated animals, shaking its charming belly, spitting at all this refinement and exposing itself."[88] Blacks become cast in a host of roles: innocents, immigrants, invaders. They embody the spirit of American modernity or, alternatively, a primitive life force. No matter what the guise, the figures are ciphers, the projective functions of German preoccupations.

It is appropriate, then, that Trenker's reckoning with Weimar Americanism accords blacks a prominent role. The first reference to life outside the homeland comes as the village teacher starts his geography lesson: "Last time we were in Africa among the blacks." The foreign prospects stimulate Tonio's imagination and ultimately compel him to leave home. Blacks will shadow him throughout his stay in Manhattan, reflecting his dissolution as if they and he were somehow related. When Tonio cannot find work, for instance, his humiliation is emphasized by the smiling black next to him who gets the job. Underlining the imaginary quality of this scenario, the figure is played by an actor in blackface whose voice has a German accent. (The New York police likewise all speak with Teutonic inflections.) As a homeless Tonio later walks about, an aimless witness of street life, we cut to a subjective shot of two blacks in front of an anonymous building, immigrants like himself who have time on their hands and nowhere to go.

Tonio's fortune turns in Madison Square Garden when he jumps into the ring and subdues an out-of-control boxer.[89] As the audience roars, his most conspicuous attendants are blacks, whom we see in repeated reaction shots, standing in the balcony and screaming with approval, gyrating wildly and ripping off their clothes. The native son regains himself, finding his way into

The Alpine hero's luck turns in Madison Square Garden when he throttles a raging bull. Tonio, the film suggests, could have been a contender.

the house of Mr. Williams and winning the heart of Lilian. Tonio could have it all. (If he wanted, the film suggests, he could even be a contender.) His decision to come home is therefore all the more momentous. Forgoing the lesser glories of America, he returns not as a repentant, but indeed a triumphant, hero.[90] Tonio's dominion above all means a reinstated identity, a reestablished presence. No more is he a homeless person or an idle spectator—that is, in the film's logic, a nonentity, the visual equivalent of a black.[91]

Anti-Americanism and racism blend in a discourse that incorporates German anxieties and projects them onto a cultural adversary, allowing audiences a pseudo-experience of otherness and the simultaneous illusion of superiority. The Manhattan episode is a Nazi *Twilight Zone,* popular fiction that betrays social truth. A nightmarish America—its every corner monitored by ubiquitous police, a land of forlorn masses, a place of constant movement and disquiet—bears much German residue. The *Rauhnacht* reveling echoes the intoxication of Madison Square Garden, the sight of shimmying berserkers and carnivalesque physiognomies. No doubt, the narrative structure means to maintain an opposition between an alienated mass culture and an organic village festival. Still, the two scenes—much like the matched dissolve between the Dolomites and skyscrapers—appear just as compelling in their affinities. Both the boxing match and the *Rauhnacht* are communal celebrations that catalyze a contagious frenzy. Boundaries between individual and mass dissolve and give way to boundless surrender before emotional spectacles.

Trenker's cultic *Rauhnacht* hallowed a community's native soul and organic soil. The spirit of the mountaintop ceremony, likewise, had much to do with the spirit of the times. Not only Tyrolean villagers resurrected primal powers in nocturnal rites with bonfires and torches. Throughout Germany masses of drunken revelers in striking costumes cheered the country's awakening, promulgating ancient myths, embracing wildness in the name of a new order. These were potent forces and constantly threatened to get out of hand. (Witness the excess imputed to the contemporaneous "Night of the Long Knives.") To the displeasure of some party officials,[92] Billinger had intimated the bloody potential of a homeland that worships blood and soil. The *Film-Kurier* notice of 4 October, an otherwise glowing review, described Trenker's *Rauhnacht* scene as strange and hard to fathom. Without question, *The Prodigal Son* is most interesting in its landscapes of the mind which explore sociopsychic disturbance: it not only reduces America to a German dream; it renders the *Heimat unheimlich.*

Rauhnacht: a blend of pagan ritual and *völkisch* celebration couched in mountain film iconography.

Nazi fantasy production endeavored—with mixed success—to occupy and control all territory in a concerted effort to eradicate alterity. In *The Prodigal Son,* there is no space that does not relate to the protagonist, no shot or object that is not narratively contained or psychologically bound. There is never a locality or a detail that exists for its own sake, an entity with a distinct presence or room of its own. We could not be further from the redemptive realism embraced by Kracauer, the direct experience of the physical world in all its haptic and phenomenological possibility. This film captures stunning shots of depression America, but these images have little to do with Neorealism, no matter what Trenker or critics would have us believe. The experience of the "other"—be it a seductive woman, men of color on the street, a shot of the Empire State Building or the Statue of Liberty—always reflects on the emigrant hero and his homegrown preoccupations. The foreign country becomes above all a space that resonates with fears—both imaginary and real—very much on the minds of Germans in 1934, fears displaced to another country, all the better to convince people they did not exist at home.[93]

The topography of *The Prodigal Son,* its demarcation between glorious native soil and peril-ridden foreign terrain, between *Heimat* and *Fremde,* resembles the imaginary order of many subsequent *Heimatfilme.*[94] In homeland films of the 1950s such as *Grün ist die Heide* (*Green Is the Heather,* 1951) and *Der Förster vom Silberwald* (*The Game Warden of the Silver Forest,* 1955), German countrysides and mountaintops become grand nature preserves untouched by wartime devastation and Allied occupation. Typically, vigilant foresters militate against outside agitators, ruthless poachers who threaten the natural order, urban intruders who disturb intact communities. Scenes of timeless landscapes and villages, however, bore topical meanings for the postwar German public; the homeland film became perhaps the most prominent popular vehicle of the Adenauer era's Cold War rhetoric.[95] Even in the subsequent attempts to reshape and subvert the genre by New German filmmakers, we encounter remnants of its binary structure, quite explicitly, for instance in Volker Vogeler's *Verflucht, dies Amerika* (*Damn This America,* 1973), a tale of fugitives from Bavaria who cross the Atlantic only to meet their doom in the Wild West.

Edgar Reitz's *Heimat* (1984) stands a half-century apart from *The Prodigal Son* but mirrors its anti-Americanism with uncanny precision. Paul Simon leaves the Hunsrück to make his fortune in Michigan. He is a *Weggeher,* an emigrant who loses his identity and integrity in a land of immigrants. The film does not depict Simon's experience in the New World; it only shows the result. Reitz's prodigal son returns to Schabbach on an afternoon in 1946. He is not alone. He arrives in a large limousine with a black chauffeur. The industrialist and his driver, their motions matched, emerge from opposite sides of the car. Simon walks down the road, and, like a shadow, the black strolls behind him. The car and the *Doppelgänger* stand out conspicuously in the all but premodern village. Simon may have flourished abroad, but the film's final episodes reveal at what price. He never finds his way back into the homeland community and to the end remains marked as an outsider.

"In our German culture," Reitz wrote in 1979, "there is hardly a more ambivalent feeling, hardly a more painful mixture of happiness and bitterness than the experience vested in the word 'Heimat.' "[96] *Heimat* is a site of emotional fixity as well as a source of conceptual slippage. An imaginary property, it possesses a fluid exchange value. The commodity served Luis Trenker well, who was, if anything, a man of fancy steps and double strategies, a person perpetually on the make and between stations. Trenker's talent lay in his skillful negotiation of *Heimat* in changing times and situations.

While receiving accolades as Nazi cinema's great hope and as a patriotic defender of German soil, Trenker pursued around-the-clock negotiations

Luis Trenker, the German homeland's ever-upbeat hero: "Alles gut gegangen."

about relocating in Hollywood.[97] Put to the test and forced to make a choice, he opted in 1940 to forsake his native Tyrol and become a resident of the Reich. He subsequently succeeded in covering his tracks, alleging he had put off making a decision and had always revered his native heritage. In the Adenauer era, he arose as a model cold warrior, a man disdainful of all ideologies and an ardent devotee of America. In Panitz's 1986 documentary of Trenker, we see the octogenarian reenact scenes from *The Prodigal Son* in original Manhattan locations. Even though garbed in the costume of Tonio Feuersinger, Trenker is, so the portrait would have us believe, immediately recognized by onlookers as the famous German filmmaker. The *völkisch* prototype thus resurfaces as a beloved foreign celebrity. The prodigal son returns to New York City, and this time America hails the conquering hero.

To this day Luis Trenker resides in German popular culture as an exemplary fate, a life of steadfastness, continuity, and good cheer: "Alles gut gegangen." More than anyone else in the postwar era, he took the bitterness and the ambivalence out of threatened emotional properties with his reassuring evocations of a home sweet *Heimat.* A high-tech romantic, an indefatigable showman, a consummate pasticheur, Trenker capitalized on primeval sentiments with calculating simulations, marketing timely fantasies in the guise of timeless moments. The director's unbroken appeal over many decades demonstrates the durable—and regressive—potential of utopian longings. *Heimat* opened doors and moved mountains. It was the prodigal son's *passe-partout.* He never left home without it.

"German film looks at America's films like a rabbit staring at a snake" (Mathias Wieman).

FOUR

Hollywood Made in Germany: *Lucky Kids* (1936)

His notions of the "American way of life" were drawn from Frank Capra's films, from the musical comedies with Fred Astaire and Ginger Rogers. They could still be seen up to 1938 in Germany. He hadn't missed any of them; some he'd seen several times, like *It Happened One Night.* He was intrigued not by the comic plot but by the unimaginable personal freedom and the American sense of humor that these films conveyed.

Karl Münch

A pie in the face of Lilian Harvey has no more political significance than one in the face of Stan Laurel.

Andreas Meyer

Spirited Abandon

Trenker's *The Prodigal Son* takes leave from a foreign inferno and spirits its hero back home. Paul Martin's *Glückskinder (Lucky Kids)* appears much more favorably disposed to America;[1] rather than *Heim ins Reich* to the *Rauhnacht,* its manifest destiny is a happy end and a Manhattan night. A German counterpart to Frank Capra's *It Happened One Night* (1934), it tours the streets of the New World and embraces Hollywood conventions, dressing up German actors in American garb, crafting Ufa sets to simulate Big Apple locations. Trenker's and Martin's films seem opposed in tone and emphasis: one provides powerful images of an urban maelstrom that engulfs the emigrant, the other shows us a world of sunny sentiments and madcap dispositions. The peppy likes of *Lucky Kids* in fact would appear to support claims that the Nazi regime created space for innocent diversions; it seems to reflect a public sphere not completely lorded over by state institutions and to exhibit an everyday with a much less sinister countenance. We cannot fully fathom film in the Third Reich unless we consider the crucial functions played by popular entertainments such as *Lucky Kids.*

Martin's 1936 production unfolds in a realm that knows nothing of Leni Riefenstahl's mass ornaments or Hans Steinhoff's paeans to self-sacrifice. As with the vast majority of films made under Goebbels, we encounter neither steeled bodies nor iron wills, no racist slurs, state slogans, or party emblems. Martin's characters dance about with zest, singing of joyful lives without responsibility:

> I wish I were a chicken!
> I wouldn't have much to do!
> I'd lay an egg in the morning
> And take the afternoon off![2]

Intrepid reporters make merry and drink great amounts of liquor. The world of *Lucky Kids*—the *New York Times* initially rendered its title as *Lucky Folks*[3]—is far from the politicized streets of Beuselkietz and the closed mountain community of St. Laurein. "Miss Nobody loves Mr. Whatever," runs a refrain we hear throughout the film, and the two live happily ever after "in a castle in the air called Nowhere." Charm and wit take the place of pathos, gravity, and obligation. The compact narrative has a classical design, unfolding swiftly and fluidly from its deft opening sequence to its upbeat romantic conclusion.

Gil Taylor, an enterprising beginner at the *New York Morning Post,* has lyrical aspirations and wants to publish his poetry in the newspaper. His two colleagues, Frank Black and Stoddard, disinclined to fill in for a drunken reporter, conspire to have Taylor cover night court, persuading him that this assignment might mean his big break. Taylor shows up as Ann Garden, charged with vagrancy, faces a stiff sentence. Meaning well, he steps forward and claims he will take care of her—he is her fiancé. To expedite matters, the judge arranges a lightning wedding and, to the cheers of the crowd and approval of the press, the two leave the courtroom, and, bickering the entire way, stop for dinner and retire to Gil's apartment. For the moment they stay together even if not as man and wife. The next morning their tale is all over the papers, except the *Morning Post,* for Gil has failed to file a story. He is promptly sacked, as are Black and Stoddard.

The trio regroup, aiming to win back their jobs and a $50,000 reward by tracking down a millionaire's missing niece, who, they are convinced, is really Ann Garden. Ann, for her part, masquerades as the kidnapped relative—to the outrage of Gil, who, having thought her a woman in distress, now considers her a conniving spoiled brat. She persuades the oil baron Mr. Jackson to play along with the ruse in hopes that the responsible party will either let the niece go or make a false move. In the attendant confusion, a burly stranger abducts Ann and drags her to the niece's hideout. The whole disappearance is a fake, Ann learns, staged to make Jackson relent and allow the niece to marry her boxer boyfriend. Jackson, Taylor, Stoddard, and Black witness Ann's capture, give hot pursuit, and appear on the scene. After some scuffling, everything falls into place: Jackson gets his niece and the niece her boxer; a sensational story written by Stoddard and Black appears in the *Morning Post,* as does Taylor's poetry. And, in the end, Gil and Ann come together—as man and wife.

Lifting key plot elements from *It Happened One Night* (the disappearance of a rich man's unruly ward, the prolonged battle of wits between a brash journalist and a spirited woman),[4] *Lucky Kids* appeared as a rarity, a domestic production that could stand up to Hollywood. Shot from May through July 1936 in the Babelsberg studios, the Ufa film reunited the popular romantic couple Lilian Harvey and Willy Fritsch in a comedy under the direction of Paul Martin. (The trio had just completed the very successful Ufa espionage drama, *Schwarze Rosen/Black Roses.*) Both Harvey and Martin had returned in 1935 from lengthy sojourns abroad. Harvey enjoyed the reputation of an international star, Martin that of someone with firsthand experience as the director of the Hollywood feature *Orient Express* (1934). Martin, throughout his career, showed a flair for elaborate traveling shots, such as the nimble track/crane through a window at the start of *Preußische Liebesgeschichte* (*Prussian Love Story,* 1938) and the extended explorations of a Bedouin camp in *Das Lied der Wüste* (*The Song of the Desert,* 1939). His musicals abound with high spirits, from the vivacious *Ein blonder Traum* (*Happy Ever After,* 1932) to the hyperexuberant *Maske in Blau* (*Mask in Blue,* 1943).[5] *Lucky Kids* rejoined fan magazines' dream couple—everyone's sweetheart Harvey ("das süßeste Mädel der Welt") and matinee idol Fritsch—with a seasoned pro fresh from a stint at 20th Century–Fox.[6]

In addition came the spunky character actors Paul Kemp and Oskar Sima, along with the well-turned dialogues of scriptwriter Curt Goetz, the snappy score by Peter Kreuder and insouciant songs by Hans Fritz Beckmann ("I Wish I Were a Chicken!" and "Miss Nobody"), and the fluid cinematography of Konstantin Irmin-Tschet. Ufa set designer Erich Kettelhut recreated a New York newsroom, a perfect copy, boasted a *Film-Kurier* observer, down to the smallest detail.[7] America was, no doubt about it, not Germany,

Lilian Harvey and Willy Fritsch, Germany's most popular romantic couple of the 1930s (from *Liebeswalzer/The Love Waltz*).

maintained the *Lichtbild-Bühne:* "People over there have a completely different mentality. But if we want to take a look at a world otherwise foreign to us, *Lucky Kids* serves as a good guide."[8]

Immediate reactions were enthusiastic. "Bravo! Bravo!" effused the *Film-Kurier* reviewer: "What the Americans can do, we can do as well." Here was a German film with lightness and verve, dialogue that "sparks and sparkles," a splendid score ("everything in rhythm, everything in sync"), a wonderful ensemble. Martin's direction scintillated: "He created a comedy that you can look at and, more important, for a change one that you can listen to as well." Waves of laughter rolled through the Gloria-Palast during the premiere screening on 18 September 1936, and long applause greeted the stars afterward.[9] "A film full of charm, spirit, and music," claimed the *Berlin Lokal-Anzeiger.* "One hasn't been so amused in the Gloria-Palast for ages," the *Völkischer Beobachter* agreed. The notice in *Das 12-Uhr-Blatt* was even more pointed: "Sincere, unceasing enthusiasm and thankful recognition were the reward for this film, which has stopped the victory parade of the American comedy."[10] *Lucky Kids,* remarked the *Variety* correspondent in Berlin, constituted Ufa's "first serious attempt to go Broadway . . . The film looks to be a smash."[11]

German Fantasies, American Dreams

Just how much influence did Hollywood have in the Third Reich?[12] Throughout the Weimar Republic, films from America had occasioned heated debate, playing the part—depending on one's persuasion—of German cinema's nemesis or its role model, and in any case demonstrating an indefatigable resilience during these years of crisis.[13] Creating a national cinema, even as artists contemplated formal alternatives and cultivated an experimental counterpraxis, meant responding to Hollywood. Despite some official reservations, German filmmakers and critics of the 1930s openly admired the professional craft, seemingly inexhaustible talent, and—all the more since the coming of sound—technical prowess behind American movies.

Commentaries accompanying the production and reception of *Lucky Kids* made it clear that American features retained a strong profile after 1933, that this foreign dream factory continued to shape domestic fantasies and impressed on German audiences—ProMi luminaries, industry observers, and everyday filmgoers alike—a painful awareness of something missing at home. A *Film-Kurier* correspondent in Brussels took in recent

Hollywood films during September 1934. Although he claimed to see through their trite love stories and sensationalistic plots, the productions still overwhelmed him with a "glowing photography that radiates from the screen." German films, he lamented, seemed dusty and wornout next to these images made under the California sun.[14] True, trade papers of the mid-1930s ran numerous articles by party officials, essays about film in the service of the German nation and the Führer, solemn treatises on the ineffable laws of the medium, fervent polemics against antiquated formulas and movies behind the times, as well as pleas for films about the present. Nonetheless, these same pages also contained one account after another about American productions.[15] A screening of Disney cartoons at the Marmorhaus in late 1934, for instance, incited squeals of delight and prompted a reviewer to repeat the often-posed—and inescapable—question: "Why can't we do this here too?"[16]

Analyses of German film culture in the mid-1930s alternated between self-assured panegyrics and less encouraging perspectives.[17] Without a doubt, the industry found itself in dire straits, a situation that had steadily worsened since 1933, a function of rising production costs,[18] insufficient ticket sales, widespread public dissatisfaction, declining export revenues, and an overall sense of crisis, which by 1937 reached alarming proportions. Prewar German box-office statistics reflect at best modest rises in attendance at a time of astronomically high production costs (see Table 2). All too often sanguine pronouncements sought to gloss over mediocre German releases. Writing during a visit to the United States in late November 1935, film journalist Ernst Jaeger addressed this discrepancy between rhetoric and reality: "People in Hollywood are neither so dumb nor so poor as to think that they can praise incompetent and self-important films as something wonderful when in the cinema all they do is produce boredom and leave the audience completely cold."[19] The official decree of 27 November 1936 banning criticism for the sake of more descriptive reviews undoubtedly intended to neutralize detractors and boost enthusiasm for domestic films.[20] Goebbels intensified his efforts to rebuild a film industry that had never really recovered since the coming of sound. In this context American successes made for double frustration: envy of what one lacked, dissatisfaction with what one had.

German audiences and critics championed films such as King Vidor's *Our Daily Bread,* Frank Lloyd's *Cavalcade,* Borzage-Lubitsch's *Desire* (the last Dietrich film shown in Nazi Germany), Henry Hathaway's *Peter Ibbetson,*

Table 2 German box-office statistics, 1929–1939

Year	Number of tickets sold	Gross income (million RM)
1929	328	273
1930	290	244
1931	273	197
1932	238	176
1933	245	117
1934	259	195
1935	304	231
1936	362	282
1937	396	309
1938	430	335
1939	624	411

Source: Hans Traub, ed., *Die Ufa. Ein Beitrag zur Entwicklungsgeschichte des deutschen Filmschaffens* (Berlin: Ufa-Buchverlag, 1943), p. 156.

and W. S. Van Dyke's *San Francisco*.[21] Among the 210 features premiered in 1934, almost 20 percent came from Hollywood; a year later, 92 German first-runs competed with 41 American releases (see Table 3).[22] Programs of Disney cartoons at the Marmorhaus (Berlin's main showcase for Hollywood films) attracted critical raves and throngs of viewers each year at Christmas. Filmgoers in the Reich's capital could also watch American (and other foreign) titles in original versions at the "Kurbel" and "Kamera unter den Linden."[23] American product remained "a necessary supplement, especially in the big cities." On 2 July 1936 the *Film-Kurier* reported in its lead article that German studios could not fill the demand of domestic theaters. This circumstance, the article went on to say, served Germany's best interests, not only economically, but artistically: "It is no disgrace to admit that recent German films have learned a lot from good American films. International cultural and artistic exchange has always been the case. Even Dürer once traveled to Venice in order to acquaint himself with the formal impulses of the Renaissance."[24] German audiences not only liked American films; German exhibitors relied on them.

Hathaway's *The Lives of a Bengal Lancer*—"a primer of manly valor"—would have a major impact on German war films. Several years later the *Völkischer Beobachter* would extol Clark Gable's heroics in *Test Pilot* along similar lines. Westerns such as *Der Kaiser von Kalifornien (The*

Table 3 Foreign feature films exhibited in the Third Reich

Year	Total features	German features No.	German features %	American features	Total foreign features
1933	206	114	55.3	64	92
1934	210	129	61.4	41	81
1935	188	92	48.9	41	96
1936	176	112	63.6	28	64
1937	172	94	54.7	39	78
1938	162	100	61.7	35	62
1939	145	111	76.6	20	34
1940	103	85	82.5	5	18
1941	81	67	82.7	—	14
1942	87	57	65.5	—	30
1943	101	78	77.2	—	23
1944	77	64	83.2	—	13

Source: Boguslaw Drewniak, *Der deutsche Film 1938–1945. Ein Gesamtüberblick* (Düsseldorf: Droste, 1987), p. 814.

Emperor of California), Sergeant Berry, and *Gold in New Frisco* reflected a German fascination with the myth of the California Gold Rush.[25] Willi Forst readily admitted how much his successful *Allotria* owed to American comedies. Hans H. Zerlett, likewise, consciously fashioned his musical production numbers after those of Busby Berkeley. Marika Rökk modeled her tapdancing in *Gasparone* after Eleanor Powell's stepping in *Broadway Melody of 1936.* Set designer Erich Kettelhut, Rökk later recalled, took many of his ideas from American revue films.[26] The New Year's Eve celebration of *San Francisco* was recast in *Wasser für Canitoga (Water for Canitoga). Lucky Kids* likewise borrowed freely from two recent Hollywood features with journalists.

Hollywood remained at once a source of embarrassment and a point of reference, an unceasing cause of frustration as well as a continuing object of German desire. "I know," said Goebbels in his programmatic Kroll Opera address of 1937, "we lack the great opportunities that other nations enjoy. We do not have America's human and material wealth. We also do not have the California sun. We have to make do with what little we have, but in critical situations the German people have always proved themselves capable of making a virtue of necessity."[27] The German film world, in other words, remained provincial and anachronistic; no one had yet found a way to modernize its aesthetic and industrial potential. The problem lay in creating a national cinema in which precision, professionalism, and popular appeal represented the guiding creative categories.[28] Talk as party officials might about the distinct character of German cinema and its promise, about its abundant talent and untapped possibilities, about film's cultural role in the shaping of a great nation, it remained clear after several years of National Socialist rule that American films still retained an enthusiastic German following.

Was there a perceived contradiction between official invocations of National Socialist cultural purity and the undeniable presence of American products? Hans Dieter Schäfer claims that Hitler's Germany was the site of an unabashed Americanism that shaped consumer habits and affected daily behavior every bit as strongly as party doctrine. In 1939, for instance, Coca-Cola had more than 2,000 German distributors as well as fifty bottlers. Ocean liners bound to New York departed every Thursday from Hamburg. Modern appliances such as electric coffeemakers, stoves, refrigerators, and washing machines, items well known from American movies and magazines, increasingly found their way into German households. Until war broke out, one could purchase a wide array of international periodicals on most big-city newsstands. Numerous books about the United States with a pro-American slant appeared in the Reich from 1933 through 1939. German movie weeklies such as *Filmwelt* and *Filmwoche* regularly featured Hollywood stars on their covers. Fashion journals contained ads for the latest American cosmetics and lingerie.[29] Despite official proscription, jazz "continued not only to exist, but to flourish in Germany after January 1933, right up to the beginning of war."[30] American mass culture, its consumer items and popular icons, offered designs for living in a modern world.[31]

Nazi Germany, argues Schäfer, was the site of a collective schizophrenia, a function of a gap between an official representative culture and an everyday popular culture that offered a variety of unpolitical, even illicit, diversions:

> From 25 to 30 September 1937, the Kurbel on the Kurfürstendamm ran a Marlene Dietrich retrospective. As Mussolini drove down the Via Triumphalis [with Hitler], one could enter the film world of *Shanghai Express*, and afterward in the Femina-Bar applaud Teddy Stauffer, who . . . in his own way denied Hitler's militarism and chauvinism as he played "Swingin' for the King" and "Goody Goody."[32]

Many Germans, according to Detlev Peuckert, led a "double life," toeing the line and fulfilling public obligations while moving in a private sphere and "pursuing non-political spare-time pleasures with minimal possible interference."[33] A film such as *Lucky Kids* would appear to pose a radical extension of what Schäfer calls a "split consciousness": an Ufa film made with official sanction which deferred to the culture and conventions of one's fiercest foreign competitor.

"If I want to watch American musicals," Goebbels said in his programmatic address of 1937, "then I'll select one and watch it. Russian films are Bolshevist, Italian films are Fascist. That's the way of the world. If people want to see German films, then they expect to see National Socialist films."[34] *Lucky Kids,* premiered a few months earlier, seemed to belie the minister's words. An editorial titled "Teacher and Pupil" in *Der SA-Mann* on 23 October 1937 complained how blindly films such as *Lucky Kids* fixated on American models. Directors and scriptwriters who turned to Hollywood for inspiration simply forgot "the essential difference" between nations and underestimated Germany's own cinematic riches, films such as *Der Rebell (The Rebel), The Emperor of California, Friesennot (Frisians in Peril), Der Schimmelreiter (The Rider on the White Steed), Fährmann Maria (Ferry Boat Woman Maria), Der alte und der junge König (The Old and the Young King),* and *Traumulus.* At best one might pick up some technical tricks from foreign colleagues, but German cameramen, composers, and set designers could more than hold their own. So much of American film's allure was a simple function of larger budgets and better facilities:

> Nothing is more senseless than to doubt one's own capacities, which after all are solidly grounded in the myriad cultural endeavors of millennia, and instead to imitate slavishly the flashy facades of a handful of foreign successes. The more German film reflects on its Germanness and takes its power, sources, and effects from the essence of the German folk, the sooner it will free itself from American film.[35]

It was one thing to chide Hollywood films for their shallowness; it was quite another thing, however, to create a popular national cinema with a loyal national following.

Goebbels from the start had promised to revive and invigorate German film, making certain that the industry at once served commerce, art, and ideology. All films, he was fond of saying, were political, most especially those that claimed not to be. His diaries espoused a popular cinema free of overt intellectualism, political heavy-handedness, artistic and technical incompetence. Contrary to *völkisch* cohorts (such as the *SA-Mann* reviewer),

Goebbels believed German films could learn from their ideological enemy, especially regarding cinema's ability to intoxicate mass audiences. "I look at and study an American film," Goebbels noted in his diary entry of 17 March 1936, "*Broadway Melody of 1936.* Fluid, made with great tempo. The Americans are good at this. The content may be utter nonsense, but the way they do things is really something."[36] It made sense, claimed a critic writing in *Der Deutsche Film,* a monthly publication of the ProMi, to scrutinize a movie such as *After the Thin Man* and figure out why it worked so well: "It's hard to say what we admire more: the dexterity with which the comic complication is put into motion or the aplomb with which it is sustained; the austere use of dialogue, or the ease and naturalness behind this compact product of labor."[37]

Contemporary observers maintained that it would be short-sighted to reject Hollywood productions as mindless fare and to chide them for their spiritless technique. "These rapid reporters, revue directors, dance-line girls, secretaries, and enterprising wheeler-dealers emanate—despite their morbid and decadent environment—a very strong vitality."[38] The strength of American film lay in its undeniable physical immediacy and visceral appeal, its grand power to enchant and enrapture, its capacity for fostering viewer identification with sights and sounds made by someone else. It could sustain interest, gripping and engrossing spectators while granting them the illusion of comfort and freedom. The cinema offered escape in the form of compelling fantasies and worlds bigger than life.

In his 1926 essay "Cult of Distraction," Siegfried Kracauer had described a new urban mass public desperately hungry for experience, seeking in the dark of cinema the stimulation and excitement that the everyday withheld. The flow of images absorbed the viewer without making intellectual demands:

> The stimulations of the senses succeed each other with such rapidity that there is no room left for even the slightest contemplation to squeeze in between them. Like *life-buoys,* the refractions of the spotlights and the musical accompaniment keep the spectator above water.[39]

Goebbels knew well that an enthralled and spellbound subject would prove much more pliable than a viewer harangued by audiovisual terror. The minister sponsored a fair number of official state productions with a distinct political slant, ensuring that newsreels yielded their desired tendentious effect. Nonetheless, given a choice, he favored subtle persuasion to the obvious touch.[40] For this reason he had lauded the imagistic strength and visual aplomb of Luis Trenker and Leni Riefenstahl and repeatedly complained about Germany's lack of talented directors and scriptwriters. His film policy sought to politicize film art in an unparalleled manner; he aimed to do nothing less than transform it into a discipline of distraction. German films would become a crucial means of dominating people from within, a vehicle to occupy psychic space, a medium of emotional remote control. And in the endeavor to create the definitive dominant cinema, Goebbels and his minions in crucial regards let Hollywood be their guide.

When speaking of American cinema, reviewers in the Third Reich often described the popular film of the ProMi's dreams. Among the successes at German box offices, nobody's films figured as strongly as those of Walt Disney. "I present the Führer with thirty of the best films from the last four years and eighteen Mickey Mouse films for Christmas," Goebbels noted in his diary on 20 December 1937. "He is very pleased."[41] Disney cartoons raised pure immanence and artistic illusion to transcendent heights. "Mickey Mouse films," claimed a critic assessing the German film crisis late in 1934, "are the best films without political content, sublime embodiments of films which could not be more different from [Eisenstein's] *Battleship Potemkin.*"[42] They suspended the laws of reality in silly symphonies and dances of ideas, expressing "the creative magic of film with complete purity and not relying in any way on the real world."[43]

Disney's *The Three Little Pigs,* said the *Film-Kurier* in May 1935, appealed to youth's naive yen for experience, awakening childish innocence in us all.[44] Here was a filmmaker who stirred imaginations every bit as vividly as the Brothers Grimm:

> When Walt Disney's creatures [in *Snow White and the Seven Dwarfs*] . . . march through the woods, run, stumble, fly, dance—this whirl of events seems to occur naturally and yet in fact is just like a fairy tale, so much so that children feel the subtle effects in their very imaginations. There are no words spoken. This is a purely visual experience, something to be taken in with the eyes and the senses, and not with the intellect.[45]

Goebbels agreed. Shortly before banishing all American films from German cinemas, he described with enthusiasm "the magnificent artistic achievement" of *Snow White and the Seven Dwarfs,* a film never to enjoy an official run in Nazi theaters: "A fairy tale for grown-ups, thought out down to the last detail and made with a great love of humanity and nature. An artistic delight!"[46]

By and large, observers mused about Hollywood delights while lamenting that the Reich's domestic cinema rarely elicited such favorable responses. The great ambition of German films contrasted markedly with the great success of Hollywood productions. Next to no German titles sparked epiphanies, those precious moments when the viewer stops thinking and, utterly transfixed by the screen spectacle, rediscovers the child's capacity for wonder. *Lucky Kids* was a noteworthy exception, in the words of the *Berliner Börsen Courier,* "the most enchanting and graceful comedy to have come out of a German film studio in a long time." "An hour and a half goes by in no time at all," proclaimed the *Berliner Tageblatt.*[47] Critics lauded the film for its moments of abandon, repeatedly using a vocabulary favoring lightness, elegance, and tempo. The vociferous attack against the film and its songs in the SS organ, *Das Schwarze Korps,* made clear just how foreign and un-German the movie seemed to less smitten *völkisch* observers: "No, this kind of artistic production bears a distinct resemblance to the behavior of certain companies that while screaming to the world that they are now 'Aryan' still maintain their Jewish methods."[48] With a similar lack of success, Nazi party organizations had chided Disney cartoons as American kitsch, calling Mickey Mouse a degenerate rat.[49] At any rate, *Lucky Kids* seemed to prove at least two things: German filmmakers could compete with Hollywood professionals and, even without Jewish cast or crew members, could also

Table 4 American feature films released in Germany, 1935–1939, by studio

Studio	1935	1936	1937	1938	1939
Burroughs-Tarzan Pictures			1		
Columbia	2		1		
20th Century–Fox	3	6	14	8	6
MGM	18	8	10	12	6
Paramount	9	11	12	15	8
RKO	4				
United Artists	1				
Universal	3	1	1		
Viking-Film		1			
Warner Bros.	1				

Source: Alexander Jason, *Das Filmschaffen in Deutschland 1935–1939. I. Teil. Die Firmen und ihre Filme* (Berlin, 1940), pp. 27–30.

craft a well-liked comedy. A modern cinema of enchantment[50] with impressive sets, seamless editing, and inspired acting, *Lucky Kids* remade an American popular fiction in an Ufa studio, transforming a foreign fantasy into a German box-office hit.

Recast Screwball Comedy

Martin's *Lucky Kids* was therefore not so much a detour from Goebbels' film policy as a step in the desired direction. It was an anomaly only insofar as it was a German comedy that pleased German audiences—including Hitler, who ordered a copy for his Berghof collection. With confidence and verve, the film presented a fantasy of America gained from the dark of cinemas, the Hollywood world celebrated in one of its two songs:

> Miss Nobody loves Mr. Anyway.
> She's happy when she's near him!
> They both live in a castle in the air called Nowhere,
> In the land of dreams on the golden sea.
> One could also be just as happy as these two,
> But sad to say that happens only in fairy tales.
> Miss Nobody loves Mr. Anyway,
> Oh wouldn't it be wonderful, if I were Miss Nobody!

The lyrics offer a précis and a program. They describe a space far removed from everyday cares and troubles, a site so inviting one wishes to share the illusion. And that was exactly the concern: how to make films like one's competitor from "the land of dreams on the golden sea," films that might shape viewers into captivated and captive audiences.[51]

Many German films of the 1930s failed in this pursuit, engendering widespread discussion about why they so seldom pleased spectators. Although light films and musicals constituted roughly half (and sometimes more) of annual feature production through 1937,[52] only Detlef Sierck's *April, April!,* Reinhold Schünzel's *Amphitryon,* Willi Forst's *Allotria,* Carl Froelich's *Wenn wir alle Engel wären (If We All Were Angels)*, and Wolfgang Liebeneiner's *Der Mustergatte (The Model Husband)* stood out as truly resonant comedies.

It was rare enough, complained journalists even after 1936, that German films allowed audiences sustained pleasure.[53] But how was one to explain repeated instances of derisive laughter at melodramas, at films that hardly set out to be funny? Although commentators suggested that ill will might offer one explanation, they readily granted that the problem could also lie in overwrought acting, unconvincing scripts, and simple differences of taste. Whatever the reason, the phenomenon haunted studios and prompted great concern, for one "false laugher" could sabotage an entire screening and unleash a disastrous word of mouth.[54] Viktor Tourjansky's *Verklungene Melodie* (*Faded Melody,* 1938), an Ufa quality production, had aroused great expectations. At the festive premiere, as Brigitte Horney solemnly declared her love to Willy Birgel ("Everyone knows—everyone except you"), a single laugh resounded. It quickly caught on, and the screening quickly turned into a fiasco, the last sequence playing to loud roars of derision. Modest applause sprinkled with whistles (most of the audience had left early) greeted the actors as they took their bows. A scene with Werner Hinz and Kristina Söderbaum in Veit Harlan's *Jugend (Youth,* 1938) fell prey to a similar devastating demonstration.[55]

Laughter—German commentators of the 1930s agreed with Henri Bergson—is a form of collective therapy; it reaffirms communal standards. Its natural environment is society: we laugh above all in groups.[56] "False laughter," in contrast,

> is anything but a spontaneous, general audience response, as for instance hearty laughter at a witty remark; rather it is an individual action that at least initially lacks a resonance among the general audience. Nonetheless, as we know, a "false laugher" can bring about a film's complete demise, for such a response both interrupts and impairs the commonality of experience in the mass psychology, the "experiential web" that holds together the entire audience.

In short, false laughter exerts a subversive effect, destroying cinematic illusion and neutralizing the "suggestive power of the film image."[57] An out-of-synch laugher is a potential terrorist in the dark, someone who refuses to let the screen cast its spell. No matter how isolated a presence, the figure lurked in the wings as a specter, an *élan vital* and dissenting voice with an incendiary potential.

The NSDAP "coordinated" institutions and organizations. The Ministry of Propaganda monitored film scripts, oversaw studio productions, and dictated press responses. Despite all these measures, one could not simply command German audiences to love German films. The challenge remained: how to find more effective ways of orchestrating what went on in the dark of cinemas. (On the street and at mass rallies, Nazi showmen had much less trouble.)[58] Goebbels envisioned a pleasure machinery capable of surefire illusions, an incomparable means of stimulating mirth and manipulating emotion. The initial endeavors, however, hardly replicated the fantasy ware he had in mind. German comedies left people cold, melodramas incited open scorn, tendentious as well as intellectual fare alienated viewers. "Many worries about film," the minister complained late in 1936. "The Führer is also extremely dissatisfied with the way things are going. But there is nothing I can do. We lack the personnel, the talent, the loyal artists."[59] As Goebbels took stock in his Kroll Opera address of 1937, he strained to sound confident and upbeat but could not deny how much there remained to accomplish: "Art is no light matter. It is inordinately hard and sometimes even brutal."[60] The art of entertainment was neither simple nor straightforward; it was, no question about it, a serious political business.

An American film such as *It Happened One Night,* on the other hand, made entertainment seem so easy. It premiered in October 1935 at the Marmorhaus in Berlin to great accolades and took other big cities by storm. Spectators in Hamburg, known for their reserve, burst out in spontaneous applause, moving the *Hamburger Tageblatt* to call the film "as invigorating as champagne," "as fresh as a morning bath."[61] Capra's film, shown initially in a subtitled and later in a dubbed version, dazzled German critics. The director, it was said, imbued the spectacle "with an effervescent vitality, so that you have no time to reflect, you are pulled along by one humorous scene after another and in the end are so out of breath and excited that all you can do is clap loudly."[62] *Lucky Kids* mimicked *It Happened One Night* and nonetheless passed for a German original, a cutout with its own shape. It relied on foreign patterns of recognition yet still proudly bore the appellation "made in Germany."

The opening moments of *Lucky Kids* provide a tour de force, a demonstration of a German film that knows the tricks of the trade. The credits roll by to breezy swing music. The camera is on the town. Seated in a limousine that eases down city avenues, it looks up with a visitor's fascination at skyscrapers and buildings, moving under train tracks, spying a cinema marquee with a film starring Joan Blondell, gliding through a sunny Central Park, glimpsing the Essex House in the distance. Unharried traveling shots segue into rapid cuts and staccato rhythms. "All the news appears first in the *Morning Post,*" reads a superimposed title, and we jerk from one sensation to another, moving actualities that freeze into still photographs and headline exclamations:

Ship Catastrophe in the Pacific!
Ohio versus Notre Dame 2–0!
Torrential Flood in Rio!
Street Fight in Chicago!
$100,000 Damages for a Broken Heart!
100 Meter Freestyle!
Seven-Alarm Fire!
New Speed Record!
Niece of Millionaire Jackson Missing after Boxing Match!

The film's first few minutes combine an efficient *mise en scène* and a breakneck montage, acquainting the viewer with a big city and a way of ordering experience. The *Morning Post* speaks a language of hyperbole and tempo, the discourse of *faits divers,* "that same old unrevealing confusion" described by Kracauer, "which does not grant insight into the world, but rather prevents it."[63] The montage sequence closes with footage from a boxing match, linking the event to the millionaire's missing niece, providing a neat transition between this whirlwind exposition and the narrative to come. As with each of the previous newspaper images, we again see the superimposed title, "*Morning Post,*" which spills off the page and covers the frame. The composition dissolves to the interior of a busy newsroom, and the camera is off and running, tracking laterally in pursuit of a messenger boy, leading us to Stoddard's desk as the reporter answers a phone and the high jinks commence.

Lucky Kids, like the *Morning Post,* embraces the new and the noteworthy, seeking to piece together scintillating tidbits in agreeable and diverting patterns. Sport events, catastrophes, domestic dramas—all become distilled into gripping images and vivid headlines. ("Is It Interesting?" reads a sign on the newsroom wall.) The opening sequence exhibits a film able to speak a foreign language fluently and fluidly,[64] changing modalities and registers, shuffling stock footage and studio takes, leading spectators on a Manhattan sightseeing tour and, in a flash, leaping across the globe. The subsequent exchanges in the *Morning Post* newsroom sustain the quick pace, one glib encounter topping the next as colleagues dash from desk to desk trying to fob off the undesired night court beat.

Curt Goetz's dialogues have all the bite of lines by Ben Hecht, if little of their venom. *Lucky Kids* celebrates journalistic enterprise, rarely casting aspersions on the profession's flimflammery and sensationalism in the manner of Nazi films such as *Togger* and *Ohm Krüger.*[65] Stoddard convinces the rookie Gil Taylor he has to move around in the real world and prove his mettle, leaving the beginner with the questionable wisdom: "You've got to get your hands dirty if you want to throw mudballs." Oskar Sima and Paul Kemp talk a mile-a-minute, the former's hard-boiled cracks bouncing off the other's nimble ripostes in sustained volleys of verbal Ping-Pong. A no-nonsense managing editor is likewise nobody's fool, a fellow with a heart of gold—to lift a phrase from Hecht—if one cares to blast for it.[66] Subsequent encounters between Ann Garden and Gil Taylor unwind with the breakneck velocity and deadly precision characteristic of screwball comedy. "Look how tender she is," Gil proclaims to Stoddard and Frank as he lifts Ann out of a chair and faces her. "You could sleep in the shadow of a telephone pole." "Go ahead and just say it," she retorts. "You think I'm skinny." "You're not skinny, you're tender." "That's the same thing." "No it's not. A beefsteak can be thick and still be tender." "I'm not your beefsteak."

The film candidly owns up to its debts as yet another way of showing off. The extended musical number, "Ich wollt', ich wär' ein Huhn," has the foursome Harvey, Fritsch, Sima, and Kemp bouncing about as they prepare breakfast, replicating the popular set piece German audiences had loved in *Broadway Melody of 1936*, a movie that played for almost a year in Ku-Damm cinemas. "Sing before Breakfast" ("Sing schon am Morgen") and several other numbers from the musical became hit tunes and popular records.[67] Gil the poet tries out various first lines before he begins his song about the joys of being a chicken:

> I wouldn't have to go to the office anymore.
> I'd be stupid, but happy.

Clowning around like a slapstick ensemble, the group behaves in a way that is frivolous, irreverent, and, it would seem, utterly un-German. One need only compare these antics with the leaden and clumsy dance numbers of a contemporaneous musical comedy such as Carl Lamac and Hans H. Zerlett's *Knock out* (1935) or with the unbearably strained levity of the same year's Paul Kemp/Fita Benkhoff vehicle, *Der schüchterne Casanova* (*The Timid Casanova*, 1936).

The quartet sits down to eat and indulges in some tag-team daydreaming. Kemp, an inimitable *Rheinländer,* imagines himself to be a hen fluttering off to a Munich beer hall. Sima, on the other hand, his Austrian timbre undeniable, speaks of being Viennese and having a servant, a wish whose topography comes a bit closer to reality. Fritsch goes on, waving his thumb like the hitchhiker from *It Happened One Night:*

> I wish I were Clark Gable
> With a mustache and a sword!
> Because then I'd be—hip hip, hurray!—
> The hero of the U.S.A.!

A German romantic hero imitates the body language and apes the appearance of an American star. Fritsch's deference nonetheless seems at least in part ironic, for he ends his turn with a grimace and a snort of defiance: "Bah!" Lilian Harvey is next, making nonsense noises and humming the tune "Who's Afraid of the Big Bad Wolf" to the occasional interruption of Donald Duck quacks. She sings, "I wish I were Mickey Mouse, because then I'd look very funny," contorting her face to mimic the cartoon figure.[68]

Lucky Kids replicated a Hollywood film on a Babelsberg studio set, imitating a generic pleasure made in a foreign dream factory, in effect creating the illusion of an already illusory world, raising artifice to a higher power by frankly admitting its own derivation and desire. "I wish I were Clark Gable," says Gil Taylor, acknowledging that Willy Fritsch is a German stand-in for the more dashing lead of Frank Capra's original. "I wish I were Mickey Mouse," sings Lilian Harvey, Germany's closest equivalent to an international star, but a comedian who enjoyed only mixed success when she tried her luck in Hollywood. Behind all this merrymaking lies what appears to be the semblance of deeper meaning. Or is this self-reflection perhaps only a smokescreen, yet another illusion?

Fond Illusions

Almost four decades later, in 1974, the Berlin Film Festival screened *Lucky Kids* as part of a Lilian Harvey retrospective. The reprise occasioned ebullient praise of the comedy as the lightest and most American feature film ever to come out of a German studio.[69] When the West German Second Channel (ZDF) aired it during prime time in February 1975, critics rejoiced: "After forty years one has to rub one's eyes," wrote Friedrich Luft. "So there was after all a time when German film actually could produce a light, frothy, and utterly elegant musical comedy."[70] *Lucky Kids,* argued Andreas Meyer, makes liars of ideologues who summarily reduce all films from the Third Reich to Nazi propaganda. If anything, Martin's comedy allows us to "discover surprising free spaces for creativity and imagination" which continued to exist even under Goebbels. Consider, for instance, how the flippant song lyrics undermine the Nazi work ethic.[71]

Critics in the mid-1970s granted *Lucky Kids* the status of a rediscovered classic (Meyer: "Perhaps the best German film comedy of all time") and went even further. It was, they submitted, an instance of anti-Nazi subversion, a work that mocked the dominant political order. If one has any doubts about its impact, Meyer pointed out, one need only look at the harsh attack against the film in *Das Schwarze Korps.* The script's glib handling of journalists had raised official hackles from the start, Hans Borgelt insisted, and Harvey later left Germany and spoke out against the state.[72] Curt Goetz, anything but a party-liner, also emigrated to America in 1939.[73] While commentators hailed the film as an anomaly, they also sought to enroll it as a paradigm, evidence of a larger truth, namely that Ufa productions in the Third Reich did not simply dance to the beat of Goebbels' drums. *Lucky Kids* thus became both an exception and the rule, a confirmation of Axel Eggebrecht's larger proposition: "Film in the Nazi state had to a great extent nothing to do with Nazi cinema!"[74]

Postwar pundits echo the praise of critics writing in 1936. Both groups stand enthralled before a perky comedy, admiring its emulation of American cinema, lauding its charming world of whimsy, claiming for it the status of a national treasure. In order to rescue the film as a subversive text, commentators now stress that it provoked wide displeasure and found an unfriendly official response. (Luft also notes that the film was closed to young audiences.) This, judging from what we know, was not quite the case. *Lucky Kids* assumed an integral role in the Nazi public sphere: a popular smash and critical hit, a film collected by Hitler, starring actors who often appeared together with party leaders, with dialogues by a writer much liked by the minister.[75] Ufa quickly sought to capitalize on the film's success with another Harvey/Fritsch vehicle directed by Martin, scripted by Goetz, and featuring Sima, *Sieben Ohrfeigen* (*Seven Slaps,* 1937), this time with an English setting. Although SA and SS spokesmen registered their dissatisfaction, everyone else, including the minister of propaganda, seems to have glimpsed in *Lucky Kids* a possible way out of a crisis, indeed hope for the future.

To say that *Lucky Kids* creates a charming world of illusion does not prove that the film—and films like it—engaged in ideological sabotage. The film, it has been noted, bears resemblance to a fairy tale.[76] Let us not forget that fairy tales typically have a moral. A celebration of wishful thinking,

Lucky Kids also affirmed official agendas. German commentators surely realized that *It Happened One Night* had deeper social meaning. For them it presented a victory of male initiative over a liberated woman, a reassertion of patriarchal privilege.[77] This was a decidedly willful reading, given how Capra's film transforms both the smug journalist and his spoiled companion, given that a great deal of its charm comes from the mutual metamorphosis that transpires during a three-day odyssey. *Lucky Kids* shifts Capra's emphasis and takes the road out of the movie. Ann appears as a vagabond, Gil as the cavalier who leaps to her rescue. Gil undergoes no transformation in the process, but rather cajoles Ann into coming around, coercing her in the end to say "please" so that the couple may consummate their already legal union.

In Nazi comedies, bitter truths often appear in very appealing shapes. Ann and Gil, for instance, meet "cute"—and they do so before the law. The felicities of *mise en scène* and agreeable actors plus the laughter of an onscreen audience reportedly delighted contemporary viewers. Ann, claims the judge, is charged with vagabondage. She has no place to live. "Is it a crime to have no money?" she asks in a stark close-up, her hair somewhat disheveled. "No," proclaims the judge framed in front of an American flag, "just forbidden. That is to say, undesirable [*unerwünscht*]. I mean unpleasant. For you as well as for us. We have no other choice but to deal with you." The "we" here extends beyond the fictional courtroom to the narrative and the film. Gil steps forward and guarantees he can take care of her. The remainder of the tale proves that, indeed, he can.[78]

Ann, whose last name is Garden, needs to be dealt with—that is to say, cultivated. The metaphorical logic extends beyond her name to the prop that separates the two each night in bed: a mobile shelf with cactus plants, quite a far cry from the blanket on a rope, the "Wall of Jericho," which stands between Gable and Colbert. Cultivating Ann means transforming a prickly vagrant into a willing partner so that Gil may clear away the cactus and have his way with Miss Garden.[79] Gable may well chide Colbert for her selfishness and impatience, but to a great extent their arguments rest on a difference in class. In *Lucky Kids,* both characters reflect decidedly petty-bourgeois predilections: Gil is orderly, quick to produce a marriage license when his landlady questions his late-night guest. Ann describes herself as "a respectable girl" and takes pride in her personal hygiene ("I always wash myself thoroughly"). No scene in *It Happened One Night* approaches the virulence of Gil's attack on Ann's sexual identity. Who are you anyway? he snaps. Where do you come from, why are you running around without a

Ann Garden's sexualized double, a vamp who speaks with a thick American accent and shares a love nest with a boxer.

home?[80] He regrets his crack about Ann's being frail. The problem is not so much "any lack in physical attributes, but rather the lack in softness of soul and femininity which makes me wonder all the more whether you really are a girl at all . . . And you will permit me to keep doubting until doubting no longer needs to be permitted."[81]

Harvey plays a second—uncredited—role, that of the vampish and heavily made-up millionaire's niece, a femme fatale who inhabits a love nest and who (unlike anyone else in the film) speaks with a distinctly American accent. Gil's doubts about Ann Garden's lacking womanliness evaporate when he confronts her sexualized double. The comedy's conclusion thus means no more trouble in paradise. It also ensures a triumph of the willy: the woman Gil brings home finally becomes Frau Taylor.

Lucky Kids cultivated Ann Garden and brought home Lilian Harvey. Much press attention followed the actress's return: it accompanied *Heim ins Reich* discourse about the misfortune of other German stars in Hollywood as well as regular caustic notices about the departed Marlene Dietrich.[82] The film rehabilitated a returned German star and director who had been given up as lost to the New World, and derived from this much ideological advantage. Their arrival meant artistic and political gains for a film industry quite eager to replicate Hollywood illusions. *Lucky Kids* recreated a mythical America, reaffirming popular prejudices about the nation's ruthless tempo. At the same time, a German production proved it could keep up with its fiercest competitor, and do so without foreign—that is to say, Jewish—help.

Emulating Hollywood, Goebbels hoped, would foster a German popular cinema that could enable the ultimate application of power, a power that worked discreetly, by signs and representations.[83] Martin's film presented a never-never land created in a studio and made for the cinema, a site of irresponsibility, reverie, and good cheer. This realm would serve as both a compromise and a consolation. People more readily accepted National Socialism because it offered them a sense of belonging as well as the illusion of a private life. This was not so much a matter of what Schäfer calls a "split consciousness" as it was a double identity; the two realms were not separate, but rather of a piece. Films crafted along American lines, engaging entertainments seemingly devoid of politics, provided a respite from the hard work increasingly demanded of Germans, the constant sacrifice, the atmosphere of threat.

If the Hitler regime expected absolute allegiance, it also offered tangible remuneration in the form of consumer goods and leisure pursuits, amenities not unlike the state-sponsored "feelies" and creature comforts of Aldous Huxley's *Brave New World*. Realizing that loyalty could not be sustained by brute force and terror alone, the Nazis struck a bargain with the German people, satisfying appetites and stimulating imaginations. "It may be all right to have power that is based on guns," Goebbels had said at the 1934

Nuremberg rally; "however, it is better and more gratifying to win the heart of a nation and to keep it."[84] As the Nazi government made its first moves toward implementing Hitler's expansionist designs, Goebbels endeavored to maximize film's seductive potential, to cloak party priorities in alluring shapes, to aestheticize politics in order to anesthetize the populace. Cinema, rather than espousing party mythologies, would become the site of grand illusions. And the grandest illusion created in studios increasingly under state control was the illusion that within this state certain spaces remained beyond control—especially the space of cinema and fantasy production.

A remake of *It Happened One Night* starring the nation's best-known romantic couple[85] became a huge success and an ideological victory, a film that transformed a Hollywood hit into a German *Schlager.* In this updated *Taming of the Shrew,* Ann Garden's submission to a domestic order echoed and confirmed a prodigal daughter's reentry to the fatherland. The narrative took an unruly woman off the streets and set her straight, offering a moral fable in the guise of upbeat entertainment.[86] Pseudo-utopias of wishful thinking such as *Lucky Kids* fostered the belief that the Hitler regime allowed room to move. When we look more carefully, though, this ostensible realm of freedom seems inordinately circumscribed. The dancers bounce about in a narrow apartment and constantly threaten to crash into walls. The semblance of animated improvisation, upon repeated viewing, looks more like assembly-line production, one activity efficiently giving way to the next function, without a trace of spontaneity or excess. Even here, in this Ufa world of whimsy, the rhythm of machines imposes itself on the workings of bodies.[87] *It Happened One Night* was a road movie that explored human desire and suggested a wider social experience. Its German ersatz, by comparison, was a chamber comedy that limited its moves to a much more confined physical and psychic space.[88]

German studios created realms of illusion which, on the surface, reflected little of everyday realities. These make-believe worlds promoted a double fiction: the persuasion that generic products such as *Lucky Kids* escaped and even resisted the Nazi status quo; and the myth that the Hitler government's policy toward cinema remained generous, liberal, and above all concerned with questions of quality and pragmatics. Many postwar commentators wish to grant films countenanced by the ProMi a dissident status. In so doing, these observers demonstrate the enduring power of Goebbels' Ministry of Illusion.

"But just try and remember that when it came to the love scenes the film was divine, an absolute dream. The political stuff, well, it was probably foisted onto the director by the government, or maybe you don't know how those things work?" (Manuel Puig, *Kiss of the Spider Woman*).

FIVE

Astray in the New World: *La Habanera* (1937)

The way Garbo looks at people these days . . . she implies that the least you can do for people in this stupid, brawling world is to keep them warm and give them a share of comfort before the end comes.

Alistair Cooke

I am regressive, very regressive.
I want women to be women.
I am as regressive as nature itself,
Which has granted women a fertile
Womb, nurturing breasts,
Domestic instincts.

Erwin Guido Kolbenheyer

"A Myth Lives"

"When we purchase Ufa today," boasted Goebbels in mid-March 1937, "we will become the world's largest film, press, theater, and radio combine . . . Now I have a very useful instrument at my disposal."[1] After studying the situation at the Ufa and Tobis installations a few weeks earlier, the media mogul had resolved "to monitor production much more carefully and make certain that artistic matters receive their due."[2] The German government owned almost three-quarters of Ufa's stock and had taken control of the Tobis, Terra, and Bavaria studios in a decisive move toward the consolidation of the film industry. (By 1939 the four companies would be responsible for 75 percent of all feature production.)[3] The Ministry of Propaganda relied on cinema to divert the masses as well as to direct their attentions; it used displaced settings to enact and resolve domestic dilemmas. *La Habanera* (1937), a film made as Germany intervened in the Spanish Civil War and geared up for larger military operations, is a particularly interesting case in point.[4]

The Prodigal Son and *Lucky Kids* were siblings; both explored a make-believe New World, rendering it as a site of, alternately, native nightmares and German dreams. In *La Habanera,* Astrée Sternhjelm visits Puerto Rico with her Aunt Ana and becomes smitten by a tropical paradise, experiencing the island as a refuge from the coldness of her native Stockholm. Charmed by a popular song, the Habanera, and overwhelmed by a chivalrous local patron, Don Pedro de Avila, she decides to stay and marry her matador hero—much to her aunt's chagrin. Ten years later, Astrée bitterly rues her reckless moment. The former paradise has lost its luster, and she lives as a veritable hostage of a man she has long since ceased loving. Her only solace is her son, little Juan, with whom she imagines a life elsewhere, singing to him of the Swedish snow. In Stockholm Aunt Ana (who has given up all hope for her wayward niece) underwrites a research expedition, a search for the cause of a virulent fever that plagues Puerto Rico. Sven Nagel, a friend and former admirer from Astrée's schooldays, heads the investigation and arrives just as the fever breaks out. Working around official attempts to cover up the epidemic, Nagel and his assistant isolate the sickness and discover a cure. An evening party at Don Pedro's residence brings Sven and Astrée together. With great effort Astrée seeks to conceal her extreme depression and dire situation. During the festivities the local police break into Nagel's hotel room and seize the serum. To placate her jealous husband, Astrée sings the Habanera. Don Pedro rejoices at the goodwill gesture—and, struck by the fever, collapses in a stupor. Nagel hastens to get the antidote but is informed that Don Pedro's minions, following his orders, have destroyed it. Soon after Don Pedro's death, Astrée and her son board a steamer with Nagel and, as islanders sing the Habanera, bid farewell to Puerto Rico.

La Habanera resembles Trenker's film, but with a gendered twist: it portrays the foreign affair of a prodigal daughter. The film can likewise be understood as an exemplary instance of the Ufa studio's own foreign affair, its conscious attempt to appropriate American patterns of recognition for Germany's domestic audiences. It starred the Swedish actress Zarah Leander, who would become Nazi cinema's most highly paid player. It was made by Detlef Sierck, a director who would go on to a notable career in the United States under the name Douglas Sirk. To a great degree, German films of the Third Reich relied on foreign talent and Hollywood formula.[5] Many of the era's female stars came from abroad—Leander and Kristina Söderbaum from Sweden, Marika Rökk and Käthe von Nagy from Hungary, Lida Baarova from Czechoslovakia, Olga Tschechowa from Russia, and Pola Negri from Poland. ("Not every foreigner," quipped Wolfgang

Liebeneiner, "who cannot speak German is born to be a star.")[6] The propaganda minister favored the stylish insouciance of Austrian filmmaker Willi Forst, his operatic reenactments of Offenbach's Paris and Strauss's Vienna, his "fashionable, immutable world of theaters, restaurants, ballrooms, and boudoirs."[7] The films of the Ukrainian director Viktor Tourjansky likewise had an undeniable romantic allure, especially sophisticated comedies such as *Der Blaufuchs* (*The Fox Fur Coat,* 1938) and *Die keusche Geliebte* (*The Chaste Lover,* 1940). "What is an illusion?" Brigitte Horney asks in the conclusion of Tourjansky's elegant opus about enamored theater people (*Illusion,* 1941). "A beautiful dream, something very beautiful."

The German "film world" *(Filmwelt)* enjoyed a reputation as a safe haven for dreams and illusions, as a sanctuary for beauty, privilege, and opportunity, as a place that prided itself on its cosmopolitan flair. Anything but prudish, its approach to morality and sex was, in the words of Arthur Maria Rabenalt, "liberal, generous, and unbourgeois." German studios, it is said, allowed filmmakers to escape from the Nazi everyday and to create fictional realms unencumbered by ideological dictates and party doctrines.[8] Chronicler David Stewart Hull goes so far as to call the film world "a hotbed—however passive—of limited resistance to the government."[9] Well into the 1930s, many other critics concur, there remained "a certain amount of freedom" in the *Filmwelt,* especially at Ufa.[10] Under Goebbels, maintains Klaus Kreimeier, "Not everything, but much, was possible."[11] Sierck left the German theater for Ufa, the filmmaker later recollected, because at the Babelsberg facilities artists could "get away with extraordinary things." There was "a certain amount of room for manoeuvre."[12] The studio needed him, and the director (for a time) felt secure that he could do what he wanted.[13]

Sierck's German endeavors are thought of today as hallmarks of aesthetic resistance. Take a typical response from the Sirk revival in Great Britain during the early 1970s:

> The surprise of the films (quite apart from their excellence) is both political—to see what could still be made in Germany in 1937—and "stylistic." The pre-1933 traditions are preserved, even enlivened, but within a highly unlikely format—one which the critics, inevitably, have failed to appreciate. Who was ready then—or now—to give attention to a (fused) combination of the traditions of Weill, Ophuls, Brecht and Sternberg, melted down and transformed by Sirk, five years after Hitler had come to power?[14]

French critic Jean Pierre Bleys celebrated the "baroque aesthetic" of Sierck's Ufa films, the way they "place the realistic world under the regard of a superior authority clearly represented as ideal and fictive." For Bleys, Sierck's authorial impetus stood out clearly among his stylistically unremarkable German peers.[15]

In the wake of his rediscovery by international cineastes,[16] Sierck became an early version of Sirk, his Ufa productions anticipating the incisive subversions of his Eisenhower-era endeavors. Critics praised his Third Reich productions in the same terms used to valorize his Universal melodramas. He became acclaimed as a left-wing intellectual and a self-conscious formalist, renowned for his displacements and discontinuities in plot construction, for "doubtful, ambiguous and uncertain characters,"[17] for the spurious harmonies of his conclusions, and in general for his use of melodrama as a means of social commentary. Above all his admirers have come to laud Sierck's ironic *mise en scène,* his stylized compositions and idiosyncratic framing, his studied use of reflective surfaces such as water and mirrors, his foregrounding of objects, his unnaturalistic lighting. Irony inheres in his mobile camera as well, which moves alternately in and away from characters, mixing emotional involvement and critical distance. In effect, summarizes William Horrigan, Sierck provides a "testament (the last?) to the embattled genius of the German cinema, which genius would come to relocate in America and there continue to dwell on the same preoccupations, work in comparable genres, and pose similar critiques."[18]

Beyond Sierck, Zarah Leander represents a strong point of interest. Her untrammeled emotions and excessive longings, according to many postwar critics, ran counter to Nazi notions of a contained and dutiful femininity. Next to her, claimed Helma Sanders-Brahms, actresses such as Kristina Söderbaum looked downright silly and superficial.[19] Goebbels reputedly had a distanced relation to Leander. Hitler openly disliked her and made certain that she did not receive commendation as an Actress of the State.[20] Leander challenged Nazi prudery; her frank eroticism brought German women a sexual self-understanding beyond that of domestic slave and deferent spouse. The Nazis could not prevent her success, but they never really welcomed it. They would have preferred a virtuous German woman to be their most celebrated heroine. In the estimation of Günther Rühle, Leander was a woman of the world, sensual and unpolitical. For a nation that sang hymns to self-sacrifice, her songs seemed disreputable and frivolous. Her kind of *femme fatale* belonged in the grand bourgeois world of a decadent *fin de siècle* and not in the Third Reich.[21]

Ufa's grandest dame worked in the Hitler regime, assert her postwar fans, without submitting to National Socialism. (It has in fact been suggested that she spied for the KGB.)[22] "Zarah Leander is an idol," effused a young German admirer recently; "even her loyalty to the Nazis could do nothing to change this. So wonderfully wicked, so harmless and so hip."[23] For German gay culture she has become, in Paul Seiler's words, "an ersatz drug for unrealized emotions."[24] In the summer of 1991, ten years after her death, Leander's films reappeared on German screens, and her songs were reissued on CD. Her legend became the object of intense media attention. "Ein Mythos lebt" ("A Myth Lives") was the title of a gala revival at the Berlin Filmbühne am Steinplatz.

Various myths thus converge in discussions of *La Habanera:* the myth of an outsider who smuggled Brechtian techniques into a film industry monitored by the Nazis, the myth of a very popular diva whose high-pitched emotional performances transported female—and gay—audiences to faraway and forbidden places. The collaboration of Sierck and Leander is also linked to a third myth, that of a classical German cinema that could persist despite Hitler. Sierck's German films would seem to offer something singular. "They show," submits an English admirer, "how German film might have looked after 1933—and how it in at least this one case actually was."[25] *La Habanera* stands out as a subversive text and a reflexive melodrama, a synthesis of noble kitsch and nuanced *Kammerspiel,* a regressive scenario outsmarted by an ironic *mise en scène.*[26] It has become all but a truism that during the 1930s the German film industry often worked at odds with the Third Reich, that the Ufa rhombus at times challenged the party swastika. Seen through the prism of commentaries from the last two decades, Detlef Sierck's endeavors with Zarah Leander offer prime examples of how German films of the 1930s undermined the Nazi state.

The Diva and the Director

When *La Habanera* premiered in the Berlin Gloria-Palast on 18 December 1937, enthusiastic critics pronounced it an exceptional film. In no way, though, did anyone claim that it took exception to the Nazi rule. Even after film criticism was superseded by "appreciation," reviewers on occasion allowed their mixed feelings to become apparent. In this case, there were no misgivings. For the film's first audiences, Zarah Leander's magnetic performance and irresistible voice provided the dominant attractions. "This woman emanates an aura of mystery," claimed the *Berliner Volks-Zeitung.*

Leander was "another Garbo" *(Leipziger Neuste Nachrichten);* she had "moments of captivating nuance when she smiles and when she muses" *(12-Uhr-Blatt);* she conquered the soul of the spectator *(Chemnitzer Tageblatt).* "Just as this voice vibrates with all our thoughts, so too does this countenance reflect all our happiness and suffering, in the way of a landscape illuminated by the sun or darkened by storm clouds—a marvelous woman and a great actress" *(Berliner Lokal-Anzeiger).*[27]

In contrast to recent Anglo-American commentators, German reviewers of 1937 granted Sierck a less exalted role. The credits likewise announced "ein Film von Gerhard Menzel," attributing authorship to the scriptwriter—a rare practice for the time.[28] The rave reviews of *Zu neuen Ufern* (*To New Shores,* 1937) contained only halting praise for the director. Writing in *Film-Kurier,* Günther Schwark commended it as "an Ufa-standard that combines all the virtues of a surefire public success. Let us mention only the most prominent elements: a gripping plot, a beautiful woman, and enchanting music!"[29] Sierck received only a few words of recognition in these contemporary notices. He was lauded for the manner in which he contrasted two very different worlds without painting in black and white. At best, he lingered in mind as the facilitator of Leander's artistic triumph.

Speaking as president of the Reich Film Chamber in its annual meeting of 1937, Oswald Lehnich openly deplored Germany's lack of capable film directors.[30] In general, Nazi film culture did not encourage authorial initiative and artistic independence. The ProMi wanted reliable, talented, and successful professionals. After the mid-1930s, a director's name generally showed up in credits as a *Spielleiter* instead of *Regisseur.* The shift in appellation reflected official attempts to cleanse the German language of foreign words. But the change of title also corresponded to a change in job description, rendering the film director an organizer of the onscreen activities whose task was to keep things moving while holding back his own personality. The most desirable authorial profile was an invisible signature. Goebbels complained about "intellectual" or "cerebral" filmmakers and scorned willful and undisciplined would-be *auteurs.*[31] "A failed avant-gardist," claimed an editorial in *Der Deutsche Film,* "can do more damage to the future of film than ten dyed-in-the-wool kitschmongers."[32] A director should concentrate on putting "his work into motion and not his own person," maintained Wolfgang Liebeneiner in 1937.[33]

Sierck was considered to be a very capable *Spielleiter.* Three of his films—*Stützen der Gesellschaft* (*Pillars of Society,* 1935), *Schlußakkord* (*Final Accord,* 1936), and *To New Shores*—were granted the state rating "artistically worthwhile." Repeatedly, Sierck received special mention for the symphonic quality of his films. *Final Accord* won a prize for the best musical film of 1936. His direction, claimed the *Film-Kurier* reviewer, "managed to blend the various emotional and affective elements of the plot into a moving musical unity," providing appropriate emphases, allowing for no dead moments, sustaining dramatic tension from start to finish.[34] Rarely does one encounter critical misgivings about Sierck. A reviewer of *Das Mädchen vom Moorhof* (*The Girl from the Marsh Croft,* 1935) observed that the urban director and his cast seemed to keep the rural setting at a distance. Their collective reserve imparted to the film a sense of "strangeness": where one expected simple feeling, one encountered intellectual heaviness.[35] More typically, though, Sierck was praised for his ability to orchestrate, to combine strong performances, expressive images, and impressive music into a *Gesamtkunstwerk,* to plot gripping stories and to catalyze strong feelings. For Nazi contemporaries, Sierck was anything but a self-reflexive or an ironic filmmaker. He was seen as a consummate illusionist, an artist who could cast a spell—and one of very few "capable" German filmmakers.

Leander's auratic presence and Sierck's expert instrumentation were not, however, *La Habanera*'s sole driving energies. Nor did the melodrama set on foreign shores function merely as an escapist entertainment. From its inception the film figured actively in political constellations and ideological campaigns. Sierck's collaborator, Gerhard Menzel, a cultural conservative, was recognized at the time as Germany's leading scriptwriter.[36] In his later utterances, Sirk downplayed Menzel's politics, referring to him as "a very gifted writer, and a very highly paid one. He had won the Kleistpreis, which was the biggest literary prize in Germany. But then he wasted his talents. He had been one of the big hopes of German literature for a time. Later on he became a big Nazi." During their work together, claimed Sirk, Menzel denied being a Nazi, "but by then it was awfully hard to know what some people were."[37] Sirk's description is in this instance disingenuous and misleading.

Menzel was a well-known party loyalist, and his fervent nationalism was no secret. He provided the scenarios for some of Nazi cinema's most strident productions. The paean to soldier males, *Morgenrot* (*Dawn,* 1933), sanctified heroic self-abandon and ushered in the Nazi era, premiering the day after Hitler became chancellor, bearing out Baldur von Schirach's claim that "In Germany, death is more alive than ever." Menzel penned the often-quoted words of the submarine commander Liers: "Perhaps we Germans do not know how to live, but how to die, this we know incredibly well." The rousing tale of Volga Germans in peril, *Flüchtlinge* (*Fugitives,* 1933), won the first Nazi National Film Prize in 1934. In *Das Mädchen Johanna* (*Young Joan of Arc,* 1935), we see Jeanne d'Arc become an instrument of state intrigue, going up in smoke so that she might better serve as a political weapon. Menzel would also do *Heimkehr* (*Homecoming,* 1941), one of the era's most repugnant features, replete with hateful images of Poles ripping a swastika necklace from a German patriot and mercilessly stoning her. Various elements of Menzel's script echoed Nazi politics: the racist separation between a civilized and a primitive world, its anticapitalism and anti-Americanism, its *Heim ins Reich* rhetoric. Menzel, like Sierck, made films concerned with displaced people as well as women who step off the beaten track.[38]

The ideological emphases of Menzel's script resonated in frequent press and radio progress reports. The film production became implicated in the Spanish Civil War as the German government threw its support to Franco's forces.[39] Location shooting took place in the Spanish-controlled Canary Islands, Tenerife and Palma. Everywhere one went, producer Bruno Duday reported, people cheered "Viva l'Allemania" and "Viva l'Ufa." Members of the Spanish Falangists proved especially helpful: "In the country's interior, on the large banana plantations, we could feel the war's effects more strongly. Particularly here because all men who were capable of bearing weapons had followed Franco's call to arms." For the film team from the North, this southern landscape had "an enchanting appeal," claimed Leander. Nonetheless, reported the star, the constant heat soon made paradise unbearable. "So you can understand that I soon had only one desire, to return to Germany and my home in Berlin."[40]

Menzel's script employs two songs in its contrast of North and South, "the tempting, seductive Habanera" and "a simple Swedish lullaby, a Christmas standard." Astrée sings the Habanera "in the singular manner with which northerners perform southern tunes; one feels the foreign undertone that grants her voice a mysterious charm." The Habanera exudes the foreign temperament of people with "dark eyes and black hair." It recalls Carmen's famous song of seduction from Bizet's opera ("Oh love was born to gypsy life"). When Astrée sings to her son about the Swedish snow, one becomes privy to her memories of home and her yearning for her lost *Heimat.* Leander's role, claimed the *Film-Kurier* commentator, is so closely allied to her own nationality that there is no question about the actress's strong personal conviction.[41] The figure of Don Pedro likewise bears out the dichotomy between two worlds, "the Spanish Central American sun-covered South and the austere Scandinavian North."[42] The plot dynamics, remarked a reviewer, demand that the conflict be resolved in Astrée's favor. Still Menzel's script does not make the husband totally unworthy of sympathy. "For a well-to-do South American woman this Don Pedro might indeed be an ideal spouse."[43]

Don Pedro is the master of the island, a country harboring an epidemic fever. In 1937 the word "fever" often cropped up in discussions of this film and its participants. Cameraman Franz Weihmayr, a frequent collaborator with Sierck, likened working in a studio with a crew to a fever, "small at first, reluctant, then a wave, which slowly comes closer and hits you higher and higher, until it grabs you and rips you away without your being able to defend yourself."[44] The cinematographer was talking about an on-set professional obsession, an immersion in one's work. A critic at the time spoke of a different kind of fever, the kind one contracts on alien shores:

> When one falls victim to a mysterious fever while exploring a tropical country, it happens because one does not know this new terrain well enough. When intelligent, decent, active people fall victim to a certain film fever that transforms their intellectual and moral constitution beyond recognition, it happens because we still do not know this new terrain well enough.[45]

But *La Habanera* remained on firm ground, in the hands of a seasoned professional and populated with a talented cast and a capable crew. Here was a film modeled along American lines which did not fall prey to foreign influences; although it went abroad, both for its locations and for its formal impulses, it still retained a distinctly national contour.

The fever would also come to bear other—clearly unintended—connotations in the contemporary context. "There is no fever," assert the island's doctors repeatedly despite dire evidence to the contrary, seeking to spare Puerto Rico's businessmen the financial disaster that a quarantine might bring. Two months before the film's premiere, President Roosevelt delivered a "quarantine speech" on 5 October in Chicago, issuing "a warning to the revisionist states, calling on all peace-loving nations to unite and threatening that lawbreakers would be expelled from the family of nations." He also intimated that in the case of foreign aggression he would activate America as a world power.[46] On 6 October Goebbels' diary mentioned Roosevelt's "infamous speech" and scorned its "hidden attacks on Japan, Italy, and Germany. Both dumb and deceitful."[47]

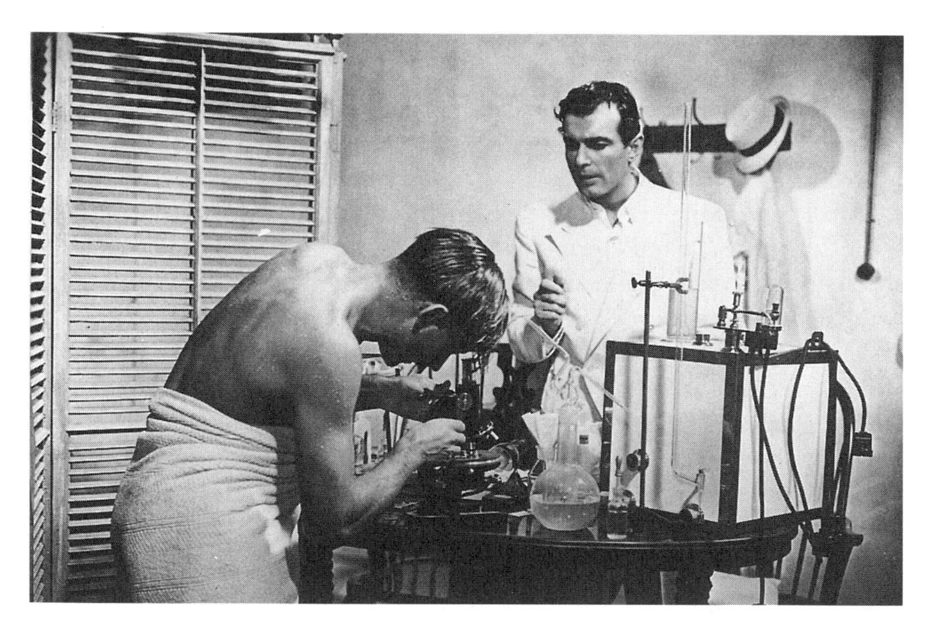

Gomez (Boris Alekin) and Nagel (Karl Martell) combat the Puerto Rico fever.

La Habanera emanated from a nation threatened with international quarantine and dramatized the fate of an island faced with a similar predicament. In this sense, the two spaces were not so distant, despite the film's attempt to mark borders between exotic Puerto Rico and Aryan Sweden. Astrée articulates the imaginary terms of this transaction when she tells her aunt, "*We* are the primitives, my dear." Puerto Rico appears as a "wild" state, a country, like Germany, that operates outside international legality. It stands under the dominion of a charismatic tyrant who controls all activities and directs a secret police force. His province seeks to be self-enclosed and to elude the control and influence of American capitalists. Foreign visitors are at once treated with courtesy and monitored carefully. Women are virtual domestic slaves, chained to their families, unable to break out. Sons are raised to be manly and athletic. The island's recreations, not unlike the Reich's diversions, are kitschy attractions and hyped-up spectacles, underwhelming and overwrought. Seen in this light, this German film about Puerto Rico embodies what it depicts: the "primitive" island becomes both the Aryan state's structured opposite and its displaced double. Without question, *La Habanera* had an ideological surplus value and an unconscious meaning. Its "subversive" qualities dominate only if we isolate our attentions and impose our own hermeneutical—and historical—quarantine. The film clearly reads differently when we bear in mind how it functioned and resonated in the Germany of late 1937.

The Perils of Zarah

Textual poachers, both in Germany and abroad, are fond of ferreting out "subversive" moments in Nazi films, assuming that these scenes somehow "slipped by" the censors or that party functionaries were so dim that irony and tongue-in-cheek escaped them. Why, though, did Goebbels cultivate Sierck and court Leander? Why would the minister wish to retain a director with a leftist past and a reputation as a nonconformist?[48] Why was Zarah Leander the highest-paid star in the Third Reich, despite Goebbels' initial impression that she was "an enemy of the Germans"?[49] Another conclusion might be that Goebbels wanted directors such as Sierck and players such as Leander, that their talents did not stand outside the party's program, but fit readily into the ProMi's designs. Contemporary recodings grant to the director and the actress a transcendent value ("testament to German genius," "so wonderfully wicked, so harmless, so hip"). In the process of inserting Sierck's films and Leander's performances into the present, one reconstructs the past and, in crucial ways, provides only a partial view. The two survive as "subversive" entities only at the price of understating or even overlooking how their roles became a part of larger functions.

On the same day Goebbels was complaining about Roosevelt's "infamous speech," he was also effusing about Zarah Leander: "Her box-office returns are enormous." Though unimpressed with her initially, the minister had warmed up quickly. His diaries contain repeated positive mention of business and social dealings with her.[50] Leander had entered Nazi cinema as a replacement for Marlene Dietrich and an ersatz for Greta Garbo. (Before her engagement by Ufa, Leander had in fact sung a Garbo parody with the words "If you want to see a star, look at me.") German film critics considered Garbo the *non plus ultra,* a sphinxlike creature who was the eternal feminine, a cinematic Mona Lisa with an auratic physiognomy: "The external perfection of her features dissolves before a second countenance, that of her soul, in which love and motherhood and suffering over human shortcomings become reflected in the larger-than-life and timeless play of light and shadow." Her poignant performance in *Anna Karenina* enacted "the ultimate tragedy of a female love."[51]

German films of the era likewise continued to make reference to Marlene Dietrich long after her departure. Luise Ullrich, for example, did an English-language imitation of the singer's throaty delivery in Werner Hochbaum's *Schatten der Vergangenheit* (*Shadows of the Past,* 1936): "I'm vaiting every night for you, vaiting." A September 1937 *Film-Kurier* report told of enthusiastic foreign press about Leander; right beside it appeared a notice that Dietrich was eagerly awaited in Vienna.[52] Several months later a headline in the same newspaper, accompanied by what appeared to be a photograph of the well-known German emigrant, heralded a "Doppelgängerin Marlene Dietrichs in Babelsberg": Karin Albihn, yet another Swedish actress, had arrived in Berlin for screen tests.[53]

Zarah Leander, brought in to fill a glaring gap, became a valued cultural icon. In the essentializing prose of the social historian Richard Grunberger: "Zara [*sic*] Leander was the Nazi cinema's flesh-and-blood monument to feminine allure—surplus flesh fuelled by calculatedly thin blood. She projected a screen-filling *décolletage* beneath which, with chaste and steady rhythm, beat a woman's heart."[54] Both a singing Garbo and a surrogate Dietrich, Leander was a stand-in whose continental fame came to rival that of the originals. A Swedish journalist likened her performance in *To New Shores* to Garbo's "authentic and natural humanity." But, the commentator continued, "Zarah Leander is no copy. She is stronger, more vital, more passionate than Garbo ever was. She is vivid."[55] By the start of World War II, Leander was earning 150,000 RM per film, more than any other actor in the Reich, male or female. (Emil Jannings received 125,000, Hans Albers 120,000, Gustaf Gründgens 80,000.)[56] She was the Nazi film industry's biggest star, an enormous box-office attraction whose face appeared everywhere, whose records sold millions and were heard constantly in public and on the radio.

Leander's distinctive contralto proved sublime and seductive; listeners swore it pierced the very depths of their souls. Critics described it as the cry of a siren or a call from the heavens. Eulogizing Leander's performance in *To New Shores,* the reviewer of the *Berliner Lokal-Anzeiger* maintained that her remarkable songs overshadowed Sierck's powerful images:

> Above all is the glow of a voice. It is as intoxicating as heavy dark wine. It can resound as mightily as the tone of an organ. Its shine is as transparent as glass, as deep as metal. In this voice is everything: jubilation, happiness, life's drunken melody and its wild pain. And this voice belongs to Zarah Leander, the great actress, the newly discovered tragic artist of German

Zarah Leander: "The singer the Germans wanted to push after Marlene Dietrich left. And like all copies she's better than the original. She doesn't drag any image around with her" (Jean Eustache's *La maman et la putain*/*The Mother and the Whore,* 1973).

> cinema. It is not overstating the case to say that she will come to mean for sound cinema what Asta Nielsen in her own way did for the silent film.[57]

Leander herself claimed that her films only provided a pretext for her songs.[58] She was a stunning sight and a stirring sound, a moving image with an animated voice—in short, the ideal medium.

In the National Socialist everyday, the media's ideal calling was envisioned as that of a Circe-like enchantress. Radios manufactured by Telefunken were not referred to as *Volksempfänger* (people's receivers), but rather bore names such as Carmen, Tosca, and Aïda. Images of women regularly figured in the firm's advertising campaigns as apparitions emanating from a table model of Radio Telefunken.[59] Film's seductive powers likewise were typically cast in a female shape. "Film," claimed Fritz Hippler, "fascinates and grips one like a beautiful and smart woman." And like a woman, film needed to be handled properly. "Just like a woman, film also wants to be regarded and treated as something unique."[60] The media could seduce and enthrall, no question. It was equally beyond question, for Hippler,

> that female representations in film influence the ideal of beauty for the mass public. For this reason the casting of film roles cannot receive too much attention. It is not just a matter of this or that woman looking attractive in this or that film. No, the right woman chosen according to her external appearance as well as her inner qualities and attributes, if used often enough in successful film roles, can exercise a favorable influence, albeit unconsciously but nonetheless with the greatest impact, on the general level of taste and the ideal of beauty among the wider male populace.[61]

Zarah Leander was treated well by the Nazi leaders who utilized the image of this beautiful woman in a variety of (usually) tragic roles. "Zarah films" were vaunted as triumphs of dramatic performance and cinematic art. The actress "was everything at once: a female, a woman, a lady, loyalty, disloyalty, a person who suffered the pangs of love. In her eyes was seduction as well as entreaty."[62]

Zarah Leander's enormous appeal derived from an ability to unite opposites: a tender physiognomy and a thick body,[63] silent suffering and animated expressivity, domestic charm and foreign allure, solemn spirituality and playful sensuality, maternal warmth and vampish sadism. She was the eternal female with a masculine voice. Jokes circulated about callers on the telephone persisting in their requests to speak to "Frau Leander" despite her protests that she *was* on the line.[64]

For many spectators her appeal was an androgynous one, and she had a wide gay following. Her favorite songwriter was the homosexual Bruno Balz, who provided *La Habanera*'s title song as well as her inimitable "Kann denn Liebe Sünde sein?"/"Can Love Be a Sin?" A fiery voice matched her red hair, claims Helma Sanders-Brahms: "It comes out of her breast and from much deeper, a voice between man and woman, a dream of snail-like bisexuality, self-engenderment that plummets one to the abyss of one's own doubleness, in every man a piece of woman, in every woman a piece of man."[65] Leander made for a singular screen presence: a woman who was seemingly "everything at once." More though than an ersatz Dietrich or a Garbo replacement, she would later come to resemble Judy Garland, working "in an emotional register of great intensity which seems to bespeak equally suffering and survival, vulnerability and strength, theatricality and authenticity, passion and irony."[66] Leander's postwar career, her appeal to gay audiences and her appropriation by female impersonators, the self-parodic pathos of her last appearances, like the older Garland's, seemed simultaneously histrionic and strongly felt.

If Leander's star image was dynamic, it was also flexible. Her powerful media profile may well have derived from a tension between seemingly contrary qualities. That did not mean that these oppositions remained eternally unresolved. During her Ufa years, from 1937 to 1943, she recorded thirty songs, twenty-six of which appear in her films, and twenty-five of which deal with love, especially the vicissitudes of love. How does this suffering woman in love respond? A recent German study describes the range of possibility: she requites herself, she hopes for miracles, she waits patiently, she suffers silently and conceals her pain, she represses memories or is consumed by yearning. In any case, she remains passive and makes no demands on her male lover, for his well-being is more important than her own and she does not want to bother him with her problems. "In not a single one of these songs," concludes Ulrike Sanders, "does one find any evidence of a woman ready to put her life in her own hands instead of waiting for destiny or her lover to intervene."[67] How, though, does this image correspond to her various willful outbursts and often-noted vampish moments? In fact, when she appears as a wayward woman, Zarah Leander invariably is playing a role at odds with her character's true person. In *Damals* (*Back Then,* 1943), for example, she feigns wanton promiscuity, singing a tune that flaunts a new conquest every night ("Jede Nacht ein neues Glück") to free herself from a relationship (one she clearly desires) for the sake of her child's welfare.

Zarah Leander made ten films at Ufa before leaving Germany in 1943. Her "song, the voice, the pose, the costume, all of these render her as something to be looked at"—but not a character whose desire is taken seriously.[68] *Die große Liebe* (*The Great Love,* 1942), an Ufa musical/melodrama, was one of the Third Reich's largest box-office hits and Leander's most celebrated role. A star vehicle featuring elaborate revue pieces and some of her most famous songs, it was also a wartime moral tale masquerading as a woman's film. The popular singer Hanna Holberg meets the on-leave aviator Paul Wendlandt, and they spend the night together. With war escalating and duty constantly calling, the couple's one night of love gives way to seemingly permanent *coitus interruptus.* Hanna despairs and revolts; the role allows Leander an elaborate showplace for masochistic contortions and emotional acrobatics. The singer learns to be patient and to suffer in silence; her great love must reconcile itself to the greater German cause.

The star's histrionic displays resembled La Jana's free dancing in *Es leuchten die Sterne* (*The Stars Are Shining,* 1938) and *Stern von Rio* (*Star of Rio,* 1940): both offered a safe and tamed eroticism, intense passion in the form of highly stylized affect. Like Marika Rökk, another leading screen actress of the era, Leander delighted in playing *femmes fatales,* but only as a strategic pose and a momentary mask. Behind the lascivious facade there abided a *femme fragile,* a determined mother, a dutiful daughter, a loyal wife, a devoted lover.[69] Nazi critics could proudly compare her to Garbo and Dietrich. She was at once racially pure and racy, a sinner in the service of the state.[70]

In *La Habanera,* Leander demonstrates what happens when a woman wanders. Astrée goes astray—and in so doing, realizes the destructive potential of her errant emotions. The Swedish traveler at first appears sympathetic, all light and spontaneity, the wild one who wants to break away from her aunt's staid notions of propriety. Astrée rebels, and the film encourages the spectator to applaud her transgression. The initial affirmation of illicit delight is rescinded, though, and we see the woman suffer—at length, indeed throughout the rest of the narrative. We cut from the island to Stockholm and witness the concerned aunt as she implores the scientist Sven Nagel to seek out her niece. The Nordic hero will deliver the foreign province from an epidemic and liberate the captive of an island. What begins as "Astrée Goes Native" becomes another installment of "The Perils of Zarah," the story of a rescue mission to save a woman in distress.

Woman in the Wind

La Habanera charts a female protagonist's stormy passage from a paradise to an inferno. Puerto Rico's attractions stir a desire for an enchanted existence; its erotic immediacy overwhelms Astrée, and she abandons ship. Distance from the homeland separates her from the authentic sources of security and stability. In Nazi fables about travelers, characters come undone in the topographies of alien cultures. Roaming about puts one's identity and person at risk. Films of the Hitler era, no matter how mobile they might appear, typically bind protagonists to constrained frameworks, to studiously choreographed and relentlessly codified scenarios. Individuals who ramble and meander are usually suspicious or tragic figures in Nazi cinema—unless they are explorers out to forge new empires and extend the Reich's domain.[71]

A preoccupation of Sierck's German films is the question of a woman's rightful place. Repeatedly women appear as objects of exchange; one thinks of the "parade of brides" in *The Girl from Marsh Croft* as well as the market of potential spouses in the Paramatta penitentiary *(To New Shores)*.[72] Music brings a couple together in the striking opening sequence of *Final Accord;* Garvenberg conducts Beethoven's Ninth Symphony in Berlin, and, in a series of dissolves across the ocean, we see the destitute emigrant Hanna listen to its radio transmission in New York. The aesthetic experience spirits the wayward mother back to Germany. The narrative will clean house, exorcising a self-indulgent wife and empowering a legitimate mother, reconstructing an authentic German family, celebrating the accomplishment as Hanna holds her child and listens to Garvenberg conduct Handel's oratorio *Judas Maccabeus.* As Goebbels expressed it, "Art and the artists are there not only to unite; their far more important task is to create a form, to expel the ill trends and make room for the healthy to develop."[73]

La Habanera portrays Astrée's fateful encounter with a song and a moment; the film ends with the painful memory of that powerful feeling as Astrée sails away on a steamship. Commentators typically remark that this is anything but a straightforward happy end, echoing Sirk's own assessment: "Well, Zarah Leander's feelings on that boat are not entirely linear. She has been in the place ten years, the ten best years of her life. As she looks back she is aware that she is getting out of rotten—*but definitely interesting*—circumstances. Her feelings are most ambiguous."[74] The film, to be sure, denies the spectator any joyful reunion in the homeland. This omission is generally claimed to be subversive, proof that Sierck's direction undermines the script's *Heim ins Reich* rhetoric. The conclusion thus anticipates the double-edged endings of Sirk's later melodramas like *All That Heaven Allows* and *Imitation of Life*.

Astrée is suspended between the harbor of Puerto Rico and the distant shores of Sweden; she has cursed the one and found existence in the other sterile. This space of abeyance is in fact to be found in other Leander films; it is hardly singular to Sierck's Ufa productions. Consider the final moments of Carl Froelich's *Heimat* (1938), a film by a director not renowned for his oppositional tendencies. (Froelich joined the Nazi party in 1933 and became president of the Reich Film Chamber in June 1939.) Here Leander plays Magda, a prodigal daughter who, having become a famous singer in America, returns to her south German homeland. She reconciles with her stubborn father, but has another falling out when she refuses to marry a local banker. The father scolds and disowns her, not knowing the businessman had earlier made her pregnant and left her in the lurch. In the end, the father learns the truth ("I think everything is clear now") and goes to watch his daughter perform the *St. Matthew's Passion.* He meets a little girl and realizes she is Magda's daughter and his grandchild. The two embrace warmly. Meanwhile, Magda sits in the church balcony and sings solemnly, knowing nothing of the good news, lamenting, "Necessity and regret tear the sinner's heart in two," tears running down her face, which we view in poignant close-ups. She remains in suspension, unaware that all is well. The last words we hear from her lips are "anxiety and pain."[75]

The space Leander occupies at the end of *La Habanera* and *Heimat* is not the actress's exclusive property. In the final moments of Eduard von Borsody's *Kongo-Express* (1939), a steamship returns from Africa and sails into the Hamburg harbor. Marianne Hoppe stands at the railing next to a companion, a man of weak constitution and fragile features. The feminized male speaks of his yearning for Africa—a sense of lack that becomes apparent as he reenters his homeland. "I think you're really homesick for Africa," she says. "Is it so hard to understand," he replies, "that it's only when you lose something forever that you realize how much you really love it?" Perhaps we might speak of this special space as a no-man's land, a refuge well known to German women who went to the era's movies.

Consider the two female spectators from the Hunsrück, Katherine and her sister Pauline, who attend a moviehouse in Simmern and watch Leander perform in *La Habanera* and *Heimat* during the course of Edgar Reitz's historical epic, *Heimat* (1984). The star transports the daughters of the homeland to a different life; she allows them to dream of a more buoyant existence. We see their tear-streaked cheeks, we hear them sing the diva's songs, we watch them do their hair and copy Astrée's curls, we partake of their dialogues about outings to purchase expensive clothing so they might dress up like their idol.

How might we explain the great powers of attraction which the cinema has for women? asked a female German critic in 1938. Women have a pronounced capacity for identification, claimed the author, for getting swept up into a story. They like to imagine lives away from the everyday. Each woman has unanswered wishes and seeks the illusion of fulfillment in the dark. Films fascinate female spectators both as narrative fantasies and as seductive fashion shows: "Film's great enchantment lasts little more than an hour and is as simple as a fairy tale. A drama, a concert, an opera, or a radio play demands concentration and a certain measure of education and comprehension. Film is much simpler, perhaps even more primitive. You don't need to reflect; you get everything served up right in front of you."[76] Women go to the movies to try on clothes, but also, by extension, to try on roles—like that of the suffering Zarah.[77] Fashion, like cinema, allows a double dream. It permits a simultaneous dream of identity (in the name of someone else) and a dream of difference (being someone other than oneself). The woman of fashion, as Roland Barthes points out, dreams of being her true self by being someone else. Quite literally, she leads a double life.[78]

To judge from contemporary fan magazines and newspapers, Zarah Leander was an important role model for women living in the Third Reich. Films of the era repeatedly confronted the prospect of difficult and unreconciled women, dealing with them in two major ways. The comedic variant ensued along the lines of *The Taming of the Shrew*—as in *Lucky Kids,* a film that takes a woman off the street, cuts her down to size, and slaps her into shape. Serious treatments employed *Madame Bovary* as their master narrative in countless melodramas about women who desire too much and dare to act on their wishes. Pola Negri played Emma in Gerhard Lamprecht's 1937 rendering of Flaubert's novel. Marianne Hoppe portrayed the fated Effi in Gustaf Gründgens' Fontane adaptation of 1939, *Der Schritt vom Wege (Effi Briest),* a film framed by images of her grave. The unfaithful wife of Helmut Käutner's *Romanze in Moll* (*Romance in a Minor Key,* 1943) asks her lover, "Do we really have a right to be happy?" knowing that the question is rhetorical. Veit Harlan's *Opfergang* (*The Great Sacrifice,* 1944) culminates in a hypnotic demonstration of sickness unto death as another transgressive heroine takes her place in Nazi cinema's procession of female martyrs. Prodigal daughters abound as well; in addition to Astrée and Magda, take the examples of Dunja in *Der Postmeister* (*The Postmaster,* 1940) and Anna in *Die goldene Stadt* (*The Golden City,* 1942). Women, almost without exception, did not travel well in Nazi era films.

Zarah Leander's performances fueled Nazi culture precisely because they appeared to offer alternative points of identification. Her disruptive outbursts and extreme longings served integrative functions. Like Leander, Detlef Sierck was neither a fascist nor a subversive. His films fit well into Nazi constellations, both as ideological affirmations and as the sites of what appeared to be transgressive designs. Aesthetic resistance was part of the system; it provided a crucial function in a larger gestalt. The liberal Sierck had an agreeable working relationship with the fascist Menzel. A film such as *La Habanera* served multiple purposes. While transporting overt political contents, the film seemed to step off track—all the better to maintain a clear ideological course.

The Ministry of Propaganda recognized the reality of needs not satisfied in everyday life. Goebbels fostered films that addressed those needs, meeting those desires halfway in an attempt to regulate errant emotions. A few days before *La Habanera* premiered, Goebbels remarked in his diary about everyday life in the Reich's capital: "Sexual morals have become a bit relaxed in this gigantic city. But there's nothing one can do. It's no Sodom and Gomorrah, but you surely could not call it a cloister."[79] This is the logic of discipline operating with dynamic efficiency, cynical reason functioning at heady heights. The cinema served the minister as a site of illusion and delusion: one got one's cake, and it tasted sweet even though it was laced with bitter ingredients. Films like *La Habanera* demonstrated that excess, irony, and distanciation could reaffirm rather than destabilize the status quo.

Leander's performances and Sierck's films tell us much about the place of women in Nazi Germany and the place of woman in the Third Reich's cinema. National Socialism, observed Ernst Bloch, managed to reintroduce "the three big K's of the good old days: *Küche, Kirche, Kinder* [kitchen, church, children]. Not in this language, of course." Party officials called for dynamism, youth, and emancipation. The Nazis "did not simply proclaim a return to the status quo for women, but rather an earthquake, a vibration of blood and soil in questions of femininity."[80] Amidst constant propaganda campaigns against the *mondaine* woman, German movies and fashion magazines celebrated sophisticated worldliness. (The journal *Die Dame* continued to play a role as an outlet for unfulfilled female fantasies until 1943.) But in fact the emancipation of the new era amounted to the return of the prodigal daughter, what Alfred Rosenberg spoke of as the "emancipation of woman from emancipation."[81]

Sierck's film leaves Astrée caught between an unbearable foreign condition and a return to a world she once renounced as oppressive. She embodies an impossible desire, a desire that becomes possible only in terms of fantasy representations and never-ceasing postponement, a desire that exists only so that it can never be satisfied, a desire one enacts on screen and thereby transforms into a source of vicarious pleasure, the pleasure of female audiences whose wish for a heightened existence will never be answered except in their dreams.

In the final moments of *La Habanera,* Astrée says she has no regrets. She looks out to the harbor, listens to the singers, and, with a dreamy look in her eyes, sighs, "La Habanera." The end of the film shows her longing gaze—and a call to order, for Sven grabs her arms and pulls her away, diverting her from the island and pointing her in a different direction. Tonio Feuersinger could return home as a conquering hero. *La Habanera*'s heroine goes astray and ends adrift, forever unreconciled. National Socialism, as Bloch pointed out, brought lasting happiness to no one—and certainly not to mothers and women.

PART III

Specters and Shadows

“I was nothing more than the faithful servant of my sovereign!”

SIX

The Elective Other: *Jew Süss* (1940)

> Has it not struck you how the Jew is the exact opposite of the German in every single respect, and yet is as closely akin to him as a blood brother?
>
> *Adolf Hitler to Hermann Rauschning*

> The oppositional, then, is sought out not as this or that specific object, not for what it contains but for the merely formal reason that it offers a distinct contrast by which one feels one's self. The Jew is conspicuous, just as Adolf Hitler is conspicuous; with him too, it is not what was in him that matters; all that matters is his conspicuousness. "Führer" and "Jew" are of the same rank; both are landmarks, points of orientation in nothingness.
>
> *Max Picard*

An Infamous Film

The prospect is dark. Nonetheless, the picture could not be clearer, there is not a shade of doubt: *Jud Süß (Jew Süss)* is Nazi cinema's most controversial and contested film, just as its director, Veit Harlan, is (next to Leni Riefenstahl) the Third Reich's most controversial and contested filmmaker.[1] Among Nazi Germany's cinematic endeavors, it is rivaled only by Fritz Hippler's *Der ewige Jude (The Eternal Jew,* 1940) for its continuing ability "to ignite fierce passions."[2] Conceived as a hate film, *Jew Süss* provided a preview of coming atrocities, preparing the German populace for the "final solution," the deportation and mass murder of European Jewry.

"Evening at the Ufa-Palast," Goebbels noted in his diary on 25 September 1940. "The premiere of *Jew Süss.* A very large audience with almost the entire Reich Cabinet. The film is an incredible success. One hears only enthusiastic responses. The whole room raves. That's exactly what I had hoped for."[3] An entry in a current German guide to classics of world cinema describes *Jew Süss* as "the most infamous, most often-quoted, and probably the most momentous propaganda film of the 'Third Reich.' Before 1945 it was shown to SS commandos before they carried out missions against Jews; after the war it was used in the Near East for anti-Israeli propaganda."[4] Critics and historians concur; it is, according to David Stewart Hull, "unquestionably the most notorious film of the Third Reich. It brought disgrace and worse on almost everyone connected with it, and . . . it became the central exhibit in Veit Harlan's postwar trial for crimes against humanity."[5]

Confronted with this film, even ardent defenders of cinema in the Third Reich will back off. It is, says the otherwise so partisan Karlheinz Wendtland, "probably the most famous Nazi propaganda film, the filmic adaptation of Hitler's anti-Semitic agitation in *Mein Kampf.* Cruel and malicious."[6] *Jew Süss* does not easily lend itself to revisionist readings. It has, however, assumed a functional role in revisionist arguments. Having confirmed traditional verdicts about *Jew Süss,* Wendtland dismisses it as an anomaly. If one looks at the epoch's output as a whole, "the number of features with National Socialist ideology is negligible; they are in fact far too isolated for one to render the entirety of the era's German feature film productions as 'bound to the Nazi cause.' "[7] For every *Jew Süss,* asserts Axel Eggebrecht, "there were ten features without the slightest trace of ideology."[8] Goebbels' most scurrilous feature thus becomes a prime witness for the defense of the Third Reich as the golden age of German cinema.

Commentators, regardless of their personal and political persuasions, single out the feature as the acme of Nazi fanaticism and revile it as one of the most hideous movies ever made. Attacked and indicted, the definitive cinematic encounter with Nazi Germany's other has itself become an other, set aside and isolated by film historians, reserved by the German government for closed screenings and educational purposes only. *Jew Süss* endures as a monstrous entity. This special status is at once deserved and deceptive. In crucial respects, the cinematic prologue to the Holocaust hardly came out of the dark. Its dramatic structure as well as its sociological and gender coding reflect, as Linda Schulte-Sasse has argued, crucial elements of the eighteenth century's venerable bourgeois tragedy.[9] The film exhibits the mechanisms of the classical Hollywood narrative in its plot construction and character motivation. Its claim to historical veracity echoes the rhetoric typical of innumerable American biographical features.

Goebbels insisted that *Jew Süss* be billed as true to the facts, just as stateside studio marketers might have told the prospective patrons of *The Life of Emile Zola* (1937) or *Marie Antoinette* (1938) "that every effort had been expended to bring them true history in the guise of spectacle, as well as suggesting that

Süss Oppenheimer brings a virtual plague upon the House of Württemberg.

the research for each film was, for the first time, bringing to the screen a true portrait, or at least a singularly true version or the accurate characterization of a person."[10] *Jew Süss*'s claim to truth sets up the film and sets the viewer straight in keeping with biopic convention. It serves as a reminder that this film is different from usual features, which "are not supposed to be taken as true."[11] "The worst of the German propaganda films"[12] reflects generic legacies of German classical drama and American classical cinema.

"The events represented in this film are based on historical occurrences," declares the title at the end of the credits.[13] The narrative begins in 1733 with the coronation of Karl Alexander as duke of Württemberg in Stuttgart. His opulent style cramped by a penny-pinching diet, the duke sends an emissary to the Frankfurt Jewish ghetto to procure a wedding gift on credit from Joseph Süss Oppenheimer. Süss exploits the monarch's desire for grandeur and luxury as a means to political power. The moneylender gains entry into Stuttgart, a city closed to Jews, and insinuates his way into the duke's court. Appointed finance minister, he transforms roads and bridges into sources of revenue. Süss's taxation schemes cause widespread hardship among the

Swabian population, and unrest grows when he persuades the duke to open the city to the Jews. Tricking his master to believe that the stars are aligned in his favor, Oppenheimer has the sovereign completely at his disposal.

With the duke's approval, Süss engineers a coup d'état that will set hired foreign soldiers upon Swabian troops and grant the head of state absolute power. Public indignation comes to a head when Süss sexually coerces Dorothea Sturm, daughter of the prominent District Councillor Sturm and wife of the young notary Faber. Stunned and shamed by the rape, Dorothea drowns herself. The discovery of her body is followed in quick order by Karl Alexander's death and the defeat of the planned revolt. Without his sovereign's protection, the Jew is punished for his crime against German blood in a public execution.[14] All Jews are to leave Stuttgart within three days, Sturm announces in the film's final shot, reinstating the ban. "May posterity honor this law so that much suffering to their property, life, and the blood of their children and their children's children might be spared them."

Jew Süss was one of the Third Reich's many historical pageants set in the eighteenth century. It was one of the era's few anti-Semitic features. Throughout the 1930s one regularly encountered anti-Jewish sentiments in German releases, to be sure. The "movement films" showed German workers threatened by Jewish Communist internationalism. The Aryan hero of *Hans Westmar* (1933) moves through bright rooms and walks under a clear sky while Jewish adversaries gather in dank cellars and on shadowy street corners. "Like rats they avoid the light, staging cowardly group attacks, murdering in the dark, and disappearing back into their holes."[15] Wilde, the red agitator of *Hitlerjunge Quex* (*Hitler Youth Quex,* 1933) has a similar visage and likewise constitutes a public menace.

In July 1935 the Ministry of Propaganda released the Swedish film *Petterson & Bendel,* granting it the rating "politically worthwhile," a rare commendation for a foreign feature. The comedy shows how a Jewish con man illegally reenters Sweden, seducing and bringing near ruin to a well-meaning unemployed worker. The film, claimed a critic in the *Völkischer Beobachter,* demonstrates "unscrupled Jewish 'business prowess,' which is repugnant to every Aryan graced with healthy common sense."[16] Under the guise of entertainment, the German government used the Scandinavian import as a means to demonstrate the wisdom of the Nuremberg Laws.

While synagogues and Jewish businesses burned on the "Crystal Night" of 10 November 1938, several anti-Semitic features were in production and others in preparation. In keeping with Goebbels' "orchestra principle," the films had a wide generic range, from broad comedies to earnest dramas, from historical features to topical documentaries. Hans H. Zerlett's *Robert und Bertram* premiered on 7 July 1939, a musical comedy with a Biedermeier era setting, based on a farce from 1865. Two vagabonds take up the cause of an honest village innkeeper pressed by a Jewish lender. They travel to Berlin and don disguises, plundering the nouveau riche household of the commercial adviser Ipelmeyer and using their ill-gotten gain to save the innkeeper and his daughter from the clutches of their venal creditor. What is most surprising and shocking about the film, Enno Patalas later observed, is the fact that the anti-Semitism of 1939 has nothing special about it; it draws on paradigms and clichés of long standing.[17] The Wien-Film production directed by Heinz Helbig, *Leinen aus Irland (Linen from Ireland),* released on 16 October 1939, meant to demonstrate that the film world of post-*Anschluß* Austria had fallen in line with Nazi priorities. A comedy set in 1909, it showed Jewish profiteers attempting to put linen weavers out of business. Once again, though, "German honesty and integrity triumph over the unscrupulousness of foreign elements." Here, claimed a reviewer in *Der Deutsche Film,* was perhaps the makings of a new genre, "the political entertainment film."[18]

The two anti-Semitic comedies of 1939 exploited racial stereotypes, employing caricatures and profiles well-known from the pages of *Der Stürmer.* Both films illustrated "that the Jew is crafty but not clever. Nordic cunning defeats Jewish guile."[19] These light approaches gave way to the harder lines of 1940's three offerings. Erich Waschneck's *Die Rothschilds (The Rothschilds)* presented a Jewish capitalist who spreads rumors that Napoleon has vanquished England and Prussia at Waterloo.[20] The misinformation creates international stock market panic and brings the manipulator enormous profits. Itself a product of misinformation and manipulation, the film was praised by critics for its careful research and historical veracity. Together with *Jew Süss* and the documentary feature *The Eternal Jew, The Rothschilds* fit into a larger second wave of Nazi propaganda efforts.[21] Whereas the initial "movement films" of 1933 had endeavored to construct the Nazi new man, the propaganda films from 1939 to 1942 constructed the Nazi adversary in a multitude of guises: spies, agitators, saboteurs, and incendiaries of various nationalities, especially British and (after mid-1941) Russian. These films repeatedly showed Germans in peril, occasioning a further profusion of *Heim ins Reich* epics.[22]

Jew Süss was part of a concerted effort to bolster the collective identity of a nation.[23] Harlan's racist images proved alluring, even outside Germany. The young Italian critic Michelangelo Antonioni responded to the film's Venice Festival showing with great enthusiasm: "We have no hesitation in saying that if this is propaganda, then we welcome propaganda. It is a powerful, incisive, extremely effective film . . . There is not a single moment when the film slows, not one episode in disharmony with another: it is a film of complete unity and balance . . . The episode in which Süss violates the young girl is done with astonishing skill."[24] Inordinately lucrative, this political entertainment film was the most popular release of the 1939–40 season. By 1943, 20.3 million viewers had seen it.[25] Period comedies and historical dramas worked together with documentaries and newsreels. *Jew Süss* functioned within a diverse array of offerings. The fabrication of an enemy served as a means of self-support. The other arose as an existential necessity: in order to feel their own existence and confirm their own reality, the Nazis needed the Jews. Nazi anti-Semitism amounted to a comprehensive advertising campaign; it turned the unconscious outward and made a "rational use of one's irrationality."[26] If we read this film as a Nazi fantasy, it tells us how Germans in the Third Reich saw the other and how they defined themselves in relation to that other.

Masks of a Monster

An anti-Semitic exhibition, *Jew Süss* portrays a shifty figure and his shifting image. Unrooted and nomadic, the Jew is all over the map, a man without a homeland, a dandy whose preferred countenance is the masquerade. Shortly before his death, Karl Alexander partakes of an evening's entertainment prepared by his court adviser:

> *Duke:* Fireworks, rockets, illuminations, and women—always the same. What's really behind this whole business?
> *Süss:* Why should there be something behind it?
> *Duke:* Always the same, Süss, always the same!—Yes, I've seen people in many different situations, on the battlefield, at the theater, and—in bed. But today it seems to me as if it had always been the same.—Hm, what kind of look is he giving me? As if his face were that of a hypocrite.
> *Süss:* What kind of face?
> *Duke:* Hm, he should take off his mask, my dear fellow!
> *Süss:* What mask?
> *Duke:* The last one, the last one! Ha, what does he really look like, what does he really look like?
> *Süss:* How am I really supposed to look?

Harlan's film penetrated surface appearances and promised to show the Jew's "real face."

The Ministry of Propaganda ordered that announcements for the film avoid any reference to its anti-Semitic bias.[27] Secret police reports noted that spectators in Nuremberg called the portrayal of Oppenheimer "frighteningly real."[28] Subsequent responses would echo this sentiment: *Jew Süss* was both horrible *and* authentic, fantastic *yet* real. This work, noted a French reviewer in *Le Parisien,* "is no fantasy product, but rather in keeping with historical facts that are more dramatic than any product of the imagination."[29] Publicity for Fritz Hippler's *The Eternal Jew* likewise proclaimed the "documentary about world Judaism" to be "unique, because it is no fantasy, but unfalsified interesting reality."

What does the Jew really look like? the Nazis had asked repeatedly since the formation of the party. The Jew was a "sadistic and cruel" creature, a master of disguises—and a manipulator of images.[30] During the first four decades of film history, claimed the authors of the 1937 pamphlet *Film-"Kunst," Film-Kohn, Film-Korruption,* Jewish influences had controlled German cinema. The book's opening pages scrutinize the unmasked Mr. Kohn, a composite representation of the Jewish film entrepreneur. It is not a pretty sight. We behold a demon whose eyes glow and whose gaze is shifty, a being who avoids the light of day. No soul or intellect emanates from him; everything is mercenary design and careful calculation. Kohn is a gambler whose ante is the life of others.[31] This "highwayman of modernity" once held the film medium hostage, abusing its considerable powers. The invention of cinema had offered the potential to present the world as it is. Jewish forces, however, took over the medium and reduced it to a crude commodity. Films under their aegis deformed reality and appealed to base instincts. The Jews "worked with exaggerations, tricks, bluffs, and swindles; the result of such filmic beginnings was nothing more than further bluff, senseless glitter, and cracked facades."[32]

A cinema under Jewish dominion, the *völkisch* agitators alleged, had been a standardized product geared to the lowest common denominator. The world of German film, its institutions and artists, had been contaminated: "A propaganda instrument of unrealized proportions and a significant site of cultural activity had in less than no time fallen into the hands of an alien tribe."[33] Jewish films had tried to conceal their lack of substance with lavish production budgets, elaborate sets, and garish costumes. For these reasons, Weimar cinema had had neither spiritual "depth" nor German character. Crafted for an international market, it had no firm contours: "Nothing could be clear, nothing could be true."[34] German film of the Weimar era had been tyrannized by wheeler-dealer Mabuses and bloodthirsty Nosferatus who produced films that ravaged reality and turned the world inside out.

Harlan's film reflects the emphases of *Film-"Kunst," Film-Kohn, Film-Korruption.* If Süss is a *metteur-en-scène,* Harlan's fantasy shows him also to be both a consummate and a malevolent master of ceremonies. *Jew Süss* revisited and at the same time refurbished the "haunted screen." Oppenheimer is a specter from Weimar cinema refracted through a Nazi prism.[35] He resembles the protagonist of Fritz Lang's *Dr. Mabuse, der Spieler* (*Dr. Mabuse, the Gambler,* 1922): he changes appearance and disguises himself, he controls a state's economy, he abducts women, he threatens to bring perdition to an entire community. A destructive force, he is a speculator and a cynic. Both Mabuse and Oppenheimer are without roots and at home anywhere. They represent "the Absolute Evil that transcends class—that is, that transcends History."[36] These powers of darkness stand "behind 'vulgar, materialist, modern culture' and, in general, all forces contributing to the decline of traditional social groupings, values and institutions."[37] Lang's Mabuse, wrote a Munich critic in 1925, is the quintessential Jew. He wants to be a master at any cost, the master of all being. No matter where and how he appears, he is "the great conqueror, always the leader." Can we not help but be reminded of the Elders of Zion? "This is the image of the Eternal Jew (whose name does not have to be Ahasvarus and who does not have to be an old man), marching through the centuries, always with the one great goal in mind: mastery of the world, even if entire nations must perish!"[38] Süss, like Mabuse, has a mobile gaze and a liminal body. His is the panoptic perspective of an omniscient camera: he peers through holes in the wall, he monitors the court from his balcony perch, he manipulates telescopes and dictates how astrologers read the stars.

Süss also can be understood as a latterday Dracula who, under the pretense of a legitimate business transaction, infects the German corpus. Like the vampire Count Orlok in F. W. Murnau's *Nosferatu* (1922), he shuffles semblances, possessing uncanny capacities of physical adaptation and visual motility: this celluloid Semite dissembles and disseminates. In Hippler's tractate, Jews appear as nomadic parasites. Like Orlok, they come from Eastern Europe, invading the world in the manner of vermin. "Wherever rats appear," the voice-over narrator informs the viewer, "they bring ruin, by destroying mankind's goods and foodstuffs. They spread disease and plague . . . They are cunning, cowardly, and cruel."[39] Süss's machinations suck the Swabian state dry. He tears down houses and preys on the community, torturing young men and ravaging female bodies. Like that of Orlok, Süss's undoing will stem from a sexual transgression against a German woman. Persons pure of heart (Ellen Hutter and Dorothea Sturm) submit to the seducer's advances, and their great sacrifice spares their loved ones a cruel fate.

Both *Nosferatu* and *Jew Süss* confront fantastic forces that issue from the realm of the shadows (be it a castle in the Carpathians or a sinister Römerberg ghetto) and that pose a challenge to German civilization's self-assurance. When Hutter enters the province of Nosferatu, we see a world gone inside-out; the screen shows us a negative image. In Max Schreck's incarnation, the vampire bears a stunning similarity to Nazi representations of degenerate Jewish physiognomies. In the same way, Süss resembles both a horror-film figure and a monster from the unconscious.

Recalling Hitler's rise to power, a critic described the party's formative years and its battles with Jewish forces. These energies, asserted the reviewer, suddenly "dissolved before our very eyes. One era receded and was replaced by another, a new one."[40] Jewish filmmakers used to pervert German reality and displace German history. Now that the film medium was no longer in the grip of flesh merchants and swindlers, a reconstituted German cinema could set the record straight. In the words of coscenarist Eberhard Wolfgang Möller:

> We have tried to be objective . . . but our objectivity is different from a previous sort, which in the name of understanding everything also excused everything. We simply let history speak. And it does not tell us that "the Jew is also a human being"; no, it makes clear that the Jew is a different kind of human being altogether, and that he utterly lacks the moral control over his actions with which we are born.

The writer denied that he and his associates were being mean-spirited or vindictive. Their intention was "to portray the great gap between Jewish and Aryan demeanor."[41]

Goebbels, recollected Harlan, wanted someone with a particularly demonic personality for the character of Süss Oppenheimer. Remembering Ferdinand Marian's performance as Iago in a Deutsches Theater production, the minister turned to the figure who had portrayed the tyrant-*torero* of *La Habanera* to assume the lead.[42] Werner Krauss, an artist lauded as a man of a thousand faces, played multiple roles. A performer graced with uncanny transformative powers, Werner Krauss was "the last great chameleon," commented director Willi Forst, "a genius who has replaced disguise with metamorphosis."[43] He could vanish into other characters, changing his physiognomy and his physique: "He can play people from all professions and walks of life, he has probably played every role possible, but he has always done so in a most unconventional manner, always allowing the quintessence, the idea of the character type, to shine through, so that his figures often move into territory where life's reality merges with fantasy, the actor's consummate art of magic."[44] Speaking at a Vienna press conference in 1941, Krauss promised that his Shylock would be so repulsive "that no one in the world will ever again accept a slice of bread from a Jew."[45] These words indicated that Krauss's appearance in *Jew Süss* was a function equally of professional aplomb and personal conviction.[46]

Süss's shifting faces would parallel Krauss's different masks. The Jew was Evil incarnate, like Mephisto, "a fluorescent being who lives entirely in his metamorphoses,"[47] an embodiment of the transformative power of cinema. *Jew Süss* might be called a monster movie in the guise of a realistic portrait and a historical reconstruction. Its central presence was a source of both alarm and comfort. Nazism had to "define 'outsiders' to safeguard its own illusions."[48] To secure the substance of Aryan identity, it reduced the Jew to an abstract entity.[49] Süss is seductive and dangerous, at once a master showman, a conniving schemer, and a front man for others of his ilk. At home in the world and yet homeless, he is a man without qualities, a person who is never what he seems to be. Not by chance did Nazi cinema create a devil of this kind, a fantastic construction who reflected German phantasms, who imparted valuable lessons about false appearances and their relation to the desired shape of things.

Dissolves and Doubles

Numerous commentators have noted that Süss was a man people loved to hate.[50] Marian, boasted Harlan, received fan mail from female spectators smitten by his portrayal of Süss. The film concentrated its attentions on his misdeeds and deceptions; the effect was to render his Swabian victims as decadent, bland, and boorish. Indeed, critics have stressed the repugnance of the duke and the film's lack of sympathetic German counterparts. Father Sturm, as portrayed by Eugen Klöpfer, is a rigid household tyrant. Young Faber, in Malte Jaeger's enactment, is a hothead and a fanatic, a character devoid of nuance. In general, the positive heroes of Nazi historical films were rarely creatures of appetite; they espoused loftier pursuits and higher goals. The most striking heroines in films of the Third Reich, from Zarah Leander to Kristina Söderbaum, were of foreign provenance rather than homegrown. It was not so much the positive points of orientation that energized Nazi films, but rather the non-German—that is to say, alien and outlandish—attractions.

Rather than crafting Siegfried-like supermen, Nazi propagandists created the disturbed great men of the genius films and fixated on the mortal enemies of the Aryan race. The Jew empowered Germans by demonstrating everything they were not; their sense of being derived more strongly from a negative image than it did from an ideal type.[51] The logic here was that of the projection: Nazis did not consider the Jew to be just a minority, but rather a racial opposite and negativity incarnate. Indeed, as Max Horkheimer and Theodor Adorno went on to say, "The portrait of the Jews that the nationalists offer to the world is in fact their own self-portrait."[52] Clearly, the formal means by which Harlan put these self-aggrandizing designs into motion warrant our careful attention.

The privileged visual technique at work in *Jew Süss*, as Marc Ferro points out, is the dissolve. It is a dissolve that takes us from the ducal emblem of Württemberg to the Hebrew writing on a Römerberg storefront. A dissolve marks Süss's metamorphosis from a bearded ghetto Jew to a cosmopolitan European countenance.[53] Another dissolve transforms gold coins tossed by Süss onto the duke's desk into a circle of dancing ballerinas. In the film's final sequence, a dissolve transmutes the court Jew's face back into his original ghetto visage.

> The Jew has two faces: his ghetto face (which does not lie about his subhuman nature) and his city face (which is no less harmful despite its deceptive appearance). By the utilization of gold, of which he is a past master, the Jew introduces into the chateau the taste for lucre, a taste intimately linked to debauchery. He perverts a society which was healthy and thereby harms the health of the race. The change from one escutcheon to another symbolizes the passage of power from Aryans to Jews.[54]

These formal emphases, claims Ferro, have an ideological significance. Harlan's art betrays him; the film's special effects, be they conscious or unconscious, define "the essence of Nazi doctrine."

Similar dissolves in Hippler's *The Eternal Jew* take the viewer from images of "the Eastern Jew, with his caftan, beard, and sideburns," to the camouflaged and grinning "clean-shaven, Western European Jew." The dissolves dramatize the Jew's feats of duplicity. "Under this mask he increased his influence more and more in Aryan nations and climbed to higher-ranking positions," noted the *Illustrierte Film-Kurier* program. "But he could not change his inner being."[55] Hippler's documentary opens eyes to acts of deception, offering before-and-after glimpses, making apparent the real face that lurks behind the mask. If there is a central impulse behind the dissolves of this anti-Semitic exercise, it involves learning to look clearly, not to be deceived by dissemblers. The Eternal Jew assumes respectable poses and comes in innocuous as well as agreeable guises. Hippler's dissolves allow us to assume the perspective of *Jew Süss*'s Faber, a zealot with x-ray eyes, letting us peer through disguises to see things for what they really are. "That's a Jew, this Herr Oppenheimer from Frankfurt," the Aryan bloodhound senses the minute Süss walks into the Sturm household.[56] The dissolve in Hippler's endeavor both mimics the Jew's treachery and at the same time allows viewers an analytical perspective, a behind-the-scenes glimpse at his trickery in action.

Speaking in general about the use of dissolves in Nazi cinema, Karsten Witte has argued that the formal device essentializes a distinct way of processing and reshaping the world. The dissolve cancels out experience in order "to rejuvenate man and to transform history into nature."[57] He cites various examples: a line of Prussian soldiers finds reconfiguration as a row of trees in the 1936 documentary *Der ewige Wald (The Eternal Forest);* Dr. Pfeiffer devolves from an accomplished writer to a schoolboy prankster in *Die Feuerzangenbowle* (*The Punch Bowl,* 1944). "Again and again," says Witte, "the fascist image operates with an assertion of eternal semblances, with a yearning for unreachable origins." Living entities evaporate into their primordial form and become divested of empirical existence and temporal being.

The Nazi use of this formal possibility, in fact, is even more dynamic than Witte suggests. The dissolve can travel back in time and evaporate history. It can also transport us forward, as Trenker's matched dissolve between the Dolomites and Manhattan skyscrapers in *Der verlorene Sohn* (*The Prodigal Son,* 1934) does in its leap from a pristine mountaintop to the scapes of high modernity. The dissolve can turn limp human shapes into waving flags and marching mass ornaments, as we witness at the end of *Hitler Youth Quex.* In a dramatic dissolve, the womb of the expired artiste Caroline Neuber gives birth to the future German national theater (G. W. Pabst's *Komödianten/Traveling Players,* 1941). Repeatedly in films of the Nazi era, we see dead bodies dissolve into death masks, gravestones, monuments, and paintings. (Junta's transfiguration in *Das blaue Licht/The Blue Light* serves as a prototype.) In Riefenstahl's *Olympia* (1938), a series of dissolves presents a dreamlike odyssey, passing from the dawn of humanity to the rise of classical antiquity and on to its Nazi revival in the 1936 Berlin Games. At the conclusion of *Carl Peters* (1941), the Brandenburg Gate will open up to Mount Kilimanjaro in an enactment of the *völkisch* hero's colonial dream.

On one level, the dissolves in *Jew Süss* mirror Oppenheimer's expansive initiatives, revealing his agile transformation from a "caftan Jew" to a courtly presence, or showing how his coins feed the duke's lecherous fantasies and fuel the monarch's visions of grandeur. (Interestingly, when contrasting the world of the court and the bourgeoisie, the film marks the class divisions by cuts.) Another dissolve from Süss's face as he speaks about money and power yields to an immediate view of his mercenary designs in action, a blocked city gate where people complain about extravagant tolls. In reflecting the Jew's desires, these shots also enlighten viewers about his true nature. And yet the dissolves also document the unconscious workings of Nazi fantasy production. The shifting images of the Jew derive from his uncertain creators, from fluid subjects and imaginary constellations: "Lack of boundaries, the projection of negative and positive energy, the new language of the state." We are, to adjust Alice Kaplan's phrase for our purposes here, in the strange territory of the Nazi dissolve.[58]

The initial matched dissolve from the oval-shaped state emblem and the duke's emphatic words ("My people! My country!") to the writing on the ghetto sign[59] asserts difference and at the same time suggests equivalence. The transition takes us from "the most blessed land under German skies" to the abject realm of the chosen people. It moves from the court of a sovereign whom we have seen leering at a woman's bared breasts to a window from which we see the community leader Rabbi Loew and the exposed bosom of the young Rebecca. In short, we become privy to a displaced version of the initial view, a virtual mirror image. The three Jews we see in this glimpse of the ghetto (Levy, who opens Oppenheimer's door; Rabbi Loew; and Aronsohn, the kosher butcher) are portrayed by the same German actor. A chameleonic player's performance emphasizes the sameness behind the changing guises of the Eternal Jew. As the butcher speaks to Rabbi Loew about Süss's intentions, what we witness is Werner Krauss simultaneously standing on the street and sitting at a window, talking to himself. The exchange discloses the Eternal Jew's essence: he is the function of a German and his double, an inner monologue and a Nazi special effect.

Images and captions from a contemporary film program: "The kosher butcher Aronsohn from the Street of the Jews . . . He is one of the different Jewish masks with which Werner Krauss demonstrates his art of transformation . . . and Rabbi Loew with his Rebekka. This splendidly interpreted figure from the Street of the Jews is also a masterful achievement of Werner Krauss. Thus the dynamic actor actually mumbles to himself in this film."

The dissolve functions on the visual and the aural level, infiltrating sights and sounds. As Régine Mihal Friedman explains, the song "All' mein Gedanken" ("All My Thoughts"), an updated version of a medieval lied, serves as a leitmotiv throughout the film:

> All the thoughts that I have
> They rest with you. You special sole
> Source of consolation, stay with me always.

We hear it six times, and in these repeated performances, both in the narrative field and as off-screen accompaniment, it comes to signify Swabian piety and temperance, a contrast to courtly indulgence and decadent appetite. The film's opening minutes offer a sound bridge that will move from the somber dirge emanating from a synagogue to heavy ominous chords to our first taste of the sentimental song. Initially presented in the narrative via Dorothea's soulful rendition for her fiancé, Faber, the reiterated tune becomes a "theme of destiny," an objective correlative to *völkisch* steadfastness and honor. We hear it last in conjunction with a close-up of the Jew's feet at the moment of his execution, a scene viewed from Faber's perspective: the tormented Süss, the shot suggests, has replaced the loving Dorothea as the object of her lover's attention and his "special source of consolation."[60] "All' mein Gedanken, die ich hab', die sind bei Dir": one could read the film's insistent refrain as a motto for National Socialism's privileged and obsessive relationship to the Jew.

In fabricating this counteridentity, the Nazis constituted a double, a self that they could acknowledge only in the form of a reverse image. The frightening reality intimated by *Jew Süss* is that under his masks the Semite is an Aryan. The dissolve, as we have seen in *The Eternal Jew,* intends to show the true nature of things. And in *Jew Süss* it indeed does: it reveals the workings of an unstable identity whose ultimate ground is a fictional monster and a monstrous fiction. The camera at one point moves in quickly to a close-up of Oppenheimer, who shifts his gaze, from a cold look at Faber to an affectionate regard of Dorothea while he speaks about owing his accuser an answer. The image then yields in a matched dissolve to a close-up of Karl Alexander with a necklace in hand, from whom the camera moves back as the duke asks Süss how much he owes. The repetition of gestures and words by different characters establishes links and dissolves borders between the Jew and his Aryan counterparts.[61]

Both a hate pamphlet and a statement of indebtedness, *Jew Süss* constructs a collective scapegoat and yet renders that figure an idealist who acts in the name of a utopian vision. Just like the man who wrote *Mein Kampf,* the leader of the Jews makes his designs known from the beginning and has no doubt that his cause will triumph: "I'll open the door for all of you," he says to Levy as he readies to leave for Stuttgart. "It may be tomorrow, it may be the next day, but it will happen!" Süss preys on a conflicted state run by a weak leader, opportunistically choosing the right moment to make his move, aligning himself with a moribund order against the people's representatives, insisting on an enabling decree that grants him special powers and allows him to open the gates for his previously proscribed comrades. He proceeds quickly to eradicate opposition and creates a private militia, monitoring all movement and maintaining a specular tyranny, murdering and terrorizing an entire population. Even at the end, Süss rehearses the fate of his double. His final words—"I was nothing more than the

National Socialists "long for total possession and unlimited power, at any price. They transfer their guilt for this to the Jews, whom as masters they despise and crucify" (Max Horkheimer and T. W. Adorno).

faithful servant of my sovereign!"—chillingly anticipate the pronouncements of condemned Nazi leaders at the Nuremberg trials.[62]

The Shadow of a Style

In Murnau's *Faust* (1926), Mephisto seduces his master by offering him an alternative self, conjuring up an attractive countenance that comes into view in a dissolve: "This is life, Faust, your youth!" Süss is a secularized devil, the spirit of negativity which assumes dynamic and dialectical guises. He grants his master's wishes for sex, prosperity, and diversion by bringing to the court of Württemberg new ways of seeing and lavish entertainments. He also brings modern business techniques, rationalized means of appreciating value and gathering capital as well as sophisticated forms of reification. In this regard the figure derives from a long tradition of anti-Semitic projections that accompanied the rise of the German bourgeoisie.

What mattered to this middle class, Rainer Werner Fassbinder once asked, more than "making money and seeing value appreciate? Nothing. So the bourgeoisie needed the Jews so as not to have to despise its own attitudes, so as to feel proud and grand and strong. The ultimate result of such unconscious self-hatred was the mass extermination of the Jews in the Third Reich; actually the bourgeoisie was trying to wipe out what it did not want to acknowledge in itself."[63] The Jew becomes a mirror image of Hitler and National Socialism—a dumping ground for German insufficiencies and excesses.[64] As a Nazi devil, the Jew is a creator of state spectacles and a master of illusion, a go-for-broke strategist and a criminal mastermind.[65] In a crucial sense, ideological distortion and racial hatred spawned an unwitting Aryan self-reflection, "a faithful servant" of German masters. Nazi cinema thereby created its own picture of Dorian Gray, a film that more than any other product of the era would come back to haunt its makers.

Jew Süss has cast long shadows, hardly surprising given its direct relation to Nazi violence and mass murder. As Erwin Leiser reminds us: "It was shown to the non-Jewish population when the Jews were about to be deported. Concentration camp guards saw it. And at the Auschwitz trial in Frankfurt former SS Rottenführer Stefan Baretzki admitted that the effect of showing the film was to instigate maltreatment of prisoners."[66] Its director's 1966 memoirs bear the title *Im Schatten meiner Filme (In the Shadow of My Films)*. In these pages Harlan aims to set the record straight. Driven by pangs of conscience, he reconstructs his private destiny. The autobiography restages the filmmaker's transactions with Goebbels as interviews with "the devil incarnate." Curiously, this image of a politician's "diabolical and demonic fury," "evil in its purest essence," bears no small resemblance to the protagonist of *Jew Süss*. "This man had charm. Maybe not always. But he had charm at moments when other people tended to lose their own. Goebbels was the embodiment of the devil not so much because of his limping foot but mainly because of his charm. It enabled him to exercise an all but irresistible power in flashes of wit and assured incisive thought."[67] Harlan's work with Goebbels would shroud his personal life in darkness long after World War II was over.

In his retrospective account the director describes his repeated attempts to avoid this assignment; he made excuses and begged Goebbels' indulgence, volunteering for war as a last resort. These were his marching orders, the minister let it be known. If Harlan resisted them, he would be shot as a deserter. Shackled with the project, Harlan vowed to create a viable depiction of a Jew, the story of a heroic challenger in contrast to what Harlan claimed was the cheat and counterfeiter of historical record. The only expression of anti-Semitism would come from the actions of anti-Semites and not from the representation of Jews. The hanging scene was also a historical fact, but this, too, Harlan wanted to make appear as a great injustice. Repeatedly, the minister intervened and interfered, running roughshod over any endeavor to modulate the material. In Harlan's recollections, Goebbels was interested only in straightforward propaganda. The minister told the director he "should produce political films and not films that one might make in peacetime."[68]

The film's contemporary resonance and infamous reputation belied any noble intentions Harlan might have had.[69] After the war he was taken to task, the only German director active in the Third Reich charged with crimes against humanity. The proceedings in Hamburg became an exercise in film analysis; the court had to discern whether *Jew Süss* constituted an unlawful act. In determining Harlan's culpability, the court had to establish the film's authorship. Who was ultimately responsible for what appeared on the screen? It also had to reconstruct the production background and probe the dynamics of the film's reception. Harlan alleged that he had constantly suffered from Goebbels' haranguing and meddling. He was neither a Nazi nor an anti-Semite. "My party is art. I am a patriot. I love my homeland . . . I'm no politician. I'm a director."[70] The film was condemned; the filmmaker was exonerated. The minister remained the heavy, not the artist. Harlan had not acted nobly, but he had worked under pressure, claimed the court.

"The 'state of distress' called fascism was held responsible for the production of the film *Jew Süss*," observes Siegfried Zielinski. And Goebbels personified this state of distress, freeing artists from responsibility for their work under National Socialism.[71] Harlan continued his career, but the shadows remained. He considered himself a scapegoat and a whipping boy, a man unfairly judged, his reputation besmirched by Communist and antifascist provocateurs. On the last page of his memoirs he speaks, a melodramatist to the end, of the "tortured hours and months" he suffered through under Goebbels and the many torments he had to endure after the war.[72]

Throughout the Adenauer era, Harlan was a source of controversy and outrage. Consensus ruled the artist to be an untouchable, an opportunist and an ideologue—and an enthusiastic one at that. This status nonetheless did not hinder him from making nine features during the 1950s, one of which—*Anders als du und ich/Different from You and Me*—was an antihomosexual tirade, whose gay seducer assumed Süss's position as tempter and undoer. *Kolberg* (1945) was revived in the mid-1960s, enhanced with an educational voice-over and newsreel footage from Nazi Germany's demise, and used as a means of exemplifying the madness of the Propaganda Ministry in the Third Reich's final hours.

Karsten Witte provided a fitting appellation for the denigrated filmmaker: "the baroque fascist." Harlan, said Witte, created the loudest, most colorful, most expensive films in the Third Reich as well as *Jew Süss,* the era's most offensive feature. His authorship was bound to the gigantic and the excessive: crowd scenes, grand parades, bombastic spectacles, and monumental settings. The nineteen features he made during the Third Reich "reflect seismographically the development of domestic and foreign politics in National Socialism."[73] Harlan for Witte was the ultimate "yea-sayer, possessed by artistic potential, politically ever-ready: a dutiful vassal."[74] His films offered powerful images and overwhelming music in the service of psychological warfare.[75]

As of late, though, Harlan has come under a new light. Many German critics have tired of assaults on films of the Third Reich, readings that seek only political meanings and ideological subtexts. One looks for Nazi propaganda or *völkisch* sentiment and, to be sure, one finds them. But these forays tell us little about "the films themselves." The time has come, wrote Norbert Grob in 1989, for new ways of seeing. People need to concern themselves with the "aesthetic quality" of films made during the Third Reich. Grob is mindful of spurious dichotomies between art and politics and takes pains to eschew such approaches. Films are always a function of their times, he argues, but they also harbor "other meanings"—and film historians dare not let obligatory agendas or politically correct priorities blind them.[76] Grob chides his colleagues for their sociological interpretations that ignore artistic subtleties. How can one judge a great melodramatist such as Harlan, a filmmaker whom one can safely mention in the same breath as von Stroheim, Dreyer, Sternberg, Sirk, and Stahl? How can one judge such a master without accepting the melodrama as an aesthetic form? It is, quips Grob, as if a radical animal activist were being called on to pass judgment on a champion hunter.

Grob's redemptive reading of Harlan constitutes a vigorous attempt to alter how critics approach films of the Third Reich. He attacks leftist know-it-alls who seem more interested in reading scripts than in looking at films. Most discussions of political subtexts in Harlan's films do not go beyond mere assertion, he submits. Just because a dog is put to sleep in *Opfergang* (*The Great Sacrifice,* 1944), do we immediately need to scream "euthanasia"?[77] Harlan may have made *Der Herrscher* (*The Leader,* 1937), *Jew Süss, Der große König* (*The Great King,* 1942), and *Kolberg,* concedes Grob, but the director also created eight melodramatic masterpieces during the Third Reich: *Die Kreutzersonate* (*The Kreutzer Sonata,* 1937), *Jugend*

(*Youth,* 1938), *Verwehte Spuren* (*Lost Traces,* 1938), *Das unsterbliche Herz* (*The Eternal Heart,* 1939), *Die Reise nach Tilsit* (*The Trip to Tilsit,* 1939), *Die goldene Stadt* (*The Golden City,* 1942), *Immensee* (1943), and *The Great Sacrifice.*[78] These are dense texts, rich and rewarding, worthy of discussion by dint of their aesthetic excellence.

If any ideology dictates Harlan's films, it is melodramatic convention, its fateful situations and treacherous objects, its exterior worlds that intervene unexpectedly in the lives of individuals. Harlan for Grob is a lord of time and space, an *auteur* blessed with a fine feeling for the rhythms of landscapes, buildings, and objects. The difference between Harlan's masterpieces and his political travesties remains in Grob's account a generic one. *Jew Süss* is concerned more with conflicts between ranks and classes than with melodramatic constellations. The same can be said of *The Great King* and *Kolberg,* in which melodramatic moments are marginal, a few private episodes upstaged by numerous grand-scale battle scenes.[79]

Veit Harlan is salvaged for film history by casting his most problematic work aside, by upgrading the artist and downplaying the propagandist, by separating projects forced upon the director from films true to the *auteur*'s heart, by distinguishing between his melodramas and his monstrosities, by divesting generic structures of their social functions and historical determinants. Grob asks us to look at the screen and turn our backs on the world, to relish the splendor of cinematic spectacles and not let outside concerns weigh on our experience.[80] He puts *Jew Süss* under quarantine, insisting it is not a melodrama, but rather a bourgeois tragedy, overlooking the historical connections between the two forms.[81] The feature in fact bears undeniable trappings of melodrama as elucidated by Peter Brooks: divisions between good and evil, an innocent woman preyed upon and ruined by a villain, a public trial, a moral verdict, a spectacle of judgment.[82] Harlan's public defense catalogues his films' ambiguities and contradictions, extolling the logic, control, and consistency behind the director's formal conception, intimating (while disavowing) that the visual and aesthetic master of "internal rhythms" and "unspoken meanings" also supplied the suggestive dissolves and the expressive sound bridges of *Jew Süss.*

It has been a half-century since Hitler's demise, and it is now time for a change, asserts Grob, unwittingly echoing other recent calls to normalize the German past. "Forty-one years have passed; soon it will be forty-two," proclaimed the conservative politician Franz Joseph Strauss in 1987, "since the end of World War II. It's high time now for us to step out of the shadow of the Third Reich and the dark clouds of Hitler and once again become a normal nation."[83] Seen through Grob's perspective, our fix on Veit Harlan is much brighter. We no longer look upon the "baroque fascist," but rather on an underappreciated *auteur,* indeed a master melodramatist. With *Jew Süss, Kolberg,* and other offensive titles shuffled aside, there is nothing wrong with the picture.

The potential ramifications of Grob's modest proposal are considerable: his call solicits a shift of paradigms, an examination of Nazi cinema with a less prejudiced regard. Let us pay attention to "films themselves," Grob urges. Let us resituate Harlan's features in more commodious surroundings so that we may appreciate their aesthetic meanings. Let us put them in a black box and allow them to unreel in the dark, in a cineaste's safe haven outside time and beyond history. How, though, are we to comprehend meanings if we view films in isolation? Only, perhaps, if we predetermine which meanings are relevant and which ones are not, if we decide which films should be valorized and which ones can be ignored. In revisionist enterprises, selective exclusion is a familiar procedure. Repressed materials, however, do not disappear so easily. In fact, even when they dissolve, they have a way of coming back to haunt us.

"To be authentic means not so much to be honest about one's self as to be all of a piece. But if the self is all tattered and torn and full of fears? Then it must be made all one, even in the act of exhibiting its wounds. And the myth which makes it so will bear the signs of its origin" (J. P. Stern).

SEVEN

The Führer's Phantom: *Paracelsus* (1943)

For we do not learn history only in order to know the past; we learn history in order to find an instructor for the future and for the continued existence of our own nationality.

Adolf Hitler

Poetry and painting thus insert death into a larger context of meaning, one that raises death from the arbitrary and triste sphere of nature into the world of values and ideals; that is to say, the fact of death itself becomes unimportant (that is a matter for medical reports), its insertion into a larger action that precedes or follows it, in relation to which it becomes necessary or fruitful; that alone is important.

Fritz Hippler

Missing in Action

A special radio announcement on 3 February 1943 stunned the German nation: "The battle for Stalingrad has come to an end. Faithful to their oath of allegiance, to their flag, fighting to their last breath, the Sixth Army, under the exemplary command of General Field Marshal von Paulus, has succumbed to superior enemy forces and adverse conditions." Of the 285,000 German soldiers committed to the campaign, over 140,000 had fallen; 91,000 had become prisoners of war.[1] War had left its marks on Hitler and made a captive of him as well. His health had become precarious: his left arm and leg trembled, and he appears to have suffered from syphilis. He complained incessantly about his physical condition and more and more relied on medication. Hitler "seems to have aged fifteen years during three and a half years of war," wrote Goebbels shortly after the surrender. "It is a tragic thing that the Führer has become such a recluse and leads so unhealthy a life."[2] As the war carried on and Germany's fortunes turned from unfavorable to disastrous, Hitler all but disappeared from sight. After Stalingrad, notes biographer Alan Bullock, "apart from the funeral addresses for Lutze and Dietl, Hitler delivered only two more speeches in public. In this same period he made no more than five broadcasts, while at the Munich anniversary celebrations of February 1943, 1944, 1945, and November 1944, his speech was read for him in his absence."[3] In a crucial way, the Führer was missing in action.

His conspicuous nonpresence posed no small problem for the Ministry of Propaganda. Hitler's image had always enjoyed a privileged, indeed auratic status. No German actor was allowed to play him; no film could dramatize his life, at least not directly.[4] The days of his commanding screen performance in Leni Riefenstahl's documentaries and his cameo appearance at the start of *Wunschkonzert* (*Request Concert,* 1940) had long since passed. His countenance showed up occasionally in feature films as paintings or photographs; at best, he was to be seen in newsreels. And even there German audiences lamented that they were being shortchanged.

The minutes of Goebbels' secret propaganda conferences reported early in 1941:

> Again and again come complaints from the populace that in newsreel coverage of the Führer's speeches one does not hear him (or get any excerpts from the speeches). This is done at the express wish of the Führer, and the minister has had no success in trying to change this. Because popular opinion unquestionably wishes to see excerpts from the Führer's speeches, one should undertake renewed attempts to bring this wish to the Führer's attention.[5]

Goebbels, speaking on the eve of Hitler's fifty-third birthday in April 1942, used a euphemism to downplay Hitler's glaring absence: "In this winter the German people have always had the Führer in their mind's eye."[6] In Wolfgang Liebeneiner's *Großstadtmelodie* (*Melody of a Big City,* 1943), set in 1938, a photographer combs Berlin, taking pictures of people at work, including cultural and political luminaries. We see Furtwängler conducting, and we see Goebbels speaking. We see people waiting to see the Führer, but we do not see Hitler. Even this retrospective view denies a personal appearance.

G. W. Pabst's *Paracelsus* premiered at a dire moment early in March 1943.[7] The elaborate Bavaria production presented a cultural icon in the service of a nation at war. *Paracelsus* honors a genius who intuitively relates to elements, nature, and folk, a thinker who questions academic orthodoxy and bookish learning. Philippus Theophrastus Aureolus Bombastus ab Hohenheim, Emerita, known to his contemporaries simply as Paracelsus (1493?–1541), stood as a forerunner of Faust, a "primordial image" in German cultural history.[8] Monumental set designs recreated sixteenth-century Basel in a film about a sorcerer and his apprentices,[9] focusing repeatedly on Paracelsus' laboratory of special devices where science and alchemy collaborate in a search for a miracle elixir. A man charged with a profound sense of his own importance, Paracelsus was a myth in his own time as well as in his own mind. A self-perpetuating medium, he became a legendary entity. National Socialists revived his myth with grand fanfare. Paracelsus served many functions; in Pabst's film, he was to stand in for an absent leader.

Werner Krauss had played an enemy of the people in *Jud Süß (Jew Süss)*. In *Paracelsus,* he played a public savior. An actor renowned for his powers of transformation, Krauss moved with ease from the Eternal Jew to a nomadic physician/healer in the two very different historical portraits. A biopic like *Jew Süss, Paracelsus* recounts a brief episode from the Swiss scientist's peripatetic life, his sojourn in Basel from 1526 through 1528. The film opens with Paracelsus intervening to spare the publisher Johann Froben an unnecessary amputation of a gouty leg. At the suggestion of the scholar Erasmus, a public debate takes place between Paracelsus and the Magister who prescribed the surgery. The unconventional healer puts his colleague to shame, eschewing the medical profession, espousing an organic view of nature, and praising the power of intuition. Paracelsus gains the confidence of civic leaders, the double position of municipal doctor and university professor, as well as admiring students and an assistant, Johannes. Soon enough, though, the physician faces the plague and orders the closing of the city's gates to prevent infection. His radical measure incurs the ire of the merchant Pfefferkorn, whose daughter, Renata, admires Paracelsus. The businessman attempts to smuggle goods into the city by night, but Paracelsus intercepts and burns Pfefferkorn's loaded wagons. Even so, the mountebank Fliegenbein, who carries the sickness, enters the city. Once more, Paracelsus intervenes, squelching the collective hysteria unleashed by Fliegenbein's dancing, combatting the specter of Death itself, and restoring order. The efforts go unappreciated, however. University officials censure Paracelsus, and he soon loses his students. Johannes, attempting to impress Renata and to emulate his master, administers a fatal drug to the relapsed Froben, prompting the city fathers to demand Paracelsus' arrest. With the combined help of Fliegenbein and Renata, Paracelsus manages to escape. In the final sequence, we see him decline an invitation to the Emperor's court in Innsbruck. He must answer a higher call: "The people need me. They cry out to me. I must serve not the Emperor, but the people."

Approaching *Paracelsus,* we confront the legend of a controversial Renaissance man and the enigma of a classical German filmmaker. In Pabst we find a rare instance of re-emigration in Nazi cinema, the most heralded case of a prominent Weimar director who was active in the studios of the Third Reich. He was in fact greeted with open arms by the Ministry of Propaganda. His wartime work raises many questions. The ProMi journal *Der Deutsche Film* contained numerous evocations of German film tradition and references to a classical legacy; did memories of the so-called haunted screen haunt Nazi cinema?[10] Is *Paracelsus,* with its mysterious laboratories and frenzied masses, perhaps an exceptional Nazi film of the fantastic? Did Pabst sell out, or did his work in the Third Reich retain a resistant potential?

Historical accounts of the Weimar Pabst present a precise and exacting artist as well as a political progressive and a social activist. He also appears as an extremely private person who did not readily divulge his thoughts, a man, in short, whom people could not pin down easily. One of the first to leave Germany before Hitler's rise to power, Pabst was considered a Jew and was denigrated by Goebbels.[11] And yet the director returned to the German Reich in the late 1930s and had no trouble finding his way back into the film industry.[12] Our images of this prodigal son remain decidedly vague. Depending on one's source, Pabst, a visitor in Austria as war broke out in 1939, allowed himself to become a purveyor of official ideology, a function of (the criteria differ) opportunism, resignation, or spinelessness.[13] Alternatively, he made films during a forced stay in Germany which, albeit artistically uneven, resisted official dictates and undermined political intentions.[14] In one view, *Paracelsus* is a conformist production: it celebrates German genius in order to bolster the Nazi leadership.[15] Seen from the other perspective, the film bears witness to a fettered director, whose *mise en scène* occasionally evidences signs of former greatness.[16] How are we to read the film? Should we privilege the influence of ideology or the power of authorship? Who made this film: a contaminated Pabst or a not fully compromised, indeed a still classical Pabst?

Outside of noting isolated moments that hark to his Weimar output, previous critics have viewed Pabst's Third Reich films as anomalies in his oeuvre. "Apart from an astonishing apparition of Death," remarks David Shipman about *Paracelsus,* "the direction indicates no directorial interest at all: one must assume that Pabst had no control over the script, or had become entirely cynical about his own work and the Nazis."[17] Continuities, however, are readily apparent, on many levels. Pabst has gone down in film history as a director who transfigured women and often granted them a powerful gaze, be they (among others) Lulu (*Die Büchse der Pandora/Pandora's Box,* 1929), Polly (*Die 3-Groschen-Oper/The Threepenny Opera,* 1931), or Antinea (*Die Herrin von Atlantis/The Mistress of Atlantis,* 1932). He has also gained notoriety for his portraits of men plagued by identity crises and ego deficiencies, for his explorations of the secrets of the male soul. Paracelsus is an object of fascination and a man on the run. Like Mack the Knife, he walks around with a blade at his side. Tormented and misunderstood, he joins Pabst's other emigrants, the peripatetic protagonists of *Don Quixote* (1933), *Komödianten* (*Traveling Players,* 1941), and *Der Prozeß* (*The Trial,* 1948).[18] *Paracelsus* also reflects the director's fascination with an enthralling female presence. The camera repeatedly caresses the countenance of Annelies Reinhold[19] in a manner that recalls the filmmaker's handling of Greta Garbo, Louise Brooks, and Carola Neher.[20]

Despite these points of similarity, Pabst's personal presence in the Third Reich and his relation to the Ministry of Propaganda confound our image of the *engagé* artist who made *Die freudlose Gasse* (*The Joyless Street,* 1925), *Kameradschaft* (1931), and *Westfront 1918* (1930).[21] "What possessed this liberal, cosmopolitan filmmaker," asked the makers of a recent documentary essay on Pabst, "to return to Austria in 1939 and direct movies for the Third Reich?"[22] Piecing together official and private documents leads to an impasse in any quest to comprehend Pabst's actual feelings about his work in Nazi Germany. He kept a careful diary during the war years, but those entries have not found the light of day.[23] In a private meeting with Lotte Eisner in 1946, Pabst insisted that he had been a prisoner of circumstance, volunteering elaborate evidence and explanations.[24] Whatever the reason may have been, the return to the German Reich of a once progressive director (the "red Pabst") with an international renown caused much controversy and would forever blemish his reputation.

During World War II Pabst made three films, *Traveling Players* and *Paracelsus* for Bavaria, *Der Fall Molander* (*The Molander Affair,* 1944–45, not completed) for Terra. He worked on a host of other projects, and his name appeared in various studio announcements.[25] Some critics have tried to portray Pabst as an inner emigrant, but no one has made a persuasive case. We have at best indications that Pabst soft-pedaled tendentious undertakings and rejected a host of projects. He openly clashed with the Bavaria front office before the production of *Paracelsus* and received official censure from the *Reichsfilmintendant,* Fritz Hippler. The director's bearing, claimed Hippler, "is not in keeping with what we expect today of a film artist." Other firms were ordered to have no dealings with Pabst until he reconciled with the studio. All things considered, Pabst did not enjoy A-list status in Nazi Germany; his salary of 30,000 RM per film compared poorly with the 80,000 received by directors Willi Forst, Carl Froelich, Gustaf Gründgens, Veit Harlan, Karl Hartl, Heinz Rühmann, and Gustav Ucicky.[26]

Despite state commendation as "politically and artistically worthwhile," *Paracelsus* was for the time a rare commercial disaster.[27] Although many critics harbor misgivings about the film's ideological provenance, they still laud the work for its aesthetic merits, insisting that we differentiate between Kurt Heuser's *völkisch* script and Pabst's subtle *mise en scène.* The director's American biographer, Lee Atwell, provides a generous assessment. "However we choose to view the ideological implications of the story," he submits, "Pabst never allows the bombastic rhetoric to overwhelm his finely shaded composition. In terms of drama and pictorial imagination, it [*Paracelsus*] ranks along with *Dreigroschenoper* and *Kameradschaft.*"[28] David Stewart Hull describes the film as "not quite so politically innocent as some would have it" before going on to applaud its technical achievements and to linger over a dance sequence with Harald Kreutzberg, lauding it as "truly one of the greatest things Pabst put on the screen."[29] These accounts make *Paracelsus* a curious hybrid, simultaneously an ideological artifact and one of Pabst's "most brilliant films" (Atwell), politically problematic but artistically worthwhile, a case in which a heavy-handed screenplay seems to have yielded somewhat under the master's graceful touch. It is hard to think of Pabst as a Nazi hagiographer.

Paracelsus Bound

Paracelsus, on the other hand, is less hard to imagine as the object of Nazi hagiography. A famous inventor and a man of the people, Paracelsus had a ready use value in the party's cult of titans. "It remained," as a critic put it in 1943, "for subsequent epochs to recognize what blessings Paracelsus had brought to all mankind."[30] Our admiration of a great deed, Hitler wrote in *Mein Kampf,* "must be bathed in pride that its fortunate performer is a member of our own people. From all the innumerable great names of German history, the greatest must be picked out and introduced to the youth so persistently that they become pillars of an unshakable national sentiment."[31] The 400th anniversary of the philosopher's death in 1941 occasioned a new edition of E. G. Kolbenheyer's three-volume epic biography,[32] Pert Peternell's novel *König der Ärzte (King of the Doctors)*,[33] Richard Billinger's play *Paracelsus*, as well as a series of memorial lectures by C. G. Jung. The inventor's 450th birthday likewise fostered renewed celebration, including Pabst's film; Billinger's drama also replaced *Jedermann (Everyman)* at that year's Salzburg Festival.

The image of Paracelsus, according to George Mosse, had circulated within a larger apocalyptic tradition concerned with "the abolition of time and the overcoming of death," a legacy of mystical utopianism shared by thinkers on the right and left.[34] In Kolbenheyer's influential and very popular trilogy, however, Paracelsus ceased to function as the popular necromancer he had been in the nineteenth century,[35] arising instead as an incarnation of post-Versailles humiliation, a visionary whose martyrdom enacts a collective destiny. Kolbenheyer divested the apocalyptical tradition of the progressive potential ascribed to it in, for instance, Ernst Bloch's *Thomas Münzer* (1921),[36] transforming Paracelsus into an embodiment of antimodern and nationalistic longings, a striver who attains "freedom from chains, though not in order to revolutionize the world but rather to restore the paradise of an eternal Germanic past. The apocalypse becomes a reactionary utopia, and so will it remain; for Kolbenheyer rather than Bloch was to be typical of the German road to utopia."[37] If Paracelsus represented a utopian construct, it was the right-wing variant that would prevail.[38]

Nazi biographical films dressed up the present in the garb of the past. Herbert Maisch, director of *Friedrich Schiller* (1940) and *Andreas Schlüter* (1942), made it clear how consciously this was done:

> "Everything past is only an allegory"—and this allegorical aspect to my mind seems to provide unquestionable confirmation that the German film's endeavors along these lines are in order. Then where could Germans better find and recognize themselves than in the mirror of their great heroes? In the midst of the nation's battle for its existence, what could move people more strongly than these heroes' battle to create this nation as a cultural and a spiritual entity? Even in its contemporary political structure the German film fulfills its role as a "moral institution."[39]

High-minded references to allegory and to Schiller simultaneously endorse a narcissistic plundering of the past,[40] what *Reichsfilmintendant* Fritz Hippler candidly described as a necessary act of "interpolation."[41] Historical films were made to serve the needs of the present, acting to emphasize a culture nation's common property and to mobilize a populace at war to defend its vital heritage.[42]

Pabst's film refurbishes the past, recasting a period setting and a cultural icon in a modern form, activating a heroic biography for a contemporary mission.[43] Although *Paracelsus* bears no express temporal or spatial markers, it draws on historical accounts of the peripatetic doctor's short residence in Basel.[44] The first long shot of the city creates a vacuum: on the left we see a church, on the right a public fountain, throughout the frame movement and people, but no organizing force that might impart stability to the community and the composition. This lack of orientation, initially evident as a formal irritation, soon reveals a political void as well.

Pfefferkorn and his entourage step out of the cathedral and into the center of the image, shunning beggars' appeals for alms, banning the mendicants from sight. The city fathers, with their self-serving interests, lack a larger vision and hence provide only a semblance of order and a sham of authority.[45] The film takes a full ten minutes to approach Paracelsus, giving rise to tension and suspense (will he appear in time to save Froben's limb?), gathering opinions about the figure (sorceror or savior? quack or genius?), alluding to larger social ills in need of redress (who will care for the sick and the poor? who will protect the city from the plague?). Paracelsus' reputation precedes him. One awaits his arrival with great expectations.

The initial sequence of the film sustains a race against time, a frantic mission to save Froben's leg from imminent dismemberment by a surgeon eager to wield his knife and collect his fee.[46] The exposition engages the audience in a play of absence and presence. The rules of the game oblige us to *hear* an array of comments about Paracelsus before we finally *see* him. He represents different things to different people, making for virulent differences of opinion.[47] Froben's charwoman is the first to speak of Paracelsus, and indeed she leads spectators to his dwelling. She forces her way past a long line of people waiting to see the doctor and pounds at his closed door, maneuvering past an assistant and charging into the chamber where Paracelsus is at work.

The first glimpse of Paracelsus (as rendered by Krauss, Pabst's definitive male lead)[48] comes in a striking composition: the physician watches a woman, looking into her eyes. Paracelsus stands to the left and faces the camera; a female subject, with her back to us and stripped to waist, poses before him; to the right sunlight spills through a window. The physician examines his patient, adjusting her arms as if she were a puppet. "Don't be

Women as objects of treatment in and by Pabst's film: Paracelsus intuits the mute woman's malady.

sad," Paracelsus tells her; "nature will help you. And we will help nature." Throughout the scene the woman behaves like a somnambulist, without a gaze, devoid of volition. She does not utter a single word and remains all but faceless. The doctor reads her mind and voices her thoughts. He gives her a prescription and sends her on her way with some coins.[49]

Paracelsus enters the film via the agency of a woman's voice and first appears in the visual field vis-à-vis an exposed female body.[50] The physician's gaze fixes on his silent patient, his hand manipulates her body, his phrase articulates her wishes: she becomes his marionette. But Paracelsus himself comes to us as the essentialized object of a camera's gaze. In the initial shot, he, too, is observed from afar and held up to scrutiny. The composition in this sense sets up a mirroring dynamics: the woman functions as a reflection of Paracelsus. The doctor's treatment of her prefigures the film's treatment of her master. He too will emerge as the product of a formative will, a mannequin worked over and recreated. The referent Paracelsus becomes divested of historical contingency, naturalized and impoverished.[51] One of the men waiting outside his lodgings describes him as "both wild and mild," a fitting designation for the unruly figure of legend as recast in this highly stylized film.[52] The narrative tames the richness of the historical Paracelsus and refines his image, rendering him the servant of an ideological elsewhere.

The Paracelsus legend presented a mélange of possibilities, lore about a scientist who viewed physical nature and human nature as organic parts of a larger whole. The historical Paracelsus was at odds with and ahead of his time. Like Faust, he stood at the crossroads of medieval magic and modern technology, pointing ahead in many directions:

> Some maintain that through his possession of ancient and oriental magic and of the cabalistic teachings of the rabbis he had prevision of such modern inventions as radio, television, and nuclear physics. Had not Paracelsus prophesied that "natural magic" would make it possible to see beyond the mountains, to hear across the ocean, to divine the future, to cure all diseases, to make gold, to gain eternal life, and even to duplicate "God's greatest miracle—the creation of man"?[53]

Kurt Heuser's script, looking to the present, made the doctor into a Teutonic champion who saves a community from perdition despite a Jewish merchant's machinations.[54] Looking into the future, the original scenario called for the film to end with images of modern laboratories, medical schools, and public clinics.[55]

Pabst's (and Heuser's) sanctification of a national hero accompanied attempts elsewhere in the nation to transform the doctor into a Nazi medium. Reich Minister of Health Leonardo Conti, for instance, praised the physician as the prototype of an advanced German medical science: "He loved his people, he knew the value of his blood, he was a warrior and an outstanding personality in the truest sense of the word."[56] During the trial scene in Wolfgang Liebeneiner's *Ich klage an* (*I Accuse,* 1941), Paracelsus' famous words (ones heard in Pabst's film as well) are quoted in defense of euthanasia: "Because medicine is a form of love." *Paracelsus* was conceived, publicized, and exhibited as a propaganda film.[57] To say that it honors a German master[58] and a self-sacrificing leader and thereby suggests a parallel with Hitler, however, is to fathom only two of this historical film's three temporal dimensions:

- It *refers* to the legend of a sixteenth-century figure.
- It *recasts* the legend as a filmic myth for the present, imputing to the material a timeless authenticity for a timely calling.[59]

- In so doing, it *reveals* for us today how the mythmaking machinery of wartime Germany overwhelmed that which it claimed to revive, how, in the name of eternalizing the present, it ravaged the past.

Paracelsus issued from an ideological apparatus charged with creating heroes larger than life. Pabst's twentieth-century actualization, however, did not fully suppress the vast possible meanings of this material.[60]

A Portrait and a Pathology

The historical Paracelsus was an earthy figure, a man who revolted against convention and authority, a thinker attuned to cosmic and elemental forces, an advocate of nature and the people, someone who preferred his native vernacular to the scholarly Latin. Charismatic and mercurial, Paracelsus deemed himself a genius and demanded absolute loyalty from his followers. He was a loner, constantly at odds with his contemporaries, a person unable to sustain a relation with a woman. The Swiss psychologist C. G. Jung lauded the psychotherapeutic premonitions and cathectic powers of his countryman.[61] In Jung's *völkisch* homage, Paracelsus abides as the constructive activator of a healthy *Volksgemeinschaft.*

Jung's portrait allows a darker side to become visible as well. Paracelsus' energy had a volatile aspect: "He was a mighty storm wind that tore up and swirled about everything not somehow tied to the ground."[62] Paracelsus' vitality repeatedly catalyzed abusive outbursts and bizarre reactions. For all his admiration, Jung cannot deny overwhelming evidence documenting the physician's erratic behavior and self-destructive ways. "Everything about him assumes the largest proportions; one could just as well say: everything about him is exaggerated."[63] As a Nazi prototype, Paracelsus was not altogether unproblematic. While sprucing up the figure for contemporary audiences, Jung could not sand off the rough edges; his partisan homage afforded momentary glimpses into a troubled mind and a conflicted person.[64] What does Pabst's portrait do with these secrets of a soul?

Commentators, with justification, generally place *Paracelsus* among other "genius films." This genre provided a distinctly Nazi variation on the Hollywood biopic. In it famous personages present historical role models and contemporary object lessons.[65] Nazi cinema designed a veritable gallery of Germanic masters: depictions of great politicians (*Fridericus,* 1937; *Bismarck,* 1940; *Carl Peters,* 1941), artists (*Friedrich Schiller,* 1940; *Andreas Schlüter,* 1942; *Rembrandt,* 1942), musicians (*Friedemann Bach,* 1941; *Wen die Götter lieben/Loved by the Gods,* 1942), and scientists (besides *Paracelsus, Robert Koch,* 1939; *Diesel,* 1942). Products above all of the early 1940s, these films offered "projections of the Führer, himself exalted in propaganda as a great general, supreme politician, artist and architect of genius."[66] Given that Hitler "embodied the true will of the German people there was no limit to his imagined protean capacity."[67] The genius film celebrated the past while rewriting history, bending facts for the sake of flattering fictions, molding German greatness in the image of the Nazi leader.

Such explanations, however, do not fully account for these films' curious dynamics. The genre does not always allow unconditional or even easy identification with its genius heroes, nor can we see all of them uniformly as embodiments of Hitler. Its protagonists are unpleasant and difficult, self-indulgent and often self-destructive, out of touch with their times and their contemporaries. As Paracelsus' youthful assistant puts it: "He has great power over things and people. Almost too much. It's not even easy to be around him." The great men of this genre can be unfair and capricious, causing confusion and—as in the cases of Diesel and Schlüter—sometimes catastrophe, transgressing conventions and breaking laws in the name of a life's mission and a higher calling. Genius films dramatize strained relations to authority and a constant undermining of established power, so much so that their privileging of willful independence might appear to contain an antiauthoritarian and incendiary potential. Rebellion in these films, however, directs itself against illegitimate power: staid experts, decadent leaders, and incompetent authorities. Paracelsus questions the limited perspectives of the Magister and the mercenary pursuits of Hans Pfefferkorn. A rebel with a larger cause and a wider vision, Paracelsus has a sovereign perspective that transcends the petty and the particular.

Interestingly and insistently, the genre consigns protagonists to failure in their own times and defers triumph to a later date. The narrative lines force characters down a gauntlet of vicissitudes, subjecting them to anguish, disappointment, and humiliation, allowing actors such as Willy Birgel *(Diesel),* Emil Jannings *(Robert Koch, Ohm Krüger),* and Heinrich George *(Andreas Schlüter)* elaborate opportunities for masochistic histrionics.[68] Conclusions bring a double victory, both for suffering genius and, by extension, the perspective that recognizes and thus appropriates revolutionary volition. The geniuses are often precarious and fated individuals: a young musician who cannot live up to the image of his mighty father, Johann Sebastian Bach, in Traugott Müller's *Friedemann Bach;* a suffering mother of the theater, Caroline Neuber, who dies in obscurity at the end of Pabst's *Traveling Players.* Works in this vein do not allow their protagonists extended enjoyment or triumph; happiness and notoriety, if any, take characters off track or come before a fall.[69] These films align the spectator with characters tormented by unappreciative and cruel contemporaries, with highstrung people at war with the world and their masters—as well as their own persons.

To see these exemplary destinies as propagandistic projections of the Führer, argues Julian Petley, is both correct and shortsighted. How do we explain "why the representation of these 'genius' figures as rebels (of a kind) remained remarkably constant throughout the period in question while Hitler himself moved from the position of 'revolutionary' to that of stable and institutionalised leader"?[70] The point is well made, for we dare not approach the genre as a static entity. If we are to understand *Paracelsus,* though, we must bear in mind that Hitler had moved out of sight when the film appeared; his power and person were less than "stable." *Paracelsus* intimates a beleaguered and uncertain surrogate Führer. It shows us a man doubted by his peers, a leader whose power constantly has to be reasserted, a person faced with a chaotic situation and an out-of-control populace. No sooner has Paracelsus cured the plague and ordered the city's gates reopened than a procession of flagellants (who seem to come out of nowhere) brings about public confusion.[71] Pabst's Paracelsus is neither omniscient nor omnipotent. He is obsessed with immortality and eternity; he craves recognition but remains misapprehended and underappreciated.

The film relentlessly circumscribes our attention and our focus on a single man; we are either looking for or seeing one individual.[72] In the words of Pfefferkorn: "Paracelsus, always Paracelsus." There is no escaping him. And, for Paracelsus, there is no denying nature and no escaping Death. Other characters represent either unconditional admirers or bitter opponents. Everything in the narrative gains importance insofar as it bears on the fate of the savior in whose hands rests a community's fortune. This radical solipsism reflects historical accounts of a commanding orator who insisted that people remain silent and listen when he spoke, a vainglorious personage who considered himself a divine mouthpiece. Paracelsus, asserted Henry Pachter, "was possessed by his genius and behaved as though he knew it. He demanded submission to the fact—incontrovertible for him—that Right and Truth were with him and that his mission was to save the world from wickedness."[73]

Lined up against Paracelsus are dogmatists, intransigents, and opportunists; in his camp stand those willing to sacrifice their persons and unconditionally serve his cause. Immortals in the German pantheon of great men likewise come forward as his allies. Erasmus of Rotterdam defends the doctor against detractors. An ailing Ulrich von Hutten seeks out Paracelsus and asks for his medical advice.[74] The film depicts the world in one man's image, an imaginary landscape peopled exclusively by friends or foes. Not surprisingly, the scenario abounds with doubles and dwells on foreign invaders. Just as the film of 1943 inhabits the historical Paracelsus, so too does his fictional extension permeate everything around him. This process becomes especially evident in three instances in which Paracelsus' character spills over into and occupies that of others.

The young Renata plays a decisive role as the physician's most ardent admirer. We first see her as a willful presence, a woman with a steady gaze, whose words call impertinent students to order: "Am I so without honor that you treat me in this way?" Repeatedly the camera stresses her erotic attraction for two suitors, even suggesting the inclination of the otherwise so preoccupied Paracelsus. Traumatized by her father's attempts to match

Paracelsus intimates to Johannes how he might best deal with Renata's illness.

Paracelsus and his soulmate, Fliegenbein (upper left): the mountebank's art is one of sensual excess and emotional abandon. The narrative will replace his initial dance of frenzy with a final performance that serves the German genius.

her with Count von Hohenried, she turns—as the dialogue puts it—"rigid and stiff," the victim of an enigmatic malady. Summoned by Pfefferkorn, Paracelsus treats her in his inimitable manner. As Renata lies supine and silent, her eyes shut, Paracelsus raises her arm, inspects her chest, and intuits the problem. He sends Johannes into her bedroom and—no fancy medicine here, just a household remedy—the assistant quickly revives her. Increasingly Renata finds herself drawn to Paracelsus, forsaking ties to her father and putting off Johannes. Her money will make possible the physician's escape from the city. She appears in the closing scene dressed as a maid in waiting, part of the wanderer's retinue, completely at his disposal.[75] Her volitionless condition recalls the silent woman of the opening sequence: what we first saw in a shot and a scene extends to Renata's mini-narrative. The two women become products of a treatment in and by the film—as does Paracelsus. Renata's path to self-sacrifice retraces the manifest destiny of her master.

The dancer Fliegenbein has much in common with Paracelsus as well. In the artist's words: "We both come from the same profession. Wanderers, vagabonds." The two nomads have firsthand knowledge of the folk and nature. Each possesses magnetic powers, the ability to captivate and command mass audiences. After Paracelsus' persuasive and entertaining performance at the university, students immediately become his followers. In the wake of Fliegenbein's invigorating leaps, bystanders are infected with his frenzy. Identities and activities dissolve. The mountebank, like Paracelsus, brings excitement and uproar into town. Paracelsus' departure recalls Fliegenbein's entry: both peer out of a wagon. Fliegenbein is saved by Paracelsus (the doctor treats him just as he has the sick woman and the daunted Renata); the dancer, in return, aids the master's flight. The performer's tightrope spectacle in the city square distracts the masses; it is literally a diversion in the service of escape. Neither autonomous nor rebellious,[76] he is anything but the Pabst surrogate critics have seen in him, nor is he a figure whose energetic presence subverts the film.[77] Fliegenbein moves within narrow confines, existing as a function of Paracelsus and his frame of reference.

A third striking presence is Death. Death, claims Paracelsus, is his worst enemy, and in the film it takes the form of the plague. The plague, though, is nothing more than a part of nature that has made itself independent and runs amuck, a vital energy that has got out of hand. The mass dance and the procession of flagellants with their sensual excess and sexual ecstasy become extensions of the malady, preceding Death's appearance and following in its wake.[78] Death constitutes a natural power that Paracelsus knows from intimate experience; like Fliegenbein, he was "always on the path of the plague." The doctor regards his traveling partner as a foreign invader to be stopped at all costs.

Acting as the civic physician, Paracelsus puts into effect extreme measures, combatting the sickness with the disciplinary mechanisms elaborated by Michel Foucault:

> The plague is met by order; its function is to sort out every possible confusion: that of the disease, which is transmitted when bodies are mixed together; that of the evil, which is increased when fear and death overcome prohibitions. It lays down for each individual his place, his body, his disease and his death, his well-being, by means of an omnipresent and omniscient power that subdivides itself in a regular, uninterrupted way even to the ultimate determination of the individual, of what characterizes him, of what belongs to him, of what happens to him. Against the plague, which is a mixture, discipline brings into play its power, which is one of analysis.[79]

Paracelsus finds both a medical and political answer to the plague, shutting the township off from the outside world and monitoring all movement, transforming Basel into a totally governed city. One man controls all comings and goings in this space, a logistic battleground on which Paracelsus combats the capitalist Pfefferkorn and faces off against his mortal enemy.[80]

Throughout the film, actions and utterances gain meaning as they relate to the protagonist. *Paracelsus* does not so much depict a popular hero as provide a case study. The character neither changes nor develops; he is set in his ways, fixed in his being. For all his travels, his world is a closed circle. His perspective resembles what Horkheimer and Adorno call "false projection." This mode of response perceives but does not reflect, either on the objects it apprehends or on its own workings: "It overflows and fades away at one and the same time. It invests the outer world boundlessly with its own content; but it invests it in fact with the void: with an overstatement of mere means, relations, machinations, and dark practice without the perspective of thought."[81] Like the intelligence described by Horkheimer and Adorno, the screen Paracelsus "makes everything in his own image. He seems to need no living being, yet demands that all serve him. His will permeates the universe and everything must relate to him. His systems know no gaps."[82] Paracelsus, a fictional character, displays the mechanisms of paranoia, just as *Paracelsus*, as a Nazi filmic fiction, offers "a delusional reconstruction of the real."[83]

The Knight of the Living Dead

Pabst's 1943 film shows us Death at work. Death hounds Paracelsus like the plague.[84] Like Fliegenbein, wherever the master goes, so too does the sickness. Death faces Paracelsus in a showdown directly after Fliegenbein's dance of abandon.[85] The doctor enters the inn "Zum Blumen" and, with a boisterous laugh, stops the mad proceedings, interrogating the artist and learning that the vagabond carries the virus. Bystanders flee the room, and the diminutive man collapses in the doctor's arms. The camera moves in on Paracelsus; at the same time, the sound of a scythe becomes increasingly louder. In the dramatic shots that follow we see:

1. The back of a dark figure, Death (medium shot) from Paracelsus' perspective.
2. A frontal medium shot of Paracelsus and the unconscious Fliegenbein; Paracelsus looks to the left and then straight ahead.
3. A medium shot of Death, who turns around suddenly to meet Paracelsus' gaze.
4. (as in 2): Paracelsus returns Death's gaze and looks directly at him.
5. (as in 3): Death stands up quickly and grabs his scythe while the camera pans to the left.
6. (as in 2 and 4) Paracelsus defends himself with his sword against Death's powerful blow.
7. A closeup of Death, who looks directly into the camera. The figure disappears, and we hear Paracelsus' hearty offscreen laughter and exclamation: "I've got you again, Grim Reaper [*Freund Hein*]!"
8. A medium shot of Paracelsus, who responds with astonishment, not believing his own eyes. He turns to the right and addresses his assistant and servant: "Quit gaping at me like that, you two!"

The confrontation is striking and macabre. Death appears here in person, screened as Paracelsus' mental distortion. The physician peers into the camera (#2) and a reverse shot reveals the steely gaze of Death (#3). Paracelsus confronts the double that obsesses and occupies him, both his undoer and his enabler, a disturbing entity in this filmed fiction—and, to be sure, a hardly unfamiliar presence in Nazi fantasy production. Death is a character's hallucination and a Führer surrogate's double, an onscreen gaze and an offscreen presence that is equated with the camera, a force that is synonymous with the plague. The cold countenance of Death gazes at the living and condemns it to perdition.[86]

Seen in this light, Paracelsus, the ostensible healer, takes on a darker aspect. His initial look at the silent woman renders her a zombie, a being devoid of independent existence. Paracelsus works with and masters nature, and a crucial measure of this mastery is his power over women. Exposed to the physician's influence, the initially pert and independent Renata is de-eroticized, her subject extinguished.[87] Under his gaze, the two women transmute into empty shells. Under the gaze of a camera, he too will become divested of life. In this way Death appears as Paracelsus' negative—but logical—counterpart, indeed the double for an alleged espouser of life. Pabst's camera and Heuser's script process the image and gaze of Paracelsus, transforming the vital and vitriolic presence, divesting him of corporeality and rendering him a death mask, lifting him out of history and into the timeless realm of the immortal.[88] This Paracelsus is a ventriloquist's dummy, an apparition whose words and gestures emanate from elsewhere. He is the product of a lethal machinery, an apparatus that in the name of higher values and historical callings transforms the larger-than-life figure into a disciplined body.

In the film's last image, Paracelsus assumes the center of the composition. The wanderer's gaze is weak, his gestures weary. He has given up all desire for power and fortune. His devotion to the folk alone determines his existence. If Paracelsus fills the formal and political void of the film's first sequence, it is a presence that takes its powers from his offscreen followers. The closing shot eradicates all traces of the legendary rebel and intransigent; the figure "shaped by the art of propaganda becomes as modeling clay—amorphous material lacking initiative of its own."[89] The volatile historical personage transmutes into the solemn servant of a different epoch and a wartime calling.

This biographical film about a walking cipher confirms rather than confounds an auteurist approach to Pabst. It fits in well with the director's other tales of males under duress, replicating the projective dynamics and paranoid scenarios of *Secrets of a Soul, The Mistress of Atlantis,* and *Don Quixote.* Here, as elsewhere in Pabst, the power of man relates to the diminished presence of woman. Here, as in *Kameradschaft, Traveling Players,* and *Der letzte Akt* (*The Last Ten Days,* 1955), we see unruly masses and uninhibited bodies. The portrait also assumes a place in Nazi cinema's gallery of self-sacrificing and suffering heroes, from Pabst's own Caroline Neuber to Robert Koch, Friedrich Schiller, Friedemann Bach, Andreas Schlüter,

Ohm Krüger, Diesel, and Rembrandt. Pabst's authorship and Nazi ideology are equal partners in *Paracelsus.*

The film, however, no more proves that Pabst was a Nazi sympathizer than it succeeded in reaffirming Hitler's greatness. Scripted to hallow the timeless authenticity of genius and by extension to support the Führer, it also depicts troubled times. Conceived to celebrate the self-anointed servant of the folk, the film leaves us with an overworked and wornout old man. The closing sequence recalls the moment in *The Wizard of Oz* (1939) when we peer behind a curtain expecting to see the "Great Oz" and instead behold the emptiness of an illusion. The Führer all along had presented himself as the embodiment of mass desire, a fiction that the expensive state production crafted by a famous director could no longer sustain in the dire wartime situation. *Paracelsus* may not be a subversive film. Nonetheless, it is a genius film that reveals much about Nazi dementia. The film served a political purpose, but in so doing it opened up an abyss in which ideological assertion displayed its own lack of substance. At a time when German audiences relied more strongly than ever on cinemas for sustenance and relief, this film left viewers with a disquieting perspective, the unsettling presentiment of a beleaguered Germany and an incapacitated Führer. A movie-hungry populace avoided *Paracelsus* like the plague.[90]

The final sequence of *Paracelsus* confirms Horkheimer and Adorno's comments about fascist leaders. Hitler and his counterparts "are not so much supermen as functions of their own propaganda machine, the focal points at which identical reactions of countless citizens intersect. In the psychology of the modern masses, the Führer is not so much a father-figure as a collective and overexaggerated projection of the powerless ego of each individual—to which the so-called 'leaders' in fact correspond." Like movie stars, they "are powerless in themselves but deputize for all the other powerless individuals, and embody the fullness of power for them, without themselves being anything other than the vacant spaces taken up accidentally by power."[91] All along Hitler had "stood out in front, visible to all, so much, in fact, that he seemed to hold the stage alone." And yet even when Hitler was present, what was really there? "Nothingness," Max Picard insists, "pure nothingness."[92] The Führer's stand-in who faces the clamoring folk can hardly stand up. His head droops, and a shadow scars his face. A tired voice responds to the cries of the sick and needy. The last shot of *Paracelsus* transfigures its hero and leaves us with a phantom, a Knight of the Living Dead.

“The true war film did not necessarily have to depict war or any actual battle. For once the cinema was able to create surprise (technological, psychological, etc.), it effectively came under the category of weapons” (Paul Virilio).

EIGHT

Self-Reflexive Self-Destruction: *Münchhausen* (1943)

> Fascist revolt promised vagabondage in infinite and eternal spaces, in new eras. Life itself seems new. One is at home and at the same time on another planet.
>
> *Gisela von Wysocki*

> Here the myth articulates itself in all its purity: what matters is to form *oneself,* to *type oneself,* and to type oneself as absolute, free creator (and consequently, as *self*-creator).
>
> *Philippe Lacoue-Labarthe and Jean-Luc Nancy*

"A Popular Film in the Truest Sense of the Term"

The German war effort had suffered a monumental setback at Stalingrad. Even the Minister of Propaganda, faced with this unthinkable defeat, confessed to a "paralyzing anxiety."[1] Speaking at the Berlin Sportpalast on 18 February 1943, Goebbels sought to transform the military debacle into a spiritual renewal. In a painstakingly choreographed and electrifying performance, he let out all the stops, rousing his listeners with a call for "total war," a comprehensive remobilization "even more total and radical than we might begin to imagine today."[2] Meanwhile Allied air strikes devastated German cities nightly. In the early hours of 2 March, British planes dropped 900 tons of bombs on Berlin, damaging thousands of buildings and causing 600 large fires, leaving 711 dead and more than 35,000 homeless.[3] "The sky is a smoky sulfur-yellow," wrote Ruth Andreas-Friedrich. "Harried people stumble through the streets. With bundles, with suitcases and houseware. Stumbling over ruins and debris."[4] Advising his staff a day later, Goebbels said the party must pay careful attention to the population, "since the problem of getting through this period of emergency is primarily a psychological one."[5]

The centerpiece for Ufa's twenty-fifth anniversary celebration, *Münchhausen* premiered at the Ufa-Palast am Zoo on 5 March, offering the shell-shocked Berlin audience a much-appreciated evening's diversion.[6] The film's state-of-the-art color cinematography and inventive special effects allowed viewers to inhabit a much more agreeable world in which constantly changing locations made for a carnivalesque bounty. The cast sported a gathering of attractive stars and beloved character actors. The male lead, Hans Albers, delighted spectators with his flamboyant charm and irrepressible vigor. Studio officials were beside themselves. They had realized their dream of a work "that unites the grandest attributes of the venerable Ufa tradition and beyond that provides the most modern example of German film art."[7] Here, publicist Curt Riess later reported, was a welcome escape, "a film like the ones people used to make in the good old days. You could at times almost forget you were living in the Third Reich."[8]

What Goebbels called "a popular film [*Volksfilm*] in the truest sense of the term," the Ufa extravaganza honored the raconteur of lore, Hieronymous Karl Friedrich, Baron von Münchhausen (1720–1797), whose fictional transfigurations in the late eighteenth and nineteenth centuries had traveled well and widely.[9] The baron's improbable first-person narratives sustain a bizarre humor and an immodest staccato, commingling hyperbole and tongue-in-cheek. They reflect copious borrowings from a host of European sources (above all, picaresque novels and popular travel literature); their author was Rudolf Erich Raspe, a German *bon vivant* who had fled creditors to settle in England. Once the adventures of Münchhausen entered the public sphere in the 1780s, they found immediate translation into German and elaboration by Gottfried August Bürger, innumerable subsequent editions, variant versions, and sequels involving multiple authors and entrepreneurs.[10] Squabbles over rights have accompanied this property into the present.

The "liar baron" would become an equally persistent presence in film history, appearing in a host of national and temporal settings, from Georges Méliès's Pathé fantasy of 1911 and animated renderings by Emile Cohl (1913), Richard Feigenbauer (1920), Paul Peroff (1929), and Karel Zeman (1962), to planned endeavors by Hans Richter as well as American features with the inimitable Jack Pearl (*Meet the Baron,* 1933, and *Hollywood Party,* 1934).[11] The baron stars in Phil Jutzi's 1936 short *Münchhausens letztes Abenteuer (Münchhausen's Last Adventure),* and rides his cannonball during a musical revue in *Es leuchten die Sterne* (*The Stars Are Shining,* 1938). His most recent appearance was in Terry Gilliam's *The Adventures of Baron Munchausen* (1988).[12]

The film of 1943 opens in what looks to be an eighteenth-century milieu. A rococo ball hosted by Münchhausen in his ancestral castle, Bodenwerder, celebrates his wife's birthday. The period setting, however, turns out to be a masquerade party: a flirtatious young woman, unsuccessful in seducing the baron, steps out of the castle and jumps into a Mercedes. We have been witness to an elaborate charade; the film's real setting is a modern world of electricity and tangos. (If we look carefully, we even glimpse a small swastika on the sports coupe.) A few days later, Münchhausen relates the tale of his famous ancestor to a student of Münchhausiana, Frederick von Hartenfeld, and his fiancée, Sophie, the vexatious coquette from the birthday party. In an extended flashback, Münchhausen traces major stations in his forebear's peripatetic biography.

The baron, accompanied by his servant, Christian Kuchenreutter, returns to his father's home in eighteenth-century Bodenwerder. The master and his valet join Prince Anton Ulrich of Brunswick, accompanying him to the court of Catherine II in Russia. Enroute Münchhausen encounters Cagliostro, a magician, scoundrel, and conniver, who unsuccessfully tries to enlist the baron in political machinations. In St. Petersburg, Münchhausen becomes the adjutant general and lover of Catherine II. Wounded in a duel, he retreats to Cagliostro, warning the former adversary of the czarina's plans to have him arrested. To express his gratitude, the illusionist offers his guest a ring of invisibility and grants him the power of eternal youth.

Serving in Russia's war against the Turks, the baron is taken prisoner and transferred to the seraglio of the sultan in Constantinople. He escapes with Princess Isabelle d'Este to Venice. During his sojourn in the lagoon city, he meets a former acquaintance, Casanova. The old man is astonished at Münchhausen's youth and vigor, wondering whether he is in league with the devil. Pursued by the Inquisition, the baron commandeers a balloon and travels with his servant to the moon. The lunar realm, the two quickly learn, follows a different temporal order. Because one moon day equals an earth year, Christian ages rapidly and soon expires. Münchhausen, saddened by his companion's death, returns to earth. Back in the narrative present, Münchhausen admits that he is the baron, a confession that shocks the young couple into a hasty departure. Alone with his aging wife, Münchhausen decides to put an end to a life of wandering and to spend his remaining days with her: "I demand everything!" he avers; "I also want—the rest!"

For its original audiences, the production offered therapeutic relief, a tale about a man who masters his own destiny and marshals the march of time.

A popular vehicle and the product of a world war, *Münchhausen* represents the Third Reich's consummate cinematic achievement.[13] More than that, though, it enacts the heroic myth central to Aryan self-fashioning. The protagonist's legendary powers became employed in Hitler's war effort, the illusory means by which the Ministry of Propaganda sought to reanimate a paralyzed nation. With its state-of-the-art wizardry, the film put German technical genius on parade and offered a compelling—and what was hoped to be reassuring—triumph of special effects. The film's central image provided its ultimate icon: Münchhausen straddles a cannonball and zooms through the air, turning toward the camera, tipping his hat and acknowledging the spectator with a smile. Hans Albers played a *Bombenrolle* in which the baron became a human projectile. The feature *Münchhausen* likewise represented a calculated feat of weapons propaganda, fashioned at a time when Goebbels needed a film that might serve as the cinematic equivalent of a V-2 rocket.

Light Fare for Hard Times

The wartime blockbuster has gone down in history as an undisputed masterpiece of European cinema, as the greatest German color film of all time. Postwar panegyrics echo and often surpass the hearty commendations of Nazi contemporaries.[14] The work fascinated David Stewart Hull so strongly that he felt moved to write an entire volume on the films of the Third Reich.[15] The prologue to a current American video copy announces "one of the great events in motion picture history." *Münchhausen* continues to be widely shown and warmly received, a production that, in the recent words of a German observer, provides "some fond memories from otherwise bad times."[16] Critics by and large view the baron as an oppositional voice rather than "a mouthpiece for the German war machine."[17] There would appear to be a clear gap between the film's wartime mission and its postwar reputation. On the one hand, we have a seminal example of how the Third Reich saw war as a total endeavor whose battleground occupied both physical spaces and fields of perception. On the other, we have a hallmark production, a cult classic, and a subversive artifact. This seeming disparity between *Münchhausen*'s instrumental design and its popular reception deserves closer scrutiny. The film is a sophisticated piece of software, a fantasy arsenal whose sights and sounds galvanize and scintillate.[18] It enjoys an undiminished renown as an exceptional film, indeed as an exception to the rule, for at least four reasons.

First, as a film meant to honor Ufa's twenty-fifth anniversary, *Münchhausen* was a high-priority production. In preparation for the event, Goebbels asked that no cost be spared. Originally budgeted at 4.57 million RM, the final price tag was almost 2 million more. Architects Emil Hasler and Otto Gülstorff were allowed to indulge their every whim. The extensive planning for their set designs necessitated more than 2,500 blueprints and drawings.[19] This occasion intended to showcase German cinema's international status and to demonstrate special effects and color technology that could rival Hollywood's.[20] Josef von Baky, relatively unknown and anything but a party enthusiast, received the directorial assignment along with virtual creative carte blanche. The Hungarian filmmaker had demonstrated his own international appeal in the German-Hungarian coproduction *Menschen vom Varieté* (*People from the Variety,* 1939). Contemporaries praised his films for their fluid visual style, emphasizing his predilection for expressive transitions and striking optical effects,[21] commending his work with Luise Ullrich in his first big success of 1941, *Annelie.* His last war effort, *Via Mala,* banned by the government in 1945 for its "gloomy atmosphere," featured the murder of a tyrant. Revived at the 1990 Berlin Film Festival, the film was lauded as a noteworthy instance of late expressionism and aesthetic resistance.[22] Among his postwar efforts, a pair of impressive "rubble films" about re-emigrants stand out, *. . . und über uns der Himmel* (*And the Sky above Us,* 1947) and *Der Ruf* (*The Last Illusion,* 1949). Von Baky subsequently adapted Erich Kästner's *Das doppelte Lottchen* (*The Two Little Lottas,* 1950), for which he received a State Film Prize. In general, Baky is thought of as a talented, reliable, and unpolitical professional whose labors spanned many different genres.

Despite official reservations, Erich Kästner, an oppositional artist disliked by the government and not allowed to publish in Germany, was enlisted to write the screenplay.[23] Kästner's scenario contains acerbic asides such as the remark on the moon that not the baron's watch, but indeed the times themselves were "kaput," as well as a disparaging reference to the "thousand eyes and arms" of the secret police: "They have the power to be just and unjust; it all depends on how they feel." The film also includes Münchhausen's caustic observation: "There are times in which one rarely takes a look in the mirror."[24] In a context in which lies were the order of the day, the baron's marvelous tales and ironic ripostes rang "truer than ever."[25] The magic powers of the baron's ring responded to many people's fantasies of escaping from the unbearable wartime situation.[26] Hans Albers, likewise, had a reputation as a dissident, a star who refused to appear in photographs with party luminaries, whose relations to the Ministry of Propaganda were anything but cordial.[27] The film's ideological nonconformity made itself evident even in Kästner's choice of a pseudonym. "Berthold Bürger" may well have evoked the eighteenth-century author who brought Münchhausen's tales into German households. The initials also recalled Bertolt Brecht, a blacklisted colleague living in exile.[28]

A second argument for the film's singular status relates to its formal shape. *Münchhausen* stands out as one of very few German films of the Third Reich with a self-reflexive framework. Most features made under Nazi rule take place in enclosed worlds and do not draw attention to their workings as a function of forces outside the text. Filmmakers shunned stylistic indulgence and formal eccentricity. A preference for transparent presentation aligns features of this era with the classical Hollywood narrative and distinguishes them from the frame stories and convoluted plots typical of Weimar's modernist cinema. *Münchhausen,* the extended retrospection of a self-conscious raconteur, is anything but straightforward. Repeatedly its hero undermines the filmic fiction, appearing in the first shot as a painted icon that winks at the camera in an animated special effect, establishing immediate contact to the offscreen spectator. This is to be a story about a hero who fabricates tales, and, mimicking the powers of cinema, incarnates a medium that traffics in illusions. The subsequent party sequence demonstrates how spectators can be deceived by cinema's imaginary properties. We take a fake world at face value, then confront the knowledge that the premodern setting is one vast simulation. The elaborately choreographed scene links the seductive wink of a protagonist to the captivating potential of the cinema, ploys hardly common to the more conventional narratives of most Third Reich features.[29]

A third point of variance concerns *Münchhausen*'s representation of sexuality. The epoch's features have a reputation for being prudish; they are hardly known for their kinetic bodies. They include little physical display or carnal proclivity; stunts and action scenes are all but lacking. According to Karsten Witte, Nazi cinema arouses desires for visual pleasures that it fails to satisfy. Fascist aesthetics are driven by an underlying fear of chaos, decadence, and sensuality, any property that might elude control, especially unharnessed eroticism.[30] Much more directly than in other German films of the Third Reich, *Münchhausen*'s characters express and act on physical desire.

Hans Albers, the blond and blue-eyed hero, is the closest one comes to a Siegfried among the Third Reich's male leads. "He is," claimed Nazi pub-

The male star as macho role model: "After an Albers film, even an apprentice hairdresser becomes like Albers: just let anybody try to give him a hard time" (Fritz Hippler).

licist Oskar Kalbus, "the embodiment of and testimony to the German idea of masculinity."[31] Albers' dynamic body language stands out amidst the controlled and contained physicality characteristic of contemporaries such as Willy Birgel (the exemplar of erect bearing), Viktor Staal, and Carl Raddatz. His suppleness and swagger are a far cry from the ungainly proportions of a Heinrich George or an Emil Jannings. In a cinema with males often plagued by deficient egos and choleric dispositions, Albers is confident, blithe, and playful. In contrast to the era's generally inhibited or downright dysfunctional romantic leads, he does not hesitate to express his libidinal longings. (In *Wasser für Canitoga/Water for Canitoga,* 1939, his Oliver Montstuart sings one bawdy song after another.) He would appear to be an anomaly in a cinema in which lusty men are in short supply, in which a sexualized male invariably bears negative markings. For his audiences, Albers embodied a sunny boy ("Hans im Glück"). As a star and a private person, Albers emanated optimism, brashness ("Hoppla-jetzt-komm-ich"/"Ready-or-not-here-I-come"), and vitality.[32]

More surprisingly yet, *Münchhausen* has a female figure, Catherine the Great (played by Brigitte Horney),[33] who candidly announces her sexual needs, who controls men with her erotic charms and determines their comings and goings—without ever being upstaged or chastened.[34] During the banquet scene in her palace, a foreign dignitary maintains that it would be an injustice to address her as Catherine "die Große," using the feminine title; rather, she should be called Catherine "*der* Große." *Münchhausen* valorizes a promiscuous hero; it contains an abundance of suggestive dialogues and intimate encounters; it has at its center a phallic woman. The film also contains some striking nude footage. For these reasons critics speak of it as "a programmatic denial of National Socialism's official policy" in its approach to sex and gender.[35]

A final consideration would seem to close the case: the production is one of very few films of the fantastic made during the Third Reich. Not since the age of silent cinema, opined a journalist in 1942, had a German film dared to indulge itself in so much magic and enchantment.[36] Organizers of a retrospective at the Berlin Film Festival in 1977 could identify only twelve films in this vein produced in Germany from 1933 to mid-1945.[37] The genre, maintained contemporaries, had a subversive potential, encompassing strange places and irrational worlds, flights of imagination and expressions of intoxication.[38] For all their deference to the romantic legacy, Nazi features rarely spirited the viewer to the realm of the exotic.[39] Films of the Third Reich did not allow for a free play in time and space; flashbacks, especially before 1941, were uncommon. If one traveled, it was with a purpose and an itinerary. Perhaps the era's true films of the fantastic remained documentaries such as *Triumph des Willens* (*Triumph of the Will*, 1935), a delirious vision of mass submission to demonic authority, a frenzied demonstration of ritual, worship, and incantation, a film that chronicled the arrival of a god from the clouds, a messianic being who brings hope and redemption to a national tribe.[40] The state created a convincing and all-encompassing fictional world, staging the fantastic in the everyday and not in the darkness of cinemas.[41]

For these reasons, *Münchhausen* stood out in its own time, just as its reputation has withstood the passage of time. The film contains a wealth of expansive designs that hark to the fabled monumental constructions of German silent cinema, set pieces such as the bustling fair in St. Petersburg, the opulent court of Catherine the Great, Cagliostro's eerie chamber, the sultan's seraglio, Carnival in Venice, a lunar phantasmagoria. The film celebrates a protagonist not subject to the laws of time, an indestructible *élan vital* whose eternal youth and unfailing energy derive from black magic. *Münchhausen* reaches back to the playfulness of Méliès, in the words of André Bazin, "to discover and make use of all the basic possibilities of this new means of expression, to endow cinema with the marvelous, the impossible, the dream."[42] A Nazi *Wizard of Oz*, it constitutes an undoubtedly international endeavor, the grand exception, so it would seem, among the feature films of the Third Reich.[43]

Nazi Cinema Incarnate

When first run in German cinemas, *Münchhausen* seemed to offer glimpses of a better world, pleasant dreams for people accustomed to sleepless nights. Its specialness derived from its unique status, a reputation carefully cultivated by the Ministry of Propaganda. *Münchhausen* was a state-sponsored film, initiated and carefully monitored by Goebbels and his coworkers, which, so it was said, nonetheless remained free from party influence and government interference. In fact *Münchhausen*'s most remarkable accomplishment resided in its ability to do double duty, to offer a fantasy of escape while holding its audiences ideologically captive. For this reason, the attributes that have made the film noteworthy to spectators, critics, and historians also attest to the film's profound political implications. Precisely the considerations that seem to mark *Münchhausen* as an *exceptional* endeavor demonstrate equally its *exemplary* status. *Münchhausen* represents not only the

Hitler era's most durable cinematic success but also its ultimate exercise in wishful thinking.

The film may have enjoyed a distinct right of exception. We dare not forget, though, the political function of the occasion that *Münchhausen* was meant to celebrate, namely the twenty-fifth anniversary of Ufa. The festive premiere in the Ufa-Palast am Zoo included all the obligatory NSDAP trappings: flags with swastikas, the "Horst Wessel Song," and the German anthem. The propaganda minister praised the spiritual power and organization of German film. Ludwig Klitzsch, general director of Ufa, reviewed the studio's history, positioning Ufa and the film within party constellations. Ufa, claimed Klitzsch, "is the creation of a world war," brought to life by the German government in an attempt to control the making of images in an embattled nation, harnessing "the economic, artistic, and technical aspects of film production in a single influential company under state leadership."[44] The history of Ufa, Germany's most renowned studio, had begun with a blend of war and cinema. Quite openly, party officials hallowed imagemaking in the service of a nation at war, reaffirming the key role of the movie industry in the state apparatus. Klitzsch, remarked Goebbels in his diary, "showed how exceedingly hard a few patriots had to fight against Jewish-American efforts at control of the German motion picture during the Weimar era."[45]

War gave rise to a new German film; after 1939, war became Nazi cinema's central mission.[46] Film and the mass media constituted crucial military instruments. In the words of ProMi luminary Fritz Hippler:

> Total war, a consequence of immense technical and sociological developments in our time, has forced us to reconsider our notions of "weapons" and "soldiers." Weapons are no longer just the means by which we physically combat our enemies, and soldiers are no longer merely the uniformed and organized bearers of weapons. In total war, nations in their entirety confront each other, and all expressions of national life become weapons of war—regardless of whether they seek to weaken the enemy's morale or to strengthen one's own, that is to say, to afford diversion, concentration, or recreation.[47]

Münchhausen dramatizes this consonance between the machinery of cinema and the machinery of war, displaying instruments such as Christian's gun with its 100-mile range, at once a lens and a weapon. The duel between Münchhausen and Count Potemkin in a darkened chamber further illustrates the connection between gunfire and camera action; pistol shots light up the black box of a room and—in a synthesis of *tableau vivant* and primitive cinema—make the spectacle visible. The famous image of Hans Albers seated on a cannonball flying through the sky essentializes the nexus between cinema's powers of illusion and war's tools of aggression.[48]

National Socialism recognized that war involved both material territories and immaterial fields of perception. Film became an explosive arsenal of surprises and effects which made minds reel and emotions surrender under a constant barrage of stimulation. As the minister of propaganda put it early in 1941, film represented "a weapon in the total struggle of our people, in the total existential battle of an entire nation which we must fight to the bitter end, where the ultimate question is to be or not to be."[49] "At the height of total war," observes Paul Virilio, "it seemed to Goebbels and to Hitler himself that the rescuing of the German cinema from black-and-white would provide it with a competitive edge against the tonic power of American productions." It was no coincidence, then, that German color production expanded after 1940 and that the Third Reich's paramount war films, *Münchhausen* and *Kolberg,* appeared in Agfacolor.[50] Color film, proclaimed Hans Albers (or perhaps a ghostwriter), "permits new possibilities and unimagined effects; now eyes really will appear blue and hair really blond."[51]

The enlistment of an oppositional writer for the production likewise facilitated rather than undermined the state-sponsored spectacle. A film choreographed by quite serious strategists, *Münchhausen* issued from a ministry whose endeavors to control all sectors of experience included alternative perspectives. The Nazi regime allowed itself the luxury of ironizing its own operations, hoping all the better to anticipate and neutralize collective dissatisfaction. The cynical asides in Erich Kästner's script provide the semblance of an oppositional voice, but they remain a calculated function in a larger design, similar in this regard to the party-sponsored criticism of the weekly *Das Reich,* a journal produced with the ProMi's blessings by non-Nazis in a consciously non-Nazi style. With so much at stake at such a crucial time, Kästner's participation in the Ufa commemoration seems to have been less an exercise in subversion than an example of how the ProMi sought to refunctionalize and thereby defuse nonconformist sensibility. Someone who suffered under the Nazis and remained an inner emigrant, Kästner nonetheless fashioned a script that proved to be precisely what the Doctor (Goebbels) ordered.

Kästner's praise of the baron's Copernican exuberance occasionally recalls the most fulsome blood-and-soil rhetoric. "Only the person," exclaims Münchhausen,

> who feels it in his blood when he rides through the forest or fights with an enemy or embraces a woman or picks a flower,—only the person who feels it deeply in his blood and knows that all of this is happening on a small star among many millions of other stars,—on a minuscule, eternally revolving ball constantly moving like a carousel around one of the glowing suns, amidst the change of beautiful seasons and hideous centuries,—only the person who always feels this is really a human being. Everyone else is just a two-legged mammal.[52]

The writer's sexual politics likewise seem remarkably of a piece with soldier male misogyny. His novel *Fabian* (1931) is a bitter exploration of deception, treachery, and fraud as central elements of modernity.[53] The narrative also contains an abundance of phantasmagoric passages that one might find in Klaus Theweleit's *Male Fantasies.*[54] Kästner's resolute moralist, Fabian, sees himself constantly pursued by sexually voracious women. Irene Moll sits across from the protagonist at one point and nibbles on pieces of candy shaped like young men. Having devoured the sweets, she crumbles the bag and turns to her interlocutor, proclaiming, "Now I'm going to eat you," moving her fingers like scissors and ripping Fabian's suit to shreds.[55]

Like Fabian, Münchhausen disdains promiscuous females. He calls Sophie a "little beast," but he spares his harshest words for the "ice-cold hussy," Louise La Tour: "Where others have a heart, she has a décolletage." The baron collects portraits of his sexual conquests in a private gallery. For all his macho posing, his bravado proves to be bluster. More often than not he eludes erotic advances; such a retreat provides the film's very point of departure. In crucial regards, then, Kästner's screenplay suggests that male fantasies do not always break down along party lines.

The second line of defense valorizes the work's formal achievement.[56] A self-reflexive film, *Münchhausen* begins with an appeal to the spectator. Self-reflexivity, however, does not necessarily diminish a film's illusory powers and expose the production of meaning. The technique is in fact employed here as a form of higher illusion, a playful facade meant both to fulfill and to camouflage the film's earnest wartime mission.[57] The baron's game displays a narrator's talent to fascinate, captivate, and control.[58] A painting's initial wink gives way to onscreen spectators enthralled by Münchhausen's presence and overwhelmed by his gaze, a look aware of its sovereignty and dominion. Curiously, the baron's identity as a sympathetic master of ceremonies remains bound to the influence of a less benevolent mesmerizer and magician. Self-reflexivity, Nazi or otherwise, is always the function of both conscious and unconscious selves.

Central to many German films from the early 1940s is an attribution of the party's own mercenary designs and malevolent behavior to clearly marked negative figures. Contrary to popular belief, the figure of the double plays every bit as strong a role in Nazi film as it does in Weimar cinema. Münchhausen comes upon another character who uses fantasy and illusion to control people, namely the power-hungry Cagliostro, a figure played by Ferdinand Marian, well-known to audiences from his performance in *Jud Süß* (*Jew Süss,* 1940).[59] Count Cagliostro, in the baron's words, "lends fools his daydreams, but at a usurious interest—he is unquestionably no gentleman."[60] The intruder is cloaked in a garb of Semitic otherness; the script describes his "greedy mouth and demonic eyes."[61] The hissing of a cat and ominous music, touches straight out of a horror film, announce the stranger's arrival. Christian curses the "weird [*unheimlich*] scoundrel" who interrupts the baron's dinner.

Cagliostro proposes that Münchhausen help him take over Courland. A tight close-up accentuates the count's shadowy profile as he broaches his larger objective, the partitioning of Poland. The image grants Cagliostro a grotesque and sinister countenance redolent of anti-Semitic iconography.[62] The baron will have no part of these schemes: "We'll never agree in one regard—the main regard! You want to rule, I want to live. Adventure, foreign lands, beautiful women—I have use for all these things. But you misuse them!"[63] The disparity between the mercenary illusionist (whose designs are in fact displaced reflections of Nazi expansionism) and the playful baron will become less apparent in their second meeting.

The sexual innuendoes and carnal explicitness of *Münchhausen* likewise deserve closer analysis, particularly in light of the affective liaison between the baron and Count Cagliostro. Many critics have lauded the film for its erotic transgressions. The sexual license here remains bound to a less permissive framework, however, for the baron's narrative serves as a moral instruction. At the end of the story, the once-capricious ingenue, Sophie, is chastened and edified. The narrative tames a shrew and trains a patriarch, empowering an uncertain suitor to take his cue from the voice of experience—which indeed recalls Münchhausen's first words, addressed to the husband-to-be, "Emulate my shining example." And yet how do we explain Catherine in this light, the remarkable power she exercises over Münchhausen, making him bow and descend if she so wills, to disappear at her command? After his encounter with the formidable monarch, the baron,

Baron Münchhausen meets Count Cagliostro, an illusionist who "lends fools his daydreams, but at a usurious interest."

with only the most tenuous motivation, will seek out his former adversary—and Catherine will never again be seen.[64]

In Cagliostro's makeshift laboratory, the two illusionists come together. The baron saves his comrade from imminent arrest. In doing so, Münchhausen betrays Catherine, who wants to hinder the count from "causing as much trouble in my kingdom as he did in Courland." Cagliostro, in return, treats Münchhausen's wounded appendage, an arm shot in a duel. The two scrutinize a painting of a nude woman posed with her back to the beholder, one of the genre, comments Kästner's script, "which makes us curious about the view from the front."[65] With a quick gesture, Cagliostro enlivens the female image, and it turns around to face the two spectators. Münchhausen, amused by his host's sleight of hand, remarks that he prefers the bare back to the exposed bosom. The animator agrees and returns the image to its former, less objectionable state. The pair sit at a piano and make music together, staring deeply into each other's eyes. Grateful for the unexpected visit, Cagliostro proceeds to offer the baron a ring that will make him invisible for an hour. He also grants his new friend's fondest wish: "To remain always as young as I am today! Until I myself ask to grow old!" Münchhausen gains control over his visual absence and presence as well as the power to preserve his body from the passage of time—capacities not unlike those of the film medium.[66] The arrangement likewise supersedes the baron's less permanent agreement to stay with Catherine "until one of us wishes to be free again." The control over his own image, as the scene bears out, remains inextricably bound to a transaction with a foreign mesmerist and to the control over women in his subsequent destiny.

The collaborative venture in a laboratory of special devices affords a glimpse at the double wish behind *Münchhausen,* the desire to manipulate one's destiny and to master those forces that—like Catherine—might hinder his unencumbered movement. Every woman we subsequently encounter is, like the painted nude figure, a contained and confined one. Female presence becomes increasingly marked by a lack of volition.[67] We partake of a sultan's seraglio, a collection of women reminiscent of the baron's private gallery.[68] We hear the baron suggest that Abdul-Hamid house his wives in a glass structure that would allow him a constant view of their every movement. We see Isabelle d'Este caged in a window frame and finally as a captive in a convent. And we end up on the moon, where people grow on trees and women no longer play a role in reproduction. Husbands carry around the heads of their spouses, whose bodies remain at home and out of mischief.[69]

The Last Action Hero

A rare Nazi film of the fantastic, *Münchhausen* is also a Nazi fantasy. The apotheosis of a virile and vital hero goes hand in hand with the exorcism of female initiative. The baron's ultimate journey takes him to the woman on the moon, whose divided self defers to her husband's authority. The arrangement pleases Münchhausen, and he lauds its practicality: "That would be something for our housewives." The scene on the moon refigures gender relations in Nazi Germany. It was both "a bad joke and a serious wish"[70] for a nation's soldiers who were anxious about what their wives or loved ones might be up to while they were off at war.[71] Sophie's request that her fiancé take her home echoes the final words of her disembodied lunar counterpart: "Carry me away." Male dominion in the Third Reich meant female servitude; the desired control over every sector of reality went together with an abiding fear of woman as the bearer of potentially disruptive energies, as a marker for untamed nature itself.[72] *Münchhausen* champions a protagonist

The moon, a world with different laws of time and space, an uncanny realm where humans grow on trees.

who controls his own image and story as well as commanding the images and actions of the women in his life.

The baron resembles other bold and brash he-men played by Hans Albers. He may come on like a ladykiller, but sensual abandon in the arms of beautiful women hardly seems to be his top priority. In the manner of the era's putative Don Juans, his sexual prowess is more often asserted than shown. Like Kästner's protagonists and many Nazi heroes, Münchhausen is an Adam who seems more eager to escape Eve than to embrace her.[73] The most erotically charged encounter remains the baron's amicable interlude with Cagliostro. His sole gesture of extended emotion takes place over the dying body of his constant companion, Christian.[74] The woman whom Münchhausen joins is more a maternal than a romantic presence, someone much older who indulges and understands him. (Kästner's Fabian, likewise, is a mother's boy.) The end of the film takes leave from the foreign and the fantastic, retreating to a domestic sanctuary and recalling the regressive trajectory of many other fearful soldier males who renounce erotic adventure.[75]

"Have you ever seen a fully mature man?" Münchhausen asks his servant Johann in the opening sequence. The film—the product of an author who later translated *Peter Pan*—shows how a man comes of age. For the baron, to grow up means to realize himself as aesthetic potential, to monitor his own image and master his own destiny, to enjoy an unfettered existence. After his transformation, the second sex appears exclusively as a pleasure unit or a pliant partner, a domestic convenience, but not an erotic threat. (It follows that the helpless Princess d'Este replaces the potent czarina as the hero's romantic interest.) The baron, as an exchange with his father makes clear, is the last of his line. He becomes a man who will reproduce himself without a woman, whose legitimate progeny will be a story and not a child.

A grand example of fantasizing fascism, *Münchhausen* enacts a male fantasy of control and likewise exhibits the fearful psyche that wants, needs, and produces such a fantasy. If National Socialism had a logic, it accorded with the logic of a dream, the dream of an unassailable identity vested in a race's transcendent power. Nazism sought to transform the mythic image of

A bad joke and a serious wish: disembodied women who function as portable appliances.

the all-powerful Aryan into a living reality. To do so, the Third Reich relied on the formative power of high art and the standardized appeal of mass culture. The Nazi myth, according to Philippe Lacoue-Labarthe and Jean-Luc Nancy, emphasized "the construction, the formation, and the production of the German people in, through, and as a work of art."[76] Münchhausen may well be, as numerous of the film's defenders have pointed out, neither a military champion nor a surrogate Hitler. He remains nonetheless a remarkable ideological fabrication and an aesthetic body par excellence. Introduced as an animated icon and a penetrating gaze, he becomes a superman whose magical powers afford him visual sovereignty and narrative dominion. As an image unbound by temporal determination and free from external control, he brings to life the Aryan dream of a self-made man.

Münchhausen's creative powers also enable him to write his own last chapter. The baron sacrifices his immortality so that he may accompany his wife to the grave. He decides when his own story will cease, blowing out a candle whose flame segues into letters of smoke spelling "Ende," an expressive instance of what Saul Friedländer has termed the "kitsch of death."[77] Münchhausen's self-reflexive wink opens the film; his self-destructive final breath provides closure. A privileged *auteur* and director of his lifescript, he stages his final act and thus determines how he will enter history. He ensures that time will not forget him, gaining the ineluctable form of everlasting life in a legendary shape of his own making. His companion Kuchenreutter and soulmate Cagliostro dissolve into thin air. In following his friends, the baron follows his own stage directions. "Man is like a cloud of smoke which rises and disappears," he muses, offering contemporary German viewers comforting intimations of mortality, what he terms a "more poetic and meaningful" way of dying. Outside cinemas, in various European theaters of war, millions of less privileged bodies also were going up in smoke. For many people, both within and outside Germany, death would neither come so easily nor prove as pleasing.

The film's temporally immune protagonist provided an inordinate source of consolation for audiences who were living through Germany's darkest hours. He was a curious hero, to be sure, in crucial respects a man without qualities, both less and more than he seems. He gains his powers from a figure of undeniably Semitic provenance[78] and wanders through the world like the Eternal Jew. "As if driven by a whip," the baron describes himself, "he constantly sought out faraway places."[79] Cagliostro and Münchhausen, despite all their apparent differences, possess a profound affinity.[80] Their bond manifests the deeper dependence of the Aryan prototype on its Jewish antipode. When Cagliostro disappears, the baron assimilates the powers of invisibility and immortality, and they radically redefine his person. Playing Faust to the count's Mephisto, the baron makes a deal, a transaction with no downside. Without Cagliostro, the baron's identity would be much less privileged; without the dark double (a figure found only in the Nazi retelling), we would have neither an omnipotent hero nor his epic tale.

If *Münchhausen* self-reflects, it also self-exposes, embodying manifest, latent, and repressed energies at work in Nazi fantasy production. In Hitler's Germany, note Lacoue-Labarthe and Nancy, "The Jew is not simply a bad race, a defective type: he is the antitype. The Jew has no *Seelengestalt,* therefore no *Rassengestalt;* his form is formless. He is the man of the universal abstract, as opposed to the man of singular, concrete identity."[81] Münchhausen, like his soulmate, appears as a shape-shifter and nomad. "Every man has only one *Heimat,* just as he only has one mother," says the baron, someone forever in transit and all but never at home, in whose father's house we see no sign of maternal presence.

Like Cagliostro and Münchhausen, Goebbels and Kästner made for an odd couple, hardly congenial but not altogether incompatible collaborators. Out of their meeting issued a hero who was an expert dissimulator and an existential innovator. In any gallery of cynics, Peter Sloterdijk reminds us, illusionists enjoy a privileged place.[82] The confidence man and the cynic resemble the fascist politician, for neither believes in his own rhetoric, but rather recognizes it for what it is: the means to an end and a swindle. The apposite gaze of the cynic is the charlatan's ironic wink, the self-reflexive acknowledgment of public deceit which allows a liar to remain credible even when lying. Cynics of modernity often appear as seductive showmen who confound any distinction between fantasy and reality. What could be more incongruous and yet appropriate in an age of rampant liars than a film about the fabled "liar baron"?[83] And would it not be more clever yet to have the prevaricator appear as a source of irony and deeper meaning?[84] "The man with a stronger imagination," observes Kästner's Münchhausen, "exacts for himself a richer world. He doesn't need deception or magic to do so."

But the baron *does* rely on magic and deception. Similarly, the Ufa dream factory systematically relied on foreign imaginations to enrich its own cinematic worlds. Just as the baron gains his powers from a despised other, so too did the creators of *Münchhausen* take their cue from Germany's adversaries. The Nazis claimed to have liberated film art from shysters who—like the self-serving illusionist, Cagliostro—had abused the medium's powers in the name of mercenary gain.[85] *Völkisch* ideologues eschewed Hollywood and Weimar cinema as the products of corrupt businessmen and degenerate artists. During the *Systemzeit,* boasted the authors of the jeremiad *Film-"Kunst," Film-Kohn, Film-Korruption,* Ufa remained the only domestic studio that partially managed to thwart Jewish manipulators.[86] *Münchhausen* borrowed freely from *Snow White and the Seven Dwarfs* (a film Goebbels admired, but barred from Germany) and *The Thief of Bagdad* (a film codirected by the exiled Jew and German director Ludwig Berger) as well as the "haunted screen" of the Weimar Republic.

The film's alien origins become dramatized when the baron seeks out his Jewish double and assimilates his powers. The scene in Cagliostro's hotel room provides trick photography equal to Hollywood's while revisiting the imaginary spaces of German silent cinema. The feature takes its impetus from the Weimar film of the fantastic, beginning with an image of an image and opening up to a world of facade and simulation. The Nazi fantasy ends with a sleight of hand indebted to Disney animation. The film's shape as a whole derives from these influences—just as Nazi cinema constantly sought to match the artistic achievements of classical German film and to rival Hollywood's industrial expertise. Nazi film was at war with German cinema's own past as well as with Hollywood competitors, many of whom were emigrants from Weimar. Together they both posed a troublesome, indeed invincible, nemesis. While attempting to show off German technological prowess, the Ufa production acknowledged Nazi cinema's larger debts as well as its inhering sense of deficit.

Münchhausen served as a medium of Nazi myth and the vehicle of wartime illusion. The film thus can be understood as a striking counterpoint and a logical supplement to Goebbels' contemporaneous call for total war. At first glance, the cheerful movie seems at odds with the shrill tone of the emergency-hour rhetoric, the minister's fervent resolution and apodictic assurance.[87] During and after the debacle of Stalingrad and in the face of nightly Allied bombings, he recognized the need for new and effective appeals, higher levels of sophistication which might counter ever-growing public dissatisfaction and collective hardship.[88] The streets of Berlin and almost every other German metropolis increasingly resembled something between an apocalyptic landscape from Hieronymus Bosch and an end-of-time image by Salvador Dali.[89] The minister of propaganda endeavored to stop the clock and to stem the tide of history.[90] His total war of illusion meant to distract Germans from painful and traumatic realities, from the presentiment of a national catastrophe and the shame of mass murder.

Suspending the laws of time and the powers of gravity, *Münchhausen* celebrates a fake world and a sham hero and invites its audiences to share the fantasy. It has enchanted and pleased viewers for more than half a century. Most observers today remain convinced that *Münchhausen* is an artistic masterpiece and an oppositional feature, "some fond memories from otherwise bad times." In early April 1991, Ilse Werner (who played Isabella d'Este) exuberantly announced *Münchhausen*'s "rebirth" on the German Second Channel (ZDF), introducing an Easter Monday primetime screening as "a little joke for April Fool's Day." It has been a central attraction in recent observations of Ufa's seventy-fifth anniversary, spectacles that have constituted a veritable springtime for the studio. Time has obscured the forces that gave rise to this cinematic extension of a world war, much less this film's participation in a nation's collective demise. An intended act of artificial resuscitation and the desperate product of an overwrought order, the work reveals artistic ambitions, logistic designs, and subterranean desires. As the Third Reich's last action hero dissolves before the viewer, he discloses the props that lay behind Nazi propaganda, leaving a void in his wake after the smoke has settled. This void represents the hollowness of special effects and the signature of an empty order whose ultimate extension could be but one thing: "the end."

Peter Pewas presents a cruel world that destroys a woman who dares to dream of a better life (Winnie Markus in *The Enchanted Day*).

Epilogue: The Testament of Dr. Goebbels

> I watch myself in a lavish film that Ufa presents to me. All my speeches since 1933. Strange and gripping. How far away things can appear to be.
>
> *Joseph Goebbels, 1936*

> All the impulses of all the media were fed into the circuitry of my dreams. One thinks of echoes. One thinks of an image made in the image and likeness of images. It was that complex.
>
> *Don DeLillo*

Feature films in the Third Reich were principally the function of a genre cinema, which in turn was part of an elaborate mass culture. This cinema sported titles, figures, and materials well-known to Weimar film which would continue in the postwar era.[1] (Indeed, until the early 1960s and the revolt of the Oberhausen activists, most West German films remained indebted to the past, the endeavors of directors, scriptwriters, and casts who had worked under Goebbels.)[2] Films in the Nazi epoch employed well-known stars, ready-made formats, standardized productions, and studio economies. Goebbels sought to create a popular domestic cinema that would be not only profitable and entertaining but also ideologically effective and politically useful, both a stabilizing force and an animating energy. The minister of propaganda announced his grand designs forthrightly: he wanted German cinema to be *the* dominant cinema. Speaking in 1940, he declared: "We must give film a task and a mission in order that we may use it to conquer the world. Only then will we also overcome American film. It will not be easily overcome. But it can be overcome."[3]

After the beginning of World War II, Nazi film became an extremely popular and lucrative entity, enjoying large audiences and enthusiastic followings. "The financial success of our films is altogether amazing," Goebbels noted soon after German troops invaded Poland. "We are becoming real war profiteers."[4] In October 1940 he wrote: "I shall not relax until the entire European film industry belongs to us."[5] Goebbels and the ProMi waged an all-out war against Hollywood, seeking to win over domestic viewers, conquer international markets, and overwhelm foreign competitors. In his diary entry of 19 May 1942, Goebbels reiterated his resolve: "We must take a similar course in our film policy as pursued by the Americans on the North American and South American continents. We must become the dominant film power in Europe. Films produced by other states should be allowed to have only local and limited character."[6]

Under Goebbels' administration, cinema became centralized and consolidated; by 1942, four state-owned studios (Bavaria, Ufa, Terra, Tobis) dominated the scene. In an attempt to control the articulation of fictional worlds, only a small proportion of films was shot outdoors or on location. Directors functioned above all as facilitators, not as distinctive *auteurs*. Film was to be artful and accessible, not intellectual or esoteric. Features of the Third Reich favored carefully crafted artificial realms and showed a predilection for studio spaces, costume design, and script logic. Films made under the Nazi regime amounted to an other-directed cinema, administered by a state apparatus that determined every aspect of production from a script treatment to a film's final shape, from its release and exhibition to its circulation in the public sphere.

In contrast to its Weimar counterpart, Nazi cinema denigrated the film of the fantastic as well as filmic realism. The former remained too open to irrational forces; the rightful place of the fantastic was to be an everyday of bright uniforms, hypnotic rituals, and dazzling spectacles. The Weimar legacy of workers' films was likewise forsaken and left behind. Nazi cinema thus shunned the extremes of Weimar's haunted screen *(Caligari, Nosferatu, Metropolis)* and its socialist realism (*Mutter Krausens Fahrt ins Glück/Mother Krause's Trip to Happiness* and *Kuhle Wampe*), assuming a middle ground of historical period pieces, costume dramas, musical revues, light comedies, melodramas, and petty-bourgeois fantasies. The film culture of the Third Reich allowed at best a limited space for experiments. Trade papers and film journals spoke only rarely about avant-garde initiatives. Modernism persisted in Nazi cinema, to be sure, not in features, but rather in short subjects and nonfiction films (for instance, in the documentaries of Leni Riefenstahl, Willy Zielke, and Walter Ruttmann).

Film narratives of the Nazi era generally privileged space over time, composition over editing, design over movement, sets over human shapes. Compared to Hollywood movies, most features of the Third Reich appeared slow and static. They were more prone to panoramas and tableaus than to close-ups, decidedly sparing in their physical displays (very little nudity, few stunts and action scenes). Nazi film theorists stressed the importance of kinetic images as well as galvanizing soundtracks.[7] Music worked together with visuals to make the spectator lose touch with conceptual logic and discursive frameworks, pulling "listener and viewer from act to act, from impression to impression ever more overwhelmingly."[8] The ideal film would spirit people away from the real world and grant viewers access to a pleasant, compelling, and convincing alternative space.

Only a minority of Nazi features displayed what one might speak of as overt propaganda. There were two waves of films with manifestly strident overtones: the "movement films" of 1933, and the anti-Semitic, anti-British, and anti-Soviet productions of 1939–1942. But to grasp how Nazi films captivated spectators and promulgated political meanings, one must comprehend the way in which films interacted with and resonated within larger social constellations. Ideology more often than not came sugar-coated, in gripping, engaging, and pleasant packages of entertainment which coexisted with other emanations of everyday culture. Films were not isolated experiences in the dark, but rather structured functions of "a variety of associations and organisations [which] locked every individual into a complicated network of apparatuses covering every sector of reality."[9] Nazi films circulated within a vast complex of orchestrated and high-tech efforts to control thought and meaning. The Third Reich constituted the first full-blown media dictatorship, a political order that sought to occupy and administer all sectors of perceptual possibility, to dominate the human subject's every waking and sleeping moment.

From its quality features to its run-of-the-mill products, Nazi film reflected the workings of the classical cinema with its deference to character motivation, the codes of realism, the strictures of dramatic development and closure. It was a cinema dedicated to illusionism. "The task that I have posed for myself as a director," claimed Veit Harlan, "consists to a great part in making spectators forget that they are sitting in cinemas."[10] Goebbels saw himself as a German David O. Selznick and sought to create a film world every bit as alluring as Hollywood. Nazi films to a great degree seemed unexceptional and resembled Anglo-European features of the era. They were steeped in Old World values and fond of traditional formulas; their favorite sites were urban localities, bourgeois interiors, and lower-middle-class settings. Government film administrators as well as studio executives eschewed films that put National Socialism directly on display. In so doing, they carefully fostered the impression that cinema was a world apart from party agendas and state priorities.

Films of the Third Reich often allowed viewers vacations from the present in fanciful spheres so that they could forget politics and civic responsibilities. With its utopian spaces sponsored by Goebbels' Ministry of Propaganda, Nazi cinema not only created illusions but also often showed illusionists at work and, on occasion, self-reflected about the power of illusions *(Der Florentiner Hut/The Florentine Hat, Capriccio, Münchhausen).* Many films thematized the fascination of aesthetic illusion (Viktor Tourjansky's 1941 film, *Illusion,* offers a programmatic title), concentrating on mesmerizers and performers as well as offering glimpses behind the scenes at film studios *(Es leuchten die Sterne/The Stars Are Shining, Die gute Sieben/The Good Seventh Wife)* or revealing tricks of magic *(Truxa).* Nazi film illusions coexisted with government oppression, political terror, and, after 1939, world war and the Holocaust. Screen illusions cushioned people against grim realities, offering the solace of worlds that were in order and seemed to allow unencumbered movement, safe havens and playgrounds where one could dream freely. Nazi escapism, however, offered only the illusion of escape from the Nazi status quo.

Despite the postwar claims of filmmakers and revisionist critics, one finds very few examples of open resistance to the party and state in films of this era. Such films either did not find their way into production or were banned after initial showings. Nonetheless, not all meaning could be controlled and various films lent themselves to alternative appropriations. To a large degree, such responses did not really run counter to official designs. Goebbels and his coworkers allowed films on occasion to transgress borders, exploring seemingly resistant potential and apparent exceptions to the rule, even subversive contents and oppositional positions, all the better to discipline distraction. Among the films made during the Third Reich, there were, however, a few notable exceptions: films from the transition era between the end of the Weimar and Hitler's rise to power, Austrian films before the *Anschluß* (especially the work of Werner Hochbaum), banned and proscribed films (from *Das letzte Testament des Dr. Mabuse/The Last Testament of Dr. Mabuse* and *Liebelei* to *Titanic* and *Große Freiheit Nr. 7/Great Freedom No. 7*), isolated instances of aesthetic resistance after 1942 (Peter Pewas' *Der verzauberte Tag/The Enchanted Day,* Helmut Käutner's *Romanze in Moll/Romance in a Minor Key,* Wolfgang Staudte's *Akrobat schö-ö-ö-n*), and films produced during the confused final months of World War II *(Unter den Brücken/Under the Bridges, Via Mala).*

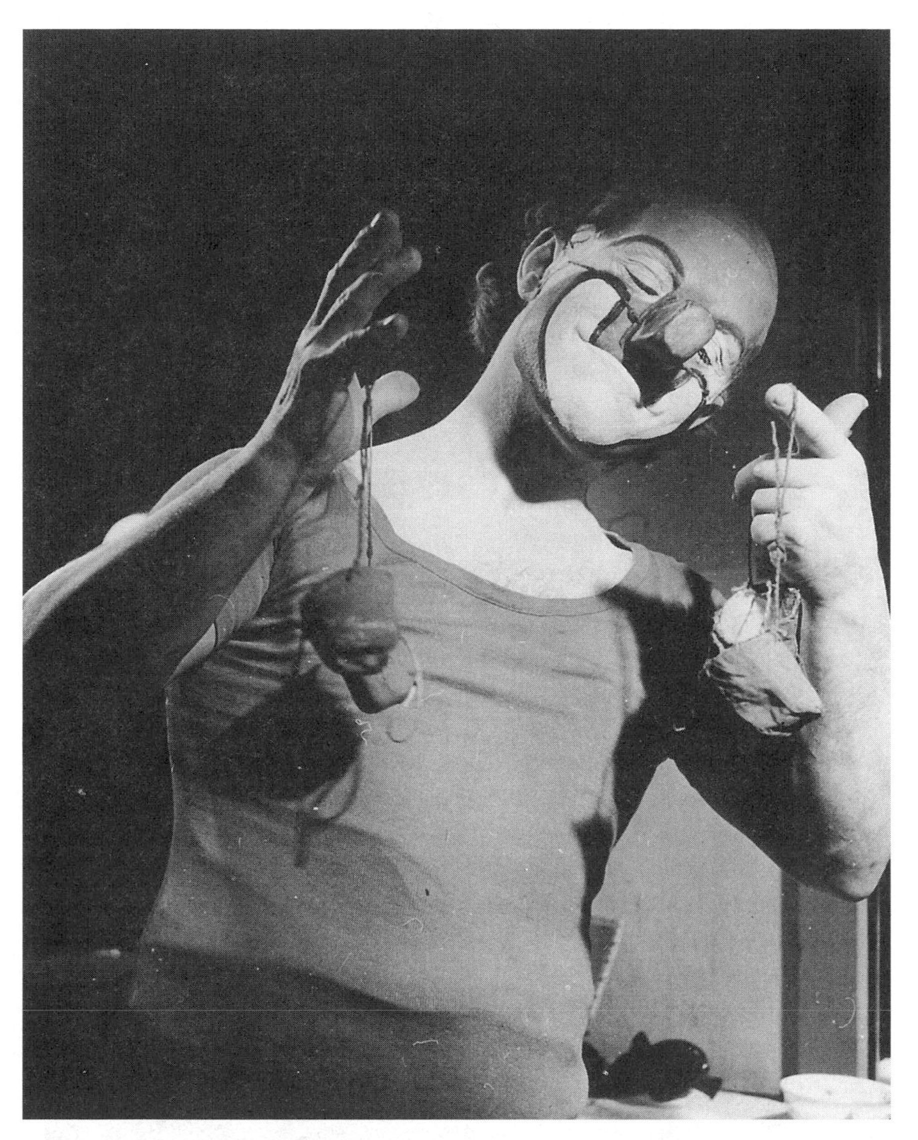

Wolfgang Staudte's analytical *Revuefilm* features an acrobat and a corporeal subversive, the antinomy of the solider male (Charlie Rivel in *Akrobat schö-ö-ö-n*).

Nazi illusions continue to exercise a hold on postwar imaginations, both in how people view Nazi images and in what they make of National Socialism. The fantasy productions of this epoch are still readily accessible—in matinee screenings, television showings, festival programs, video catalogues, and university curricula. They offer testimony from the Third Reich which would seem to suggest a less oppressive everyday. Many of them abide as classics and evergreens, objects of reverie and nostalgia; they circulate widely and remain problematic. Goebbels' tools of political affirmation have undergone transformation to become national monuments and vehicles of subversion. Nazi films such as *Glückskinder (Lucky Kids), La Habanera,* and *Münchhausen* as well as memories of Ufa's grandeur fuel fond German dreams; they energize reassuring fantasies of how, even in a cinema watched over by Hitler and his minions, the better part of the nation resisted the Third Reich. Many critics and observers persist today in holding onto National Socialism's prime illusions, namely that the imaginary worlds and fantasy scenarios created under a state-administered film industry had little to do with that state's operations.

Young German Film and its extension, New German Cinema, once turned against the Nazi legacy and "its demagogic treatment of images,"

Under the Bridges, Helmut Käutner's subtle study of needy men and their makeshift images of women.

castigating its products as "the most despicable meters of celluloid ever shot."[11] The New German directors declared war on their elders, seeking to liberate German film history from a fatal heritage of abuse. Over the years, though, as the history of the Third Reich was integrated into a larger German history, a rapprochement between New German Cinema and Nazi cinema became increasingly apparent. Hans Jürgen Syberberg recycled Ufa stars, Werner Herzog sought to revive Arnold Fanck's mountain films, Helma Sanders-Brahms celebrated Leni Riefenstahl's *Tiefland (Lowlands),* Edgar Reitz affectionately cited Carl Froelich's *Heimat* of 1938 in his own *Heimat* of 1984, and a current Wim Wenders feature *(In weiter Ferne so nah!/Far Away and Yet So Close)* poignantly exonerated the Nazi collaborator Heinz Rühmann. Niklaus Schilling insisted on maintaining a sense of German tradition which incorporated films made during the Third Reich. "Without them," Schilling asserted, "we ignore an important part of our film tradition."[12] In Reitz's recent *Die Nacht der Regisseure* (*The Night of the Directors,* 1995), Leni Riefenstahl takes her place amidst contemporary Germany's most prominent directors. Even filmmakers—and critics—whose look back in anger spawned a New German Cinema have increasingly come to gaze on the sights and sounds of the Third Reich with a kinder and gentler regard.

Watching *Jud Süß (Jew Süss)* today is unlikely to turn anyone into an anti-Semite, people often claim, so why should it be banned along with several dozen other feature films from the Third Reich? No official list of these proscribed titles (so-called *Vorbehaltsfilme*) exists; such a list could only demonstrate that the German government considers the populace of its democracy in crucial ways politically immature. Right-wing radicals and neofascist groups still partake of Nazi films, and there is a substantial German black market for banned war movies, newsreels, and Hitler documentaries.[13] One wonders how these films now resonate in a climate of violence toward foreigners, in a nation casting about for a new collective self-understanding.

Surely the continuing and largely unquestioned presence of entertainment films from the Nazi era in the German public sphere shapes popular feelings about that past. Comedies with Heinz Rühmann and Hans Moser hardly threaten to undermine civic values, but they do influence how people look back at the Third Reich, granting it a more agreeable countenance. Films of the Nazi era are easy to enlist in campaigns to normalize and neutralize the Nazi legacy. "We are what we remember," says the narrator of Don DeLillo's *Americana.* "The past is here, inside this black clock, more devious than night or fog, determining how we see and what we touch at this irreplaceable instant in time."[14] Films can preserve memory and function as vehicles of history. They can also serve as a means of forgetting, a medium to stylize, distort, or erase the past.

Cinema under the aegis of Goebbels blended sensory plenitude and sensual deprivation.[15] Film images defined the good and the beautiful while vitiating the capacity for spontaneity and the desire for experience. Perhaps the most striking thing about life in National Socialism was its vicarious quality. A vanguard site, Nazi mass culture reformed the living in the shape of the mediated; the everyday was defined above all by mechanically reproduced sights and sounds, by simulations and special effects meant to generate strong emotions while systematically militating against the aptitude to think in terms of continuities. Nazi cinema exploited the limitations of human imagination, seeking to obliterate first-person consciousness and to replace it with a universal third person.[16] Even as a leisure being, this other-directed creature was to remain a loyal state servant, a modern golem cast in the shape of mass-produced images. The Nazis used the cinema as their fictional Cagliostro employed magic; they granted Germans their dreams, but at a usurious interest.

The Nazis recognized well that political effects could never derive from political expressions alone. Entertainment, spectacle, and diversion lent themselves remarkably to instrumental endeavors. Hitler and Goebbels were consummate narcissists enamored of their media images, the Third Reich a grand production, the world war a continuing movie of the week. Standardized mass culture, Goebbels realized, was the secret formula for successful mass manipulation.[17] Mass culture also became a crucial precondition for mass murder. The media enabled Germans to withstand awful truths and ignore hideous presentiments, serving as a shield and a blindfold, audiovisual instruments that ensured uplifting fictions no matter how bitter the realities. Nazi feature films—both as entities that circulated in German cinemas during the Third Reich and as entities that still enjoy much public attention today—teach us above all one thing: entertainment can be far more than innocent pleasure.

Nazi media culture demonstrated just how potent and destructive the powers of fascination and fantasy can be, especially when systematically appropriated by a modern state and strategically implemented by advanced technology. A nation faced with material hardship and a spiritual void hailed Hitler's promises of a better life while shunning enlightened rhetoric. The Führer's order propped up spirits with artificial means and strived to hyperstylize the subjects of a new Germany. Simulations supplanted direct experience, and illusions superseded reality. In this endeavor, the Third Reich granted a preview of postmodern attractions. Abusing the utopian possibilities of mass-produced representations, the ProMi also exhibited their dystopic potential. The National Socialist state's production of death and devastation would not have been possible without Goebbels' dream machinery.[18]

The unprecedented historical example of the Nazi media dictatorship lingers as a very disturbing prospect, especially now, as sophisticated and pervasive technologies for the transmission and manipulation of audiovisual materials increasingly define who we are and how we exist. We refer to Hitler and Goebbels as madmen and demons, consigning them to the shadows. No matter how studiously we cloak these figures in darkness, however, they are clearly more than just ghouls or phantoms. Indeed, one might speak of Nazi Germany's irrepressible imagemakers as postmodernity's secret sharers, as grasping entrepreneurs who profited from the industrialized means of enchantment, as master showmen who staged extravagant spectacles as the ultimate political manifestations.[19] These real-life Mabuses have enacted the worst nightmares of any community whose social viability and collective identity depend on the media and mass culture. More than fifty years since the demise of National Socialism, the testament of Dr. Goebbels continues to haunt us.

APPENDIX A

Films and Events, 1933–1945

For a comprehensive and detailed inventory of daily occurrences during the Third Reich, see Manfred Overesch, ed., *Chronik deutscher Zeitgeschichte. Politik—Wirtschaft—Kultur,* 2 vols. (Düsseldorf: Droste, 1982); also Heinz Bergschicker, *Deutsche Chronik 1933–1945,* 5th rev. ed. (Berlin: Verlag der Nation, 1990). A useful English-language source of information is Tim Kirk, *The Longman Companion to Nazi Germany* (London: Longman, 1995). For an elaborate chronology of German film and cinema culture during the era, see the entries in Hans Helmut Prinzler, *Chronik des deutschen Films 1895–1994* (Stuttgart/Weimar: Metzler, 1995).

From 30 January 1933 to 7 May 1945, 1,086 German feature films passed the censors and premiered in the Reich's cinemas. (Three of these were rereleased Weimar era films.) An additional 8 films were submitted to the censors before 30 January 1933 but were not released until after that date. The total of 1,094 features also includes a few films that were banned after their first public screenings. It does not include 26 films that were banned and never premiered; nor does it take into account 67 international coproductions, films made in Austria before the *Anschluß,* or the films that were banned in Germany but premiered abroad. Reference sources that incorporate these latter productions into their reckonings consequently reflect higher figures.

The following lists are not exhaustive; they present each year's most important films, the names of directors and studios, and release dates. Asterisks indicate films that were initially prohibited by the Allied High Commission after May 1945.

■ ■ ■

1933 (109 German premieres after 30 January)

Morgenrot (G. Ucicky, Ufa, 31 January)*
Der Choral von Leuthen (C. Froelich/A. von Cserépy/W. Supper, Froelich-Film, 3 February)*
Ich und die Kaiserin (F. Hollaender, Ufa, 22 February)

Der Läufer von Marathon (E. A. Dupont, Matador, 24 February)
Lachende Erben (M. Ophüls, Ufa, 6 March)
Liebelei (M. Ophüls, Elite, 10 March)*
Brennendes Geheimnis (R. Siodmak, Tonal, 20 March)
Anna und Elisabeth (F. Wysbar, Kollektiv/Terra, 12 April)
Schleppzug M 17 (H. George/W. Hochbaum, Orbis, 19 April)
Unter der schwarzen Sturmfahne (R. von Sonjevski-Jamrowski, Vortrupp/Sonja/Czerny, 26 April)*
Ein Lied geht um die Welt (R. Oswald, Rio, 9 May)
Arbeit macht glücklich/Acciaio (W. Ruttmann, Cines-Film, 16 May)
SA-Mann Brand (F. Seitz, Bavaria, 14 June)*
Kleiner Mann—was nun? (F. Wendhausen, RN, 3 August)*
Morgen beginnt das Leben (W. Hochbaum, Ethos, 4 August)
Der Judas von Tirol (F. Osten, Stark, 26 August)*
S.O.S. Eisberg (A. Fanck, Deutsche Universal-Film/Universal Pictures, 30 August)
Leise flehen meine Lieder (W. Forst, Cine-Allianz, 8 September)
Hitlerjunge Quex (H. Steinhoff, Ufa, 11 September)*
Reifende Jugend (C. Froelich, Froelich-Film, 22 September)*
Ein Unsichtbarer geht durch die Stadt (H. Piel, Ariel, 29 September)
Hans Westmar (F. Wenzler, Volksdeutsche Film, 3 October)*
Walzerkrieg (L. Berger, Ufa, 4 October)
Der Tunnel (K. Bernhardt, Vandor/Bavaria, 27 October)*
Du sollst nicht begehren . . . (R. Schneider-Edenkoben, Ufa, 31 October)*
Ihre Durchlaucht, die Verkäuferin (K. Hartl, Cine-Allianz, 4 November)
Drei Kaiserjäger (R. Land and F. Hofer, ABC, 15 November)*
Flüchtlinge (G. Ucicky, Ufa, 8 December)*
Des jungen Dessauers große Liebe (A. Robison, Ufa, 22 December)
Viktor und Viktoria (R. Schünzel, Ufa, 23 December)

Banned:

Das Testament des Dr. Mabuse (F. Lang, Nero, 29 March 1933, premiered 21 April 1933 in Paris; first German screening, 24 August 1951)
Ganovenehre (R. Oswald, Rio, 15 May 1933)
Moral und Liebe (G. Jacoby, Glass/Kristall, 3 March 1934)
Spione am Werk (G. Lamprecht, Cine-Allianz, 9 October 1935)
Hände aus dem Dunkel (E. Waschneck, Fanal, 24 January 1936)

Wege zur guten Ehe (A. Trotz, Gnom, 7 March 1936)
Lachende Erben (M. Ophüls, Ufa, 1 October 1937)

During the year, 59 studios produce films, and 23 distributors circulate them. Sixty-five percent of German films derive from original screenplays; 19 percent are based on novels or novellas, 15 percent on plays and operettas. Twenty-seven European films open in Germany along with 65 American features (in contrast to 54 from the United States in 1932 and 80 in 1931). The most active scriptwriter is Walter Wassermann, who provides the screenplays for 10 features. Forty-eight German features premiere in the United States.

30 January: President Hindenburg appoints Adolf Hitler chancellor; Hitler holds the new administration's first cabinet meeting.

2 February: Premiere of the Ufa film *Morgenrot* in the Ufa-Palast am Zoo. "It was in equal measure a demonstration of the German military's commitment to the spirit of World War I and a recognition of film's ability to serve as a valuable form of national historiography" (Hans Traub).

23 February: Proscription of homosexual rights groups.

27 February: The Reichstag burns; the Nazis hold the Communists responsible.

28 February: Hitler is granted emergency powers by presidential decree "for the Protection of People and State."

11 March: Hitler's cabinet establishes the Ministry for Popular Enlightenment and Propaganda (Reichsministerium für Volksaufklärung und Propaganda; RMVP), to be divided into six departments: radio, press, film, propaganda, theater, and administration.

13 March: Joseph Goebbels, thirty-five, propaganda head of the NSDAP, is appointed minister of propaganda.

21 March: The Reichstag convenes in Potsdam in the Garrison Church ("Tag von Potsdam"). A Malicious Practices Law *(Heimtückegesetz)* condemns criticism of the new government and its leaders.

22 March: A Department of Racial Hygiene is established in the Ministry of the Interior.

23 March: Ratification of the Enabling Act *(Ermächtigungsgesetz)* provides the legal basis for Hitler's dictatorship. On the same day Hitler announces in the *Völkischer Beobachter* "a systematic campaign to restore the nation's moral and material health. The whole educational system, theater, film, literature, the press, and broadcasting—all these will be used as a means to this end. They will be harnessed to help preserve the eternal values that are part of the integral nature of our people."

25 March: Goebbels addresses the heads of German radio stations.

28 March: Goebbels speaks to leading representatives of the German film industry at the Berlin Hotel Kaiserhof about the crisis of German cinema, calling for radical reforms and productions with distinctive national contours.

29 March: Fritz Lang's *Das Testament des Dr. Mabuse* is banned by the Berlin film censors as "a danger to public order and security." The Ufa board of directors dismisses Jewish employees.

April: Fritz Lang emigrates to France. Contrary to his postwar claims, he will return to Germany on several occasions during the next months.

1–3 April: Boycott of Jewish shops and businesses throughout Germany.

27 April: Goebbels speaks to party members of Ufa at their invitation.

4 May: Establishment of the "Gestapo," the secret state police.

10 May: Goebbels writes in the *Völkischer Beobachter:* "The Ministry's task is to bring about a spiritual mobilization in Germany. It seeks to do for the German spirit what the Ministry of Defense does for German weaponry." On the same day Goebbels is present as Nazi student activists in Berlin burn books containing "un-German" writings.

19 May: Goebbels speaks in the Sporthallen (Berlin-Wilmersdorf) to a mass meeting of film employees. He announces a generous project to restore the German film industry: "One should dispel the illusion that the current crisis is a material one; the film crisis is above all a spiritual one; it will continue as long as we lack the courage to reform German film from the roots up."

1 June: Legislation is passed which lowers the average entertainment tax rate of films from 11.5 percent to 8 percent. The Film Credit Bank (Filmkreditbank GmbH; FKB) is established to stimulate film production. During 1933 the FKB will help finance 22 shorts and features; in 1934, 49 features; in 1935, 65; in 1936, 82 (over 70 percent of German feature film production).

Late June: Hitler decrees that the RMVP is responsible "for all tasks related to the spiritual guidance of the nation, to the promotion of the state, culture, and the economy, to the promulgation of information to domestic and foreign sources about the nation as well as the administration of all the agencies responsible for these endeavors."

30 June: The Aryan Clause *(Arierparagraph)* forbids Jews to work in the film industry. "German films should in the future be made only by Germans . . . Only those films that are made by a German company in German studios with German ideas, a German author, German composers, and German film crews will be recognized as German films" (Hans Traub).

14 July: Announcement of the Law Regarding the Establishment of a Provisional Reich Film Chamber (Reichsfilmkammer; RFK), which replaces the

previous professional organizations (SPIO and Dacho). The Film Chamber is a state body created "to promote the German film branch within the framework of the overall economy, to represent the interests of the individual groups within the industry as well as in relation to the Reich, states, and communities." The Ministry of Propaganda will appoint the RFK's board of directors. A film can be screened publicly only if all its cast and crew are members of the Film Chamber. Admission to the Chamber will be denied to "undesirable and destructive elements."

The NSDAP is officially declared to be the only political party in Germany.

The Law for the Prevention of Hereditarily Sick Progeny is passed; it will legitimate over 360,000 sterilizations during the next twelve years.

22 September: The Reich Culture Chamber Law (*Reichskulturkammergesetz;* RKKG) organizes the entirety of German cultural activity within seven Cultural Chambers, of which the provisional RFK becomes one, alongside literature, theater, music, fine arts, press, and radio.

5 October: The Reich Film Organization (Reichsfachschaft Film) is created to bring together all employees of the film industry.

9 October: Goebbels: "We National Socialists have no great desire to watch Storm Troopers march on stages or cinema screens. They belong on the street."

14 October: Germany withdraws from the League of Nations.

15 November: Festive opening of the Reich Chamber for Culture in the Berlin Philharmonie. Goebbels delivers an address titled "German Culture at a New Beginning": "What we want is more than just a dramatized party program. What we have in mind is a profound bond between the spirit of a heroic world view and the eternal laws of art."

27 November: The German Labor Service (DAF) introduces two new organizations: "Strength through Joy" (Kraft durch Freude), a leisure and recreation program; and "Beauty of Labor" (Schönheit der Arbeit).

1 December: Leni Riefenstahl's *Der Sieg des Glaubens* premieres in the Berlin Ufa-Palast am Zoo. According to an announcement in *Film-Kurier,* the film of the 1933 Reich Party Congress "does not provide a chronological compilation of single events, but rather an artistic presentation of selected film footage."

▪ ▪ ▪

1934 (130 German premieres)

Volldampf voraus! (C. Froelich, Froelich-Film, 3 January)*
Mutter und Kind (H. Steinhoff, Tofa, 5 January)*
Wenn ich König wär'! (J. Alexander Hübler-Kahla, KMR, 9 January)*
Die Finanzen des Großherzogs (G. Gründgens, Tofa, 10 January)

Der Polizeibericht meldet (G. Jacoby, Majestic, 12 January)*
Der Schimmelreiter (C. Oertel/H. Deppe, R. Fritsch Tonfilm, 12 January)
Wilhelm Tell (H. Paul, Terra, 12 January)*
Rivalen der Luft (F. Wysbar, Ufa, 19 January)*
Das alte Recht (I. Martin-Andersen, Deutsche Universal-Film, 27 January)*
Der Flüchtling aus Chicago (J. Meyer, Atlanta/Bavaria, 31 January)
So ein Flegel (R. A. Stemmle, Cicero, 13 February)
Stoßtrupp 1917 (H. Zöberlein/L. Schmid-Wildy, Arya, 20 February)*
Die Welt ohne Maske (H. Piel, Ariel, 9 March)
Gold (K. Hartl, Ufa, 29 March)*
Zu Straßburg auf der Schanz (F. Osten, Ideal, 13 April)*
Die Bande von Hoheneck (H. Wilhelm, Czerny, 25 April)*
Die vier Musketiere (H. Paul, Terra, 27 April)*
Die Töchter ihrer Exzellenz (R. Schünzel, Ufa, 17 May)
Grenzfeuer (H. Beck-Gaden, Arnold & Richter, 27 May)*
Die Csardasfürstin (G. Jacoby, Ufa, 29 June)
Ein Mann will nach Deutschland (P. Wegener, Ufa, 26 July)*
Musik im Blut (E. Waschneck, Fanal, 1 August)
Der Herr der Welt (H. Piel, Ariel, 11 August)
Krach um Jolanthe (C. Froelich, Froelich-Film, 18 August)
Maskerade (W. Forst, Tobis-Sascha, 21 August)
Die Sporck'schen Jäger (R. Randolf, Randolf-Filmproduktion, 30 August)*
Schwarzer Jäger Johanna (J. Meyer, Terra, 6 September)*
Der verlorene Sohn (L. Trenker, Deutsche Universal-Film, 6 September)*
Der junge Baron Neuhaus (G. Ucicky, Ufa, 14 September)
Fürst Woronzeff (A. Robison, Ufa, 2 October)
Der Fall Brenken (C. Lamac, Westofi, 12 October)*
So endete eine Liebe (K. Hartl, Cine-Allianz, 18 October)
Die Reiter von Deutsch-Ostafrika (H. Selpin, Terra, 19 October)*
Die englische Heirat (R. Schünzel, Cine-Allianz, 31 October)
Heldentum und Todeskampf unserer Emden (L. Ralph, Herzog/Tobis, 13 November)*
Der ewige Traum (A. Fanck, Cine-Allianz, 20 November)
Ich für Dich—Du für mich (C. Froelich, Froelich-Film, 30 November)*
Peer Gynt (F. Wendhausen, Bavaria/Tofa, 17 December)
Liebe, Tod und Teufel (H. Hilpert/R. Steinbicker, Ufa, 21 December)
Um das Menschenrecht (H. Zöberlein, Arya, 28 December)*
Hohe Schule (E. Engel, ABC, 31 December)

Banned:

Frühlingsstimmen (P. Fejos, Wolf-Film, 27 July 1934)
Die Liebe siegt (G. Zoch, Westropa, 12 January 1935)
Ein Kind, ein Hund, ein Vagabund (A. M. Rabenalt, Lloyd-Film, 12 January 1935, recut and rereleased as *Vielleicht war's nur ein Traum,* 12 July 1935)
Die Reiter von Deutsch-Ostafrika (H. Selpin, Terra, 19 December 1939)*

The three most successful films of the 1933–34 season are *Flüchtlinge, Gold,* and *Krach um Jolanthe.* Fifty-nine German features have American premieres.

6 January: *Film-Kurier* discusses the German response to foreign films in 1933: "A considerable number of them have been highly successful. The French films *La maternelle* and *Poil de carotte* as well as *Cavalcade* were accepted with great applause. The Italian films *Sky Fleet* and *Black Shirts* got the title of education films."

3 February: Goebbels appoints Willi Krause, editor of *Der Angriff,* as Reich Film director *(Reichsfilmdramaturg).* Krause's tasks include the review of scripts and outlines for prospective films and the prevention of productions not in keeping with the priorities of the new order.

9 February: Goebbels speaks again to the Reichsfachschaft Film in the Kroll Opera, describing the initial successes of his new film directives: "Our work has found its most gratifying rewards in the confidence granted to us by the German art world." "We are convinced," he goes on, "that film is one of the most modern and comprehensive means of mass influence." The government must not let the film world guide itself. The new order intends to give German film a German countenance. "We do not want representations of National Socialism to be a matter of choosing the correct material, but rather of granting this material a proper shape."

1 March: A new Reich Cinema Law *(Lichtspielgesetz)* goes into effect, replacing the old one from 12 May 1920 and entailing:

- Evaluation *(Vorzensur)* of all feature film scripts under the auspices of the Reich Film adviser, an officer of the ProMi, who is "to prevent the presentation of contents that run counter to the spirit of the times."
- Required official certification by the Film Censorship Board before public screenings. Films will not be approved if they endanger "essential interests of the state or public order" or if they violate "National Socialist, religious,

moral, or artistic sensibilities, or have a brutalizing or immoral effect, or jeopardize German prestige or German foreign relations."
- Scrutiny of images, titles, and both written and spoken words.
- Expansion of the rating system, including the new rating "politically especially worthwhile" as the highest honor with "artistically especially worthwhile."

30 March: Founding of the Reich Film Archive (Reichsfilmarchiv).

1 May: *Flüchtlinge* is the first film to receive the new State Film Prize.

Workers for all film companies (including Ufa's 5,000 employees) swear an oath of loyalty to the new legislation "for the Organization of National Labor."

26 June: A decree of the Reich minister of education officially implements film in school education.

30 June–2 July: Hitler purges the SA in a move to eliminate opposition both inside and outside the party. Among the many victims of the "Night of the Long Knives" are 170 prominent Nazis, including SA leader Ernst Röhm and oppositional elements within the conservative right.

2 August: Hindenburg dies and Hitler merges the offices of *Reichskanzler* and *Reichspräsident*. The German Army (Reichswehr) pledges its loyalty to Hitler.

19 August: Hitler declares himself "Führer" and Reich chancellor.

6–9 September: The sixth annual Nazi Party Congress takes place in Nuremberg, an event captured on camera by Leni Riefenstahl and a production staff of 172 people, including 36 cinematographers and camera assistants.

20 September: The first annual meeting of the RFK takes place in Munich. The new emphasis in German production is to be "artistic films with an international appeal."

October–November: Widespread arrests of homosexuals in Germany.

13 December: The Cinema Law is amended to allow the Reich Film adviser to support scripts deemed worthy of encouragement. "At the request of the firm, he can advise and assist in the production of the script and film. The film is then bound to follow his directions."

■ ■ ■

1935 (93 German premieres)

Regine (E. Waschneck, Fanal, 7 January)
Lockspitzel Asew (P. Jutzi, Atlantis/Maxim, 10 January)
Hermine und die sieben Aufrechten (F. Wysbar, Terra, 11 January)
Oberwachtmeister Schwenke (C. Froelich, Froelich-Filmproduktion, 14 January)*
Vorstadtvarieté (W. Hochbaum, Styria, 17 January)

Nur nicht weich werden, Susanne! (A. von Cserépy, Cserépy Tonfilm/Normaton, 24 January)*
Der alte und der junge König (H. Steinhoff, Deka, 29 January)*
Der stählerne Strahl (F. Wenzler, Pallas, 29 January)
Warum lügt Fräulein Käthe? (G. Jacoby, Majestic, 29 January)
Der rote Reiter (M. Wallner/H. Vietzke, Randolf-Film, 1 February)*
Mein Leben für Maria Isabell (F. D. Andam/E. Hasselbach, Lloyd-Film, 7 February)*
Alles um eine Frau (A. Abel, K. U.-Filmproduktion/Delta, 14 February)*
Frischer Wind aus Kanada (H. Kenter/E. Holder, Ufa, 22 February)
Barcarole (G. Menzel, Ufa, 4 March)
Artisten (H. Piel, Ariel, 12 March)
Zigeunerbaron (K. Hartl, Ufa, 17 April)
Das Mädchen Johanna (G. Ucicky, Ufa, 26 April)*
Wunder des Fliegens (H. Paul, Terra, 14 May)*
Ehestreik (G. Jacoby, Ufa, 31 May)
Nacht der Verwandlung (H. Deppe, Itala, 31 May)*
Mach' mich glücklich (A. Robison, Ufa, 5 July)
Amphitryon (R. Schünzel, Ufa, 18 July)
Liselotte von der Pfalz (C. Froelich, Froelich-Filmproduktion, 8 August)
Der Werft zum grauen Hecht (F. Wysbar, Pallas, 22 August)
Episode (W. Reisch, Viktoria, 23 August)
Stradivari (G. von Bolvary, Boston, 26 August)*
Pygmalion (E. Engel, Klagemann-Film, 2 September)
Das Einmaleins der Liebe (C. Hoffmann, Minerva, 6 September)
Ein idealer Gatte (H. Selpin, Terra, 6 September)
. . . nur ein Komödiant (E. Engel, Horus, 20 September)
Königswalzer (H. Maisch, Ufa, 23 September)
Der grüne Domino (H. Selpin, Ufa, 4 October)
Leichte Kavallerie (W. Hochbaum, FDF, 14 October)
April, April! (D. Sierck, Ufa, 24 October)
Das Mädchen vom Moorhof (D. Sierck, Ufa, 30 October)
Einer zuviel an Bord (G. Lamprecht, Ufa, 31 October)
Mazurka (W. Forst, Cine-Allianz, 14 November)
Viktoria (C. Hoffmann, Minerva, 27 November)
Der Ammenkönig (H. Steinhoff, Fritzsche, 5 December)
Der Student von Prag (A. Robison, Cine-Allianz, 10 December)
Henker, Frauen und Soldaten (J. Meyer, Bavaria, 19 December)*
Krach im Hinterhaus (V. Harlan, ABC, 20 December)*

Stützen der Gesellschaft (D. Sierck, RN, 21 December)
Schwarze Rosen (P. Martin, Ufa, 23 December)*
Die weiße Hölle vom Piz Palü (A. Fanck/G. W. Pabst, H. T.-Film, 23 December)
Der höhere Befehl (G. Lamprecht, Ufa, 30 December)*

Banned:

Das Stahltier (W. Zielke, 25 July 1935, released in a shortened version, 6 January 1954)
Die Katz' im Sack (R. Eichberg, Société-Internationale Cinématographique, 7 September 1939)
Varieté (N. Farkas, Les Films E. F./Bavaria, 7 September 1939)
Friesennot (P. Hagen, Delta, 7 September 1939)*

The three most successful films of the 1934–35 season are *Maskerade, So endete eine Liebe,* and *Ein Mann will nach Deutschland.*

4 February: Opening of the Reich Film Archive, a collection of German and international films. American films will continue to be collected and shown to political officials and members of the film industry even after Goebbels bans Hollywood productions from German screens in 1940.

16 March: General conscription is reintroduced in Germany and the disarmament clauses of the Treaty of Versailles are repudiated.

22 March: The German postal service (Reichspost) begins regular transmission of television programs, initially ninety minutes an evening, three days a week.

17 April: German rearmament endeavors are officially rebuked by the League of Nations.

25 April–3 May: An International Film Congress in Berlin brings together representatives from twenty national film industries. On 27 April in Babelsberg, Ufa studio officials greet 1,800 visitors.

1 May: *Triumph des Willens* receives the year's State Film Prize. Goebbels commends the film as "a great cinematic vision of the Führer, here seen with a forcefulness that has not been previously revealed. The film has successfully avoided the danger of being merely a politically slanted film. It has translated the strong rhythm of these great times into convincing artistic terms; it is an epic, beating the tempo of marching formations, steel-like in its conviction, fired by a passionate artistry."

26 June: Compulsory labor service for young men from ages eighteen to twenty-five is introduced *(Reichsarbeitgesetz).*

28 June: A further amendment to the Cinema Law grants the minister for popular enlightenment and propaganda the ability to ban a licensed film for reasons of public welfare.

15 September: The Nuremberg Race Laws ("for the protection of German blood and honor") deny German Jews their civil rights; marriages and sexual relations between Germans and Jews become crimes punishable by imprisonment.

2 December: Special showings of MGM films are held for exhibitors in the Berlin Marmorhaus. The screenings are also open to the general public, but tickets are a steep 15 RM. The day's program includes *Vagabond Lady* (10 A.M.), *Broadway Melody of 1936* (11:30 A.M.), and *China Seas* (2:30 P.M.); the following day's screenings are *Murder in the Fleet* (9 A.M.), *Bonnie Scotland* (10:30 A.M.), *No More Ladies* (noon), and *Anna Karenina* (3 P.M.).

■ ■ ■

1936 (109 German premieres)

Fährmann Maria (F. Wysbar, Pallas, 7 January)
Die ewige Maske (W. Hochbaum, Progress, 8 January)
August der Starke (P. Wegener, Nerthus, 17 January)*
Traumulus (C. Froelich, Froelich-Filmproduktion, 23 January)*
Donogoo Tonka (R. Schünzel, Ufa, 24 January)
Herbstmanöver (G. Jacoby, FDF, 24 January)*
Junges Blut (K. Skalden, Skalden-Filmgesellschaft, 24 January)*
Die Leuchter des Kaisers (K. Hartl, Gloria, 14 February)*
Kater Lampe (V. Harlan, RN, 19 February)*
Der Favorit der Kaiserin (W. Hochbaum, Itala, 21 February)
Mädchenjahre einer Königin (E. Engel, Klagemann-Film, 28 February)
Der müde Theodor (V. Harlan, Majestic, 13 March)
Savoy-Hotel 217 (G. Ucicky, Ufa, 7 April)
Allotria (W. Forst, Cine-Allianz, 12 June)
Schlußakkord (D. Sierck, Ufa, 27 June)
Weiberregiment (K. Ritter, Ufa, 9 July)
Schatten der Vergangenheit (W. Hochbaum, Donau, 17 July)
Der Kaiser von Kalifornien (L. Trenker, Trenker-Film, 21 July)*
Boccaccio (H. Maisch, Ufa, 31 July)
Standschütze Bruggler (W. Klingler, Tonlicht, 21 August)*
Der Bettelstudent (G. Jacoby, Ufa, 1 September)
Eskapade (E. Waschneck, Fanal, 1 September)

Verräter (K. Ritter, Ufa, 9 September)*
Glückskinder (P. Martin, Ufa, 18 September)
Neunzig Minuten Aufenthalt (H. Piel, Ariel, 25 September)
Maria, die Magd (V. Harlan, Minerva, 2 October)*
Das Mädchen Irene (R. Schünzel, Ufa, 9 October)
Wenn wir alle Engel wären (C. Froelich, Froelich-Tonfilm, 9 October)
Stadt Anatol (V. Tourjansky, Ufa, 16 October)
Eine Frau ohne Bedeutung (H. Steinhoff, Majestic, 26 October)
Annemarie (F. P. Buch, Witt-Film, 10 November)*
Hannerl und ihre Liebhaber (W. Hochbaum, Favorit, 10 November)
Die Unbekannte (F. Wysbar, Paul-Film, 12 November)
Burgtheater (W. Forst, Forst-Film, 13 November)
Das Veilchen vom Potsdamer Platz (J. A. Hübler-Kahla, Stark-Film, 16 November)
Alles für Veronika (V. Harlan, Berna, 8 December)
Das Hofkonzert (D. Sierck, Ufa, 18 December)
Donner, Blitz und Sonnenschein (E. Engels, NFK, 22 December)
Die Nacht mit dem Kaiser (E. Engel, Klagemann-Film, 22 December)
Unter heißem Himmel (G. Ucicky, Ufa, 23 December)

Banned:

August der Starke (P. Wegener, Nerthus, 7 September 1939)
Die klugen Frauen (J. Feyder/A. M. Rabenalt, Films Sonores Tobis, 7 September 1939)
Der Kurier des Zaren (R. Eichberg, Ermolieff/Eichberg-Film, 7 September 1939)

During 1936, 58 directors make German feature films. The most active filmmakers are Hans Deppe (five features), Carl Boese (four), and Veit Harlan (four). Forty-one companies produce films; Ufa heads the list with eighteen German-language titles and four French features. The most successful films for the 1935–36 season are *Schwarze Rosen, Allotria,* and *Krach im Hinterhaus.*

7 March: In defiance of the provisions of the Treaty of Locarno, German troops march into and reclaim the Rhineland; a plebiscite on 29 March approves the action with a 99 percent majority.

1 April: Jürgen Nierentz replaces Willi Krause as *Reichsfilmdramaturg.* Nierentz will be succeeded by Ewald von Demandowsky in 1937.

1 May: Carl Froelich's *Traumulus,* starring Emil Jannings, receives the State Film Prize.

July: The first groups of gypsies are sent to a concentration camp at Dachau.

17 July: After a military putsch, the Spanish Civil War begins. On 25 July Hitler will intervene on the side of Franco.

1 August: Hitler opens the Eleventh Modern Olympic Games in Berlin.

4 August: The first German color production, a short film, is premiered, *Das Schönheitsfleckchen,* starring Lil Dagover as the Marquise de Pompadour.

25 October: The Berlin-Rome Axis is proclaimed in a treaty between Germany and Italy.

1 November: Announcement of the Berlin-Rome Axis.

25 November: Anti-Comintern Pact between Germany and Japan.

27 November: Goebbels bans all film criticism. From now on critics will act as servants *(Kunstdiener)* rather than judges of art *(Kunstrichter):* "The critic is to be replaced by the arts editor. Coverage of the arts should not concern itself with evaluation, but should confine itself to description. Such coverage should give the public a chance to draw its own conclusions—it should stimulate people to use their own attitudes and feelings in evaluating artistic achievements."

28 November: Goebbels' press chief, Alfred Berndt, defends the new measures at the annual gathering of the Central German Press Chamber: "Art works can be evaluated in the National Socialist state only on the basis of National Socialist cultural perspectives. Only the party and the state are in a position to determine artistic values by appealing to the artistic standpoint of National Socialism."

▪ ▪ ▪

1937 (89 German premieres)

Weiße Sklaven (K. Anton, Lloyd-Film, 5 January)*
Die Frau des anderen/Romanze (H. Selpin, Patria, 8 January)
Ritt in die Freiheit (K. Hartl, Ufa, 14 January)*
Und Du, mein Schatz, fährst mit (G. Jacoby, Ufa, 15 January)
Truxa (H. H. Zerlett, Tobis-Magna, 19 January)
Ball im Metropol (F. Wysbar, Neucophon, 26 January)
Gleisdreieck (R. A. Stemmle, FDF, 27 January)*
Fridericus (J. Meyer, Diana, 8 February)*
Die Kreutzersonate (V. Harlan, Witt-Film, 11 February)
Lumpacivagabundus (G. von Bolvary, Styria/Hade, 12 February)
Togger (J. von Alten, Minerva, 12 February)*
Premiere (G. von Bolvary, Gloria, 25 February)
Menschen ohne Vaterland (H. Maisch, Ufa, 6 March)*

Der Etappenhase (J. Stöckel, Astra, 16 March)*
Der Herrscher (V. Harlan, Tobis-Magna, 17 March)*
Die göttliche Jette (E. Waschneck, Fanal, 18 March)
Die Tochter des Samurai (A. Fanck, Fanck-Film/J. O. Studio/Towa Shoji-Film, 23 March)*
Condottieri (L. Trenker/W. Klingler, Tobis, 24 March)*
Man spricht über Jacqueline (W. Hochbaum, Deka, 16 April)
Madame Bovary (G. Lamprecht, Euphono, 23 April)
Die ganz grossen Torheiten (C. Froelich, Tonfilmstudio Froelich, 30 April)
Land der Liebe (R. Schünzel, Witt-Film, 10 June)
Mein Sohn, der Herr Minister (V. Harlan, Ufa, 6 July)*
Der Mann, der Sherlock Holmes war (K. Hartl, Ufa, 15 July)
Husaren, heraus! (G. Jacoby, Pallas, 22 July)*
Karussell (A. Elling, Astra, 2 August)
Sieben Ohrfeigen (P. Martin, Ufa, 3 August)
Kapriolen (G. Gründgens, Forst-Filmproduktion, 10 August)
Alarm in Peking (H. Selpin, Minerva, 20 August)*
Versprich mir nichts! (W. Liebeneiner, Meteor, 20 August)
Pan (O. Fjord, Fjord-Film, 27 August)
Zu neuen Ufern (D. Sierck, Ufa, 31 August)
Heimweh (J. von Alten, Minerva, 3 September)
Die Warschauer Zitadelle (F. P. Buch, ABC, 6 September)*
Unternehmen Michael (K. Ritter, Ufa, 7 September)*
Patrioten (K. Ritter, Ufa, 24 September)*
Zauber der Bohème (G. von Bolvary/Alfred Gerasch, Intergloria, 8 October)
Der Mustergatte (W. Liebeneiner, Imagoton, 13 October)
Der zerbrochene Krug (G. Ucicky, Tobis-Magna, 19 October)
Brillanten (E. von Borsody, Ufa, 22 October)
Ein Volksfeind (H. Steinhoff, FDF, 26 October)*
Fanny Elßler (P. Martin, Ufa, 4 November)
Serenade (W. Forst, Forst-Filmproduktion, 26 November)
Der Biberpelz (J. von Alten, FDF, 3 December)
Gasparone (G. Jacoby, Ufa, 17 December)
La Habanera (D. Sierck, Ufa, 18 December)

Banned:

Starke Herzen (H. Maisch, Ufa, rejected by the censors on 7 December 1937, released 3 January 1953 as *Starke Herzen im Sturm*)*

Andere Welt (M. Allegret/A. Stöger, Regina, 7 September 1939)

Of the 89 German films that premiere in Berlin cinemas this year, 58 (61.8 percent) derive from literary sources (in contrast to 45.7 percent in 1936 and 52.7 percent in 1935). Eighty percent of all German features are distributed by three firms: Ufa, Tobis, and Terra. Thirty-six German producers make feature films in 1937. Hans Deppe, Georg Jacoby, and Carl Lamac are the most active among 55 directors: each completes four features. The biggest box-office successes of the 1936–37 season are *Verräter* and *Truxa.*

20 January: Willi Forst, Gustaf Gründgens, and Emil Jannings become Tobis-Film board members. Later in the year Veit Harlan and Hans Zerlett join them.

30 January: At the recommendation of Goebbels, the ProMi awards Carl Froelich a professorship and grants the title "State Actor" to Heinrich George, Ernst Karchow, Theodor Loos, Paul Otto, Jakob Tiedtke, and Mathias Wieman.

The "Enabling Act" is extended for four years.

5 March: Goebbels speaks to the RFK in the Berlin Kroll Opera at its annual meeting. He outlines priorities for German film, describing his role as that of a "neutral observer, someone bound to no political party, but rather an enthusiastic friend of film art." During the year Goebbels will take decisive measures to place the film industry under state control.

6 March: Ufa head Ludwig Klitzsch reports to a committee of the RFK that feature film production costs have doubled over the last five years. *Film-Kurier* recalls Goebbels' seven theses about film which he presented at the closing meeting of the International Film Congress in 1933, claiming they still are valid:

1. Film, declares the minister, like every other art, has its own laws, and one must obey them. These are not the same as those of theater; each medium has its own language. Film must struggle against the century-long power of theater if it is to gain its own legitimacy.
2. Film must free itself from the vulgar banality of a simple mass amusement but must not lose its strong inner connection with people. Mass taste can be educated; film as an art can play a crucial role in educating the masses.
3. But this does not mean that film should pursue solely aesthetic goals. In fact, given its larger range, film is duty bound to be a popular art [*Volkskunst*] in the best sense of the word. *Volkskunst* should grant artistic form to the joys and sorrows of the masses. It should not avoid the troubles of the day and escape into a never-never land.
4. No art can take care of itself; it needs material support. It must be clear that the State should support film as it does the other arts; only in this way can film's development as an art be guaranteed.

5. Film must keep in touch with current events if it is to have an effect on them. It must reflect the spirit of the times if it is to speak to them.
6. Film gives expression to national identity and, in so doing, creates understanding among nations. It bridges different cultures and enhances mutual understanding.
7. Film should develop its innermost natural essence. Foreign to it are empty pathos and kitschy razzle-dazzle. The honest and natural film that grants the present a vital and plastic expression can serve as a valuable means of creating a better, purer, and more realistic world of artistic possibility. If film realizes these principles, it will conquer the world as a new artistic possibility.

7 March: Dr. Oswald Lehnich complains in a meeting of the Reich Film Chamber that German film production has dropped off since 1933.

18 March: Represented by the Cautio Treuhandsgesellschaft, the government buys a controlling interest of Ufa (72.6 percent), paying full market value for Alfred Hugenberg's shares (21,250,000 RM) and 8 million RM for shares held by the Deutsche Bank. Engineer of the transaction is Goebbels' emissary, Max Winkler. Cautio Treuhand GmbH will ultimately procure the Ufa, Tobis, Terra, and Bavaria studios for the Reich government.

25 March: Goebbels introduces a new film rating system.

4 April: The *New York Times* reports that American film companies are pulling back from the German market. Censors in the Reich refuse to admit good American box-office attractions. "American distributors have discovered that the censor shows a conscious and obvious preference for American films that are second-rate and unlikely to appeal to the public."

1 May: Veit Harlan's *Der Herrscher,* scripted by Thea von Harbou and Curt J. Braun, starring Emil Jannings, receives the year's State Film Prize.

17 June: Goebbels takes a tour of the Siemens-Schaltwerk and inquires about the progress of color film technology.

26 June: A new Terra company comes into being with plans to make twenty-five films a year.

12 July: Under new regulations regarding the exhibition of foreign films in Germany, distributors of foreign films are required to register films with the Kontingentstelle Berlin (until June 1942 an organ of the RFK, afterward of the Film Censorship Board). To be passed on for inspection by the censorship board, a film must receive preliminary approval *(Unbedenklichkeitsbescheinigung)* from the ProMi.

18 July: Hitler opens the House of German Art in Munich, a space meant to

exhibit officially sanctioned artwork: "For 'modern art' National Socialism wishes to substitute a 'German' art and an eternal art. This House of German Art is designed for the art of the German people—not for an international art. . . . There can be no standard of yesterday and today, of modern or unmodern: there can be only the standard of 'valueless' or 'valuable,' or 'eternal' or 'transitory.' "

19 July: The exhibition "Decadent Art" *(Entartete Kunst)* is opened in Munich.

August: Berlin celebrates its 700th anniversary.

25 September: Mussolini comes to Germany on his first state visit.

October: *Der Kongress tanzt* is banned by the Filmprüfstelle because of its large number of Jewish, politically objectionable, and emigrated cast and crew.

8 October: The popular actress Renate Müller, star of *Viktor und Viktoria* and *Allotria,* dies under mysterious circumstances in a sanatorium.

1 December: The German government assumes total control of Tobis-Film.

■ ■ ■

1938 (99 German premieres)

Das Geheimnis um Betty Bonn (R. A. Stemmle, Ufa, 4 January)*
Der Berg ruft (L. Trenker, Trenker-Film, 6 January)
Der Tiger von Eschnapur (R. Eichberg, Eichberg-Film, 7 January)
Der Katzensteg (F. P. Buch, Euphono, 11 January)
Urlaub auf Ehrenwort (K. Ritter, Ufa, 11 January)*
Mit versiegelter Order (K. Anton, Majestic, 14 January)*
Petermann ist dagegen (F. Wysbar, Neucophon, 14 January)*
Das indische Grabmal (R. Eichberg, Eichberg-Film, 28 January)
Die Umwege des schönen Karl (C. Froelich, Tonfilmstudio Froelich, 31 January)
Frau Sylvelin (H. Maisch, FDF, 2 February)
Der Maulkorb (E. Engel, Tobis, 10 February)
Heiratsschwindler (H. Selpin, ABC, 15 February)
Verklungene Melodie (V. Tourjansky, Ufa, 25 February)
Revolutionshochzeit (H. H. Zerlett, Euphono, 7 March)*
Kameraden auf See (H. Paul, Terra, 12 March)*
Ihr Leibhusar (H. Marischka, Hunnia, 14 March)*
Es leuchten die Sterne (H. H. Zerlett, Tobis, 17 March)
Musketier Meier III (J. Stöckel, Germania, 17 March)*
Yvette (W. Liebeneiner, Meteor, 25 March)
Fünf Millionen suchen einen Erben (C. Boese, Majestic, 1 April)
Das Mädchen von gestern Nacht (P. P. Brauer, Ufa, 2 April)

Jugend (V. Harlan, Tobis, 12 April)*
Großalarm (G. Jacoby, FDF, 16 April)
Der unmögliche Herr Pitt (H. Piel, Ariel, 16 April)
Olympia (L. Riefenstahl, Olympia, 20 April)*
Anna Favetti (E. Waschneck, Fanal, 28 April)
Die kleine und die große Liebe (J. von Baky/U. Bettac, Klagemann-Film, 29 April)*
Dreiklang (H. Hinrich, Witt-Film, 24 May)
Spiegel des Lebens (G. von Bolvary, Vienna, 8 June)
Mordsache Holm (E. Engels, NFK, 18 June)*
Heimat (C. Froelich, Tonfilmstudio Froelich, 25 June)*
Fahrendes Volk (J. Feyder, Tobis, 1 July)
Ich liebe Dich (H. Selpin, Meteor, 21 July)
Eine Frau kommt in die Tropen (H. Paulsen, Terra, 28 July)
Der Fall Deruga (F. P. Buch, Witt-Film, 1 August)
Geheimzeichen LB 17 (V. Tourjansky, Terra, 9 August)*
Capriccio (K. Ritter, Ufa, 11 August)
Fortsetzung folgt (P. Martin, Ufa, 26 August)
Verwehte Spuren (V. Harlan, Majestic, 26 August)*
Gastspiel im Paradies (K. Hartl, Ufa, 6 September)
Du und Ich (W. Liebeneiner, Minerva, 14 September)*
Eine Nacht im Mai (G. Jacoby, Ufa, 14 September)
13 Stühle (E. W. Emo, Emo-Film, 16 September)
Nordlicht (H. B. Fredersdorf, Ufa, 20 September)
Am seidenen Faden (R. A. Stemmle, Ufa, 23 September)*
Ein Mädchen geht an Land (W. Hochbaum, Ufa, 30 September)
Die vier Gesellen (C. Froelich, Tonfilmstudio Froelich, 1 October)
Fracht von Baltimore (H. Hinrich, Terra, 14 October)
Liebelei und Liebe (A. M. Rabenalt, Terra, 21 October)
Steputat & Co. (C. Boese, Terra, 21 October)*
Kautschuk (E. von Borsody, Ufa, 1 November)
Nanon (H. Maisch, Ufa, 15 November)
Napoleon ist an allem schuld (C. Goetz, Tobis, 29 November)
Tanz auf dem Vulkan (H. Steinhoff, Majestic, 30 November)*
Ziel in den Wolken (W. Liebeneiner, Terra, 1 December)*
Liebesbriefe aus dem Engadin (L. Trenker/W. Klingler, Trenker-Film, 5 December)
Der Blaufuchs (V. Tourjansky, Ufa, 14 December)
In geheimer Mission (J. von Alten, Cine-Allianz, 16 December)

Dreizehn Mann und eine Kanone (J. Meyer, Bavaria, 22 December)*
Pour le Mérite (K. Ritter, Ufa, 22 December)*
Sergeant Berry (H. Selpin, Euphono, 22 December)
Lauter Lügen (H. Rühmann, Terra, 23 December)
Menschen, Tiere, Sensationen (H. Piel, Ariel, 23 December)
Frauen für Golden Hill (E. Waschneck, Fanal, 30 December)

Banned:

Der Spieler (G. Lamprecht, Euphono, 30 October 1938)
Das Leben kann so schön sein (R. Hansen, Tonfilmstudio Froelich, premiered in Vienna after 20 December 1938, banned 3 January 1939, released 9 February 1950 as *Eine Frau fürs Leben*)
Abenteuer in Warschau (C. Boese, Nerthus, 7 September 1939)
Ab Mitternacht (C. Hoffmann, Ermolieff/Tobis, 7 September 1939)
Preußische Liebesgeschichte (P. Martin, Ufa, banned in December 1938, premiered 12 April 1950 as *Liebeslegende*)
Altes Herz geht auf die Reise (C. Junghans, Witt-Film for Ufa, banned March 1939; shown in the U.S. after 1945 and premiered on West German television, 27 September 1978)

The box-office hits of the 1937–38 season are *Der Mustergatte, Olympia: Fest der Völker,* and *Gasparone.*

11 February: The Bavaria Filmkunst GmbH is founded in Munich, replacing the bankrupt Bavaria AG.

4 March: Goebbels dedicates a German Film Academy on the Ufa grounds at Babelsberg: "Anyone in the future who seeks admittance to the German Film Academy, must—regardless of the film sector in which he wishes to be active—demonstrate signs of genius." Wolfgang Liebeneiner heads the Film Art faculty.

4–5 March: Annual meeting of the RFK in Berlin; in his main address, Goebbels calls for productions with greater verisimilitude *(Lebensnähe);* film should hold up a mirror to the world and everyday life.

12–13 March: German troops march into Austria; the annexation *(Anschluß)* is declared, and Austria becomes incorporated into the German Reich; a plebiscite provides popular support for the measure on 10 April.

20 April: Leni Riefenstahl's two-part *Olympia* premieres in Berlin. It will become the most highly decorated film of the Third Reich; on 1 May it receives the year's State Film Prize.

13 May: An interview with director Karl Ritter appears in the weekly magazine *Filmwelt:* "The pure entertainment film is only one aspect of our world view. The modern film [*Zeitfilm*] is about tanks, aircraft, and the troops at the front. It must bear the characteristics of contemporary Germany; it must be heroic as our fate at this time demands. At the same time, it must show humor and a positive approach to life in accordance with our newfound beliefs."

14 May: The ProMi issues a decree stipulating that German stars can act in foreign productions only with approval of the Reich Culture Chamber (Reichskulturkammer).

21 May: Under the direction of Slatan Dudow, Bertolt Brecht's play *Furcht und Elend des Dritten Reiches* premieres in Paris.

15 June: All provisions of the RKKG are extended to Austria, including the German Cinema Law and restrictions regarding the exhibition of foreign films.

23 June: The boxer Joe Louis defeats Max Schmeling in a world heavyweight championship fight.

1 July: A kilogram of bread costs 31 pfennigs, a liter of milk 23 pfennigs. A kilogram of veal is 2.06 RM, a kilogram of butter 3.13 RM.

17 July: Robert Wiene, director of *Das Cabinet des Dr. Caligari,* dies in Paris exile while working on *Ultimatum,* an espionage drama starring Erich von Stroheim.

1 August: The ProMi sharply criticizes the Berlin *Katholisches Kirchenblatt* for its attack on Veit Harlan's *Jugend,* a film whose representation of the clergy provokes widespread controversy among Germany's Catholics.

5 August: Goebbels announces the production of a small radio that will be available for 35 RM. He also speaks of endeavors to produce affordable televisions and functional car radios (for installation in Volkswagens).

10 August: The first German nonstop flight to America embarks from Berlin-Staaken. The "Condor" makes the trip in twenty-five hours.

25 September: The *New York Times* publishes an article on exiled German filmmakers; directors who are now working in Hollywood include Erik Charell, Wilhelm Dieterle, E. A. Dupont, Karl Freund, Henry Koster, Fritz Lang, Ernst Lubitsch, Joe May, Hanns Schwarz, and Wilhelm Thiele.

30 September: The Munich Agreement between Britain, France, Italy, and Germany brings about the cession of the Sudetenland to Germany.

1 October: German troops march into the Sudeten area of Czechoslovakia.

15 October: Ufa provides an account of its fiscal year's production: 34 German features, 6 foreign-language features, 28 German short features, 21 German culture films, 14 foreign-language culture films, 156 newsreel installments, and 127 commercial and industrial films.

3 November: The joint Boycott Council of the American Jewish Congress and the Jewish Labor Committee send a telegram to leading film distributors and exhibitors in the United States: "Seeking your cooperation as in the past to stop possible showings of Nazi Olympic film brought to this country by Leni Riefenstahl. This production is part of Nazi propaganda attack on American institutions and American democracy. Council will picket all houses booking this Fascist picture."

9 November: "Kristallnacht" ("the Night of Broken Glass") is the occasion of anti-Jewish violence throughout Germany: 91 people are murdered, 191 synagogues destroyed, and many Jewish cemetaries desecrated. Mass arrests of Jews follow. Jews are held responsible, and a compensation fine of one billion RM is imposed on them.

16 November: With Hitler in attendance, the Berlin Schillertheater is reopened.

6 December: A French-Germany nonaggression treaty is signed in Paris.

16 December: Wien-Film is established; it becomes Germany's fifth-largest studio, headed by Paul Hack, Fritz Hirtz, and Karl Hartl.

31 December: 654,062 marriages take place in Germany during 1938; more than 1.3 million births are recorded, the highest number since 1922.

■ ■ ■

1939 (108 German premieres)

Wir fahren nach Amerika (K. Engel, Boehner-Film, 15 January)
Drei wunderschöne Tage (F. Kirchhoff, Bavaria, 27 January)*
Im Namen des Volkes (E. Engels, Terra, 27 January)*
Das unsterbliche Herz (V. Harlan, Tobis, 31 January)*
Der Schritt vom Wege (G. Gründgens, Terra, 9 February)
Bel ami (W. Forst, Forst-Film, 21 February)
Aufruhr in Damaskus (G. Ucicky, Terra, 24 February)*
Wasser für Canitoga (H. Selpin, Bavaria, 10 March)
Hotel Sacher (E. Engel, Ufa, 15 March)
Männer müssen so sein (A. M. Rabenalt, Terra, 16 March)
Liebe streng verboten! (H. Helbig, Aco, 28 March)
Drei Unteroffiziere (W. Hochbaum, Ufa, 31 March)*
Der Florentiner Hut (W. Liebeneiner, Terra, 4 April)
Die Hochzeitsreise (K. Ritter, Ufa, 4 April)
Menschen vom Varieté (J. von Baky, Hunnia-Pictura, 14 April)
Salonwagen E 417 (P. Verhoeven, Deka, 14 April)*
Der Gouverneur (V. Tourjansky, Terra, 21 April)*

Die Stimme aus dem Äther (H. Paulsen, Terra, 10 May)*
Frau am Steuer (P. Martin, Ufa, 20 June)
Hallo Janine (C. Boese, Ufa, 1 July)
Robert und Bertram (H. H. Zerlett, Tobis, 7 July)*
Die Frau ohne Vergangenheit (N. Malasomma/C. Klein, Euphono, 18 July)
Fräulein (E. Waschneck, Ufa, 20 July)
Mann für Mann (R. A. Stemmle, Ufa, 21 July)*
Die Geliebte (G. Lamprecht, Ufa, 28 July)*
Paradies der Junggesellen (K. Hoffmann, Terra, 1 August)
Flucht ins Dunkel (A. M. Rabenalt, Terra, 8 August)*
Sensationsprozeß Casilla (E. von Borsody, Ufa, 8 August)
Ich bin Sebastian Ott (W. Forst/V. Becker, Forst-Filmproduktion, 11 August)
Es war eine rauschende Ballnacht (C. Froelich, Tonfilmstudio Froelich, 15 August)
Schneider Wibbel (V. de Kowa, Majestic, 18 August)*
Renate im Quartett (P. Verhoeven, Tobis, 24 August)
Kitty und die Weltkonferenz (H. Käutner, Terra, 25 August)
Irrtum des Herzens (B. Hofmann, Bavaria, 29 August)
Fasching (H. Schweikart, Bavaria, 14 September)
Robert Koch, der Bekämpfer des Todes (H. Steinhoff, Tobis, 26 September)
Gold in New Frisco (P. Verhoeven, Bavaria, 3 October)
Frau im Strom (G. Lamprecht, Wien, 13 October)
Leinen aus Irland (H. Hilbig, Styria, 16 October)*
Eine Frau wie Du (V. Tourjansky, Bavaria, 19 October)
D III 88 (H. Maisch/Hans Bertram, Tobis, 26 October)*
Die Reise nach Tilsit (V. Harlan, Majestic, 2 November)
Johannisfeuer (A. M. Rabenalt, Terra, 3 November)
Alarm auf Station III (P. L. Mayring, Terra, 10 November)*
Das Lied der Wüste (P. Martin, Ufa, 17 November)*
Der Stammbaum des Dr. Pistorius (K. G. Külb, Ufa, 5 December)*
Das Gewehr über (J. von Alten, Germania, 7 December)*
Maria Ilona (G. von Bolvary, Terra, 14 December)*
Kongo-Express (E. von Borsody, Ufa, 15 December)
Eine kleine Nachtmusik (L. Hainisch, Tobis, 18 December)
Mutterliebe (G. Ucicky, Wien, 19 December)*
Befreite Hände (H. Schweikart, Bavaria, 20 December)
Ihr erstes Erlebnis (J. von Baky, Ufa, 22 December)
Opernball (G. von Bolvary, Terra, 22 December)

Wir tanzen um die Welt (K. Anton, Tobis, 22 December)

Banned:

Wer küßt Madeleine? (V. Janson, Terra, 7 September 1939)
Kitty und die Weltkonferenz (H. Käutner, Terra, banned in late 1939)

The box-office hits of the 1938–39 season are *Heimat, Es war eine rauschende Ballnacht,* and *Robert Koch, der Bekämpfer des Todes.*

15 January: *Wir fahren nach Amerika,* a docudrama about a trip through the United States, has its premiere in Hamburg. The film is limited to guests with written invitations and is shown only in special matinees.

23 January: Quoting a "source close to the government," a *New York Times* correspondent reports from Berlin: "It is pointed out that the American film industry stands under predominating Jewish influence and it may be stated that the number of American films in Germany has declined."

27 January: Leni Riefenstahl returns from a controversial and unsuccessful trip to the United States with *Olympia.* Goebbels describes her personal report to him about the chances of German films on the American market, "an exhaustive description, and one that is far from encouraging. We shall get nowhere there. The Jews rule by terror and bribery. But for how much longer?"

30 January: Speaking in the Reichstag, Hitler declares that a new war will bring "the extermination of the Jewish race in Europe."

February: Production head Ernst Hugo Correll leaves Ufa.

2 February: The Reichfachschaftfilm's membership of 6,435 (4,010 men and 2,425 women) includes 3,371 actors (1,682 men and 1,689 women), 503 cinematographers (497 men and 6 women), 168 directors (167 men and one woman).

6 February: The Central Publishing House of the Nazi Party announces a luxury edition of *Mein Kampf* (bound in leather with gold embossment) to be sold for 32 RM.

13 February: Hitler places a wreath on Bismarck's grave in Friedrichsruh.

15 February: According to a survey, Germany has 6,667 movie houses with a total of 2.4 million seats. In 1938 more than 500 million admissions are counted; the average German attends the cinema eight times a year.

21 February: Heinrich Himmler visits Warsaw.

10–12 March: Annual meeting of the RFK; Goebbels calls for film to function as a "popular art" *(Volkskunst),* as a representation of collective joy and suffering in tune with everyday reality.

15 March: As Hitler's troops occupy Czechoslovakia, the German protectorate appropriates the Barrandov Studio facilities in Prague.

Lichtbild-Bühne carries an article that asks readers, "How Long Do You Mull Over a Film?" Cinema is not just a source of distraction, the editorial claims. Some films offer more than entertainment. For people living in small towns, an evening at the movies can in fact provide a rich experience. Spectators take films seriously; they talk and write about them intensely.

23 March: German troops invade and reannex the Memel region.

25 March: Membership in the Hitler Youth becomes compulsory for all German boys from age ten to eighteen.

22 April: A ten-year military and political alliance between Germany and Italy, the "Pact of Steel," is formalized.

1 May: Goebbels announces that Carl Froelich's *Heimat,* starring Zarah Leander and Heinrich George, is the recipient of the annual State Film Prize.

18 May: Princeton University awards Thomas Mann an honorary doctorate.

22 May: Exiled expressionist dramatist Ernst Toller commits suicide in a New York hotel.

30 June: The director and producer Carl Froelich becomes president of the RFK.

1 July: Painter Oskar Kokoschka is barred from the Prussian Academy of Art.

14 July: In Munich the "Day of German Art" begins with a festive celebration.

28 July: During an exhibition in Berlin, the first German television *(Volksfernseher)* is introduced at a price of 650 RM.

29 July: The German National Tourist Organization celebrates the "Day of the Guest."

8 August: The Seventh Mostra Internationale del Cinema begins in Venice with films from eighteen nations. The German film, *Robert Koch, der Bekämpfer des Todes,* opens the festival and later wins the grand prize.

23 August: The Nazi-Soviet Nonaggression Pact is concluded; secret clauses stipulate the terms of Poland's partition.

27 August: Food is rationed in the Reich.

31 August: Since January, 22,706 Jews have left Germany.

1 September: German troops invade Poland and annex Danzig.

3 September: France and Great Britain declare war on Germany, and World War II begins.

7 September: The weekly newsreel Ufa-Tonwoche runs at twice the customary length.

27 September: The Reich Main Security Office (Reichssicherheitshauptamt, RSHA) brings together the Gestapo, Kripo, and the Sicherheitsdienst. Headed

by Reinhard Heydrich, the RSHA becomes a mighty instrument of police terror.

Warsaw surrenders.

1 October: Hitler's signature, backdated to 1 September 1939, authorizes mercy killings, effectively legalizing euthanasia in Germany.

14 October: Clothing coupons are introduced in Germany.

21 October: Goebbels writes in his diary: "The financial success of our films is altogether amazing. We are becoming real war profiteers."

25 October: Goebbels records his thoughts about film, radio, and theater, promising directives to intensify work in these sectors. "The people need them, now more than ever. Apart from anything else, people must have something to spend their money on at a time when there is not much else available."

30 October: Cinema pioneer Max Skladanowsky, age seventy-six, dies in Berlin.

5 November: Goebbels opens the first weekly Sunday film matinee to expose the Hitler Youth to National Socialist productions.

8 November: Georg Elser makes an unsuccessful attempt on Hitler's life in a Munich beerhall.

31 December: Hitler speaks to the German Army: "Before us lies the hardest battle ever for the existence or nonexistence of the German people! With great optimism I and the entire nation look to you, because if Germany has such soldiers, it most certainly will victor!"

▪ ▪ ▪

1940 (86 German premieres)

Zwei Welten (G. Gründgens, Terra, 5 January)*
Der ewige Quell (F. Kirchhoff, Bavaria, 19 January)
Nanette (E. Engel, Klagemann-Film, 23 January)
Der Weg zu Isabel (E. Engel, Tobis, 26 January)
Zwielicht (R. van der Nass, Ufa, 2 February)
Aus erster Ehe (P. Verhoeven, Tobis, 12 February)*
Ein Mann auf Abwegen (H. Selpin, Euphono, 16 February)
Die gute Sieben (W. Liebeneiner, Terra, 27 February)
Fahrt ins Leben (B. Hofmann, Bavaria, 29 February)*
Der Feuerteufel (L. Trenker, Trenker-Film, 5 March)*
Stern von Rio (K. Anton, Tobis, 20 March)
Frau nach Maß (H. Käutner, Terra, 23 March)
Der Fuchs von Glenarvon (M. W. Kimmich, Tobis, 24 April)*
Der Postmeister (G. Ucicky, Wien, 24 April)

Ein Robinson (A. Fanck, Bavaria, 25 April)*
Liebesschule (K. G. Külb, Ufa, 3 May)
Bal paré (K. Ritter, Ufa, 22 May)
Mädchen im Vorzimmer (G. Lamprecht, Ufa, 31 May)*
Die Rothschilds (E. Waschneck, Ufa, 17 July)*
Die 3 Codonas (A. M. Rabenalt, Tobis, 1 August)
Die Geierwally (H. Steinhoff, Tobis, 13 August)
Trenck, der Pandur (H. Selpin, Tobis, 23 August)*
Wie konntest Du, Veronika! (M. Harbich, Ufa, 29 August)
Achtung! Feind hört mit! (A. M. Rabenalt, Terra, 3 September)*
Kleider machen Leute (H. Käutner, Terra, 16 September)
Das sündige Dorf (J. Stöckel, Bavaria, 17 September)
Die unvollkommene Liebe (E. Waschneck, Ufa, 20 September)
Jud Süß (V. Harlan, Terra, 24 September)*
Ein Leben lang (G. Ucicky, Wien, 9 October)
Das Fräulein von Barnhelm (H. Schweikart, Bavaria, 18 October)*
Traummusik (G. von Bolvary, Itala, 25 October)
Der dunkle Punkt (G. Zoch, Deka, 26 October)*
Herz modern möbliert (T. Lingen, Majestic, 29 October)
Das Herz der Königin (C. Froelich, Tonfilmstudio Froelich for Ufa, 1 November)*
Feinde (V. Tourjansky, Bavaria, 7 November)*
Friedrich Schiller (H. Maisch, Tobis, 13 November)*
Falschmünzer (H. Pfeiffer, Terra, 13 November)*
Kora Terry (G. Jacoby, Ufa, 27 November)
Rosen in Tirol (G. von Bolvary, Terra, 5 December)
Bismarck (W. Liebeneiner, Tobis, 6 December)*
Im Schatten des Berges (A. J. Lippl, Bavaria, 17 December)
Der liebe Augustin (E. W. Emo, Wien, 17 December)
Die keusche Geliebte (V. Tourjansky, Ufa, 18 December)
Der Kleinstadtpoet (J. von Baky, Ufa, 20 December)
Operette (W. Forst, Forst-Film for Wien, 20 December)
Unser Fräulein Doktor (E. Engel, Klagemann-Film, 20 December)
Wunschkonzert (E. von Borsody, Cine-Allianz-Film der Ufa, 30 December)*

The box-office hits of the 1939–40 season are *Jud Süß* (20.3 million admissions), *Mutterliebe* (19.4 million), and *Der Postmeister* (18.1 million). Sixty filmmakers complete films; the most active director is Géza von Bolvary, who does four features. Jacob Geis, Kurt Heuser, Felix Lützendorf, and Kurt E. Walten are each responsible for the scripts of four films. The last American features released in the Third Reich are *The Case against Mrs. Ames, The Great Gambini, Murder with Pictures, The Plainsman,* and *The Return of the Cisco Kid.*

8 January: The Berlin publishing house Spaeth und Linde publishes Edith-Sylvia Burgmann's book, *Gut gekocht—gern gegessen,* which offers 444 recipes and tips on how to prepare nourishing and tasty meals with modest means.

18 January: German filmmaker Otto Rippert, director of *Homunculus* (1916), dies at age seventy-one in Berlin.

24 January: Goebbels notes: "Ufa is in a very good position, Terra the same, good at Bavaria and Wien-Film, still bad at Tobis . . . The number of productions at Ufa, Tobis, and Terra will be halved. I am looking for a few experienced, able men to handle entertainment film production. Apart from this, we intend to establish a Society for Electro-Acoustic Research to improve the technical aspect of our films . . . We have only good films and bad films. We lack the serviceable middle range."

25 January: Goebbels checks the year's production schedules: "Entertainment films remain the only real source of worry. There is still a lot to do in that area. The industry's box-office receipts are splendid. Millions in profits."

30 January: Hitler speaks in the Berlin Sportpalast, commenting on Soviet-German relations: "For centuries Germany and Russia have lived in friendship and in peace. Why should this not be possible again in the future? I think it will be possible because both nations wish it to be so."

2–13 February: First deportations of Jews.

8 February: Goebbels: "I keep impressing my people with one basic truth: repeat everything until the last, most stupid person has understood."

13 March: The actress and dancer La Jana dies as a result of a lung infection contacted while on tour performing for German troops.

29 March: Speaking at a working meeting of the RFK, Goebbels stresses the important political role of comedies and musicals.

9 April: Germany invades Norway and Denmark.

27 April: Heinrich Himmler orders that a concentration camp be established at Auschwitz.

30 April: An article in the *Völkischer Beobachter* by ProMi film administrator Fritz Hippler describes at length how the war has activated German film culture, both in the Reich and in occupied countries. Many films now run for weeks in sold-out houses. German films are replacing American, French, and English films in foreign countries.

10 May: German troops march into Holland, Belgium, and Luxemburg without an official declaration of war.

June: Production and distribution of *Kulturfilme* are centralized under the auspices of the Deutsche Kulturfilm-Zentrale.

20 June: The first German cinema to screen newsreels around the clock opens in Berlin. Many such cinemas will open in subsequent months throughout the Reich.

22 June: France and Germany sign an armistice.

28 July: Goebbels' address at the Haus der deutschen Kunst is broadcast on the radio: "National Socialism as an idea and a world view encompasses the life of our people in its entirety and precisely in this total encompassing of life and the world, it has taken on the role of a system that marches on all fronts from one success to the next."

10 August: Goebbels calls on all German artists, especially actors and musicians, to put themselves at the disposal of the war effort. "Anyone who would shirk this responsibility is not worthy of living in this great historical moment and of being a part of its blessings."

13 August: The Battle of Britain begins with intensive German bomb raids on England.

14 August: MGM is ordered to close its German offices.

5 September: Producer, director, and president of the RFK Carl Froelich celebrates his sixty-fifth birthday. "In his many years of work as a creator of films, he has always maintained a high artistic level, which he was able to combine with his unquestioned mastery of the cinema's technical possibilities" (Goebbels).

20 September: *Film-Kurier* notes that the actor Rudolf Forster has returned from America and has signed on for future film projects with Ufa.

26 October: Lead headline in *Film-Kurier:* "The New Season Began with Remarkable Successes: The German People's Interest in Good Films Is Now Stronger than Ever." The domestic strength of national productions, claims the article, is a crucial factor in German cinema's position on the world market. Recent events make clear that German cinema "stands on the threshold of a great development whose consequences simply cannot be overlooked."

November: German newsreel companies become state-run under the Deutsche Wochenschau GmbH.

2 November: Goebbels receives prominent members of the film industry, promising them "extra payments for especially valuable and successful work." He screens *Gone with the Wind,* "which arouses general admiration. Rightly so," remarks Goebbels, "because it deserves it. But some doubtful opinions too."

9 November: Under Hitler's sponsorship, an exhibition titled "German Greatness," featuring scenes and representations from the highlights of German history, opens in Munich. Materials on display include paintings, documents,

maps, sculptures, and found objects. This exhibit accompanies the release and production of historical films such as *Der große König*, *Bismarck*, and *Ohm Krüger*.

11 November: *Film-Kurier* runs an article claiming that Walt Disney is a Spaniard, not an American; his real name is José Luis Guirao Zamora, born in Mojacar in 1901.

14 November: The propaganda minister calls for more humor in the mass media: "This is the best thing to see us through difficult times. We are taking everything so dreadfully seriously. It harms morale."

2 December: From Goebbels' diary: "Fiftieth Request Concert. A very big affair. I give a short speech. To great applause. Thanks to the radio and its people. General Dietl speaks. Short, folksy, and effective . . . A complete success. And the entire nation, at the front and in the homeland, is glued to its radios. I am very satisfied with this magnificent achievement."

9 December: Goebbels appeals to all studio heads, insisting on the importance of maintaining a high artistic quality of film production if Germany is to win the war. He calls on members of the German film industry to uphold strict discipline and to do everything possible so that all projects achieve maximal results.

12 December: Hitler signs a directive ordering an attack on the Soviet Union ("Operation Barbarossa"); preparations are to be completed by mid-May of 1941.

▪ ▪ ▪

1941 (71 German premieres)

Blutsbrüderschaft (P. L. Mayring, Terra, 3 January)*
Das Mädchen von Fanö (H. Schweikart, Bavaria, 24 January)
Alarm (H. B. Fredersdorf, Aco, 31 January)*
Am Abend auf der Heide (J. von Alten, Cine-Allianz, 11 February)
Mein Leben für Irland (M. W. Kimmich, Tobis, 17 February)*
Kampfgeschwader Lützow (H. Bertram, Tobis, 28 February)*
Kopf hoch, Johannes (V. de Kowa, Majestic, 11 March)*
Über alles in der Welt (K. Ritter, Ufa, 19 March)*
Carl Peters (H. Selpin, Bavaria, 21 March)*
Hauptsache, glücklich! (T. Lingen, Bavaria, 3 April)
Ohm Krüger (H. Steinhoff et al., Tobis, 4 April)*
Die schwedische Nachtigall (P. P. Brauer, Terra, 9 April)
. . . reitet für Deutschland (A. M. Rabenalt, Ufa, 11 April)*
Liebe ist zollfrei (E. W. Emo, Wien, 17 April)*
Auf Wiedersehen, Franziska! (H. Käutner, Terra, 24 June)*
Jungens (R. A. Stemmle, Ufa, 2 May)*

Der Weg ins Freie (R. Hansen, Tonfilmstudio Froelich for Ufa, 7 May)
U-Boote westwärts! (G. Rittau, Ufa, 9 May)*
Das leichte Mädchen (F. P. Buch, Witt-Film for Ufa, 27 May)
Venus vor Gericht (H. H. Zerlett, Bavaria, 4 June)*
Wir erinnern uns gern (W. Malbran, Tobis, 20 June)
Dreimal Hochzeit (G. von Bolvary, Wien, 24 June)*
Friedemann Bach (T. Müller, Terra, 25 June)
Stukas (K. Ritter, Ufa, 27 June)*
Pedro soll hängen (V. Harlan, Majestic, 11 July)*
Frau Luna (T. Lingen, Majestic/Müllereisen & Tapper, 22 July)
Aufruhr im Damenstift (F. D. Andam, Algefa, 29 July)
Der Gasmann (C. Froelich, Ufa, 1 August)*
Immer nur . . . Du! (K. Anton, Tobis, 22 August)
Ich klage an (W. Liebeneiner, Tobis, 29 August)*
Komödianten (G. W. Pabst, Bavaria, 5 September)
Clarissa (G. Lamprecht, Aco, 8 September)
Annelie (J. von Baky, Ufa, 9 September)*
Kameraden (H. Schweikart, Bavaria, 26 September)*
Sechs Tage Heimaturlaub (J. von Alten, Cine-Allianz, 3 October)*
Heimkehr (G. Ucicky, Wien, 10 October)*
Leichte Muse (A. M. Rabenalt, Terra, 10 October)
Jakko (F. P. Buch, Tobis, 12 October)*
Wetterleuchten um Barbara (W. Klingler, Randolf-Film, 17 October)*
Frauen sind doch bessere Diplomaten (G. Jacoby, Ufa, 31 October)
Was geschah in dieser Nacht? (T. Lingen, Majestic/Mülleneisen & Tapper, 31 October)
Das andere Ich (W. Liebeneiner, Tobis, 21 November)
Jenny und ihr Herr im Frack (P. Martin, Bavaria, 25 November)
Kadetten (K. Ritter, Ufa, 2 December)*
Quax, der Bruchpilot (K. Hoffmann, Terra, 16 December)*
Menschen im Sturm (F. P. Buch, Tobis, 19 December)*
Tanz mit dem Kaiser (G. Jacoby, Ufa, 19 December)
Alarmstufe V (A. J. Lippl, Bavaria, 22 December)*
Illusion (V. Tourjansky, Ufa, 30 December)

Banned:

Dreimal Hochzeit (G. von Bolvary, Wien, banned shortly after premiere, 24 June 1941)

The biggest hits of the 1940–41 season are *Wunschkonzert* (26.5 million tickets), *Frauen sind doch bessere Diplomaten* (24.7 million), and *Die Entlassung* (20 million). Seventy-eight percent of all Berlin households now have a radio.

3 January: After extensive location work, Leni Riefenstahl's production *Tiefland* moves to studio shooting.

11 January: An editorial by Wolfgang Liebeneiner in *Film-Kurier,* "Scripts Are in Reality Shooting Scripts," initiates a lively debate about the creative role of directors and screenwriters. Liebeneiner claims that scripts at best represent the raw material for a film production.

15 February: Goebbels speaks to the film industry: "Now that film has come into the possession of the Reich, we have essentially experienced the following change: whereas film used to be governed by majority shareholders, it now is governed by the national leadership."

21 March: Goebbels writes in his diary: "I plan to introduce a new rating for quality productions such as *Ohm Krüger.* Something like 'National Film.' Coupled with the award of an honorary ring for the main creators. This will engender even more ambition. German film is on the march." Only four other films will receive the recognition: *Heimkehr, Der große König, Die Entlassung,* and *Kolberg.*

29 March: The lead story in *Film-Kurier* speaks of "Women's Films in a Manly Era." Heroic times call for manly stories, claims the editorial. Still, that does not mean women are being neglected altogether: "Among 'women's films'—if we give them this name we do not want to suggest that they lack male spirit—*Heimkehr,* the new Wien Film distributed by Ufa, especially stands out. Its focal point is the fate of a German woman living abroad played by Paula Wessely."

3 April: The ProMi announces the creation of its highest distinction, "Film of the Nation," meant to recognize works "of especially great national, political, and artistic significance." A few days earlier Emil Jannings proclaims, "For a long time now I have felt that the classical era of the German national film is about to begin."

11 April: German war planes bomb Coventry.

May: By order of the Reich Press Chamber, 550 newspapers are closed down in Germany.

10 May: On a secret mission, Rudolf Hess flies to Scotland, where he is taken captive; in his absence, Martin Bormann becomes head of the party chancellery.

Summer: Widespread complaints in the Reich about fruit, vegetable, and bread shortages.

22 June: Operation Barbarossa brings the German invasion of the Soviet

Union. Special police units *(Einsatzgruppen)* follow the army troops, liquidating Communists, Jews, and gypsies.

31 July: Goering orders Heydrich to prepare a "comprehensive solution" of the Jewish question.

1 August: *Der Gasmann,* Carl Froelich's comedy starring Heinz Rühmann about a rebellious petit bourgeois, opens at the Gloria-Palast in Berlin.

11 August: The Atlantic Charter is signed by the United States and Great Britain.

29 August: The Tobis production *Ich klage an,* an apologia for euthanasia, opens at the Berlin Capitol am Zoo. It receives the rating "artistically especially worthwhile."

1 September: All Jewish citizens in Germany aged six years and older are now required to wear a yellow star.

2 September: Establishment of Berlin Film GmbH as a catchall company for the few remaining independent producers.

3 September: The first experimental gassings with Zyklon B take place at Auschwitz, where a concentration camp has been readied during the summer.

7 September: Paramount's German office is closed by government decree.

19 September: German troops take Kiev. The Battle for Moscow will begin several weeks later and last until December.

3 October: In a radio address, Hitler declares that the enemy "has already been broken."

12 October: In a public address, Goebbels celebrates German film's box-office success. "Art has the duty to render the highest service to the nation by developing its artistic character to the fullest. This has in fact happened here. In the last two years German film has taken an almost astonishing upturn. Last winter and summer our film theaters have been full to overflowing as never before. The German people are streaming in by the millions and, as with the German theater, seeking edification, instruction as well as enlightenment."

14 October: The mass deportation of Jews from the German Reich begins; they are relocated to ghettoes in Kovno, Lodz, Minsk, and Riga.

15 October: Walter Ruttmann, the director of modernist film experiments (*Berlin, die Sinfonie der Großstadt* and *Melodie der Welt*), dies in Berlin at age fifty-three.

16 October: *Film-Kurier* announces that *Ohm Krüger* has been awarded the Mussolini Cup for the best foreign film at the Venice Film Festival. Eight other German productions also have received major recognitions. The festival is seen as "a great success for German film."

31 October: Berlin premiere of Ufa's first color feature, Georg Jacoby's

Frauen sind doch bessere Diplomaten, starring Marika Rökk and Willy Fritsch. Subsequent German color features during the era are *Die goldene Stadt* (Ufa, 1942), *Das Bad auf der Tenne* (Tobis, 1943), *Münchhausen* (Ufa, 1943), *Immensee* (Ufa, 1943), *Opfergang* (Ufa, 1944), *Die Frau meiner Träume* (Ufa, 1944), *Große Freiheit Nr. 7* (Terra, 1944), and *Kolberg* (Ufa, 1945). *Die Fledermaus* (Terra), *Wiener Mädeln* (Wien-Film), and *Das kleine Hofkonzert* (Tobis) are completed after the war. *Ein toller Tag* (Ufa), *Wir beide liebten Katharina* (Terra), *Shiva und die Galgenblume* (Prag), and *Pole Poppenspäler* (Ufa) will remain fragments.

7 November: Joachim Gottschalk, a prominent actor, prevents the deportation of his Jewish wife and child by killing them and taking his own life. His suicide is not made known to the general public.

21 November: Establishment of Prag-Film AG.

5 December: The Soviets launch a massive counteroffensive.

7 December: Japanese bombing of Pearl Harbor. On the same day Hitler enacts the "Night and Fog" *(Nacht und Nebel)* decree by which those committing hostile acts against German occupation forces may be arrested and liquidated.

8 December: The United States and Great Britain declare war against Japan.

11 December: Germany and Italy declare war on the United States.

■ ■ ■

1942 (52 German premieres)

Zwei in einer großen Stadt (V. von Collande, Tobis, 23 January)*
Geheimakte WB 1 (H. Selpin, Bavaria, 26 January)*
Das heilige Ziel (K. Nomura/S. Ofuna, Cocco, 5 February)*
Viel Lärm um Nixi (E. Engel, Klagemann-Film, 19 February)
Himmelhunde (R. von Normann, Terra, 20 February)*
Der große König (V. Harlan, Tobis, 3 March)*
Schicksal (G. von Bolvary, Wien, 18 March)*
Zwischen Himmel und Erde (H. Braun, Ufa, 26 March)*
Anuschka (H. Käutner, Bavaria, 27 March)
Wiener Blut (W. Forst, Forst-Film for Wien, 2 April)
Der Fall Rainer (P. Verhoeven, Tobis, 12 May)*
Kleine Residenz (H. H. Zerlett, Bavaria, 28 May)
Hochzeit auf Bärenhof (C. Froelich, Ufa, 8 June)*
Die große Liebe (R. Hansen, Ufa, 12 June)*
Rembrandt (H. Steinhoff, Terra, 17 June)
Vom Schicksal verweht (N. Malasomma, FDF, 24 July)
GPU (K. Ritter, Ufa, 14 August)*
Anschlag auf Baku (F. Kirchhoff, Ufa, 25 August)*

Fronttheater (A. M. Rabenalt, Terra, 24 September)*
Der große Schatten (P. Verhoeven, Tobis, 25 September)
Die Entlassung (W. Liebeneiner, Tobis, 6 October)*
Wir machen Musik (H. Käutner, Terra, 8 October)
Hände hoch! (A. Weidenmann, Deutsche Filmherstellungs- und Verwertungs-GmbH, 25 October)*
Stimme des Herzens (J. Meyer, Berlin, 27 October)
Geliebte Welt (E. Burri, Bavaria, 30 October)
Mit den Augen einer Frau (K. G. Külb, Aco, 30 October)
Dr. Crippen an Bord (E. Engels, Terra, 6 November)
Einmal der liebe Herrgott sein (H. H. Zerlett, Bavaria, 10 November)
Diesel (G. Lamprecht, Ufa, 13 November)
Andreas Schlüter (H. Maisch, Terra, 19 November)
Meine Freundin Josefine (H. H. Zerlett, Tobis, 20 November)
Die goldene Stadt (V. Harlan, Ufa, 24 November)*
Sommerliebe (E. Engel, Wien, 26 November)
Wen die Götter lieben (K. Hartl, Wien, 5 December)
Hab mich lieb (H. Braun, Ufa, 8 December)

Banned:

Der 5. Juni (F. Kirchhoff, Ufa, November 1942)*
Die See ruft (H. F. Köllner, Propagandaamt der Deutschen Arbeitsfront, November 1942)

Box-office hits of 1942 are *Die große Liebe, Die goldene Stadt, Wiener Blut, Der große König,* and *Die Entlassung.* German audiences throughout the Reich now attend the movies on the average of fourteen times a year. The German Reich has 6,537 cinemas with 2.6 million seats; 8 theaters have capacities of more than 2,000. Berlin has 400 screens, Vienna 221. Ufa has gone from 97 cinemas (with 106,302 seats) in 47 cities in 1933 to a 1939 figure of 130 cinemas (with 148,371 seats) in 56 cities to a 1942 figure of 159 cinemas (162,171 seats) in 69 cities. Ufa's largest houses are in Berlin: Ufa-Palast am Zoo (2,314 seats), Capitol am Zoo (1,279), Gloria-Palast (1,197), Tauentzien-Palast (1,052), and Marmorhaus (600).

2 January: All film distribution now comes under the central authority of the Deutsche Filmvertriebs GmbH (DFV). Smaller private firms may offer only previously released titles or foreign films. The first season's release schedule

includes 60 features (Ufa 12, Tobis 12, Terra 11, Bavaria 8, Berlin 8, Wien 6, Prag 3), 12 foreign films, and 72 *Kulturfilme.*

10 January: The establishment of the Ufa-Film GmbH brings together the six major film studios (the old Ufa, Tobis, Terra, Bavaria, Wien-Film, Berlin-Film). To avoid confusion with the old Ufa, one refers to this new body as "Ufi." All copy works also became state-controlled agencies.

17 January: The old Ufa studio now becomes Ufa-Filmkunst GmbH.

20 January: The "final solution" *(Endlösung)* regarding the fate of European Jewry is decided at the Wannsee Conference, a meeting convened by RSHA head Heydrich and attended by chief officials of the most important ministries.

February: Deportations of Jews to the death camps begin.

February 28: Goebbels speaks in Berlin, announcing measures to streamline German production and to enable an increased number of feature films:

- All German production companies are to be centralized under the firm Ufa-Film GmbH (later called Ufi). It will combine production, economic, and technical concerns.
- Ufa-Film GmbH will bring together Bavaria, Berlin-Film, Prag-Film, Terra-Filmkunst, Tobis-Filmkunst, Ufa-Filmkunst, Wien-Film, and Deutsche Zeichenfilm GmbH.
- The new position of *Reichsfilmintendant* is to be assumed by Fritz Hippler.
- Wartime feature productions are in the main to be entertainment films (80 percent). Costs are to be cut wherever possible. With few exceptions, budgets are not to exceed one million RM.
- Studios are to create stable communities of artists to allow for greater continuity and efficiency in production.

1 March: Goebbels writes in his diary: "Even entertainment can be politically of special value, because the moment a person is conscious of propaganda, propaganda becomes ineffective. However, when propaganda as a tendency, as a characteristic, as an attitude remains in the background and becomes apparent through human beings, then propaganda becomes effective in every respect."

16 April: Herbert Selpin and W. Zerlett-Olfenius publish two ironic and polemic letters in *Film-Kurier,* intervening in a debate about whether German actors playing the roles of foreigners should speak German or, when appropriate, the native language. They sign their contribution, "With Massive Arrogance" ("in massiver Überheblichkeit").

26 April: The Reichstag recognizes Hitler as the "supreme judicial authority."

30–31 May: Major RAF bomb attack on Cologne.

1 June: Under the direction of Wilhelm Furtwängler, the Berlin Philharmonie gives concerts in Switzerland.

2 June: Deportation of German Jews to Theresienstadt begins.

23 June: At Auschwitz the systematic gassing of Jewish prisoners commences.

30 June: Müller Verlag in Dresden publishes Heinz Halter's account of corruption in America, *Der Polyp von New York.*

4 July: In Munich the Sixth German Art Exhibition opens; 690 artists present 1,213 works.

25 July: In honor of Gerhart Hauptmann's eightieth birthday, Suhrkamp Verlag announces an eighteen-volume edition of his work (price: 185 RM).

1 August: The director Herbert Selpin takes his life in a Berlin prison cell after being arrested for disparaging remarks about the German army.

29 August: Over 400,000 admissions have been registered at the Berlin Ufa-Palast am Zoo since the opening of *Die große Liebe* on June 12; this is an all-time record.

30 August: The Venice Film Festival begins; six films represent Germany: *Der große König, Wiener Blut, Die große Liebe, Die goldene Stadt, Andreas Schlüter,* and *Der große Schatten. Der große König* will receive the Mussolini Cup for the best foreign film.

5 September: German troops enter Stalingrad.

9 September: Countermanding the ProMi's recommendation, Hitler denies Zarah Leander recognition as an Actress of the State *(Staatsschauspielerin).*

11 September: The 1937 film *Der zerbrochene Krug* is rereleased and shown at the Ufa-Palast am Zoo. On this occasion Emil Jannings delivers a public address titled "Film and Theater Are Two Different Things."

October: The ProMi orders the press to ignore Lilian Harvey's expatriation. Harvey had already left Germany in 1939.

November: Himmler declares that all the Reich's concentration camps must become "free of Jews" *(judenrein).*

11–12 November: German troops occupy Vichy France.

19 November: Soviet counteroffensive at Stalingrad begins; within four days the German Sixth Army is surrounded and trapped by Stalin's troops.

16 December: Goebbels' journal describes a discussion with Leni Riefenstahl about her film-in-progress, *Tiefland:* "It has become involved in innumerable complications. Already more than five million RM have been wasted on this film, and it will take another whole year before it is finished. Frau Riefenstahl has become very ill from overwork and worry, and I urged her earnestly to go on leave before resuming work. I am glad I have nothing to do with the unfortunate case and hence bear no responsibility."

23 December: The German press informs citizens: "When the time comes, be sure to darken carefully! Save energy during the day and let the daylight in!"

▪ ▪ ▪

1943 (74 German premieres)

Maske in Blau (P. Martin, NFK, 15 January)
Der dunkle Tag (G. von Bolvary, Bavaria, 10 February)
Späte Liebe (G. Ucicky, Wien, 16 February)
Sophienlund (H. Rühmann, Terra, 26 February)
Damals (R. Hansen, Ufa, 2 March)
Du gehörst zu mir (G. Lamprecht, Ufa, 2 March)
Liebesgeschichten (V. Tourjansky, Ufa, 3 March)*
Nacht ohne Abschied (E. Waschneck, Ufa, 4 March)*
Münchhausen (J. von Baky, Ufa, 5 March)
Paracelsus (G. W. Pabst, Bavaria, 12 March)
Kohlhiesels Töchter (K. Hoffmann, Tobis, 18 March)
Gefährtin eines Sommers (F. P. Buch, Berlin, 22 March)
Frauen sind keine Engel (W. Forst, Wien, 23 March)
Karneval der Liebe (P. Martin, Berlin, 1 April)
Altes Herz wird wieder jung (E. Engel, Tobis, 2 April)
Ich vertraue Dir meine Frau an (K. Hoffmann, Terra, 2 April)
Symphonie eines Lebens (H. Bertram, Tobis, 21 April)
Das Ferienkind (K. Leiter, Wien, 22 April)*
Der kleine Grenzverkehr (H. Deppe, Ufa, 22 April)*
Germanin (M. W. Kimmich, Ufa, 15 May)*
Liebespremiere (A. M. Rabenalt, Terra, 11 June)
Romanze in Moll (H. Käutner, Tobis, 25 June)
Der zweite Schuß (M. Fritsch, Prag, 2 July)*
Tonelli (V. Tourjansky, Bavaria, 12 July)
Das Bad auf der Tenne (V. von Collande, Tobis, 30 July)
Der unendliche Weg (H. Schweikart, Bavaria, 24 August)
Wien 1910 (E. W. Emo, Wien, 26 August)*
Die Gattin (G. Jacoby, Ufa, 31 August)
Zirkus Renz (A. M. Rabenalt, Terra, 10 September)
Man rede mir nicht von Liebe (E. Engel, Bavaria, 17 September)
Großstadtmelodie (W. Liebeneiner, Berlin, 4 October)*
Der weiße Traum (G. von Cziffra/K. Hartl, Wien, 5 October)
Ich werde Dich auf Händen tragen (K. Hoffmann, Tobis, 19 October)
Reise in die Vergangenheit (H. H. Zerlett, Bavaria, 5 November)

Gabriele Dambrone (H. Steinhoff, Terra, 11 November)
Ein Mann mit Grundsätzen? (G. von Bolvary, Terra, 11 November)
Akrobat schö-ö-ö-n (W. Staudte, Tobis, 1 December)
Johann (R. A. Stemmle, Bavaria, 3 December)
Immensee (V. Harlan, Ufa, 17 December)
Wildvogel (J. Meyer, Berlin, 21 December)*
Die goldene Spinne (E. Engels, Terra, 23 December)*

Banned:

Titanic (H. Selpin/W. Klingler, Tobis, premiered in Paris, 10 November; banned in Germany, 9 November 1944 or earlier)*
Alles aus Liebe (H. Marischka, Aco, banned October 1943, premiered 17 February 1950)
Panik (H. Piel, FDF, banned October 1943, premiered 16 October 1953 as *Gesprengte Gitter*)
Besatzung Dora (K. Ritter, Ufa, banned in early November 1943; ban confirmed, 9 November 1944; presented in a closed screening to members of the Luftwaffe, 2 February 1945)*
Am Ende der Welt (G. Ucicky, Wien, first banned December 1943, banned again in mid-1944, premiered 4 July 1947)

The most successful films of the year are *Immensee, Das Bad auf der Tenne, Gabriele Dambrone, Tonelli,* and *Zirkus Renz.* The average production cost for a feature film now runs 1,161,600 RM. Fifty-three directors make features during the year. In cities and communities with local cinemas, Germans attend the movies on the average of twenty times a year (as opposed to twelve times in 1939); in Vienna, the average is more than thirty times a year (as opposed to fifteen times in 1933). During the 1942–43 season, there are approximately 45,300 Hitler Youth Film Hours, which attract 11 million viewers.

14–25 January: At the Casablanca Conference, Churchill and Roosevelt demand "unconditional surrender."

31 January–2 February: Surrender of the Sixth Army under General von Paulus at Stalingrad.

16 February: The German press complains about an alarming rise of public requests for autographs from film stars. These requests clog the mail; they also overwhelm artists, who should be devoting their energies to answering fan letters from soldiers on the front.

18 February: In a rousing speech at the Berlin Sportpalast, Goebbels calls for

"total war," "more total, more radical, than we could ever have imagined." According to Albert Speer, "Except for Hitler's most powerful public meetings, I had never seen an audience so effectively roused to fanaticism. Back in his home, Goebbels astonished me by analyzing what had seemed to be a purely emotional outburst in terms of its psychological effects—much as an experienced actor might have done. He was also satisfied with his audience that evening. 'Did you notice? They reacted to the smallest nuance and applauded at just the right moments. It was the politically best-trained audience you can find in Germany.' "

22 February: Hans and Sophie Scholl, prominent members of the "White Rose" resistance group, are executed.

3 March: Festive celebration of Ufa's twenty-fifth anniversary and premiere of *Münchhausen* at the Ufa-Palast am Zoo. Dr. Ludwig Klitzsch, executive director of Ufa, speaks about the history of the studio, describing the struggle against Jewish-American attempts to control the film industry during the Weimar era. Goebbels announces a number of awards, including an Eagle Shield to Alfred Hugenberg and honorary professorships to Veit Harlan and Wolfgang Liebeneiner. Later Goebbels visits Carl Froelich and various prominent figures from Ufa.

4 March: A Security Service of the SS report observes that "newsreels have been unable to regain their former popularity. It has been confirmed from wide sections of the population that people no longer want to go to the cinema just to see the newsreel. It is only seldom now that people make spontaneous comments about newsreels."

11 March: Goebbels notes in his diary: "The English papers make no bones about admitting that German propaganda constitutes a truly inspired force liable to cause great confusion in England and the U.S.A."

13 March: The military resistance movement makes an unsuccessful attempt on Hitler's life in Berlin; another attempt will take place on March 21.

April: Wolfgang Liebeneiner becomes production head of Ufa-Filmkunst GmbH.

20 April: Jews are massacred in the Warsaw ghetto.

8 May: Goebbels writes in his diary: "We naturally cannot accept questions of right and wrong even as a basis of discussion. The loss of this war would constitute the greatest wrong to the German people, victory would give us the greatest right. After all, only the victor will have the possibility of proving to the world the moral justification for his struggle."

13 May: Surrender of German and Italian troops in Tunisia.

15 May: "A lot of criticism is contained in the letters reaching us," writes Goebbels. "Morale among the masses is so low as to be rather serious. Even

people of goodwill are now worried about further developments. The man in the street no longer sees any way out of the military dilemma. As a result there is criticism of the leaders, in some cases even of the Führer himself."

19 May: Berlin is declared "free of Jews."

24–30 July: Massive Allied air attacks on Hamburg ("Operation Gomhorrah") with casualties of more than 30,000 civilians and vast destruction.

28 July: Italian radio announces the end of Fascism. Mussolini is arrested.

August: An inhouse Ufa communiqué provides studio employees with guidelines for behavior after air raids. "What am I to do if my workplace should be destroyed?" the memo asks. The first of ten points elaborates: "If it becomes apparent that my place of employment has been destroyed by a bomb attack, I will nevertheless try to get to work; I will not give up until it is clear that there is no way to get through." The final point reads: "In total war my service at work is as important as the service on the front of comrades in uniform, my war service is the workplace. This dare not remain unoccupied, and for that reason I will take no independent actions before checking with my superiors."

1 August: So far Allied bombings have destroyed 237 of the Reich's cinemas.

6 August: Goebbels calls for the partial evacuation of Berlin's citizenry.

2 September: Albert Speer creates a centralized Ministry for Armaments and War Production.

11 September: The German people, reflects Goebbels, "are waiting for a speech by the Führer. Everybody realizes that a totalitarian decision must be made. Nobody doubts any longer that this is a war to be or not to be. The Eastern Front is causing the German people considerably greater worry now than in past weeks. The state of depression because of air raids has increased as a result of the most recent heavy attacks."

24 November: Goebbels drives through a Berlin devastated by heavy bomb raids: "The whole Tiergarten quarter is destroyed, likewise the section around the Zoo . . . How beautiful Berlin was at one time and how run-down and woebegone it now looks!"

28 November–1 December: At the Tehran Conference, Roosevelt, Stalin, and Churchill deliberate about war strategy and consider Germany's future.

7 December: German entrepreneuer, inventor, and film pioneer Oskar Messter dies at age seventy-seven in Berlin.

31 December: 6,561 of Germany's cinemas remain in operation.

■ ■ ■

1944 (62 German premieres)

Ein schöner Tag (P. L. Mayring, Tobis, 27 January)*

Die Feuerzangenbowle (H. Weiss, Terra, 28 January)
In flagranti (H. Schweikart, Bavaria, 31 January)
Herr Sanders lebt gefährlich (R. A. Stemmle, Tobis, 14 February)
Nora (H. Braun, Ufa, 14 February)
Familie Buchholz (C. Froelich, Ufa, 3 March)
Schrammeln (G. von Bolvary, Wien, 3 March)
Neigungsehe (C. Froelich, Ufa, 24 March)
Der Verteidiger hat das Wort (W. Klingler, Tobis, 6 April)
Eine Frau für 3 Tage (F. Kirchhoff, Ufa, 28 April)
Träumerei (H. Braun, Ufa, 3 May)
Ich brauche Dich (H. Schweikart, Bavaria, 12 May)
Der große Preis (K. Anton, Tobis, 19 May)*
Es lebe die Liebe (E. Engel, Bavaria, 24 May)
Junge Adler (A. Weidenmann, Ufa, 24 May)*
Der Täter ist unter uns (H. B. Fredersdorf, Bavaria, 27 May)
Sommernächte (K. Ritter, Ufa, 26 June)
Die Degenhardts (W. Klingler, Tobis, 6 July)
Der gebieterische Ruf (G. Ucicky, Wien, 11 July)
Die Affäre Roedern (E. Waschneck, Berlin, 14 July)*
Ich hab' von Dir geträumt (W. Staudte, Tobis, 21 July)
Die Frau meiner Träume (G. Jacoby, Ufa, 25 August)
Die schwarze Robe (F. P. Buch, Berlin, 4 September)*
Musik in Salzburg (H. Maisch, Terra, 8 September)
Ein Blick zurück (G. Menzel, Wien, 1 December)
Orient-Express (V. Tourjansky, Bavaria, 1 December)
Philharmoniker (P. Verhoeven, Tobis, 4 December)
Opfergang (V. Harlan, Ufa, 8 December)*
Große Freiheit Nr. 7 (H. Käutner, Terra, 15 December in Prague; not shown in Germany until 6 September 1945)
Das Herz muß schweigen (G. Ucicky, Wien, 19 December)
Das Leben ruft (A. M. Rabenalt, Terra, 20 December)*
Der grüne Salon (B. Barlog, Terra, 27 December)

Finished but unreleased features (14):

Die heimlichen Bräute (J. Meyer, Berlin, shelved 10 August 1944, banned November 1944)
Eine kleine Sommermelodie (V. von Collande, Tobis, shelved 10 August 1944)*

Erzieherin gesucht (U. Erfurth, Ufa, shelved 10 August 1944, banned January 1945, premiered 29 October 1950)

Jan und die Schwindlerin (H. Weissbach, Ufa, shelved 10 August 1944, premiered 4 March 1947)

Jugendliebe (E. von Borsody, Tobis, banned October 1944, premiered 27 February 1947 as *Über's Jahr, wenn die Kornblumen blühen*)

Der verzauberte Tag (P. Pewas, Terra, banned October 1944; premiered in Zürich, September 1947)

Moselfahrt mit Monika (R. von Norman, Terra, banned October 1944, shelved 4 April 1945, premiered 19 August 1952)

Freunde (E. W. Emo, Wien, banned November 1944, premiered 25 July 1950)

Schuß um Mitternacht (H. H. Zerlett, Bavaria, approved 10 November 1944, premiered 28 April 1950)

Melusine (H. Steinhoff, Terra, banned December 1944, shelved 4 April 1945)

Intimitäten (P. Martin, Berlin, banned December 1944, premiered 3 February 1948)

Am Abend nach der Oper (A. M. Rabenalt, Terra, approved 21 December 1944, premiered 31 August 1945)

Freitag, der 13. (E. Engels, Terra, passed the censor December 1944, premiered 9 November 1949)

Zwischen Nacht und Morgen/Augen der Liebe (A. Braun, Terra, passed the censor December 1944, premiered 26 October 1951)

The most successful films of the season are *Der weiße Traum, Die Frau meiner Träume, Die Feuerzangenbowle,* and *Die Affäre Roedern.*

March: SS Group Leader Hans Hinkel succeeds Fritz Hippler as *Reichsfilmintendant.* Goebbels had discharged Hippler in March 1943 after differences of opinion.

31 March: 6,517 cinemas continue to show movies in Germany.

19 April: At a concert on the eve of Hitler's birthday, Goebbels offers best wishes: "We want to assure him that he is able to rely on his people absolutely in this great struggle, that he is as he always was, our Führer!"

6 June: Allied troops storm the beaches of Normandy.

1 July: Renowned screenwriter Carl Mayer dies at age fifty in London.

20 July: Unsuccessful attempt on Hitler's life at his headquarters in Rastenburg, East Prussia, by Colonel Claus von Stauffenberg; abortive coup attempts in Paris and Berlin.

1 September: The Warsaw Uprising begins.

All theaters, operas, night clubs, and cabarets are closed throughout the Reich; film and radio remain the major vehicles of diversion and entertainment.

8 September: Germany fires V-2 rockets on England.

11 September: U.S. troops reach the German border.

3 October: The Warsaw Uprising is crushed.

18 October: An order by Hitler is made public which calls on all able-bodied men from age sixteen to sixty, regardless of class or occupation, to serve in the militia *(Volkssturm)*.

21 October: Allied troops capture Aachen.

Late October: "In recognition of the gravity and status of our times," the ProMi orders the rerelease of "films of soldierly and national import." The list includes thirty-nine titles, most of them *Staatsfilme* made after the outbreak of war; only eleven of the films are from 1933–1939.

November: A newsreel (Deutsche Wochenschau) shows Himmler proclaiming Hitler's decree regarding the formation of a *Volkssturm*.

13 November: A confidential government report names the most successful films of the Third Reich. The top ten titles are *Die goldene Stadt* (12.5 million RM box office, 31 million admissions in domestic screenings), *Der weiße Traum, Immensee, Die große Liebe, Wiener Blut, Wunschkonzert, Schrammeln, Zirkus Renz, Die Frau meiner Träume,* and *Münchhausen.*

27 November: Himmler ceases the gassing at Auschwitz and orders that the crematoria be destroyed.

16–24 December: The Battle of the Bulge begins; the Germans wage the Ardennes offensive.

■ ■ ■

1945 (12 German premieres)

Solistin Anna Alt (W. Klingler, Tobis, 22 January)
Kolberg (V. Harlan, Ufa, 30 January)*
Bravo, kleiner Thomas (J. Fethke, Bavaria, ? February)
Die Jahre vergehen (G. Rittau, Tobis, 6 February)
Meine Herren Söhne (R. A. Stemmle, Tobis, 20 February)
Die Brüder Noltenius (G. Lamprecht, Ufa, 23 February)
Eines Tages (F. Kirchhoff, Berlin, 26 February)
Der stumme Gast (H. Braun, Ufa, ? March)
Die falsche Braut (J. Stöckel, Bavaria, 3 March)
Ein Mann wie Maximilian (H. Deppe, Bavaria, 13 March)
Das alte Lied (F. P. Buch, Berlin, 30 March)
Der Erbförster (A. J. Lippl, Tobis, ? April)

Finished productions not released before May 1945 (18):

Spuk im Schloß (H. H. Zerlett, Bavaria, 20 February 1947)
Via Mala (J. von Baky, Ufa, shelved 19 March 1945, premiered 16 January 1948)
Mit meinen Augen (H. H. Zerlett, Bavaria, 27 February 1948)
Fahrt ins Glück (E. Engel, Ufa, 6 August 1948)
Frech und verliebt (H. Schweikart, Bavaria, 25 December 1948)
Münchnerinnen (P. L. Mayring, Bavaria, 10 February 1949)
Wie sagen wir es unseren Kindern? (H. Deppe, Ufa, 21 December 1949)
Der Posaunist (C. Boese, Ufa, 23 December 1949)
Das Gesetz der Liebe (H. Schweikart, Bavaria, 30 December 1949)
Vier Treppen rechts (K. Werther, Ufa, 21 July 1950)
Regimentsmusik (A. M. Rabenalt, Bavaria, 1 September 1950)*
Unter den Brücken (H. Käutner, Ufa, passed the censor March 1945, premiered September 1946 in Locarno and 15 May 1950 in Göttingen)
Liebe nach Noten (G. von Cziffra, Wien, 13 October 1950)
Erzieherin gesucht (U. Erfurth, Ufa, 29 October 1950)
Das fremde Leben (J. Meyer, Berlin, 16 March 1951)
Umwege zu Dir (H. Thimig, Wien, 15 June 1951)
Quax in Fahrt/Quax in Afrika (H. Weiss, Terra, 22 May 1953)*
Wir seh'n uns wieder (P. L. Mayring, Tobis, never shown)*

Works still in progress before May 1945, finished/released after May 1945 (*Uberläufer*) (27):

Peter Voß, der Millionendieb (K. Anton, Tobis, 27 September 1946)
Monte miracolo/Im Banne des Monte Miracolo (L. Trenker, Tirol-Film, 19 November 1948)
Die Nacht der Zwölf (H. Schweikart, Bavaria, 7 January 1949)
Dreimal Komödie (V. Tourjansky, Bavaria, 4 March 1949)
Wiener Mädeln (W. Forst, Forst-Film for Wien, 19 August 1949)
Ich glaube an Dich (R. Hansen, Berlin-Film, premiered 9 June 1950 as *Mathilde Möhring*, aka *Mein Herz gehört Dir*)
Frau über Bord (W. Staudte, Tobis, premiered 16 May 1952 as *Das Mädchen Juanita*)
Tiefland (L. Riefenstahl, Riefenstahl-Film der Tobis, 11 February 1954)
Ein toller Tag (O. F. Schuh, Ufa, 27 September 1954)
Der Puppenspieler (V. Harlan, Ufa, unfinished)

Unfinished productions (22).

12 January: In a confidential document, the ProMi lists the biggest box-office flops of recent years; these include *Wien 1910*, *Die Degenhardts*, *Paracelsus*, *Junge Adler*, and *Romanze in Moll*.

27 January: Soviet troops liberate Auschwitz.

30 January: Vice Admiral Schirlitz speaks on German radio: "The premiere of the color film *Kolberg* took place in La Rochelle before soldiers of all units in our defense corps. Deeply moved by the artistic presentation of the Kolberg fortress's heroic actions, we add our gratitude for the dispatch of the film on 30 January and pledge that we will emulate the courageous struggle at home." On the same day Hitler speaks for the last time on the radio, urging Germans to hold out to the bitter end.

4–11 February: The Yalta Conference.

5 February: Goebbels declares: "The great hour has arrived for German propaganda."

12 February: Women are drafted into war as auxiliaries to the *Volkssturm*.

13–14 February: Fire bombings of Dresden by Allied aircraft.

March: The second-to-last German weekly newsreel shows Goebbels addressing a mass rally at Görlitz: "As the Führer has achieved victories in the past, so he will in the future. Of this I am firmly convinced. Only the other day he said to me: 'I believe so much that we will overcome this crisis. By placing our forces on to new offenses, we will beat the enemy and push him back. And I believe as I have never believed in anything that one day we will raise our flags in victory.' "

19 March: Hitler issues his "Scorched Earth" command, ordering that all industry potentially useful to the enemy be destroyed.

23 March: Goebbels acknowledges public expressions of "profound apathy and resignation. All refer quite openly to the leadership crisis . . . Even the Führer is now more frequently referred to in critical terms. I get off somewhat lightly in the letters I receive but that must not be overestimated . . . I think that my work too is no longer totally effective today. A fateful development seems to me to be that now neither the Führer himself nor the National Socialist concept nor the National Socialist movement is immune from criticism."

27 March: The last film document of Hitler made during the Third Reich, Deutsche Wochenschau No. 755/10, shows him awarding Iron Crosses to young boys in front of the Reich Chancellery.

12 April: Roosevelt dies and is succeeded by Harry Truman.

17 April: Goebbels attempts to rouse his staff after a special screening of *Kolberg:* "Gentlemen, in a hundred years' time, they will be showing another

fine color film describing the terrible days we are undergoing now. Don't you want to play a part in this film, to be brought back to life in a hundred years' time? Every one of you has the chance to choose the role that he will play in the film a hundred years from now. I can assure you it will be a tremendous film, exciting and beautiful, and worth holding steady for a fine and an elevating picture. Hold out now, so that a hundred years from now the audience does not hoot and whistle when you appear on the screen."

18 April: As British troops march into the Lüneburger Heide, Wolfgang Liebeneiner stops production work on the wartime epic *Das Leben geht weiter.*

20 April: Soviet troops reach Berlin. Hans Steinhoff, director of *Hitlerjunge Quex,* dies in a plane crash at sixty-three.

24 April: The Ufa studio grounds in Babelsberg are occupied by Red Army troops.

25 April: Soviet and American troops meet on the Elbe.

28 April: Italian partisans kill Mussolini.

29 April: American troops liberate the concentration camp at Dachau.

30 April: Hitler, together with Eva Braun, commits suicide in the bunker of the Reich Chancellery. He is replaced by Admiral Dönitz.

1 May: German radio broadcasts news of Hitler's death: "It is reported from the Führer's Headquarters that this afternoon our Führer Adolf Hitler fell in his command post in the Reich Chancellery, fighting with his last breath for Germany against Bolshevism." On the same day Goebbels kills his children and wife before committing suicide.

2 May: Surrender of Berlin to Allied occupiers.

8 May: Unconditional surrender of Germany and end of war in Europe ("V-E Day").

20 September: The Allies legally confiscate the holdings of Ufi.

28 September: Allied forces in a quadripartite meeting determine guidelines for postwar censorship of German films. German films may not be screened in German cinemas

> which:
>
> (1) Glorify ideology of Fascism, Nazism or racial distinction.
>
> (2) Glorify or idealise war or militarism.
>
> (3) Politically subvert or pervert German history.
>
> (4) Glorify or idealise the German Army.
>
> (5) Ridicule, or seem derogatory or uncomplimentary of, Allied peoples, their governments, their political or national leaders.
>
> (6) Deal with German revenge.

(7) Ridicule or criticise the religious feelings and religious attitudes of others.

(8) Glorify or idealise the thoughts and/or acts of German leaders whose opinions or actions or political philosophy was imperialistic at the expense of the Allies.

(9) Originate in a book or script of a known Nazi Party member or supporter.

(10) Originate through the creative efforts of known Nazi Party members or proven active supporters. Those whose creative efforts contribute to the making of a picture shall be: producer, director, production chief, author, scenario writer, actors and actresses, composer, musical score adapter and film editor.

It was agreed upon that point (10) above should, however, be applied with reasonable elasticity.

The Allies initially ban 700 films. During the postwar years German self-censorship authorities (the Freiwillige Selbstkontrolle, founded in July 1949) assume responsibility for the removal of individual films from the proscribed list and their commercial rerelease, responding to the requests of petitioners. Some titles are taken off without conditions, others only if offensive or questionable passages are deleted. In June 1953, 340 German films from 1930–1945, including some documentaries and short subjects, appear on an updated inventory. By January 1954, 275 films remain on the list; by August 1977 there are 176. As of mid-1995, between 30 and 35 feature films *(Vorbehaltsfilme)* from the Third Reich are still barred to the German public, available only for special screenings and closed seminars. This figure, however, is misleading; some titles remain on the list only because rightholders, for whatever reasons, have not petitioned for the release of films.

APPENDIX B

Directorial Filmographies

Films are listed in order of their first public showings. Information has been consulted and cross-checked in the following sources: Gerd Albrecht, *Nationalsozialistische Filmpolitik* (Stuttgart: Enke, 1969); Christa Bandmann and Joe Hembus, *Klassiker des deutschen Tonfilms 1930–1960* (Munich: Goldmann, 1980); Alfred Bauer, *Deutscher Spielfilm Almanach 1929–1950*, rev. enl. ed. (Munich: Winterberg, 1976); Hans-Michael Bock, ed., *CineGraph. Lexikon zum deutschprachigen Film* (Munich: edition text + kritik, 1984–); Felix Bucher and Leonhard H. Gmür, *Screen Series: Germany* (London/New York: Zwemmer/Barnes, 1970); Bogusław Drewniak, *Der deutsche Film 1938–1945. Ein Gesamtüberblick* (Düsseldorf: Droste, 1987); Herbert Holba, Günter Knorr, and Peter Spiegel, *Reclams deutsches Filmlexikon* (Stuttgart: Reclam, 1984); Klaus Kanzog, *"Staatspolitisch besonders wertvoll." Ein Handbuch zu 30 deutschen Spielfilmen der Jahre 1934 bis 1945* (Munich: Schaudig und Ledig, 1994); Ulrich J. Klaus, *Deutsche Tonfilme 4. Jahrgang 1933* (Berlin/Berchtesgarden: Klaus, 1992) and *Deutsche Tonfilme 5. Jahrgang 1934* (Berlin/Berchtesgarden: Klaus, 1993); Hans-Peter Kochenrath, ed., *Der Film im Dritten Reich. Dokumentation zu dem Seminar im SS 1963* (Cologne: Universität zu Köln, 1963); and Karlheinz Wendtland, *Geliebter Kintopp. Sämtliche deutsche Spielfilme von 1929–1945*, 10 vols. (Berlin: Wendtland, 1987–1991).

The following film ratings were used in the Third Reich as of:

30 Jan. 1933						kü		vb	kuw		
7 June 1933		bw			sw	kü		vb	kuw		
16 Feb. 1934		bw			sw	kü		vb	kuw		
5 Nov. 1934	skbw				sw		küw	vb	kuw		
1 April 1939	skbw		sbw	kbw	sw		küw	vb	kuw	vw	
1 Sept. 1942			sbw	kbw	sw		küw	vb	kuw	vw	aw

aw *anerkennenswert* (commendable)
bw *besonders wertvoll* (especially worthwhile)

jw *jugendwert* (worthwhile for young audiences, as of 21 November 1938)
kbw *künstlerisch besonders wertvoll* (artistically especially worthwhile)
kuw *kulturell wertvoll* (culturally worthwhile)
kü *künstlerisch* (artistic)
küw *künstlerisch wertvoll* (artistically worthwhile; replaced "artistic")
sbw *staatspolitisch besonders wertvoll* (politically especially worthwhile)
skbw *staatspolitisch und künstlerisch besonders wertvoll* (politically and artistically especially worthwhile)
sw *staatspolitisch wertvoll* (politically worthwhile)
vb *volksbildend* (educational)
vw *volkstümlich wertvoll* (nationally worthwhile)

In addition, two film prizes were established: the Staatspreis für Film (State Film Prize, SP) in 1933, and the Film der Nation (Film of the Nation, FN) in 1941.

Josef von Baky (1902–1966)

1936: *Intermezzo*
1938: *Die kleine und die große Liebe* (codir. with Ulrich Bettac)
Die Frau am Scheidewege
1939: *Menschen vom Varieté/A varieté csillagai*
Ihr erstes Erlebnis (küw)
1940: *Der Kleinstadtpoet*
1941: *Annelie* (skbw, vw)
1943: *Münchhausen* (color) (kbw, vw)
1944: *Via Mala* (banned in Germany, 1945; premiered in 1948)

Géza von Bolvary (1897–1961)

1933: *Was Frauen träumen*
Die Nacht der großen Liebe
Skandal in Budapest (codir. with Istvan Székely)
Das Schloß im Süden/Château de rêve (French version codir. with Henri-Georges Clouzot)
Mindent a nöért (sequence in Hungarian episode film with Géza von Cziffra and B. Gaál)
1934: *Ich kenn' Dich nicht und liebe Dich/Toi, que j'adore* (French version codir. with Albert Valentin)
Abschiedswalzer/La chanson de l'adieu (French version codir. with Albert Valentin)

1935: *Frühjahrsparade/Tavoszi parádé* (codir. with Erwin Wratschko)
Winternachtstraum
Stradivari/Stradivarius (French version codir. with Albert Valentin)
Es flüstert die Liebe (aka . . . *und es flüstert die Liebe*)
1936: *Die Entführung*
Das Schloß in Flandern
Mädchenpensionat
Die Julika (aka *Ernte*)
1937: *Lumpacivagabundus*
Premiere
Der Unwiderstehliche
Zauber der Bohème (codir. with Alfred Gerasch)
1938: *Finale* (aka *Die unruhigen Mädchen*)
Spiegel des Lebens
1939: *Zwischen Strom und Steppe/Tiszavirag* (Hungarian version)
Maria Ilona
Opernball (küw)
1940: *Wiener Geschichten* (aka *Wiener G'schichten*) (küw, vw)
Traummusik/Ritorno (Italian version)
Rosen in Tirol
1941: *Dreimal Hochzeit* (küw)
1942: *Schicksal*
Die heimliche Gräfin (küw, vw)
1943: *Der dunkle Tag*
Ein Mann mit Grundsätzen?
1944: *Schrammeln* (küw, vw)
Die Fledermaus (color) (finished as a Defa production, premiered in 1946)
1945: *Die tolle Susanne* (unfinished)

Eduard von Borsody (1898–1970)

1935: *Schnitzel fliegt* (short)
1936: *Früh übt sich* (short)
Was ein Häkchen werden will (short)
Stradivaris Schülergeige (short)
Die Hochzeitsreise (short)
Rosen und Liebe (short)
Du bist so schön, Berlinerin (short)
In 40 Minuten (short)

Das Patentkunstschloß (short)
1937: *Die Bombenidee* (short)
Jürgens riecht Lunte (short) (vb)
Brillanten
1938: *Kautschuk* (küw, sw)
1939: *Sensationsprozeß Casilla*
Kongo-Express
1940: *Wunschkonzert* (jw, küw, sw, vw)
1944: *Jugendliebe* (banned, released in 1947 as *Über's Jahr, wenn die Kornblumen blühen*)
1945: *Die Kreuzlschreiber* (finished by Defa and premiered in 1950)

Harald Braun (1901–1960)

1942: *Zwischen Himmel und Erde*
Hab mich lieb (küw, vw)
1944: *Nora*
Träumerei (küw)
1945: *Der stumme Gast*

Erich Engel (1891–1966)

1933: *Inge und die Millionen*
1934: *Pechmarie*
Hohe Schule
1935: *Pygmalion* (küw)
. . . nur ein Komödiant
1936: *Mädchenjahre einer Königin*
Ein Hochzeitstraum
Die Nacht mit dem Kaiser
1937: *Gefährliches Spiel*
1938: *Der Maulkorb*
1939: *Ein hoffnungsloser Fall* (küw)
Hotel Sacher (küw)
1940: *Nanette* (küw)
Der Weg zu Isabel
Unser Fräulein Doktor
1942: *Viel Lärm um Nixi/Non mi sposo più* (Italian version codir. with Giuseppe Amato) (küw)
Sommerliebe

1943: *Altes Herz wird wieder jung* (kbw)
Man rede mir nicht von Liebe (küw)
1944: *Es lebe die Liebe*
Fahrt ins Glück (premiered in 1948)
1945: *Wo ist Herr Belling?* (unfinished)

Arnold Fanck (1889–1974)

1933: *S.O.S. Eisberg* (English version codir. with Tay Garnett) (kü)
1934: *Der ewige Traum* (aka *Der König des Montblanc*)/*Rêve éternel* (French version codir. with Henri Chomette) (kü)
1937: *Die Tochter des Samurai* (aka *Die Liebe der Mitsu*) (küw, sw)
1938: *Kaiserbauten in Fernost* (doc. short)
1939: *Hänschen klein* (short)
1940: *Ein Robinson* (kuw)
1943: *Josef Thorak—Werkstatt und Werk* (doc. short codir. with Hans Cürlis)
1944: *Arno Breker* (doc. short codir. with Hans Cürlis)
Atlantik-Wall (doc. short)

Willi Forst [Wilhelm Fross] (1903–1980)

1933: *Leise flehen meine Lieder*/*The Unfinished Symphony* (English version codir. with Anthony Asquith)
1934: *Maskerade*
1935: *Mazurka* (küw)
1936: *Allotria* (küw)
Burgtheater
1937: *Serenade*
1939: *Bel ami*
Ich bin Sebastian Ott (codir. with Victor Becker)
1940: *Operette* (küw, kuw)
1942: *Wiener Blut* (kbw, kuw)
1943: *Frauen sind keine Engel* (küw)
1945: *Wiener Mädeln* (color) (premiered in 1949)

Carl Froelich (1875–1953)

1933: *Der Choral von Leuthen* (codir. with Arsen von Cserépy and Walter Supper) (vb)
Reifende Jugend (kbw)

1934: *Volldampf voraus!* (sw)
Schlagerpartie (short)
Frühlingsmärchen (aka *Verlieb' dich nicht in Sizilen*) (kü)
Krach um Jolanthe (kbw)
Ich für Dich—Du für mich (kü, sbw)
1935: *Oberwachtmeister Schwenke*
Liselotte von der Pfalz (skw)
Ich war Jack Mortimer
1936: *Traumulus* (skbw, SP)
Wenn der Hahn kräht (küw)
Wenn wir alle Engel wären (skbw)
1937: *Die ganz großen Torheiten* (küw)
1938: *Die Umwege des schönen Karl* (küw)
Heimat (skw, SP)
Die vier Gesellen (kw)
1939: *Es war eine rauschende Ballnacht* (kbw, kw)
1940: *Das Herz der Königin* (küw, kuw)
1941: *Der Gasmann*
1942: *Hochzeit auf Bärenhof* (küw)
1943: *Familie Buchholz* (küw, vw)
Neigungsehe (küw, vw)

Gustaf Gründgens (1899–1963)

1933: *Eine Stadt steht Kopf*
1934: *Die Finanzen des Großherzogs* (kü)
1937: *Kapriolen*
1939: *Der Schritt vom Wege* (küw)
1940: *Zwei Welten* (küw)

Rolf Hansen (1904–1990)

1935: *Der Traum vom großen Los* (short) (kbw)
1936: *Das Schönheitsfleckchen* (first German color short)
1937: *Gabriele eins, zwei, drei*
1938: *Das Leben kann so schön sein* (banned, released in 1950 as *Eine Frau für's Leben*)
1939: *Sommer, Sonne, Erika* (vw)
1941: *Der Weg ins Freie* (küw)

1942: *Die große Liebe* (skw, vw)
1943: *Damals* (küw)
1945: *Ich glaube an Dich* (finished as a Defa production and released in 1950 as *Mathilde Möhring;* aka in the FRG as *Mein Herz gehört Dir*)

Veit Harlan (1899–1964)

1935: *Die Pompadour* (codir. with Willy Schmidt Gentner)
Krach im Hinterhaus
1936: *Kater Lampe* (küw)
Der müde Theodor
Maria, die Magd
Alles für Veronika (aka *Fräulein Veronika*)
1937: *Die Kreutzersonate* (küw)
Der Herrscher (skbw, SP)
Mein Sohn, der Herr Minister (küw)
1938: *Jugend* (küw)
Verwehte Spuren (küw)
1939: *Das unsterbliche Herz* (küw)
Die Reise nach Tilsit
1940: *Jud Süß* (jw, skbw)
1941: *Pedro soll hängen* (made in 1939)
1942: *Der große König* (jw, kuw, skbw, vb, vw, FN)
Die goldene Stadt (color) (kbw)
1943: *Immensee* (color) (kuw, küw, vw)
1944: *Opfergang* (color) (kbw)
1945: *Kolberg* (color) (aw, jw, kuw, skbw, vb, vw, FN)
Der Puppenspieler (color) (unfinished)

Karl Hartl (1899–1978)

1933: *Ihre Durchlaucht, die Verkäuferin/Caprice de princesse* (French version codir. with Henri-Georges Clouzot)
1934: *Gold/L'or* (French version codir. with Serge de Poligny) (kü)
So endete eine Liebe
1935: *Zigeunerbaron/Le Baron Tzigane* (French version codir. with Henri Chomette) (küw)
1936: *Die Leuchter des Kaisers*
1937: *Ritt in die Freiheit*
Der Mann, der Sherlock Holmes war (küw)

1938: *Gastspiel im Paradies*
1942: *Wen die Götter lieben* (skbw)
1943: *Der weiße Traum* (codir. with Géza von Cziffra) (küw)

Werner Hochbaum (1899–1946)

1933: *Schleppzug M 17* (codir. with Heinrich George)
Morgen beginnt das Leben
1935: *Vorstadtvarieté*
Leichte Kavallerie/Cavalerie légère (French version codir. with Roger Vitrac)
1936: *Die ewige Maske*
Der Favorit der Kaiserin
Schatten der Vergangenheit
Hannerl und ihre Liebhaber
1937: *Man spricht über Jacqueline*
1938: *Ein Mädchen geht an Land*
1939: *Drei Unteroffiziere* (sw, vb)

Kurt Hoffmann (1910–)

1938: *Wochenendfrieden* (short)
Der Skarabäus (short)
Andere Länder, andere Sitten (short)
1939: *Paradies der Junggesellen*
Hurra! Ich bin Papa!
1941: *Quax, der Bruchpilot* (jw, küw, vw)
1943: *Kohlhiesels Töchter* (vw)
Ich vertraue Dir meine Frau an (küw, vw)
Ich werde Dich auf Händen tragen (vw)

Georg Jacoby (1882–1965)

1933: *Der große Bluff* (Austria: *Alles ist Komödie/Schüsse in der Nacht*)
Moral und Liebe (Austria: *Die heilige Dirne;* banned in 1934)
Sag' mir, wer Du bist (Austria: *Madonna, wo bist Du?*)
Die Wette (short)
Ist mein Mann nicht fabelhaft? (Austria: *Ich bin von meinem Mann entzückt*)
Eine ideale Wohnung (short)

Zwei im Sonnenschein (Austria: *Wenn der Mensch verliebt ist*)
Der streitbare Herr Kickel (short)
Das 13. Weltwunder (short)
Der Störenfried (short)
1934: *Liebe und Zahnweh* (short)
Hochzeit am 13. (short)
Der Polizeibericht meldet (Austria: *Die Dame mit dem Schleier*)
Ein Mädel wirbelt durch die Welt
Die Csardasfürstin/Princesse Czárdás (French version aka *Sérénade*)
Der kühne Schwimmer
G'schichten aus dem Wienerwald
Der letzte Walzer (Austria: *Hofball in St. Petersburg*)
Besuch am Abend
1935: *Warum lügt Fräulein Käthe?*
Ehestreik
Ein Teufelskerl (Austria: *Leutnant Bobby, der Teufelskerl*)
1936: *Herbstmanöver*
Heißes Blut/Les deux favoris (French version codir. with André Hornez)
Der Bettelstudent (küw)
1937: *Und Du, mein Schatz, fährst mit*
Die Kronzeugin
Husaren, heraus! (Austria: *Das Liebesregiment*)
Spiel auf der Tenne (Austria: *Die reuigen Sünder*)
Gasparone
1938: *Großalarm*
Eine Nacht im Mai
1939: *Der Vorhang fällt*
1940: *Kora Terry*
1941: *Frauen sind doch bessere Diplomaten* (color) (vw)
Tanz mit dem Kaiser (küw, vw)
1943: *Die Gattin*
1944: *Die Frau meiner Träume* (color)

Helmut Käutner (1908–1980)

1939: *Kitty und die Weltkonferenz* (premiered 25 August, banned in late 1939)
1940: *Frau nach Maß*
Kleider machen Leute

1941: *Auf Wiedersehen, Franziska!* (küw)
1942: *Anuschka* (küw, vw)
Wir machen Musik (aw, küw, vw)
1943: *Romanze in Moll* (kbw)
1944: *Große Freiheit Nr. 7* (color) (banned in Germany, premiered in Prague, 15 December)
1945: *Unter den Brücken* (premiered 1946 in Locarno, 1950 in Göttingen)

Gerhard Lamprecht (1897–1974)

1933: *Was wissen denn Männer*
Spione am Werk
Ein gewisser Herr Gran/ Un certain M. Grant (French version codir. with Roger Le Bon)
1934: *Einmal eine große Dame sein/ Un jour viendra* (French version codir. with Serge Veber)
Prinzessin Turandot/ Turandot, princesse de Chine (French version codir. with Serge Veber)
1935: *Barcarole/ Barcarolle* (French version codir. with Roger Le Bon)
Einer zuviel an Bord/ Un homme de trop à bord (French version codir. with Roger Le Bon)
Der höhere Befehl (skbw)
1936: *Ein seltsamer Gast*
1937: *Madame Bovary*
Die gelbe Flagge
1938: *Der Spieler/ Le joueur* (French version codir. with Louis Daquin) (küw)
1939: *Die Geliebte* (küw)
Frau im Strom
1940: *Mädchen im Vorzimmer*
1941: *Clarissa*
1942: *Diesel* (skw, vw)
1943: *Du gehörst zu mir*
1945: *Die Brüder Noltenius*
Kamerad Hedwig (unfinished)

Wolfgang Liebeneiner (1905–1987)

1937: *Versprich mir nichts!* (küw)
Der Mustergatte (küw)

1938: *Yvette*
Du und Ich (küw)
Ziel in den Wolken (küw, sw)
1939: *Der Florentiner Hut* (küw)
1940: *Die gute Sieben*
Bismarck (jw, skbw)
1941: *Ich klage an* (kbw, vb)
Das andere Ich (küw)
1942: *Die Entlassung* (rereleased in 1954 as *Schicksalswende*) (aw, jw, kuw, skbw, vb, vw, FN)
1943: *Großstadtmelodie* (küw)
1945: *Das Leben geht weiter* (unfinished)

Herbert Maisch (1890–1974)

1935: *Königswalzer*
1936: *Liebeserwachen*
Boccaccio
1937: *Menschen ohne Vaterland*
Starke Herzen (not released; premiered in 1953 as *Starke Herzen im Sturm*)
1938: *Frau Sylvelin*
Andalusische Nächte
Nanon
1939: *D III 88* (codir. withh Hans Bertram) (jw, sbw)
1940: *Friedrich Schiller* (jw, küw, sw)
1941: *Ohm Krüger* (with Karl Anton and Hans Steinhoff) (jw, kuw, skbw, vb, vw, FN)
1942: *Andreas Schlüter* (jw, skbw)
1944: *Musik in Salzburg*
Die Zaubergeige (küw)
Der Freischütz (unfinished)

Paul Martin (1899–1967)

1935: *Schwarze Rosen* (French version: *Roses noires,* codir. with Jean Boyer; English version: *Did I Betray?*) (küw)
1936: *Glückskinder* (French version: *Les gais lurons,* codir. with Jacques Natanson) (küw)

1937: *Sieben Ohrfeigen* (küw)
Fanny Elßler (küw)
1938: *Fortsetzung folgt*
Preußische Liebesgeschichte (banned, released in 1950 as *Liebeslegende*)
1939: *Frau am Steuer*
Das Lied der Wüste
1941: *Was will Brigitte?*
Jenny und der Herr im Frack (vw)
1943: *Maske in Blau*
Karneval der Liebe (vw)
Geliebter Schatz (vw)
1944: *Das war mein Leben*
Intimitäten (banned, released in 1948)
1945: *Das seltsame Fräulein Sylvia* (unfinished)

Georg Wilhelm Pabst (1885–1967)

1933: *Don Quichotte/Don Quixote* (French-English production)
Du haut en bas
1934: *A Modern Hero*
1937: *Mademoiselle docteur* (aka *Salonique, nid d'espions*)
1938: *Le drame de Shanghai*
1939: *Jeunes filles en détresse*
1941: *Komödianten* (kuw, skbw, vb)
1943: *Paracelsus* (skw)
1945: *Der Fall Molander* (unfinished)

Peter Pewas [Walter Schultz] (1904–1984)

1934: *Alexanderplatz überrumpelt* (unfinished)
1939: *Zwischen Abend und Morgen* (unfinished)
1941: *Eine Stunde* (short)
1942: *Zweiklang* (short)
1944: *Der verzauberte Tag* (banned, premiered in 1947)

Harry [Heinrich] Piel (1892–1963)

1933: *Sprung in den Abgrund* (aka *Spuren im Schnee*)
Ein Unsichtbarer geht durch die Stadt

1934: *Die Welt ohne Maske*
Der Herr der Welt (vb)
1935: *Artisten* (küw)
1936: *Der Dschungel ruft* (aka *Dschungel*) (küw, vb)
90 Minuten Aufenthalt (aka *Abenteuer in Lissabon*) (küw)
1937: *Sein bester Freund*
1938: *Der unmögliche Herr Pitt* (rereleased in the FRG as *Die Nacht der 1000 Sensationen*)
Menschen, Tiere, Sensationen
1943: *Panik* (preliminary version banned in October 1943, premiered in 1953 as *Gesprengte Gitter*)
1945: *Mann im Sattel* (codir. with Werner Klingler, unfinished)

Arthur Maria Rabenalt (1905–1993)

1934: *Pappi*
Was bin ich ohne Dich?
Eine Siebzehnjährige
Ein Kind, ein Hund, ein Vagabund (banned, rereleased 12 July 1935 as *Vielleicht war's nur ein Traum*)
1936: *Die klugen Frauen* (French version with Jacques Feyder: *La kermesse heroïque*)
Die weiße Frau des Maharadscha (aka *Die Liebe des Maharadscha;* Italian version with Goffredo Alessandrini: *Una donna tra due mondi*)
Das Frauenparadies
1937: *Millionenerbschaft*
1938: *Liebelei und Liebe*
Rosemarie will nicht mehr lügen (short)
Schwarz und Weiß (short, banned)
1939: *Männer müssen so sein* (küw)
Modell Lu, der Lebensweg eines Hutes (short)
Flucht ins Dunkel (küw)
Johannisfeuer (küw)
1940: *Weißer Flieder*
Die 3 Codonas
Achtung! Feind hört mit! (sw)
1941: *. . . reitet für Deutschland* (jw, sw)
Leichte Muse (rereleased in 1950 as *Was eine Frau im Frühling träumt*) (vw)

1942: *Fronttheater* (sw, vw)
Meine Frau Teresa (küw)
1943: *Liebespremiere*
Zirkus Renz (küw, vw)
1944: *Das Leben ruft*
Am Abend nach der Oper (premiered in 1945)
1945: *Regimentsmusik* (premiered in 1950 as *Die Schuld der Gabriele Rottweil*)
Wir beide liebten Katharina (unfinished)

Leni [Helene] Riefenstahl (1902)

1933: *Der Sieg des Glaubens* (doc.)
1935: *Triumph des Willens* (doc.) (küw, sw, vb, SP)
Tag der Freiheit!—Unsere Wehrmacht (doc. short) (küw, sw, vb)
1938: *Olympia* (two-part doc.) (kuw, küw, sw, vb, SP)
1954: *Tiefland*

Karl Ritter (1888–1977)

1936: *Weiberregiment*
Verräter (skbw, vb)
1937: *Patrioten* (skbw)
Unternehmen Michael (skw)
1938: *Urlaub auf Ehrenwort* (skbw)
Capriccio
Pour le Mérite (jw, skbw)
1939: *Die Hochzeitsreise*
Im Kampf gegen den Weltfeind. Deutsche Freiwillige in Spanien (doc.) (sw, vb)
Kadetten (originally to be premiered on 5 September, not released until 2 December 1941)
Legion Condor (unfinished)
1940: *Bal paré*
1941: *Über alles in der Welt* (jw, sw)
Stukas (jw, küw, sw, vw)
1942: *GPU*
1943: *Besatzung Dora* (banned in November)
1944: *Sommernächte*

Walter Ruttmann (1887–1941)

1933: *Acciaio/Arbeit macht glücklich* (aka *Stahl*)
1934: *Altgermanische Bauernkultur* (short) (vb)
1935: *Metall des Himmels* (doc. short) (küw, vb)
Kleiner Film einer großen Stadt . . . der Stadt Düsseldorf am Rhein (doc. short) (küw)
Stuttgart, die Großstadt zwischen Wald und Reben—die Stadt des Auslanddeutschtums (doc. short) (küw, vb)
Stadt Stuttgart. 100. Cannstatter Volksfest (doc. short)
1936: *Schiff in Not* (doc. short) (sw, vb)
1937: *Helden der Küste* (doc. short) (sw, vb)
Mannesmann. Ein Film des Mannesmannröhren-Werke (doc.) (küw)
1938: *Mannesmann. Ein Ufa-Kulturfilm nach dem international preisgekrönten Film* (doc. short) (küw, vb)
Im Zeichen des Vertrauens. Ein Bayer-Film (doc. short)
Im Dienste der Menschheit (doc. short) (küw)
Weltstraße See—Welthafen Hamburg (doc. short) (küw, vb)
Henkel. Ein deutsches Werk in seiner Arbeit (doc. short)
1940: *Deutsche Waffenschmieden* (doc. short) (küw, sw, vb)
Deutsche Panzer (doc. short) (sw, vb)
Aberglaube (doc. short) (sw, vb)
Ein Film gegen die Volkskrankheit Krebs (doc. short) (küw, sw, vb)

Reinhold Schünzel (1888–1954)

1933: *Saison in Cairo/Idylle au Caire* (French version codir. with Claude Heymann) (kü)
Viktor und Viktoria/Georges et Georgette (French version codir. with Roger Le Bon) (kü)
1934: *Die Töchter Ihrer Exzellenz/La jeune fille d'une nuit* (French version codir. with Roger Le Bon)
Die englische Heirat
1935: *Amphitryon/Les dieux s'amusent* (French version codir. with Albert Valentin) (küw)
1936: *Donogoo Tonka/Donogoo* (French version codir. with Henri Chomette)
Das Mädchen Irene
1937: *Land der Liebe*
1938: *Rich Man, Poor Girl*

1939: *The Ice Follies of 1939*
Balalaika
1941: *New Wine*

Hans Schweikart (1895–1975)

1938: *Das Mädchen mit dem guten Ruf* (Austria: *Mirandolina, das Mädchen mit dem schlechten Ruf*)
1939: *Fasching* (küw, vw)
Befreite Hände (kbw, kuw)
1940: *Das Fräulein von Barnhelm* (küw)
1941: *Das Mädchen von Fanö*
Kameraden (aka *Ritt zwischen den Fronten*) (jw, küw, skw, vb)
1943: *Der unendliche Weg* (jw, skbw)
1944: *In flagranti* (küw)
Ich brauche Dich (küw)
1945: *Das Gesetz der Liebe* (premiered in 1949)
Frech und verliebt (premiered in 1948)
Die Nacht der Zwölf (premiered in 1949)

Herbert Selpin (1902–1942)

1933: *Der Traum vom Rhein* (Austria: *Was wär' die Welt ohne Liebe*)
Mädels von heute
1934: *Zwischen zwei Herzen*
Der Springer von Pontresina
Die Reiter von Deutsch-Ostafrika (vb)
1935: *Ein idealer Gatte*
Der grüne Domino/Le domino vert (French version codir. with Henri Decoin)
1936: *Skandal um die Fledermaus*
1937: *Die Frau des Anderen* (aka *Romanze*)
Alarm in Peking
1938: *Heiratsschwindler* (aka *Die rote Mütze*) (küw)
Ich liebe Dich
Sergeant Berry
1939: *Wasser für Canitoga* (küw)
1940: *Ein Mann auf Abwegen*
Trenck, der Pandur (jw, vw)
1941: *Carl Peters* (jw, kuw, skw, vb)

1942: *Geheimakte WB 1* (jw, skw)
1943: *Titanic* (finished by Werner Klingler, banned in Germany; premiered in the FRG, 1950)

Detlef Sierck (1897–1987)

1934: *Zwei Genies* (short, banned on 14 December)
1935: *Der eingebildete Kranke* (short)
Dreimal Ehe (short)
April, April!/'t was 1 April (Dutch version codir. with Jacques van Tol)
Das Mädchen vom Moorhof
Stützen der Gesellschaft (küw)
1936: *Schlußakkord* (küw)
Das Hofkonzert/Le chanson du souvenir (French version codir. with Serge de Poligny)
1937: *Zu neuen Ufern* (küw)
La Habanera
1938: *Accord final* (artistic direction; directed by I. R. Bay, aka Ignacy Rosenkranz)
1939: *Boefje*
1943: *Hitler's Madman*
1944: *Summer Storm*

Wolfgang Staudte (1906–1984)

1933: *Ein jeder hat mal Glück* (short)
1938: *Deutsche Siege in drei Erdteilen* (doc.)
1941: *Ins Grab kann man nichts mitnehmen* (short)
1942: *Aus eins mach' vier* (short)
1943: *Akrobat schö-ö-ö-n*
1944: *Ich hab' von Dir geträumt*
Der Mann, dem man den Namen stahl (banned, redone as *Die seltsamen Abenteuer des Herrn Fridolin B.* and premiered in 1948)
1945: *Frau über Bord* (premiered in 1952 as *Das Mädchen Juanita*)

Hans Steinhoff (1882–1945)

1933: *Madame wünscht keine Kinder/Madame ne veut pas d'enfants*
Liebe muß verstanden sein
Hitlerjunge Quex (kbw)

1934: *Mutter und Kind* (sw)
Freut Euch des Lebens
Die Insel/ Vers l'abîme (French version codir. with Serge Veber)
Lockvogel/ Le miroir aux alouettes (French version codir. with Roger Le Bon)
1935: *Der alte und der junge König* (skbw, vb)
Der Ammenkönig (küw)
1936: *Eine Frau ohne Bedeutung* (küw)
1937: *Ein Volksfeind* (küw)
1938: *Tanz auf dem Vulkan* (küw)
1939: *Robert Koch, der Bekämpfer des Todes* (kuw, skbw, vw)
1940: *Die Geierwally* (küw, vw)
1941: *Ohm Krüger* (with Herbert Maisch and Karl Anton) (jw, kuw, skbw, vb, vw, FN)
1942: *Rembrandt* (küw)
1943: *Gabriele Dambrone* (küw)
1944: *Melusine* (banned)
1945: *Shiva und die Galgenblume* (color) (unfinished)

Viktor Tourjansky (1891–1976)

1935: *Die ganze Welt dreht sich um Liebe*
1936: *Stadt Anatol/ Puits en flammes* (küw)
1938: *Verklungene Melodie* (Austria: *Der weite Weg*) (küw)
Geheimzeichen LB 17 (küw)
Der Blaufuchs
1939: *Der Gouverneur* (küw)
Eine Frau wie Du
1940: *Feinde* (jw, küw, sw)
Die keusche Geliebte
1941: *Illusion*
1943: *Liebesgeschichten* (küw)
Tonelli (küw)
1944: *Orient-Express* (küw)
1945: *Dreimal Komödie* (premiered in 1949 as *Liebeswirbel*)

Luis Trenker (1892–1990)

1933: *5 Minuten Skikurs* (doc. short)
1934: *Der verlorene Sohn* (kbw)

1936: *Der Kaiser von Kalifornien* (skbw)
1937: *Condottieri* (German version codir. with Werner Klingler) (skbw)
Der Berg ruft/The Challenge (Eng. version codir. with Milton Rosmer) (küw)
1938: *Liebesbriefe aus dem Engadin* (codir. with Werner Klingler)
1939: *Urlaub im Schnee* (doc. short)
1940: *Der König der Berge* (doc. short, made in 1938) (vb)
Der Feuerteufel
1941: *Unsere Gebirgspioniere* (doc. short) (sw, vb)
1942: *Pastor Angelicus* (artistic direction; doc. directed by Romolo Marcellini)
1945: *Monte miracolo/Im Banne des Monte Miracolo* (German-language version premiered 1948 in Innsbruck and 1949 in Stuttgart; aka *Der verrufene Berg*)

Gustav Ucicky (1899–1961)

1933: *Morgenrot* (kü)
Flüchtlinge/Au bout du monde (French version codir. with Henri Chomette) (kbw, SP)
1934: *Der junge Baron Neuhaus/Nuit de mai* (French version codir. with Henri Chomette) (kü)
1935: *Das Mädchen Johanna* (skbw)
1936: *Savoy-Hotel 217* (rereleased in 1950 as *Mord im Savoy*) (küw)
Unter heißem Himmel
1937: *Der zerbrochene Krug* (skw)
1938: *Wort und Tat* (doc. short codir. with Fritz Hippler, Ottoheinz Jahn, and Eugen York) (sw, vb)
Frau Sixta (küw)
1939: *Aufruhr in Damaskus* (küw, sw)
Mutterliebe (skbw)
1940: *Der Postmeister* (kbw)
Ein Leben lang (küw)
1941: *Heimkehr* (jw, skbw, FN)
1943: *Späte Liebe* (küw)
Am Ende der Welt (banned, premiered in 1947; rereleased in the FRG in 1956 as *Die Erbin der Wälder*)
1944: *Der gebieterische Ruf* (kbw)
Das Herz muß schweigen (kbw)

Erich Waschneck (1887–1970)

1933: *Hände aus dem Dunkel* (Austria: *Das Mädchen mit dem gewissen Etwas;* banned in 1936)
Abel mit der Mundharmonika (Austria: *Eine Frau fällt vom Himmel*) (kü)
1934: *Abenteuer im Südexpress*
Musik im Blut (kü)
1935: *Regine* (küw)
Mein Leben für Maria Isabell
Liebesleute (aka *Hermann und Dorothea heute*) (küw)
1936: *Eskapade* (Austria: *Seitensprung*)
Onkel Bräsig (Austria: *Der Dorfonkel*)
1937: *Die göttliche Jette* (Austria: *Die Göttliche*)
Streit um den Knaben Joe
Gewitterflug zu Claudia (küw)
1938: *Anna Favetti*
Frauen für Golden Hill
1939: *Fräulein* (küw)
Kennwort Machin
1940: *Die Rothschilds*
Die unvollkommene Liebe
Zwischen Hamburg und Haiti
1943: *Nacht ohne Abschied*
Die beiden Schwestern (vw)
1944: *Die Affäre Roedern* (jw, sw)
1945: *Eine reizende Familie* (aka *Danke, es geht mir gut;* finished by Defa and released in 1948)

Paul Wegener (1874–1948)

1934: *Die Freundin eines großen Mannes* (kü)
Ein Mann will nach Deutschland (kü)
Der rote Tod von Riga (unfinished)
1936: *August der Starke*
Die Stunde der Versuchung
Moskau—Shanghai (rereleased in 1949 as *Der Weg nach Shanghai*)
1937: *Krach und Glück um Künnemann*
Unter Ausschluß der Öffentlichkeit

Frank Wysbar (1899–1967)

1933: *Anna und Elisabeth* (kü)
1934: *Rivalen der Luft* (vb)
1935: *Hermine und die sieben Aufrechten* (skbw)
Die Werft zum grauen Hecht (küw)
1936: *Fährmann Maria* (küw, vb)
Die Unbekannte
1937: *Ball im Metropol* (küw)
1938: *Petermann ist dagegen*
1945: *Stranger of the Swamp*

Hans H. Zerlett (1892–1962)

1934: *Da stimmt was nicht* (Austria: *Der Heiratsschwindler*)
1935: *Knock out* (codir. with Carl Lamac, aka *Ein junges Mädchen—Ein junger Mann;* Austria: *Liebe und Knock out*)
Die selige Exzellenz (aka *Das Tagebuch der Baronin W.*) (küw)
1936: *Arzt aus Leidenschaft* (küw)
Moral
Diener lassen bitten
Max Schmelings Sieg—ein deutscher Sieg (doc.)
1937: *Truxa*
Liebe geht seltsame Wege
Die Fledermaus (codir. with Paul Verhoeven) (küw)
1938: *Revolutionshochzeit* (küw)
Es leuchten die Sterne
Zwei Frauen
Verliebtes Abenteuer
1939: *Robert und Bertram*
Die goldene Maske
1940: *Meine Tochter tut das nicht*
1941: *Venus vor Gericht* (vw)
1942: *Kleine Residenz* (küw, vw)
Einmal der liebe Herrgott sein
Meine Freundin Josefine
1943: *Reise in die Vergangenheit* (aw)
1944: *Liebesbriefe*
Schuß um Mitternacht (approved 1944, not premiered until 1950)
1945: *Spuk im Schloß* (premiered in 1947)
Mit meinen Augen (premiered in 1948)

APPENDIX C

American Film and Videotape Sources for German Features, 1933–1945

Facets Video (FV)
1517 W. Fullerton Avenue
Chicago, IL 60614
Tel. 800-331-6197

Films Incorporated (FI)
5547 North Ravenswood Avenue
Chicago, IL 60640-1199
Tel. 800-323-4222, ext. 42
Fax 312-878-8648

German Language Video Center (GLVC)
Division of Heidelberg Haus Imports
7625 Pendleton Pike
Indianapolis, IN 46226-5298
Tel. 800-252-1957 or 317-547-1257
Fax 317-547-1263

International Historic Films Inc. (IHT)
P.O. Box 29035
Chicago, IL 60629
Tel. 312-927-2900
Fax 312-927-9211

The Museum of Modern Art (MOMA)
Circulating Film Library
11 West 53rd Street
New York, NY 10019
Tel. 212-708-9530
Fax 212-708-9351

The Rohauer Collection (Rohauer)
239 South High Street, no. 310
Columbus, OH 43215
Tel. (614) 469-0720
Fax (614) 469-1607

Trans-World Films, Inc. (TW)
332 South Michigan Avenue
Chicago, IL 60604
Tel. 312-922-1530

West Glen Communications (WG)
German Feature Films
1430 Broadway, 9th Floor
New York, NY 10018
Tel. 212-921-0966
Fax 212-944-9055

Unless otherwise noted, the following entries are German-language original versions without subtitles.

Achtung! Feind hört mit! (video: GLVC, IHF)
Die Affäre Roedern (video: GLVC)
Akrobat schö-ö-ö-n (16mm with subtitles: TW; video: GLVC)
Der alte und der junge König (16mm with subtitles: TW, WG; video with subtitles: FV)
Andreas Schlüter (16mm with subtitles: TW; video: GLVC)
Anuschka (video: GLVC)
Arzt aus Leidenschaft (video: IHF)
Aufruhr in Damaskus (video: GLVC, IHF)
Auf Wiedersehen, Franziska! (video: GLVC)
Barcarole (video: FV, GLVC)
Bel ami (video: GLVC)
Der Berg ruft (video: GLVC)
Besuch am Abend (video: GLVC, IHF)
Der Bettelstudent (16mm with subtitles: TW)
Bismarck (video: GLVC, IHF)
Carl Peters (video: GLVC, IHF)
Condottieri (video: GLVC)
Die Csardasfürstin (video: GLVC)
Damals (video: GLVC, IHF)

Die Degenhardts (video: GLVC, IHF)
Diesel (video: GLVC, IHF)
Die vom Niederrhein (video: GLVC, IHF)
Dr. Crippen an Bord (video: GLVC, IHF)
Du bist mein Glück (video: GLVC, IHF)
Einmal der liebe Herrgott sein (video: GLVC, IHF)
Das Ekel (video: GLVC)
Die Entlassung (video: GLVC, IHF)
Es gibt nur eine Liebe (video: GLVC, IHF)
Eskapade (video: GLVC, IHF)
Es leuchten die Sterne (video: GLVC)
Es war eine rauschende Ballnacht (video: GLVC)
Eva (video: GLVC)
Familie Schimek (video: GLVC)
Der Feuerteufel (video: FV, GLVC, IHF)
Der Florentiner Hut (video: GLVC)
Flüchtlinge (video: GLVC, IHF)
Die Frau am Scheidewege (video: GLVC)
Frauen sind doch bessere Diplomaten (video: GLVC, IHF)
Das Fräulein von Barnhelm (16mm with subtitles: TW)
Die Frau meiner Träume (video: GLVC)
Fridericus (video: GLVC, IHF)
Friedemann Bach (16mm with subtitles: TW, WG; 16mm without subtitles: WG; video with subtitles: GLVC)
Friedrich Schiller (16mm with subtitles: TW; video: GLVC, IHF)
Fünf Millionen suchen einen Erben (video: GLVC)
Geheimakte WB 1 (video: GLVC, IHF)
Geheimzeichen LB 17 (video: GLVC, IHF)
Die Geierwally (video: GLVC)
Germanin (video: GLVC, IHF)
Glückskinder (video: GLVC, IHF)
Gold (video: GLVC, IHF)
Die goldene Spinne (video: GLVC, IHF)
Die goldene Stadt (video: FV, GLVC, IHF)
Die göttliche Jette (video: GLVC)
Der Gouverneur (video: GLVC, IHF)
GPU (video: GLVC)
Große Freiheit Nr. 7 (video: GLVC, IHF)
Der große König (video: GLVC, IHF)
Die große Liebe (video: GLVC, IHF)
G'schichten aus dem Wienerwald (video with subtitles: FV)

Hallo Janine (video: GLVC)
Hans Westmar (16mm fragment: MOMA)
Das häßliche Mädchen (video: GLVC, IHF)
Hauptsache glücklich! (video: GLVC, IHF)
Himmel auf Erden (video: GLVC)
Hitlerjunge Quex (16mm with partial intertitles: MOMA; video with partial intertitles: FV, IHF).
Der höhere Befehl (video: GLVC, IHF)
Hohe Schule (video: GLVC, IHF)
Hotel Sacher (video: GLVC, IHF)
Ich klage an (video: GLVC, IHF)
Ich sehne mich nach Dir (video: GLVC)
Ich sing' mich in Dein Herz hinein (video: GLVC, IHF)
Ihr Leibhusar (video: GLVC)
Immensee (video: GLVC, IHF)
Immer nur . . . Du! (video: GLVC)
Irrtum des Herzens (video: GLVC)
Jud Süß (video with subtitles: IHF)
Junge Adler (video: GLVC, IHF)
Der Kaiser von Kalifornien (video: FV, GLVC, IHF)
Kameraden (video: GLVC, IHF)
Karneval der Liebe (video: GLVC)
Kautschuk (video: GLVC, IHF)
Kleider machen Leute (video with subtitles: FV)
Kolberg (video with subtitles: FV, GLVC, IHF)
Komödianten (16mm with subtitles: TW)
Kongo-Express (video: GLVC, IHF)
La Habanera (16mm with subtitles: WG; video: GLVC, IHF)
Das leichte Mädchen (video: GLVC)
Liebesbriefe aus dem Engadin (video: GLVC, IHF)
Das Lied der Wüste (video: GLVC)
Ein Lied geht um die Welt (video with subtitles: GVLC)
Lumpacivagabundus (video: GLVC, IHF)
Das Mädchen Johanna (video: GLVC, IHF)
Made in Germany (video: GLVC)
Der Mann, der Sherlock Holmes war (16mm with subtitles: Rohauer; video: GLVC)
Ein Mann will nach Deutschland (video: GLVC, IHF)
Maria Ilona (video: GLVC, IHF)
Maskerade (16mm: WG)
Der Maulkorb (video: GLVC, IHF)

Mazurka (16mm: WG)
Mein Leben für Irland (video: GLVC, IHF)
Der Meisterdetektiv (video: GLVC, IHF)
Menschen im Sturm (video: GLVC)
Menschen ohne Vaterland (video: GLVC, IHF)
Der Millionär (video: GLVC, IHF)
Morgenrot (video: FV, GLVC, IHF)
Münchhausen (16mm with subtitles: WG; video with subtitles: FV, GLVC)
Musik im Blut (video: GLVC, IHF)
Nanu, Sie kennen Korff noch nicht! (video: GLVC)
. . . nur ein Komödiant (video: GLVC, IHF)
Ohm Krüger (video: GLVC)
Olympia (16mm, English-language version: FI; video, English-language version: FV, GLVC, IHF)
Opfergang (video: GLVC, IHF)
Orient-Express (video: GLVC, IHF)
Paracelsus (16mm with subtitles: TW; video: GLVC, IHF)
Patrioten (video: GLVC, IHF)
Peterle (video: GLVC)
Peter Voß, der Millionendieb (video: GLVC, IHF)
Der Postmeister (video: GLVC, IHF)
Quax, der Bruchpilot (video: GLVC)
Quax in Afrika (video: GLVC, IHF)
Regine (video: GLVC, IHF)
Die Reiter von Deutsch-Ostafrika (video: GLVC, IHF)
. . . reitet für Deutschland (video: GLVC, IHF)
Rembrandt (video: GLVC, IHF)
Robert Koch, der Bekämpfer des Todes (16mm with subtitles: TW; video: GLVC)
Robert und Bertram (video: GLVC)
Romanze in Moll (16mm with subtitles: WG; video with subtitles: FV)
Rosen in Tirol (video: GLVC)
Die Rothschilds (video: IHF)
Die Sache mit Styx (video: GLVC)
S.A. Mann Brand (video: GLVC)
Savoy-Hotel 217 (video: GLVC, IHF)
Schlußakkord (video: GLVC, IHF)
Schrammeln (video: GLVC)
Der Schritt vom Wege (16mm with subtitles: WG)
Schwarz auf Weiß (video: GLVC)
Schwarze Rosen (video: GLVC)
Schwarzer Jäger Johanna (video: GLVC, IHF)

Seinerzeit zu meiner Zeit (video: GLVC)
Sensationsprozeß Casilla (video: GLVC, IHF)
So endete eine Liebe (video: GLVC)
S.O.S. Eisberg (video: GLVC, IHF)
Spiel auf der Tenne (video: GLVC)
Standschütze Bruggler (video: GLVC, IHF)
Stern von Rio (video: GLVC, IHF)
Die Stimme des Herzens (video: GLVC)
Stradivari (video: GLVC)
Stukas (video: GLVC, IHF)
Tanz auf dem Vulkan (video: GLVC, IHF)
Tiefland (16mm with subtitles: FI; video with subtitles: FV, GLVC)
Titanic (video: GLVC, IHF)
Triumph des Willens (16mm with subtitles: FI; video with subtitles: FV, GLVC, IHF)
Truxa (video: GLVC)
Der Tunnel (video: GLVC, IHF)
U-Boote westwärts! (video: GLVC, IHF)
Das unsterbliche Herz (video: GLVC, IHF)
Unter den Brücken (16mm with subtitles: WG; video with subtitles: FV, GLVC)
Urlaub auf Ehrenwort (video: GLVC, IHF)
Verklungene Melodie (video: GLVC, IHF)
Der verlorene Sohn (video: FV, GLVC, IHF)
Verräter (video: GLVC, IHF)
Versprich mir nichts! (video: GLVC, IHF)
Verwehte Spuren (video: GLVC, IHF)
Vorstadtvarieté (video: GLVC)
Walzerkrieg (16mm: WG)
Wasser für Canitoga (video: GLVC, IHF)
Wo die Lerche singt (video: GLVC)
Wunder des Fliegens (video: GLVC, IHF)
Wunschkonzert (video: GLVC, IHF)
Zauber der Bohème (video with subtitles: GLVC)
Der zerbrochene Krug (16mm with subtitles: TW; video with subtitles: FV, GLVC)
Ziel in den Wolken (video: GLVC, IHF)
Zu neuen Ufern (video: FV, GLVC, IHF)
Zwei in einer großen Stadt (video: GLVC)

NOTES

Introduction

1. Don DeLillo, *Running Dog* (New York: Vintage, 1979), p. 52.

2. Recall Albert Speer's final speech at the Nuremberg trials: "The instruments of technology made it possible to maintain a close watch over all citizens and to keep criminal operations shrouded in a high degree of secrecy"; *Inside the Third Reich: Memoirs* (New York: Macmillan, 1970), p. 520.

3. See the script for Hans Jürgen Syberberg's 1977 seven-hour opus, *Hitler: A Film from Germany,* trans. Joachim Neugroschel (New York: Farrar, Straus & Giroux, 1982).

4. Wim Wenders, "That's Entertainment: Hitler (1977)," in *West German Filmmakers on Film: Visions and Voices,* ed. Eric Rentschler (New York/London: Holmes & Meier, 1988), p. 128.

5. A recent example is Rebecca Lieb's "Nazi Hate Movies Continue to Ignite Fierce Passions," *New York Times,* 4 August 1991. Do Nazi propaganda films, asks Lieb, still possess the power to stir up hate? "Are they dangerous or should they be shown? If they are to be shown, who will show them and under what circumstances? Is there anything to be learned from them or are they too horrifying even to contemplate?" More than two decades ago, Amos Vogel posed impassioned questions regarding the reception and exhibition of Leni Riefenstahl's films in his essay "Can We Now Forget the Evil That She Did?" *New York Times,* 13 May 1973. For a German contribution that articulates similar concerns, see Hilmar Hoffmann, *Es ist noch nicht zu Ende. Sollen Nazikunst und Nazifilme wieder öffentlich gezeigt werden?* (Badenweiler: Oase, 1988).

6. See Kraft Wetzel and Peter Hagemann's *Liebe, Tod und Technik. Kino des Fantastischen 1933–1945* (Berlin: Spiess, 1977) and *Zensur. Verbotene deutsche Filme 1933–1945* (Berlin: Spiess, 1978); also Helga Belach, ed., *Wir tanzen um die Welt. Deutsche Revuefilme 1933–1945* (Munich: Hanser, 1979).

7. See the two volumes edited by Hans Helmut Prinzler: *Europa 1939. Filme aus zehn Ländern* (Berlin: Stiftung Deutsche Kinemathek, 1989) and *Das Jahr 1945. Filme aus fünfzehn Ländern* (Berlin: Stiftung Deutsche Kinemathek, 1990); also Wolfgang Jacobsen, ed., *Babelsberg. Das Filmstudio,* 3rd rev. ed. (Berlin: Stiftung Deutsche Kinemathek/Argon, 1994).

8. See Anja Henningsmeyer, "Interview mit Ufa-Ausstellungsleiter Dr. Rainer Rother," *zitty,* 26 November 1992, p. 227. Rother, a film historian and chief director of

the exhibit, spoke of the organizers' conscious resolve "to create a situation that quotes the reality of the studios without seeking to imitate it. The main idea is to bring the viewer into ever new artificial worlds that do not remain intact, but are shattered and destroyed, in essence a direct confrontation with the dream world." Jubilation and exuberance prevailed in press accounts and television reports; the exhibit ended up on the "Hit List of Berlin Exhibits for 1992." *Die Berliner Zeitung,* for instance, ran a series of unabashedly nostalgic pieces under the title "Das gab's nur einmal—die deutsche Traumfabrik im Spiegel persönlicher Erinnerungen" (That Happened Only Once—The German Dream Factory in the Mirror of Personal Memories). Installments bore headlines such as "No One Had Such Glowing Blue Eyes as He Did" (on Hans Albers) and "They [Ufa films] Were Meant to Further German Spirit" (the Third Reich recollections of a former Ufa extra).

9. A sampling of responses with a political edge is documented in "Kontroverses aus dem Besucherbuch der Ufa-Ausstellung," *SDK-Newsletter* 4 (June 1993): 27.

10. See Oksana Bulgakowa, "Bilderschlachten," *Der Freitag,* 18 December 1992; and William Uricchio, "An Image Empire Remembered: Ufa between Memory and History," *Historical Journal of Film, Radio and Television* 13.2 (1993): 229–235.

11. Wim Wenders, "Reden über Deutschland," *Film und Fernsehen* 20.2 (1992): 44–49.

12. In the fall of 1987, members of the Berlin "Alternative List" took the cinema to task for trivializing the Nazi era. The criticism in turn gave rise to much hostile response. See Susann Mietzner's report "Seniorenfilm-Programm verteidigt. Lieber Raddatz und Röck [sic] als Schwarzenegger," *Berliner Morgenpost,* 22 September 1987. In 1993 the Eva matinee screenings of old movies were cut back to once a month.

13. Alfons Arns, "Die halbe Wahrheit. Zum Umgang mit NS-Spielfilmen in Fernsehen und Kritik," *Medium* 21.4 (1991): 35. See also Friedrich Knilli, " 'Perlen' der Leinwand. Zur Rezeption von NS-Filmen in der Bundesrepublik," *Film und Fernsehen* 8.8 (1980): 20–22.

14. The down-and-out protagonist of Klaus Schlesinger's novel *Alte Filme. Eine Berliner Geschichte* (Frankfurt am Main: Fischer, 1979) lives in East Berlin and eagerly awaits such reprises on television: "His preference for old films extended to the kind of works that generally were shown without any introductory comments and that came from the realm of light entertainment" (p. 22).

15. See the inventories of academic courses and scholarly endeavors compiled by Hans-Bernhard Moeller, "Der deutsche Film in amerikanischer Forschung und Lehre," *Film und Fernsehen in Forschung und Lehre* 7 (1984): 96–110; 9 (1986): 97–115; 11 (1988): 162–182; 14 (1991): 187–215.

16. Regarding Hitler's enthusiasm for *The Broken Jug,* see Kurt Wortig, "Realien zum Film im Dritten Reich," *dif: filmkundliche mitteilungen* 3.3 (September 1970): 27. Other commentators insist that Hitler's alltime favorite was Fred Sauer's *Die beiden Seehunde* (*The Two Seals,* 1934), starring the Bavarian character actor Weiss-Ferdl. The comedy, in which a prince switches identities with a lookalike so that he might mingle

with the common folk, presented a fantasy that neatly complemented Hitler's self-styled double role as Führer and man of the people; Thomas Brandlmeier, "Das Kino der Diktatoren. Stalin, Hitler, Mussolini," *epd Film* 10.7 (July 1993): 28, 30. See the inventory presented by Hitler's projectionist, Ellerkamp: "Two or three movies every day, *Broadway Melody* with Fred Astaire, Walt Disney's *Snow White, An Ideal Husband* with Heinz Rühmann, *The Two Seals* with Weiss Ferdl, and almost anything with Weiss Ferdl or Moser or Rühmann, and Fritz Lang's *Nibelungen* over and over again, *The Hot Punch, Quax the Hard Luck Pilot, The Finances of the Grand Duke,* operettas, *The Trouble with Iolanthe*"; Syberberg, *Hitler: A Film from Germany,* p. 109.

17. Kevin Brownlow, "Leni Reifenstahl [*sic*]," *Film* 47 (Winter 1966–67): 19.

18. See Alvin H. Rosenfeld, *Imagining Hitler* (Bloomington: Indiana University Press, 1985), p. xiv: "It is not that Nazism has been altogether denuded of its aspect of terror (although sometimes it has) but that its aura of destructive power has been turned into sexual and political fantasies, religious allegories, pseudohistories, science fictions. Nazism, in other words, has been lifted from its historical base and transmuted into forms of entertainment and political bad faith."

19. Don DeLillo, *White Noise* (New York: Viking, 1985), p. 63.

20. Promiscuous recyclings of fascist phantasms and expressive reenactments of Nazi images constitute for Saul Friedländer a "new discourse" about the Third Reich. In reflecting on Nazism, emanations of the new discourse unwittingly reflect and reproduce Nazi emphases. A postwar gathering of prominent films, novels, and essays reveals "a deep structure based on the coexistence of the adoration of power with a dream of final explosion . . . a particular kind of bondage nourished by the simultaneous desires for absolute submission and total freedom"; *Reflections of Nazism: An Essay on Kitsch and Death,* trans. Thomas Weyr (New York: Harper & Row, 1984), p. 19.

21. See Kristine McKenna, "Gotham Owes Its Look to the Third Reich," *Los Angeles Times,* 14 June 1992. In preparing *Batman Returns,* claimed production designer Bo Welch, "the first question I asked myself was how can I create a visual expression of corruption and greed? That got me thinking about the fascistic architecture employed at world's fairs—that feels corrupt because it's evocative of oppressive bureaucracies and dictatorships—so I looked at a lot of Nazi art and images from world's fairs." Welch's sets had conscious recourse to fascist architecture; the film's scenario, claimed other commentators, also contained an anti-Semitic subtext. See Rebecca Roiphe and Daniel Cooper's editorial, "Batman and the Jewish Subtext," *New York Times,* 2 July 1992.

22. See Jochen Schulte-Sasse, "Electronic Media and Cultural Politics in the Reagan Era: The Attack on Libya and Hands across America as Postmodern Events," *Cultural Critique* 8 (Winter 1987–88): 123–152.

23. J. Hoberman, *Vulgar Modernism: Writing on Movies and Other Media* (Philadelphia: Temple University Press, 1991), p. 8.

24. Compare Paul A. Cantor, " 'Adolf, We Hardly Knew You,' " in *New Essays on White Noise,* ed. Frank Lentricchia (Cambridge: Cambridge University Press, 1991), p.

58: "Do we resemble the Nazis in their devotion to dark powers or in their theatrical phoniness?"

25. See "Simulacra and Simulations," in Jean Baudrillard, *Selected Writings,* ed. Mark Poster (Stanford: Stanford University Press, 1988), pp. 166–184.

26. See the fiercely partisan commentaries in Karlheinz Wendtland, *Geliebter Kintopp. Sämtliche deutsche Spielfilme von 1929–1945,* 10 vols. (Berlin: Wendtland, 1987–1991); see also Arthur Maria Rabenalt, *Film im Zwielicht* (Hildesheim: Olms, 1978). They, like other writers, celebrate Nazi cinema as a "golden era" in German film history. See also Curt Riess, *Das gab's nur einmal. Die große Zeit des deutschen Films* (Vienna/Munich: Molden, 1977); Géza von Cziffra, *Es war eine rauschende Ballnacht. Eine Sittengeschichte des deutschen Films* (Frankfurt am Main: Ullstein, 1987); and Michele Sakkara, ed., *Die große Zeit des deutschen Films 1933–1945* (Leoni am Starnberger See: Druffel, 1980).

27. Gerd Albrecht, *Nationalsozialistische Filmpolitik* (Stuttgart: Enke, 1969), pp. 96–97. In generating these figures, Albrecht relies chiefly on the generic descriptions of the Nazi Reichsfilmarchiv. He distinguishes between films with manifest (intended and recognized) and latent (neither intended nor recognized) propaganda, that is, between political and nonpolitical films. In crucial and problematic ways, Albrecht's statistics reflect Nazi categories and conceptions.

28. Wolfgang Becker, *Film und Herrschaft. Organisationsprinzipien und Organisationsstrukturen der nationalsozialistischen Filmpropaganda* (Berlin: Spiess, 1973), pp. 118–119. See also Peter Nowotny, *Leni Riefenstahls "Triumph des Willens"* (Dortmund: Nowotny, 1981), p. 80: paraphrasing Becker, the author concludes that "entertainment feature films corresponded in this way every bit as much to political and ideological intentions as those productions that were explicitly produced as propaganda films."

29. Erwin Leiser, *Nazi Cinema,* trans. Gertrud Mander and David Wilson (New York: Collier, 1975), pp. 16–17. Note Leiser's statement of intent: "My purpose is to demonstrate, as clearly as I can, the mechanics by which film became part of the propaganda machine" (p. 8).

30. Richard Grunberger, *The 12-Year Reich: A Social History of Nazi Germany, 1933–1945* (New York: Holt, Rinehart and Winston, 1971), p. 376.

31. Ibid., p. 378. Regarding the discrepancies between National Socialist policy and everyday culture in the Third Reich, see Hans Dieter Schäfer, *Das gespaltene Bewußtsein. Über deutsche Kultur und Lebenswirklichkeit 1933–1945* (Munich/Vienna: Hanser, 1981).

32. Klaus Kreimeier, *Die Ufa-Story. Geschichte eines Filmkonzerns* (Munich/Vienna: Hanser, 1992), pp. 253, 268.

33. Ibid., p. 270.

34. David Stewart Hull, *Film in the Third Reich* (New York: Simon and Schuster, 1973), p. 7. Julian Petley takes violent exception to this thesis in *Capital and Culture: German Cinema 1933–45* (London: British Film Institute, 1979), p. 4: "Hull's particular combination of special pleading, wishful thinking and political innocence can be ex-

plained partly by his naive reliance on interviews with and statements by the likes of Veit Harlan, Leni Riefenstahl and Luis Trenker, who have clearly taken this as a welcome opportunity to remove black (or brown) spots from their pasts."

35. See, for instance, Riess, *Das gab's nur einmal;* Cziffra, *Es war eine rauschende Ballnacht;* as well as almost every single memoir written by film artists who worked in the Third Reich.

36. A recent American commentator, for instance, comes to the following conclusion: "While only about 10 percent of the thirteen hundred features made in National Socialist Germany can be claimed to have substantial propaganda content, only about 10 percent—a different 10 percent—can be claimed as masterpieces of filmmaking"; William Moritz, "Film Censorship during the Nazi Era," in *"Degenerate Art": The Fate of the Avant-Garde in Nazi Germany,* ed. Stephanie Barron (Los Angeles: Los Angeles County Museum of Art, 1991), p. 188.

37. Maxim Biller, *Die Tempojahre* (Munich: Deutscher Taschenbuch Verlag, 1991), pp. 37–38.

38. Axel Eggebrecht, *Der halbe Weg. Zwischenbilanz einer Epoche* (Reinbek bei Hamburg: Rowohlt, 1975), p. 308.

39. PEM, "The Nazis Return," *Films and Filming* 12.7 (April 1966): 39.

40. Leiser, *Nazi Cinema,* p. 12.

41. Compare Peter Reichel, *Der schöne Schein des Dritten Reiches. Faszination und Gewalt des Faschismus* (Munich/Vienna: Hanser, 1991), p. 16. Christian Metz distinguishes between a fascist cinema of compulsion and a capitalist/liberal cinema that relies on the popularity of commodities. Nazi cinema would seem to be under discussion when Metz speaks of political regimes "in which certain direct propaganda films are practically 'obligatory' for members of the movement or of the official youth organizations"; *The Imaginary Signifier: Psychoanalysis and the Cinema,* trans. Celia Britton et al. (Bloomington: Indiana University Press, 1982), p. 9. Thus even at this sophisticated theoretical level, fascist film's public sphere is seen in contrast to "normal" forms of circulation: it would seem to involve command performances that obviate the viewer's free choice. In this way, one likens the effect of feature films to that of overtly political documentaries. The latter, argues Siegfried Kracauer in his exemplary analysis of wartime propaganda, "treated souls like prisoners of war; they endeavored to duplicate in the field of psychology Germany's achievements in Europe"; "Supplement: Propaganda and the Nazi War Film," in *From Caligari to Hitler: A Psychological History of the German Film* (Princeton: Princeton University Press, 1947), p. 288.

42. Kreimeier, *Die Ufa-Story,* p. 331.

43. David Welch, *Propaganda and the German Cinema 1933–1945* (Oxford: Oxford University Press, 1983), p. 1. There is a curious similarity between how some critics look at the place of propaganda within Nazi culture at large and how they glimpse the place of propaganda in Nazi films. In both cases one assumes certain contents as given and speaks of their insidious qualities while failing to consider the functional and formal constitution of Nazi culture and Nazi film culture. Propaganda is not just a political

message but also the product of the systematic implementation of modern media within various sectors of the public sphere.

44. Ibid., p. 3: "I must stress that this investigation still excludes the majority of 'escapist' films that were produced during the Third Reich principally for entertainment purposes." This is a characteristic approach to entertainment films of the era. See also Louis Marcorelles, "The Nazi Cinema (1933–1945)," *Sight and Sound* 25.2 (Autumn 1955): "Where, then, was the national-socialist line in these resolutely escapist films? It seemed to exist solely in providing the best kind of recreation for a populace long deprived of so many of the charms of life, and drawn more and more inexorably towards total war" (p. 67).

45. See Francis Courtade and Pierre Cadars, *Geschichte des Films im Dritten Reich,* trans. Florian Hopf (Munich/Vienna: Hanser, 1975): one must, claim the authors, consider Steinhoff and Ritter "among the Third Reich's most talented filmmakers" (p. 179). A rave review of this book appeared in the radical right-wing West German newspaper *Deutsche Nationalzeitung* on 26 November 1976. For a sustained critique of Courtade/Cadars's cineastic celebration of Nazi film, see Karl Stamm, "Rezension. Courtade, François [*sic*] und Pierre Cadars: *Geschichte des Films im Dritten Reich,*" *Kritische Berichte* 5–6 (1976): 54–62.

46. Rabenalt, *Film im Zwielicht;* and Karlheinz Wendtland, *Deutsche Spielfilmproduktion 1933–1945. Blüte des deutschen Films oder Ideologiefabrik der Nazis* (Berlin: Wendtland, n.d.). For an East German critique of such rehabilitation attempts, see Günter Netzeband, "D. St. Hull und die Folgen. Korrekturen zur Nazifilm- und Geschichtsschreibung," *Film und Fernsehen* 7.1 (January 1979): 33–38.

47. See historian David Weinberg's comments regarding crucial gaps in Nazi film studies: "There have been few attempts at indepth analysis of film content . . . There is a need to go beyond the manifest messages of films produced under nazism to explore their subtle impact upon the psychology of the individual viewer. Such an exploration necessitates not only interpretation of the film dialogue but also an awareness of the various visual techniques employed by film-makers to create specific audience responses"; "Approaches to the Study of Film in the Third Reich: A Critical Appraisal," *Journal of Contemporary History* 19.1 (January 1984): 117.

48. Richard Meran Barsam, *Filmguide to Triumph of the Will* (Bloomington: Indiana University Press, 1975), p. 18.

49. "Fascinating Fascism" first appeared in the 6 February 1975 issue of the *New York Review of Books;* it was reprinted in Susan Sontag, *Under the Sign of Saturn* (New York: Vintage, 1981), pp. 71–105.

50. Many of Kracauer's most important essays of the 1920s and early 1930s are available in *The Mass Ornament: Weimar Essays,* trans. and ed. Thomas Y. Levin (Cambridge, Mass.: Harvard University Press, 1995). Benjamin's essay is to be found in *Illuminations,* ed. Hannah Arendt, trans. Harry Zohn (New York: Schocken, 1969), pp. 217–251.

51. Karsten Witte, "Visual Pleasure Inhibited: Aspects of the German Revue Film,"

trans. J. D. Steakley and Gabriele Hoover, *New German Critique* 24–25 (Fall/Winter 1981–82): 262.

52. Ibid., p. 257. Witte offers an incisive analytical overview of Nazi film culture in his essay "Film im Nationalsozialismus. Blendung und Überblendung," in *Geschichte des deutschen Films,* ed. Wolfgang Jacobsen, Anton Kaes, and Hans Helmut Prinzler (Stuttgart: Metzler, 1993), pp. 119–170.

53. Witte, "Visual Pleasure Inhibited," p. 261.

54. It is all but a cliché of the secondary literature that directors such as Willi Forst, Gustav Ucicky, and Wolfgang Liebeneiner were skilled professionals who could have pursued equally successful careers in Hollywood.

55. Petley, *Capital and Culture;* Régine Mihal Friedman, *L'image et son juif. Le juif dans le cinéma nazi* (Paris: Payot, 1983); and Stephen Lowry, *Pathos und Politik. Ideologie in Spielfilmen des Nationalsozialismus* (Tübingen: Niemeyer, 1991).

56. Commentators, especially in Germany, have frequently called for studies along these lines. Take, for instance, Fernand Jung's recent demand that we bear in mind contemporary media culture when we study fascist propaganda, because "one can find no better way of sensitizing eyes and ears to false tones than the film of the Third Reich"; "Zwei Bücher zum Nazifilm," *epd Film* 7.3 (March 1990): 8.

57. Patrice Petro, *Joyless Streets: Women and Melodramatic Representation in Weimar Germany* (Princeton: Princeton University Press, 1989); Miriam Hansen, "Early Silent Cinema: Whose Public Sphere?" *New German Critique* 29 (Spring–Summer 1983): 147–184.

58. See, among other contributions, Gertrud Koch, "Der höhere Befehl der Frau ist ihr niederer Instinkt. Frauenhaß und Männer-Mythos in Filmen über Preußen," in *Preußen im Film,* ed. Axel Marquardt and Heinz Rathsack (Reinbek bei Hamburg: Rowohlt, 1981), pp. 219–233; Heide Schlüpmann, "Faschistische Trugbilder weiblicher Autonomie," *Frauen und Film* 44–45 (October 1988): 44–66; Ute Bechdolf, *Wunsch-Bilder? Frauen im nationalsozialistischen Unterhaltungsfilm* (Tübingen: Tübinger Vereinigung für Volkskunde, 1992); and Dora Traudisch, *Mutterschaft mit Zuckerguß? Frauenfeindliche Propaganda im NS-Spielfilm* (Pfaffenweiler: Centaurus, 1993).

59. I share Marc Ferro's desire to fathom film's dynamic historical meaning potential. See his valuable essay "Film as an Agent, Product and Source of History," *Journal of Contemporary History* 3 (July 1983): 357–363.

60. Enno Patalas, "Reise in die Vergangenheit," *Filmkritik* 9.11 (November 1965): 650.

61. Compare B. Ruby Rich, "Leni Riefenstahl: The Deceptive Myth," in *Sexual Stratagems: The World of Women in Film,* ed. Patricia Erens (New York: Horizon, 1979), p. 207: "For if the hypnotic manipulation of the audience, encouraging identification with the distorted characters within the world of film and manipulating that identification for ideologically potent ends, is a cinema of latent fascism, then just such a cinema dominates our screens today."

62. "Appell an die Disziplin der Parteischaffenden," *Film-Kurier,* 21 December 1940.

63. Among the era's numerous trade paper discussions about mass audiences and spectator responses, see, for instance, the lead articles W. P., "Suggestion und Beifall. Es spricht für den Film, wenn geklatscht wird," *Film-Kurier,* 29 March 1939; and Hermann Meyer, "Der falsche Lacher," *Film-Kurier,* 4 May 1937. Also see Meyer's long essay "Mundpropaganda und Film," *Film-Kurier,* 19 and 20 February 1937: word of mouth reflects the opinions of individuals. One would do well to pay careful attention to such feedback "because, as a legitimate private response, it has a decisive influence on a film's potential success."

64. See Fritz Hippler, *Betrachtungen zum Filmschaffen* (Berlin: Hesse, 1942), p. 15: film must extend its interests to encompass the widest range of topics and materials. Hippler speaks explicitly of a "film encyclopedia" as a collective endeavor to be undertaken by all the production companies. The enterprise is to be conceived of as a comprehensive lexicon. This would lead to an index of names, concepts, elements, all of which would be considered in terms of their filmic possibility.

65. See Peter Brückner et al., "Perspectives on the Fascist Public Sphere," *New German Critique* 11 (Spring 1977): 94–132.

66. The phrase is taken from Max Horkheimer and Theodor W. Adorno, *Dialectic of Enlightenment,* trans. John Cumming (New York: Seabury, 1972), p. 163.

67. See Goebbels' diary entry of 30 January 1938, *Tagebücher 1924–1945,* ed. Ralf Georg Reuth, 5 vols. (Munich: Piper, 1992), vol. 3, p. 1191.

68. The proportion of American features premiered in Germany declined steadily throughout the 1930s; Bogusław Drewniak, *Der deutsche Film 1938–1945. Ein Gesamtüberblick* (Düsseldorf: Droste, 1987), p. 814.

69. Hans-Hubert Gensert, "Die neue Kunstanschauung und ihr Ausdruck," *Der Deutsche Film* 2.12 (June 1938): 323–326.

70. Fritz Aeckerle, "Wohin steuern wir? Der Film am Kreuzweg," *Der Deutsche Film* 2.4 (October 1937): 98.

71. Veit Harlan's *Der Herrscher (The Ruler),* with its apotheosis of a leader's iron will and German industrial might, was one of few strident exceptions among the year's releases.

72. Hans Spielhofer, "Vom Kostümfilm zum Gegenwartsfilm," *Der Deutsche Film* 2.4 (October 1937): 109.

73. See, for instance, Hans Spielhofer, "Die Eindruckskraft des Bildes," *Der Deutsche Film* 2.6 (December 1937): 160–162; or Walter Berten, "Musik durch Film, Funk und Schallplatte," *Der Deutsche Film* 1.7 (January 1937): 200–203, 207.

74. Gert Eckert, "Filmtendenz und Tendenzfilm," *Wille und Macht. Führerorgan der nationalsozialistischen Jugend* 6.4 (15 February 1938): 19–25.

75. As quoted in Gerd Rühle, *Das Dritte Reich. Dokumentarische Darstellung des Aufbaus der Nation, das erste Jahr. 1933* (Berlin: Hummel, 1934), p. 82.

76. Gert Berghoff, "Die Spielfilmproduktion 1933–1945," in *Der Spielfilm im Dritten*

Reich, ed. Manfred Dammeyer (Oberhausen: XII. Westdeutsche Kurzfilmtage, 1966), p. 50. This trend remained constant throughout the Third Reich. The seven most successful films of the 1941–42 season, for instance, combined melodramas, musicals, anti-Semitic agitation, and a historical war film: *Die große Liebe,* 8 million RM box-office; *Wunschkonzert,* 7.6 million RM; *Frauen sind doch bessere Diplomaten,* 7.0 million RM; *Wiener Blut,* 7.0 million RM; *Annelie,* 6.5 million RM; *Jud Süß,* 6.2 million RM; *Der große König,* 6.0 million RM; Lowry, *Pathos und Politik,* p. 271.

77. "Ufa verpflichtet Lilian Harvey/Schule Riefenstahl," lead stories in *Film-Kurier,* 25 January 1936.

78. A foreign visitor to prewar Hamburg provided an intriguing and detailed account of an evening at the Ufa-Palast in "Hamburg Cinema: A Typical German Programme Described by Winifred Holmes," *Sight and Sound* 8 (Spring 1939): 18–20.

79. Hartmut Bitomsky, "Der Kotflügel eines Mercedes Benz. Nazikulturfilme, Teil I. Filme von 1933 bis 1938," *Filmkritik* 27.10 (October 1983): 445.

80. An uncustomarily frank commentary from the era supplies an ironic appreciation of the interaction between different program offerings. Before the Zarah Leander film, *Der Blaufuchs* (*The Fox Fur Coat,* 1938), "ran a culture film, a film with culture, about the certainty of animal instinct. Then followed a feature about the shortcomings of human instinct"; Werner Fiedler, "Vom Blaufuchs und anderen Tieren. Ufa-Film im Gloria-Palast," *Deutsche Allgemeine Zeitung,* 15 December 1938. For comments regarding Werner Fiedler's reviews and critical praxis during the Third Reich in general, see Theo Fürstenau, "Eskapismus und Camouflage," *Internationale Zeitschrift für Kommunikationsforschung* 1.3 (1974): 366–382.

81. *The Goebbels Diaries: 1939–1941,* trans. and ed. Fred Taylor (Harmondsworth: Penguin, 1984), p. 84.

82. Philippe Lacoue-Labarthe, *Heidegger, Art and Politics,* trans. Chris Turner (Oxford: Blackwell, 1990), p. 64.

83. Sontag "Fascinating Fascism," p. 91.

84. Hannah Arendt, *The Origins of Totalitarianism* (New York: World, 1958), p. 325.

85. Compare Frieda Grafe, "Leni Riefenstahl. Falsche Bauern, falsche Soldaten und was für ein Volk," *Süddeutsche Zeitung,* 13–14 September 1975: "There are no definitive criteria for fascist style, there is art that has gone to the dogs, which publicizes ideas."

86. See Berthold Hinz, *Art in the Third Reich,* trans. Robert Kimber and Rita Kimber (New York: Pantheon, 1979), p. 21: "The National Socialists created continuity by making central figures out of peripheral ones. The constant falling back on nineteenth-century art and particularly on what was not the best art of that century amounts to an attempt to link it with the present by enlisting the aid of provincial art."

87. The German notion of the *Gesamtkunstwerk* was even extended to describe the totalizing effect of Hollywood movies. See, for instance, H. Ch. M., "Amerikanische Filme," *Die Tat* 28.2 (May 1936): "Whereas German features manage to present only a few good dramatic performances with cinematic allure, good American films are total works of art. The spiritual quality, the richness of sensibility and emotion in a single

dramatic role of a German film, is larger and deeper than all the roles in an entire American film. But because American films are total works of art, even if very primitive ones, they have a significance that deserves future consideration" (p. 151). The author concludes with a discussion of the overwhelming effect of Leni Riefenstahl's short, *Tag der Freiheit!—Unsere Wehrmacht* (*Day of Freedom,* 1935). Its high drama and artistic pyrotechnics achieve the same ends as its Hollywood counterparts but remain decidedly less subtle. "As a means of expression, film surely comes much more easily to the American" (p. 153).

88. Thomas Elsaesser, "Film History and Visual Pleasure: Weimar Cinema," in *Cinema Histories, Cinema Practices,* ed. Patricia Mellencamp and Philip Rosen (Frederick, Md.: University Publications of America, 1984), p. 72.

89. See, for instance, Klaus Staeck, ed., *Nazi-Kunst ins Museum?* (Göttingen: Steidl, 1988); and the special issue "Nazikunst ins Museum?" *tendenzen* 157 (January–March 1987).

90. Rosenfeld, *Imagining Hitler,* p. xvi.

1. A Legend for Modern Times

1. Stephen Schiff, "Leni's Olympia," *Vanity Fair,* September 1992, pp. 252–261, 291–296. The same issue contains a short portrait of Riefenstahl's adversary, also by Schiff, "Prodigal Sontag."

2. John Simon, "The Führer's Movie Maker," *New York Times Book Review,* 26 September 1993, pp. 1, 26–29.

3. Richard Corliss, "Riefenstahl's Last Triumph," *Time,* 18 October 1993, pp. 91–92.

4. See Ernst Jaeger's account, "How Leni Riefenstahl became Hitler's Girlfriend," *Hollywood Tribune,* 28 April through 17 July 1939 (weekly installments). Jaeger, former editor-in-chief of *Film-Kurier,* defected to the United States while accompanying Riefenstahl on her 1938 tour through America.

5. Budd Schulberg, "Nazi Pin-Up Girl: Hitler's No. 1 Movie Actress," *Saturday Evening Post,* 30 March 1946, p. 11.

6. See Glenn B. Infield, *Leni Riefenstahl: The Fallen Film Goddess* (New York: Crowell, 1976).

7. Bianca Jagger, "Leni's Back & Bianca's Got Her," *Interview* 5 (January 1975): 35–37.

8. Quoted in Georg Seesslen, "Die Krieger, der Tanz, das Mädchen und der Führer," *Blimp* 22/23 (Spring 1993): 23. See her response in Leni Riefenstahl, *A Memoir* (New York: St. Martin's, 1993), p. 650: "I would love to have met this unusually gifted as well as controversial director and to have worked with him—especially after he wrote to me how keenly he looked forward to our collaboration." Fragile health, however, prevented her from accepting the offer.

9. Kevin Brownlow, "Leni Reifenstahl [*sic*]," *Film* (London) 47 (Winter 1966–67): 15.

10. The secondary literature on Riefenstahl's career and films is massive and ever-growing. A useful albeit outdated initial guide is Sandra Bernstein and Michael MacMillan, "Leni Riefenstahl: A Selected Annotated Bibliography," *Quarterly Review of Film Studies* 2.4 (November 1977): 439–457. Recent career studies include David B. Hinton, *The Films of Leni Riefenstahl* (Metuchen, N.J.: Scarecrow, 1978); Charles Ford, *Leni Riefenstahl* (Paris: La Table Ronde, 1978); Renata Berg-Pan, *Leni Riefenstahl* (Boston: Twayne, 1980); and Leonardo Quaresima, *Leni Riefenstahl* (Florence: La Nuova Italia, 1984). The most comprehensive account of her early films as actress and director is Peggy Ann Wallace, "An Historical Study of the Career of Leni Riefenstahl from 1923 to 1933" (Diss. University of Southern California, 1975). For analyses of *Triumph of the Will,* see Richard Meran Barsam, *Filmguide to Triumph of the Will* (Bloomington: Indiana University Press, 1975); Peter Nowotny, *Leni Riefenstahls "Triumph des Willens"* (Dortmund: Nowotny, 1981); Martin Loiperdinger, *Der Parteitagsfilm "Triumph des Willens" von Leni Riefenstahl. Rituale der Mobilmachung* (Opladen: Leske + Budrich, 1987); and Linda Deutschmann, *Triumph of the Will: The Image of the Third Reich* (Wakefield, N.H.: Longwood, 1991). For close studies of *Olympia,* see Cooper C. Graham, *Leni Riefenstahl and Olympia* (Metuchen, N.J.: Scarecrow, 1986); and Taylor Downing, *Olympia* (London: British Film Institute, 1992).

11. Susan Sontag, "Fascinating Fascism," *New York Review of Books,* 6 February 1975; reprinted in Sontag, *Under the Sign of Saturn* (New York: Vintage, 1981), p. 97.

12. Ibid., p. 91.

13. Karsten Witte, "Visual Pleasure Inhibited: Aspects of the German Revue Film," trans. J. D. Steakley and Gabriele Hoover, *New German Critique* 24–25 (Fall/Winter 1981–82): 261.

14. Riefenstahl also produced two short films about the most prominent fascist artists, both directed by Arnold Fanck: *Josef Thorak—Werkstatt und Werk* (1943) and *Arno Breker* (1944).

15. Thomas Elsaesser, "Portrait of the Artist as a Young Woman," *Sight and Sound* 3.2 (February 1993): 18.

16. *Das blaue Licht,* 1932. Produced by L. R.-Studio-Film and H. R. Sokal-Produktion, Berlin. Producers: Leni Riefenstahl and Heinrich Sokal (uncredited). Production Assistance: Waldi Traut. Director: Leni Riefenstahl. Script: Leni Riefenstahl, Béla Balázs, Hans Schneeberger, and Carl Mayer (uncredited). Cinematography: Hans Schneeberger. Assistant Cameraman: Heinz von Jaworski. Publicity Still Photographer: Walter Riml. Original Score: Giuseppe Becce. Song Texts: Hedy Knorr. Set Design: Leopold Blonder. Sound: Hans Bittmann. Sound Editing: Hanne Kuyt. Editing: Leni Riefenstahl and Arnold Fanck (uncredited).

The Players: Leni Riefenstahl (Junta), Mathias Wieman (Vigo, a painter), Franz Maldacea (Guzzi, a shepherd boy), Max Holzboer (innkeeper), Beni Führer (Tonio, his son), Martha Mair (Lucia), peasants from the Sarn Valley.

Original length: 2,341 meters (85 minutes). Premiered on 24 March 1932 in Berlin (Ufa-Palast am Zoo). Rating: "Artistic."

A subtitled 16mm copy is available from Films Incorporated and Kit Parker Films; a subtitled videocassette can be purchased from Facets Video, the German Language Video Center, and International Historic Films.

17. Hans Barkhausen provides evidence regarding the Nazi government's support of the two *Olympia* films; "Footnote to the History of Riefenstahl's *Olympia*," *Film Quarterly* 28.1 (Fall 1974): 8–12.

18. For a detailed account of Balázs' work on *The Blue Light,* see Joseph Zsuffa, *Béla Balázs: The Man and the Artist* (Berkeley: University of California Press, 1987), esp. pp. 203–206, 214–215. According to Zsuffa, Balázs' influence was central to the film's conception and ultimate shape. Carl Mayer assisted Balázs in writing the script and also participated in the editing, clashing violently with Fanck, who also played a key role in the cutting of the film (p. 219). Zsuffa's reconstruction of the production and division of labor provides a dynamic sense of collaboration, cooperation, and conflict. His discussion, though sympathetic to Balázs, is meticulously documented, drawing on private correspondence, archival materials, and contemporary reviews, all of which renders it more credible than Riefenstahl's self-serving and contradictory recollections. See also John Ralmon, "Béla Balázs in German Exile," *Film Quarterly* 30.3 (Spring 1977): 12–19.

19. During the mid-1980s the German journalist and filmmaker Nina Gladitz engaged in a vigorous campaign against Riefenstahl, claiming the director willingly exploited gypsy inmates from a concentration camp during her wartime work on *Tiefland* (*Lowlands*), offering help if they cooperated, but in the end failing to make good on her promise. These allegations were denied by the filmmaker in an ensuing court battle, when Riefenstahl again argued that she stood unfairly accused. See, for instance, Wolfgang Rumpf, "Infame Lügen," *Tip,* 14 December 1984, pp. 56–57; and Ulrich Enzensberger, "KZ-Zigeuner tanz' mit mir," *Konkret,* February 1985, pp. 12–17. Also see Gladitz's film about Riefenstahl and *Lowlands,* the WDR production that prompted the legal proceedings, *Zeit des Schweigens und der Dunkelheit (Time of Silence and Darkness).* For an analysis of the documentary see Andreas Seltzer, "Bildbanditen," *Merkur* 39 (July 1985): 621–625. After Riefenstahl appealed the initial verdict, a second trial confirmed Gladitz's claims that the director had selected 60 gypsies from a group of 250 concentration camp inmates and forced them to act in *Lowlands* without pay. Among the many press accounts, see Hanno Kühnert's critical essay, "Wenn Juristen Vergangenheit klären," *Die Zeit,* 27 March 1987.

20. Siegfried Kracauer, in *From Caligari to Hitler: A Psychological History of the German Film* (Princeton: Princeton University Press, 1947), described Junta "as a sort of gypsy girl" (p. 258).

21. Riefenstahl, *A Memoir,* p. 89. An identical translation appeared in Great Britain under the title *The Sieve of Time* (London: Quartet, 1992). The German original edition, *Memoiren* (Munich/Hamburg: Knaus, 1987), is more than 250 pages longer.

22. Michel Delahaye's interview with the director appeared in the September 1965 number of *Cahiers du cinéma.* The passage is quoted from Rose Kaplin's awkward English translation in *Interviews with Film Directors,* ed. Andrew Sarris (New York: Avon, 1967), p. 468.

23. Barsam, *Filmguide to Triumph of the Will,* p. 9. See also Simon, "The Führer's Movie Maker," p. 29: "Perhaps we should look to the character with whom Riefenstahl most closely identifies herself: Junta, the mountain girl in *The Blue Light,* who was willing to die for her aspirations. Riefenstahl, too, was ready to sacrifice all in pursuit of her obsessions."

24. See David Gunston, "Leni Riefenstahl," *Film Quarterly* 14.1 (Fall 1960): *The Blue Light* is "the one film above all others that was to settle her fate as a director" (p. 12).

25. Invitations to the Ufa-sponsored gala premiere of 1932 announce a 6:45 P.M. curtain. The program began with Ufa sound newsreel no. 81. Guiseppe Becce conducted the Ufa Symphony Orchestra in a live performance of Tchaikovsky's *Capriccio italien,* followed by a stage prologue to *The Blue Light* (a solo dance by Igor Schwezoff choreographed by Percy Athos with original music by Becce) before the actual feature. The 1952 German reprise, in contrast, was preceded by the 21-minute short *Wunder der Bienenwelt* (*Wonders of the Bee World*), a *Kulturfilm* that promised "unforgettable insights into the deeper meaning of miraculous creation." The publicity brochure lists the length of *The Blue Light* as 2,000 meters (73 minutes). The information file on *The Blue Light* in the Stiftung Deutsche Kinemathek, Berlin, also contains the program for the 1938 release and the National-Verleih press booklet for the 1952 version.

26. Riefenstahl, *A Memoir,* p. 384.

27. Postwar apologias of Riefenstahl echo a previous century's romantic celebrations of the artist-genius. Take, for instance, Rühle von Lilienstern's special plea for Caspar David Friedrich: "All genius is of an infinite nature and is, to itself and for all others, the measure and plumbline and substitute for all finite experience. It is safest to let it flourish freely, where and when it is encompassed within the process of creation . . . It behoves genius to break new ground everywhere, and to ripen according to its own experience, just as it allows no rules from without to intrude upon it, preferring rather to err in the heights and depths than to remain content in the false ground of impoverished certainty. 'Can genius really err?' *Genius,* never!—insofar as it is understood as the divine, creative principle"; quoted in Joseph Leo Koerner, *Caspar David Friedrich and the Subject of Landscape* (London: Reaktion, 1990), p. 61.

28. Berg-Pan, *Leni Riefenstahl,* p. 82.

29. National Film press booklet for the 1952 German release, Stiftung Deutsche Kinemathek.

30. See Zsuffa, *Béla Balázs,* p. 454: "Arnold Fanck was familiar with Renker's novels; in fact he used the title, with a slight change, of one of Renker's novels, *Heilige Bergen* [*sic*] *(Holy Mountains),* for the first film in which Riefenstahl acted, *Der heilige Berg (The Holy Mountain).* Thus it is most likely that Riefenstahl became acquainted with Renker's works at the very beginning of her film career."

31. Riefenstahl quoted in Wallace, "Riefenstahl from 1923 to 1933," p. 285. Compare the director's similar allegation regarding *Triumph of the Will* in a letter to the editor of *Film Library Quarterly* 5.3 (Summer 1972): "Since, right down to the premiere of the film no one from the party, neither Hitler nor Goebbels nor others, got to see as much as one meter of the film, nothing can be said, consequently, of the intention or interference of the political leaders. Just as the film is still to be seen today, it came into being from out of my imagination alone" (p. 5).

32. Gustav Renker, *Bergkristall,* 4th ed. (Gütersloh: Bertelsmann, 1943), p. 45.

33. Riefenstahl speaks of her work in evocative terms reminiscent of Friedrich's notion that art is "the language of our feeling, or disposition, indeed, even our devotion and our prayers"; quoted in William Vaughan, *German Romantic Painting* (New Haven: Yale University Press, 1980), p. 74.

34. Likewise, the iconography of the final sequence brings to mind Friedrich's "Morning" and "Morning Mist in the Mountains" as well as "Two Men Contemplating the Moon" and "Rocky Gorge in *Elbesandsteingebirge.*"

35. Consistently, we encounter a use of silhouetting characteristic of Friedrich, with solitary bodies shaded in dark contours posing before luminescent and vague backdrops, a strategy often found as well in Fanck's mountain films. Elsewhere we glimpse, as in Friedrich, figures who stand with their backs to the viewer and stare into the distance, small dots against vast expanses, characters who embody yearning, persons wishing to merge with the grandeur before them.

36. Alice A. Kuzniar, "The Temporality of Landscape: Romantic Allegory and C. D. Friedrich," *Studies in Romanticism* 28.1 (Spring 1989): 74. Compare Philippe Lacoue-Labarthe and Jean-Luc Nancy, *The Literary Absolute: The Theory of Literature in German Romanticism,* trans. Philip Barnard and Cheryl Lester (Albany: State University of New York Press, 1988), p. 4: A landscape before which one feels the "sentiment of nature" is romantic. "But romantic, as well, is the sensibility capable of responding to the spectacle, and of imagining, or better, recreating—*phantasieren*—what it evokes."

37. Vigo was played by Mathias Wieman, a strident Nazi activist, one of the first to receive Hitler's commendation as a state actor *(Staatsschauspieler)* in 1937.

38. The version currently in American distribution is the 1952 German one. A fragmentary copy of the original version released in the United States also exists. Although it is silent (with English-language intertitles) and runs far less than an hour, it does have the initial (though not the final) framing passage.

39. The couple's entry to the village parallels that of another traveler from the outside world in the embedded story, namely Vigo.

40. Compare Immanuel Kant, *Observations on the Feeling of the Beautiful and Sublime,* trans. John T. Goldthwait (Berkeley: University of California Press, 1965), p. 48.

41. See Martin Swales, *The German Novelle* (Princeton: Princeton University Press, 1977), p. 28: "I would argue that the mainspring of much novelle writing is the contact between an ordered and reliably interpreted human universe on the one hand and an

experience or set of experiences that would appear to conflict utterly with any notion of order or manageable interpretation on the other. Hence, the novelle derives its peculiar and insistent energy from what one can best describe as a hermeneutic gamble, as a shock confrontation with marginal events. Implicitly, the attempt to make an ordered statement of that which by definition resists the ordering intention is one of the central undertakings within the narrative universe of the novelle."

42. Representative examples include *Das Cabinet des Dr. Caligari* (*The Cabinet of Dr. Caligari,* 1920), *Chronik von Grieshuus* (*Chronicle of the Gray House,* 1925), and *Geheimnisse der Orients* (*Secrets of the Orient,* 1928).

43. See Leni Riefenstahl, *Kampf im Schnee und Eis* (Leipzig: Hesse & Becker, 1933), for her earliest recollections of *The Holy Mountain, Der große Sprung* (*The Great Leap,* 1927), *Die weiße Hölle vom Piz Palü* (*The White Hell of Pitz Palü,* 1929), *Stürme über dem Montblanc* (*Avalanche,* 1930), *Der weiße Rausch* (*The White Frenzy,* 1931), *The Blue Light,* and *S.O.S. Eisberg* (1933). For a useful collection of materials on the mountain film, see Klaus Kreimeier, ed., *Fanck—Trenker—Riefenstahl. Der deutsche Bergfilm und seine Folgen* (Berlin: Stiftung Deutsche Kinemathek, 1972). See also the special issue of *Film und Kritik* 1 (June 1992) titled "Revisited Der Fall Dr. Fanck. Die Entdeckung der Natur im deutschen Bergfilm."

44. Kracauer, *From Caligari to Hitler,* p. 111. Throughout his exegesis Kracauer has little to say about sexual difference. In talking about mountain films, he reduces women to secondary factors in his terse and frequently ironic plot descriptions, desisting from any sustained comment about their constant and conspicuous appearance. He overlooks Junta's erotic attraction and the sexual frenzy she catalyzes in the community's young males. Instead, Kracauer explains the villagers' active hostility toward her as a result of superstition alone: because the strange woman enjoys sole access to the blue light, residents of Santa Maria consider her a witch (p. 258).

45. Herman Weigel, "Interview mit Leni Riefenstahl," *Filmkritik* 16.8 (August 1972): 396.

46. Kracauer described the genre's intended audience harshly in his notice "*Der Heilige Berg,*" *Frankfurter Zeitung,* 4 March 1927, reprinted in *Von Caligari zu Hitler,* ed. Karsten Witte (Frankfurt am Main: Suhrkamp, 1979), p. 400: "There may be here and there in Germany small youth groups that attempt to counter everything that they call mechanization, by means of an overrun nature worship, i.e., by means of a panic-stricken flight into the foggy brew of vague sentimentality. As an expression of their particular manner of not existing, the film is a masterpiece."

47. Vaughan, *German Romantic Painting,* p. 66.

48. See Hans Feld, "Der Fanck-Film der Aafa," *Film-Kurier,* 3 February 1931. See also the cinematographer Sepp Allgeier's account, *Die Jagd nach dem Bild,* 2nd rev. ed. (Stuttgart: Engelhorns, 1931), especially his description of location shooting on *The Holy Mountain:* "Sometimes we had to lend a bit of a helping hand when nature did not provide us with camera-ready footage" (p. 62). Compare Joachim Kroll, "Die filmische Landschaft," *Der Deutsche Film* 3.6 (December 1938), for whom landscapes maintained

a photographic interest only to the degree to which they reflected human presence (p. 148).

49. Riefenstahl, *A Memoir*, p. 89. Riefenstahl also describes Fanck's editing room as a "magic workshop."

50. For a detailed account of the film's production background (whose privileged source of information is Riefenstahl), see Peggy A. Wallace, " 'The Most Important Factor Was the Spirit': Leni Riefenstahl during the Filming of *The Blue Light*," *Image* 17.1 (March 1974): 17–29.

51. F. W. Murnau, "Films of the Future," *McCall's*, September 1928; quoted in Richard Koszarski, ed., *Hollywood Directors, 1914–1940* (Oxford: Oxford University Press, 1976), p. 217.

52. The phrase comes from Balázs' review of *Nosferatu*, which appeared in *Der Tag* on 9 March 1923 and was included in his collection of notices and essays, *Der sichtbare Mensch;* reprinted in Helmut H. Diederichs et al., eds., *Schriften zum Film* (Munich: Hanser, 1982), vol. 1, pp. 175–176.

53. Frieda Grafe, "Leni Riefenstahl. Falsche Bauern, falsche Soldaten und was für ein Volk," *Süddeutsche Zeitung*, 13–14 September 1975.

54. See Robin Wood's exemplary reading of *Nosferatu*, "F. W. Murnau," *Film Comment* 12.3 (May–June 1976): 7–8.

55. See ibid., p. 8: "One is tempted toward a straight psychoanalytical interpretation: Nosferatu is the symbol of neurosis resulting from the repressed sexuality (repressed nature); when the neurosis is revealed to the light of day it is exorcised, but the process of its emergence and recognition has been so terrible that positive life . . . is destroyed with it."

56. Earlier Vigo contemplates the sleeping Junta as if he were Count Orlok, leering at her exposed bosom and hovering over her body.

57. Vincent Canby, "Leni Riefenstahl in a Long Close-Up," *New York Times*, 14 October 1993.

58. Kracauer, *From Caligari to Hitler*, p. 259.

59. Sontag, "Fascinating Fascism," p. 77. Sontag's essay occasioned spirited debate in West Germany when it appeared in *Die Zeit* on 2 and 9 March 1975. See Hans Egon Holthusen, "Leni Riefenstahl in Amerika. Zum Problem einer 'faschistischen Ästhetik,' " *Merkur* 29.7 (July 1975): 569–578; see also the special issue of *Frauen und Film* devoted to the "Riefenstahl Renaissance," 14 (December 1977).

60. Andrew Sarris, "Notes on the Fascination of Fascism," *Village Voice*, 30 January 1978, p. 33. Riefenstahl also is struck by Sontag's reliance on *From Caligari to Hitler*, but she chides the American critic above all for branding "thousands of mountain climbers as Nazis or Fascists"; *A Memoir*, p. 622.

61. Sontag, "Fascinating Fascism," p. 77.

62. Ibid., p. 93.

63. Junta's metamorphosis mirrors quite poignantly the blend of kitsch and death which Saul Friedländer considers central to the frisson of Nazi aesthetics. See *Reflections of Nazism: An Essay on Kitsch and Death*, trans. Thomas Weyr (New York: Harper &

Row, 1984), p. 29: "The juxtaposition of these two contradictory elements represents the foundation of a certain religious aesthetic, and, in my opinion, the bedrock of Nazi aesthetics as well as the new evocation of Nazism."

64. See Ludwig Giesz's comments about kitsch art and tourism, "Der 'Kitsch-Mensch' als Tourist," in *Der Kitsch,* ed. Gillo Dorfies, trans. Birgid Mayr (Tübingen: Wasmuth, 1969), p. 170.

65. The later version begins with Vigo's voice-over, which was recorded after the war by Mathias Wieman: "Locked in the pathless valleys of Santa Maria, the legend of Junta lives on. On quiet evenings, the taciturn peasant tells the wanderer the story of the 'Blue Light.' It is long since extinguished, but on silvery moonlit nights, the secret of beautiful Junta entices the lonely mountaineer to Monte Cristallo's rocky walls."

66. Oskar Kalbus, *Vom Werden deutscher Filmkunst,* vol. 2: *Der Tonfilm* (Altona-Bahrenfeld: Cigaretten-Bilderdienst, 1935), p. 66. The high regard for the power of human physiognomy is, of course, a central concern in Balázs' theory of film. Compare the manner in which the villagers in *Lowlands,* played by concentration camp inmates, generally appear in group configurations rather than in sympathetic close-ups.

67. Arnold Berson, "The Truth about Leni: Nazi Collaborator—or Independent Artist," *Films and Filming* 11 (April 1965): 16.

68. Kracauer, *From Caligari to Hitler,* p. 259.

69. Ernst Bloch, "Nonsynchronism and the Obligation to Its Dialectics," trans. Mark Ritter, *New German Critique* 11 (Spring 1977): 27, 30.

70. See Jeffrey Herf, *Reactionary Modernism: Technology, Culture and Politics in Weimar and the Third Reich* (Cambridge: Cambridge University Press, 1984).

71. Compare Klaus Theweleit, *Male Fantasies,* vol. 1: *Women Floods Bodies History,* trans. Stephen Conway, Erica Carter, and Chrus Turner (Minneapolis: University of Minnesota Press, 1987), p. 215, where he discusses the fascist "language of occupation" and how "it acts imperialistically against any form of independently moving life." One might also compare this scene with the transformation of Maria into the vamp robot in Fritz Lang's *Metropolis.*

72. Upon the second release, Riefenstahl still spoke of the film as a collective effort, but her account (as well as the film's credit sequence and advertisements) left out the names of significant collaborators such as Balázs, Sokal, and Mayer; "Gespräch mit Leni Riefenstahl. 'So entstand *Das blaue Licht,*' " *Film-Kurier,* 24 September 1938. The postwar German version reinstates Balázs as a collaborator, although Riefenstahl continues to claim primary credit for the screenplay—as well as for the direction and cinematography.

73. *Triumph of the Will* would likewise change its shape over time. Its release version of March 1935 was 3,109 meters; on 2 January 1939 the film was cut back to 3,030 meters, and on 28 January 1942 to 2,358. In early September 1935 a 16mm version of 1,237 meters was also released; Klaus Kanzog, *"Staatspolitisch besonders wertvoll." Ein Handbuch zu 30 deutschen Spielfilmen der Jahre 1934 bis 1945* (Munich: Schaudig & Ledig, 1994), p. 24.

74. Hermann Sinsheimer, "Zwei Legenden. *Das blaue Licht* im Ufapalast am Zoo," *Film-Kurier,* 26 March 1932. The Vienna correspondent for the film journal *Close Up* was equally underwhelmed: "Certainly there are mountains, and water-falls, and moonlight, and clouds and very characteristic old peasants (I have never seen so many wrinkled faces in my life), but it is all so disconnected, and you cannot help thinking that someone feels obliged to show you everything which in his opinion belongs to a perfect legendary mountain film"; Trude Weiss, *"The Blue Light," Close Up* 9.2 (June 1932): 121. "Magnus," the *Variety* reviewer in Berlin, also expressed mixed feelings in his notice of 19 April 1932: "The picture could have been a worldwide hit but story appeal was ignored. The story does not grip and it is the photography, beautiful in the extreme, and fine production that carry the subject." Riefenstahl, both as director and as actress, was unimpressive. "In directing she is lost in repetitions." For a more upbeat assessment of *The Blue Light*'s resonance in the United States, see "Bahnbrechender Erfolg in den Vereinigten Staaten. Amerikanische Pressestimmen über *Das blaue Licht,*" *Film-Kurier,* 6 November 1934.

75. Coproducer Harry Sokal maintains that Riefenstahl threw a temper tantrum, chiding Jewish critics as aliens who lacked all understanding of German mentality and spirit. "Thank God," she exclaimed in 1932, "this won't last much longer!"; cited in Harry R. Sokal, "Über Nacht Antisemitin geworden?" *Der Spiegel,* 8 November 1976, p. 14. See also Goebbels' diary entry of 5 February 1939: "In the evening, Leni Riefenstahl reports to me on her trip to America. She gives me an exhaustive description, and one that is far from encouraging. We shall get nowhere there. The Jews rule by terror and bribery"; *The Goebbels Diaries: 1939–1941,* trans. and ed. Fred Taylor (Harmondsworth: Penguin, 1984), p. 9.

76. "Gespräch mit Leni Riefenstahl. 'So entstand *Das blaue Licht,*' " *Film-Kurier,* 24 September 1938. Also see Günther Schwark's review, "*Das blaue Licht*/Kurbel," *Film-Kurier,* 28 September 1938: "The film, whose artistic merit will remain unforgettable, had a very strong resonance." The January 1939 issue of *Der Deutsche Film* ran an editorial about a German national cinematography, "Gibt es einen deutschen Kamerastil?" pp. 176–177. *The Blue Light* is singled out as an exemplar of a distinctly German camera style.

77. Riefenstahl file, Berlin Document Center. The Kaiserhof hotel was a favorite gathering place for Nazi luminaries.

78. Riefenstahl, *A Memoir,* p. 135.

79. The original negative of *The Blue Light* had either been lost or, depending on the account, confiscated by the French or stolen by producer Harry Sokal.

80. Riefenstahl, *A Memoir,* p. 100.

81. Negotiations regarding the ballet version resulted in a contract signed on 27 October 1958, in which Riefenstahl granted rights for a dance adaptation that would premiere in Paris and tour Europe. For reasons unknown to Riefenstahl, the undertaking fell through. The film remake was to have been produced in England and directed by Riefenstahl. According to Wallace, "Riefenstahl from 1923 to 1933," pp. 401–403,

public controversy in England, including unfavorable articles in the *Daily Express* and other newspapers, led to cancellation of the project.

82. Dietrich Kuhlbrodt, "Leni Riefenstahl wieder offiziell," *Die Zeit,* 24 July 1964.

83. See, among other essays and articles, the special issue of *Film Comment* 3.1 (Winter 1965), "1965—Comeback for Leni Riefenstahl." The lead piece by Gordon Hitchens, "Interview with a Legend," unabashedly declares the writer's admiration: "One doesn't *interview* Riefenstahl. One listens. And watches. No question—she's a remarkable woman" (p. 6). The number gave rise to lively responses, mainly pro-Riefenstahl, in a subsequent issue of *Film Comment* 3.3 (Summer 1965): 82–87. Kevin Brownlow also published a passionate defense of the director, "Leni Reifenstahl [*sic*]." See also Jeffrey Richards, "Leni Riefenstahl: Style and Structure," *Silent Picture* 8 (Autumn 1970): 17–19. Gordon Hitchens played a key role in another American homage to Riefenstahl, a special issue devoted to the director, *Film Culture* 56–57 (Spring 1973). Almost two decades later he provided the "American Intelligence Report on Leni Riefenstahl—May 30th, 1945" for *Film Culture* 77 (Fall 1992): 34–38. WCBS "Camera Three" in New York aired a two-part program on Riefenstahl in mid-1973. See Amos Vogel's critical commentary, "Can We Now Forget the Evil That She Did?" *New York Times,* 13 May 1973: "The program was created with the active participation of Miss Riefenstahl, whose charisma has already previously inspired other impressionable men to smooth her attempt to transform herself into an innocent, apolitical artist." The international wave of enthusiasm also gave rise to *Filmkritik*'s special issue on the director in August 1972, replete with a sympathetic interview, notes from the filmmaker's Penthesilea project, an admiring portrait of Riefenstahl, and a comprehensive filmography. The issue prompted much critical discussion. See, for instance, Rudolph Ganz, "Leni Riefenstahls fragwürdige Renaissance," *Frankfurter Rundschau,* 25 August 1972; Klaus Kreimeier, "Zum Riefenstahl-Heft der '*Filmkritik,*' " *epd Kirche und Film* 25.9 (September 1972); and Gerd Albrecht, "Nochmals. Der Fall Riefenstahl. Gedanken über die Propaganda und ihre Bewunderer," *epd Kirche und Film* 25.11 (November 1972): 18–19.

84. Corliss, "Riefenstahl's Last Triumph," pp. 91–92. Compare J. Hoberman, "Triumph of the Swill," *Premiere* 7.4 (December 1993): he wryly terms the homage "something like the *Sunset Boulevard* of the Third Reich" (p. 56).

85. Sarris, *Interviews with Film Directors,* p. 456.

86. Riefenstahl, *A Memoir,* p. 89.

87. Helma Sanders-Brahms, "*Tiefland.* Tyrannenmord," in *Das Jahr 1945,* ed. Hans Helmut Prinzler (Berlin: Stiftung Deutsche Kinemathek, 1990), p. 176.

88. J. Hoberman, "Far from Lincoln Center," *Village Voice,* 7 October 1981, p. 44. The critic provides a striking characterization of Riefenstahl's "narcissistic performance" in *Lowlands:* "Clumsily sexy, she's less Marlene Dietrich in *The Devil Is a Woman* than Maria Montez in *Gypsy Wildcat.*"

89. Riefenstahl's memoirs at times read like the perils of Leni. There are repeated scenes in which she, an unwary soul, confronts male aggression and unwanted sexual

advances. The minister of propaganda harasses her in hot-and-heavy tableaus straight out of Harlequin Romances: "He grabbed my breast and tried to force himself on me. I had to wrestle my way out of his arms and dashed to the door, with Goebbels pursuing me. Besides himself with rage, he held me against the wall and tried to kiss me. His eyes were wide open and his face completely distorted"; *A Memoir,* p. 142. Later Hitler makes a pass at her, and French journalists tear off her clothes.

90. See Riefenstahl's account of her "fateful meeting" with Hitler, ibid., p. 106.

91. Gisela von Wysocki, "Die Berge und die Patriarchen. Leni Riefenstahl," in *Die Fröste der Freiheit. Aufbruchsphantasien* (Frankfurt am Main: Syndikat, 1980), p. 75.

92. The filmmaker, to be sure, was the object of much envy and idle gossip as well as abusive humor. Contemporaries called her a *Bergziege* (mountain goat-bitch) or, even worse, the *Reichsgletscherspalte* (the Reich's Glacial Crack); see, for instance, "Lachen," *Film-Kurier,* 31 March 1934; and Brigitte Jeremias, "Das Jahr 1945," *epd Film* 7.4 (April 1990): 26.

93. *Triumph of the Will,* she tells Michel Delahaye, was "only a documentary. I showed what everyone was witness to or had heard about"; Sarris, *Interviews with Film Directors,* p. 458. Later she insisted that she made the film as a documentary and it was only after the film left her hands that it became propaganda. "But what I make with *Triumph of the Will* is normally like newsreels, but I make it in my artistic way"; "Leni Riefenstahl Interviewed by Gordon Hitchens, October 11th, 1971, Munich," *Film Culture* 56–57 (Spring 1973): 102.

94. Quoted by Gunston, "Leni Riefenstahl," p. 13. See Claudia Koonz, *Mothers in the Fatherland: Women, the Family, and Nazi Politics* (New York: St. Martin's, 1987), p. 6: "The separation between masculine and feminine spheres, which followed logically and psychologically from Nazi leaders' misogyny, relegated women to their space—both beneath and beyond the dominant world of men."

95. Wysocki, *Die Froste der Freiheit,* p. 80. Riefenstahl represents, in the words of B. Ruby Rich, "a sort of Amazon among the Nazis, the token exceptional woman who was granted 'permission' by the patriarchy to be privileged in its power in exchange for adopting its values"; "Leni Riefenstahl: The Deceptive Myth," in *Sexual Stratagems: The World of Women in Myth,* ed. Patricia Erens (New York: Horizon, 1979), p. 208. Rich also argues against critics who would look to Riefenstahl as a feminist role model.

96. Margarete Mitscherlich, "Triumph der Verdrängung," *Stern,* 8 October 1987, p. 82.

97. Béla Balázs, *Theory of the Film,* trans. Edith Bone (New York: Dover, 1970), p. 33.

98. Compare Klaus Wolbert, *Die Nackten und die Toten des "Dritten Reiches"* (Giessen: anabas, 1982), p. 234: "The beauty of the nude figure in National Socialist sculpture contained . . . a mandate of death. Its excessiveness condemned anyone whose aesthetic claims could not suffice . . . The fascists murdered programmatically in the name of beauty!"

99. Compare Manohla Dargis, "Queen of Denial: The Life and Lies of Leni Riefen-

stahl," *Voice Literary Supplement* 123 (March 1994): "Riefenstahl and her defenders would rescue the director and her films from the very history and aesthetics of hate she helped create" (p. 10).

100. Joseph Goebbels, "Rede bei der ersten Jahrestagung der Reichsfilmkammer am 5.3.1937 in der Krolloper, Berlin," reprinted in Gerd Albrecht, *Nationalsozialistische Filmpolitik* (Stuttgart: Enke, 1969), p. 449.

2. Emotional Engineering

1. *Hitlerjunge Quex. Ein Film vom Opfergeist der deutschen Jugend,* 1933. Produced by Universum-Film A.-G, Production Group Karl Ritter. Director: Hans Steinhoff. Script: Karl Aloys Schenzinger and Bobby E. Luethge, based on Schenzinger's novel. Cinematography: Konstantin Irmen-Tschet. Assistant Camera: Fred Fernau and Erich Rudolf Schmidke. Publicity Photography: Otto Schulz. Editing: Milo Harbich. Set Design: Benno von Arent and Arthur Günther. Makeup: Waldemar Jabs. Clothing: Berta Grützmacher and Paul Haupt. Sound: Walter Tjaden and Erich Leistner. Music: Hans-Otto Borgmann. Lyrics for the Hitler Youth Song: Baldur von Schirach.

The Players: A Hitler Youth [Jürgen Ohlsen] (Heini Völker), Heinrich George (Father Völker), Berta Drews (Mother Völker), Claus Clausen (Brigade Leader Cass), a Hitler Youth (Fritz Dörries), a Hitler *Mädchen* (Ulla Dörries), Rotraut Richter (Gerda), Hermann Speelmans (Stoppel), Hans Richter (Franz), a Hitler Youth (Grundler), Ernst Behmer (Kowalski), Hans Joachim Büttner (doctor), Franziska Kinz (nurse), Rudolf Platte (carnival singer), Reinhold Bernt (barker), Hans Deppe (furniture dealer), Anna Müller-Lincke (neighbor of the Völker family), Karl Meixner (Wilde), Karl Hannemann (grocer), Ernst Rotmund (desk sergeant), Hans Otto Stern (bartender), Hermann Braun, Heinz Trumper, members of the Berlin Hitler Youth.

Original length: 2,609 meters (95 minutes). Premiered on 11 September 1933 in Munich (Ufa-Phoebus-Palast) and on 19 September 1933 in Berlin (Ufa-Palast am Zoo). Rating: "Artistically especially worthwhile." The film may not be screened publicly in the Federal Republic of Germany.

A 16mm copy with partial English intertitles (summaries and commentary by Gregory Bateson) can be rented from the Museum of Modern Art; a video copy with English intertitles is available from Facets Video and International Historic Films.

2. This film, claimed an enthusiastic reviewer, provided "a fanfare for Germany's youth and in so doing one for Germany's future"; "Unsere Fahne ist die neue Zeit," *Der Kinematograph,* 12 September 1933.

3. Gerhard Paul discusses the development of a party propaganda apparatus before 1933 in *Aufstand der Bilder. Die NS-Propaganda vor 1933* (Bonn: Dietz, 1990). The propaganda minister's most important programmatic addresses on film are reprinted in Gerd Albrecht, *Nationalsozialistische Filmpolitik* (Stuttgart: Enke, 1969), pp. 439–500. For general approaches to Nazi propaganda, see Robert Edwin Herzstein, *The War That Hitler Won: The Most Infamous Propaganda Campaign in History* (New York: Putnam,

1978); and Michael Balfour, *Propaganda in War, 1939–1945: Organisations, Policies and Publics in Britain and Germany* (London: Routledge & Kegan Paul, 1979).

4. Goebbels, speech in the Kaiserhof, Berlin, 28 March 1933, in Albrecht, *Nationalsozialistische Filmpolitik,* p. 439.

5. Karsten Witte, *Lachende Erben, Toller Tag. Filmkomödie im Dritten Reich* (Berlin: Vorwerk 8, 1995), p. 49.

6. Goebbels, speech in the Tennishallen, Berlin, 19 May 1933, in Albrecht, *Nationalsozialistische Filmpolitik,* pp. 442–443.

7. Goebbels, speech in the Kaiserhof, p. 440.

8. For a harsh reckoning with Weimar cinema characteristic of the transition period, see "The New German Cinema," *Film-Kurier,* 1 December 1933: "One has learned to realise that the former 'concessions to the public taste' have been much more to the detriment than to the advantage of a film and of the film business as a whole." See also a fierce polemic against Weimar cinema's alleged esoteric experiments, foreign sensibilities, and self-indulgent artists: Robert Volz, "Der Ruf nach Filmen aus dem Leben," *Film-Kurier,* 22 December 1933. The most vehement sustained attack on Weimar cinema written during the Third Reich, an extension of the campaign against "decadent art" into film culture, is to be found in Carl Neumann, Curt Belling, and Hans-Walther Betz, *Film-"Kunst," Film-Kohn, Film-Korruption* (Berlin: Scherping, 1937).

9. Goebbels, speech in the Kaiserhof, p. 441.

10. Goebbels, speech in the Tennishallen, pp. 442, 444.

11. Jay W. Baird, *To Die for Germany: Heroes in the Nazi Pantheon* (Bloomington: Indiana University Press, 1990) p. 119. This source provides a meticulously researched account of Norkus' life, death, and transfiguration. Throughout his book, Baird mimics National Socialist perspectives, simulating its virulent anti-Semitism, anti-Communism, and misogyny. This discursive ploy is undoubtedly meant to be critical; at times, though, it gives way to an unwitting affective alignment. A description of the character Wilde, for instance, actually embellishes what we see in Steinhoff's film: "When the devil took human form, he came as Wilde, and his followers are the gangsters and shadowy figures who compose the neighborhood KPD. His physiognomy is calculated to reflect an inner nature of decomposition; here, indeed, was a 'subhuman,' the product of miscegenation, venereal disease, and criminality. Unshaven, squint-eyed, and repulsive, he was the incarnation of Bolshevism. The gutter was his proper milieu" (p. 123). The Communist Gerda's "raw sexuality," we read, "is devoid of Nordic refinement"; a "painted street girl," she provides "a walking catalogue of Berlin vice" (ibid.).

12. *Film-Kurier* published and distributed the lyrics to the theme song of *Hitler Youth Quex,* "Unsere Fahne flattert uns voran," text by von Schirach, music by Hans-Otto Bergmann, available for 1.50 RM.

13. Gerd Albrecht, ed., *Hitlerjunge Quex. Ein Film vom Opfergeist der deutschen Jugend* (Frankfurt am Main: Deutsches Institut für Filmkunde, 1983), p. 16. Theater critic Rudolf Ramlow's *Herbert Norkus?—Hier! Opfer und Sieg der Hitler-Jugend* (1933), according to George L. Mosse, likewise "went through no less than twenty-five editions

in six years"; *Nazi Culture: Intellectual, Cultural, and Social Life in the Third Reich* (New York: Schocken, 1981), p. 266. Mosse's collection includes a short selection from Ramlow's book (pp. 286–287) as well as a passage from Baldur von Schirach's influential manual of 1934, *Die Hitler Jugend. Idee und Gestalt* (pp. 294–303). In Hans W. Geissendörfer's *Gudrun* (1992), a period piece couched in *Heimatfilm* iconography, we see the young Hitler Youth Fritz avidly reading Schenzinger's novel. On the book cover is a photograph of Heini Völker from Steinhoff's film.

14. For a dramatic description of the festive evening, see Oskar Kalbus, *Vom Werden deutscher Filmkunst,* vol. 2: *Der Tonfilm* (Altona-Bahrenfeld: Cigaretten-Bilderdienst, 1935), pp. 121–123. The film premiered in the United States on 6 July 1934 in the Yorkville Theatre, New York City. The 75-minute version ran under the title *Unsere Fahne flattert uns voran (Our Flag Flutters before Us).* For an account of the Manhattan response, see "*Hitlerjunge Quex* in New York. Erste Pressestimmen," *Film-Kurier,* 24 July 1934.

15. "Dr. Goebbels über *Hitlerjunge Quex,*" *Der Angriff,* 25 September 1933.

16. Reprinted in Ulrich Kurowski, ed., *Deutsche Spielfilme 1933–1945. Materialien III,* 2nd rev. ed. (Munich: Stadtmuseum Munich and Münchner Filmzentrum, 1980), p. 207.

17. Albrecht, *Hitlerjunge Quex,* pp. 8–10. The film took in 190,000 RM during its first three weeks and by the end of 1935 had reached a domestic box office of 800,000 RM.

18. Gert Berghoff, "Die Spielfilmproduktion 1933–1945," in *Der Spielfilm im Dritten Reich,* ed. Manfred Dammeyer (Oberhausen: XII. Westdeutsche Kurzfilmtage, 1966), p. 34. A two-day seminar held in Düsseldorf early in 1988 scrutinized the three martyr films. See Wilhelm Bettecken's report, "Der Film im Dienst der Propaganda," *Film-Korrespondenz* 34.4 (16 February 1988): 3–6. For extended historical analyses of these films, see Martin Loiperdinger, ed., *Märtyrerlegenden im NS-Film* (Opladen: Leske + Budrich, 1991).

19. See Herbert Marcuse, "The Struggle against Liberalism in the Totalitarian View of the State," in *Negations: Essays in Critical Theory,* trans. Jeremy J. Shapiro (Boston: Beacon, 1968). Such a call stresses historical exigency but in truth ignores the real forces of history, appealing instead to "self-evident" claims of existence: "A secularized theological image of history emerges. Every folk receives its historical mandate as a 'mission' that is the first and last, the unrestricted obligation of existence" (p. 35).

20. Taken from the original press booklet copy, Stiftung Deutsche Kinemathek, Berlin. See also Karsten Witte, "Der Apfel und der Stamm. Jugend und Propaganda am Beispiel *Hitlerjunge Quex* (1933)," in *Schock und Schöpfung—Jugendästhetik im 20. Jahrhundert,* ed. Willi Bucher and Klaus Pohl (Darmstadt: Luchterhand, 1986): as the Hitler Youths stand around a piano and sing their anthem, we glimpse a helmet (*Stahlhelm*) from World War I hanging on the wall. "The future," claims Witte, "into which these choirboys want to march, as their song announces 'man for man,' is their fathers' past" (p. 304). Compare Walther Gottfried Klucke's contemporary drama,

Einsiedel (1934), in which the ghosts of fallen front soldiers appear before a wounded veteran, now a graveyard attendant, ten years after Germany's defeat. Full of energy, they insist that their deaths served a grand national cause—and that youth must carry on their legacy.

21. In order to enhance the fictional impact of *Quex,* film officials suppressed the name of the Hitler Youth who played Heini Völker. Thus, both in its story and in its production, the film depersonalized its leading player for the sake of a larger cause.

22. Compare the expressive deathbed tableau in Karl Aloys Schenzinger, *Der Hitlerjunge Quex* (Berlin: Zeitgeschichte-Verlag, 1932), p. 255: "Heini sits up in bed with his eyes wide open. His gaze flickers, fixes on no one, peers into emptiness before it slowly fades out again. The nurse lays the sick boy down. His mouth opens. His comrades hear something, but they can't recognize the words. Then terror overcomes them. Heini is singing. They stand there paralyzed. They don't know the words, but they recognize the melody that oozes, chimes, and rattles in his throat. They sing it almost every day, every evening, on every march, on every outing. They've sung it with Quex, just recently. It's terrible to hear him singing like this.

"The nurses bid them silent leave. They sneak away, upset, disturbed, desperate. They feel it. No one talks about it. Everyone knows: this is the song of death."

23. Gottfried Benn, *Nach dem Nihilismus* (Berlin: Kiepenheuer, 1932), p. 20; cited in Walter H. Sokel, *The Writer in Extremis: Expressionism in Twentieth-Century German Literature* (New York: McGraw-Hill, 1964), p. 115.

24. Ibid., p. 116.

25. See Ernst Jünger's 1932 study, *Der Arbeiter. Herrschaft und Gestalt* (reprint, Stuttgart: Klett, 1981). The film actor's task, according to Jünger, is to represent the type. "For that reason one does not ask that he be unique, but rather obvious. One does not expect him to express the endless harmony of a human life, but rather its precise rhythm" (p. 134).

26. "The priority and primacy of the whole over its 'members' (parts)," argues Marcuse, is basic to Nazi doctrine. The whole constitutes "the unity that unifies the parts, a unity which is the precondition for the fulfillment and completion of each part"; "Struggle against Liberalism," pp. 19–20.

27. Rust delivered the address to schoolteachers on 22 June 1934; it was reprinted a day later in the *Völkischer Beobachter.* Quoted in John Altman, "Movies' Role in Hitler's Conquest of German Youth," *Hollywood Quarterly* 3.4 (Summer 1948): 381; and David Welch, "Educational Film Propaganda and the Nazi Youth," in *Nazi Propaganda: The Power and the Limitations,* ed. David Welch (London: Croom Helm, 1983), p. 69. Compare Erik Homburger Erikson, "Hitler's Imagery and German Youth," *Psychiatry* 5 (1942): 475–493.

28. Quoted in Peter Loewenberg, "The Psychohistorical Origins of the Nazi Youth Cohort," *American Historical Review* 76.5 (December 1971): 1469–70.

29. Axel Eggebrecht, "Rückblicke ins Dritte Reich," *Nordwestdeutsche Hefte* 1.1 (1946): 8.

30. Heini reenters the world as the "true child of the drill-machine" spoken of by Klaus Theweleit, an automaton "created without the help of a woman, parentless"; *Male Fantasies,* vol. 2: *Male Bodies: Psychoanalyzing the White Terror,* trans. Erica Carter, Chris Turner, and Stephen Conway (Minneapolis: University of Minnesota Press, 1989), p. 161.

31. In the novel, the father sends the police to look for his son, who has disappeared following the mother's suicide. Except for a short chat with Stoppel, the father vanishes from the film after his meeting with Cass. The lengthy plot summary in the Reichsfilmarchiv handbook of 1935–36 does not mention the father at all. Theweleit notes the general absence of fathers in the *Freikorps* literature: "Whether heroes or chief opponents, fathers are categorically denied a voice in these books. To a remarkable extent, they are simply dispensed with . . . Patriarchy secures its dominance under fascism in the form of a 'filiarchy'—that much is clear. Nothing but sons as far as the eye can see—Hitler too is one of their number"; *Male Fantasies,* vol. 1: *Women Floods Bodies History,* trans. Stephen Conway, Erica Carter, and Chris Turner (Minneapolis: University of Minnesota Press, 1987), p. 108.

32. Theweleit, *Male Fantasies,* vol. 2, pp. 252–253.

33. See Wilhelm Reich, *The Mass Psychology of Fascism,* trans. Vincent R. Carfagno (New York: Farrar, Straus & Giroux, 1970), p. 46n.: "By *identification,* psychoanalysis understands the process whereby a person begins *to feel at one with* another person, adopts that person's characteristics and attitudes, and in his fantasy puts himself in the other's place; this process entails an actual change in the identifying person, inasmuch as the latter 'internalizes' characteristics of his model." Heini turns away from his father and Stoppel, finding in neither a desirable focus for his energies and aligning himself with the party, an entity much larger than a single individual. As he says to Stoppel: "I believe in my Führer and my comrades; that's why I'm with them."

34. Oskar Mazerath, the young protagonist of another famous German tale of education, experiences the same period from a much different perspective. Both an antihero and an anti-Heini, he sits under a rostrum and laments, "Poor Hitler Youth Quex, you have died in vain," proceeding to disrupt a party mass rally and to transform it into a raucous counter-Nuremberg; Günter Grass, *The Tin Drum,* trans. Ralph Manheim (New York: Vintage, 1964), p. 120.

35. Walter Benjamin, "The Work of Art in the Age of Mechanical Reproduction," in *Illuminations,* ed. Hannah Arendt, trans. Harry Zohn (New York: Schocken, 1969), p. 242. See also Hannah Arendt, *The Origins of Totalitarianism* (New York: World, 1958), p. 308, where she discusses complete absorption by a totalitarian movement: "The fanaticized members can be reached by neither experience nor argument; identification with the movement and total conformism seem to have destroyed the very capacity for experience, even if it be as extreme as torture or the fear of death."

36. Grundler sings "Die Liebe der Matrosen," well-known to contemporary audiences from Hanns Schwarz's 1931 Ufa musical, *Bomben auf Monte Carlo (Monte Carlo Madness),* a film starring Hans Albers and Heinz Rühmann. The song was written by the prominent composer Werner R. Heymann.

37. Gregory Bateson, "Cultural and Thematic Analysis of Fictional Films," *Transactions of the New York Academy of Sciences* 2.5 (February 1943): 77.

38. Karl-Heinz Huber, *Jugend unterm Hakenkreuz* (Frankfurt am Main: Ullstein, 1986), p. 19.

39. See Max Horkheimer and Theodor W. Adorno, *Dialectic of Enlightenment,* trans. John Cumming (New York: Seabury, 1972), p. 255. Propaganda "fixes the condition of men . . . by setting them in motion. It counts on being able to count on them."

40. Michele Sakkara, ed., *Die große Zeit des deutschen Films 1933–1945* (Leoni am Starnberger See: Druffel, 1980), p. 28. The editor applauds the film's realism and authenticity, claiming it anticipates Italian Neorealism and the French Nouvelle Vague.

41. See H. Sp., "Deutsche Filmregisseure. IV. Hans Steinhoff," *Der Deutsche Film* 2.4 (October 1937): 110: "Anyone who has followed Hans Steinhoff's work through the silent period and into the sound era has witnessed a development that with increasing purity and beauty has crystallized the ideal of a dramatic film, substantial and tactful, mature in its characters and its artistry." See the interview portrait "Hans Steinhoff spricht sich aus," *Film-Kurier,* 15 January 1935. For recent career evaluations of Steinhoff, see Herbert Holba, Günter Knorr, and Peter Spiegel, *Reclams deutsches Filmlexikon* (Stuttgart: Reclam, 1984), pp. 364–365; and the alphabetical entry in Hans-Michael Bock, ed., *CineGraph. Lexikon zum deutschsprachigen Film,* installment 9 (Munich: edition text + kritik, 1987), pp. D1–D2. Billy Wilder, coauthor of the script for Steinhoff's *Scampolo, ein Kind der Straße* (*Scampolo, a Child of the Streets,* 1932), later spoke of Steinhoff as "a shithead" and "an idiot," a "very bad director," a filmmaker "without a lick of talent"; Neil Sinyard and Adrian Turner, *Billy Wilders Filme* (Berlin: Spiess, 1980), p. 21.

42. See *The Goebbels Diaries: 1939–1941,* trans. and ed. Fred Taylor (Harmondsworth: Penguin, 1984), p. 16. On 10 October 1939 the minister noted: "Old film, *The Threepenny Opera.* Typical Jewish humbug. This is the kind of thing that they were allowed to set before the German people with impunity. To our credit that we have got rid of all this rubbish."

43. Steinhoff was sympathetic to the Nazi party before Hitler assumed power. After the success of *Quex,* the director became an important figure in youth film activities, overseeing many 16mm short and medium-length political productions for the Hitlerjugend such as *Der Marsch zum Führer* (*The March to the Führer,* 1939).

44. See Leif Fuhrhammar and Folke Isaksson, *Politics and Film,* trans. Kersti French (New York: Praeger, 1971), p. 102: "It is one of the earliest Nazi feature films produced while it was still necessary to build a National Socialist spirit on what was left of the values of the Weimar Republic."

45. Heinrich George, a former Communist who became a stage and screen luminary in Nazi Germany, played both roles. His onscreen change from red to brown thus paralleled his real-life transformation. Curt Riess (in his inimitably sensationalistic manner) describes George's participation here as an act of desperation and accommoda-

tion, an attempt to save his career and reestablish himself; *Das gab's nur einmal. Die große Zeit des deutschen Films,* vol. 2 (Vienna/Munich: Molden, 1977), pp. 230–233. No matter what George's motives might have been, it was useful to the Nazis that a prominent ex-Communist publicly enact his political conversion.

46. Fuhrhammar and Isaksson, *Politics and Film,* p. 102. Jutzi, the erstwhile proponent of a realistic film for working-class audiences, fell into obscurity during the Third Reich. In 1933 the Nazis censored his documentary *Um's tägliche Brot (For Our Daily Bread)* and banned *Mother Krause's Trip to Happiness.* His subsequent productions were limited to short features, generally comedies and detective films. Recently his entire career has come under reexamination; during late October 1993 the Historisches Museum in Berlin presented a comprehensive retrospective.

47. Francis Courtade and Pierre Cadars, *Geschichte des Films im Dritten Reich,* trans. Florian Hopf (Munich/Vienna: Hanser, 1975), p. 46. See also David Welch, *Propaganda and the German Cinema 1933–1945* (Oxford: Oxford University Press, 1983), p. 63; and Lotte H. Eisner, *The Haunted Screen,* trans. Roger Greaves (Berkeley: University of California Press, 1969), p. 333: "The cinema of the Nazi era, which portrays men and societies 'as they are in reality,' is not vastly different from its predecessors; with regard to style, for example, *Hitlerjunge Quex* (1938) [*sic*] is not a great way away from its political opposite *Berlin-Alexanderplatz* (1931)."

48. See Alice Yaeger Kaplan, *Reproductions of Banality: Fascism, Literature, and French Intellectual Life* (Minneapolis: University of Minnesota Press, 1986), p. 30: "Fascism recuperates modern man's lost rituals with the help of the very factor that has threatened them in the first place: technology. And this is precisely how fascist art can appear both nostalgic and avant-garde, how it can construct by representing destruction."

49. See Frank D. McConnell, *The Spoken Seen: Film & the Romantic Imagination* (Baltimore: Johns Hopkins University Press, 1975), p. 31.

50. Schenzinger, *Der Hitlerjunge Quex,* p. 14.

51. See Ernst Bloch's trenchant commentary on the derivative character of Nazi discourse: "After all, the Nazi did not even invent the song with which he seduces. Nor even the gunpowder with which he makes his fireworks, nor even the firm in whose name he deceives"; "On the Original History of the Third Reich," in *Heritage of Our Times,* trans. Neville Plaice and Stephen Plaice (Berkeley: University of California Press, 1991), p. 117.

52. In the Nazi calendar, the summer solstice (21 June) served as an occasion to recruit new Hitler Youth members. See Klaus Vondung, *Magie und Manipulation. Ideologischer Kult und politische Religion des Nationalsozialismus* (Göttingen: Vandenhoeck & Ruprecht, 1971), p. 81: "The summer solstice celebrations lent themselves particularly well to ritual presentations in which, before a deeply symbolic fire and against a nocturnal nature backdrop, one evoked religious states of mind and feelings in the service of National Socialist ideology." Compare the opening sequence of Edward

Dmytryk's *Hitler's Children* (1943) with its stylized studio replication of a Nazi summer solstice ceremony, replete with a stirring speaker, an ornamental mass, and chiaroscuro lighting.

53. See the compelling recollections of Peter Brückner, *Das Abseits als sicherer Ort. Kindheit und Jugend zwischen 1933 und 1945* (Berlin: Wagenbach, 1980). Brückner describes his youth during the Third Reich and his ongoing attempts to find pockets of fresh air not controlled by the party or the state. He notes that Hitler Youth outings transformed forests and countrysides into spaces "to be entered either as an exercise ground or as a site of loud games, and one could hardly withdraw from either" (p. 31). For a scene redolent of Brückner's description, see Schenzinger, *Der Hitlerjunge Quex,* pp. 181–183. As the government increasingly closed its net to ensure that all youth joined party organizations, there was some level of resistance, especially after 1938. See Detlev J. Peuckert, *Die Edelweißpiraten. Protestbewegungen jugendlicher Arbeiter im Dritten Reich. Eine Dokumentation,* 2nd rev. ed. (Cologne: Bund, 1983); also Arno Klönne, "Jugendliche Subkulturen im Dritten Reich," in *Schock und Schöpfung—Jugendästhetik im 20. Jahrhundert,* ed. Willi Bucher and Klaus Pohl (Darmstadt: Luchterhand, 1986), pp. 308–313.

54. Compare Theweleit, *Male Fantasies,* vol. 2, p. 67.

55. Bateson quoted in Margaret Mead and Rhoda Métraux, "An Analysis of the Nazi Film *Hitlerjunge Quex:* Gregory Bateson," in *The Study of Culture at a Distance* (Chicago: University of Chicago Press, 1953), p. 302.

56. Ibid., p. 311.

57. Ibid., p. 310: Bateson describes a compositional contrast between Communists and Nazis as if it were a verbal one, maintaining that "we are told almost in so many words that this contrast is a part of the emotional dynamics upon which Nazism rests."

58. Erwin Leiser, *Nazi Cinema,* trans. Gertrud Mander and David Wilson (New York: Collier, 1975), p. 36.

59. Welch, *Propaganda and the German Cinema,* p. 48.

60. Welch collapses the two, defining propaganda rather fuzzily as "a means of conversion of one kind or another. However, it should also be remembered that it can be used as a means of maintaining the status quo, of reinforcing already held beliefs, by way of various psychological defence mechanisms"; ibid., p. 55.

61. Ibid., p. 48. Compare the verdict of the *Variety* critic (Kauf.) in his notice of 7 July 1934 (following the Yorkville screening of an unsubtitled version): "It's frank propaganda and no bones about it." Nonetheless, it demonstrates "how good German film technique is."

62. Thomas Doherty, *Projections of War: Hollywood, American Culture, and World War II* (New York: Columbia University Press, 1993), pp. 29–30.

63. Ibid., p. 35.

64. Bateson's analysis is used in Leiser, *Nazi Cinema,* pp. 36–38; it has reappeared in almost every subsequent discussion of the film, for instance in Courtade and Cadars, *Geschichte des Films im Dritten Reich,* pp. 45–46; Welch, *Propaganda and the German*

Cinema, pp. 68–70; Albrecht, *Hitlerjunge Quex,* pp. 17–20; Baird, *To Die for Germany,* p. 124; Loiperdinger, *Märtyrerlegenden im NS-Film,* p. 161. See also Hanno Möbius, "Heimat im nationalsozialistischen Stadtfilm," *Augen-Blick* 5 (March 1988): 35. Analyzing the scene, Möbius stresses the role of the park backdrop to the confrontation, how the green space suggests Nazism's ideological project of renaturalization. Linda Schulte-Sasse both cites the passage and recapitulates Möbius' reading; "Retrieving the City as *Heimat:* Berlin in Nazi Cinema," in *Berlin: Culture and Metropolis,* ed. Charles W. Haxthausen and Heidrun Suhr (Minneapolis: University of Minnesota Press, 1990), pp. 172–173. See as well Siegfried Kracauer's notes from 1941 about the scene: "For no reason the father develops from a stubborn communist into a tolerant and stupid person. The over-simplified method: 'Where are you born? In o-u-r Germany, Think about it.' like a hypnotic order"; reprinted in David Culbert, "The Rockefeller Foundation, the Museum of Modern Art Film Library, and Siegfried Kracauer, 1941," *Historical Journal of Film, Radio and Television* 13.4 (1993): 509.

65. Witte's analysis ("Der Apfel und der Stamm") poses the sole exception. His reading studies a production still from the scene and elucidates its body language (p. 304.)

66. Theweleit, *Male Fantasies,* vol. 2, p. 261.

67. The shot numbers are taken from Thomas Arnold, Jutta Schöning, and Ulrich Schröter, eds., *Hitlerjunge Quex. Einstellungsprotokoll* (Munich: Filmland Presse, 1980), pp. 171–175.

68. The young actor who played Heini was reportedly the lover of Baldur von Schirach. See the intriguing memoirs of an HJ member, Hans Siemsen's *Hitler Youth,* trans. Trever Blewitt and Phyllis Blewitt (London: Drummond, 1940), p. 213: "There was a lot of talk . . . about Schirach's relations with a certain boy with whom he was seen about everywhere over a long period. Even at official functions this boy either stood next to him or was a member of his escort." "No one," he concedes, "thought any the worse of Baldur von Schirach for loving this boy. We all loved him and quite understood how it was that the Reich Youth Leader had singled him out." For this reason, the verb "to quex" *(quexen)* became "part of the vocabulary of Hitler Youth. It is easy to imagine what it means." Schirach was hardly the exception, maintains the author. "Among the sixty to seventy Hitler Youth Leaders with whom I came into close contact practically half were considered by us boys to be homosexuals." Siemsen describes a popular contemporary booklet, *Deutsches Jungvolk,* with "admirable photographs of boys, marching, camping, eating and bathing; and two full-size portraits of two particularly good-looking boys. It can be seen at once (I don't mean this ironically) that the leaders who compiled the booklet are very susceptible to good looks in their boys" (p. 146).

69. The scene—in both its verbal shape and its patriotic project—recalls Heinrich von Kleist's *Katechismus der Deutschen* (*German Catechism,* 1809), lessons in national identity which unfold as a dialogue between a father and his son. See, for instance, the opening lines of the first section:

Question: Speak, child, who are you?
Answer: I am a German.
Question: A German? You must be joking. You were born in Meissen, and the country to which Meissen belongs is called Saxony.
Answer: I was born in Meissen, and the country to which Meissen belongs is called Saxony; but my fatherland, the country to which Saxony belongs, is Germany, and your son, my father, is a German.

70. See Horkheimer and Adorno, *Dialectic of Enlightenment,* p. 154: "But the miracle of integration, the permanent act of grace by the authority who receives the defenseless person—once he has swallowed his rebelliousness—signifies Fascism."

71. Konstantin Irmen-Tschet, "Objektiv am Objektiv. Filmschaffende berichten von ihrer Arbeit," *Filmwelt,* 25 November 1942.

72. Schenzinger, *Der Hitlerjunge Quex,* p. 160.

73. Ibid., p. 207.

74. Philippe Lacoue-Labarthe and Jean-Luc Nancy, "The Nazi Myth," trans. Brian Holmes, *Critical Inquiry* 16.2 (Winter 1990): 311.

75. Reinhold Conrad Muschler, "Nationalsozialistischer Film?" *Deutsche Kulturwacht* 21 (1933): 7.

76. See Karlheinz Schmeer, *Die Regie des öffentlichen Lebens im Dritten Reich* (Munich: Pohl, 1956), p. 52: "The NS leaders were determined to occupy all remaining islands of individuality within the public sphere and to transform them into political spaces. In this endeavor one attempted to create a new type of *Volksfest* as a replacement for the traditional forms of public amusement."

77. Jürgen Ohlsen in fact was the unnamed Hitler Youth. He would later appear as an enthused admirer of the aviator Ernst Udet in Heinz Paul's *Wunder des Fliegens* (*The Miracle of Flying,* 1935). "The children of cinema are growing up," proclaimed a 1934 holiday headline in *Film-Kurier.* A collection of Christmas greetings included a message from Ohlsen: "What more could I possibly wish for than to pass my pilot's examination as soon as possible?"; "Quex will Flieger werden," *Film-Kurier,* 22 December 1934.

78. For an extended analysis of the different ways in which Nazi films functionalized flags, see Hilmar Hoffmann, *"Und die Fahne führt uns in die Ewigkeit." Propaganda im NS-Film* (Frankfurt am Main: Fischer, 1988).

79. *Hitler Youth Quex* was often reprised during the Nazi Youth Film Hours from 1940 through 1942—and received with much enthusiasm; see Gerd Albrecht's comments in Dammeyer, *Der Spielfilm im Dritten Reich,* p. 52. Alfred Weidenmann's *Junge Adler* (*Young Eagles,* 1944) was consciously intended as a continuation of *Quex,* a film for young audiences which built on the earlier success. A father gives his son over to the Hitler Youth after his own attempts at raising the child have failed. We see how a youth collective regulates itself, how boys educate other boys (much as in the 1938 Hollywood film *Boys Town*). The production in fact issued from government concern that youths were becoming restive and out of control during the war years, reacting negatively to

the hard labor (e.g., ten-hour workdays, graveyard shifts), discipline, and sacrifice demanded of them, while being forbidden to go out at night, visit bars, smoke in public, or attend cinemas alone. The working title for *Young Eagles* was "Schritt ins Leben" (Path to Life): here again, one meant to show the way. For an analysis of the film, see Rolf Seubert, "*Junge Adler.* Retrospektive auf einen nationalsozialistischen Jugendfilm," *Medium* 18.3 (July–September 1988): 31–37.

80. Max Picard, *Hitler in Our Selves,* trans. Heinrich Hauser (Hinsdale, Ill.: Regnery, 1947), p. 54.

3. Home Sweet *Heimat*

1. *Das Prinzip Hoffnung* (Frankfurt: Suhrkamp, 1973) vol. 3, p. 1628. For a historical study of the term, see Celia Applegate, *A Nation of Provincials: The German Idea of Heimat* (Berkeley: University of California Press, 1990).

2. Roland Barthes, "Wine and Milk," in *Mythologies,* trans. Annette Lavers (New York: Farrar, Straus & Giroux, 1972), p. 58. Manuel Puig has his raconteur Molina connect the two intoxicants while recreating an apocryphal wartime Nazi melodrama set in Paris. A German officer entertains a French chanteuse in his luxurious apartment, asking her, "Won't she have a glass of champagne, the very best from her own France, like the nation's blood streaming up from its very soil"; *Kiss of the Spider Woman,* trans. Thomas Colchie (New York: Vintage, 1980), p. 55.

3. *Der verlorene Sohn,* 1934. Produced by Deutsche Universal-Film AG. Producer: Paul Kohner. Production Head: Fred Lyssa. Production Manager: Rudolf Fichtner. Direction: Luis Trenker. Assistant Director: Werner Klingler. Script: Luis Trenker, Arnold Ulitz, and Reinhart Steinbicker, based on Trenker's novel. Cinematography: Albert Benitz and Reimar Kuntze. Assistant Cinematography: Klaus von Rautenfeld. Editing: Waldemar Gaede and Andrew Marton. Set Design: Fritz Maurischat. Sound: Hans Grimm. Music: Giuseppe Becce. Song Lyrics: Hedy Knorr. Costumes: Martin Gericke and Adolf Braun. Props: Max Klar and Paul Gaebele.

The Players: Luis Trenker (Tonio Feuersinger), Maria Anderngast (Barbl Gudauner), Albert Schultes (Barbl's father, a wood sculptor), Marian Marsh (Lilian Williams), Franz W. Schröder-Schrom (Mr. Williams, Lilian's father), Jimmy Fox (Jimmy, Tonio's American friend), Paul Henckels (schoolteacher), Eduard Köck (Father Feuersinger), Melanie Horeschowsky (Rosina Unverdorben, grocery store proprietor), Emmerich Albert, Hans Jamnik, Luis Gerold (woodcutters and mountain guides), Lore Schützendorf (Rauhnacht maiden), Lucie Euler (landlady), Borwin Walth (Mr. Williams' butler), Hans Kettler, Theo Lingen.

Original length: 2,800 meters (102 minutes). Premiered on 6 September 1934 in Stuttgart (Universum der Schwäbischen Urania) and on 3 October 1934 in Berlin (Capitol). Rating: "Artistically especially worthwhile."

An unsubtitled video copy is available from Facets Video, the German Language

Video Center, and International Historic Films. A subtitled 16mm print is available from Inter Nationes, Bonn.

4. The Oedipal dynamics in *The Old and the Young King* offer a variation on an expressionist theme similar to Fritz Lang's *Metropolis* (1927), another film scripted by Thea von Harbou. See Karin Bruns, *Kinomythen 1920–1945. Die Filmentwürfe der Thea von Harbou* (Stuttgart: Metzler, 1995), pp. 118–119.

5. A psychoanalytical critic could hardly find a more literal variation on a Lacanian scenario: at one point the old king pushes the crown prince in front of a mirror and compels the son to despise the reflection before him. The narrative as a whole processes Frederick so that he can become a gaze that stands scrutiny, the fierce and inexorable countenance that sustains the camera's attention for several minutes in the film's mesmerizing closing shot.

6. Ernst Bloch, "Nazi-Filme oder Der Zauber der Persönlichkeit," in *Vom Hasard zur Katastrophe. Politische Aufsätze aus den Jahren 1934–1939* (Frankfurt am Main: Suhrkamp, 1972), p. 14.

7. Ibid., p. 15.

8. Oskar Kalbus, *Vom Werden deutscher Filmkunst,* vol. 2: *Der Tonfilm* (Altona-Bahrenfeld: Cigaretten-Bilderdienst, 1935), p. 70.

9. The film was based on Kleist Prize–winner Gerhard Menzel's novel, which first appeared in serialized form as *Deutsche wollen heim (Germans Want to Go Home).*

10. Bloch, "Nazi-Filme," p. 14.

11. See Kalbus, *Vom Werden deutscher Filmkunst,* vol. 2, p. 104: "This gathering of inner turmoil and torment, full of hopelessness and weakness, full of insecurity, without energy and courage: this is Germany! . . . And these Volga Germans, who are Germany, would have fallen prey to their desperation and divisiveness—if fate had not sent them a Führer, a fellow who turned his back on the milquetoastish likes of November Germany with its whining, procrastination, and petitioning, a person who still believes wholeheartedly in an authentic Germany."

12. See Karsten Witte, *Lachende Erben, Toller Tag. Filmkomödie im Dritten Reich* (Berlin: Vorwerk 8, 1995), p. 83.

13. Early in this otherwise unexceptional feature directed by Karl Heinz Martin and starring Attila Hörbiger, Punks (whose nickname comes from a Karl May novel and refers to a primitive lighter) arrives from America, then travels from Heidelberg to Berlin. During the trip we view no cities, no streets, only native soil that accumulates on the clothes of the hitchhiker. Here, too, an eager new arrival applies American know-how and mass-marketing techniques to the German situation.

14. The shots echo the opening five minutes of Trenker's earlier feature, *Der Rebell* (*The Rebel,* 1932), a symphonic sequence devoid of dialogue, the only ambient sound being the ringing of cowbells. See Ulrich Kurowski's obituary, "Luis Trenker. 4.10.1892–13.4.1990," *epd Film* 7.6 (June 1990): 3–4. Kurowski places Trenker's work within a tradition of German film symphonies stretching from Walter Ruttmann's portrait of Berlin to mountain films and World War II documentaries.

15. A contemporary observer in fact complained that Tonio's journey seems insufficiently motivated; Karl August Götz, *Der Film als journalistisches Phänomen* (Düsseldorf: Nolte, 1937), pp. 117–118.

16. This adage is also quoted in Veit Harlan's tale of a prodigal daughter, *Die goldene Stadt* (*The Golden City,* 1942), a film based on Richard Billinger's drama *Der Gigant.*

17. The title sequence anticipates the film's narrative trajectory, moving from a picture of the Sun King mask to a high-angle shot of Manhattan before going back to a vista of the mountain village and a second glimpse of the *Rauhnacht* mask.

18. See, for instance, films from the period in which wishes cause catastrophes, works scripted (or coscripted) by Kurt Heuser: *Liebe, Tod und Teufel* (*Love, Death, and Devil,* 1934) and *Die unheimlichen Wünsche* (*The Uncanny Wishes,* 1939).

19. On this occasion (1 October 1982 at 9:15 P.M.) the West German Second Channel (ZDF) screened a tribute to Trenker. Two days later, ZDF presented *Der Berg ruft* (*The Challenge,* 1937) as a matinee. The birthday celebration lasted four days and catalyzed innumerable newspaper and magazine articles. For an incisive—and atypical—critical report, see Fritz Rumler, "Nur ein Phantom der Medien?" *Der Spiegel,* 4 October 1982, p. 283: "One can't help but wonder if there really is a Luis Trenker or whether he's not just a phantom created by the media, someone like the Marlboro cowboy, the 100-year-old Kirghizian garlic eater, or Donald Duck, existent only in the gray cells where we tuck away myths and advertising slogans."

20. See Trenker and Walter Schmidkunz's richly illustrated panegyric to blood and soil, *Berge und Heimat. Das Buch von den Bergen und ihren Menschen* (Berlin: Knaur, 1935).

21. See, for instance, the lead article, "Geht Luis Trenker für längere Zeit nach Hollywood?" *Film-Kurier,* 17 October 1934. Trenker's directorial debut, *Berge in Flammen* (codirected with Karl Hartl), appeared in an American version, *The Doomed Battalion. The Rebel* (codirected with Curtis Bernhardt) was dubbed into English for American release. Contrary to popular belief, the vast majority of *Der Kaiser von Kalifornien* (*The Emperor of California,* 1936) was shot in Italy and not the United States. As a result of a cutback in Universal's financing, only a very few sequences derive from American locations.

22. "Gestern im Rundfunk. Luis Trenker über seine Filmarbeit in Amerika," *Film-Kurier,* 29 December 1933. *Der verlorene Sohn* also would appear as a novel of the same title by Trenker (Berlin: Ullstein, 1934). All quotations from the novel are taken from this edition.

23. BeWe, "Luis Trenker im Jofa-Atelier. 'Wer nie fortkommt, kommt nie heim,' " *Film-Kurier,* 6 April 1934.

24. Trenker's voluminous correspondence with the famous producer and agent is part of the Paul Kohner-Sammlung, which was recently acquired by the Stiftung Deutsche Kinemathek, Berlin. The correspondence in the collection spans twenty years, from 1933 to 1953, and is, quite fittingly, framed by negotiations about *The Prodigal Son.* It provides invaluable details regarding Trenker's business dealings, his many

different projects and plans, as well as offering insight into the filmmaker's mercurial personality, his political naïveté, his unabashed opportunism. The letters put Trenker's inimitable energy and contagious enthusiasm on display; they also bear witness to a calculating, resourceful, and compulsive self-promoter, a man of undeniably ruthless ambition. For depictions of Paul Kohner, see Frederick Kohner, *The Magician of Sunset Boulevard* (Palos Verdes, Calif.: Morgan, 1977); and Gundolf S. Freyermuth, *Reise in die Verlorengegangenheit. Auf den Spuren deutscher Emigranten (1933–1940)* (Hamburg: Rasch und Röhring, 1990).

25. "Zwei Aufführungen im Reich erfolgreich. Trenker in Stuttgart," *Film-Kurier,* 7 September 1934.

26. Trenker quoted in Kalbus, *Vom Werden deutscher Filmkunst,* vol. 2, p. 114. Compare Trenker's much different postwar recollections of his trip to the New World in *Mutig und heiter durchs Leben* (Munich: Bertelsmann, 1982), pp. 98–101. See also the Manhattan memories of another famous German director during the mid-1920s: Fritz Lang, "Was ich in Amerika sah. Neuyork—Los Angeles," *Film-Kurier,* 11 December 1924.

27. G. H., *"Der verlorene Sohn," Film-Kurier,* 4 October 1934.

28. Trenker quoted in Kalbus, *Vom Werden deutscher Filmkunst,* vol. 2, p. 115. Even a less smitten New York reviewer conceded that the American scenes were "remarkable." He shared the conclusion of his overseas colleagues, if not their enthusiasm: the film proved "that the old home is best for all good little German boys"; Stern., *"Verlorene Sohn ['Prodigal Son']," Variety,* 29 January 1935).

29. R. L., "Festliche Trenker-Premiere im Dresdner 'Capitol,' " *Lichtbild-Bühne,* 25 September 1934.

30. "Wettkampf der Filme. Trenkers *Verlorener Sohn* hinterläßt starken Eindruck in Venedig," *Film-Kurier,* 15 August 1935. *The Prodigal Son* received the Venice Prize of the Ministry for Folk Culture. *The Emperor of California* won the Mussolini Cup as the best foreign entry at the 1937 Venice Festival.

31. "Billingers Rauhnacht wird Trenkers Rauhnacht," *Film-Kurier,* 24 April 1934. Other prominent contemporary feature-length celebrations of the German homeland included Rolf von Sonjewski-Jamrowski's *Blut und Boden. Grundlagen zum neuen Reich* (*Blood and Soil: Foundations of a New Reich,* 1933), a film notable for Walter Ruttmann's cinematography and sound montage; also, Carl Heinz Wolff's *Heideschulmeister Uwe Karsten* (*Village Schoolmaster Uwe Karsten,* 1933), starring, among others, Marianne Hoppe and Brigitte Horney. In Ruttmann's 1934 short, *Altgermanische Bauernkultur* (*Ancient Germanic Peasant Culture*), a student speaks directly to spectators, imploring them to "help us revive the German people's pride in its many-century-long tradition of peasant culture."

32. S-k., "Der beste Film des Jahres. *Der verlorene Sohn,*" *Lichtbild-Bühne,* 4 November 1934.

33. See "An der Jahreswende. Erfolge und Ziele des deutschen Films," *Film-Kurier,* 29 December 1933.

34. The Nazis quickly realized that, as Bloch noted in 1934, "one can also lie more subtly"; "Nazi-Filme," p. 13. This awareness also influenced their use of other mass media. Speaking to radio officials in March 1933, Goebbels insisted: "By all means don't be boring. Don't be tedious. Don't just dish out propaganda. Don't think for a moment that you can serve the national government well just by playing loud march music"; *Goebbels-Reden. 1932–1939,* ed. Helmut Heiber, vol. 1 (Düsseldorf: Droste, 1971), p. 82.

35. Joseph Goebbels, "Rede im Kaiserhof, Berlin, am 28.3.1933," reprinted in Gerd Albrecht, *Nationalsozialistische Filmpolitik* (Stuttgart: Enke, 1969), p. 439. See also Goebbels, *Vom Kaiserhof zur Reichskanzlei* (Munich: Eher, 1934), p. 244, where the minister praises *The Rebel* as an "exemplary achievement in film art . . . One can learn here what is possible with film if people know what they're doing. All of us are stirred to the depths of our souls."

36. G. H., "*Der verlorene Sohn.*"

37. Martin Behnke, "Endlich vollsaftige Filmkunst," *Der Angriff,* 4 October 1934.

38. Riefenstahl describes her liaison with Trenker during the filming of Fanck's *Der heilige Berg* (*The Holy Mountain,* 1926) in great detail, relating as well their strained subsequent relations. In her life's story, Trenker increasingly becomes a nemesis; Leni Riefenstahl, *A Memoir* (New York: St. Martin's, 1993). Trenker's postwar letters contain numerous scathing remarks about Riefenstahl, letters that Kohner passed on to *Variety* reporters. News about Riefenstahl, transmitted in Trenker's note of 3 November 1945, reappeared in the front-page *Variety* article "Hitler's Girl Friend Resumes Film-Making" on 25 January 1946; its source was identified as "a letter from a resident of the Tyrol."

39. See Trenker's "Gedanken zum deutschen Film," *Intercine* (Rome) 7.8–9 (1935): 200. Here he maintains that film must return to the boundless visual possibility of silent cinema and find the appropriate tonal and musical accompaniment to create a poetic totality. See his comments about the craft of impressive visual effects in the pamphlet *Hinter den Kulissen der Filmregie* (Munich: Bruckmann, 1938). Also see the young Michelangelo Antonioni's recommendation of Trenker, "Nuvole fotogeniche," *Cinema* (Rome) 48 (August 1942).

40. See *Mutig und heiter durchs Leben,* pp. 111–122, for Trenker's account of how he came into disfavor with Goebbels, why he refused to betray his Tyrolean homeland for the sake of Nazi Germany. (In actuality Trenker flipflopped, initially opting for South Tyrol before giving way to pressure and changing his mind.) Pointing to an entry in Goebbels' diary, Trenker often maintained (in interviews, on talk shows, in his books) that not only did the propaganda minister blacklist him and force him to work in Italy, but also that Goebbels had plans to liquidate him. Clearly, Trenker's initial decision put the minister into a rage. See Goebbels' diary entry of 18 January 1940: "The South Tyrolean business has been sorted out. Trenker, spineless creature, has chosen Italy. We shall settle his hash. The Führer never thought much of him, and I have also cautioned people against him"; *The Goebbels Diaries: 1939–1941,* trans. and ed. Fred Taylor (Harmondsworth: Penguin,

1984), p. 98. Compare Riefenstahl's claims about Trenker in her *Memoir,* p. 340: "In no way was Trenker persecuted by the Nazis, as he liked to represent himself as having been after the war . . . If he had been unpopular with the Nazis, they wouldn't have allowed him to make a national film like *The Fire Devil,* which he both directed and starred in. Then, in 1942–3, he played the male lead in *The Germanic Woman* [*sic*], which was directed by W. [*sic*] Kimmich, Goebbels' brother-in-law." (Max W. Kimmich, director of *Germanin,* was the husband of Goebbels' sister, Maria.)

41. See Karl Lukan, "Der große Luis hat Berge verkauft," *Stuttgarter Zeitung,* 30 September 1972. Trenker, claimed the amused journalist, "has found just the right package in which to market mountains to the masses."

42. Luis Trenker, *Alles gut gegangen. Geschichten aus meinem Leben,* 2nd rev. ed. (Munich: Bertelsmann, 1979).

43. The various television series included *Luis Trenker erzählt* (thirty-three installments), *Alles gut gegangen,* and *Luftsprünge,* as well as numerous documentary shorts and travelogues. For a detailed filmography, see the entry for Trenker in Hans-Michael Bock, ed., *CineGraph. Lexikon zum deutschsprachigen Film,* installment 22 (Munich: edition text + kritik, 1993), pp. F1–F20.

44. Fritz Weber claimed to have ghostwritten various Trenker novels (including *Der Feuerteufel, Hauptmann Ladurner, Sterne über den Gipfeln*), receiving only 5,000 RM per book, although Trenker earned far more. Trenker later maintained that Weber was at best an occasional collaborator. See the interview with Felix Schmidt, "Immer alles gutgegangen. Ein Gespräch mit dem Mann, der die Berge als eine Art Wallfahrtsstätte entdeckte," *Die Zeit,* 30 September 1977.

45. Compare Riefenstahl's account, "Trenker and Eva Braun's Diary," in *A Memoir,* pp. 338–352.

46. A typical example of such tongue-wagging is Raimund le Viseur, "Luis Trenker. Sex-Gipfel in der Sauna—mit 95?" *Bild-Zeitung,* 30 September 1992. An accompanying photograph showing ninety-three-year-old Trenker and his six-decades-younger companion, Martina Höller, bears the caption: "Millions of men envied him. His young woman. His potency at a biblical age. They did it in the sauna—or did they?"

47. Hans-Horst Skupy, "Ein ausgeprägter Individualist. Gespräch mit dem 90jährigen Luis Trenker," *Süddeutsche Zeitung,* 4 October 1982. Trenker's negotiations with Kohner clearly bear out, though, how limited the director's appeal for foreign markets actually was.

48. From an address delivered by Trenker at a conference in Munich on "Literature and Human Rights," 6 April 1978; quoted in *Mutig und heiter durchs Leben,* pp. 155–156.

49. The film was at best anti-Napoleonic. It received a warm review in *Film-Kurier,* 6 March 1940. Contemporary media accounts hardly depict Trenker as a man out of favor. See "Luis Trenker. Kamerad unter Kameraden," *Filmwoche* 9 (1940): "Luis Trenker ranks today without question among the most popular and beloved people, both in Germany and far beyond its borders."

50. In fact 86 percent of the South Tyrolean population would opt for the German

Reich. See Reinhold Messner, ed., *Die Option. 1939 stimmten 86% der Südtiroler für das Aufgeben ihrer Heimat,* 2nd rev. ed. (Munich/Zürich: Piper, 1995).

51. In a hand-written note to Hans Hinkel of 25 February 1940 signed with the notation "Heil Hitler," Trenker enclosed a copy of his letter to Thorak. Copies of both missives are available in the Trenker file, Berlin Document Center. Quoted as reprinted in Florian Leimgruber, ed., *Luis Trenker, Regisseur und Schriftsteller. Die Personalakte Trenker im Berlin Document Center* (Bozen: Frasnelli-Keitsch, 1994), pp. 54, 57–58.

52. Ibid., p. 63.

53. Ibid., p. 88.

54. William K. Everson, "Luis Trenker," *Films in Review* 33.5 (May 1984): 275. One might, however, also recall the official approval enjoyed by *The Prodigal Son* and remember that the film was rereleased in 1941, at a time when Trenker, according to his own accounts, had long fallen out of favor with Goebbels. *The Emperor of California* enjoyed its premiere at the Reich Ministry with Hitler in attendance. It received the official rating "politically and artistically especially worthwhile." It later appeared among the "Great National Films" reprised during the *Volkssturm* at the end of 1944. For additional particulars regarding the production and reception of the film, see Jan-Christopher Horak, "Luis Trenker's *The Kaiser of California:* How the West Was Won, Nazi Style," *Historical Journal of Film, Radio and Television* 6.2 (1986): 181–188. Hitler's select private collection of films included copies of *The Rebel* and *The Emperor of California.* Compare David Shipman's assertion in *The Story of Cinema* (New York: St. Martin's, 1982), p. 315: "Trenker had begun to challenge the Nazis in *Der Kaiser von Kalifornien,* with its clear warning that self-made dictators can well end up powerless and lonely."

55. On various occasions in the 1930s, Kohner admonished Trenker to desist from public appearances as well as photo opportunities with Nazi party leaders. Such exposure, feared Kohner, might well ruin Trenker's career chances abroad. Writing to Trenker from his Hollywood office on 29 October 1937, Kohner noted: "Incidentally, in all of your letters you ask me to give regards to Fritz Lang. I just want you to know that Lang is not a friend of yours. He thinks you are a Nazi. So, from now on don't send any more regards to him." Lang, of course, had cofounded the Hollywood Anti-Nazi League in 1936. Three years earlier, on 27 March 1933, Lang—together with Trenker, Carl Boese, and Victor Janson—also had organized German film directors in the Nazi party organization, the Nationalsozialistische Betriebsorganisation (NSBO); Gösta Werner, "Fritz Lang and Goebbels: Myth and Facts," *Film Quarterly* 43.3 (Spring 1990): 26.

56. In his polite but formal letter to Trenker of 17 June, Kohner described a subsequent meeting with the former Ufa producer: "He feels that if you will now apply for permission to work in Germany in the American Zone, or if you will have one of the leasing companies apply for you, there will be no objection raised to your getting the necessary clearance."

57. Hans-Horst Skupy, "Ein ausgeprägter Individualist," *Süddeutsche Zeitung,* 4 October 1982.

58. Ronald Holloway, "Interview: Bill & Stella Pence. Telluride Film Festival," *Kino: German Film* 19 (Summer 1985): 38. Pence extols Telluride's showcasing of an unbroken German film history from Riefenstahl and Trenker "to the New German Cinema of Wenders and Schloendorff and Herzog and Gabrea." See William K. Everson, "Trenker at 91 Still a Hit: Verbal Salvos re 'Art' Mark 10th Telluride," *Variety,* 14 September 1983. Sheila Benson, also in attendance at Telluride, observed how differently Trenker's films played months later in "Another View of Trenker's Mountains," *Los Angeles Times,* 25 January 1984: "If there was ever the suspicion that Telluride casts a hallucinatory spell, part attitude, part altitude, proof is seeing the 50-year old films of little-known Bavarian [*sic*] director/actor Luis Trenker down here at sea level on an overcast Thursday morning . . . Out of that rarefied atmosphere, although they certainly have an arresting look, the films are at times enough to try the patience of an oyster."

59. Everson's account in fact closely follows Trenker's own postwar recollections.

60. A typewritten copy of the original dialogue from *The Prodigal Son* is available in the Kohner papers at the Stiftung Deutsche Kinemathek.

61. The materials on file at the Stiftung Deutsche Kinemathek also include an invitation from Unitas-Film to a special screening of *The Prodigal Son* on 19 January 1953 at the Filmtheater Berlin am Kurfürstendamm. The West German Catholic Film Commission recommended the film upon its postwar release as "still worth seeing for audiences 14 years old and up." See Klaus Brüne, ed., *6000 Filme. Kritische Notizen aus den Kinojahren 1945–1958,* 4th ed. (Cologne/Düsseldorf: Katholische Filmkommission für Deutschland, 1980), p. 460.

62. See, for instance, the prose used in a 1982 advertisement by Reelife Productions, American distributor of Trenker's films: "Luis Trenker is one of the first all-around talents of the European cinema. As a director, actor, producer, and author, he always tried to present the highest human standards, which are still valid today. The subjects of his films presented variations of the fight for liberty, patriotism, the courage of the loner against all odds to help the underdog, and the comradeship which developed through danger to life and limb." Globus Film rereleased six Trenker films in the Federal Republic on the occasion of his ninetieth birthday. A brochure provides marketing guidelines, defending *The Fire Devil* as a film that deals with "freedom and love of the homeland . . . Luis Trenker was never an accomplice to those in power, but rather an independent producer—and when that was not possible—an author and actor who demonstrated for freedom."

63. Lulu von Strauss und Torney, *Erde der Väter* (Jena: Diederichs, 1939), p. 64; reprinted in Ernst Loewy, *Literatur unterm Hakenkreuz. Das Dritte Reich und seine Dichtung* (Frankfurt am Main: Fischer, 1983), p. 118.

64. Ernst Bloch, *Heritage of Our Times,* trans. Neville Plaice and Stephen Plaice (Berkeley: University of California Press, 1991), p. 48.

65. Herbert Marcuse, "The Struggle against Liberalism in the Totalitarian View of the State," in *Negations: Essays in Critical Theory,* trans. Jeremy J. Shapiro (Boston: Beacon, 1968), p. 23.

66. Ibid., p. 6. See Arthur Moeller van den Bruck, *Das dritte Reich* (quoted by Marcuse, p. 272, n. 39): "In the history of a folk, with time, things may change as they will: the immutable, which remains, is more powerful and important than the mutable, which consists only in something being added or subtracted. The immutable is the presupposition of all changes, and whatever may change returns, when its time has come, to the immutable."

67. Compare Ulrich Kurowski's formulation in "Luis Trenker. 4.10.1892–13.4.1990": "A typical composition from a Trenker film: high on an Alpine peak, the hero Trenker, behind him a chain of large mountains. Naturally not only as a background, but as a dramatic backdrop. The hero/director/author/showoff/star/architect/mountain expert partakes of nature in order to tell a story and to stage his symphonic *Gesamtkunstwerk*" (p. 4).

68. Leo Löwenthal, "Knut Hamsun, 1860–1952," in *Literature and the Image of Man* (New Brunswick, N.J.: Transaction, 1986), p. 194.

69. Ibid., p. 195.

70. Trenker particularly dwells on Tonio's allure for the opposite sex. At the festivity following the ski competition, the camera shows Lilian gazing longingly at Toni while he converses with Barbl. As if granting the American woman's wish, the image dissolves to a shot of Toni dancing with Lilian. The subsequent scene yet again changes partners: Barbl gazes at Tonio with the American, and a dissolve places Barbl at a table next to him. In his Alpine comedy of 1938, *Liebesbriefe aus dem Engadin* (*Love Letters from the Engadine Valley*, codirected with Werner Klingler), Trenker appears as the ski instructor Tonio, a man desired by throngs of women who flock from all over Europe to be near him. "They only come here to stare at you," complains Tonio's possessive sister. See also Heide-Marie Scheuering, "Erst 78 Jahre alt!" *Berliner Morgenpost*, 10 October 1970: "He [Trenker] has an extraordinary effect on women."

71. The novel describes Tonio's dizziness as he looks down from the edifice: "Damn if that wasn't a different world altogether. And he remembers the Dolomite towers at home. One feels the money, the competition, the tempo!" (p. 174). Later in the film the former king of the mountains becomes a construction worker on a skyscraper, a faceless function of a capitalist order subject to the logic of the mass ornament. Compare Siegfried Kracauer, *The Mass Ornament: Weimar Essays*, trans. and ed. Thomas Y. Levin (Cambridge, Mass.: Harvard University Press, 1995): "A system oblivious to differences in form leads on its own to the blurring of national characteristics and to the production of worker masses that can be employed equally well at any point on the globe" (p. 78).

72. These shots occasioned spontaneous applause during the premiere screening in Berlin.

73. Compare the formulation of a contemporary reviewer, "Das Hohelied der Heimat. Erfolgreiche Aufführung im Berliner Capitol," *Völkischer Beobachter*, 5 October 1934: "America, the country with houses that climb to the sky, with its millions of unemployed, with its grotesque contrasts, does not receive him [Tonio] well."

74. See Karsten Witte, "Der Gipfel bin ich. Zum Tode Luis Trenkers," *Frankfurter*

Rundschau, 14 April 1990. Witte speaks of how the director used avant-garde techniques to produce regressive images. Rudolf Arnheim complained in 1933 about the loose ordering of images in *The Rebel;* "Zweierlei Rebellen," *Die Weltbühne,* 24 January 1933, pp. 135–136. For an insightful analysis of the montage in *The Rebel,* see Lothar Schwab, "Deutschland 1932. Die Einheit von genretypischer Ahistorizität und reaktionärer Propaganda in Luis Trenkers *Der Rebell,*" *Diskurs* (Cologne) 3.3–4 (1973): 51–64. Trenker, according to Barry Salt, cut far more rapidly than his French and German contemporaries. The average shot length for *The Prodigal Son* was 5.5 seconds, for *The Emperor of California,* 6.0 seconds—much less than the mean of 10.6 seconds for German films of the 1930s and 1940s; "Continental Manners: Formal and Stylistic Features of French and German Cinema of the 30's and 40's," in *European Cinema Conference Papers,* ed. Susan Hayward (Aston: AMLC Publications, 1985), pp. 56–57.

75. For a valuable representative sampling of Weimar debates about Americanism, see the materials collected in Anton Kaes, Martin Jay, and Edward Dimendberg, eds., *Weimar Republic Sourcebook* (Berkeley: University of California Press, 1994).

76. The book version portrays New York as a city of unceasing noise and constant movement, a place—similar to Fritz Lang's *Metropolis*—controlled by an unseen subterranean machinery. Characterizing Manhattan as a maelstrom, Trenker makes frequent use of metaphors involving water and flow, streams, channels, and currents. See, for instance, the description of Tonio's job at a skyscraper construction site: "No question, the tempo of this job was murderous. Everything went so quickly, everyone was at everyone else's throat, as if a great flood were just about to happen and they were charged with building Noah's ark" (pp. 206–207).

77. "The National Film Is the International Film," *Film-Kurier,* 1 January 1934.

78. For a typical contemporaneous instance of anti-Americanism in the German print media, see "Wie Amerika sich um die Wohlfahrt und Sicherheit sorgt," *Die Woche,* 18 February 1936, p. 10. Accompanying the article is a photograph of what purports to be everyday reality in urban America, a street scene of overflowing garbage cans and loitering tramps. Anti-American touches can be found throughout Nazi cinema, in propaganda features such as *Hans Westmar* (1933) as well as in Trenker's *The Emperor of California* and *Love Letters from the Engadine Valley.* See as well the documentaries, *Rund um die Freiheitsstatue* (*A Trip around the Statue of Liberty,* 1942) and *Herr Roosevelt plaudert* (*Mr. Roosevelt Chats,* 1943). A flighty millionaire lures Marika Rökk to New York in *Und Du, mein Schatz, fährst mit* (*And You, My Dear, Will Come with Me,* 1937). Treacherous and mercenary Americans appear frequently in later features such as *Fünf Millionen suchen einen Erben* (*Five Million in Search of an Heir,* 1938), *Sensationsprozeß Casilla* (*The Sensational Casilla Trial,* 1939), and the revue film *Liebespremiere* (*Love Makes Its Debut,* 1943). Compare the untenable conclusion of David Stewart Hull, *Film in the Third Reich* (New York: Simon and Schuster, 1973), p. 260: "It has often been asked if the Nazi film industry turned out any anti-American pictures. With certain qualifications, the answer would have to be no. This was a reflection of Hitler's strange attitude toward the United States."

79. Compare Hull's enthusiastic recommendation of *The Prodigal Son,* p. 66: "The scenes of depression New York put similar American efforts to shame. Rarely has the atmosphere of the period been so utterly convincingly conveyed. We see the United States through the eyes of a stranger, and the effect is extraordinary."

80. See Tonio's return to his father's house in the novel: "Across from him stood the old clock on the wall and its constant tick-tock tick-tock, as if nothing, absolutely nothing, had happened during the whole long while" (p. 287). Trenker's films of the 1930s prefer premodern settings. When modernity does appear (as in *The Prodigal Son* and *Love Letters from the Engadine Valley*), it has negative associations. In this regard, Trenker's mountain films (unlike his western about a modernizer, *The Emperor of California*) do not share the curious mixture of premodern sentiment and modern machinery found in the work of Arnold Fanck. See Eric Rentschler, "Mountains and Modernity: Relocating the *Bergfilm,*" *New German Critique* 51 (Fall 1990): 137–161.

81. Trenker's novel describes how ritual continuity suffered because of the world war, how the *Rauhnacht* lost its importance during the postwar era. The mask of the Sun King has gathered dust in the workshop of Barbl's father.

82. For accounts of the function of the winter solstice in the Nazi calendar, see Karlheinz Schmeer, *Die Regie des öffentlichen Lebens im Dritten Reich* (Munich: Pohl, 1956), pp. 91–93; and Klaus Vondung, *Magie und Manipulation. Ideologischer Kult und politische Religion des Nationalsozialismus* (Göttingen: Vandenhoeck & Ruprecht, 1971), pp. 85–87. For an overview of Nazi holidays and celebrations, see Peter Reichel, *Der schöne Schein des Dritten Reiches. Faszination und Gewalt des Faschismus* (Munich: Hanser, 1991), pp. 209–221.

83. Billinger received the prestigious Kleist Prize for *Rauhnacht.* The play premiered at the Schauspielhaus München on 10 October 1931 and at the Staatliches Schauspielhaus Berlin on 17 December 1931 under the direction of Jürgen Fehling (subsequently Billinger's favorite stage collaborator). The Berlin cast included Werner Krauss as Simon and Luise Ullrich (whose first feature film role would be in Trenker's *The Rebel*); Rochus Gliese (who had worked on F. W. Murnau's *Sunrise*) served as set designer. For background materials and representative contemporary notices, see Günther Rühle, *Theater für die Republik im Spiegel der Kritik,* vol 2: *1926–1933* (Berlin: Henschel, 1988), pp. 1086–92. One finds repeated claims that Billinger helped write the script of *The Prodigal Son.* See "Billingers *Rauhnacht* wird Trenkers *Rauhnacht,*" *Film-Kurier,* 24 April 1934; also "Richard Billinger 40 Jahre," *Film-Kurier,* 20 July 1934. The dramatist, however, receives no mention in the film's credits. He went on to become a successful and productive scriptwriter during the Third Reich.

84. Rolf Nürnberg's review of the Staatliches Schauspielhaus Berlin performance, *12-Uhr-Blatt* (Berlin), 18 December; reprinted in Rühle, *Theater für die Republik,* p. 1092.

85. Rudolf Kayser, "Amerikanismus," *Vossische Zeitung,* 27 September 1925; as rendered in Kaes, Jay, and Dimendberg, *Weimar Republic Sourcebook,* p. 395.

86. Compare Béla Balázs' comments from 1923, reprinted in *Theory of the Film: Character and Growth of a New Art,* trans. Edith Bone (New York: Dover, 1970), p. 42:

"In the epoch of word culture we made little use of the expressive powers of our body and therefore partly lost that power. The gesturing of primitive peoples is frequently more varied and expressive than that of the educated European whose vocabulary is infinitely richer." During Leni Riefenstahl's 1938 tour to America, she commented on a black revue in New York: "It is all breath-taking jungle ability, but no brains and no inspiration. Did a Negro ever make a great invention?"; Ernst Jaeger, "How Leni Riefenstahl became Hitler's Girlfriend," *Hollywood Tribune,* 2 June 1939.

87. Yvan Goll, "Die Neger erobern Europa," *Die literarische Welt* 2.3 (15 January 1926); as rendered in Kaes, Jay, and Dimendberg, *Weimar Republic Sourcebook,* p. 560.

88. Theodor Lessing, "Josephine," *Das Stachelschwein,* November/December 1928, excerpted in Anton Kaes, ed., *Weimarer Republik. Manifeste und Dokumente zur deutschen Literatur 1918–1933* (Stuttgart: Metzler, 1983), p. 259.

89. Later critics would promote the popular legend that Tonio's ring triumph offered audiences of 1934 fictional compensation for Schmeling's knockout at the hands of Joe Louis; D. A., "Weltheil. Luis Trenker," *Deutsches Allgemeines Sonntagsblatt,* 3 October 1982. The famous two-minute fight, of course, did not take place until 1938. Schmeling's victory over Louis in their initial bout of 1936 offered *völkisch* ideologues conclusive evidence of white superiority. The German documentary film about the fight, *Max Schmelings Sieg—ein deutscher Sieg* (*Max Schmeling's Victory—a German Victory,* Hans H. Zerlett, 1936) is a particularly vicious example of racist propaganda.

90. Compare J. Hoberman, "Franz Kafka's Bogus Journey," *Village Voice,* 4 February 1992, p. 51: "Tonio rejects the New World (including those decadent Americans who want to revitalize themselves on German energy)."

91. See Luis Trenker, *Das große Luis Trenker Buch* (Gütersloh: Bertelsmann, 1974): Trenker describes a trip with a German television crew to New York in 1972 to take footage for his eightieth birthday celebration. Reporters gathered around him along with a bunch of children who "carried on in the liveliest manner, they were mainly black boys and girls who all wanted my autograph" (p. 175).

92. For a discussion of Rosenberg's disdain for Billinger, see Bogusław Drewniak, *Das Theater im NS-Staat* (Düsseldorf: Droste, 1983), p. 223.

93. See the director's reflections about the Statue of Liberty in *Das große Luis Trenker Buch:* "In 1932 [*sic*—the location shooting took place well after Hitler's rise to power] I sat here as the starving son of a lost homeland. In 1972 I greeted this consoling image of the American will to freedom with gratitude for the generous help which we Europeans received from this great nation in our years of need." In the retrospective reading, New York, "despite its shadowy sides," now appears as an incarnation of "American spirit, American energy, and the American pursuit of liberty" (p. 176).

94. See Willi Höfig's voluminous genre study, *Der deutsche Heimatfilm 1947–1960* (Stuttgart: Enke, 1973).

95. At the beginning of Trenker's *Lightning around Maria* (1957), the director's voice-over commentary accompanies images of grazing mountain animals: "After the

war Germans were forbidden to bear arms. Poachers refused to obey the law and in many regions decimated the entire stock of game." Read symptomatically, the virulent conflict of interest between forest rangers and armed invaders resembles Cold War concerns about threats from abroad and affirms the need for German rearmament.

96. Edgar Reitz, "The Camera Is Not a Clock (1979)," reprinted in *West German Filmmakers on Film: Visions and Voices,* ed. Eric Rentschler (New York/London: Holmes & Meier, 1988), p. 139.

97. Trenker repeatedly wrote Kohner that if the price was right, he would be ready to relocate immediately: "I'm always willing to consider a substantial offer, and any company would suit me fine as long as it is solvent and generous" (12 January 1937). Clearly, Goebbels and his coworkers from the start did not harbor illusions about Trenker's loyalty. It would seem that the ideological use value of Trenker's films outweighed his potential as a political liability. An undated letter of 1934 to the Reich Film Division from Fred Lyssa, a party member charged with production tasks on *The Prodigal Son,* provided the following confidential assessment of Trenker: "T. is always letting people know that he can do what he wants in Germany, otherwise he'll go to Hitler and then there will be hell to pay. T. is neither a National Socialist nor a German. He is a businessman at *any* price, even if it means stepping on the party"; *Die Personalakte Trenker,* p. 18. "Trenker makes national films," Goebbels noted in his diary on 16 February 1940, "but he is and always was a real dirt-bag [*Miststück*]."

4. Hollywood Made in Germany

1. *Glückskinder,* 1936. Produced by Ufa-Film, Production Group Max Pfeiffer. Production Head: Dietrich von Theobald. Direction: Paul Martin. Assistant to the Director: Paul Zils. Script: Robert A. Stemmle and Paul Martin, based on Brian Marlow and Thyra Samter Winslow's film novella *Lady Beware.* Dialogue: Curt Goetz. Cinematography: Konstantin Irmen-Tschet. Editing: Carl-Otto Bartning. Set Design: Erich Kettelhut. Costume Design: Manon Hahn. Sound: Fritz Thiery and Erich Leistner. Music: Peter Kreuder. Song Lyrics: Hans Fritz Beckmann.

The Players: Lilian Harvey (Ann Garden), Willy Fritsch (Gil Taylor), Paul Kemp (Frank Black), Oskar Sima (Stoddard), Fred Goebel (Bill), Erich Kestin (Hopkins), Otto Stoeckel (Manning, Editor of the *Morning Post*), Paul Bildt (judge), Albert Florath (Mr. Jackson, oil magnate), ***[Lilian Harvey] (his niece), Thomas Cziruchin (the boxer), Peter Lau (butler), Jac Diehl, Arno Ebert, Max Hiller, Fred Koester, Hermann Meyer-Falkow, Carl Merznicht, Paul Rehkopf, Kurt Seifert, Walter Steinweg.

Original length: 2,558 meters (93 minutes). Premiered on 18 September 1936 in Berlin (Gloria-Palast). Rating: "Artistically worthwhile."

French-language version: *Les gais lurons.* Produced by Universum-Film A. G. and Alliance Cinématographique Européene, Paris. Codirected by Paul Martin and Jacques Natanson. Dialogue: Jacques Natanson. Song Lyrics: Jean Boyer. The Players: Lilian Harvey (Ann Garden), Henri Garat (Gil Taylor), Stéphane Pizella (Frank), Henri

Guisol (Stoddard), Jean Toulot (judge), Paul Ollivier (Jackson), Pierre Magnier (Manning), Marcel Duhamel (Hopkins), Pierre Labry (bartender), Thomas Cziruchin (the boxer), André Siméon, Bill-Bocketts, Aimos. Premiered on 6 October 1936 in Paris (Marivaux).

An unsubtitled video copy of *Lucky Kids* is available from the German Language Video Center and International Historic Films.

2. The song was a big hit in 1936. The Ufaton record release was sung by Harvey and Fritsch, accompanied by the Odeon Tanzorchester under the direction of Friedrich Schröder. The tune can be heard in the 1939 Ufa comedy *Hallo Janine,* but it seems to have lost its luster: a listless pianist (played by Rudi Godden) grinds it out mechanically in a nearly empty nightclub.

3. H. T. S., "At the 86th St. Garden Theatre," *New York Times,* 5 June 1937. The film played in a subtitled version.

4. For a cogent comparison of *It Happened One Night* and *Lucky Kids,* see Karsten Witte, "Die Filmkomödie im Dritten Reich," in *Die deutsche Literatur im Dritten Reich,* ed. Horst Denkler and Karl Prümm (Stuttgart: Reclam, 1976), pp. 354–355.

5. *Mask in Blue* was revived in Berlin during the summer of 1991, touted by the cinema Babylon-Mitte as a wild and crazy Nazi musical. The film's exuberance resides above all in the frenetic stepping and effervescent performance of Clara Tabody, an actress who blends the attributes of Kristina Söderbaum, Marika Rökk, and Lilian Harvey.

6. For details about Harvey's sojourn in Hollywood as well as her romantic and professional relationships with Martin and Fritsch, see Christiane Habich, ed., *Lilian Harvey* (Berlin: Haude & Spener, 1990).

7. Schu, "Presseleute besuchen amerikanische Redaktion. *Glückskinder* am ersten Tag," *Film-Kurier,* 26 May 1936.

8. BvM, "Was ist interessant?" *Lichtbild-Bühne,* 18 September 1936.

9. S-k., *"Glückskinder," Film-Kurier,* 19 September 1936.

10. Quotations from an advertisement for the film in *Film-Kurier,* 22 September 1936.

11. *" 'Glueckskinder' ('Children of Fortune')," Variety,* 21 October 1936.

12. Regarding Nazi influences in Hollywood, see Anthony Slide, "Hollywood's Fascist Follies," *Film Comment* 27.4 (July–August 1991): 62–67.

13. For an exhaustive and lucid account of this cross-cultural drama, see Thomas J. Saunders, *Hollywood in Berlin: American Cinema and Weimar Germany* (Berkeley: University of California Press, 1994). See also Anton Kaes, "Mass Culture and Modernity: Notes toward a Social History of Early American and German Cinema," in *America and the Germans: An Assessment of a Three-Hundred-Year History,* ed. Frank Trommler and Joseph McVeigh (Philadelphia: University of Pennsylvania Press, 1985), vol. 2, pp. 317–331. For general perspectives on European reactions to American film interests, see Victoria de Grazia, "Mass Culture and Sovereignty: The American Challenge to European Cinemas, 1920–1960," *Journal of Modern History* 61.1 (March 1989): 53–87.

14. H. N., "Abstecher nach Brüssel. Fim-Eindrücke—das 'helle Bild' des USA-Films," *Film-Kurier,* 26 September 1934.

15. Ernst Jaeger of *Film-Kurier* published a series of long articles describing a trip to the United States in the fall of 1935, expressions of fascination and admiration.

16. "Zivilisationsmärchen, Filmfabeln als Extrakt der Zeit," *Lichtbild-Bühne,* 24 December 1934.

17. The definitive expression of these mixed feelings came in Joseph Goebbels' speech of March 1937 to the First Meeting of the Reich Film Chamber; "Rede bei der ersten Jahrestagung der Reichsfilmkammer am 5. 3. 1937 in der Krolloper, Berlin," reprinted in Gerd Albrecht, *Nationalsozialistische Filmpolitik* (Stuttgart: Enke, 1969), pp. 447–465. This creative crisis was also felt in the German theater world. The Reich did not lack new plays in 1935, said one critic. What it lacked were any good ones; Wilhelm von Schramm, "Praktische Dramaturgie. Erfahrungen im Bühnenvertrieb," *Deutsche Allgemeine Zeitung,* 27 January 1935.

18. According to a confidential Ufa document from 1944 (provided by Gero Gandert, Stiftung Deutsche Kinemathek, Berlin), German feature films cost on the average 248,000 RM in 1934. The largest outlays went for studio facilities (35 percent) and actors' salaries (20 percent). For the 1935–36 season, an average Ufa feature was budgeted at 550,000 RM. (By these standards *Lucky Kids* was exorbitant; it cost 1.2 million RM.) By 1944 the Ufa figure rose to 1,450,000 RM, a sum topped by Berlin-Film (almost 2 million per film) and Wien-Film (1.6 million). For detailed assessments of Nazi cinema's political economy from a materialist perspective, see Wolfgang Becker, *Film und Herrschaft. Organisationsprinzipien und Organisationsstrukturen der nationalsozialistischen Filmpropaganda* (Berlin: Spiess, 1973); and Jürgen Spiker, *Film und Kapital. Der Weg der deutschen Filmwirtschaft zum nationalsozialistischen Einheitskonzern* (Berlin: Spiess, 1975). The best overview in English (in great part dependent on Becker and Spiker) is Julian Petley, *Capital and Culture: German Cinema, 1933–45* (London: British Film Institute, 1979), pp. 47–94.

19. Ernst Jaeger, "Herbst im Hollywood III. Viel Licht—also auch Schatten," *Film-Kurier,* 16 November 1935.

20. It was the task of the critic, claimed Goebbels in 1936, to encourage rather than to condemn. See Theo Fürstenau's discussion of film criticism in the Third Reich, "Eskapismus und Camouflage," *Internationale Zeitschrift für Kommunikationsforschung* 1.3 (1974): 366–368.

21. See, for instance, the large advertisement for MGM films (among others, *Vagabond Lady, China Seas, Murder in the Fleet, Bonnie Scotland, No More Ladies,* and *Anna Karenina*) in *Film-Kurier,* 2 December 1935: "The whole world can't be wrong! Everywhere these films played they were among the hits of the season!"

22. *Jahrbuch der Reichsfilmkammer* 3 (1939): 199. Goebbels sought to drive American films not only out of Germany, but eventually out of Europe; by 1939, only 20 American films would play in Germany. During the Third Reich, 600 foreign features found their way onto German screens; Bogusław Drewniak, *Der deutsche Film 1938–1945. Ein*

Gesamtüberblick (Düsseldorf: Droste, 1987), p. 814. According to Drewniak, American distributors did not suffer losses in Germany until 1939. From 1933 to March 1940, Paramount released 141 titles in Germany, MGM 153 (p. 820).

23. See Schu., "Berlin sieht Auslands-Versionen," *Film-Kurier,* 29 April 1936. The Kurbel also screened foreign-language versions of German films during the Olympics, among others Martin's *Black Roses* and Reinhold Schünzel's *Amphitryon.* Through June 1940, both the Kurbel and the Kamera unter den Linden presented weekly screenings of American films in the original versions. Goebbels occasionally allowed films to be shown in the Kamera which otherwise were forbidden, including *Mädchen in Uniform;* Peter F. Gallasch, "Filmvorführungen als Ventilfunktion. Ein Beispiel der NS-Kulturpolitik. Die Kamera zeigte offiziell verbotene Filme," *Der Tagesspiegel,* 2 December 1984.

24. S-k., "Noch einmal. Die Amerikaner," *Film-Kurier,* 2 July 1936.

25. For a brief but insightful discussion of Nazi Westerns, see Christopher Frayling, *Spaghetti Westerns: Cowboys and Europeans from Karl May to Sergio Leone* (London: Routledge & Kegan Paul, 1981), pp. 29, 32–33.

26. Karsten Witte, "Visual Pleasure Inhibited: Aspects of the German Revue Film," trans. J. D. Steakley and Gabriele Hoover, *New German Critique* 24–25 (Fall/Winter 1981–82): 253.

27. Albrecht, *Nationalsozialistische Filmpolitik,* p. 462.

28. Hermann Gressieker, "Amerikanische Leistungsprinzipien. II. Maßstäbe," *Der Deutsche Film* 2.10 (April 1938): 273.

29. Hans Dieter Schäfer, *Das gespaltene Bewußtsein. Über deutsche Kultur und Lebenswirklichkeit 1933–1945* (Frankfurt am Main: Ullstein, 1984), pp. 146–208.

30. Michael H. Kater, *Different Drummers: Jazz in the Culture of Nazi Germany* (Oxford: Oxford University Press, 1992), p. 57.

31. Fascist Italy's response to American mass culture, in crucial ways, proceeded along similar lines, even if it did not exclusively associate the United States with progress, modernity, and the new. According to James Hay, Italian audiences found "in America a celebration, in *modern* images, of spiritual community and conservative values. America's mythical status produced both desire and fear—emotions which for about twenty years helped transform Italy into a stage for ideological conflict"; *Popular Film Culture in Fascist Italy: The Passing of the Rex* (Bloomington: Indiana University Press, 1987), p. 98.

32. Schäfer, *Das gespaltene Bewußtsein,* p. 184. Regarding Nazi Berlin's rich array of dance halls and nightclubs, see Knud Wolffram, *Tanzdielen und Vergnügungspaläste. Berliner Nachtleben in den dreißiger und vierziger Jahren* (Berlin: Edition Hentrich, 1992).

33. Detlev J. K. Peuckert, *Inside Nazi Germany: Conformity, Opposition, and Racism in Everyday Life,* trans. Richard Deveson (New Haven: Yale University Press, 1987), p. 79.

34. Kroll Opera address of March 1937, reprinted in Albrecht, *Nationalsozialistische Filmpolitik,* p. 456. See Goebbels' speech in the Tennishallen, Berlin, 19 March 1933:

"When someone from America watches a German film, he does not expect to see a film that just as easily could have been made in America. When he goes to watch a German film, he expects to see something typically German. When I go to see a Chinese film, I expect to see how the Chinese live in China, because I already know well how we Germans live"; ibid., p. 446.

35. "Lehrer und Schüler," *Der SA-Mann,* 23 October 1937. See also the actor Mathias Wieman's programmatic attack on American film in general and specifically on the box-office hit *San Francisco:* "Diesseits und jenseits des Erreichten," *Film-Kurier,* 29 April 1937.

36. Joseph Goebbels, *Tagebücher,* vol. 3: *1935–1939,* ed. Ralf Georg Reuth (Munich: Piper, 1992), p. 942. See also Goebbels' entry of 4 April 1937, where he describes the Sonja Henie vehicle *One in a Million* as "very precise, bright, and funny . . . How effortlessly the Americans do these things. One can only admire them" (p. 1063).

37. Hermann Gressieker, "Amerikanische Leistungsprinzipien," *Der Deutsche Film* 2.7 (January 1938): 185.

38. H. Ch. M., "Amerikanische Filme," *Die Tat* 28.2 (May 1936): 152.

39. Siegfried Kracauer, "Cult of Distraction: On Berlin's Picture Palaces," trans. Thomas Y. Levin, *New German Critique* 40 (Winter 1987): 94.

40. See his often-quoted pronouncement of 1937: "When propaganda is perceived as such it becomes ineffective. When propaganda, political message, bias, attitude remain in the background and appear only as a function of plot, sequence, action, or contrast between characters, then they become effective in every conceivable way"; Albrecht, *Nationalsozialistische Filmpolitik,* p. 446.

41. Goebbels' diary entry of 20 December 1937, quoted in J. P. Storm and M. Dressler, *Im Reiche der Micky Maus. Walt Disney in Deutschland 1927–1945* (Berlin: Henschel, 1991; cited hereafter as Storm/Dressler), p. 11.

42. Paul Scheffer, "Potemkin und Micky Maus. Zur Krise des deutschen Films," *Berliner Tageblatt,* 2 December 1934; quoted in Storm/Dressler, p. 76. See Laurence A. Rickels, *The Case of California* (Baltimore: Johns Hopkins University Press, 1991), p. 7: "Mickey Mouse is not an indifferent or altogether innocent emblem of humanistic transformation . . . With Mickey Mouse, Disney had invented not only the totally American product but also the first in that category to circulate with unequalled international appeal." See also Miriam Hansen, "Of Mice and Ducks: Benjamin and Adorno on Disney," *South Atlantic Quarterly* 92.1 (Winter 1993): 27–61.

43. *"Die lustige Palette," Berliner Tageblatt,* 21 December 1934; quoted in Storm/Dressler, p. 81.

44. *"Rottkäppchen," Film-Kurier,* 3 May 1935.

45. "Märchenfilme," *Film-Kurier,* 16 December 1938.

46. *The Goebbels Diaries: 1939–1941,* trans. and ed. Fred Taylor (Harmondsworth: Penguin, 1984), p. 120.

47. Quotations from an advertisement for the film in *Film-Kurier,* 22 September 1936.

48. " 'Ich wollt', ich wär' ein Huhn . . .," *Das Schwarze Korps,* 26 November 1936; reprinted in Ulrich Kurowski, ed., *Deutsche Spielfilme 1933–1945. Materialien III,* 2nd rev. ed. (Munich: Stadtmuseum Munich and Münchner Filmzentrum, 1980), pp. 175–177.

49. Storm/Dressler, p. 10.

50. Its title recalls the well-known Grimm Brothers fairy tales "Goldkinder" and "Hans im Glück."

51. See S-k., "Auch das ist Weltanschauung!" *Film-Kurier,* 16 February 1937. Rather than fussing about what constitutes a correct world view, filmmakers should promote a "healthy contemporary sense of reality and an authentic feeling for life"—especially in the plots and roles of "so-called entertainment fare." Here in particular, claimed the critic, German artists had much to learn from their American counterparts.

52. Albrecht, *Nationalsozialistische Filmpolitik,* p. 110.

53. See, for instance, "Das Recht auf Humor. Über das 'Heitere' des deutschen Films," *Film-Kurier,* 23 May 1936; M. R. M., "Mehr Humor im Film. Ein wichtiges Thema," *Film-Kurier,* 17 August 1936; S-k., "Angst vor Humor? Wir brauchen nach wie vor Lustspiele, Schwänke und Unterhaltungsfilme," *Film-Kurier,* 22 May 1937.

54. See Hermann Meyer, "Der falsche Lacher. Methodische Untersuchung," *Film-Kurier,* 4 May 1937.

55. W. P., "Der 'falsche Lacher.' Betrachtungen über die Psychologie des Publikums," *Film-Kurier,* 6 July 1938.

56. Henri Bergson, "Laughter," in *Comedy,* ed. Wylie Sypher (Garden City, N.Y.: Doubleday, 1956), p. 65.

57. W. P., "Der 'falsche Lacher.' "

58. See Peter Reichel, *Der schöne Schein des Dritten Reiches. Faszination und Gewalt des Faschismus* (Munich/Vienna: Hanser, 1991), esp. pp. 114–156; Klaus Vondung, *Magie und Manipulation. Ideologischer Kult und politische Religion des Nationalsozialismus* (Göttingen: Vandenhoeck & Ruprecht, 1971); and Karlheinz Schmeer, *Die Regie des öffentlichen Lebens im Dritten Reich* (Munich: Pohl, 1956).

59. Goebbels, *Tagebücher,* vol. 3, p. 1007 (entry of 10 November 1936).

60. Goebbels, Kroll Opera address, reprinted in Albrecht, *Nationalsozialistische Filmpolitik,* p. 462.

61. Advertisement in *Film-Kurier,* 9 December 1935.

62. S-k., "*Es geschah in einer Nacht*/Marmorhaus. Triumph amerikanischer Lustspieltechnik," *Film-Kurier,* 16 October 1935.

63. Siegfried Kracauer, "Wochenschau-Theater [1931]," in *Kino. Essays, Studien, Glossen zum Film,* ed. Karsten Witte (Frankfurt am Main: Suhrkamp, 1974), p. 15.

64. In the film's attempt to mimic Americana, it occasionally betrays a foreign accent. The messenger boy at the *Morning Post* is dressed like a bellhop. The football score 2–0 is not altogether unlikely, but a game between Ohio (and not Ohio State) and Notre Dame is. (The original script calls it a rugby match—an even less likely prospect for a headline story.) A soda jerk at a Manhattan drugstore counter dispenses beer and dishes

up herring! The cutting between German localities and American locations likewise gives rise to amusingly bizarre blends of Berlin suburbs and the boulevards of Manhattan. The final chase sequence also has a striking continuity error; we see Paul Kemp arrive at the niece's love nest in two different cars.

65. Compare Richard Corliss' discussion of Ben Hecht's newsroom environments in *Talking Pictures: Screenwriters in the American Cinema* (New York: Penguin, 1975), p. 10.

66. Hecht's screenplay for William Wellman's *Nothing Sacred* (1937) describes a managing editor as "sort of a cross between a ferris wheel and a werewolf—but with a lovable streak, if you care to blast for it."

67. For a year-by-year inventory of hit songs in the Third Reich, see Bernd Polster, ed., *"Swing Heil." Jazz im Nationalsozialismus* (Berlin: Transit, 1989), pp. 231–238.

68. In Anny Ondra's first sound film, the 1930 feature directed by Carl Lamac, *Die vom Rummelplatz/Das Micky-Maus-Girl* (*The Girl from the Fairground/The Mickey Mouse Girl*), the actress (whom the critic Rudolf Arnheim once described as the "Girl-Golem") sang and danced like the Disney cartoon figure.

69. Thomas Brandlmeier, "Lilian Harvey und Jacques Feyder. Die Retrospektive der Berlinale," *Film-Korrespondenz,* no. 8 (1974): 179.

70. Friedrich Luft, *"Glückskinder," Die Welt,* 6 February 1975.

71. Andreas Meyer, "19.30 Uhr. ZDF. *Glückskinder,*" *Medium* 5.1 (January 1975): 26.

72. Hans Borgelt, "*Glückskinder* mit Lilian Harvey und Willy Fritsch," *Berliner Morgenpost,* 4 February 1975.

73. The German press announced Goetz's imminent return to the Reich in June 1940 for an engagement at the Kurfürstendamm Theater and the Komödie in Berlin; the writer, however, remained in the United States until 1946; Drewniak, *Der deutsche Film 1938–1945,* p. 510.

74. Axel Eggebrecht, *Der halbe Weg. Zwischenbilanz einer Epoche* (Reinbek bei Hamburg: Rowohlt, 1975), p. 308.

75. See the entry for 30 May 1939, *The Goebbels Diaries: 1939–1941,* p. 14: "Yesterday: Read a little in the morning. Curt Goetz, always pleasant and amusing." Also see *Tagebücher,* vol. 3, p. 1182: "Meeting with Curt Goetz . . . Request that he work on film dialogue. He is very useful, witty, and clever" (26 January 1938).

76. See "Märchenfilme, eine deutsche Angelegenheit," *Film-Kurier,* 30 June 1938.

77. See "Wirklichkeitssinn im Film. Etwas über das Wesen des amerikanischen Lustspiels," *Lichtbild-Bühne,* 6 December 1937.

78. *Lucky Kids* provides an updated variation on Martin's *Ein blonder Traum* (*Happy Ever After,* 1932), an Ufa depression comedy in which Harvey plays Jou-Jou, an itinerant actress who dreams of fame and fortune in Hollywood. Homeless after being swindled out of her money by a bogus American film producer, she moves in with a pair of window washers named Willy (Willy Fritsch and Willi Forst), ultimately deciding to settle down in Germany with Willy I.

79. In the end Ann will say "Bitte?" which in the context means "I beg your pardon?" Gil willfully misconstrues her response, insisting that her "bitte" is not a question, but rather the answer to his wish ("please"). The closing tableau, then, leaves us with a woman who is not taken at her word.

80. The cause of Ann's homelessness is not divulged in the film until the very end, when all problems have been resolved. To do so earlier (as the script does) might have taken the narrative even more strongly in the direction of the depression comedy. The original screenplay contains a handwritten addition in which Ann tells her hard-luck story to Mr. Jackson: "As of yesterday I've been in New York exactly five weeks. I spent the first three weeks with pencil and notepad, then the company went broke. Two weeks looking for work." Soon she was out of money and without a room; typescript in the Stiftung Deutsche Kinemathek, pp. 209–210.

81. The film later opens up briefly, and the foursome head for the racetrack. As they study the day's lineup, Stoddard insists they not "bet on [the horse named] Virgin, that's always an uncertain business," reasserting in jest the film's underlying anxiety about unbound women. Frank does, however, and, sure enough, they lose their shirts.

82. See, for instance, Chaparral, "Der Fall Dorothea Wieck," *Film-Kurier,* 15 June 1934: "One wonders whether it was a good idea to transplant Dorothea Wieck to Hollywood. Such valuable property, which this artist undoubtedly is, does not seem to receive proper handling over there. Her case is anything but an exception." For a more general reflection, see Oskar Kalbus, *Vom Werden deutscher Filmkunst,* vol. 2: *Der Tonfilm* (Altona-Bahrenfeld: Cigaretten-Bilderdienst, 1935), p. 99: almost all the German film artists who tried their luck in Hollywood have returned, "disappointed and chagrined about what happened to them over there." In Georg Jacoby's revue film *Und Du, mein Schatz, fährst mit* (*And You, My Dear, Will Come with Me,* 1937), the female protagonist (played by an ever-perky Marika Rökk) sacrifices a successful career on Broadway to return with her German lover to Europe.

83. At the same time, Cinecittà arose as an attempt to revive the Italian film industry by emulating American lines of production and Hollywood formulas. See Hay, *Popular Film Culture in Fascist Italy,* p. 72: "On the other hand, Cinecittà was also seen as an antidote to American cultural forms, i.e., as a means of expressing and disseminating a national spirit and as a *weapon* for combatting media imperialism."

84. These words from Goebbels' comments at the opening congress of delegates appear as a soundbite in Leni Riefenstahl's *Triumph des Willens* (*Triumph of the Will,* 1935). At times Goebbels seemed to be a curious synthesis between a Dr. Mabuse and a well-meaning therapist. Speaking at the Kroll Opera on 10 March 1939, he said: "A smart, prescient leadership must from the very start secure all the means by which one can or might be able to educate the will power of the masses, to guide or to strengthen it."

85. German filmgoers wanted to believe that the screen couple were actually married: "What are we to say about this conceptual confusion of the audience, which wants to project what it sees on the unreal space of the screen into reality?"; U. Konstantin, "'Lilian' oder der Wunschtraum," *Der Deutsche Film* 2.2 (August 1937): 44. According to

Géza von Cziffra, Nazi officials forced Fritsch and Harvey to appear together in public, "holding hands, smiling, signing autographs," maintaining the popular illusion of this representative couple's private liaison; *Es war eine rauschende Ballnacht. Eine Sittengeschichte des deutschen Films* (Frankfurt am Main: Ullstein, 1987), p. 37.

86. Hitler's police likewise made certain that prostitutes and panhandlers disappeared from big-city streets. For a discussion of loitering's subversive potential, see Susan Buck Morss, "The Flaneur, the Sandwichman and the Whore: The Politics of Loitering," *New German Critique* 39 (Fall 1986): 136 f.

87. Compare Hartmut Bitomsky, "Der Kotflügel eines Mercedes Benz. Nazikulturfilme, Teil I. Filme von 1933 bis 1938," *Filmkritik* 27.10 (October 1983): 471.

88. The short that preceded the first screenings of *Lucky Kids* explored the heavens. Martin Rikli's Ufa *Kulturfilm* bore the title *Unendlicher Weltraum (The Infinite Universe)* and "included photographs of the stars from prominent observatories."

5. Astray in the New World

1. Joseph Goebbels, *Tagebücher*, vol. 3: *1935–1939*, ed. Ralf Georg Reuth (Munich: Piper, 1992), p. 1057.

2. Ibid., pp. 1041–42 (entry of 15 February 1937).

3. See Jeffrey Herf, *Reactionary Modernism: Technology, Culture, and Politics in Weimar and the Third Reich* (Cambridge: Cambridge University Press, 1984): the Third Reich's second four-year-plan of 1937 stressed the larger goal "of reducing German dependence on the world economy through technical innovation"—meaning as well liberation from Jewish finance (p. 201). In the film world this brought about a radical consolidation and concentration of production in a handful of major studios, a situation decidedly in contrast to that of 1933, when 59 different companies released feature films.

4. *La Habanera*, 1937. Produced by Universum-Film AG (Ufa), Berlin. Producer: Bruno Duday. Production Manager: Erich Holder. Direction: Detlef Sierck. Assistant Director: Fritz Andelfinger. Script: Gerhard Menzel. Cinematography: Franz Weihmayr. Editing: Axel von Werner. Set Design: Anton Weber and Ernst H. Albrecht. Costumes: Annemarie Heise. Sound: Hermann Fritzsching. Music: Lothar Brühne. Song Lyrics: Detlef Sierck, Bruno Balz, Franz Baumann.

The Players: Zarah Leander (Astrée Sternhjelm), Julia Serda (Ana Sternhjelm, her aunt), Ferdinand Marian (Don Pedro de Avila), Karl Martell (Dr. Sven Nagel), Boris Alekin (Dr. Luis Gomez), Paul Bildt (Dr. Pardway), Edwin Jürgensen (Shumann), Carl Kuhlmann (prefect), Michael Schulz-Dornburg (little Juan), Rosita Alcaraz (Spanish dancer), Lisa Helwig (old servant), Geza von Földessy (chauffeur), Franz Arzdorf, Roma Bahn, Günther Ballier, Bob Bauer, Werner Finck, Karl Hannemann, Harry Hardt, Max Wilhelm, Hans Kettler, Werner Kepich, Carl Merznicht, Ernst Rotmund, Werner Scharf, Franz Stein.

Original length: 2,692 meters (98 minutes). Premiered on 18 December 1937 in Berlin (Gloria-Palast).

A subtitled 16mm copy is available from West Glen Films; a videocassette without subtitles can be purchased from the German Language Video Center and International Historic Films.

5. See Arthur Maria Rabenalt, *Joseph Goebbels und der "Großdeutsche" Film* (Munich: Herbig, 1985), p. 68: Goebbels, claims Rabenalt, was willing to accept new ideas and impulses about film only if they came from abroad.

6. Wolfgang Liebeneiner, "Im entscheidenden Augenblick darf man nur sich selber fragen. Wege zum filmischen Kunstwerk," *Film-Kurier,* 31 December 1937.

7. John Gillett, "Germany: A Lost Decade," *Sight and Sound* 41.4 (Autumn 1972): 225.

8. Arthur Maria Rabenalt, *Film im Zwielicht* (Hildesheim: Olms, 1978), pp. 26, 43. Rabenalt stresses how film artists posed "mental resistance" against the Nazi leadership; the German film world in fact offered asylum to political refugees (p. 18).

9. David Stewart Hull, *Film in the Third Reich* (New York: Simon and Schuster, 1973), p. 7.

10. Jon Halliday, "Notes on Sirk's German Films," in *Douglas Sirk,* ed. Laura Mulvey and Jon Halliday (Edinburgh: Edinburgh Film Festival, 1972), p. 15.

11. Klaus Kreimeier, *Die Ufa-Story. Geschichte eines Filmkonzerns* (Munich/Vienna: Hanser, 1992), p. 270.

12. Jon Halliday, *Sirk on Sirk* (New York: Viking, 1972), p. 41. Ufa, the director argues, remained a privately owned entity in the mid-1930s. "And there weren't any Nazis in it at the time—there didn't have to be, because the Hugenberg people were very right-wing anyway" (p. 35).

13. Ibid., p. 35.

14. Halliday, "Notes on Sirk's German Films," pp. 20–21. See also Mulvey and Halliday, *Douglas Sirk;* the special issue on Sirk in *Screen* 12.2 (Summer 1971); Paul Willemen, "Towards an Analysis of the Sirkian System," *Screen* 13.4 (Winter 1972–73): 128–134; William James Horrigan, "An Analysis of the Construction of an Author: The Example of Douglas Sirk" (Diss. Northwestern University, 1980).

15. Jean Pierre Bleys, "Quand Douglas Sirk s'appelait Detlef Sierck," *Cahiers de la cinémathèque* 32 (Spring 1981): 82.

16. Contrary to myth, it was not Fassbinder alone who rediscovered Sirk for Germany. A group of cineastes in Cologne was already watching and discussing his films avidly in the late 1960s, as was Ulrich Kurowski in Munich. The Cinemathek Köln (at the time still operating as the Arbeitsgemeinschaft für Filmfragen an der Universität zu Köln) sponsored a weekend series in the Wallraf-Richartz-Museum in 1969 dedicated to the American melodramas with an elaborate documentation by Hartmut Engmann. Also during that year in Cologne there was a weekend screening of Sirk's entire oeuvre, from his Ufa films to his Universal productions. From 1958 through 1973 not a single article on Sirk appeared in the leading West German cinema journal, *Filmkritik.* It took the famous melodrama seminar in Toulouse during the summer of 1971 to bring Sirk to the attention of the German media. For additional details about Sirk's reception in the FRG, see Sebastian Feldmann, "Leserbrief," *epd Film* 3.10 (October 1986): 14.

17. Halliday, *Sirk on Sirk,* p. 48.

18. Horrigan, "Analysis of Construction of an Author," p. 130. Horrigan maintains that the Anglo-American myth of Sirk "manages effectively to deny the existence of Nazi repressiveness altogether by claiming a strong continuity—with no fundamental differences recognized—between that [German] work and the work in America in the 1950s." Sirk became the prototype for a transcendent *auteur,* a figure whose subjectivity and vision remained intact no matter where and when he worked (pp. 130–131).

19. Helma Sanders-Brahms, "Zarah," in *Jahrbuch Film 81/82,* ed. Hans Günther Pflaum (Munich: Hanser, 1981), p. 171.

20. Bogusław Drewniak, *Der deutsche Film 1938–1945. Ein Gesamtüberblick* (Düsseldorf: Droste, 1987), p. 135.

21. Günther Rühle, "Die ganz große Geliebte. Das Leben und die Rollen der Zarah Leander," *Frankfurter Allgemeine Zeitung,* 24 June 1981.

22. See Paul Seiler, *Ein Mythos lebt. Zarah Leander* (Berlin: Graphische Werkstätten, 1991), p. 17.

23. *zitty* (Berlin), 7 January 1993, p. 172.

24. Paul Seiler, *Zarah Leander. Ein Kultbuch* (Reinbek bei Hamburg: Rowohlt, 1985), p. 8. Rosa von Praunheim also insists that she was an identification figure for gay men during the Third Reich, "escape from a bad dream that for many ended in a concentration camp"; "Die Baßamsel singt nicht mehr," *Der Spiegel,* 29 June 1981, p. 158.

25. Halliday, "Notes on Sirk's German Films," p. 22.

26. Kreimeier, *Die Ufa-Story,* p. 352.

27. The excerpts are taken from a page-long Ufa advertisement for *La Habanera* which appeared in German trade papers in early February 1938.

28. In Halliday, *Sirk on Sirk,* the director claims that Ufa "took my name off the films I had made in Germany—so they sometimes appeared without any director's credit at all" (p. 57). His claim, however, is not validated by extant prints from the era of *Final Accord, To New Shores,* or *La Habanera.*

29. Günther Schwark, *"Zu neuen Ufern," Film-Kurier,* 1 September 1937.

30. Prof. Dr. Lehnich, " 'Die Eigengesetzlichkeit des Films,' " *Film-Kurier,* 6 March 1937.

31. Goebbels clashed with Gustaf Gründgens over *Zwei Welten* (*Two Worlds,* 1939). See the minister's diary entry of 27 December 1939: "A film set in the present and about helping with the harvest—or at least supposedly so. It has totally missed the point. Too intellectual and almost entirely cerebral in its demands on the audience. Gründgens cannot get out of his own skin"; *The Goebbels Diaries: 1939–1941,* trans. and ed. Fred Taylor (Harmondsworth: Penguin, 1984), p. 75. On 12 January 1940 Goebbels noted: "I am a little depressed by the way our directors start with a few successes and then always go off the rails and become intellectual. But I shall do something about it" (p. 93).

32. Hermann Gressieker, "Die Film-Circe oder Die Normung des Geistes durch die Routine," *Der Deutsche Film* 2.5 (November 1937): 134.

33. Liebeneiner, "Im entscheidenden Augenblick." Liebeneiner provides an exemplary case study of a filmmaker who successfully negotiated his directorial presence by carefully modulating his authorial identity. See H. Gr., "Wolfgang Liebeneiner," *Der Deutsche Film* 2.5 (November 1937): "This is the lesson that the career of the actor and director Wolfgang Liebeneiner teaches us: intelligence and expertise, intellectual self-assertion against the temptations of stardom need not hinder one's road to success.—To have character is not necessarily a liability. We should heed his lesson" (p. 138). Later approaches to authorship, however, occasionally cast directors in the role of artist-genius. See, for instance, Günther Sawatzki, "Vom Stil des Spielleiters," *Filmwelt* 17 (26 April 1940): the director must have "a special gift," "a power of imagination that grasps the totality even while it is in a state of becoming, and an expressive talent and ability to communicate which impress his formal will on everybody, from the lead actor to the lighting man" (p. 6).

34. S-k., *"Schlußakkord," Film-Kurier,* 25 July 1936.

35. Schu, *"Das Mädchen vom Moorhof," Film-Kurier,* 31 October 1935.

36. An essay by the editors of the ProMi-sponsored film monthly characterized Menzel as "the quintessential film poet"; "Mehr Dialog? Eine Antwort an Gerhard Menzel," *Der Deutsche Film* 1.3 (September 1936): 65. See Goebbels' diary entry of 10 December 1940: "The film writer Gerhard Menzel is to receive 50,000 marks from me as a bonus for his excellent achievements. He is overjoyed"; *The Goebbels Diaries: 1939–1941,* p. 199.

37. Halliday, *Sirk on Sirk,* p. 50.

38. Menzel, together with Georg Marischka, also wrote the screenplay for the controversial postwar film about a wayward woman, *Die Sünderin* (*The Sinner,* 1951).

39. A series of contemporary German films supported Franco's cause, newsreels and short documentary subjects as well as compilation films and features. In the Terra film *Kameraden auf See* (*Comrades at Sea,* 1938), a German torpedo boat liberates a Spanish steamer captured by Republican forces, demonstrating the necessity of the Reich's participation without mention of the secret air mission of the "Legion Condor." See also the documentary compilation film, *Helden in Spanien* (*Heroes in Spain,* 1938). The real enemy lay in Moscow, claimed Karl Ritter's *Im Kampf gegen den Weltfeind. Deutsche Freiwillige in Spanien* (*At War against the Universal Enemy: German Volunteers in Spain,* 1939), a film made after Franco's victory which now mentioned the Legion Condor; Helmut Regel, "Han pasado—Sie sind durchgekommen. Der Spanische Bürgerkrieg im NS-Kino," in *Bilder schreiben Geschichte. Der Historiker im Kino,* ed. Rainer Rother (Berlin: Wagenbach, 1991), pp. 129–132.

40. S. Pfannkuch, "Die Duday-Produktion kehrte mit Zarah Leander aus Teneriffa zurück," *Lichtbild-Bühne,* 28 September 1937.

41. S-k., "Habanera gegen Weihnachtslied. Filmdramatik aus natürlichen Begebenheiten," *Film-Kurier,* 10 December 1937.

42. Max Stoll, "Ferdinand Marian. Gegen Einförmigkeit und Typisierung," *Lichtbild-Bühne,* 18 December 1937.

43. Georg Herzberg, *"La Habanera,"* *Film-Kurier,* 20 December 1937. Marian had also played the seducer Boulanger in Gerhard Lamprecht's 1937 rendering of *Madame Bovary.* One critic ventured to suggest that Menzel might have overlooked—that is, been unaware of—the problematic racial implications of "the marriage between a Swedish woman and a West Indian grandee"; Fritz Aeckerle, "Ufa-Groß-Film *La Habanera* im Gloria-Palast," *Deutsche Allgemeine Zeitung,* 20 December 1937.

44. Hans Spielhofer, "An der Kamera. Franz Weihmayr," *Der Deutsche Film* 2.10 (April 1938): 278.

45. Gressieker, "Die Film-Circe oder Die Normung des Geistes," pp. 133–134.

46. K. Hildebrand, *The Third Reich,* trans. P. S. Falla (London: Allen & Unwin, 1984), p. 28.

47. Goebbels, *Tagebücher,* vol. 3, pp. 1136–37.

48. Even after Sierck made his break with Germany and fled to Paris, Goebbels still wanted him, according to the director. The Ufa producer Bruno Duday took Sierck out to lunch: "He tried to persuade me to go back to Germany. 'Your career is in Germany. You belong in Germany, and the Nazis are here to stay; they will soon control the whole of Europe,' he told me. So I said I did not want to go back, and I told him about the letter I'd written to [Ufa head] Mr. Correll. 'Don't worry,' he said, 'no-one knows about that—Correll didn't show it to anyone. In fact, I've got a personal letter for you from Dr Goebbels." This letter, which Sierck claims to have flushed down the toilet, said all would be forgiven if he were to return. Though written "in an almost military tone," it stressed that Sierck "had a great future as a director in Germany"; Halliday, *Sirk on Sirk,* p. 50.

49. Goebbels, *Tagebücher,* vol. 3, p. 1029.

50. When Leander worried about her children and possible war in Sweden early in 1940, Goebbels sought to calm her, observing, "Women are completely apolitical"; *The Goebbels Diaries: 1939–1941,* p. 92. The minister mentioned her often in 1940: for instance, 29 January and 8 October (visits from director Carl Froelich and the actress), 24 November (a tea party for the cast of *Das Herz der Königin/The Heart of the Queen*), and 2 December (the singer's performance for the fiftieth Request Concert: "A complete success").

51. S-k., *"Anna Karenina,"* *Film-Kurier,* 1 February 1936.

52. *Film-Kurier,* 22 September 1937.

53. S-k., "Doppelgängerin Marlene Dietrichs in Neubabelsberg," *Film-Kurier,* 11 December 1937. Albihn was known to German audiences from her Swedish screen debut in the anti-Semitic feature *Petterson & Bendel,* a film that ran with great success in Germany.

54. Richard Grunberger, *The 12-Year Reich: A Social History of Nazi Germany, 1933–1945* (New York: Holt, Rinehart and Winston, 1971), p. 381.

55. "*Zu neuen Ufern* in der Heimat Zarah Leanders. Die ersten Pressestimmen," *Film-Kurier,* 22 September 1937.

56. Drewniak, *Der deutsche Film 1938–1945,* p. 153. In 1940 Leander's earnings totaled 262,937 RM; in 1941 she took in 461,538 RM (p. 167).

57. Quoted in Seiler, *Zarah Leander,* p. 43.

58. Zarah Leander, *Es war so wunderbar! Mein Leben* (Hamburg: Hoffmann & Campe, 1973), p. 127.

59. Uwe Westphal, *Werbung im Dritten Reich* (Berlin: Transit, 1989), pp. 56–59.

60. Fritz Hippler, *Betrachtungen zum Filmschaffen* (Berlin: Hesse, 1942), p. vii.

61. Ibid., p. 102.

62. Seiler, *Zarah Leander,* p. 44.

63. Commentators often speak of her body in decidedly contrastive terms, admiring her "legendary décolletage" and making fun of her "plowhorse's behind"; see, for instance, Seiler, *Ein Mythos lebt,* p. 32.

64. Herbert A. Frenzel, "Der Zauber einer dunklen Stimme," *Film-Kurier,* 2 December 1937. Another popular anecdote involved an admirer's surprise at a signed photograph of the female star in response to a fan letter: "Dear Mr. Leander, I have all your records; could you please send me an autograph?"

65. Sanders-Brahms, "Zarah," p. 168.

66. Richard Dyer, *Heavenly Bodies: Film Stars and Society* (New York: St. Martin's, 1986), p. 155.

67. Ulrike Sanders, *Zarah Leander—Kann denn Schlager Sünde sein?* (Cologne: Pahl-Rugenstein, 1988), p. 27.

68. Renate Helker, "Körper in der Stimme. Zarah Leander," in *Das Ufa-Buch. Kunst und Krisen, Stars und Regisseure, Wirtschaft und Politik,* ed. Hans-Michael Bock and Michael Töteberg (Frankfurt am Main: Zweitausendeins, 1992), p. 386.

69. Rökk likewise feigns being a coquette, staging rebellions only to return to patriarchy's fold. Compare her different countenance in the two revue numbers that frame the musical *Die Frau meiner Träume (The Woman of My Dreams):* "The Woman without a Heart" and "The Woman of My Dreams." The 1940 production *Kora Terry* proves who is the better mother, a nurturing figure or a soulless vamp (both of whom are played by Rökk), by killing off the latter.

70. Hans Mayer claims that the Nazis exorcised the cinema of female outsiders, figures such as Garbo, Dietrich, and Elisabeth Bergner, any woman who might pose a threat. "No woman with a weapon, because man carries the weapons around here." Nazi cinema, he claims, privileged the girl-next-door as an object of affection, binding erotic dreams to healthy collective frameworks; *Außenseiter* (Frankfurt am Main: Suhrkamp, 1975), p. 145. Mayer does not take into account the wide range of fantasy offerings in Nazi cinema, much less its sophisticated strategies of dealing with erotic desire. Zarah Leander, in any case, can hardly be accounted for by Mayer's explanation.

71. Compare the peril- and vicissitude-ridden fates of Germans abroad in other films released in the months just before and after the premiere of *La Habanera:* Herbert Selpin's *Alarm in Peking,* Karl Ritter's *Patrioten (Patriots),* Richard Eichberg's *Das indische Grabmal (The Indian Tomb),* even the comedy *Fünf Millionen suchen einen Erben (Five Million in Search of an Heir).*

72. As the male suitors wait for the female prisoners to present themselves, a drunken lout speaks up. Women should have broad hips, he says, "and meat, that's the important thing. That's what makes them different from men, and that's the way nature wanted it. Young people around here are so skinny. Degeneration [*Entartung*], that's what it is, degeneration." This would seem to be a clear reflection of the concept's contemporary importance; the fact that an inebriated crank invokes the term undermines its significance. Here indeed is an exchange that can be said to have had a subversive contemporary meaning.

73. Open letter from Goebbels to Wilhelm Fürtwangler, *Berliner Lokal-Anzeiger,* 11 April 1933; quoted in Viktor Reimann, *Goebbels,* trans. Stephen Wendt (Garden City, N.Y.: Doubleday, 1976), p. 171.

74. Halliday, *Sirk on Sirk,* pp. 51–52.

75. Zarah Leander shows up in a recent film by Wolfgang Kohlhaase, *Inge, April und Mai* (1992). It is near war's end in a small town outside Berlin. Teenagers take in a reprise of Carl Froelich's *Heimat.* Watching Leander sing moves a young boy to tears. Her pathos, though, is not only contagious; it is a turn-on. The sensitized male catches the attention of a female peer.

76. Christine Grossmann, "Worin besteht die Wirkung des Films auf die Frauen?" *Lichtbild-Bühne,* 1 April 1938.

77. The dramatic moments of Froelich's *Heimat* gripped female spectators so strongly that they "could not hold back their tears"; Günther Schwark, "*Heimat*/Ufa-Palast am Zoo," *Film-Kurier,* 2 September 1938.

78. Roland Barthes, *The Fashion System,* trans. Matthew Ward and Richard Howard (New York: Hill and Wang, 1983), pp. 255–256.

79. Goebbels, *Tagebücher,* vol. 3, p. 1167.

80. Ernst Bloch, "Die Frau im Dritten Reich," in *Vom Hasard zur Katastrophe. Politische Aufsätze aus den Jahren 1934–1939* (Frankfurt am Main: Suhrkamp, 1972), pp. 130–131.

81. Alfred Rosenberg quoted in Leila J. Rupp, *Mobilizing Women for War: German and American Propaganda, 1939–1945* (Princeton: Princeton University Press, 1978), p. 16.

6. The Elective Other

1. *Jud Süß,* 1940. Produced by Terra Filmkunst GmbH, Production Group Otto Lehmann. Director: Veit Harlan. Assistant Direction: Wolfgang Schleif and Alfred Braun. Script: Harlan, Eberhard Wolfgang Möller, Ludwig Metzger. Cinematography: Bruno Mondi. Music: Wolfgang Zeller. Sound: Gustav Bellers. Set Design: Otto Hunte and Karl Vollbrecht. Dance Choreography: Sabine Ress. Editing: Friedrich Carl von Puttkammer and Wolfgang Schleif.

The Players: Ferdinand Marian (Jew Süss), Heinrich George (Duke Karl Alexander), Hilde von Stolz (his wife), Werner Krauss (Rabbi Loew, Aronsohn, and Levy, Süss's secretary), Eugen Klöpfer (Sturm), Kristina Söderbaum (Dorothea Sturm), Malte

Jaeger (Faber), Albert Florath (Röder), Theodor Loos (von Remchingen), Walter Werner (Fiebelkorn), Charlotte Schulz (Mrs. Fiebelkorn), Anny Seitz (Minchen Fiebelkorn), Ilse Buhl (Friedericke Fiebelkorn), Jacob Tiedtke (Konsistorialrat), Erna Morena (his wife), Else Elster (Luziana, Süss's mistress), Emil Hess (Hans Bogner, a smith), Käte Jöken-König (his wife), Ursula Deinert (prima ballerina), Erich Dunskus (master of the guild of smiths), Otto Henning (head judge), Heinrich Schroth (von Neuffer), Hannelore Benzinger (maid in Sturm household).

Original length: 2,663 meters (97 minutes). Premiered on 5 September 1940 in Venice (Cinema San Marco) and on 24 September 1940 in Berlin (Ufa-Palast am Zoo). Rating: "Politically and artistically especially worthwhile." The film may not be screened publicly in the Federal Republic of Germany.

An unlicensed video copy with English intertitles is available from the German Language Video Center and International Historic Films. Worldwide rights for the film are owned by Transit-Film in Germany.

2. See Rebecca Lieb, "Nazi Hate Movies Continue to Ignite Fierce Passions," *New York Times,* 4 August 1991.

3. As quoted in Klaus Kanzog, *"Staatspolitisch besonders wertvoll." Ein Handbuch zu 30 deutschen Spielfilmen der Jahre 1934 bis 1945* (Munich: Schaudig und Ledig, 1994), p. 220.

4. Dieter Krusche and Jürgen Labenski, *Reclams Filmführer,* 9th rev. ed. (Stuttgart: Reclam, 1993), p. 287.

5. David Stewart Hull, *Film in the Third Reich* (New York: Simon and Schuster, 1973), p. 160.

6. Karlheinz Wendtland, *Geliebter Kintopp. Sämtliche deutsche Spielfilme von 1929–1945 mit zahlreichen Künstlerbiographien. Jahrgang 1939 und 1940* (Berlin: Wendtland, n.d.), p. 149.

7. Wendtland, *Geliebter Kintopp. Jahrgang 1943, 1944 und 1945,* p. 199.

8. Axel Eggebrecht, *Der halbe Weg. Zwischenbilanz einer Epoche* (Reinbek bei Hamburg: Rowohlt, 1975), p. 308.

9. Linda Schulte-Sasse, "The Jew as Other under National Socialism: Veit Harlan's *Jud Süß*," *German Quarterly* 61.1 (Winter 1988): "*Jud Süß* borrows the basic scenario of the bourgeois tragedy; its plot likewise revolves around the disruption of social harmony and the invasion of familial bliss by figures initiating courtly intrigue" (p. 24).

10. George F. Custen, *Bio/Pics: How Hollywood Constructed Public History* (New Brunswick, N.J.: Rutgers University Press, 1992), p. 35. The Danish writer Isak Dinesen visited the Babelsberg atelier at the time and recorded her observations in "Letters from a Land at War": "Inside the studio, in rooms as high-ceilinged as a cathedral, they were arranging large, magnificent interiors from the eighteenth century, and it was interesting to see how carefully and conscientiously all the details were designed and assembled by UFA's scene-painters and laborers; it was a handsome piece of craftsmanship, though the material was of an ephemeral nature. To my surprise, it was *Jud' Süss*

that was to be filmed there"; *Daguerreotypes and Other Essays* (Chicago: University of Chicago Press, 1979), p. 122.

11. Custen, *Bio/Pics,* p. 51.

12. Roger Manvell and Heinrich Fraenkel, *The German Cinema* (New York: Praeger, 1971), p. 87.

13. The best discussion of the film's liberties with historical fact and its debts to literary sources is to be found in Régine Mihal Friedman, *L'image et son juif. Le juif dans le cinéma nazi* (Paris: Payot, 1983), pp. 118–152. For biographical studies of Joseph Süss Oppenheimer, see Curt Elwenspoeck, *Joseph Süß Oppenheimer. Der große Finanzier und galante Abenteurer des 18. Jahrhunderts* (Stuttgart: Süddeutsches Verlagshaus, 1926); Selma Stern, *Jud Süß. Ein Beitrag zur deutschen und zur jüdischen Geschichte* (Berlin: Akademie, 1929). For recent perspectives, see the ZDF production *Joseph Süß Oppenheimer* (Rainer Wolffhardt, 1984) and the accompanying brochure, *Joseph Süß Oppenheimer. Geschichte und Geschichten um eine historische Gestalt. Sendung am 14. Februar 1984, 19.30 Uhr;* also Rolf Schneider, *Süß und Dreyfus* (Göttingen: Steidl, 1991). For an overview of Süss adaptations, see Friedrich Knilli and Siegfried Zielinski, "Der Jude als Sittenverderber. Kleine Mediengeschichte des Joseph Süß Oppenheimer, 1737/38 bis 1984," in the ZDF program brochure, pp. 15–21. According to Knilli, there have been more than one hundred literary treatments of Süss's story, one-third of them sympathetic to the protagonist, the rest anti-Semitic. The most crucial literary source for Harlan's film was Wilhelm Hauff's novella *Jud Süß* (1827), and not, as is often maintained, Leon Feuchtwanger's novel *Jud Süß* (1925). For evidence of the importance of Hauff's novella in Nazi anti-Semitic circles, see *Jud Süß. Mit einer Betrachtung im Lichte der erwachenden Welt von Eduard Gerber* (Berlin: Deutsche Kulturwacht, 1935). For further information regarding Harlan's use of literary and historical sources, see Kanzog, *"Staatspolitisch besonders wertvoll,"* pp. 227–229.

14. *Reichsfilmintendant* Fritz Hippler spoke of this brutal scene as a "happy ending." See his poetics of cinema, *Betrachtungen zum Filmschaffen* (Berlin: Hesse, 1942), p. 107.

15. Dorothea Hollstein, *"Jud Süß" und die Deutschen. Antisemitische Vorurteile im nationalsozialistischen Spielfilm* (Frankfurt am Main: Ullstein, 1983), p. 35.

16. Ibid., p. 39. *Petterson & Bendel* was also rereleased in 1938 in German cinemas.

17. Enno Patalas quoted in Manfred Dammeyer, ed., *Der Spielfilm im Dritten Reich* (Oberhausen: XII. Westdeutsche Kurzfilmtage, 1966), p. 72.

18. Ilse Wehner, "Filme des Monats," *Der Deutsche Film* 4.5 (November 1939): 110.

19. Erwin Leiser, *Nazi Cinema,* trans. Gertrud Mander and David Wilson (New York: Collier, 1975), p. 75.

20. The plot line recalls Eberhard Wolfgang Möller's drama *Rothschild siegt bei Waterloo* (*Rothschild's Victory at Waterloo,* 1934), which depicts how Rothschild uses insider information regarding Napoleon's famous defeat to make a killing on the stock exchange. Rothschild becomes the ultimate victor in the war between England and France. Möller, of course, also provided the original script for *Jew Süss.*

21. Other Nazi films from 1940 and after with prominent anti-Semitic scenes ana-

lyzed by Hollstein include *Ein Robinson (A German Robinson Crusoe), . . . reitet für Deutschland (Ride for Germany), Der ewige Quell (The Eternal Source), Bismarck, Über alles in der Welt (Above Everything in the World), Carl Peters, Ohm Krüger, Der Weg ins Freie (The Path to Freedom), Venus vor Gericht (Venus on Trial), Heimkehr (Homecoming), GPU, Die Entlassung (The Dismissal),* and *Wien 1910 (Vienna 1910).* Regarding Goebbels' change of course in the early 1940s, see notes from a meeting of the Tobis-Filmkunst Executive Board on 23 April 1940: "The Minister wishes political films *(Bismarck, Ohm Krüger, Friedrich Schiller)* even at the risk of financial loss. Program is 50-50 political and entertainment films. A sufficient reserve of scripts is available"; Berlin Document Center, quoted in Gerd Albrecht, *Nationalsozialistische Filmpolitik* (Stuttgart: Enke, 1969), p. 143.

22. These include *Homecoming, Menschen im Sturm (People in the Storm), Menschen ohne Vaterland (People without a Fatherland), A German Robinson Crusoe.*

23. See Hannah Arendt, *The Origins of Totalitarianism* (New York: World, 1958), pp. 355–356: "The Nazis placed the Jewish issue at the center of their propaganda in the sense that antisemitism was no longer a question of opinion about people different from the majority, or a concern of national politics, but the intimate concern of every individual in his personal existence." Thus Nazi propaganda made anti-Semitism "a principle of self-definition."

24. Michelangelo Antonioni, "La settimana cinematografica di Venezia. L'ebreo Süss e Il cavaliere di Kruja," *Corriere Padano,* 6 September 1940; quoted and translated in Sam Rohdie, *Antonioni* (London: British Film Institute, 1990), p. 29. Writing in *Cinema* later that month (on 25 September), Antonioni would temper his praise, criticizing the unconvincing cruelty of the film's lead character.

25. Dammeyer, *Der Spielfilm im Dritten Reich,* p. 49. The other top films of the 1939–40 season were directed by Gustav Ucicky, *Mutterliebe (A Mother's Love)* and *Der Postmeister (The Postmaster),* with 19.4 and 18.1 million viewers respectively; figures from *Das deutsche Filmschaffen im vierten Kriegsjahr* (Berlin: Ufa, 1943), unpaginated.

26. T. W. Adorno, "Freudian Theory and the Pattern of Fascist Propaganda," in *The Essential Frankfurt School Reader,* ed. Andrew Arato and Eike Gebhardt (New York: Urizen, 1978), p. 133.

27. See the confidential press dispatch from the Reich Office of Propaganda dated 27 April 1940, reprinted in Joseph Wulf, ed., *Theater und Film im Dritten Reich. Eine Dokumentation* (Frankfurt am Main: Ullstein, 1983), p. 448.

28. Quoted in David Welch, *Propaganda and the German Cinema 1933–1945* (Oxford: Oxford University Press, 1983), p. 291.

29. "Les nouveaux films. *Le juif Süss,*" *Le Parisien,* 21 February 1941; excerpted in Wulf, *Theater und Film im Dritten Reich,* p. 454.

30. See the reprint of a contemporary advertisement for *The Eternal Jew* in Yizhak Ahren, Stig Hornshøj-Møller, and Christoph B. Melchers, *"Der ewige Jude." Wie Goebbels hetzte* (Aachen: Alano, 1990), p. 23. To accompany the "Degenerate Art"

exhibit, a compilation film was made which bore the title *Juden ohne Maske (Jews without a Mask)* (p. 18).

31. Carl Neumann, Curt Belling, and Hans-Walther Betz, *Film-"Kunst," Film-Kohn, Film-Korruption* (Berlin: Scherping, 1937), pp. 7–9.

32. Ibid., p. 14.

33. Ibid., p. 40.

34. Ibid., p. 29. See the director William Dieterle's postwar review of this book, "Made in Germany," *Hollywood Quarterly* 1.1 (October 1945): "The Jews, so the authors maintain, hate to work. They have no talent for anything but smoking cigars, lending money, and raping girls—innocent German girls, of course" (p. 125).

35. Harlan's *Die Reise nach Tilsit (The Trip to Tilsit)* drew on the same Hermann Sudermann novel that had provided the basis for Murnau's *Sunrise.*

36. Noël Burch, "Notes on Fritz Lang's First *Mabuse,*" *Ciné-tracts* 13 (Spring 1981): 6.

37. Moishe Postone, "Anti-Semitism and National Socialism: Notes on the German Reaction to *Holocaust,*" *New German Critique* 19 (Winter 1980): 106.

38. stb., *"Dr. Mabuse der Spieler," Völkischer Kurier,* 1 September 1925; quoted in Norbert Jacques and Fritz Lang, *Dr. Mabuse der Spieler. Roman/Film/Dokumente,* ed. Günter Scholdt (St. Ingbert: Röhrig, 1987), p. 149. For a subsequent Nazi reading of *Dr. Mabuse* along similar lines, see Otto Kriegk, *Der deutsche Film im Spiegel der Ufa. 25 Jahre Kampf und Vollendung* (Berlin: Ufa-Buchverlag, 1943), p. 86.

39. For an extensive analysis of the numerous correspondences between *Nosferatu* and *The Eternal Jew,* see Régine Mihal Friedman, "Juden-Ratten. Von der rassistischen Metonymie zur tierischen Metapher in Fritz Hipplers *Der ewige Jude,*" *Frauen und Film* 47 (September 1989): 24–35. Anti-Semitic discourse of the 1920s regularly depicted Jews as a plague upon the German corpus, systematically invoking hygienic figures of speech. See, for instance, the point of departure in Walter Liek's jeremiad *Der Anteil des Judentums am Zusammenbruch Deutschlands* (Munich: Lehmanns, 1924), p. 1: "The influence of Judaism constitutes the true breeding ground of sickness for the German national body."

40. Paul Gerhart Dippel, "Die innere Machtergreifung," *Der Deutsche Film* 7.7 (1943): 2.

41. E. F., "Jud Süß unmaskiert vor der Kamera. Eberhard Wolfgang Möller zu seinem ersten Filmdrehbuch," *Lichtbild-Bühne,* 25 October 1939.

42. Veit Harlan, *Im Schatten meiner Filme* (Gütersloh: Mohn, 1966), p. 103. Marian went so far as to distance himself from the role in public declarations. See Max Weinheber, "Ferdinand Marian als Jud Süß. Der Schauspieler hat der Kunst und nicht seinen eigenen Wünschen zu dienen," *Tonfim, Theater, Tanz* 9.12 (1939): this time, the actor stated, he would play an "irredeemably evil and cynical criminal."

43. Robert Dachs, *Willi Forst. Eine Biographie* (Vienna: Kremayr & Scherlau, 1986), p. 81. See also Florian Kienzl, "Das Genie der Verwandlung. Die Darstellungskunst Werner Krauß'," *Film-Kurier,* 23 June 1941.

44. Felix Henseleit, "Magische Schauspielkunst. Werner Krauß 60 Jahre. Ein Bild des Künstlers," *Film-Kurier,* 23 June 1944. Krauss's peer and competitor Jannings was praised in similar terms. See Frank Maraun, "Emil Jannings," *Der Deutsche Film* 2.11 (May 1938): "He constantly transforms himself. He becomes a different person in every role" (p. 300). Friedman observes that Krauss's status as the greatest expressionistic actor "seemed to predispose him to play Jewish roles"; *L'image et son juif,* p. 219.

45. Quoted in Hollstein, *"Jud Süß" und die Deutschen,* p. 111. An Ufa production based on Shakespeare's *The Merchant of Venice* was scheduled to begin shooting late in 1944. Harlan was to direct; Krauss and Kristina Söderbaum were to play the leading roles; Hans-Christoph Blumenberg, *Das Leben geht weiter. Der letzte Film des Dritten Reichs* (Berlin: Rowohlt, 1993), p. 130.

46. See Harlan's press release of January 1940: Krauss, claims the director, would demonstrate "that all of the different temperaments and personalities: the pious patriarch, the crafty swindler, the sly businessmen, etc., they all stem from a single origin"; quoted in Friedman, *L'image et son juif,* p. 181.

47. Peter Sloterdijk, *Critique of Cynical Reason,* trans. Michael Eldred (Minneapolis: University of Minnesota Press, 1987), p. 175.

48. Alice Yaeger Kaplan, *Reproductions of Banality: Fascism, Literature, and French Intellectual Life* (Minneapolis: University of Minnesota Press, 1986), p. 31.

49. Compare Postone, "Anti-Semitism and National Socialism," p. 113.

50. See, for instance, Thomas Brandlmeier and Heidi Pillhatsch, "Der Krieg der Kameras. Filmpropaganda 1933–1946," *Medium* 9.8 (August 1979): Marian's Süss is sympathetic, whereas his counterpart, played by Conrad Veidt in the 1934 English production *Jew Süss,* despite all noble intentions, is not. The Jew in the British film "is a sterile, cardboard figure who lacks the human dimension." Marian's Süss, on the other hand, brought "the entrance of a figure with human failings into a cinematic landscape populated by false feelings, spurious heroism, and an unbearable nobility of spirit" (p. 7).

51. "This counterimage, the antitype, the antirace, in a word, the Jew," points out Friedman, "was present and visible in Germany, as opposed to the hard-to-find fictive archetype"; *L'image et son juif,* p. 67.

52. Max Horkheimer and Theodor W. Adorno, *Dialectic of Enlightenment,* trans. John Cumming (New York: Seabury, 1972), p. 168.

53. Compare a similar scene in Hippler's *The Eternal Jew* and the voice-over narrator's commentary: "Hair, beard, skullcap, and caftan make the Eastern Jew recognizable to all . . . It is an intrinsic trait of the Jew that he always tries to hide his origin when he is among non-Jews."

54. Marc Ferro, "Dissolves in *Jud Süss,*" in *Cinema and History,* trans. Naomi Greene (Detroit: Wayne State University Press, 1988), p. 140.

55. Quoted in Stig Hornshøj-Møller and David Culbert, "*Der ewige Jude* (1940): Joseph Goebbels' Unequaled Monument to Anti-Semitism," *Historical Journal of Film, Radio and Television* 12.1 (1992): 47.

56. Characters who instinctively see through Jewish disguises are stock presences in Nazi anti-Semitic features. Take, for instance, the Lina Carstens figure in *The Eternal Source* or Lilly in *Linen from Ireland*; see Hollstein, *"Jud Süß" und die Deutschen,* p. 59.

57. Karsten Witte, "Wie faschistisch ist *Die Feuerzangenbowle?* Bemerkungen zur Filmkomödie im Dritten Reich," *epd Kirche und Film* 29.7 (July 1976): 2.

58. Kaplan, *Reproductions of Banality,* p. 8. Kaplan is talking about literature in this context; her concern is with echoing effects in fascist discourse which are a function of voice.

59. Discussants in the Oberhausen seminar of 1965 saw a similarity between this dissolve and a transition in *The Eternal Jew* from the Star of David at the top of a synagogue to state edifices in London, Paris, Washington, and Berlin; Dammeyer, *Der Spielfilm im Dritten Reich,* p. 99.

60. Friedman, *L'image et son juif,* pp. 212–216.

61. See, for instance, a scene from the original script which does not appear in the finished film. Having fallen into a river while illegally crossing the border, Süss splashes water around while looking at the opposite shore. "This splashing of water dissolves into splashing of water that comes from the bathroom of the duke"; original script, *Jud Süß. Ein historischer Film,* p. 32; copy in Stiftung Deutsche Kinemathek, Berlin.

62. The logic of the double allows us to see Nosferatu and Mabuse as prefigurations of Hitler (in keeping with Kracauer's teleology), but also as projections of collective anti-Semitic stereotypes. Offering further testimony to the historical persistence of this logic, the Jew's closing speech both anticipates the indicted Nazi leaders and echoes the deranged Beckert's appeal to his accusers at the conclusion of Fritz Lang's *M:* "I'm innocent! I'm only a poor Jew! Spare my life! I want to live!" The child murderer, in Peter Lorre's memorable enactment, also makes a brief appearance in *The Eternal Jew* as an example of Jewish degeneracy.

63. Rainer Werner Fassbinder, "Credited Debit, Debited Credit: On Gustav Freytag's Novel *Debit and Credit* and the Aborted Television Version," in *The Anarchy of the Imagination,* ed. Michael Töteberg and Leo A. Lensing, trans. Krishna Winston (Baltimore: Johns Hopkins University Press, 1992), p. 117. Fassbinder's own use of Jewish figures in his work also occasioned much controversy, debate, and scandal. See, for instance, Elisabeth Kiderlen, ed., *Deutsch-jüdische Normalität . . . Fassbinders Sprengsätze* (Frankfurt am Main: Pflasterstrand, 1985); Heiner Lichtenstein, ed., *Die Fassbinder-Kontroverse oder Das Ende der Schonzeit* (Königstein: Athenäum, 1986); in English, see Gertrud Koch, "Torments of the Flesh, Coldness of the Spirit: Jewish Figures in the Films of Rainer Werner Fassbinder," *New German Critique* 38 (Spring/Summer 1986): 28–38. In Koch's analysis, Fassbinder's cinematic Jews dramatize the aporias of postwar West German relations to German history and its Jewish victims. In effect, Fassbinder's Jews "are not merged into the suffering cosmos; they remain bearers of symbols or distanced observers" (p. 36).

64. According to Harlan, Goebbels praised Hitler's attempts to apply the lessons of Jewish history in Germany's racial policies. The Jews had instrumentalized anti-Semi-

tism as a means of fortifying themselves against the goyim. Hitler now aimed to enact laws in Germany which would no longer allow anti-Semitism to work for the Jews. "The destiny of the Jews," argued Goebbels, "was similar to the destiny of the Germans, and for that reason Germans must learn from Moses and Jews those things that the Germans lack because of their sentimentality"; Harlan, *Im Schatten meiner Filme,* pp. 98–99. Also see E. M. Cioran, *Dasein als Versuchung,* trans. Kurt Leonhard (Stuttgart: Klett, 1983), p. 104: "The Germans despised the Jews' *realized* dream of universality, which they could not achieve themselves. They too wanted to be the chosen people, but nothing predestined them for this status. After they had tried to force history, hoping they might escape and overcome it, they ultimately only became more deeply mired in it."

65. Compare Jeffrey Herf, *Reactionary Modernism: Technology, Culture, and Politics in Weimar and the Third Reich* (Cambridge: Cambridge University Press, 1984), p. 229: "If the Jews were the physical embodiment of abstraction or rationalization, then their elimination would be synonymous with the victory of a cultural revolution that restored feeling and immediacy to a world threatened by soulless rationality."

66. Leiser, *Nazi Cinema,* pp. 84–85.

67. Harlan, *Im Schatten meiner Filme,* pp. 28, 7, 208–209.

68. Ibid., p. 143.

69. Likewise, repeated passages in the memoirs espouse anti-Nazi sentiments, but do so in fascist language. See, for instance, Harlan's description of Gerhart Hauptmann's hatred of National Socialism and the "unspeakable disdain" the writer "had for the spiritually inferior people who were in power. He did not speak of specific people—but anyone capable of feeling the aura of this great mind also sensed the heights from which he looked down upon 'the porcupines' "; ibid., pp. 52–53.

70. Quoted in Siegfried Zielinski, *Veit Harlan* (Frankfurt am Main: R. G. Fischer, 1981), p. 56. Particulars regarding the Hamburg trials are taken in great part from this source.

71. Ibid., p. 58.

72. Harlan, *Im Schatten meiner Filme,* p. 245.

73. Karsten Witte, "Der barocke Faschist. Veit Harlan und seine Filme," in *Intellektuelle im Bann des Nationalsozialismus,* ed. Karl Corino (Hamburg: Hoffmann und Campe, 1980), pp. 150–151.

74. Ibid., p. 155.

75. Ibid., p. 157.

76. Norbert Grob, "Veit Harlan," in *CineGraph,* installment 15 (Munich: edition text + kritik, 1989), p. E4.

77. Ibid., p. E13.

78. In an apparent typographical error, Grob's text claims that Harlan made eight melodramatic masterpieces "between 1939 [*sic*] and 1943"; ibid., p. E4.

79. Ibid., p. E15.

80. Grob's intervention catalyzed a spirited exchange in Germany, especially in numbers 26 (1993) and 27 (1994) of *journal film,* published by the Kommunales Kino in

Freiburg. Several of the articles take vehement exception to Grob's essay, particularly Barbara Schierese, "Offener Brief an Norbert Grob und Anmerkungen zu fünf Artikeln," *journal film* 27 (1994): 81–82; and Holger Torstmann, "Im luftleeren Raum? Wie man die Filme Veit Harlans falsch versteht," ibid., pp. 83–84.

81. Regarding the historical links between the German bourgeois tragedy and cinematic melodrama, see Thomas Elsaesser, "Tales of Sound and Fury," *monogram* 4 (1972): 2–15. Speaking of Lessing's *Emilia Galotti* and Schiller's *Kabale und Liebe (Intrigue and Love)*, Elsaesser observes: "The melodramatic elements are clearly visible in the plots, which revolve around family relationships, star-crossed lovers and forced marriages. The villains (often of noble birth) demonstrate their superior political and economic power invariably by sexual aggression and attempted rape, leaving the heroine no other way than to commit suicide or take poison in the company of her lover" (p. 3). Linda Schulte-Sasse points out the film's central point of departure from the bourgeois tragedy: it "displaces the source of evil usually ascribed to the aristocracy to the Jew"; "The Jew as Other under National Socialism," p. 24.

82. See Peter Brooks, *The Melodramatic Imagination: Balzac, Henry James, Melodrama, and the Mode of Excess* (New York: Columbia University Press, 1985).

83. Franz Joseph Strauss quoted in Eike Hennig, *Zum Historikerstreit. Was heißt und zu welchem Ende studiert man Faschismus?* (Frankfurt am Main: Athenäum, 1988), p. 100.

7. The Führer's Phantom

1. Viktor Reimann, *Goebbels,* trans. Stephen Wendt (Garden City, N.Y.: Doubleday, 1976), pp. 262–263.

2. *The Goebbels Diaries 1942–1943,* trans. and ed. Louis P. Lochner (Garden City, N.Y.: Doubleday, 1948), p. 266.

3. Alan Bullock, *Hitler: A Study in Tyranny,* rev. ed. (New York: Harper & Row, 1964), p. 722.

4. In this regard Hitler's relationship to film differed markedly from Stalin's. The Soviet leader, more a man of the written word than—like Lenin—a man of speech, shied away from newsreel cameras. Stalin did, though, appear in a host of feature films, usually portrayed by the actor Mikhail Gelovani. Historical epics, likewise, such as *Peter the First* (1938), provided allegorical portraits of the leader. For discussions of the various cinematic representations of Stalin, see Enno Patalas and Oksana Bulgakowa's documentary, *Stalin, eine Mosfilmproduktion* (1993); also Thomas Brandlmeier, "Das Kino der Diktatoren. Stalin, Hitler, Mussolini," *epd Film* 10.7 (July 1993): 22–30.

5. Notation from 28 February 1941, reprinted in Willi A. Boelcke, ed., *Kriegspropaganda 1939–1941. Geheime Ministerkonferenzen im Reichspropagandaministerium* (Stuttgart: Deutsche Verlags-Anstalt, 1966), p. 630.

6. *Goebbels-Reden,* vol. 2: *1939–1945,* ed. Helmut Heiber (Düsseldorf: Droste, 1972), p. 117. The minister comments at length in this address on Veit Harlan's *Der*

große König (*The Great King,* 1942), drawing explicit parallels between the film's beleaguered Frederick II and the persevering Nazi leader.

7. *Paracelsus,* 1943. Produced by Bavaria Filmkunst GmbH. Production Manager: Fred Lyssa. Unit Manager: Willy Laschinsky. Directed by G. W. Pabst. Assistant Director: Auguste Barth-Reuss. Script: Kurt Heuser. Cinematography: Bruno Stephan. Assistant Cinematography: Herbert Stephan. Art Direction: Herbert Hochreiter and Walter Schlick. Costumes: Herbert Ploberger. Editing: Lena Neumann. Sound: Emil Specht. Music: Herbert Windt.

The Players: Werner Krauss (Paracelsus), Mathias Wieman (Ulrich von Hutten), Harald Kreutzberg (Fliegenbein), Martin Urtel (Johannes), Harry Langewisch (Pfefferkorn), Annelies Reinhold (Renata Pfefferkorn), Fritz Rasp (the Magister), Josef Sieber (Bilse, Paracelsus' servant), Herbert Hübner (Count von Hohenried), Rudolf Blümner (Froben), Karl Skraup (surgeon), Franz Schafheitlin (Erasmus of Rotterdam), Erich Dunskus (innkeeper), Victor Janson (mayor), Hilde Sessak (waitress), Egon Vogel (Urias), Arthur Wiesner (horse doctor), Franz Stein (doctor), Hans von Uritz (captain), Bernhard Goetzke, Oskar Höcker, Maria Hofen, Klaus Pohl, Joachim Wedekind.

Original length: 2,919 meters (107 minutes). Premiered on 12 March 1943 in Salzburg (Festspielhaus) and on 6 May 1943 in Berlin (Capitol am Zoo, Roxy Palast in Friedenau). Rating: "Politically and artistically worthwhile."

A subtitled 16mm copy can be rented from Trans-World Films, Chicago; unsubtitled video copies are available from Facets Video, the German Language Video Center, and International Historic Films.

For a description of the 12 March debut, see the front-page report by Otto Th. Kropsch, "*Paracelsus* im Salzburger Festspielhaus," *Film-Kurier,* 13 March 1943. Before the sold-out screening the Mozarteum-Orchestra performed the overture to *Der fliegende Holländer (The Flying Dutchman).* The showing gave rise to the "strongest impression." Pabst and the players Werner Krauss, Annelies Reinhold, Herbert Hübner, and Martin Urtel received a long ovation.

8. Jacob Burckhardt, quoted in C. G. Jung, *Paracelsica. Zwei Vorlesungen über den Arzt und Philosophen Theophrastus* (Zürich/Leipzig: Rascher, 1942), p. 55. See also Jung's "Psychology and Literature," reprinted in *The Spirit in Man, Art, and Literature,* trans. R. F. C. Hull (Princeton: Princeton University Press, 1966), p. 103: "This image has lain buried and dormant in the unconscious since the dawn of history; it is awakened whenever the times are out of joint and a great error deflects society from the right path. For when people go astray they feel the need of a guide or teacher, and even of a physician. The seductive error is like a poison that can also act as a cure, and the shadow of a saviour can turn into a fiendish destroyer."

9. Compare the short commentary about Paracelsus and his willful student, Johannes: z. E., "Lehrer und Schüler," *Filmwoche* 37/38 (7 October 1942): 292–293. Among numerous production reports before the film's release, see Felix Henseleit, " '—geh'n viel Geschichten um von seiner Hände Segen.' Blick auf die Aufnahmen des Paracelsus-Films in Prag," *Film-Kurier,* 16 October 1942.

10. Numerous critics have commented that the film revives memories of classical German cinema. Julian Petley elaborates on the connection in *Capital and Culture: German Cinema 1933–45* (London: British Film Institute, 1979), p. 144: "With its 'atmospheric' and 'Romantic' medieval background *Paracelsus* recalls a certain strain of German silent cinema . . . It is one of the few German films of the Third Reich which relates so directly to that particular current of cinematic mysticism and irrationalism . . . a relationship which, however, casts a good deal of light on the ideological dimension of the 'classics' of the German silent screen."

11. See Bogusław Drewniak, *Der deutsche Film 1938–1945. Ein Gesamtüberblick* (Düsseldorf: Droste, 1987), p. 66: "Every reader of the *Philo Lexikon* (Berlin 1935) knew that the director Pabst was of pure Jewish ancestry." Pabst is also spoken of as a Jew in Carl Neumann, Curt Belling, and Hans-Walther Betz, *Film-"Kunst," Film-Kohn, Film-Korruption* (Berlin: Scherping, 1937), p. 38. Such claims, of course, were not true. As late as 1939, the minister cast aspersions on the director, calling *Die 3-Groschen-Oper (The Threepenny Opera)* "pure Jewish humbug"; *The Goebbels Diaries: 1939–1941,* trans. and ed. Fred Taylor (Harmondsworth: Penguin, 1984), p. 16.

12. For a careful reconstruction of the facts regarding Pabst's movements during this time, see Hans-Michael Bock, "Georg Wilhelm Pabst: Documenting a Life and a Career," in *The Films of G. W. Pabst: An Extraterritorial Cinema,* ed. Eric Rentschler (New Brunswick, N.J.: Rutgers University Press, 1990), pp. 231–233. For one of the first extended journalistic encounters with the returned Pabst, see Dr. Gessner, "Wiedersehen mit G. W. Pabst," *Filmwoche* 39/40 (1941): 776–778. The portrait describes the director's work on *Traveling Players,* stressing his optical emphasis and how, after his stint in Hollywood, he has had to readjust himself to filmmaking in Germany.

13. See, for instance, Paul Rotha and Richard Griffith, *The Film till Now: A Survey of World Cinema* (London: Spring, 1967), p. 582; Guido Aristarco, "Il cinema tedesco e il passato nazista," *Cinestudio* 7 (March 1963); reprinted in Barthélemy Amengual, *G. W. Pabst* (Paris: Seghers, 1966), p. 137; Freddy Buache, *G. W. Pabst* (Lyons: Serdoc, 1965), pp. 90–91; Edgardo Cozarinsky, "G. W. Pabst," in *Cinema: A Critical Dictionary. The Major Film-makers,* vol. 2: *Kinugasa to Zanussi,* ed. Richard Roud (New York: Viking, 1980), p. 759.

14. Among the attempts to vindicate Pabst's wartime endeavors, see Leo Lania, "In Defense of Pabst," *New York Times,* 2 April 1950: "The two films he directed were historical pictures without any Nazi tinge. He neither directed nor produced propaganda films. He did not let himself be used for any glorification of the Nazi regime." See also Lee Atwell, *G. W. Pabst* (Boston: Twayne, 1977), pp. 121–128.

15. Erwin Leiser, *Nazi Cinema,* trans. Gertrud Mander and David Wilson (New York: Collier, 1975), p. 107; David Welch, *Propaganda and the German Cinema 1933–1945* (Oxford: Oxford University Press, 1983), p. 224.

16. See Louis Marcorelles, "The Nazi Cinema (1933–1945)," *Sight and Sound* 25.4 (Autumn 1955): "If Pabst finds obvious difficulty in transcending nationalistic claptrap, if he lacks the candour and conviction of Harlan or a Steinhoff, he at least extracts some

magical effects from medieval costumes and settings, and the completely mimed sequence of the appearance of Death would in itself justify the mediocrity of the rest" (p. 68); see also Christa Bandmann and Joe Hembus, *Klassiker des deutschen Tonfilms 1930–1960* (Munich: Goldmann, 1980), p. 231; Wilhelm Roth, "Ein Großer ist noch nicht entdeckt. Zum 80. Geburtstag des Regisseurs Georg Wilhelm Pabst," *Spandauer Volksblatt,* 27 August 1965.

17. David Shipman, *The Story of Cinema* (New York: St. Martin's, 1982), p. 314.

18. See Eric Rentschler, "The Problematic Pabst: An *Auteur* Directed by History," in *The Films of G. W. Pabst,* pp. 1–3.

19. For a contemporary profile of the actress, see m., "Annelies Reinhold," *Filmwelt,* 16 February 1940, p. 12.

20. See Lotte H. Eisner's discussion of Pabst's work with Louise Brooks in *The Haunted Screen,* trans. Roger Greaves (Berkeley: University of California Press, 1969), p. 296.

21. See, for instance, Pabst's words regarding film and personal conviction, "Film und Gesinnung," in *Der Film und seine Welt. Reichsfilmblatt—Almanach 1933,* ed. Felix Henseleit (Berlin: Photokino, 1933), p. 99: "Film is the art form that belongs to the future. It is a revolutionary art form. The masses can learn through film much better, more thoroughly and quickly, *how* their lives look and *what* they should look like, than by reading millions of political pamphlets." Film must be liberated and become the property of the people.

22. From the press booklet for Johanna Heer and Werner Schmiedel's biographical inquiry about Pabst, *Der andere Blick* (*The Other Eye,* 1991).

23. In *The Other Eye,* we see the director's journal in the hands of his son, Michael Pabst, and we hear short quotations from the source.

24. Obituaries of both Pabst's father and father-in-law demonstrated why he had returned to Vienna and Berlin shortly before the outbreak of war. When hostilities appeared imminent during the Munich Conference, the director fled to Basel. A doctor's bill and hospital statement documented that Pabst had suffered a hernia and could not leave with his family for New York on a previously booked passage from Rome. Eisner remained convinced that even if Pabst was not a Nazi, he surely had been an opportunist. She considered his Third Reich productions to be "mediocre, smooth, and insignificant"; Lotte H. Eisner, *Ich hatte einst ein schönes Vaterland. Memoiren* (Heidelberg: Das Wunderhorn, 1984), pp. 94–95.

25. Pabst was scheduled by Terra to direct *Die große Entscheidung (The Great Decision)* in 1940. Bavaria announced *Geheimnisvolle Tiefe (Mysterious Depths),* starring Brigitte Horney and Ferdinand Marian, in its 1941–42 schedule. A Terra advertisement for the same season which appeared in the October/November 1941 issue of *Der Deutsche Film* also highlighted "a Brigitte Horney film" directed by Pabst under the production group Walter Tost. After finishing *Paracelsus,* he was to have done *Regimentsmusik (Regimental Music)* with Bavaria, but this assignment was given to Arthur Maria Rabenalt. Pabst negotiated with Prag-Film regarding *Theresa Lasotta,* for which shooting was slated early

in 1944. When this project did not materialize, Pabst went to Terra and started work on *The Molander Case.* Another unrealized project was "Heinrich I., genannt der Vogeler" (Bock, "Georg Wilhelm Pabst," pp. 231–233; Drewniak, *Der deutsche Film 1938–1945,* pp. 91–92). Leni Riefenstahl hired Pabst in the early 1940s to direct the acting sequences for *Tiefland (Lowlands).* She claims the collaboration initially fell through when "Goebbels, who so greatly disliked Pabst, made him a generous offer to do two major features . . . I didn't have the heart to hinder this wonderful opportunity, and Pabst was grateful to me." Riefenstahl's memory and chronology fail her when she describes how Pabst, having "completed his obligations," joined her on a sound stage shortly after Rudolf Hess's ill-fated mission to Scotland (which was in May 1941). Hollywood had not agreed with Pabst, Riefenstahl observes, insinuating that the sojourn abroad in the early 1930s had ruined him for all time: "His present approach was a routine more consistent with run-of-the-mill commercial movies and I tried in vain to discover traces of his once pronounced originality"; *A Memoir* (New York: St. Martin's, 1993), pp. 264, 273.

26. Pabst received an additional 12,000 RM for his work on the script of *Paracelsus.* Regarding Pabst's clash with Hippler, see Drewniak, *Der deutsche Film 1938–1945,* p. 92; for an inventory of directors' salaries in the Third Reich, see ibid., pp. 165–166.

27. Given the reduced production schedules and large public demand for movies, almost every wartime feature found an audience. *Paracelsus,* however, flopped altogether. It ranked among the Third Reich's largest box-office disasters, taking in only 3.5 million RM despite a very elaborate advertising campaign and a carefully orchestrated press buildup. Veit Harlan's *Die goldene Stadt* (*The Golden City,* 1942), in contrast, had a return of 12.5 million RM (Drewniak, *Der deutsche Film 1938–1945,* pp. 630–632). A confidential Ufa document from 1944 (provided by Gero Gandert, Stiftung Deutsche Kinemathek, Berlin) contains a list of box-office figures for features released from June 1942 through May 1943. By October 1943, *Paracelsus* had grossed only 1,995,000 RM against production costs of 2,794,000. Only one other film on this list is shown as being in the red, namely the Tobis production *Symphonie eines Lebens* (*Symphony of a Life,* 1943).

28. Atwell, *G. W. Pabst,* p. 127.

29. David Stewart Hull, *Film in the Third Reich* (New York: Simon and Schuster, 1973), p. 246.

30. *Der Deutsche Film 1942/43* (yearbook), p. 5. See also the Paracelsus portrait, P. I., "Jedem Krankheitsbild entspricht ein Heilmittel, sagte Theophrastus Paracelsus," *Filmwoche* 31/32 (26 August 1942): 239–242.

31. Adolf Hitler, *Mein Kampf,* trans. Ralph Manheim (Boston: Houghton Mifflin, 1971), p. 426.

32. The three parts appeared originally as *Paracelsus' Kindheit, Das Gestirn des Paracelsus,* and *Das Dritte Reich des Paracelsus.* For a contemporary appreciation of Kolbenheyer's trilogy by a prominent Germanist, see Erich Trunz, "Kolbenheyers Roman der deutschen Mystik," *Das Innere Reich* 5.7 (October 1938): 817–829. When Kolbenheyer learned of the plans for a Paracelsus film, he wrote the Ministry of Propaganda an angry letter, claiming the rights to the material and demanding appro-

priate remuneration. See Boelcke, *Kriegspropaganda 1939–1941,* p. 684. The notation of 10 April 1941 describes Goebbels' response to the writer's "presumptuous" letter. An official is charged with telling Kolbenheyer that the order for the Bavaria production came from Goebbels himself. The minister, not having read the author's books, in no way appropriated Kolbenheyer's intellectual property; the claim was therefore groundless.

33. Atwell lists the novel as the inspiration for Kurt Heuser's script without any further explanation or reference; *G. W. Pabst,* p. 125. One scene that surely does derive from Peternell's novel is Paracelsus' tumble down the stairs after Froben's death. See Peternell's *Der König der Ärzte. Ein Paracelsus-Roman* (Vienna/Munich: Petrei/Rain, 1964), pp. 201–202. For a more informed perspective regarding the likely sources for the script, see Udo Benzenhöfer, " 'Propaganda des Herzens.' Zum *Paracelsus*-Film von Georg W. Pabst," in *Medizin im Spielfilm des Nationalsozialismus,* ed. Udo Benzenhöfer and Wolfgang U. Eckart (Tecklenburg: Burgverlag, 1990), pp. 60–62. Benzenhöfer argues that Heuser relied considerably on Kolbenheyer's novel, taking the flagellant procession from that source, a scene not found in other biographies of Paracelsus.

34. George L. Mosse, *Masses and Man: Nationalist and Fascist Perceptions of Reality* (Detroit: Wayne State University Press, 1987), p. 70.

35. See Kurt Goldammer, *Paracelsus in der deutschen Romantik* (Vienna: Verband der Wissenschaftlichen Gesellschaften Österreichs, 1980).

36. See also Bloch's lecture on Paracelsus in *Vorlesungen zur Philosophie der Renaissance* (Frankfurt am Main: Suhrkamp, 1972), pp. 58–68.

37. Mosse, *Masses and Man,* p. 72.

38. An exceptional Paracelsus biography from the Third Reich is Bodo Sartorius von Waltershausen's *Paracelsus. Am Eingang der deutschen Bildungsgeschichte* (Leipzig: Meiner, 1935). The author stressed "the humanist and theosophical aspects of Parcelsus' philosophy" and "denied the Nazis the right to usurp Paracelsus as their precursor"; Henry M. Pachter, *Magic into Science: The Story of Paracelsus* (New York: Schuman, 1951). p. 280. See also Alexander Koyré's valuable analysis, "Paracelsus 1933," in *Mystiques, spirituels, alchimistes au XVIe siècle allemand* (Paris: Idées-Gallimard, 1971), pp. 75–129.

39. Herbert Maisch, "Die historische Gestalt im Film," *Film-Kurier,* 12 April 1941.

40. The Schiller text in question is his programmatic early essay, "Die Schaubühne als moralische Anstalt betrachtet." See also Felix Henseleit, "Die geschichtliche Persönlichkeit im Film," *Film-Kurier,* 2 April 1941: "For the film artist, the larger picture [*die große Linie*] remains the crucial concern."

41. Fritz Hippler, *Betrachtungen zum Filmschaffen* (Berlin: Hesse, 1942), p. 77: one has to prepare history so that the contemporary viewer (who often possesses only a vague notion of the past) can comprehend and appreciate it. Figures such as Paracelsus stir up strong emotions because they represent "mythical presence in human form"; Paul Gerhardt Dippel, "Filmgewordene Geschichte," *Der Deutsche Film* 7.6 (1942/43): 7.

42. See Paul Gerhardt Dippel, "Die innere Machtergreifung," *Der Deutsche Film* 7.7

(1943): with Germany at war, the stakes had risen. Facing enemies both to the east and to the west, the Reich "must defend its culture's great accomplishments, the work of Bach and Kant, Beethoven and Schiller, Rembrandt and Goethe, Mozart and Schopenhauer, Kleist and Nietzsche, Richard Wagner and Stefan George" (p. 2).

43. According to the Polish film historian Jerzy Toeplitz, *Paracelsus* approaches "dangerous sectors of a philosophical conception not far removed from the official Nazi ideology"; *Geschichte des Films,* vol. 4: *1939–1945,* trans. Lilli Kaufman (Berlin: Henschel, 1983), p. 239. Hull calls the protagonist "a sort of substitute Faust with Nazi attributes"; "Forbidden Fruit: The Harvest of the German Cinema, 1939–1945," *Film Quarterly* 14.4 (Summer 1961): 25.

44. Kurt Heuser's script sets the action at "around 1526." A copy of the original screenplay is available in the Film Studies collection at Dartmouth College. I am grateful to Gerd Gemünden for providing me access to this invaluable document. For a detailed account of Paracelsus' sojourn in Basel, see Henry Pachter, *Magic into Science*, pp. 144–171.

45. See how Heuser's script describes the city council, p. 58: there is little dignity in their proceedings; "rather, turbulence and disturbance reign, just as one might otherwise find in a modern democratic parliament."

46. "Pabst and his knife fetishism," observes Karsten Witte, "offers an iconography worthy of careful scrutiny"; "China and Not Yet China: *Shanghai Drama* (1938)," in Rentschler, *The Films of G. W. Pabst,* p. 173.

47. Bloch's characterization of Paracelsus captures his carnivalesque aspect: "Magus, phantasus, natural scientist, empiricist, cosmosoph, he was all of these at once"; *Vorlesungen zur Philosophie der Renaissance,* p. 59.

48. The actor appeared in numerous films by Pabst: *Der Schatz* (*The Treasure,* 1923), *The Joyless Street, Geheimnisse einer Seele* (*Secrets of a Soul,* 1926), and *Man spielt nicht mit der Liebe* (*Don't Play with Love,* 1926).

49. Compare a similar scene at the beginning of Kolbenheyer's *Das dritte Reich des Paracelsus,* in *Paracelsus. Roman-Trilogie* (Munich: Lehmanns, 1964), in which the physician cures a hopelessly afflicted woman, the victim of much abuse by unknowing doctors. Repeatedly the patient praises Paracelsus for his mild hands (p. 622).

50. One of the earliest scenes in Hans Steinhoff's *Robert Koch, der Bekämpfer des Todes* (*Robert Koch, the Enemy of Death,* 1939) shows the doctor at the deathbed of a little girl. The advertisement for the film likewise pictures a bespectacled Emil Jannings (as Koch) standing over a prone and half-naked female corpse.

51. Compare Roland Barthes's comments on the signifying dynamics of myths, in *Mythologies,* trans. Annette Lavers (New York: Hill and Wang, 1972), p. 117.

52. "What distinguishes this film," said a contemporary reviewer, "is the uncompromising seriousness with which this material has been given form—a seriousness that not only finds visual shape for the theme's mighty force, but furthermore lets it also gain expression in the editing"; Paul Ickes, "*Paracelsus.* Capitol am Zoo, Roxy-Palast Friedenau," *Film-Kurier,* 10 May 1943.

53. Pachter, *Magic into Science,* p. 4.

54. Pfefferkorn is explicitly identified as a Jew in Conrad Ferdinand Meyer's *Huttens letzte Tage (The Last Days of Hutten),* which Kurt Heuser read before writing his screenplay for *Paracelsus;* hr, "*Paracelsus.* Gespräch über die Probleme des historisch-biographischen Films mit Kurt Heuser," *Der Deutsche Film* 7 (1942/43): 6. The script describes Pfefferkorn simply as "the Rich Man." See also how Paracelsus reproaches the merchant (script, p. 115): "So it is indeed true what one reads about the rich, that they are heartless, corrupt, and always ready to sell out their brother." Commentators have noted that Heuser refused to work on the script of *Jew Süss* despite strong pressure from the ProMi; M. R.-R., "Historisches Nein. Kurt Heuser gestorben," *Frankfurter Allgemeine Zeitung,* 27 June 1975. Heuser, however, did collaborate on the script for *Ohm Krüger* (1941)—as well as *Rembrandt* (1942), a film with many anti-Semitic barbs.

55. See Heuser's script, pp. 269–270: the tableau of the sick and suffering yields to contemporary images of "farmers, workers, wounded soldiers." A series of dissolves brings us to a modern laboratory, "an operation room sparkling with chrome and cleanliness—in it physicians in white smocks move among nurses and assistants." We see a modern ampitheater for medical students and "the garden of a rest home, healthy mothers at play with their children; a happy and healthy new generation is growing up." The script insistently links Paracelsus' sober and professional bedside manner with the praxis of modern medicine (pp. 36, 160).

56. Brochure quoted in Benzenhöfer, " 'Propaganda des Herzens,' " p. 57.

57. See the contemporary brochure, *Paracelsus* (Berlin: Vertriebs-Presse-Referat der Deutschen Filmvertriebs-Gesellschaft, 1943). This valuable source is discussed at length by Benzenhöfer, " 'Propaganda des Herzens,' " pp. 55–58.

58. See Leiser's chapter on genius films, "Honour Your German Masters," in *Nazi Cinema,* pp. 106–111.

59. See Hippler's comments on the dramaturgy of the historical film, *Betrachtungen zum Filmschaffen,* pp. 76–80.

60. Compare Barthes, *Mythologies,* p. 118: "But the essential point in all this is that the form does not suppress the meaning, it only impoverishes it, it puts it at a distance, it holds it at one's disposal . . . The meaning will be for the form like an instantaneous reserve of history, a tamed richness, which it is possible to call and dismiss in a sort of rapid alternation."

61. A similar emphasis can be found in Arthur Schnitzler's one-act play *Paracelsus* (1898). The physician hypnotizes a woman, enabling her to articulate her deepest wishes. Like Freud, Paracelsus is a person who claims to know "what the woman wants."

62. Jung, *Paracelsica,* p. 9.

63. Ibid., p. 10.

64. Ibid., p. 59: "For in the unconscious nature of his [Paracelsus'] conflict he does not realize that deep down inside someone else rules his own house and militates against everything that he himself wants. This is in keeping with all unconscious conflicts: one hinders and undermines oneself."

65. For an incisive discussion of the "genius film" and an analytical application, see Linda Schulte-Sasse, "National Socialism's Aestheticization of Genius: The Case of Herbert Maisch's *Friedrich Schiller—Triumph eines Genies*," *Germanic Review* 66.1 (Winter 1991): 4–15.

66. Leiser, *Nazi Cinema*, p. 106.

67. Welch, *Propaganda and the German Cinema*, p. 146.

68. See a contemporary appraisal of *Diesel:* "[The actor] Birgel demonstrates for us the tragedy of this person, who during his whole life never settled down, whose achievement was so immense that even in his final hours he could not consider his work completed"; Georg Herzberg, "*Diesel.* Ufa-Palast am Zoo/Alhambra-Seestraße," *Film-Kurier*, 10 February 1943.

69. "The way fame is linked to misfortune and, in turn, happiness, is one of the most powerful instructive lessons [Hollywood] biopics display," remarks George F. Custen. With great gifts comes great vicissitude. The American biographical film evinces "a rhetoric of suffering," but unlike its Nazi extension, it locates salvation as "just around the corner in the form of the very institutions that the famous share with most members of the audience: family, community, and home"; *Bio/Pics: How Hollywood Constructed Public History* (New Brunswick, N.J.: Rutgers University Press, 1992), pp. 75–76.

70. Petley, *Capital and Culture*, pp. 138–139. Irmbert Schenk makes a similar point in an essay about Nazi historical films, "Geschichte im NS-Film. Kritische Anmerkungen zur filmwissenschaftlichen Suggestion der Identität von Propaganda und Wirkung," *montage/av* 3.2 (1994): 75–76.

71. For an acute analysis of this passage as a point of textual rupture and a "zone of disturbance," see Régine Mihal Friedman, "'*Ecce Ingenium Teutonicum*': *Paracelsus* (1943)," in Rentschler, *The Films of G. W. Pabst*, pp. 185–196.

72. Compare Steve Neale's comments about Hitler's visual appeal in *Triumph of the Will:* "Hitler's status *in the film* derives from, and is motivated and signalled by, the fact that he is structured and marked as the privileged object of the gaze, that he himself is the ultimately significant spectacle—for the crowds *in* the film and for the spectators *of* the film"; "*Triumph of the Will:* Notes on Documentary and Spectacle," *Screen* 20.1 (Spring 1979): 69–70.

73. Pachter, *Magic into Science*, p. 192.

74. This meeting is apocryphal; it is apparently taken from C. F. Meyer's *Hutten's Last Days.*

75. See the description in Heuser's script, p. 264: she wears "a cape that makes her look like a nun."

76. Both Fliegenbein and Johannes resemble their master, but both fall short of his greatness, both cause people to dance in wild abandon, both become subject to the physician's treatment and teaching, and in the end both serve his cause. Fliegenbein's final dance does not stir up the masses, but rather diverts their attention and aids the master's escape; Johannes becomes an unquestioning follower.

77. Sheila Johnson attempts to read Fliegenbein's various appearances as resistant moments in her essay "Ideological Ambiguity in G. W. Pabst's *Paracelsus,*" *Monatshefte* 83.2 (Summer 1991): 104–126. Fliegenbein becomes Paracelsus' (and Pabst's) better half, "the carnivalized *Führer,* a leader without ideological goals, without real substance in himself, and therefore immune to censors' attack" (p. 120). Johnson's notions of textual norms both within Pabst's work and in Nazi cinema as a whole are narrow and schematic. To say that the film contains "ideological ambiguity" is to state the obvious; many Nazi productions build in oppositional voices and offer ostensible counterpositions as part of their textual strategies. Johnson's interpretation remains myopic in its insistence that we see the Fliegenbein scenes in isolation rather than as a part of a narrative process.

78. For a compelling study of the historical conjunction between the plague, flagellation, and anti-Semitism, see Frantisek Graus, *Pest—Geissler—Judenmorde* (Göttingen: Vandenhoeck & Ruprecht, 1987); also see Arthur Hübner, *Die deutschen Geisslerlieder. Studien zum geistlichen Volksliede des Mittelalters* (Berlin/Leipzig: De Gruyter, 1931).

79. Michel Foucault, *Discipline & Punish: The Birth of the Prison,* trans. Alan Sheridan (New York: Vintage, 1979), p. 197.

80. An intriguing intertext in this regard is F. W. Murnau's *Nosferatu* (1922), a film that also shows a German city visited by a plague bearing a human countenance, a township whose most prominent physician is the Paracelsian Doctor Bulwer, whom we see teaching his students about the nature of carnivorous plants.

81. Max Horkheimer and Theodor W. Adorno, *Dialectic of Enlightenment,* trans. John Cumming (New York: Seabury, 1972), p. 190.

82. Ibid., pp. 190–191.

83. The phrase is taken from Jacqueline Rose, "Paranoia and the Film System," *Screen* 17.4 (Winter 1976/77): 89–90.

84. In Richard Billinger's drama of 1943, a portrait of the last year in the physician's life set in Salzburg, Paracelsus also has a privileged relationship to Death:

> I'm not afraid of him.
> I've battled him on many occasions.
> I've put a dent in his grim reaper's blade,
> He has no power over me.

Richard Billinger, *Paracelsus,* in *Gesammelte Werke. Dramen* (Graz/Vienna: Stiasny, 1959), vol. 4, p. 67.

85. Harald Kreutzberg had also fascinated a crowd of many thousands in a dance of death at the Festival Play *Olympische Jugend (Olympic Youth)* in conjunction with the opening festivities of the Berlin Olympics on 1 August 1936. The *Festspiel* was written by Carl Diem with music by Werner Egk and Carl Orff. See the program *Olympische Jugend Festspiel* (Berlin: Reichssportverlag, 1936) for an account of Kreutzberg's performance in the series of dances "Heroic Struggle and Death Lament": "The words of the speaker, calling to mind the spiritual significance of all games, the supreme sacrifice

for one's native land, introduce a sword dance that is performed by Harald Kreutzberg, Werner Stammer, and a chorus of sixty other dancers and that ends in the death of the two protagonists. The dead warriors are then carried from the field in a solemn procession, after which Mary Wigman and her troupe depict the death lament" (p. 24). Contemporary notices repeatedly document how Kreutzberg's dances reflected the spirit of the times. See, for instance, Schu., "Harald Kreutzberg. Volksbühne," *Film-Kurier,* 1 October 1934; or E. T., "Harald Kreutzberg und seine Kunst. Dritter Abend der Tanzfestspiele," *Film-Kurier,* 8 November 1935. Regarding his role in *Paracelsus,* see Georg Speckner, "Gaukler, Tänzer und Spielmann Fliegenbein," *Film-Kurier,* 5 August 1942. For recent perspectives on Kreutzberg, see the career appreciations in a special issue of *Tanzdrama Magazin* 21 (1992).

86. Compare Klaus Theweleit, *Male Fantasies,* vol. 1: *Women Floods Bodies History,* trans. Stephen Conway, Erica Carter, and Chris Turner (Minneapolis: University of Minnesota Press, 1987), p. 217.

87. See Horkheimer and Adorno, *Dialectic of Enlightenment,* p. 191, where the authors, not unproblematically, describe how women succumb to the power of the paranoiac: "In the devotees themselves, paranoia is rendered unto the paranoiac as to a demon; qualms of conscience are offered to the man without conscience, to whom they owe their thanks. They follow a man who looks through them, who takes them not as individuals but as material for any purpose . . . He simply inflames them."

88. After Froben's demise, an angry mob throws Paracelsus down a stairway, and we fear for his life. He pulls himself up and faces his tormentors: "You can murder me, but you can't kill me." His spirit is eternal, he claims, vowing to fight his adversaries even without a body. (These words appear verbatim in Peternell's novel, p. 202.) Shortly thereafter, a closeup of his wounded forehead and closed eyes lends the impression of a death mask, a wan physiognomy linked in a cut from the solemnly transfigured Renata.

89. The phrase is taken from Siegfried Kracauer's 1942 essay "Propaganda and the War Film," reprinted in *From Caligari to Hitler: A Psychological History of the German Film* (Princeton: Princeton University Press, 1947), p. 299.

90. Compare the reaction of Karl Eugen Gass, a student of Ernst Curtius and a sympathizer with the national conservative opposition. On 22 January 1944 he notes: "Afterward I saw the Paracelsus film. It does not give rise to a compelling response, but what nonetheless moved me was the difference between the staleness of our contemporary world and the vitality of the sixteenth century, of which one saw a lot, even if it was contrived." Gass characterizes Krauss's performance as "strangely unfocused" but observes with amazement how the figure "increasingly came to life"; Karl Eugen Gass, *Pisaner Tagebuch. Aufzeichnungen, Briefe aus dem Nachlaß eines Frühvollendeten,* ed. Paul Egon Hübinger, 2nd ed. (Heidelberg: Schneider, 1962), p. 328.

91. Horkheimer and Adorno, *Dialectic of Enlightenment,* p. 236.

92. Max Picard, *Hitler in Our Selves,* trans. Heinrich Hauser (Hinsdale, Ill.: Regnery, 1947), p. 79. For an idiosyncractic analysis of Nazi necrophilia, see Wilfred Mairgünther, *Morbus Hitler. Ein Essay* (Kiel: Neuer Malik, 1989).

8. Self-Reflexive Self-Destruction

1. Viktor Reimann, *Goebbels,* trans. Stephen Wendt (Garden City, N.Y.: Doubleday, 1976), p. 264.

2. *Goebbels-Reden,* vol. 2: *1939–1945,* ed. Helmut Heiber (Düsseldorf: Droste, 1972), p. 205.

3. Manfred Overesch, ed., *Chronik deutscher Zeitgeschichte,* vol. 2/II: *Das Dritte Reich 1939–1945* (Düsseldorf: Droste, 1983), p. 347.

4. Ruth Andreas-Friedrich, *Der Schattenmann. Tagebuchaufzeichnungen 1938–1945* (Frankfurt am Main: Suhrkamp, 1986 [1947]), p. 103.

5. Willi A. Boelcke, ed., *The Secret Conferences of Dr. Goebbels: The Nazi Propaganda War 1939–43,* trans. Ewald Osers (New York: Dutton, 1970), p. 337.

6. *Münchhausen,* 1943. Ufa-Filmkunst GmbH, Berlin. Director: Josef von Baky. Dialogue Direction: Fritz Thiery. Screenplay: Berthold Bürger [Erich Kästner]. Cinematography (Agfacolor): Werner Krien. Trick Photography: Konstantin Irmen-Tschet. Editing: Milo Harbich and Walter Wischniewsky. Art Direction: Emil Hasler and Otto Gülstorff. Costume Design: Manon Hahn. Choreography: Maria Sommer. Music: Georg Haentzschel.

The Players: Hans Albers (Baron Münchhausen), Brigitte Horney (Catherine the Great), Wilhelm Bendow (the Man in the Moon), Michael Bohnen (Duke Karl of Brunswick), Hans Brausewetter (Frederick von Hartenfeld), Marina von Ditmar (Sophie von Riedesel), Andrews Engelmann (Prince Potemkin), Käthe Haack (Baroness Münchhausen), Hermann Speelmans (Christian Kuchenreutter), Walter Lieck (the runner), Ferdinand Marian (Count Cagliostro), Leo Slezak (Sultan Abdul-Hamid), Gustav Waldau (Casanova), Ilse Werner (Princess Isabella d'Este), Hilde von Stolz (Louise La Tour), Eduard von Winterstein (Münchhausen's father), Waldemar Leitgeb (Prince Grigori Orlov), Hubert von Meyerinck (Prince Anton Ulrich of Brunswick), Jaspar von Oertzen (Count Lanskoi), Werner Scharf (Prince Francesco d'Este), Armin Schweizer (Johann), Marianne Simson (Woman in the Moon), Franz Weber (Prince von Ligne), Bernard Goetzke, Harry Hardt, Victor Janson, Leopold von Ledebur, Franz Schafheitlin, Ewald Wenck.

Original length: 3,662 meters (134 min.). Color. Premiered on 5 March 1943 in Berlin (Ufa-Palast am Zoo). Rating: "Artistically especially worthwhile" and "nationally worthwhile."

A subtitled videocassette version is available from Facets Video and the German Language Video Center.

7. Otto Heinz Jahn, production chief of Ufa, described the studio's hopes for the film in these words; "Das Programm der Ufa-Filmkunst," *Der Deutsche Film 1942/43* (yearbook), p. 68.

8. Curt Riess, *Das gab's nur einmal. Die große Zeit des deutschen Films* (Vienna/Munich: Molden, 1977), vol. 3, p. 178.

9. For a comprehensive survey of the many different (and multimedial) renderings

of the Münchhausen-legend, see Werner R. Schweizer, *Münchhausen und Münchhausiaden. Werden und Schicksale einer deutsch-englischen Burleske* (Bern/Munich: Francke, 1969). See also Z. E., "Dichter und Nachdichter formen Münchhausen," *Filmwoche* 25/26 (1 July 1942): 191–192.

10. On the proliferation of Münchhausen texts, see John Carswell's introduction to *The Singular Adventures of Baron Munchausen by Rudolph Raspe and others,* ed. John Carswell (New York: Heritage, 1952), pp. ix–xxxviii; and Max Lüthi's afterword to Gottfried August Bürger, *Wunderbare Reisen zu Wasser und Lande, Feldzüge und lustige Abenteuer des Freiherrn von Münchhausen* (Zürich: Manese, 1978), pp. 203–215. See also Ruth P. Dawson, "Rudolf Erich Raspe and the Munchausen Tales," *Lessing Yearbook* 16 (1984): 205–220.

11. Jewish comedian Pearl came to renown as an airwave Münchhausen. The radio personality's tag line ("Vass you dere, Sharlie?") for a time was a pet phrase of American popular culture.

12. The multimillion-dollar production bears some similarity to its 1943 precursor. Both involve an extended flashback and a story-within-a-story framework. Each exhibits a profusion of fantastic worlds and exotic sites. Gilliam's contribution features a late eighteenth-century setting with nations at war and a city under siege, where bombings and food shortages are the order of the day, where the specter of death constantly lurks in the wings.

13. The film ran in Germany through the last weeks of Hitler's reign, filling cinemas in Berlin as late as March 1945, registering approximately 25 million admissions through the end of the Third Reich.

14. See, for instance, Ronald Holloway, "*Muenchhausen (The Adventures of Baron Muenchhausen),*" *Variety,* 21 June 1978: "The result is a German highpoint in comedy, action and witty dialog; it's a relaxed, easy-flowing thespian tour-de-force for both Albers and Brigitte Horney, as Catherine the Great."

15. David Stewart Hull, *Film in the Third Reich* (New York: Simon and Schuster, 1973), p. ix: "This study of the Nazi-era film originated sometime in late 1959 when James Card, curator of motion pictures at the George Eastman House, Rochester, New York, showed me a print of *Münchhausen.* I was intrigued with the film, and wanted to find some more information about it and about a film industry which, in the middle of a terrible war, could produce such an epic."

16. I. B., "Pomp und Prunk entstand auf Pump," *Abend,* 22 June 1978. Another German critic lauds the work's charm and irony, maintaining that its fantastic vigor renders it "a film against its times"; Volker Baer, "Im Widerspruch zur Zeit. Zur Wiederaufführung des Films *Münchhausen* von 1942/43," *Der Tagesspiegel,* 25 June 1978.

17. Don Leifert, "*Baron Muenchhausen,*" *Video Times,* March 1985.

18. The premiere version ran 134 minutes but was cut back to 118 minutes by 17 June. The videocassette commercially available in the United States today runs 104 minutes. (The most recent German release, though 3 minutes shorter, has a far better color resolution. The version typically shown on German television today, whose color

is splendid, runs 110 minutes.) The copies that circulated in West Germany during the early 1950s, shorn of the framing passages, were only 90 minutes; Gunter Groll, "Wiedersehen mit *Münchhausen,*" *Süddeutsche Zeitung,* 19 July 1954. The elaborate 1978 reconstruction, undertaken by the Murnau-Stiftung in Wiesbaden, restored missing footage and the original tones of the Agfacolor. The film played with great success at the Cannes Festival in May 1978, opening shortly thereafter, likewise to accolades, in West German cinemas. Interestingly, the Neue Constantin Film press booklet contains documents and descriptions lifted verbatim or paraphrased (without attribution) from the Ufa publicity materials of 1943, including an erroneous plot summary that claims Münchhausen remains alive at the film's end, ever-immortal and still active. *Münchhausen* has appeared frequently in German special screenings, e.g., in the film series accompanying the "Berlin, Berlin" exhibition celebrating the city's 750th anniversary in 1987 and the festival retrospective devoted to color films at the 1988 *Berlinale.* It also played to many thousands of viewers during the summer of 1988 in the open-air *Waldbühne* (where Nazi *Thingspiele* had been performed in the early 1930s).

19. Heinrich Miltner, "Gespräch mit Emil Hasler und Otto Gülstorff. Die Bauten zum 'Münchhausen'-Film," *Film-Kurier,* 21 July 1942.

20. See, for instance, Riess, *Das gab's nur einmal,* p. 173: "Goebbels wants to prove that an Ufa color film can be every bit as good as the great American color films. That's the whole point of the exercise." Initial plans had called for Josef Winckler's novel *Der tolle Bamberg* to serve as the source for the film. Erich Kästner apparently was the one to suggest *Münchhausen* for the event; Ingo Tornow, *Erich Kästner und der Film* (Munich: Filmland Presse, 1989), p. 18. The actors Werner Krauss and Eugen Klöpfer had written a comedy titled *Münchhausens Abenteuer* in 1940, intending it for both stage and film versions; Bogusław Drewniak, *Der deutsche Film 1938–1945. Ein Gesamtüberblick* (Düsseldorf: Droste, 1987), p. 672.

21. G. H., "Josef von Baky," *Film-Kurier,* 21 August 1942. A penchant for visual opulence and formal razzle-dazzle also marked the work of the Hungarian filmmaker Géza von Bolvary, for whom Baky served as assistant director during the 1930s.

22. Norbert Grob, "Die Vergangenheit, sie ruht aber nicht," in *Das Jahr 1945. Filme aus fünfzehn Ländern,* ed. Hans Helmut Prinzler (Berlin: Stiftung Deutsche Kinemathek, 1990), p. 33.

23. For a consideration of Kästner's work in the Nazi film industry, see Tornow, *Erich Kästner und der Film,* pp. 17–24; also Dieter Mank, *Erich Kästner im nationalsozialistischen Deutschland—Zeit ohne Werk?* (Frankfurt am Main: Lang, 1981); and Elisabeth Lutz-Kopp, *"Nur wer Kind bleibt . . ." Erich Kästner-Verfilmungen* (Frankfurt am Main: Bundesverband Jugend und Film, 1993), pp. 183–198. See "Ich hole Erich Kästner zur Ufa," in Fritz Hippler's memoirs, *Die Verstrickung. Einstellungen und Rückblenden* (Düsseldorf: Mehr Wissen, 1981), pp. 227–228; also see Hippler's letter of 14 August 1974 to the editor of *Die Welt,* in which he maintains that as the *Reichsfilmintendant* and head of the Propaganda Ministry's Film Division, he interceded and, against

Goebbels' express wishes, managed to secure Kästner's appointment. Hippler goes on to criticize the recently deceased Kästner for never having publicly acknowledged the wartime assistance.

24. Erich Kästner, *Münchhausen. Ein Drehbuch* (Frankfurt am Main: Fischer, 1960), p. 111.

25. Hans-Christoph Blumenberg, *In meinem Herzen, Schatz . . . Die Lebensreise des Schauspielers und Sängers Hans Albers* (Frankfurt am Main: Fischer, 1991), p. 79.

26. Heike Klapdor, "Berthold Bürger," in *Münchhausen* (*Ufa Magazin* no. 19), ed. Michael Töteberg and Klaus Kreimeier (Berlin: Deutsches Historisches Museum, 1992), p. 8.

27. See, for instance, Henning Harmssen, "Die Unbekümmertheit des Hans Albers," *Neue Zürcher Zeitung,* 13 April 1976; "Meister des Stilbruchs," *Der Spiegel,* 11 January 1982, pp. 130–134; and schw, "Vom Halunken mit Herz zum Helden," *Die Welt,* 17 November 1987: "In an age of oppression he was a free man, independent and irrepressible; that was every bit as important as his voice and his good looks." For a recent celebration of the figure, see Hans-Joachim Neumann, "Ein Star wider die Zeit," *zitty,* 3 October 1991, p. 62. The mythical notion of Albers as an oppositional presence conveniently ignores or consciously overlooks his starring roles in political productions such as Gustav Ucicky's *Flüchtlinge* (*Fugitives,* 1933) and Herbert Selpin's *Carl Peters* (1941). A recent critical biography provides a more differentiated portrait of the actor's inimitable blend of opportunism, obstinacy, and accommodation: Michaela Krützen, *Hans Albers. Eine deutsche Karriere* (Weinheim: Quadriga, 1995).

28. The contractual arrangement between Ufa and Kästner was never put to paper. Neither Kästner's name nor his pseudonym appeared in the original film credits. The transaction between the writer and the Ministry of Propaganda has been the object of radically divergent and often wildly speculative accounts. See Helga Bemman, *Humor auf Taille. Erich Kästner—Leben und Werk* (Berlin: Verlag der Nation, 1983), pp. 35lff. For reviews lauding Kästner's script, see Heino Eggers, "Die Zeit ist ganz kaputt. Neu aufgelegt. *Münchhausen*—eine Filmlegende und die Wirklichkeit," *Vorwärts,* 27 July 1978; and Dietmar Schmidt, "Unpolitisch?" *Neue Osnabrücker Zeitung,* 8 July 1978.

29. An interesting comparison text demonstrating a different kind of commanding gaze, a visual regime more in keeping with state-sanctioned political productions, is the closing sequence of Hans Steinhoff's *Der alte und der junge König* (*The Old and the Young King,* 1935). The scene focuses on the Prussian prince who in the course of the narrative learns to identify with his father. He assumes the dying monarch's gaze, adopting a regal pose, staring, like a mesmerizer, unflinching and inexorable. All energy in the film frame is organized around this steely gaze. Frederick stands as the ultimate and unquestioned source of power, a countenance that turns in the final shot to face the spectator as the camera lingers in a prolonged close-up. Both on- and offscreen spectators are called upon to defer to this gaze, to assume a relationship in a design at whose center stands the commanding presence of unquestioned authority.

30. Karsten Witte, "Visual Pleasure Inhibited: Aspects of the German Revue Film," trans. J. D. Steakley and Gabriele Hoover, *New German Critique* 24–25 (Fall/Winter 1981–82): 244.

31. Oskar Kalbus, *Vom Werden deutscher Filmkunst,* vol. 2: *Der Tonfilm* (Altona-Bahrenfeld: Cigaretten-Bilderdienst, 1935), p. 110. This motif recurs in discussions of Albers' appeal to audiences and, above all, of his allure for female spectators. See the contemporary brochure by Hans-Joachim Schlamp, *Frauen um Hans Albers* (Berlin: Mölich, 1938). See also Harald Juhnke's description in a boulevard press tribute that uses a rhetoric characteristic of much writing on the actor, " 'Der kam, sah die Mieze—schon war es passiert,' " *Bild am Sonntag,* 13 July 1978: "Hans Albers died twenty years ago. No one has forgotten him. The fascination he exercises over women was singular." Another recurring preoccupation of Albers literature is the luminous gaze emanating from his piercing blue eyes. Among the many star portraits, see Eberhard Spiess, *Hans Albers. Eine Filmographie* (Frankfurt am Main: Kommunales Kino, 1977); Otto Tötter, ed., *Hans Albers. Hoppla, jetzt komm ich* (Zürich: Rasch und Röhring, 1986); Knuth Weidlich, ed., *Der blonde Hans—Mosaiksteine eines Lebens* (Hamburg: Historika Photoverlag, 1992). See as well Hans-Christoph Blumenberg's film tribute, *In meinem Herzen, Schatz . . .*

32. Detlef Kühn, "Der Erfolg des schönen Zaubers. Zum 25. Todestag von Hans Albers," *epd Film* 2.7 (July 1985): 20. Compare Siegfried Kracauer's characterization of how Albers, the "film actor, who had once portrayed adulterers and well-dressed rogues, suddenly turned into Germany's No. 1 screen favorite, the incarnation of Prince Charming"; *From Caligari to Hitler: A Psychological History of the German Film* (Princeton: Princeton University Press, 1947), p. 214. For Ernst Bloch, the "Hans-in-Boots" who starred in Ucicky's *Fugitives,* was "at first glance from head to toe a shining star. From head to toe a Nazi Führer, or what people in Cologne mean when they speak of a vile [*fieser*] monarch"; "Nazi-Filme oder Der Zauber der Persönlichkeit," in *Vom Hasard zur Katastrophe. Politische Aufsätze aus den Jahren 1934–1939* (Frankfurt am Main: Suhrkamp, 1972), p. 14. Rudolf Arnheim characterized the Albers of the early 1930s as a compelling gaze that seemed afraid of its own powers. The actor manifested "a sort of weakness toward his own strength," a comforting gesture given his sizable muscles. "He is a heavyweight even if at times he seems too light"; "Hans Albers," *Die Weltbühne* 36 (8 September 1931): 384.

33. Enno Patalas speaks of Horney (daughter of the famous psychologist Karen Horney and, after October 1940, the wife of the prominent cinematographer Konstantin Irmen-Tschet) as someone who kept the regime at a distance, starring mainly in unpolitical productions and working abroad before the war in English productions such as *Secret Life; Sozialgeschichte der Stars* (Hamburg: Schröder, 1963), p. 87. This is not completely the case, for she did appear in some nationalistic films, including *Ein Mann will nach Deutschland* (*A German Wants to Go Home,* 1934), *Ziel in den Wolken* (*Up into the Clouds,* 1938), *Der Gouverneur* (*The Governor,* 1939), and *Feinde* (*Enemies,* 1940).

34. Our first glimpse of her comes along with an otherwise unmotivated image of a caged man, Pugachev, a rebellious soldier imprisoned by Catherine for leading a mutiny

of Cossacks who refuse to shave their beards. We also hear a rumor that the czarina has had her husband murdered. In this way, she is introduced via fearful conjectures about her castrating powers.

35. Wilfried Wiegand, "Die Wahrheit des Scheins. Der *Münchhausen*-Film des Jahres 1943 wird wieder aufgeführt," *Frankfurter Allgemeine Zeitung,* 5 July 1978.

36. H. F., "Wer war Münchhausen?" *Film-Kurier,* 8 August 1942.

37. See Kraft Wetzel and Peter Hagemann, *Liebe, Tod und Technik. Kino des Phantastischen 1933–1945* (Berlin: Spiess, 1977).

38. *Film-Kurier* published a debate in May 1942 about the relation between fantasy and reality in film, exchanges that accompanied regular progress reports on the *Münchhausen* production. Also see Fritz Theodor Fabius, "Phantasie und Wirklichkeit. Anmerkungen anlässlich einer Unterhaltung mit dem Spielleiter Josef von Baky," *Film-Kurier,* 3 March 1944.

39. Contemporary commentators in the Third Reich spoke of the genre in terms of peril and challenge: the fantastic demands intense creative control, a decisive formal will that might harness its destructive potential; if filmmakers allow the irreal to get out of hand, narrative lines become blurry and story logic suffers. See, for instance, Hans-Hubert Gensert, "Dämonie und Phantastik im Film," *Film-Kurier,* 22 May 1942.

40. See Peter Hagemann, "Eine fast erfolgreiche Unterdrückung der Affenliebe zum Filmwechselbalg," in *Liebe, Tod und Technik,* p. 42.

41. See Hannah Arendt's general comments on how totalitarian leaders create convincing alternative worlds, in *The Origins of Totalitarianism* (New York: World, 1958), p. 362: "Their art consists in using, and at the same time transcending, the elements of reality, of verifiable experiences, in the chosen fiction, and in generalizing them into regions which then are definitely removed from all possible control by individual experience. With such generalizations, totalitarian propaganda establishes a world fit to compete with the real one, whose main handicap is that it is not logical, consistent, and organized."

42. André Bazin, "Marcel L'Herbier's *La Nuit Fantastique,*" in *French Cinema of the Occupation and Resistance,* ed. François Truffaut, trans. Stanley Hochman (New York: Ungar, 1981), p. 77. During the film's initial Paris run, it broke box-office records, according to a review in *Je suis partout* cited in *Film-Kurier,* 4 April 1944; Drewniak, *Der deutsche Film 1938–1945,* p. 674.

43. See Frederick W. Ott, *The Great German Films* (Secaucus, N.J.: Citadel, 1986), pp. 217–218: "Von Baky and his technical staff studied the special effects of numerous color productions, including Walt Disney's *Snow White and the Seven Dwarfs* (1938) and David O. Selznick's *Gone with the Wind* (1939), but particular attention was given to Alexander Korda's 1940 film, *The Thief of Bagdad,* which Goebbels much admired and hoped to surpass in special effects and color artistry." See Hull, *Film in the Third Reich,* pp. 252–260. His account of the production has dominated the subsequent literature on *Münchhausen,* from newspaper criticism to film historiography, even finding its way into the Neue Constantin Film press booklet for the 1978 rerelease.

44. Ludwig Klitzsch, "Die Ansprache von Generaldirektor Dr. Klitzsch," *Film-Kurier,* 5 March 1943.

45. *The Goebbels Diaries 1942–1943,* trans. and ed. Louis P. Lochner (Garden City, N.Y.: Doubleday, 1948), p. 273 (translation slightly modified).

46. See Goebbels' public address, "Der Krieg schuf den neuen deutschen Film," reprinted in *Der Deutsche Film* 5.9 (March 1941): 169–170.

47. Fritz Hippler, "Ein Vorwort," *Nationalsozialistische Monatshefte* 13 (June 1942): 337.

48. See Paul Virilio, *War and Cinema: The Logistics of Perception,* trans. Patrick Camiller (London: Verso, 1989), pp. 7–8: "War consists not so much in scoring territorial, economic or other material victories as in appropriating the 'immateriality' of perceptual fields. As belligerents set out to invade those fields in their totality, it became apparent that the true war film did not necessarily have to depict war or any actual battle. For once the cinema was able to create surprise (technological, psychological, etc.), it effectively came under the category of weapons."

49. Joseph Goebbels, "Rede anläßlich der Kriegstagung der Reichsfilmkammer am 15.2.1941 in Berlin," reprinted in Gerd Albrecht, *Nationalsozialistische Filmpolitik* (Stuttgart: Enke, 1969), p. 479.

50. Virilio, *War and Cinema,* p. 8.

51. Hans Albers, "Der Schauspieler und die Farbe," *Berliner Lokal-Anzeiger,* 25 December 1942. As the piece continues, one becomes privy to a striking appreciation of film technique's panoptic capacity. New laws, claimed Albers, dominate studio endeavors. The camera monitors an actor's every move. The microphone listens to everything people say. The even more refined technical capability of film captures people "in all their turbulent splendor and colorful magnificence." Filmmakers must now, he concluded, serve the interests of color.

52. Kästner, *Münchhausen,* pp. 37–38.

53. See Peter Sloterdijk, *Critique of Cynical Reason,* trans. Michael Eldred (Minneapolis: University of Minnesota Press, 1987), pp. 477–479, where he uses a passage from *Fabian* to exemplify Kästner's acute awareness of Weimar's cynical zeitgeist.

54. See Klaus Theweleit, *Male Fantasies,* vol. 1: *Women Floods Bodies History,* trans. Stephen Conway, Erica Carter, and Chris Turner (Minneapolis: University of Minnesota Press, 1987).

55. Erich Kästner, *Fabian. Die Geschichte eines Moralisten* (Frankfurt am Main: Ullstein, 1986 [1931]), p. 117. For a feminist reading of *Fabian,* see Marianne Bäumler, *Die aufgeräumte Wirklichkeit des Erich Kästner* (Cologne: Prometh, 1984), pp. 108–130. Another of Kästner's anxious males, the hero of the 1943 script and film *Der kleine Grenzverkehr (A Salzburg Comedy),* is a linguist specializing in laugh research. The loud laughter of a vampish woman summons up disturbing mental images of a cruel cannibal.

56. A temporal leap from an eighteenth-century castle to a modern setting also provides the dramatic framework for Phil Jutzi's Münchhausen short of 1936. As the baron emerges from the realm of ghosts and enters the present-day world, the first

person he encounters is a costumed woman in a sports car who is on her way to a masquerade ball. The avuncular baron, a walking anachronism, is alternately amused and bewildered by trains, radios, and movies.

57. See Robert Stam, *Reflexivity in Film and Literature: From Don Quixote to Jean-Luc Godard* (New York: Columbia University Press, 1992), p. 16: "The self-referentiality of commercials that parody themselves or other commercials . . . is calculated to mystify rather than disenchant. The self-referential humor signals to the spectator that the commercial is not to be taken seriously, and this relaxed state of expectation renders the viewer more permeable to its image. The self-referentiality, far from demystifying the product or exposing hidden codes, conceals the deadly seriousness of the commercial—the fact that it is after the spectator's money."

58. The historical spectator, well aware of the Münchhausen legend, is thus positioned simultaneously as a member of an in-group privy to his tricks and an object of the film's own technical—and discursive—trickery.

59. See Helma Sanders-Brahms, "*Münchhausen* oder Lügen haben lange Beine," *epd Kirche und Film* 31.8 (August 1978), especially her witty and lucid description of Marian as "the most brilliant malevolent presence" *(Brunnenvergifter)* in Nazi cinema (p. 14). Alfons Arns also sees a continuity between Marian's roles as Süss and Cagliostro. It is, claims Arns, as if the elegant and erotic heavy simply walked from one film into the other, serving in both cases as an "anti-Semitic object of projection," a villain who lusts after money and power; "Die halbe Wahrheit. Zum Umgang mit NS-Spielfilmen in Fernsehen und Kritik," *Medium* 21.4 (1991): 38. Compare the contemporary production report by L. Krabbe, "Münchhausen-Casanova-Cagliostro," *Film-Kurier,* 29 May 1942, whose title suggests an affinity between the trio, even if the article takes pains to elucidate their differences.

60. In this way, *Münchhausen*'s anti-Semitism is indirect, a function of innuendo. See Theodor W. Adorno, "Anti-Semitism and Fascist Propaganda," in *The Stars Down to Earth,* trans. Stephen Crook (London: Routledge, 1994), p. 169: "For example, the agitator says, 'those dark forces, you know whom I mean,' and the audience at once understands that his remarks are directed against the Jews. The listeners are thus treated as an in-group who already know everything the orator wishes to tell them and who agree with him before any explanation is given." National Socialist orators regularly employed innuendo as a ploy to unite audiences, positioning listeners as attuned to insider knowledge, thereby confirming a "concord of feeling and opinion" and suggesting a "basic identity between leader and followers."

61. Kästner, *Münchhausen,* p. 75. The figure's Semitic physiognomy becomes more explicit in another script passage that was altered for the film. Asked why he does not want to become the Duke of Courland himself, Cagliostro replies: "I would be a very handsome man if I were not so ugly. My profile would not look particularly attractive on gold coins" (p. 79). Cagliostro is Kästner's own striking addition to the Münchhausen legends. Neither the figure nor Münchhausen's immortality (much less women) plays a role in Kästner's subsequent postwar retelling for children, *Des Freiherrn von*

Münchhausen wunderbaren Reisen und Abenteuer zu Wasser und zu Lande. Nacherzählt (Zürich: Atrium, 1951).

62. The historical Cagliostro, a prominent albeit controversial Freemason, was neither a Jew nor a megalomaniac. As Peter G. Christensen points out, Cagliostro "went to Kurland in March 1789 because he felt that there he would have strong support for the branch of Egyptian Freemasonry which he wished to establish in lodges all over Europe"; "The Representation of the Late Eighteenth Century in the von Baky/Kästner *Baron Münchhausen:* The Old Regime and Its Links to the Third Reich," *German Life and Letters* 44.1 (October 1990): 15. Cagliostro was a consummate confidence man, an illusionist who indulged the wishes and desires of gullible contemporaries. Goethe's drama *Der Groß-Cophta* ridiculed the figure's charlatanism; Catherine the Great also made light of him in three comedies. See Gregor Eisenhauer's portrait of Cagliostro (born Joseph Balsamo) in *Scharlatane. Zehn Fallstudien* (Frankfurt am Main: Eichborn, 1994), pp. 137–166. One of the count's many scams involved his claim that he could produce the " 'physical means by which one might live for centuries'—without showing any signs of age" (p. 142). See as well Carl Neumann, Curt Belling, and Hans-Walther Betz, *Film-"Kunst," Film-Kohn, Film-Korruption* (Berlin: Scherping, 1937), pp. 9–10: the *völkisch* propagandists describe Cagliostro as a "pirate with intelligence" and view him as an antithesis to the crude and ruthless Jewish "highwayman of modernity." The most extensive biography on the figure is W. R. H. Trowbridge's *Cagliostro* (New Hyde Park, N.Y.: University Books, 1960).

63. The pronouncement moved a West German critic to express astonishment at how the script, written at a time of Nazi expansionism, could nonetheless "propagate the peaceful individualistic adventurism of a man who only wants to visit foreign countries to conquer their women"; Wiegand, "Die Wahrheit des Scheins."

64. She will be out of sight but not fully out of mind, banished from the narrative as a visual presence but nevertheless not utterly repressed. The baron, we learn from the script, is discarded for a younger lover and goes on to serve as an officer in Catherine's war against the Turks. We later *hear* of her attempt to ransom Münchhausen from the Sultan; the convalesced hero, however, uses his power of invisibility to escape.

65. Kästner, *Münchhausen,* p. 106.

66. Compare André Bazin, "The Ontology of the Photographic Image," in *What Is Cinema?* trans. and ed. Hugh Gray (Berkeley: University of California Press, 1967), vol. 1, pp. 9–16.

67. Compare Tornow, *Erich Kästner und der Film,* p. 22: Kästner's "personal image of women is not exactly unproblematic, but it plays no essential role in *Münchhausen.* In no way can one speak here of a fascist image of women."

68. The film shows the registration of new arrivals to the harem, a processing of human material which in light of contemporaneous realitites brings to mind disturbing associations: "One looks into the ladies' eyes, measures their pulses, appraises their teeth, etc."; *Münchhausen,* p. 136.

69. Compare Francis Courtade and Pierre Cadars, *Histoire du cinéma nazi* (Paris:

Losfeld, 1972), pp. 297–298. In an otherwise enthusiastic appreciation of the film (one that relies heavily on Hull), the authors note that its exotic topography recalls "the disquieting phantasmagorias" of Odilon Rédon. Compare as well Alice Yaeger Kaplan's discussion of F. T. Marinetti's *Mafarka le Futuriste* (1909) and *Les mots en liberté futuristes,* in *Reproductions of Banality: Fascism, Literature, and French Intellectual Life* (Minneapolis: University of Minnesota Press, 1986), p. 87: "As man 'humanizes' nature, he reinvents it in a form he can control. Yet only the distance permitted by modern technology allows this foreshortened perspective—this visual version of uneven development—whereby countries become feet, and boulders become crouching natives. Technology gives to man the impression of having created nature, but also of having killed it. This is where misogyny comes in."

70. Karsten Witte, "Das Braun von Agfacolor. Hans Albers als *Münchhausen,*" *Frankfurter Rundschau,* 4 July 1978.

71. The wife on the moon thus is literally a woman made to the measure of male desire, recalling another Kästner script, *Frau nach Maß* (*A Woman Made to Measure,* 1940), directed by Helmut Käutner, a comedy of errors in which a female performer sings: "I want to be just what you want me to be." Interestingly, the film's titles unreel over the close-up image of a woman seen from behind—a shot that points ahead to the painted lady in Cagliostro's hotel room.

72. See Theweleit, *Male Fantasies,* vol. 1, p. 215n.: " 'Women' is a code word for the whole complex of nature, for anything at all having to do with 'feelings' and the unconscious."

73. In the film's opening sequence, Sophie pursues the baron to a private room. She grabs a red billard ball from a pool table and makes it known that she is available, prompting Münchhausen to exclaim: "You're standing there like Eve with an apple. But I'll be damned if I'll bite into a billard ball." Calling her a child, he leads her away. An earlier Nazi production that even more explicitly recycles the Adam and Eve myth is Herbert Selpin's screwball comedy, *Ich liebe Dich* (*I Love You,* 1938), starring Viktor de Kowa and Luise Ullrich.

74. Other intense demonstrations of affection between Albers and male comrades are to be found in *Fugitives, Der Mann, der Sherlock Holmes war* (*The Man Who Was Sherlock Holmes,* 1937), and *Water for Canitoga.*

75. In *Carl Peters,* Albers played perhaps the most mother-fixated character in all of Nazi cinema. A painting of his parent accompanies the colonial hero wherever he goes. Contrary to history's infamous philanderer and sadist, Albers' Peters has no affective attachment to any other woman, black or white. He ultimately forsakes the world and in the film's last shot walks off into the horizon at the side of his maternal companion. In Rudolf Jugert's 1952 film *Nachts auf den Strassen (Nights on the Streets),* Albers plays a stoic truck driver who finds a large sum of money, gains a new lease on life, and falls in love with a much younger woman. In the end, he returns to his faithful wife and decides to grow old with her rather than enjoy an ill-gained material well-being.

76. Philippe Lacoue-Labarthe and Jean-Luc Nancy, "The Nazi Myth," trans. Brian Holmes, *Critical Inquiry* 16.2 (Winter 1990): 303.

77. See Saul Friedländer, *Reflections of Nazism: An Essay on Kitsch and Death,* trans. Thomas Weyr (New York: Harper & Row, 1984), p. 27: "But faced with a kitsch representation of death, everyone knows that here two contradictory elements are amalgamated: on the one hand, an appeal to harmony, to emotional communion at the simplest and most immediate level; on the other, solitude and terror. It has often been said that one of the characteristics of kitsch is precisely the neutralization of 'extreme situations,' particularly death, by turning them into some sentimental idyll . . . The juxtaposition of these two contradictory elements represents the foundation of a certain religious aesthetic, and, in my opinion, the bedrock of Nazi aesthetics."

78. In a similar way, Fritz Lang's Siegfried (in the first part of the 1924 epic, *Die Nibelungen*) derives his ability to become invisible and to change appearance from the misshapen and treacherous Alberich, a magician who lords over a realm that resembles at once a film studio and an underground cinema. Siegfried likewise uses these powers to conquer and seduce a woman, to overcome Brunhild's threatening femininity. (Her collection of damaged male armor is comparable to Münchhausen's gallery of miniatures; it documents her successes in encounters with members of the opposite sex.) *Die Nibelungen,* like *Münchhausen,* represented a concerted German attempt to compete with Hollywood on an international scale. The monumental Ufa film of 1924 propagated a national myth and sought to invigorate a devastated postwar populace. Even though Lang had fled Germany, *Siegfried* (edited, synchronized, and retitled as *Siegfrieds Tod/Siegfried's Death*) would be reprised in May 1933. See Goebbels' diary entry of 31 December 1936, where he states that Hitler, having rescreened Lang's *Siegfried,* "was deeply impressed by it"—so impressed that he wanted to recast the *Nibelungen* epic in an even more mammoth and extravagant color version, a film that would become a primer for schoolchildren and a "standard work" for Nazi Germany; *Tagebücher,* vol. 3: *1935–1939,* ed. Ralf Georg Reuth (Munich: Piper, 1992), pp. 1023–24.

79. Without drawing further consequences, Gunter Groll recognizes the nomadic baron's resemblance to the Wandering Jew when he describes Münchhausen as "half fairy-tale hero, half Ahasver"; *Süddeutsche Zeitung,* 19 July 1954.

80. See Cagliostro's comment in the script version: "We resemble each other like dissimilar brothers. I always believed that we were brothers. And you always believed that we were not alike." The baron replies: "One can resemble another person in almost every respect and still be essentially different"; Kästner, *Münchhausen,* p. 106. Critic Eckhart Schmidt, reviewing the film's 1978 revival, was troubled that Münchhausen's dealings with the diabolical count are emphasized so strongly, complaining that these scenes pose sources of irritation; "Münchhausens lange Reise zum Mond. Eine Filmlegende in ihrer ursprünglichen Fassung," *Deutsche Zeitung,* 9 June 1978.

81. Lacoue-Labarthe and Nancy, "The Nazi Myth," p. 307.

82. See Sloterdijk, *Critique of Cynical Reason,* p. 484, where he cites such modern examples as Thomas Mann's Felix Krull, the international thief Manolescu, and the

Captain of Köpenick. This gallery of cynics might also include Fritz Lang's Mabuse and Haghi, Pabst's Khalibiew and Mackie Messer, and the sinister Wenzel of Karl Grune's *Brüder Schellenberg* (*Two Brothers*, 1926).

83. Volker Baer, "Im Widerspruch zur Zeit. Zur Wiederaufführung des Films *Münchhausen* von 1942/43," *Der Taggespiegel*, 25 June 1978.

84. Contemporary critics lauded the film's artful play of deception. See, for instance, Paul Beyer, "*Münchhausen*. Der neue Ufa-Farbfilm mit Hans Albers im Capitol," *Leipziger Neueste Nachrichten*, 24 July 1943: "The laws of our more sober world are suspended. A cheerful bluff rules. For two hours you believe the unbelievable and joyfully submit to the magician's magic."

85. This endeavor is part of what Jeffrey Herf describes as the Nazi design to deliver technology from Jewish materialism and abstraction in the name of "a cultural revolution that restored feeling and immediacy to a world threated by soulless rationality"; *Reactionary Modernism: Technology, Culture, and Politics in Weimar and the Third Reich* (Cambridge: Cambridge University Press, 1984), p. 229.

86. See Neumann, Belling, and Betz, *Film-"Kunst," Film-Kohn, Film-Korruption*, p. 10: "The first four decades of German film history are to the greatest and definitive degree the history of Jewish 'art' in all its different shapes, the history of its Kohns in their various shades and of corruption in its every conceivable fashion. This history is one of tyranny and decline, of boundless mediocrity."

87. See J. P. Stern, *Hitler: The Führer and the People* (Berkeley: University of California Press, 1975), p. 35: "The histrionic self is indeed 'committed': not, however, to an idea or an ideal, nor to anything outside itself, but to the performance of its own act of commitment."

88. Contemporary studio advertisements heralded the film as "born from the yearning of the German heart," unwittingly suggesting the urgency behind the production. See as well Georg Herzberg, "*Münchhausen*," *Film-Kurier*, 5 March 1943: on the surface, the film is like a colorful and amusing picturebook. On a more profound level, though, it is a creation "that appeals to our hearts and causes us to contemplate our very being."

89. The journalist Ursula von Kardorff described how in April 1944 German film actors and staff from the Foreign Office holed up in the Berlin Hotel Adlon and passed the hours during air raids with a popular charade game known as "Hollywood": "Aribert Wäscher as the Sphinx, Paul Hartmann as Venus in fur, Wilfried Seyffert as [Grillparzer's] *Ahnfrau*—all of them are fantastic"; von Kardorff, *Berliner Aufzeichnungen 1942–1945*, ed. Peter Hartl (Stuttgart: Deutscher Taschenbuch Verlag, 1994), p. 176. Von Kardorff's war diaries record the different survival strategies that Germans employed in a situation of constant threat. For a valuable collection of wartime responses, see also Hans Dieter Schäfer, ed., *Berlin im Zweiten Weltkrieg*, 2nd rev. ed. (Munich/Zürich: Piper, 1991); and Walter Kempowski, *Das Echolot. Ein kollektives Tagebuch Januar und Februar 1943* (Munich: Knaus, 1993).

90. After 1941, flashbacks abound in German productions, quite in contrast to films from 1933 to the end of the decade, in which temporal detours are rare. In *Die Feuer-*

zangenbowle (*The Punch Bowl,* 1944), the Heinz Rühmann protagonist dresses up as his younger self and masquerades as a high school student. The film allows him literally to flash back in time and to regain his lost youth. Similar to *Münchhausen,* a dissolve transforms the character's image, and the conclusion casts his countenance in flames. The preponderance of films dealing with something lost (a loss often put on display in flashbacks) is apparent in many films released in 1943. Note the numerous film titles that bear temporal referents or narratives that manifest flashback structures: *Späte Liebe (Late Love), Damals (Back Then), Liebesgeschichten* (*Love Stories,* a film that features images of an intact Berlin before World War I), *Nacht ohne Abschied (Night with no Goodbye), Gefährtin eines Sommers (One Summer's Companion), Altes Herz wird wieder jung (An Old Heart Grows Young Again), Liebe, Leidenschaft und Leid (Love, Passion, and Sorrow), Symphonie eines Lebens (Symphony of a Life), Romanze in Moll (Romance in a Minor Key), Wien 1910 (Vienna 1910), Reise in die Vergangenheit (Journey to the Past), Gefährlicher Frühling (The Perils of Spring),* and *Immensee.*

Epilogue

1. Various Weimar films were remade during the Third Reich, including *Schloß Vogelöd* (1936), *Der Student von Prag* (1935), *Das indische Grabmal* (1938), *Kohlhiesels Töchter* (1943), *Die Geierwally* (1940), and *Die Finanzen des Großherzogs* (1934). Willi Forst and Viktor Tourjansky provided ersatz Lubitsch fare, and passages of Karl Ritter's *Verräter* (1936) resembled Lang's *Das Testament des Dr. Mabuse* (1933). Numerous Weimar generic legacies continued without a break in the Third Reich: Prussia films (especially military dramas featuring Frederick the Great and starring Otto Gebühr), *Heimat-* and mountain films, costume films with historical settings, musicals with matinee idols such as Lilian Harvey and Willy Fritsch, action films with Harry Piel, Ufa *Kulturfilme,* and big-city symphonies by Walter Ruttmann.

2. See Hans-Peter Kochenrath, "Kontinuität im deutschen Film," in *Film und Gesellschaft in Deutschland. Dokumente und Materialien,* ed. Wilfried von Bredow and Rolf Zurek (Hamburg: Hoffmann und Campe, 1975), pp. 286–292. Remakes of Nazi films in the postwar period include Wolfgang Liebeneiner's . . . *und ewig bleibt die Liebe* (1954, based on *Johannisfeuer), Urlaub auf Ehrenwort* (1955), *Waldwinter* (1956), and *Franziska* (1957, based on the Käutner film *Auf Wiedersehen, Franziska!*). Hans Deppe remade *Heideschulmeister Uwe Karsten* in 1954 with Claus Holm, Barbara Rütting, and Katharina Mayberg. Carl Froelich's *Krach um Jolanthe* became Rudolf Schündler's *Das fröhliche Dorf* (1955). Some other recasts are *Bel ami* (1955), *Dunja* (1955, Josef von Baky's variation on *Der Postmeister*), *Das Bad auf den Tenne* (Paul Martin, 1956), *Kitty und die große Welt* (1956, based on *Kitty und die Weltkonferenz*), *Wenn wir alle Engel wären* (1956, a new version of *Die Feuerzangenbowle*), *Der Maulkorb* (1958), and *Robert und Bertram* (1961).

3. Joseph Goebbels, "Rede vor den Filmschaffenden am 28.2.1942 in Berlin,"

quoted in Gerd Albrecht, *Nationalsozialistische Filmpolitik* (Stuttgart: Enke, 1969), p. 500.

4. *The Goebbels Diaries: 1939–1941,* trans. and ed. Fred Taylor (Harmondsworth: Penguin, 1984), p. 26.

5. Ibid., p. 149.

6. *The Goebbels Diaries 1942–1943,* trans. and ed. Louis P. Lochner (Garden City, N.Y.: Doubleday, 1948), p. 221.

7. See Hermann Wanderscheck's lead article, "Die Macht der Musik im Film," *Film-Kurier,* 19 January 1942. Many scenes in leading films prove, claim the author, "that music can often be more essential than dialogues, actors, or visuals. It can compete with the soul of the image—the image remains silent, but music resounds, roars, paints, rings out in major and minor keys, spreading itself out like a rug over the image or flickering upward like a flame to provide the most powerful expression of redemption and liberation."

8. Leni Riefenstahl, *Hinter den Kulissen des Reichsparteitag-Films* (Munich: Eher, 1935), p. 28.

9. Nicos Poulantzas, *Fascism and Dictatorship* (London: Humanities Books, 1974), p. 347.

10. Veit Harlan, "Der Farbfilm marschiert," in *Der Deutsche Film 1943/44. Kleines Handbuch für die deutsche Presse,* ed. Karl Klär (Berlin: Deutsche Filmvertriebs-Gesellschaft, 1943), p. 77.

11. Wim Wenders, "That's Entertainment: Hitler (1977)," in *West German Filmmakers on Film,* ed. Eric Rentschler (New York/London: Holmes & Meier, 1988), p. 128.

12. Niklaus Schilling, "Tradition im Kino, 15.10.78," *Filmforum* (Düsseldorf), December 1978, p. 61.

13. See André Gerely's survey, "Rechter Geschmack am NS-Film," *Medium* 13.10 (October 1983): 35–37.

14. Don DeLillo, *Americana* (1971; reprint, New York: Penguin, 1989), p. 299.

15. See, for instance, Walter Berten, "Musik durch Film, Funk und Schallplatte," *Der Deutsche Film* 1.7 (January 1937): "Without question the majority of the populace finds its desire for entertainment and its hunger for music to a great degree satisfied by radio, films, and records." The possibilities of mass reproduction, though, would not be fully realized until the popular media succeeded in "freeing people from time and space so as to free up more time for spiritual and intellectual life" (p. 200).

16. See the discussion about modern media advertising in DeLillo, *Americana,* pp. 270–271.

17. See T. W. Adorno, "Freudian Theory and the Pattern of Fascist Propaganda," in *The Essential Frankfurt School Reader,* ed. Andrew Arato and Eike Gebhardt (New York: Urizen, 1978), p. 134: "It may well be the secret of fascist propaganda that it simply takes men for what they are: the true children of today's standardized mass culture, largely robbed of autonomy and spontaneity, instead of setting goals the realization of which would transcend the psychological *status quo* no less than the social one.

Fascist propaganda has only to *reproduce* the existent mentality for its own purposes;—it need not induce a change—and the compulsive repetition which is one of its foremost characteristics will be at one with the necessity for this continuous reproduction."

18. In the fall of 1944 Adorno described an American war documentary that dehumanized the enemy in a manner redolent of Nazi propaganda: "Cinema newsreel: the invasion of the Marianas, including Guam. The impression is not of battles, but of civil engineering and blasting operations undertaken with immeasurably intensified vehemence, also of 'fumigation,' insect-extermination on a terrestrial scale. Works are put in hand, until no grass grows. The enemy acts as patient and corpse. Like the Jews under Fascism, he features now as merely the object of technical and administrative measures, and should he defend himself, his own action immediately takes on the same character. Satanically, indeed, more initiative is in a sense demanded here than in old-style war: it seems to cost the subject his whole energy to achieve subjectlessness. Consummate inhumanity is the realization of Edward Grey's humane dream, war without hatred"; *Minima Moralia: Reflections from Damaged Life,* trans. E. F. N. Jephcott (London: Verso, 1978), p. 56. These are chilling words; in the light of American media coverage of the Persian Gulf War, they have become even more chilling.

19. "In a totalitarian state," observes J. Hoberman, "entertainment is an obvious function of politics. But in the American mediacracy, where TV has hopelessly blurred the distinction between art and life, private and public, great and petty, it would seem that the reverse is closer to the truth"; "The Star Who Fell to Earth," in *Vulgar Modernism: Writing on Movies and Other Media* (Philadelphia: Temple University Press, 1991), p. 64.

BIBLIOGRAPHY

For a valuable earlier research and source guide, see Richard Alan Nelson's three-part inventory, "Germany and the German Film, 1930–1945: An Annotated Research Bibliography," which appeared in the *Journal of the University Film Association:* "Part I. Books, Dissertations, and Pamphlets," 29.1 (Winter 1977): 45–66; "Part II. Articles and Periodicals," 29.2 (Spring 1977): 67–80; "Part III. Research Libraries, Archives, and Other Sources," 30.1 (Winter 1978): 53–72.

Periodicals

Der Bildwart
Cahiers du cinéma
Der Deutsche Film
Deutsche Filmzeitung
Der deutsche Kulturfilm
dif: filmkundliche mitteilungen
epd Film
epd Kirche und Film
F-Filmjournal
Film
Der Film
Film-Atelier
Film Comment
Film Culture
Der Film heute und morgen
Film-Korrespondenz
Filmkritik
Der Film-Kurier
Film-Kurier Index
Film-Nachrichten
Film Quarterly
Films and Filming
Films in Review
Der Filmspiegel
Filmstudio
Film und Bild
Film und Fernsehen
Filmwärts
Filmwelt
Filmwoche
Frauen und Film
Hollywood Quarterly
Die Information
Das Innere Reich
Kinematograph
Lichtbild-Bühne
Medium
Monthly Film Bulletin
Nationalsozialistische Monatshefte
New German Critique
New York Times
Prisma
Das Reich
Sight and Sound
Ufa Feldpost
Variety

Film and Cinema in the Nazi Public Sphere

Bagier, Guido. *Das tönende Licht.* Berlin: Gross, 1943.

Belling, Curt. *Der Film im Dienste der Partei. Die Bedeutung des Films als publizistischer Faktor.* Berlin: Lichtspielbühne, 1936.

——— *Der Film in Staat und Partei.* Berlin: Verlag "Der Film," 1936.

Belling, Curt, and Alfred Schultze. *Der Film in der Hitler-Jugend.* Berlin: Limpert, 1937.

Betz, Hans-Walther. *Weißbuch des deutschen Films.* Berlin: Verlag "Der Film," 1936.

Boehmer, Henning von, and Helmut Reitz. *Der Film in Wirtschaft und Recht: Seine Herstellung und Verwertung.* Berlin: Heymanns, 1933.

Böttcher, Ilse. *Film und Tageszeitung: Vergleich ihrer Struktur und Wirkungsmöglichkeit.* Borna-Leipzig: Noske, 1937.

Das deutsche Filmschaffen im vierten Kriegsjahr. Berlin: Ufa, 1943.

Funk, Alois. *Film und Jugend.* Munich: Reinhardt, 1934.

Giese, Hans-Joachim. *Die Film-Wochenschau im Dienste der Politik.* Dresden: Dittert, 1940.

Goebbels, Joseph. *Final Entries 1945: The Diaries of Joseph Goebbels.* Ed. Hugh Trevor-Roper. Trans. Richard Barry. New York: Putnam, 1978.

——— *The Goebbels Diaries: 1939–1941.* Ed. and trans. Fred Taylor. Harmondsworth: Penguin, 1984.

——— *The Goebbels Diaries 1942–1943.* Ed. and trans. Louis P. Lochner. Garden City, N.Y.: Doubleday, 1948.

——— *Tagebücher 1924–1945.* Ed. Ralf Georg Reuth. 5 vols. Munich: Piper, 1992.

Götz, Karl August. *Der Film als journalistisches Phänomen.* Düsseldorf: Nolte, 1937.

Groll, Gunter. *Film. Die unentdeckte Kunst.* Munich: Beck, 1937.

Günther, Walther. *Der Film als politisches Führungsmittel.* Leipzig: Noske, 1934.

Hippler, Fritz. *Betrachtungen zum Filmschaffen.* Berlin: Hesse, 1942.

Iros, Ernst. *Wesen und Dramaturgie des Films.* Zürich/Leipzig: Niehans, 1938.

Kalbus, Oskar. *Vom Werden deutscher Filmkunst.* 2 vols. Altona-Bahrenfeld: Cigaretten-Bilderdienst, 1935.

Kauer, Edmund Th. *Der Film. Vom Werden einer neuen Kunstgattung.* Berlin: Deutsche Buch-Gemeinschaft, 1943.

Klär, Karl, ed. *Der Deutsche Film 1942/43. Erste Staffel. Uebersicht der Filmproduktion. Struktur des Filmschaffens in Deutschland.* Berlin: Deutsche Filmvertriebs-Gesellschaft, 1942.

——— *Der Deutsche Film 1943/44. Kleines Film-Handbuch für die deutsche Presse.* Berlin: Deutsche Filmvertriebs-Gesellschaft, 1943.

——— *Der Deutsche Film 1945. Kleines Film-Handbuch für die deutsche Presse.* Berlin: Deutsche Filmvertriebs-Gesellschaft, 1944.

Klitzsch, Ludwig. *Bekenntnis zum deutschen Film.* Berlin: Privatdruck, 1941.

Koch, Heinrich, and Heinrich Braune. *Von deutscher Filmkunst. Gehalt und Gestalt.* Berlin: Scherping, 1943.

Kolb, Richard, and Heinrich Siekmeier, eds. *Rundfunk und Film im Dienste nationaler Kultur.* Düsseldorf: Floeder, 1933.

Kriegk, Otto. *Der deutsche Film im Spiegel der Ufa. 25 Jahre Kampf und Vollendung.* Berlin: Ufa-Buchverlag, 1943.

Kullmann, Max. "Die Entwicklung des deutschen Lichtspieltheaters." Diss. Univ. Nürnberg, 1935.

Lehnich, Oswald, ed. *Jahrbuch der Reichsfilmkammer 1937.* Berlin: Hesse, 1937.

——— *Jahrbuch der Reichsfilmkammer 1938.* Berlin: Hesse, 1938.

——— *Jahrbuch der Reichsfilmkammer 1939.* Berlin: Hesse, 1939.

Müller, Gottfried. *Dramaturgie des Theaters und des Films.* Würzburg: Triltsch, 1941.

Neumann, Carl, Curt Belling, and Hans-Walther Betz. *Film-"Kunst," Film-Kohn, Film-Korruption.* Berlin: Scherping, 1937.

Oertel, Rudolf. *Filmspiegel. Ein Brevier aus der Welt des Films.* Vienna: Frick, 1941.

Panofsky, Walter. *Die Geburt des Films.* Würzburg-Aumühle: Triltsch, 1940.

Rabenalt, Arthur Maria. *Mimus ohne Maske. Über die Schauspielkunst im Film.* Düsseldorf: Merkur, 1945.

Rehlinger, Bruno. *Der Begriff Filmisch.* Emsdetten: Lechte, 1938.

Reichsfilmkammer, ed. *Almanach der deutschen Filmschaffenden 1938/39.* Berlin: Hesse, 1938.

Retschlag-Zimmermann, Eve. "Geschichtliche Entwicklung und Bedeutung des Problemfilms." Diss. Univ. Leipzig, 1944.

Riefenstahl, Leni. *Hinter den Kulissen des Reichsparteitag-Films.* Munich: Eher, 1935.

——— *Kampf im Schnee und Eis.* Leipzig: Hesse und Becker, 1933.

——— *Schönheit im Olympischen Kampf.* Berlin: Deutscher Verlag, 1937.

Rohwer-Kahlmann, Harry. *Die Reichsfilmkammer. Ständischer Aufbau und Hoheitsmacht.* Leipzig: Noske, 1936.

Sander, A. U. *Jugendfilm im Nationalsozialismus.* Berlin: Jugend und Film, 1944.

Sattig, Ewald. *Die deutsche Filmpresse.* Breslau: Brehmer & Minuth, 1937.

Schamoni, Victor. *Das Lichtspiel. Möglichkeiten des absoluten Films.* Hamm: Reimann, 1936.

Schubert, Walter. *Das Filmrecht des nationalsozialistischen Staates.* Würzburg: Triltsch, 1939.

Serda, Charlotte. *Das Farbfoto-Buch vom Film.* Leipzig: Breitkopf & Härtel, 1941.

Siska, Heinz W., ed. *Wunderwelt Film. Künstler und Werkleute einer Weltmacht.* Heidelberg: Hüthig, 1943.

Taussig, Hans. *Entschleierte Filmwelt. Erlebtes aus fünfzehn Jahren Filmarbeit.* Brünn: Stil-Verlag, 1936.

Traub, Hans. *Der Film als politisches Machtmittel.* Munich: Münchener Druck- und Verlagshaus, 1933.

——— *Die Ufa-Lehrschau. Der Weg des Films von der Planung bis zur Vorführung.* Berlin: Ufa-Buchverlag, 1941.

———, ed. *Die Ufa. Ein Beitrag zur Entwicklungsgeschichte des deutschen Filmschaffens.* Berlin: Ufa-Buchverlag, 1943.

Traub, Hans, and Hanns Wilhelm Lavies, eds. *Das deutsche Filmschrifttum.* Leipzig: Hiersemann, 1940.

Ufa-Lehrschau, ed. *25 Jahre Wochenschau der Ufa.* Berlin: Illustrierte Filmwoche, 1939.

Weinschenk, Harry E. *Schauspieler erzählen.* Berlin: Limpert, 1941.

——— *Wir von Bühne und Film.* Berlin: Limpert, 1939.

Werder, Peter von. *Trugbild und Wirklichkeit. Aufgaben des Films im Umbruch der Zeit.* Leipzig: Schwarzhäupter, 1943.

Wortig, Kurt. *Der Film in der deutschen Tageszeitung.* Frankfurt am Main: Diesterweg, 1940.

Memoirs, Star Studies, and Nostalgia

Ball, Gregor, and Eberhard Spiess. *Heinz Rühmann und seine Filme.* Munich: Goldmann, 1982.

Belach, Helga, ed. *Henny Porten. Der erste deutsche Filmstar 1880–1960.* Berlin: Haude & Spener, 1986.

Berger, Erich M. *Heinrich George im Film seiner Zeit.* Wiesbaden: Deutsche Gesellschaft für Filmdokumentation, 1975.

Bergmann, Werner. *Das verwundete Objektiv. Ein Bericht aus Briefen und Notizen 1939–1943.* Berlin: Aufbau, 1992.

Beyer, Friedemann. *Die Gesichter der UFA. Starportraits einer Epoche.* Munich: Heyne, 1992.

——— *Die UFA-Stars im Dritten Reich. Frauen für Deutschland.* Munich: Heyne, 1991.

Bie, Richard. *Emil Jannings. Eine Diagnose des deutschen Films.* Berlin: Frundsberg, 1936.

Blumenberg, Hans-Christoph. *In meinem Herzen, Schatz . . . Die Lebensreise des Schauspielers und Sängers Hans Albers.* Frankfurt am Main: Fischer, 1991.

Bock, Hans-Michael, and Wolfgang Jacobsen, eds. *Olga Tschechowa. Film-Materialien* 4 (June 1993).

Borgelt, Hans. *Grete Weiser. Herz mit Schnauze.* Berlin: Blanvalet, 1971.

——— *Das süßeste Mädel der Welt. Die Lilian-Harvey-Story.* Bayreuth: Hestia, 1974.

Brandlmeier, Thomas. "Hans Moser." In *CineGraph,* installment 7. Munich: edition text + kritik, 1987. Pp. E1–E4.

——— "Heinz Rühmann." In *CineGraph,* installment 8. Munich: edition text + kritik, 1987. Pp. E1–E6.

——— "Willy Birgel." In *CineGraph,* installment 19. Munich: edition text + kritik, 1992. Pp. E1–E2.

Braun, Harald. *Ein Buch des Gedenkens.* Witten: Eckart, 1961.

Brinker, Käthe. *Nordische Filmsterne. Zarah Leander, Kristina Söderbaum, Ingrid Bergman, Greta Garbo.* Berlin: Mölich, 1938.

Cadenbach, Joachim. *Hans Albers.* Berlin: Universitas, 1975.

Cichocki, Max, and Ingeborg Jessultat. *Die großen Zwei. Hans Albers, Harry Piel.* Berlin: Selbstverlag, 1972.

Cziffra, Géza von. *Das Beste aus meiner Witz- und Anekdotensammlung vom Film.* Munich: Heyne, 1977.

——— *Es war eine rauschende Ballnacht. Eine Sittengeschichte des deutschen Films.* Frankfurt am Main: Ullstein, 1987.

——— *Kauf dir einen bunten Luftballon. Erinnerungen an Götter und Halbgötter.* Munich: Herbig, 1975.

Dachs, Robert. *Willi Forst. Eine Biographie.* Vienna: Kremayr & Scherlau, 1986.

Dagover, Lil. *Ich war die Dame. Autobiographie.* Munich: Schneekluth, 1979.

Dahlke, Paul. *Heiteres Sternbild.* Stuttgart: Blüchert, 1958.

Dombrowski, Inge, and Rudolf Borchert. *Johannes Heesters.* Bergisch-Gladbach: Lübbe, 1993.

Drews, Berta. *Heinrich George. Ein Schauspielerleben.* Reinbek bei Hamburg: Rowohlt, 1959.

Eckardt, Felix von. *Ein unordentliches Leben. Lebenserinnerungen.* Düsseldorf/Vienna: Econ, 1967.

Eggebrecht, Axel. *Der halbe Weg. Zwischenbilanz einer Epoche.* Reinbek bei Hamburg: Rowohlt, 1975.

Eser, Willibald. *Helmut Käutner. "Abblenden." Sein Leben, seine Filme.* Munich: Moewig, 1981.

——— *Theo Lingen. Komiker aus Versehen.* Munich/Vienna: Langen Müller, 1986.

Fanck, Arnold. *Er führte Regie mit Gletscher, Stürmen und Lawinen. Ein Filmpionier erzählt.* Munich: Nymphenburger, 1973.

Fernau, Rudolf. *Als Lied begann's. Lebenstagebuch eines Schauspielers.* Berlin: Ullstein, 1972.

Fischer, Helmar Rudolf. " 'Was gestrichen ist, kann nicht durchfallen.' Trauerarbeit, Vergangenheitsverdrängung oder sentimentalische Glorifizierung? Wie sich Schauspieler an ihre Arbeit im Dritten Reich erinnern." *Theater heute* 9 (September 1989): 1–21.

Fontana, Oskar Maurus. *Hans Moser. Volkskomiker und Menschendarsteller.* Vienna: Kremayr & Scherlau, 1965.

Forster, Rudolf. *Das Spiel—mein Leben.* Berlin: Propyläen, 1967.

Fritsch, Willy . . . *das kommt nicht wieder. Erinnerungen eines Filmschauspielers.* Zürich/Stuttgart: Classen, 1963.

Fröhlich, Gustav. *Waren das Zeiten. Mein Film-Heldenleben.* Munich: Herbig, 1984.

Goertz, Heinrich. *Gustaf Gründgens.* Reinbek bei Hamburg: Rowohlt, 1982.

Goetz, Wolfgang. *Werner Krauß.* Hamburg: Hoffmann und Campe, 1954.

Gregor, Joseph. *Meister deutscher Schauspielkunst. Krauß, Klöpfer, Jannings, George.* Bremen/Vienna: Schünemann, 1939.

Haack, Käthe. *In Berlin und anderswo.* Munich: Herbig, 1971.

Habich, Christiane, ed. *Lilian Harvey.* Berlin: Haude & Spener, 1990.

Harlan, Veit. *Im Schatten meiner Filme.* Gütersloh: Mohn, 1966.

Heesters, Johannes. *Ich bin gottseidank nicht mehr jung.* Munich: Ferenczy/Bruckmann, 1993.

Heinzlmeier, Adolf, Jürgen Menningen, and Berndt Schulz. *Die großen Stars des deutschen Kinos.* Herford: Busse + Seewald, 1985.

Heinzlmeier, Adolf, Bernd Schulz, and Karsten Witte. *Die Unsterblichen des* Kinos. Vol. 2: *Glanz und Mythos der Stars der 40er und 50er Jahre.* Frankfurt am Main: Fischer, 1980.

Henckels, Paul. *Ich war kein Musterknabe. Eines Lebenskünstlers lachende Weisheit.* Berlin: Blanvalet, 1956.

Herzog, Peter, and Gene Vazzana. *Brigitte Helm: From Metropolis to Gold.* New York: Corvin, 1994.

Hindermann, Aenny. *Lied eines Lebens. Wegstrecken mit Paul Wegener.* Minden: Bruns, 1950.

Hippler, Fritz. *Die Verstrickung. Einstellungen und Rückblenden.* Düsseldorf: Mehr Wissen, 1981.

Holba, Herbert. *Emil Jannings.* Ulm: Knorr, 1979.

Holt, Hans. *Jeder Tag hat einen Morgen. Erinnerungen.* Munich: Herbig, 1990.

Hörbiger, Paul. *Ich hab für euch gespielt. Erinnerungen.* Munich: Herbig, 1979.

Horney, Brigitte. *So oder so ist das Leben. Eine unvergeßliche Schauspielerin erzählt ihr Leben.* Munich: Scherz, 1992.

Ihering, Herbert. *Emil Jannings. Baumeister seines Lebens und seiner Filme.* Heidelberg: Hüthig, 1941.

——— *Käthe Dorsch.* Munich: Zinnen, 1944.

——— *Von Josef Kainz bis Paula Wessely.* Heidelberg: Hüthig, 1942.

Ihering, Herbert, and Eva Wisten. *Eduard von Winterstein.* Berlin: Henschel, 1961.

Jacobsen, Wolfgang, and Klaus Nothnagel. "Karl Valentin." In *CineGraph,* installment 3. Munich: edition text + kritik, 1985. Pp. E1–E2.

Jannings, Emil. *Theater, Film—Das Leben und ich.* Berchtesgaden: Zimmer & Herzog, 1951.

Jary, Micaela. *Ich weiß, es wird einmal ein Wunder gescheh'n. Die große Liebe der Zarah Leander.* Berlin: edition q, 1993.

Joachim Gottschalk. Dem Gedenken eines deutschen Schauspielers. Cottbus: Nationale Front des demokratischen Deutschland, 1956.

Kalbus, Oskar. *Die besten Jahre eines Lebens für den Film. Eine Rückblende auf sieben Jahrzehnte (1890–1960).* Wiesbaden: Film-Echo, 1961.

Kästner, Hans-Gerd, and Wolf-Rüdiger Ohlhoff, eds. *Günther Lüders. Materialien zur Gedenkstunde und Retrospektive.* Lübeck: Amt für Kultur, 1985.

Käutner, Helmut. *Abblenden.* Munich: Moewig, 1981.

Kemp, Paul. *Blühendes Unkraut. Heiteres aus meinem Leben.* Bonn: Athenäum, 1953.

Kirst, Hans Hellmut, and Matthias Forster. *Das große Heinz-Rühmann Buch.* Grünwald: Greil, 1990.

Knudsen, Hans. *O. E. Hasse.* Berlin: Rembrandt, 1960.

Knuth, Gustav. *Mit einem Lächeln im Knopfloch.* Hamburg: Glöss, 1974.

Koch, Heinrich. *Heinrich George.* Berlin: Curtius, 1940.

Koselka, Fritz. *Ein kleiner großer Mann. Hans Moser.* Vienna: Eberle, 1946.

Kowa, Viktor de. *Achduliebzeit. Aus dem Libretto meines Lebens.* Stuttgart: Deutsche Verlagsanstalt, 1971.

Kratochvil, Antonín. *Abendgespräche mit Luis Trenker.* Munich: Athos, 1980.

Krauss, Werner. *Das Schauspiel meines Lebens. Einem Freund erzählt.* Ed. Hans Weigel. Stuttgart: Goverts, 1958.

Kreuder, Peter. *Nur Puppen haben keine Tränen. Ein Lebensbericht.* Bergisch-Gladbach: Lübbe, 1973.

Krützen, Michaela. *Hans Albers. Eine deutsche Karriere.* Weinheim: Quadriga, 1995.

Kuhlbrodt, Dietrich. "Otto Gebühr." In *CineGraph,* installment 4. Munich: edition text + kritik, 1985. Pp. E1–E2.

Kühn, Detlev. "Der Erfolg des schönen faulen Zaubers: Zum 25. Todestag von Hans Albers." *epd Film* 2.7 (July 1985): 20–21.

Kurowski, Ulrich. "Zum 90. Geburtstag von Heinz Rühmann." *epd Film* 9.3 (March 1992): 5.

Kurowski, Ulrich, et al., eds. *Karl Valentin. Fundsachen.* 4 vols. Munich: Münchner Filmzentrum/Münchner Filmmuseum, 1976, 1977, 1982.

Leander, Zarah. *Es war so wunderbar! Mein Leben.* Hamburg: Hoffmann & Campe, 1973.

Lenssen, Claudia. "Sinnlichkeit abstrakt." *epd Kirche und Film* 34.8 (August 1981): 23–24. (on Zarah Leander)

Luft, Friedrich. *Grete Weiser. Herz mit Schnauze.* Berlin: Blanvalet, 1971.

——— *Gustaf Gründgens.* Berlin: Rembrandt, 1958.

Lundquist, Gunnar. "Hans Albers." *Films in Review* 16 (March 1965): 150–167.

Maisch, Herbert. *Helm ab—Vorhang auf. Siebzig Jahre eines ungewöhnlichen Lebens.* Emsdetten: Lechte, 1968.

Martens, Valérie von, ed. *Das große Curt Goetz-Album. Bilder eines Lebens.* Stuttgart: Deutsche Verlagsanstalt, 1968.

Mertens, Eberhard, ed. . . . *reitet für Deutschland. Das Willy Birgel—Erinnerungsbuch.* Hildesheim/New York: Olms, 1979.

Mesalla, Horst. "Heinrich George. Versuch einer Rekonstruktion der schauspielerischen Leistung unter besonderer Berücksichtigung der zeitgenössischen Publizistik." Diss. Freie Universität Berlin, 1969.

Mihelic, Dagmar. "Paul Hartmann." Diss. Univ. Wien, 1959.

Milde, Maria. *Berlin Glienicker Brücke. Als Hiller-Girl um die Welt. Die Ufa-Zeit in Babelsberg.* Munich: Universitas, 1978.

Nottebohm, Rudolf. *Fast ein Jahrhundert. Luis Trenker.* Munich: Herbig, 1987.

Peipp, Matthias, and Bernhard Springer, eds. *Ich bin ein Anhänger der Stille. Ein Gespräch mit Heinz Rühmann.* Munich: belleville, 1994.

Rabenalt, Arthur Maria. "Die eherne Zeit. Erinnerungen von Arthur Maria Rabenalt." In *Europa 1939. Filme aus zehn Ländern.* Ed. Hans Helmut Prinzler. Berlin: Stiftung Deutsche Kinemathek, 1989. Pp. 61–64.

——— *Film im Zwielicht.* Hildesheim: Olms, 1978.

——— *Joseph Goebbels und der "Großdeutsche" Film.* Munich: Herbig, 1985.

Reiht-Zanthier, Jobst von. *Sie machten uns glücklich. Erinnerungen an große Schauspieler in goldenen und nicht nur goldenen Jahren.* Munich: Ehrenwirth, 1967.

Riefenstahl, Leni. *A Memoir.* New York: St. Martin's, 1993.

Riess, Curt. *Die Frau mit den hundert Gesichtern. Requiem für Heidemarie Hatheyer.* Düsseldorf: Droste, 1991.

——— *Das gab's nur einmal. Die große Zeit des deutschen Films.* Vienna/Munich: Molden, 1977.

——— *Gustaf Gründgens. Eine Biographie.* Hamburg: Hoffmann und Campe, 1965.

Rökk, Marika. *Herz mit Paprika.* Berlin: Universitas, 1974.

Rühmann, Heinz. *Das war's. Erinnerungen.* Frankfurt: Ullstein, 1982.

Sakkara, Michele, ed. *Die große Zeit des deutschen Films 1933–1945.* Leoni am Starnberger See: Druffel, 1980.

Sanders, Ulrike. *Zarah Leander—Kann denn Schlager Sünde sein?* Cologne: Pahl-Rugenstein, 1988.

Sanders-Brahms, Helma. "Ein kleiner Mann. Anmerkungen zu einem deutschen Publikumsliebling." In *Jahrbuch Film 82/83.* Ed. Hans Günther Pflaum. Munich: Hanser, 1982. Pp. 52–60. (on Heinz Rühmann)

——— "Zarah." In *Jahrbuch Film 81/82.* Ed. Hans Günther Pflaum. Munich: Hanser, 1981. Pp. 165–172.

Sandrock, Adele. *Mein Leben.* Ed. Wilhelmine Sandrock. Berlin: Buchwarte Blanvalet, 1940.

Scherzer, Ulrich. "Eugen Klöpfer. Sein Leben—sein Wirken." Diss. Univ. Wien, 1960.

Schlamp, Hans-Joachim. *Brigitte Horney.* Berlin: Mölich, 1939.

——— *Frauen um Hans Albers.* Berlin: Mölich, 1938.

——— *Lida Baarova.* Berlin: Mölich, 1938.

Schmeling, Max. *Erinnerungen.* Berlin: Ullstein, 1977.

Schmitz, Ludwig. *Verschmitztes.* Mühlhausen/Leipzig: Bergwald, 1941.

Schneider, Ute. "Brigitte Helm." In *CineGraph,* installment 4. Munich: edition text + kritik, 1985. Pp. E1–E2.

Schoenhals, Albrecht, and Anneliese Born. *Immer zu zweit. Erinnerungen.* Wiesbaden: Limes, 1977.

Schönböck, Karl. *Wie es war durch achtzig Jahr. Erinnerungen.* Munich: Langen Müller, 1988.

Schöning, Jörg. "Ernst Udet." In *CineGraph,* installment 7. Munich: edition text + kritik, 1986. Pp. E1–E2.

Schroth, Carl-Heinz. *Keine Angst vor schlechten Zeiten. Geschichte meines Lebens.* Berlin: Herbig, 1984.

Schulte, Michael. *Karl Valentin.* Reinbek bei Hamburg: Rowohlt, 1968.

Schulte, Michael, and Peter Syr, eds. *Karl Valentins Filme.* Munich/Zürich: Piper, 1989.

Schulz, Heidi. *Hans Moser. Der große Volksschauspieler wie er lebte und spielte.* Vienna: Molden, 1980.

Seesslen, Georg. "Theo Lingen." In *CineGraph,* installment 11. Munich: edition text + kritik, 1988. Pp. E1–E6.

——— "Zarah Leander." In *CineGraph,* installment 15. Munich: edition text + kritik, 1989. Pp. E1–E3.

Seiler, Paul. *Ein Mythos lebt. Zarah Leander.* Berlin: Graphische Werkstätten, 1991.

——— *Zarah Leander. Ein Kultbuch.* Reinbek bei Hamburg: Rowohlt, 1985.

Söderbaum, Kristina. *Nichts bleibt immer so. Rückblenden auf ein Leben vor und hinter der Kamera.* Bayreuth: Hestia, 1983.

Spiess, Eberhard. *Hans Albers. Eine Filmographie.* Frankfurt am Main: Kommunales Kino, 1977.

Stuhlemmer, Rupert. *Chrom, Lack und Leder. Automobile der Ufa-Stars.* Berlin: transpress, 1991.

Till, Wolfgang, ed. *Karl Valentin. Volkssänger? Dadaist?* Munich: Schirmer/Mosel: 1982.

Tötter, Otto, ed. *Hans Albers. Hoppla, jetzt komm ich!* Hamburg/Zürich: Rasch und Röhring, 1986.

Trenker, Luis. *Alles gut gegangen. Geschichten aus meinem Leben.* 2nd rev. ed. Munich: Bertelsmann, 1979.

——— *Das große Luis Trenker Buch.* Gütersloh: Bertelsmann, 1974.

Trenker, Luis, and Walter Schmidkunz. *Berge und Heimat. Das Buch von den Bergen und ihren Menschen.* Berlin: Knaur, 1935.

Uhlig, Anneliese. *Rosenkavaliers Kind. Eine Frau und drei Karrieren.* Munich: Herbig, 1977.

Ullrich, Luise. *Komm auf die Schaukel, Luise. Balance eines Lebens.* Percha: Schulz, 1973.

Weidlich, Knuth, ed. *Der blonde Hans—Mosaiksteine eines Lebens.* Hamburg: Historika Photoverlag, 1992.

Weissensteiner, Friedrich. *Publikumslieblinge. Von Hans Albers bis Paula Wessely.* Vienna: Kremayr & Scherlau, 1993.

Werner, Ilse. *So wird's nie wieder sein. Ein Leben mit Pfiff.* Bayreuth: Hestia, 1982.

Werner, Paul. *Die Skandalchronik des deutschen Films.* Vol. 1: *Von 1900 bis 1945.* Frankfurt am Main: Fischer, 1990.

Wichmann, Karin. *Hans Moser. Seine Filme—sein Leben.* Munich: Heyne, 1980.
Zumkeller, Cornelia. *Zarah Leander. Ihre Filme—ihr Leben.* Munich: Heyne, 1988.

Postwar Studies

Albrecht, Gerd. "Meisterwerke deutscher Tonfilmkunst der Jahre 1940–41." *Film-Echo/Filmwoche* 34.27 (17 May 1980): 13–16.

——— *Nationalsozialistische Filmpolitik.* Stuttgart: Enke, 1969.

———, ed. *Der Film im Dritten Reich. Eine Dokumentation.* Karlsruhe: Schauburg & Doku, 1979.

Albrecht, Gerd, Johanna Bardili, and Peter Uhlig, eds. *NS-Feiertage in Wochenschauen.* Stuttgart: Landeszentral für politische Bildung Baden-Württemberg, n.d.

Altman, John. "Movies' Role in Hitler's Conquest of German Youth." *Hollywood Quarterly* 3.4 (Summer 1948): 379–386.

Amedeo, Michael. "Frightening 'Illusions': 'Lighthearted' Nazi Films Hid Subtle Propaganda." *Chicago Sun-Times,* 30 April 1995.

Aurich, Rolf, and Heiner Behring. "Nationalsozialistische Propagandafilme. Ein Filmseminar in der Erwachsenenbildung." *medien praktisch* 4 (December 1989): 13–17.

Bandmann, Christa, and Joe Hembus. *Klassiker des deutschen Tonfilms 1930–1960.* Munich: Goldmann, 1980.

Barkhausen, Hans. "Deutsche Filme in den USA. Rückführung im Austausch." *Der Archivar* 3 (July 1966): 269–274.

——— *Filmpropaganda für Deutschland im Ersten und Zweiten Weltkrieg.* Hildesheim/Zürich/New York: Olms, 1982.

——— "Die NSDAP als Filmproduzentin." In *Zeitgeschichte im Film-und Ton-dokument.* Ed. Günter Moltmann and Karl Friedrich Reimers. Göttingen: Musterschmidt, 1970. Pp. 145–176.

Bauer, Alfred. "Die Bevormundung des deutschen Filmschaffens im Dritten Reich. Film in Ketten." *F-Filmjournal* 17 (November 1979): 17–22, 48.

——— *Deutscher Spielfilm Almanach 1929–1950.* Rev. enl. ed. Munich: Winterberg, 1976.

Beaumont, Roger. "Images of War: Films as Documentary History." *Military Affairs* 35 (February 1971): 5–7.

Bechdolf, Ute. *Wunsch-Bilder? Frauen im nationalsozialistischen Unterhaltungsfilm.* Tübingen: Tübinger Vereinigung für Volkskunde, 1992.

Becker, Wolfgang. *Film und Herrschaft. Organisationsprinzipien und Organisationsstrukturen der nationalsozialistischen Filmpropaganda.* Berlin: Spiess, 1973.

Beckley, Paul V. "Nothing Grand about Illusions in Nazi Films." *New York Herald Tribune,* 10 July 1960.

Belach, Helga, ed. *Wir tanzen um die Welt. Deutsche Revuefilme 1933–1945.* Munich: Hanser, 1979.

Benzenhöfer, Udo, and Wolfgang U. Eckart, eds. *Medizin im Spielfilm des Nationalsozialismus.* Tecklenburg: Burgverlag, 1990.

Berg-Ganschow, Ute, and Wolfgang Jacobsen, eds. . . . *Film . . . Stadt . . . Kino . . . Berlin.* Berlin: Argon, 1987.

Bitomsky, Hartmut. "Der Kotflügel eines Mercedes Benz. Nazikulturfilme, Teil I: Filme von 1933 bis 1938." *Filmkritik* 27.10 (October 1983): 443–474.

——— "Der Kotflügel eines Mercedes Benz. Nazikulturfilme, Teil II: Filme von 1939 bis 1945." *Filmkritik* 27.12 (December 1983): 543–581.

Blobner, Helmut, and Herbert Holba. "Jackboot Cinema: The Political Propaganda Film in the Third Reich." *Films and Filming* 8.3 (December 1962): 12–20.

Blum, Heiko R. *Dreißig Jahre danach. Dokumentation zur Auseinandersetzung mit dem NS in Film 1945 bis 1975.* Cologne: Freie Filmkritik-AG unabhängiger Filmjournalisten, 1975.

Bock, Hans-Michael, and Michael Töteberg, eds. *Das Ufa-Buch. Kunst und Krisen, Stars und Regisseure, Wirtschaft und Politik.* Frankfurt am Main: Zweitausendeins, 1992.

Borgelt, Hans. *Die Ufa—ein Traum.* Berlin: edition q, 1993.

Brandlmeier, Thomas, and Heidi Pillhatsch. "Der Krieg der Kameras. Filmpropaganda 1933–1946. I. Fragen der Ästhetik." *Medium* 9.8 (August 1979): 37–41.

——— "Der Krieg der Kameras. Filmpropaganda 1933–1946. II. Die Ebene der Auseinandersetzung." *Medium* 9.9 (September 1979): 35–38.

——— "Der Krieg der Kameras. Filmpropaganda 1933–1946. III. Mobilmachung. Wirkungsgeschichte." *Medium* 9.10 (October 1979): 32–36.

Brandt, Hans-Jürgen. *NS-Filmtheorie und dokumentarische Praxis. Hippler, Noldan, Junghans.* Tübingen: Niemeyer, 1987.

Bulgakowa, Oksana. "Film der totalitären Epoche (1933–1945). Stenogramm eines Kolloquiums." *Kunst und Literatur* 38.5 (September/October 1990): 516–532.

Burleigh, Michael. "Selling Murder: The Killing Films of the Third Reich." In *Death and Deliverance: "Euthanasia" in Germany 1900–1945.* Cambridge: Cambridge University Press, 1994. Pp. 183–219.

Cadars, Pierre. "L'enfer aux rideaux de soie (quelques réflexions à propos et à partir du mélodrame nazi)." *Cahiers de la cinémathèque* 28 (1979): 70–71.

Chalmers, Martin. "Notes on Nazi Propaganda." *Screen Education* 40 (Autumn/Winter 1981/82): 34–47.

Chanjutin, Juri. "Der Film im System der Propaganda des deutschen Faschismus." *Filmwissenschaftliche Beiträge* 14 (1973): 172–206.

Chrystal, William G. "Nazi Party Election Films, 1927–1938." *Cinema Journal* 15.1 (Fall 1975): 28–47.

Cornelius, Marion, and Sabine Steig, eds. *Die Ufa 1917–1945. Das deutsche Bilderimperium. Die Ausstellung* (*Ufa Magazin* no. 22). Berlin: Deutsches Historisches Museum, 1992.

Coultass, Clive. "The German Film 1933–1945." *Screen* 12.2 (Summer 1971): 38–41.

Courtade, Francis. "Die deutsch-französischen Koproduktionen." In *Kameradschaft—Querelle. Kino zwischen Deutschland und Frankreich.* Ed. Heike Hurst and Heiner Gassen. Munich: Institut Français de Munich/CICIM, 1991. Pp. 159–172.

Courtade, Francis, and Pierre Cadars. *Histoire du cinéma nazi* (Paris: Losfeld, 1972). Abridged German ed.: *Geschichte des Films im Dritten Reich.* Trans. Florian Hopf. Munich/Vienna: Hanser, 1975.

Dammeyer, Manfred. "Nationalsozialistische Filme im historisch-politischen Unterricht." *Aus Politik und Zeitgeschichte. Beilage zur Wochenzeitung Das Parlament* B 16/77 (23 April 1977): 3–16.

———, ed. *Der Spielfilm im Dritten Reich.* Oberhausen: XII. Westdeutsche Kurzfilmtage, 1966.

Dargis, Manohla. "The Damned: Confronting Cinema of the Third Reich." *LA Weekly,* 13 January 1995.

Delage, Christian. *La vision nazie de l'histoire: Le cinéma documentaire du Troisième Reich.* Lausanne: L'Age d'Homme, 1989.

Denzer, Kurt. "Untersuchungen zur Filmdramaturgie des Dritten Reiches." Diss. Univ. Kiel, 1970.

Dieterle, William. "Made in Germany." *Hollywood Quarterly* 1.1 (October 1945): 124–126.

Dolezel, Stefan. *German Newsreels 1933–1947.* Trans. Peter Green. Munich: Goethe-Institut, 1984.

Drewniak, Bogusław. *Der deutsche Film 1938–1945. Ein Gesamtüberblick.* Düsseldorf: Droste, 1987.

Dworkin, Martin S. "Clean Germans and Dirty Politics." *Film Comment* 3.1 (Winter 1965): 36–42.

Eisenstein, S. M. "On Fascism, German Cinema, and Real Life: Open Letter to the German Minister of Propaganda, Dr. Goebbels." In *Eisenstein: Writings 1922–1934.* Ed. Richard Taylor. London/Bloomington: BFI/Indiana University Press, 1988. Pp. 280–284.

Elsaesser, Thomas. "Moderne und Modernisierung. Der deutsche Film der dreißiger Jahre." *montage/av* 3.2 (1994): 23–40.

Estes, Jim. "Nazi Film—A Triumph of Evil Genius." *San Francisco Chronicle,* 28 July 1959.

"Faschismus." *Frauen und Film,* special issue, 44/45 (October 1988).

Filgers, Ulrike, et al., eds. *Nationalsozialismus. Eine Filmauswahl.* Düsseldorf: Landeszentrale für politische Bildung, 1994.

Fledelius, Karsten. "Bekehrung und Bestätigung im Spielfilm des Dritten Reichs." *Text und Kontext* 8.2 (1980): 395–410.

Ford, Charles. "Grandeur and Decadence of Ufa." *Films in Review* 4 (June–July 1953): 266–268.

Franzos, Friedel. "Wie sich die Bilder gleichen. Zur Kontinuität deutscher Filmbilder." *Filme* 8 (March–April 1981): 36–39.

Frey, Rainer. "Zum Tod im Film des Dritten Reiches." *Filmfaust* 17/18 (February 1980): 40–45.

Friedländer, Saul. *Reflections of Nazism: An Essay on Kitsch and Death.* Trans. Thomas Weyr. New York: Harper & Row, 1984.

Friedman, Régine Mihal. *L'image et son juif. Le juif dans le cinéma nazi.* Paris: Payot, 1983.

Fritz, Walter, ed. *Der Wiener Film im Dritten Reich.* Vienna: Österreichisches Filmarchiv, 1988.

Furhammar, Leif, and Folke Isaksson. *Politics and Film.* Trans. Kersti French. New York: Praeger, 1971.

Fürstenau, Theo. "Eskapismus und Camouflage." *Internationale Zeitschrift für Kommunikationsforschung* 1.3 (1974): 366–382.

——— *Propagandastrukturen im Film des Dritten Reiches.* Wiesbaden: Deutsches Institut für Filmkunde, n.d.

Gallasch, Peter F. "Kamera obskura oder Wie man aus der Not eine Untugend macht. Doppelzüngige Filmpolitik der Nazis. 'Jüdische' Filme bis 1942 in deutschen Kinos." *Film-Korrespondenz* 30.22 (23 October 1984): 6–10.

Gast, Wolfgang. "Treue und Gehorsam. Fritz Langs *Nibelungen* und die NS-Filmpropaganda." *Medium* 18.3 (July–September 1988): 18–22.

Gerely, André. "Rechter Geschmack am NS-Film." *Medium* 13.10 (October 1983): 35–37.

Gietinger, Klaus. "Ideologie im nationalsozialistischen Spielfilm." *medien + erziehung* 26.2 (1982): 84–92.

Gillett, John. "Germany: A Lost Decade." *Sight and Sound* 41.4 (Autumn 1972): 225–226.

Gleber, Anke. " 'Only Man Must Be and Remain a Judge, Soldier and Ruler of State': Female as Void in Nazi Film (*The Old and Young King, The Broken Jug, Fräulein von Barnheim*)." In *Gender and German Cinema: Feminist Interventions.* Vol. 2. Ed. Sandra Frieden et al. Providence/Oxford: Berg, 1993. Pp. 105–116.

Grunsky, Konrad. *Deutsche Volkskunde im Film. Gesellschaftliche Leitbilder im Unterrichtsfilm des Dritten Reiches.* Munich: Minerva, 1978.

Hachmeister, Sylke. *Kinopropaganda gegen Kranke.* Baden-Baden: Nomos, 1992.

Hagge, Hans. *Das gab's schon zweimal . . . Auf den Spuren der Ufa.* Berlin: Henschel, 1959.

Hanlon, Lindley P. "Film Document and the Myth of Horst Wessel: A Sampler of Nazi Propaganda." *Film and History* 5.3 (1975): 16–18.

Happel, Hans-Gerd. *Der historische Film im Nationalsozialismus.* Frankfurt am Main: R. G. Fischer, 1984.

Harms, Gerhard, and Marion Schmidt. "Tod als Gage. Kurt Gerron und das schwärzeste Kapitel der deutschen Filmgeschichte." *epd Film* 3.7 (July 1986): 16–21.

Harmssen, Henning. "Presse in der Zwangsjacke. Zur Lage der Presse und Filmkritik im Dritten Reich." *Film-Korrespondenz* 25.2 (13 February 1979): 19–23.

Hauptmann, Carl. "Der Film in totalitären Staaten." *Politische Studien* 124 (1960): 532–542.

Hausmanninger, Thomas. *Kritik der medienethischen Vernunft. Die ethische Diskussion über den Film in Deutschland im 20. Jahrhundert.* Munich: Fink, 1992.

Heinzlmeier, Adolf. *Nachkriegsfilm und Nazifilm. Anmerkungen zu einem deutschen Thema.* Badenweiler: Oase, 1988.

Hitchens, Gordon. "Nazi Films in the American Archive." *Film Library Quarterly* 5.2 (Spring 1972): 16–20.

Hoffmann, Hilmar. *Es ist noch nicht zu Ende. Sollen Nazikunst und Nazifilme wieder öffentlich gezeigt werden?* Badenweiler: Oase, 1988.

——— "Manipulation of the Masses through the Nazi Film." *Film Comment* 3.4 (Fall 1965): 34–39.

——— *The Triumph of Propaganda: Film and National Socialism 1933–1945.* Oxford: Berghahn, 1995.

——— *"Und die Fahne führt uns in die Ewigkeit." Propaganda im NS-Film.* Frankfurt am Main: Fischer, 1988.

Hoffmann, Hilmar, and Peter Kress. "German Cinema of the Nazi Period." *Film Library Quarterly* 5.2 (Spring 1972): 8–15.

Hollstein, Dorothea. *"Jud Süß" und die Deutschen. Antisemitische Vorurteile im nationalsozialistischen Spielfilm.* Frankfurt am Main: Ullstein, 1983.

Horak, Jan-Christopher. "Eros, Thanatos, and the Will to Myth: Prussian Films in German Cinema." In *Framing the Past: The Historiography of German Cinema and Television.* Ed. Bruce A. Murray and Christopher J. Wickham. Carbondale: Southern Illinois University Press, 1992. Pp. 121–139.

——— "Zionist Film Propaganda in Nazi Germany." *Historical Journal of Film, Radio and Television* 4.1 (1984): 49–58.

Huemer, Andrea. "Von der 'ewigen Hüterin' und einem Steuerungsinstrument des 'Unbewußten.' Frau und Film—Frau im Film, als Objekte der nationalsozialistischen Propaganda. Ein Erkundungsversuch." Diss. Univ. Wien, 1985.

Hull, David Stewart. *Film in the Third Reich.* 1969; reprint, New York: Simon and Schuster, 1973.

——— "Forbidden Fruit: The Harvest of the German Cinema, 1939–1945." *Film Quarterly* 14.4 (Summer 1961): 16–30.

Jacobs, Arthur. "Foreign Policy and Cinema." *Sight and Sound* 15.2 (Autumn 1946): 102–105.

Jacobsen, Wolfgang, ed. *Babelsberg. Das Filmstudio.* 3rd rev. ed. Berlin: Stiftung Deutsche Kinemathek/Argon, 1994.

Jaeger, Klaus, et al., eds. *Der Weg ins Dritte Reich. Deutscher Film und Weimars Ende. Eine Dokumentation.* Oberhausen: Laufen, 1974.

Jung, Werner. "Kunst als 'Selbstgestaltung des gesamten Zeitgeistes.' Eine Nachbemerkung zu Adam Kuckhoffs Beiträgen zur Filmästhetik." *Juni* 3.1 (March 1989): 97–100.

Kagan, Norman. "Nazi Cinema." *Filmmakers' Newsletter* 5.7 (May 1972): 30–33.

Kahlenberg, Friedrich P. "*Von deutschem Heldentum:* A 1936 Compilation Film for Television." *Historical Journal of Film, Radio and Television* 10.2 (1990): 187–192.

Kanzog, Klaus. *"Staatspolitisch besonders wertvoll." Ein Handbuch zu 30 deutschen Spielfilmen der Jahre 1934 bis 1945.* Munich: Schaudig und Ledig, 1994.

Kasten, Jürgen. "Entmündigung als Schreibprogramm. Der Autor in der NS-Filmproduktion." In *Film Schreiben. Eine Geschichte des Drehbuchs.* Vienna: Hora, 1990. Pp. 115–127.

Kayser, Erika. "Deutsche Unterhaltungsfilme der zwanziger und dreißiger Jahre." Diss. Univ. Osnabrück, 1983.

Klaus, Ulrich J. *Deutsche Tonfilme 4. Jahrgang 1933.* Berlin/Berchtesgarden: Klaus, 1992.

——— *Deutsche Tonfilme 5. Jahrgang 1934.* Berlin/Berchtesgarden: Klaus, 1993.

——— *Deutsche Tonfilme 6. Jahrgang 1935.* Berlin/Berchtesgarden: Klaus, 1995.

Klooss, Reinhard, and Thomas Reuter. *Körperbilder. Menschenornamente in Revuetheater und Revuefilm.* Frankfurt am Main: Syndikat, 1980.

Knietzsch, Horst. "Wirklichkeit und Illusionen. Zu Filmen aus dem Jahr 1937." *Prisma* 18 (1988): 209–230.

Knilli, Friedrich. " 'Perlen' der Leinwand. Zur Rezeption von NS-Filmen in der Bundesrepublik." *Film und Fernsehen* 8.8 (1980): 20–22.

Kochenrath, Hans-Peter. "Filme für den Führer. Seminarreihe über Nazi-Propaganda in der Cinemathek." *Kölner Stadt-Anzeiger,* 3 February 1973.

———, ed. *Der Film im Dritten Reich. Dokumentation zu dem Seminar im SS 1963.* Cologne: Universität zu Köln, 1963.

Konlechner, Peter, and Peter Kubelka, eds. *Propaganda und Gegenpropaganda im Film 1933–1945.* Vienna: Österreichishes Filmmuseum, 1972.

Kraatz, Karl L., ed. *Deutscher Film Katalog, 1930–1945. Ufa, Tobis, Bavaria.* Frankfurt am Main: Transit-Film, 1966.

Kracauer, Siegfried. "Supplement: Propaganda and the Nazi War Film." In *From Caligari to Hitler: A Psychological History of the German Film.* Princeton: Princeton University Press, 1947. Pp. 273–331.

Kramer, Thomas, and Dominik Siegrist. *Terra. Ein Schweizer Filmkonzern im Dritten Reich.* Zürich: Chronos, 1991.

Krebstakies, Marlies, ed. *Die UFA—auf den Spuren einer großen Filmfabrik.* Berlin: Elefanten, 1987.

Kreimeier, Klaus. "Aufmarsch im Bildfeld. Ambivalente Beobachtungen zur Konstruktion eines Mythos in deutschen Filmen der 30er und 40er Jahre." *Arnoldshainer Filmgespräche* 9 (1992): 21–37.

——— *Die Ufa-Story. Geschichte eines Filmkonzerns.* Munich/Vienna: Hanser, 1992.

———, ed. *Fanck-Trenker-Riefenstahl. Der deutsche Bergfilm und seine Folgen.* Berlin: Stiftung Deutsche Kinemathek, 1972.

Kurowski, Ulrich, ed. *Deutsche Spielfilme 1933–1945. Materialien.* 5 vols. Munich: Filmmuseum, 1978–1983.

——— "Fahrt in den deutschen Untergrund. Verbotene Film aus der Nazizeit." *Film + Ton* 24 (June 1978): 60–62.

Kuschel, Thomas. "Darstellung der Mittel, mit denen im Unterhaltungsfilm faschistische Ideologie erzeugt wurde." *Filmwissenschaftliche Mitteilungen* special issue, 1 (1965): 288–297.

Lange, Gabriele. *Das Kino als moralische Anstalt. Soziale Leitbilder und die Darstellung gesellschaftlicher Realität im Spielfilm des Dritten Reiches.* Frankfurt am Main: Lang, 1994.

Laqua, Carsten. *Wie Micky unter die Nazis fiel. Walt Disney und Deutschland.* Reinbek bei Hamburg: Rowohlt, 1992.

Leiser, Erwin. *"Deutschland, erwache!" Propaganda im Film des Dritten Reiches.* 2nd rev. ed. Reinbek bei Hamburg: Rowohlt, 1978.

——— "Legitime Manipulation. Dokumentarfilm und Geschichte am Beispiel der NS-Vergangenheit." *Medium* 22.2 (April–June 1992): 24–28.

——— *Nazi Cinema.* Trans. Gertrud Mander and David Wilson. New York: Collier, 1975.

Lieb, Rebecca. "Nazi Hate Movies Continue to Ignite Fierce Passions." *New York Times,* 4 August 1991.

Liebe, Ulrich. *Verehrt, verfolgt, vergessen. Schauspieler als Naziopfer.* Weinheim: Beltz Quadriga, 1992.

Loiperdinger, Martin. "*Why We Fight* contra *Triumph des Willens.* Feind-Bilder in der amerikanischen Gegenpropaganda." In *Widergänger. Faschismus und Antifaschismus im Film.* Ed. Joachim Schmitt-Sasse. Münster: MAkS, 1993. Pp. 76–90.

———, ed. *Märtyrerlegenden im NS-Film.* Opladen: Leske + Budrich, 1991.

Lowry, Stephen. *Pathos und Politik. Ideologie in Spielfilmen des Nationalsozialismus.* Tübingen: Niemeyer, 1991.

Lueken, Verena. *Zur Erzählstruktur des nationalsozialistischen Films. Versuch einer strukturellen Analyse.* Siegen: Universität-Gesamthochschule Siegen, 1981.

Luft, Herbert G. "The Screen as a Propaganda Weapon." *Cinema* (Beverly Hills) 5.2 (1969): 24–26.

——— "Shadow of the Swastika." *Films and Filming* 7.2 (November 1960): 10–11.

Lymberopoulos, Christopher. "Rundfunk und Film als Propagandamittel im Dritten Reich." Aachen: Historisches Institut der RWTH Aachen, 1989.

Maiwald, Klaus-Jürgen. *Filmzensur im NS-Staat.* Dortmund: Nowotny, 1983.

Malek-Kohler, Ingeborg. *Im Windschatten des Dritten Reiches. Begegnungen mit Filmkünstlern und Widerstandskämpfern.* Freiburg im Breisgau: Herder, 1986.

Manvell, Roger, and Heinrich Fraenkel. *The German Cinema.* New York: Praeger, 1971.

Manz, Peter. *Ufa und der frühe deutsche Film.* Zürich: Sanssouci, 1963.

Marcorelles, Louis. "The Nazi Cinema (1933–1945)." *Sight and Sound* 25.4 (Autumn 1955): 65–69.

Margry, Karel. " 'Theresienstadt' (1944–1945): The Nazi Propaganda Film Depicting the Concentration Camp as Paradise." *Historical Journal of Film, Radio and Television* 12.2 (1992): 145–162.

Marquardt, Axel, and Heinz Rathsack, eds. *Preußen im Film.* Reinbek bei Hamburg: Rowohlt, 1981.

Melchers, Christoph Bernhard. "Untersuchungen zur Wirkungspsychologie nationalsozialistischer Propagandafilme." Diss. Univ. Köln, 1977.

Mertens, Eberhard, ed. *Filmprogramme. Ein Querschnitt durch das deutsche Filmschaffen.* 4 vols. Hildesheim: Olms, 1977.

———, ed. *Die großen deutschen Filme. Ausgewählte Kinoprogramme 1930–1945.* Hildesheim: Olms, 1995.

Möbius, Hanno. "Heimat im nationalsozialistischen Stadtfilm." *Augen-Blick* 5 (March 1988): 31–44.

Monaco, Paul. "Motion Pictures and Ideology: Plumbing the Depths of Nazi Germany." *Quarterly Review of Film Studies* 5.2 (Spring 1980): 287–290.

Mühl-Benninghaus, Wolfgang. "The German Film Credit Bank, Inc.: Film Financing during the First Years of National-Socialist Rule in Germany." *Film History* 3.4 (1989): 317–332.

Myrick, Howard A. "The Reichsfilmkammer: A Study of Film Propaganda Management in Nazi Germany." M.A. thesis University of Southern California, 1967.

Neale, Steve. "Propaganda." *Screen* 18.3 (Autumn 1977): 9–40.

Netzeband, Günter. "D. St. Hull und die Folgen. Korrekturen zur Nazifilm-und Geschichtsschreibung." *Film und Fernsehen* 7.1 (January 1979): 33–38.

Niehl, Wiltrud, ed. *Musik, Theater, Literatur und Film zur Zeit des Dritten Reichs.* Düsseldorf: Kulturamt der Stadt Düsseldorf, 1987.

NS-Filme in der Diskussion. Wie wirkt heute das Goebbels-Gift? Frankfurt am Main: Evangelischer Pressedienst, 1977.

Papen, Manuela von. "Franziska, Agnes, Gisela und ihre Schwestern. Beobachtungen zum nationalsozialistischen Heimatfrontfilm." *Film-Dienst* 48.10 (9 May 1995): 12–16.

Patalas, Enno. "Reise in die Vergangenheit." *Filmkritik* 9.11 (November 1965): 647–650.

Paul, Gerhard. *Aufstand der Bilder. Die NS-Propaganda vor 1933.* Bonn: Dietz, 1990.

PEM. "The Nazis Return." *Films and Filming* 12.7 (April 1966): 36–39.

Petley, Julian. *Capital and Culture: German Cinema 1933–45.* London: British Film Institute, 1979.

Phillips, Baxter. *Swastika: Cinema of Oppression.* New York: Warner, 1976.

Phillips, M. S. "The German Film Industry and the New Order." In *The Shaping of the Nazi State.* Ed. Peter D. Strachura. London: Croom Helm, 1978. Pp. 257–281.

——— "The Nazi Control of the Film Industry." *Journal of European Studies* 1.1 (1971): 37–68.

Prinzler, Hans Helmut, ed. *Das Jahr 1945. Filme aus fünfzehn Ländern.* Berlin: Stiftung Deutsche Kinemathek, 1990.

———, ed. *Europa 1939. Filme aus zehn Ländern.* Berlin: Stiftung Deutsche Kinemathek, 1989.

Projektgruppe deutscher Heimatfilm. *Der deutsche Heimatfilm. Bildwelten und Weltbilder.* Tübingen: Tübinger Vereinigung für Volkskunde, 1989.

Quaresima, Leonardo. "Der Film im Dritten Reich. Moderne, Amerikanismus, Unterhaltungsfilm." *montage/av* 3.2 (1994): 5–22.

Raack, R. C. "Nazi Film Propaganda and the Horrors of War." *Historical Journal of Film, Radio and Television* 6.2 (1986): 189–195.

Regel, Helmut. "Autoritäre Muster." *Filmkritik* 10.11 (November 1966): 643–653.

——— "Zur Topographie des NS-Films." *Filmkritik* 10.1 (January 1966): 5–18.

Regel, Helmut, and Rudolf Weichsel, eds. *Der "gute" deutsche Film. Versuch einer Chronik seiner Untugenden.* Aachen: Filmstudio an der Technischen Hochschule Aachen, 1965.

Reiss, Tom. "How the Nazis Created a Dream Factory in Hell." *New York Times,* 6 November 1994.

Rentschler, Eric. "German Feature Films 1933–1945." *Monatshefte* 82.3 (Fall 1990): 257–266.

——— "Ministry of Illusion: German Films 1933–1945." *Film Comment* 30.6 (November—December 1994): 34–42.

——— "Remembering Not to Forget: A Retrospective Reading of Kluge's *Brutality in Stone.*" *New German Critique* 49 (Winter 1990): 23–41.

——— "Springtime for Ufa." *Quarterly Review of Film and Video* 15.2 (Spring 1994): 75–87.

Richards, Jeffrey. *Visions of Yesterday.* London: Routledge & Kegan Paul, 1973.

Romani, Cinzia. *Stato Nazista e Cinematografica.* Rome: Bulzoni, 1983.

——— *Tainted Goddesses: Female Film Stars of the Third Reich.* Trans. Robert Connolly. New York: Sarpedon, 1992.

Rost, Karl Ludwig. *Sterilisation und Euthanasie im Film des "Dritten Reiches."* Husum: Matthiesen, 1987.

Roth, Karl Heinz. "Filmpropaganda für die Vernichtung der Geisteskranken und Behinderten im Dritten Reich." Diss. Univ. Hamburg, 1986.

Salt, Barry. "Continental Manners: Formal and Stylistic Features of French and German Cinema of the 30's and 40's." In *European Cinema Conference Papers.* Ed. Susan Hayward. Aston: AMLC Publications, 1985. Pp. 53–70.

Schebera, Jürgen. *Damals in Neubabelsberg . . .* Leipzig: Edition Leipzig, 1990.

Schenk, Irmbert. "Geschichte im NS-Film. Kritische Anmerkungen zur filmwissenschaftlichen Suggestion der Identität von Propaganda und Wirkung." *montage/av* 3.2 (1994): 73–98.

Schettler, Holger. *Arbeiter und Angestellte im Film. Die Darstellung der sozialen Lage von Arbeitern und Angestellten im deutschen Spielfilm 1918–1939.* Bielefeld: Verlag für Regionalgeschichte, 1992.

Schlüpmann, Heide. "Faschistische Trugbilder weiblicher Autonomie." *Frauen und Film* 44–45 (October 1988): 44–66.

Schmidt-Sasse, Joachim, ed. *Widergänger. Faschismus und Antifaschismus im Film.* Münster: MAkS, 1993.

Schoenberner, Gerhard. "Ideologie und Propaganda im NS-Film. Von der Eroberung der Studios zur Manipulation ihrer Produkte." In *Der deutsche Film. Aspekte seiner Geschichte von den Anfängen bis zur Gegenwart.* Ed. Uli Jung. Trier: Wissenschaftlicher Verlag, 1993. Pp. 91–110.

Schöning, Jörg, ed. *66 Programmblätter. Filmhistorische Retrospektive 1992. Babelsberg. Ein Filmstudio. 1912–1992.* Berlin: Stiftung Deutsche Kinemathek, 1992.

Schrenk, Helene. "Die Produktion der Wien-Film zwischen 1939 und 1945." Diss. Univ. Wien, 1984.

Schulte-Sasse, Linda. "The Never Was as History: Portrayals of the 18th Century in the National Socialist Film." Diss. Univ. of Minnesota, 1985.

——— "Retrieving the City as *Heimat:* Berlin in Nazi Cinema." In *Berlin: Culture and Metropolis.* Ed. Charles W. Haxthausen and Heidrun Suhr. Minneapolis: University of Minnesota Press, 1990. Pp. 166–186.

Schurig, Michael, and Thomas Worschech. " 'Der Geist der neuen Zeit.' Kino und Film unter dem Hakenkreuz." In *Lebende Bilder einer Stadt. Kino und Film in Frankfurt am Main.* Ed. Rudolf Worschech et al. Frankfurt am Main: Deutsches Filmmuseum, 1995. Pp. 142–155.

Seesslen, Georg. *Tanz den Adolf Hitler. Faschismus in der populären Kultur.* Berlin: Bittermann, 1994.

Silberman, Marc. "Shooting Wars: German Cinema and the Two World Wars." In *1914/1939: German Reflections of the Two World Wars.* Ed. Reinhold Grimm and Jost Hermand. Madison: University of Wisconsin Press, 1992. Pp. 116–136.

Singer, Hans-Jürgen. " 'Tran und Helle': Aspekte unterhaltender 'Aufklärung' im Dritten Reich." *Publizistik* 3–4 (1986): 346–356.

Slide, Anthony. "Hollywood's Fascist Follies." *Film Comment* 27.4 (July–August 1991): 62–67.

Spiker, Jürgen. *Film und Kapital. Der Weg der deutschen Filmwirtschaft zum nationalsozialistischen Einheitskonzern.* Berlin: Spiess, 1975.

Stein, Elliott. "The Adolf Hitler Picture Show." *Village Voice,* 15 November 1994.

Stein, Ruthe. "Directed by . . . the Third Reich." *San Francisco Chronicle,* 26 February 1995.

Stock, Walter, ed. *Nationalismus und Sexualität. Filmseminar zur Zeitgeschichte.* Regensburg: Arbeitskreis Film, 1987.

Storm, J. P., and M. Dressler. *Im Reiche der Micky Maus. Walt Disney in Deutschland 1927–1945.* Berlin: Henschel, 1991.

Syberberg, Hans Jürgen. *Hitler: A Film from Germany.* Trans. Joachim Neugroschel. New York: Farrar, Straus & Giroux, 1982.

Taylor, Richard. *Film Propaganda: Nazi Germany and Soviet Russia.* London: Croom Helm, 1979.

Töteberg, Michael. "Ernst Hugo Correll." In *CineGraph,* installment 19. Munich: edition text + kritik, 1992. Pp. E1–E6.

Traubner, Richard. "Escapist Movies from Wartime Germany." *New York Times,* 11 March 1979.

——— "The Sound and the Führer." *Film Comment* 14.4 (July–August 1978): 17–23.

Traudisch, Dora. *Mutterschaft mit Zuckerguß? Frauenfeindliche Propaganda im NS-Spielfilm.* Pfaffenweiler: Centaurus, 1993.

Turan, Kenneth. "Reflections of the Third Reich." *Los Angeles Times,* 8 January 1995.

Der Unterhaltungsfilm im 3. Reich. Gerolzhofen: LAG Film Bayern, 1989.

Vas, Robert. "Sorcerers or Apprentices: Some Aspects of Propaganda Films." *Sight and Sound* 32.4 (Autumn 1963): 199–204.

Virilio, Paul. *War and Cinema: The Logistics of Perception.* Trans. Patrick Camiller. London: Verso, 1989.

Vogelsang, Konrad. *Filmmusik im 3. Reich.* Hamburg: Facta, 1990.

Wehling, Will, ed. *Der Weg ins Dritte Reich. Deutscher Film und Weimars Ende. Eine Dokumentation.* Oberhausen: Laufen, 1974.

Weihsmann, Helmut. "*Das Wort aus Stein*—eine Welt aus Schein. Architektur im Medium des NS-Propagandafilms." *Cinema* 36 (1990): 137–150.

Weinberg, David. "Approaches to the Study of Film in the Third Reich: A Critical Appraisal." *Journal of Contemporary History* 19.1 (January 1984): 105–126.

Welch, David. *Propaganda and the German Cinema 1933–1945.* Oxford: Oxford University Press, 1983.

———, ed. *Nazi Propaganda: The Power and the Limitations.* London: Croom Helm, 1983.

Welzel, Brigitta. *Die Beliebigkeit der Botschaft aufgewiesen am "ideologischen" Gehalt von 120 NS-Spielfilmen.* Rheinfelden: Schäuble, 1994.

Wendtland, Karlheinz. *Deutsche Spielfilmproduktion 1933–1945. Blüte des deutschen Films oder Ideologiefabrik der Nazis.* Berlin: Wendtland, n.d.

——— *Geliebter Kintopp. Sämtliche deutsche Spielfilme von 1929–1945.* 10 vols. Berlin: Wendtland, 1987–1991.

Wetzel, Kraft, and Peter Hagemann. *Liebe, Tod und Technik. Kino des Fantastischen 1933–1945.* Berlin: Spiess, 1977.

——— *Zensur. Verbotene deutsche Filme 1933–1945.* Berlin: Spiess, 1978.

Wilting, Bernd. "Ein düsteres Kapitel deutscher Filmgeschichte. Propagandafilme für die Euthanasie im Dritten Reich." *Film-Korrespondenz* 32.8 (15 April 1986): 13–16.

Winkler, Andrea. *Starkult als Propagandamittel. Studien zum Unterhaltungsfilm im Dritten Reich.* Munich: Ölschläger, 1992.

——— "Starkult auf germanisch. Goebbels und Hippler hielten sich an die Rezepte Hollywoods." *Medium* 18.3 (July–September 1988): 27–30.

Witte, Karsten. "Film im Nationalsozialismus. Blendung und Überblendung." In *Geschichte des deutschen Films.* Ed. Wolfgang Jacobsen, Anton Kaes, and Hans Helmut Prinzler. Stuttgart: Metzler, 1993. Pp. 119–170.

——— "Die Filmkomödie im Dritten Reich." In *Die deutsche Literatur im Dritten Reich.* Ed. Horst Denkler and Karl Prümm. Stuttgart: Reclam, 1976. Pp. 347–365.

——— *Lachende Erben, Toller Tag. Filmkomödie im Dritten Reich.* Berlin: Vorwerk 8, 1995.

——— "Politik als Nebenhandlung. Zu einer Theorie des faschistischen Films." *Politik und Kultur* 2.9 (1982): 32–41.

——— "Visual Pleasure Inhibited: Aspects of the German Revue Film." Trans. J. D. Steakley and Gabriele Hoover. *New German Critique* 24–25 (Fall/Winter 1981–82): 238–263.

Wortig, Kurt. "Realien zum Film im Dritten Reich." *dif: filmkundliche mitteilungen* 3.3 (September 1970): 23–28.

Wulf, Joseph, ed. *Theater und Film im Dritten Reich. Eine Dokumentation.* Frankfurt am Main: Ullstein, 1983.

Ziegler, Gert. "Agfacolor—Wie der deutsche Film farbig wurde." *F-Filmjournal* 19 (January 1980): 42–52.

Films and Filmmakers

Josef von Baky

Arns, Alfons. "Die halbe Wahrheit. Zum Umgang mit NS-Spielfilmen in Fernsehen und Kritik." *Medium* 21.4 (1991): 36–41. (on *Münchhausen*)

Christensen, Peter G. "The Representation of the Late Eighteenth Century in the von Baky/Kästner *Baron Münchhausen:* The Old Regime and Its Links to the Third Reich." *German Life and Letters* 44.1 (October 1990): 13–24.

Dillmann, Claudia. "Ewige Jugend. Der Jubiläumsfilm *Münchhausen.*" In *Das Ufa-Buch.* Ed. Hans-Michael Bock and Michael Töteberg. Frankfurt am Main: Zweitausendeins, 1992. Pp. 434–437.

Fuchs, W. J. "Integral rekonstruiert und diese Farben! Was Filmkritiker so alles bei *Münchhausen* auffiel." *medien + erziehung* 22.3 (1978): 217–218.

Kurowski, Ulrich. "*Münchhausen.*" *Medium* 8.8 (August 1978): 30–31.

Lefévre, Raymond. "*Les aventures du Baron Münchhausen.*" *La revue du cinéma* 284 (May 1974): 112–114.

Rentschler, Eric. "The Triumph of Male Will: *Münchhausen* (1943)." *Film Quarterly* 43.3 (Spring 1990): 14–23.

Sanders-Brahms, Helma. "*Münchhausen* oder Lügen haben lange Beine." *epd Kirche und Film* 31.8 (August 1978): 12–14.

Sudendorf, Werner. "*Via Mala.* Kein Richter und kein Henker." In *Das Jahr 1945. Filme aus fünfzehn Ländern.* Ed. Hans Helmut Prinzler. Berlin: Stiftung Deutsche Kinemathek, 1990. Pp. 165–167.

Töteberg, Michael, and Klaus Kreimeier, eds. *Münchhausen* (*Ufa Magazin* no. 19). Berlin: Deutsches Historisches Museum, 1992.

Giuseppe Becce

Simeon, Ennio. "Giuseppe Becce." In *CineGraph,* installment 10. Trans. Claudia Hoff. Munich: edition text + kritik, 1988. Pp. E1–E4.

Hans Bertram

Aurich, Rolf. "Der Adler ist gelandet. Wer war Hans Bertram?" *Filmwärts* 28 (December 1993): 48.

Carl Boese

Töteberg, Michael, and Klaus Kreimeier, eds. *Hallo Janine* (*Ufa Magazin* no. 16). Berlin: Deutsches Historisches Museum, 1992.

Géza von Bolvary

Dumont, Etienne. "Geza von Bolvary, un maître de la comédie musicale allemande." *Travelling* 42 (May/June 1974): 2–30.

Holba, Herbert. "Bolvary & Reisch. Cineasten fürs Publikum." *F-Filmjournal* 5 (August/September 1978): 11–24.

Schlüpmann, Heide. "Politik als Schuld. Zur Funktion des historischen Kostümfilms in Weiblichkeitsbildern der Filme *Maria Ilona* (1939) und *Königin Luise* (1956)." *Frauen und Film* 38 (1985): 47–57.

Eduard von Borsody

Silberman, Marc. "The Fascist Discourse in the Cinema: A Reading of Eduard von Borsody's *Wunschkonzert*." In *Intertextuality: German Literature and Visual Art from the Renaissance to the Twentieth Century*. Ed. Ingeborg Hoesterey and Ulrich Weisstein. Columbia, S.C.: Camden, 1993. Pp. 188–200.

Töteberg, Michael, and Klaus Kreimeier, eds. *Wunschkonzert* (*Ufa Magazin* no. 17). Berlin: Deutsches Historisches Museum, 1992.

Erich Engel

Arnold, Frank. "*Fahrt ins Glück*. Ohne Tränen." In *Das Jahr 1945. Filme aus fünfzehn Ländern*. Ed. Hans Helmut Prinzler. Berlin: Stiftung Deutsche Kinemathek, 1990. Pp. 161–162.

Göttler, Fritz. "*Hotel Sacher.* Zeit zu lieben, Zeit zu sterben." In *Europa 1939. Filme aus zehn Ländern.* Ed. Hans Helmut Prinzler. Berlin: Stiftung Deutsche Kinemathek, 1989. Pp. 114–115.
Holba, Herbert, Günter Knorr, and Helmut Dan. *Erich Engel. Filme 1923–1940.* Vienna: Action, 1977.

Hanns Heinz Ewers

Keiner, Reinhold. *Hanns Heinz Ewers und der Phantastische Film.* Hildesheim: Olms, 1988.
Loiperdinger, Martin, ed. *Hans Westmar. Einstellungsprotokoll.* Munich: Filmland Presse, 1980.

Arnold Fanck

"Arnold Fanck." *Filmhefte,* special issue, 2 (Summer 1976).
Brandlmeier, Thomas. "Arnold Fanck." In *CineGraph,* installment 4. Munich: edition text + kritik, 1985. Pp. E1–E4.
Fanck, Arnold. "Der Kultur-Spielfilm." *Nationalsozialistische Monatshefte* 147 (June 1942): 361ff.
"Der Mensch in der Natur. Die Filmarbeit Dr. Arnold Fancks." *Der Deutsche Film* 3.1 (July 1938): 3–5.
Rentschler, Eric. "Mountains and Modernity: Relocating the *Bergfilm.*" *New German Critique* 51 (Fall 1990): 137–161.
"Revisited Der Fall Dr. Fanck. Die Entdeckung der Natur im deutschen Bergfilm." *Film und Kritik* 1 (June 1992).

Willi Forst

Arnold, Frank. "*Bel Ami.* Der Mann, den die Frauen liebten." In *Europa 1939. Filme aus zehn Ländern.* Ed. Hans Helmut Prinzler. Berlin: Stiftung Deutsche Kinemathek, 1989. Pp. 106–107.
Gillett, John. "Willi Forst." *Film Dope* 17 (April 1979): 20–21.
Holba, Herbert. "Frauenheld seitenverkehrt." *F-Filmjournal* 2 (April 1978): 13–20. (on *Bel ami*)
Lippert, Renate. " 'Was wißt denn ihr, was Liebe ist.' Pola Negri in *Mazurka,* 1935." *Frauen und Film* 44–45 (October 1988): 77–89.
Sierek, Karl. "/Wien/?—Wien!" *Kinoschriften* 1 (1988): 103–139. (on *Wiener Mädeln*)
Stanzl, Karl. "Willi Forsts Bühnen- und Filmarbeit." Diss. Univ. Wien, 1947.

Carl Froelich

Klasen, Bernadette. " 'Eine Frau wird erst schön durch die Liebe.' Ein Paradox. Zarah Leander in *Heimat.*" In *Widergänger. Faschismus und Antifaschismus im Film.* Ed. Joachim Schmitt-Sasse. Münster: MAkS, 1993. Pp. 38–58.

Kleinert, Franz-Jürgen. *Das Herz der Königin—Maria Stuart. Die Adaption des klassischen Dramas im Spielfilm des Dritten Reiches.* Cologne: Pahl-Rugenstein, 1987.

Littrow, Dorothea von. "Vergleich zwischen Drama und Film *Heimat.* (Ein Beitrag zur Wesensbestimmung des Films)." Diss. Univ. Wien, 1939.

Lowry, Stephen. "Überlegungen zur NS-Unterhaltung an Hand eines Rühmann-Films." *Medium* 20.3 (July–September 1990): 27–30. (on *Die Umwege des schönen Karl*)

Lueken, Verena. "Die unmögliche Frau. Ingrid Bergmann in *Die vier Gesellen.*" *Frauen und Film* 44–45 (October 1988): 90–102.

Gustaf Gründgens

Bechdolf, Ute. "Erwünschte Weiblichkeit? Filmische Konstruktionen von Frauenbildern im nationalsozialistischen Unterhaltungsfilm." *Augen-Blick* 15 (August 1993): 49–64. (on *Kapriolen*)

Dumont-Lindemann-Archiv, ed. *Gustaf-Gründgens-Ausstellung anläßlich seines 80. Geburtstags am 22. December 1979.* Düsseldorf: Theaterarchiv der Landeshauptstadt Düsseldorf, 1980.

Goertz, Heinrich. *Gustaf Gründgens.* Reinbek bei Hamburg: Rowohlt, 1982.

Holba, Herbert, Günter Knorr, and Peter Spiegel. *Gustaf Gründgens Filme.* Vienna: Action, 1978.

Luft, Friedrich. "Gustaf Gründgens. Geschichte eines Aufstiegs in drei Phasen." *Der Monat* (May 1958): 59–66.

Rischbieter, Henning, ed. *Gustaf Gründgens. Schauspieler, Regisseur, Theaterleiter.* Velber: Friedrich, 1963.

Schmid, Eva M. J. "War Effi Briest blond? Bildbeschreibungen und kritische Gedanken zu vier *Effi Briest*-Verfilmungen." In *Literaturverfilmungen.* Ed. Franz-Josef Albersmeier and Volker Roloff. Frankfurt am Main: Suhrkamp, 1989. Pp. 122–154.

Töteberg, Michael. "Gustaf Gründgens." In *CineGraph,* installment 13. Munich: edition text + kritik, 1989. Pp. E1–E8.

Rolf Hansen

Hansen, Rolf, and Alexander Lernet-Holenia. *Die große Liebe.* Ed. Lars Badram. Copenhagen: Gjellerup & Gad, 1986.

Loiperdinger, Martin, and Klaus Schönekäs. "*Die große Liebe*—Propaganda im Unterhaltungsfilm." In *Bilder schreiben Geschichte. Der Historiker im Kino.* Ed. Rainer Rother. Berlin: Wagenbach, 1991. Pp. 143–153.

Sanders-Brahms, Helma. "*Mathilde Möhring.* Eine preußische Liebesgeschichte." In *Das Jahr 1945. Filme aus fünfzehn Ländern.* Ed. Hans Helmut Prinzler. Berlin: Stiftung Deutsche Kinemathek, 1990. Pp. 168–169.

Thiele, Jens, and Fred Ritzel. "Politische Botschaft und Unterhaltung—die Realität im NS-Film. *Die große Liebe* (1942)." In *Fischer Filmgeschichte.* Vol. 2: *Der Film als gesellschaftliche Kraft 1925–1944.* Ed. Werner Faulstich and Helmut Korte. Frankfurt am Main: Fischer, 1991. Pp. 310–323.

Töteberg, Michael, and Klaus Kreimeier, eds. *Die große Liebe* (*Ufa Magazin* no. 18). Berlin: Deutsches Historisches Museum, 1992.

Thea von Harbou

Bruns, Karin. *Kinomythen 1920–1945. Die Filmentwürfe der Thea von Harbou.* Stuttgart: Metzler, 1995.

Haentsch, Wolf-Ulrich. "Thea von Harbou und der Film im Dritten Reich. Eine Autorin zwischen Politik und Unterhaltung." Magisterarbeit J. W. von Goethe Universität Frankfurt, 1986.

Töteberg, Michael. "Thea von Harbou." In *CineGraph,* installment 1. Munich: edition text + kritik, 1984. Pp. E1–E4.

Veit Harlan

Ahren, Yizak, and Christoph Melchers. "Zur Psychologie des Propagandafilms. Film und Beeinflussung am Beispiel *Jud Süß.*" *Medium* 9.4 (April 1979): 29–35.

Aurich, Rolf. "Film als Durchhalteraktion. *Kolberg* von Veit Harlan." In *Das Ufa-Buch.* Ed. Hans-Michael Bock and Michael Töteberg. Frankfurt am Main: Zweitausendeins, 1992. Pp. 462–465.

Bollmann, Yvonne. "Subversion de l'art cinématographique au service de la propaganda nazie. Les films *Jud Süss* (Veit Harlan) et *Ich klage an* (Wolfgang Liebeneiner)." In *Subversion et création dans les pays de langue allemande.* Saint-Etienne: Univ. Jean Monnet, 1992. Pp. 119–129.

Cadars, Pierre, and Francis Courtade. "Veit Harlan 1899–1964." In *Anthologie du cinéma,* no. 8. Paris: L'Avant-Scène, 1973.

Culbert, David. "*Kolberg:* Film, Filmscript and Kolobrzeg Today." *Historical Journal of Film, Radio and Television* 14.4 (1994): 449–454.

Drössler, Stefan. "Harlan und die FSK." *journal film* 26 (1993): 34–37.

Fledelius, Karsten. "Verfilmung oder Zerfilmung. Überlegungen zum Film *Jud Süß.*" In *Verfilmte Literatur.* Ed. Sven-Aage Jørgenson and Peter Schepelern. Kopenhagen: Text & Kontext, 1993. 121–129.

Friedman, Mihal Régine. "Male Gaze and Female Reaction: Veit Harlan's *Jew Süss* (1940)." In *Gender and German Cinema: Feminist Interventions.* Vol. 2. Ed. Sandra Frieden et al. Providence/Oxford: Berg, 1993. Pp. 117–133.

Göttler, Fritz. "*Kolberg.* Nichts geht mehr." In *Das Jahr 1945. Filme aus fünfzehn Ländern.* Ed. Hans Helmut Prinzler. Berlin: Stiftung Deutsche Kinemathek, 1990. 188–189.

——— "*Die Reise nach Tilsit.* Der Gesang der Sirenen." In *Europa 1939. Filme aus zehn Ländern.* Ed. Hans Helmut Prinzler. Berlin: Stiftung Deutsche Kinemathek, 1989. Pp. 120–121.

Grob, Norbert. " 'Dann kommt es eben, wie es kommt!' Noch einmal. Veit Harlan—seine deutschnationalen Melodramen." *journal film* 27 (1994): 85–91.

——— "Veit Harlan." In *CineGraph,* installment 15. Munich: edition text + kritik, 1989. Pp. E1–E20.

Knilli, Friedrich, et al. *"Jud Süß." Filmprotokoll, Programmheft und Einzelanalysen.* Berlin: Spiess, 1983.

Koltan, Michael. "Die Demonstration gegen Veit Harlans *Hanna Amon* im Jahr 1952. 'Wir haben vor Begeisterung geheult.' " *journal film* 26 (1993): 20–25.

Kothenschulte, Daniel. "Zur Aesthetik des Melodramatischen bei Veit Harlan. Verwehte Spuren, verklärte Landschaften." *journal film* 26 (1993): 29–33.

Kugelmann, Cilly, and Fritz Backhaus. *Jüdische Figuren in Film und Karikatur. Die Rothschilds und Joseph Süß Oppenheimer.* Sigmaringen: Thorbecke, 1995.

Laudien, Alexander. "Die Appellstruktur in Veit Harlans Film *Der große König.*" Magisterarbeit Univ. München, 1993.

Möller, Olaf. "Die Konsequenz." *journal film* 26 (1993): 26–28.

Mozer, Isolde. "*Opfergang.*" *Arnoldshainer Filmgespräche* 4 (1987): 38–46.

Pardo, Herbert, and Siegfried Schiffner. *"Jud Süß." Historisches und juristisches Material zum Fall Veit Harlan.* Hamburg: Auerdruck, 1949.

Paret, Peter. "*Kolberg* (1945) as Historical Film and Historical Document." *Historical Journal of Film, Radio and Television* 14.4 (1994): 433–448.

Patalas, Enno. "*Der 30. Januar 1945* (*Kolberg*)." *Filmkritik* 9.12 (December 1965): 689–691.

Pertsch, Dietmar. "Dreimal *Jud Süß.* Die filmische Verwertung der Literatur über den Hoffaktor Joseph Süß Oppenheimer." In *Jüdische Lebenswelten in Spielfilmen und in Fernsehspielen.* Tübingen: Niemeyer, 1992. Pp. 63–111.

Rother, Rainer. "Suggestion der Farben. Die Doppelproduktion *Immensee* und *Opfergang.*" In *Das Ufa-Buch.* Ed. Hans-Michael Bock and Michael Töteberg. Frankfurt am Main: Zweitausendeins, 1992. Pp. 452–455.

Schick, Petra. "Vom Überleben und Sterben. Zur Unsichtbarkeit des Bösen in Veit Harlans *Opfergang.*" *Arnoldshainer Filmgespräche* 4 (1987): 47–55.

Schmieding, Walther. "Der Fall *Kolberg.*" *Filmstudio* 48 (January 1966): 41–44.

Schoenberner, Gerhard. "Nochmals. Soll man Nazifilme spielen? Ein Nachwort zum Fall *Kolberg.*" *epd Kirche und Film* 19.2 (February 1966): 7–9.

Schulte-Sasse, Linda. "The Jew as Other under National Socialism: Veit Harlan's *Jud Süß*." *German Quarterly* 61.1 (Winter 1988): 22–49.
Seesslen, Georg. "*Ich werde Dich auf Händen tragen* oder die Todessehnsucht als wiederkehrendes Element." *journal film* 26 (1993): 13–19.
Spurgat, Günter. *Theodor Storm im Film. Die Kino- und Fernsehverfilmungen seiner Werke*. Lübeck: Graphische Werkstätten, 1987. (on *Immensee* and *Der Puppenspieler*)
Stettner, Herbert. "*Kolberg*—ein Antinazifilm?" *epd Kirche und Film* 18.12 (December 1965): 2–4.
Tegel, Susan. *Jud Süß: A Study*. Trowbridge: Flicks, 1996.
Torstmann, Holger. "Im luftleeren Raum? Wie man die Filme Veit Harlans falsch versteht." *journal film* 27 (1994): 83–84.
Töteberg, Michael. "Karriere im Dritten Reich. Der Regisseur Veit Harlan." In *Das Ufa-Buch*. Ed. Hans-Michael Bock and Michael Töteberg. Frankfurt am Main: Zweitausendeins, 1992. Pp. 458–461.
——— "Triumph im Gerichtssaal. Wie Veit Harlan wieder gesellschaftsfähig wurde." In *Filmstadt Hamburg*. Hamburg: VSA, 1990. Pp. 120–126.
Töteberg, Michael, and Klaus Kreimeier, eds. *Kolberg* (*Ufa Magazin* no. 20). Berlin: Deutsches Historisches Museum, 1992.
Witte, Karsten. "Der barocke Faschist. Veit Harlan und seine Filme." In *Intellektuelle im Bann des Nationalsozialismus*. Ed. Karl Corino. Hamburg: Hoffmann und Campe, 1980. Pp. 150–164.
Zielinski, Siegfried. *Veit Harlan*. Frankfurt am Main: R. G. Fischer, 1981.

Karl Hartl

Dörfler, Goswin. "An Austrian Director: Karl Hartl." *Focus on Film* 29 (March 1978): 35–48.
Grünseid, Gerhard. "Das Filmschaffen Karl Hartls." Diss. Univ. Wien, 1949.

Fritz Hippler

Ahren, Yizhak, Stig Hornshøj-Møller, and Christoph B. Melchers. "*Der ewige Jude.*" *Wie Goebbels hetzte*. Aachen: Alano, 1990.
Avisar, Ilan. "The Historical Significance of *Der ewige Jude*." *Historical Journal of Film, Radio and Television* 13.3 (1993): 363–365.
Barkhausen, Hans. "Offener Brief an Dr. Fritz Hippler." *epd Kirche und Film* 34.8 (August 1981): 26–27.
Bucher, Peter. "Die Bedeutung des Films als historische Quelle. *Der ewige Jude* (1940)." In *Festschrift für Eberhard Kessel zum 75. Geburtstag*. Ed. Heinz Duchhardt and Manfred Schlenke. Munich: Fink, 1982. Pp. 300–329.

Burghardt, Jutta. "Zum Beispiel—*Der ewige Jude*." *Filmstudio* 48 (January 1966): 31–40.

Friedman, Régine Mihal. "Juden-Ratten. Von der rassistischen Metonymie zur tierischen Metapher in Fritz Hipplers *Der ewige Jude*." *Frauen und Film* 47 (September 1989): 24–35.

Hornshøj-Møller, Stig. "Kultfilm der Nazis. *Der ewige Jude* verbreitet immer noch 24 Lügen pro Sekunde." *Medium* 24.3 (July–September 1994): 31–33.

Hornshøj-Møller, Stig, and David Culbert. "*Der ewige Jude* (1940): Joseph Goebbels' Unequaled Monument to Anti-Semitism." *Historical Journal of Film, Radio and Television* 12.1 (1992): 41–67.

Netzeband, Günter. "Hippler-eine Karriere oder die Rhetorik des Verschweigens." *Film und Fernsehen* (Beilage) 10.3 (March 1982): I–XII.

Siegert, Michael. "*Der ewige Jude*." In *Propaganda und Gegenpropaganda im Film 1933–1945*. Ed. Peter Konlechner and Peter Kubelka. Vienna: Österreichishes Filmmuseum, 1972. Pp. 63–79.

——— "Fritz Hippler—Goebbels Reichsfilmintendant." In *Propaganda und Gegenpropaganda im Film 1933–1945*. Ed. Peter Konlechner and Peter Kubelka. Vienna: Österreichishes Filmmuseum, 1972. Pp. 51–62.

Walker, Gila. "An Analysis of *Der ewige Jude:* Its Relationship to Nazi Anti-Semitic Ideas and Policies." *Wide Angle* 3.4 (1980): 48–53.

Werner Hochbaum

Arnold, Frank. "*Drei Unteroffiziere*. Geregeltes Leben." In *Europa 1939. Filme aus zehn Ländern*. Ed. Hans Helmut Prinzler. Berlin: Stiftung Deutsche Kinemathek, 1989. Pp. 108–110.

Aurich, Rolf. "Vom Fahren beim Stehenbleiben. *Leichte Kavallerie* von Werner Hochbaum." In *Das Ufa-Buch*. Ed. Hans-Michael Bock and Michael Töteberg. Frankfurt am Main: Zweitausendeins, 1992. Pp. 356–358.

Holba, Herbert, and David Robinson. "The Enigma of Werner Hochbaum." *Sight and Sound* 45.2 (Spring 1976): 98–103.

Kurowski, Ulrich. " 'Halt es fest, das Glück . . .' " *Film- & Ton-Magazin* 6 (June 1977): 69–73.

——— "Werner Hochbaum." In *CineGraph*, installment 2. Munich: edition text + kritik, 1984. Pp. E1–E2.

Lichtenstein, Manfred. "Der Filmregisseur Werner Hochbaum." *Prisma* 9 (1978): 263–280.

Spiegel, Peter, ed. *Werner Hochbaum. Filme 1929–1939. Viennale-Retrospektive 1976*. Vienna: Action, 1976.

Töteberg, Michael. "Morgen beginnt das Leben. Die späte Wiederentdeckung des Regisseurs Werner Hochbaum." In *Filmstadt Hamburg*. Hamburg: VSA, 1990. Pp. 68–74.

Kurt Hoffmann

Koschnitzki, Rüdiger. *Filmographie Kurt Hoffmann.* Wiebaden-Biebrich: Deutsches Institut für Filmkunde, 1980.

Tornow, Ingo. *Piroschka und Wunderkinder. Oder, von der Unvereinbarkeit von Idylle und Satire. Der Regisseur Kurt Hoffmann.* Munich: Filmland Presse, 1990.

Wenk, Michael. "Der Meister, der vom Himmel fiel. Die Filme von Kurt Hoffmann." *Filmwärts* 29 (March 1994): 11–16.

Georg Jacoby

Ellwanger, Karen, and Eva-Maria Warth. "*Die Frau meiner Träume.* Weiblichkeit und Maskerade. Eine Untersuchung zu Form und Funktion von Kleidung als Zeichensystem im Film." *Frauen und Film* 38 (May 1985): 58–71.

Lowry, Stephen. "Der Ort meiner Träume? Zur ideologischen Funktion des NS-Unterhaltungsfilms." *montage/av* 3.2 (1994): 54–72. (on *Die Frau meiner Träume*)

Warth, Eva-Maria. "The Reconceptualisation of Women's Roles in War-Time National Socialism: An Analysis of *Die Frau meiner Träume.*" In *The Nazification of Art: Art, Design, Music, Architecture and Film in the Third Reich.* Ed. Brandon Taylor and Wilfried van der Will. Winchester, U.K.: Winchester, 1990. Pp. 219–230.

Carl Junghans

Dan, Helmut. "Carl Junghans. Dokumentation." *F-Filmjournal* 7 (November 1978): 11–16.

Holba, Herbert. "*Altes Herz geht auf die Reise.*" *F-Filmjournal* 7 (November 1978): 4–10.

Phil Jutzi

Bock, Hans-Michael, and Wolfgang Jacobsen, eds. *Phil Jutzi. Film-Materialien* 5 (September 1993).

Knorr, Günter. "Phil Jutzi und der Kurztonfilm." *F-Filmjournal* 3 (May 1978): 13–19.

Erich Kästner

Lutz-Kopp, Elisabeth. *"Nur wer Kind bleibt . . ." Erich Kästner-Verfilmungen.* Frankfurt am Main: Bundesverband Jugend und Film, 1993.

Mank, Dieter. *Erich Kästner im nationalsozialistischen Deutschland 1933–1945. Zeit ohne Werk?* Frankfurt am Main: Lang, 1981.

Tornow, Ingo. *Erich Kästner und der Film.* Munich: Filmland Presse, 1989.

Helmut Käutner

Arnold, Frank. "*Kitty und die Weltkonferenz.* Das fehlende 1%." In *Europa 1939. Filme aus zehn Ländern.* Ed. Hans Helmut Prinzler. Berlin: Stiftung Deutsche Kinemathek, 1989. Pp. 118–119.

Cornelsen, Peter. *Helmut Käutner. Seine Filme—sein Leben.* Munich: Heyne, 1980.

Friedman, Mihal Régine. "Die Ausnahme ist die Regel. Zu *Romanze in Moll* (1943) von Helmut Käutner." *Frauen und Film* 43 (December 1987): 48–58.

Jacobsen, Wolfgang, and Hans Helmut Prinzler, eds. *Käutner.* Berlin: Spiess, 1992.

Koschnitzki, Rüdiger. *Filmographie Helmut Käutner.* Wiesbaden: Deutsches Institut für Filmkunde, 1978.

Kuhlbrodt, Dietrich. "*Große Freiheit Nr. 7.* Bleib oder komm." In *Das Jahr 1945. Filme aus fünfzehn Ländern.* Ed. Hans Helmut Prinzler. Berlin: Stiftung Deutsche Kinemathek, 1990. Pp. 183–185.

Marcorelles, Louis. "Kautner le Dandy." *Cahiers du cinéma* 73 (July 1957): 26–29.

Rundell, Richard J. "Keller's *Kleider machen Leute* as Novelle and Film." *Die Unterrichtspraxis* 13.2 (Fall 1980): 156–165.

Schütte, Jan. "*Unter den Brücken.* Die Viererbande." In *Das Jahr 1945. Filme aus fünfzehn Ländern.* Ed. Hans Helmut Prinzler. Berlin: Stiftung Deutsche Kinemathek, 1990. Pp. 170–172.

Seesslen, Georg. "Helmut Käutner." In *CineGraph,* installment 13. Munich: edition text + kritik, 1989. Pp. E1–E12.

Silberman, Marc. "The Illusion of Escapism: Helmut Käutners' *Romance in a Minor Key.*" In *German Cinema: Texts in Context.* Detroit: Wayne State University Press, 1995. Pp. 81–96.

Töteberg, Michael. "Die Tränen sind vergebens. *Große Freiheit Nr. 7.* Von den Nazis verboten, von den Sittenwächtern bekämpft." In *Filmstadt Hamburg.* Hamburg: VSA, 1990. Pp. 76–81.

Töteberg, Michael, and Klaus Kreimeier, eds. *Unter den Brücken* (*Ufa Magazin* no. 21). Berlin: Deutsches Historisches Museum, 1992.

Wischnewski, Klaus. "Ein Augenblick der Freiheit oder Helmut Käutners *Romanze in Moll.*" In *Mitten ins Herz. 66 Liebesfilme.* Ed. Helga Hartmann and Ralf Schenk. Berlin: Henschel, 1991. Pp. 170–173.

Witte, Karsten. "Ästhetische Opposition? Käutners Filme im Faschismus." *Sammlung. Jahrbuch für antifaschistische Literatur und Kunst* 2 (1979): 113–123.

Max W. Kimmich

Eckart, Wolfgang U. "*Germanin*—Fiktion und Wirklichkeit in einem nationalsozialistischen Propagandafilm." In *Medizin im Spielfilm des Nationalsozialismus.* Ed. Udo Benzenhöfer and Wolfgang U. Eckart. Tecklenburg: Burgverlag, 1990. Pp. 69–82.

Ernst Kunstmann

Fleischer, Uwe, and Rolf Aurich. "Der Trickser. Ernst Kunstmann—ein Pionier der Special Effects." *Filmwärts* 23 (August 1992): 53–60.

Gerhard Lamprecht

Holba, Herbert. "Deutsches Filmmelodram I. *Die Geliebte.*" *F-Filmjournal* 11 (March 1979): 21–26.

Wolfgang Liebeneiner

Anschlag, Dieter. "Tödliche Propaganda. Zur Uraufführung des Films *Ich klage an* vor 50 Jahren." *Film-Dienst* 44.18 (3 September 1991): 14–15.

Blumenberg, Hans-Christoph. *Das Leben geht weiter. Der letzte Film des Dritten Reichs.* Berlin: Rowohlt, 1993.

Brandt, H. J. "Der Propagandakern (W. Liebeneiner. *Ich klage an*)." In *Widergänger. Faschismus und Antifaschismus im Film.* Ed. Joachim Schmitt-Sasse. Münster: MAkS, 1993. Pp. 15–35.

Fischer, Kurt Joachim. "Auf eigenwilligen Wegen—Wolfgang Liebeneiner." *Film und Frau* 10.7 (1958): 110–115.

Fürstenau, Theo. "Zum Beispiel *Großstadtmelodie:* Noch werden NS-Filme 'ehrbar gemacht.' " *epd Kirche und Film* 33.8 (August 1980): 16–18.

Huttner, Stephan. "Die 'Euthanasie'-Argumente in Wolfgang Liebeneiners Film *Ich klage an* (1941)—Aus heutiger Sicht." Diss. Univ. Erlangen, 1988.

Kuhlbrodt, Dietrich. "Der Kult des Unpolitischen. Produktionschef Wolfgang Liebeneiner." In *Das Ufa-Buch.* Ed. Hans-Michael Bock and Michael Töteberg. Frankfurt am Main: Zweitausendeins, 1992. Pp. 446–449.

Rost, Karl Ludwig. "*Ich klage an*—ein historischer Film?" In *Medizin im Spielfilm des Nationalsozialismus.* Ed. Udo Benzenhöfer and Wolfgang U. Eckart. Tecklenburg: Burgverlag, 1990. Pp. 52–68.

Roth, Karl Heinz. "*Ich klage an*—Aus der Entstehungsgeschichte eines Propaganda-Films." In *Aktion T-4 1939–1945. Die "Euthanasie"-Zentrale in der Tiergartenstrasse 4.* Ed. Götz Aly. Berlin: Hentrich, 1987. Pp. 93–116.

Witte, Karsten. "Die Wirkgewalt der Bilder. Zum Beispiel Wolfgang Liebeneiner." *Filme* 8 (March/April 1981): 24–35.

Herbert Maisch

Popp, Christian. "Der 'vorbildliche Offizier' im Kriegsfilm. Untersuchung zur Rollentypologie in den Filmen *Die andere Seite* (1931) und *D III 88* (1939)." Magisterarbeit Univ. München, 1992.

Reis, Thomas, ed. *Drehbuch zu dem Film "Friedrich Schiller. Der Triumph eines Genies" (1940).* Frankfurt am Main: R. G. Fischer, 1983.

Schulte-Sasse, Linda. "National Socialism's Aestheticization of Genius: The Case of Herbert Maisch's *Friedrich Schiller—Triumph eines Genies.*" *Germanic Review* 66.1 (Winter 1991): 4–15.

Wegschneider, Michael. "Genie und Mythos. Der heroische Künstlertyp und seine Ästhetisierung im NS-Film." Magisterarbeit Univ. München, 1993. (on *Friedrich Schiller*)

Paul Martin

Aurich, Rolf. "Glückskekse. Lilian Harvey und Willy Fritsch." In *Das Ufa-Buch.* Ed. Hans-Michael Bock and Michael Töteberg. Frankfurt am Main: Zweitausendeins, 1992. Pp. 366–367.

Heinzlmeier, Adolf, and Berndt Schulz. "Lilian Harvey und Willy Fritsch. *Glückskinder.*" In *Happy-End. Berühmte Liebespaare der Leinwand.* Frankfurt am Main: Fischer, 1981. Pp. 96–105.

Rentschler, Eric. "Eigengewächs à la Hollywood." In *Babelsberg. Das Filmstudio.* Ed. Wolfgang Jacobsen. 3rd rev. ed. Berlin: Stiftung Deutsche Kinemathek/Argon, 1994. Pp. 207–222. (on *Glückskinder*)

Töteberg, Michael, and Kreimeier, Klaus, eds. *Glückskinder* (*Ufa Magazin* no. 13). Berlin: Deutsches Historisches Museum, 1992.

G. W. Pabst

Amengual, Barthélemy. *G. W. Pabst.* Paris: Seghers, 1966.

Atwell, Lee. *G. W. Pabst.* Boston: Twayne, 1977.

Benzenhöfer, Udo. " 'Propaganda des Herzens.' Zum *Paracelsus*-Film von Georg W. Pabst." In *Medizin im Spielfilm des Nationalsozialismus.* Ed. Udo Benzenhöfer and Wolfgang U. Eckart. Tecklenburg: Burgverlag, 1990. Pp. 52–68.

Friedman, Régine Mihal. "'*Ecce Ingenium Teutonicum*': *Paracelsus* (1943)." In *The Films of G. W. Pabst: An Extraterritorial Cinema.* Ed. Eric Rentschler. New Brunswick, N.J.: Rutgers University Press, 1990. Pp. 184–196, 264–267.

Gleber, Anke. "Masochism and Wartime Melodrama: *Komödianten* (1941)." In *The Films of G. W. Pabst: An Extraterritorial Cinema.* Ed. Eric Rentschler. New Brunswick, N.J.: Rutgers University Press, 1990. Pp. 175–183, 261–264.

Groppali, Enrico. *Georg W. Pabst.* Florence: La Nuova Italia, 1983.

Johnson, Sheila. "Ideological Ambiguity in G. W. Pabst's *Paracelsus.*" *Monatshefte* 83.2 (Summer 1991): 104–126.

Rentschler, Eric. "Pabst, Paracelsus und der Blick des Todes." In *G. W. Pabst.* Ed.

Gottfried Schlemmer, Bernhard Riff, and Georg Haberl. Münster: MAks, 1990. Pp. 208–226.

——— "Pabsts umfunktionierter Paracelsus." *Germanic Review* 66.1 (Winter 1991): 16–24.

Ruppelt, Susanne. "Analyse des nationalsozialistischen Spielfilms *Paracelsus.*" Magisterarbeit Freie Universität Berlin, 1980.

Schulte-Sasse, Linda. "A Nazi Herstory: The Paradox of Female 'Genius' in Pabst's Neuberin Film *Komödianten* (1941)." *New German Critique* 50 (Spring–Summer 1990): 57–84.

Witte, Karsten. "Flügelkämpfe." *Kinemathek* 78 (March 1992): 50–55. (on *Paracelsus*)

Peter Pewas

Kreimeier, Klaus. "Peter Pewas 22.3.1904–13.9.1984." *epd Film* 1.10 (September 1984): 2–3.

Kurowski, Ulrich, and Andreas Meyer. *Der Filmregisseur Peter Pewas.* Berlin: Spiess, 1981.

Thie, J. M. "Kleine revolutionäre Anstriche. *zitty* Gespräch mit Peter Pewas." *zitty* 4 (1981): 52–53.

Harry Piel

Bleckman, Matias. "Harry Piel." In *CineGraph,* installment 14. Munich: edition text + kritik, 1989. Pp. E1–E8.

——— *Harry Piel. Ein Kino-Mythos und seine Zeit.* Düsseldorf: Filminstitut der Landeshauptstadt Düsseldorf, 1992.

Hohwiller, Heinz. "Harry Piel. Ein Besessener des Films." *Retro-Filmjournal* 7 (January/February 1981): 5–15.

Arthur Maria Rabenalt

Bachorski, Hans-Jürgen. *Filmhistoriker, Theaterwissenschaftler, Pornologe. Arthur Maria Rabenalts künstlerische und wissenschaftliche Arbeiten der Jahre 1933–1985.* Bayreuth: Markgrafbuchhandlung, 1989.

Göttler, Fritz. "*Johannisfeuer.* Spurenlese." In *Europa 1939. Filme aus zehn Ländern.* Ed. Hans Helmut Prinzler. Berlin: Stiftung Deutsche Kinemathek, 1989. Pp. 116–117.

Köhler, Otto. ". . . stiftet für Deutschland. Hat sich der 83jährige Film-Regisseur und Soft-Porno-Produzent Arthur Maria Rabenalt eine Professur 'gekauft'?" *Die Zeit,* 5 May 1989.

Seesslen, Georg. "Arthur Maria Rabenalt. 25.6.1905–26.2.1993." *epd Film* 10.6 (June 1993): 6.

Wetzel, Kraft. "Faschismus und Kino. Ein Beitrag zur politischen Psychologie des Faschismus am Beispiel des Films . . . *reitet für Deutschland*." Diplomarbeit Freie Universität Berlin, 1978.

Herbert Reinecker

Pöttker, Horst, and Rolf Seubert. "Glückseliger Dämmerzustand. Herbert Reinecker über *Junge Adler* und seine Vergangenheit im Nationalsozialismus im Gespräch." *Medium* 18.3 (July–September 1988): 37–42.

Leni Riefenstahl

Barsam, Richard Meran. *Filmguide to Triumph of the Will.* Bloomington: Indiana University Press, 1975.

Berg-Pan, Renata. *Leni Riefenstahl.* Boston: Twayne, 1980.

Berman, Russell A. "Written Right across Their Faces: Leni Riefenstahl, Ernst Jünger, and Fascist Modernism." In *Modern Culture and Critical Theory: Art, Politics, and the Legacy of the Frankfurt School.* Madison: University of Wisconsin Press, 1989. Pp. 99–119.

Bernstein, Sandra, and Michael MacMillan. "Leni Riefenstahl: A Selected Annotated Bibliography." *Quarterly Review of Film Studies* 2.4 (November 1977): 439–457.

Corliss, Richard. "Leni Riefenstahl: A Bibliography." *Film Heritage* 5.1 (Fall 1969): 27–36.

Dargis, Manohla. "Queen of Denial: The Life and Lies of Leni Riefenstahl." *Voice Literary Supplement* 123 (March 1994): 8–10.

Deutschmann, Linda. *Triumph of the Will: The Image of the Third Reich.* Wakefield, N.H.: Longwood Academic, 1991.

Downing, Taylor. *Olympia.* London: British Film Institute, 1992.

Elsaesser, Thomas. "Portrait of the Artist as a Young Woman." *Sight and Sound* 3.2 (February 1993): 15–18.

Fabe, Marilyn. *Triumph of the Will: The Arrival of Hitler. Notes and Analysis.* Mount Vernon, N.Y.: Macmillan Films, 1975.

Ford, Charles. *Leni Riefenstahl.* Paris: La Table Ronde, 1978.

Grafe, Frieda. "Leni Riefenstahl. Falsche Bauern, falsche Soldaten und was für ein Volk." *Süddeutsche Zeitung* 13–14 September 1975.

Graham, Cooper C. *Leni Riefenstahl and Olympia.* Metuchen, N.J.: Scarecrow, 1986.

Grenier, Richard. "The Fuehrer's Filmmaker." *Commentary* 98.2 (August 1994): 48–51.

Hinton, David B. *The Films of Leni Riefenstahl.* Metuchen, N.J.: Scarecrow, 1978.

Hoffmann, Hilmar. *Mythos Olympia. Autonomie und Unterwerfung von Sport und Kultur.* Berlin: Aufbau, 1993.

Infield, Glenn B. *Leni Riefenstahl: The Fallen Film Goddess.* New York: Crowell, 1976.

Ishioka, Eiko. *Leni Riefenstahl Life.* Tokyo: Kyuryudo Art, 1992.

Lenssen, Claudia. "Die fünf Karrieren der Leni Riefenstalh." *epd Film* 13.1 (January 1996): 26–31.

Loiperdinger, Martin. *Der Parteitagsfilm "Triumph des Willens" von Leni Riefenstahl. Rituale der Mobilmachung.* Opladen: Leske + Budrich, 1987.

Neale, Steve. "*Triumph of the Will:* Notes on Documentary and Spectacle." *Screen* 20.1 (Spring 1979): 63–86.

Nowotny, Peter. "Leni Riefenstahl." In *CineGraph,* installment 2. Munich: edition text + kritik, 1984. Pp. E1–E4.

Pohlmann, Ulrich. "Nur die Sieger zählen. Die Funktion der Schönheit bei Leni Riefenstahl." *Tendenzen. Zeitschrift für engagierte Kunst* 154 (1986): 69–76.

Quaresima, Leonardo. "Kino als rituelle Erfahrung. *Triumph des Willens* im Ufa-Palast." In *Das Ufa-Buch.* Ed. Hans-Michael Bock and Michael Töteberg. Frankfurt am Main: Zweitausendeins, 1992. Pp. 372–374.

——— *Leni Riefenstahl.* Florence: La Nuova Italia, 1984.

Rentschler, Eric. "The Elemental, the Ornamental, the Instrumental: *The Blue Light* and Nazi Film Aesthetics." In *The Other Perspective in Gender and Culture.* Ed. Juliet Flower MacCannell. New York: Columbia University Press, 1990. Pp. 161–188.

——— "Fatal Attractions: Leni Riefenstahl's *The Blue Light.*" *October* 48 (Spring 1989): 47–68.

Rich, B. Ruby. "Leni Riefenstahl: The Deceptive Myth." In *Sexual Stratagems: The World of Women in Film.* Ed. Patricia Erens. New York: Horizon, 1979. Pp. 202–209.

Sanders-Brahms, Helma. "*Tiefland.* Tyrannenmord." In *Das Jahr 1945. Filme aus fünfzehn Ländern.* Ed. Hans Helmut Prinzler. Berlin: Stiftung Deutsche Kinemathek, 1990. Pp. 173–176.

Schulte-Sasse, Linda. "Leni Riefenstahl's Feature Films and the Question of a Fascist Aesthetic." *Cultural Critique* 18 (Spring 1991): 123–148.

Seesslen, Georg. "Die Krieger, der Tanz, das Mädchen und der Führer." *Blimp* 22/23 (Spring 1993): 20–28.

Sontag, Susan. "Fascinating Fascism." In *Under the Sign of Saturn.* New York: Vintage, 1981. Pp. 71–105.

Stupp, Vicki O'Donnell. "Myth, Meaning, and Message in *The Triumph of the Will.*" *Film Criticism* 2.2–3 (Winter/Spring 1978): 40–49.

Vogel, Amos. "Can We Now Forget the Evil That She Did?" *New York Times,* 13 May 1973.

Wallace, Peggy Ann. "An Historical Study of the Career of Leni Riefenstahl from 1923 to 1933." Diss. University of Southern California, 1975.

Wood, Robin. "Fascism/Cinema." *CineAction!* 18 (Fall 1989): 45–50. (on *Triumph of the Will*)

Wysocki, Gisela von. "Die Berge und die Patriarchen. Leni Riefenstahl." In *Die Fröste der Freiheit. Aufbruchsphantasien.* Frankfurt am Main: Syndikat, 1980. Pp. 70–85.

Karl Ritter

Altman, John. "The Technique and Content of Hitler's War Propaganda Films. Part I: Karl Ritter and His Early Films." *Hollywood Quarterly* 4.4 (Summer 1950): 385–391.

——— "The Technique and Content of Hitler's War Propaganda Films. Part II: Karl Ritter's 'Soldier Films.' " *Hollywood Quarterly* 5.1 (Fall 1950): 61–72.

Baird, Jay W. "Karl Ritter and the Heroic Nazi Cinema." In *To Die for Germany: Heroes in the Nazi Pantheon.* Bloomington: Indiana University Press, 1990. Pp. 172–201.

Petley, Julian. "Karl Ritter." In *CineGraph,* installment 1. Munich: edition text + kritik, 1984. Pp. E1–E5.

Rother, Rainer. "Grauen Panik Untergang. Karl Ritters Propagandafilm *GPU.*" In *Das Ufa-Buch.* Ed. Hans-Michael Bock and Michael Töteberg. Frankfurt am Main: Zweitausendeins, 1992. Pp. 430–432.

——— " 'Hier erhält der Gedanke eine feste Form.' Karl Ritters Regie-Karriere im Nationalsozialismus." In *Das Ufa-Buch.* Ed. Hans-Michael Bock and Michael Töteberg. Frankfurt am Main: Zweitausendeins, 1992. Pp. 422–427.

Töteberg, Michael, and Klaus Kreimeier, eds. *Urlaub auf Ehrenwort* (*Ufa Magazin* no. 15). Berlin: Deutsches Historisches Museum, 1992.

Walter Ruttmann

Brandt, Hans Jürgen. "Walter Ruttmann. Vom Expressionismus zum Faschismus. 3. Teil (Schluß)." *Filmfaust* 51 (February/March 1986): 42–54.

Fulks, Barry A. "Walter Ruttmann, the Avant-Garde Film, and Nazi Modernism." *Film and History* 14.2 (1984): 26–35, 46.

Goergen, Jeanpaul, ed. *Walter Ruttmann. Eine Dokumentation.* Berlin: Freunde der deutschen Kinemathek, 1989.

Milkert, Angelika. "Avantgardist und Propagandist." *Neue Zürcher Zeitung,* 25 December 1987.

Quaresima, Leonardo, ed. *Walter Ruttmann: Cinema, pittura, ars acustica.* Calliano (Trento): Manfrini, 1994.

Schenk, Irmbert. "Ruttmann und die Moderne." In *Film, Fernsehen, Video und die Künste.* Ed. Joachim Paech. Stuttgart/Weimar: Metzler, 1994. Pp. 89–102.

Reinhold Schünzel

Aurich, Rolf. "Lachen mit Sondererlaubnis." In *Das Ufa-Buch.* Ed. Hans-Michael Bock and Michael Töteberg. Frankfurt am Main: Zweitausendeins, 1992. Pp. 350–355.

Bock, Hans-Michael. "Aus den Wolken. Technische Neuerungen bei *Amphitryon.*" In *Das Ufa-Buch.* Ed. Hans-Michael Bock and Michael Töteberg. Frankfurt am Main: Zweitausendeins, 1992. Pp. 368–371.

Schöning, Jörg, ed. *Reinhold Schünzel. Schauspieler und Regisseur.* Munich: edition text + kritik, 1989.

Theis, Wolfgang. "Reinhold Schünzel." In *CineGraph,* installment 6. Munich: edition text + kritik, 1986. Pp. E1–E8.

Töteberg, Michael, and Klaus Kreimeier, eds. *Amphitryon* (*Ufa Magazin* no. 12). Berlin: Deutsches Historisches Museum, 1992.

Hans Schweikart

Gleber, Anke. "Das Fräulein von Tellheim. Die ideologische Funktion der Frau in der nationalsozialistischen Lessing-Adaption." *German Quarterly* 59.4 (Fall 1986): 547–568. (on *Das Fräulein von Barnhelm*)

Nau, Peter. "*Die Nacht der Zwölf.* Die Reise nach Fürstenberg." In *Das Jahr 1945. Filme aus fünfzehn Ländern.* Ed. Hans Helmut Prinzler. Berlin: Stiftung Deutsche Kinemathek, 1990. Pp. 163–164.

Witte, Karsten. "How Nazi Cinema Mobilizes the Classics: Schweikart's *Das Fräulein von Barnhelm* (1940)." In *German Film and Literature: Adaptations and Transformations.* Ed. Eric Rentschler. New York: Methuen, 1986. Pp. 103–116.

Franz Seitz

Schriefer, Uwe, ed. *SA-Mann Brand. Einstellungsprotokoll.* Munich: Filmland Presse, 1980.

Herbert Selpin

Maurischat, Fritz. "Selpin und *Titanic.*" *dif: filmkundliche mitteilungen* 3.2 (June 1970): 4–28; 3.3 (September 1970): 4–22.

Detlef Sierk (= Douglas Sirk)

Babington, Bruce. "Written by the Wind: Sierck/Sirk's *La Habanera* (1937)." *Forum for Modern Language Studies* 31.1 (January 1995): 24–36.

Bleys, Jean Pierre. "Quand Douglas Sirk s'appelait Detlef Sierck." *Cahiers de la cinémathèque* 32 (Spring 1981): 79–84.

Bourget, Jean-Loup. *Douglas Sirk.* Paris: Edilig, 1984.

Brandlmeier, Thomas. "Das Glück der Bürger. Zum Werk des Filmregisseurs Douglas Sirk." *Medium* 17.3 (July–September 1987): 9–14.

Brown, Geoff. "*La Habanera.*" *Monthly Film Bulletin* 48 (January 1981): 13.

Coates, Paul. "Melodrama contra the Fantastic: Petro, Elsaesser, and Sirk." In *The Gorgon's Gaze.* Cambridge: Cambridge University Press, 1991. Pp. 229–236. (on *La Habanera*)

Halliday, Jon. *Sirk on Sirk.* New York: Viking, 1972.

Holba, Herbert. "Deutsches Filmmelodram II. *Zu neuen Ufern.*" *F-Filmjournal* 23 (May 1980): 39–43.

Koch, Gertrud. "Von Detlef Sierck zu Douglas Sirk." *Frauen und Film* 44/45 (October 1988): 109–129.

Läufer, Elisabeth. *Skeptiker des Lichts. Douglas Sirk und seine Filme.* Frankfurt am Main: Fischer, 1987.

Meyer-Wendt, Jochen. " 'Ich brauche etwas mehr Kino.' Detlef Siercks deutsche Melodramen." In *Das Ufa-Buch.* Ed. Hans-Michael Bock and Michael Töteberg. Frankfurt am Main: Zweitausendeins, 1992. Pp. 382–384.

Petley, Julian. "Detlef Sierck." In *CineGraph,* installment 8. Munich: edition text + kritik, 1987. Pp. E1–E19.

——— "Sirk in Germany." *Sight and Sound* 57.1 (Winter 1987–88): 58–61.

Pithon, Remy. "Les constances d'un style: Sur quelques films allemands de Douglas Sirk." *Cinema* 3 (1978): 13–25.

Silberman, Marc. "Zarah Leander in the Colonies." In *Medien/Kultur. Schnittstellen zwischen Medienwissenschaft, Medienpraxis und gesellschaftlicher Kommunikation.* Ed. Knut Hickethier and Siegfried Zielinski. Berlin: Spiess, 1991. Pp. 247–253.

Töteberg, Michael, and Klaus Kreimeier, eds. *Zu neuen Ufern* (*Ufa Magazin* no. 14). Berlin: Deutsches Historisches Museum, 1992.

Trumpener, Katie. "Puerto Rico Fever: Douglas Sirk, *La Habanera* (1937) and the Epistemology of Exoticism." In *"Neue Welt"/"Dritte Welt." Interkulturelle Beziehungen Deutschlands zu Lateinamerika und der Karibik.* Ed. Sigrid Bauschinger and Susan Cocalis. Tübingen/Basel: Francke, 1994. Pp. 115–140.

Wolfgang Staudte

Fürstenau, Theo. "Staudte, Eggebrecht und der Film des 'Dritten Reichs.' " *epd Kirche und Film* 33.2 (February 1980): 11–12.

Grunwald, Gabriela. "Wolfgang Staudte." In *CineGraph,* installment 20. Munich: edition text + kritik, 1992. Pp. E1–E10.

Netenjakob, Egon, et al. *Staudte.* Berlin: Edition Filme/Spiess, 1991.

Orbanz, Eva, ed. *Wolfgang Staudte.* 3rd rev. ed. Berlin: Spiess, 1977.

Hans Steinhoff

Albrecht, Gerd, ed. *Hitlerjunge Quex. Ein Film vom Opfergeist der deutschen Jugend.* Frankfurt am Main: Deutsches Institut für Filmkunde, 1983.

Arnold, Thomas, Jutta Schöning, and Ulrich Schröter, eds. *Hitlerjunge Quex. Einstellungsprotokoll.* Munich: Filmland Presse, 1980.

Bateson, Gregory. "An Analysis of the Nazi Film *Hitlerjunge Quex.*" In *The Study of Culture at a Distance.* Ed. Margaret Mead and Rhoda Métraux. Chicago: University of Chicago Press, 1953. Pp. 302–314.

——— "Cultural and Thematic Analysis of Fictional Films." *Transactions of the New York Academy of Sciences* 2.5 (February 1943): 72–78.

Bettecken, Wilhelm. "Der Film im Dienst der Propaganda." *Film-Korrespondenz* 34.4 (16 February 1988): 3–6. (on *Hitlerjunge Quex*)

Cadars, Pierre, and Francis Courtade. "Hans Steinhoff." In *L'avant scène du cinéma,* Supplément Anthologie 87 (March 1976).

Horak, Jan-Christopher. "Wo liegt Deutschland? *Hitlerjunge Quex* von Hans Steinhoff." In *Das Ufa-Buch.* Ed. Hans-Michael Bock and Michael Töteberg. Frankfurt am Main: Zweitausendeins, 1992. Pp. 332–333.

Koch, Friedrich. "Heini Völker und der Kampf um Deutschlands Ewigkeit." In *Schule im Kino. Autorität Erziehung vom "Blauen Engel" bis zur "Feuerzangenbowle."* Weinheim/Basel: Beltz, 1987. Pp. 127–143.

——— "*Hitlerjunge Quex* und der hilflose Faschismus. Zum nationalsozialistischen Jugendfilm." *Zeitschrift für Pädagogik* 31 (1993): 163–179.

Oms, Marcel. "*Le jeune hitlérien Quex:* Un moment de l'histoire du cinéma allemand." *Cahiers de la cinémathèque* 32 (Spring 1981): 102–105.

Pöttker, Horst. "Ressentiments gegen die Moderne. Hans Steinhoffs Propagandafilm *Ohm Krüger* von 1941." *Arnoldshainer Filmgespräche* 9 (1992): 88–102.

Reim, Ulrike. "Probleme filmischer Darstellung medizin-historischer Sachverhalte am Beispiel des Robert-Koch-Films." Diss. Univ. Bochum, 1989.

——— "Der *Robert-Koch*-Film (1939) von Hans Steinhoff. Kunst oder Propaganda?" In *Medizin im Spielfilm des Nationalsozialismus.* Ed. Udo Benzenhöfer and Wolfgang U. Eckart. Tecklenburg: Burgverlag, 1990. Pp. 22–33.

Töteberg, Michael, and Klaus Kreimeier, eds. *Hitlerjunge Quex* (*Ufa Magazin* no. 11). Berlin: Deutsches Historisches Museum, 1992.

Witte, Karsten. "Der Apfel und der Stamm. Jugend und Propaganda am Beispiel *Hitlerjunge Quex* (1933)." In *Schock und Schöpfung—Jugendästhetik im 20. Jahrhundert.* Ed Willi Bucher and Klaus Pohl. Darmstadt: Luchterhand, 1986. Pp. 302–307.

R. A. Stemmle

"Denn er war wer,—und er konnte was!" Ein Magdeburger erobert die Filmwelt. Magdeburg: R.-A.-Stemmle-Kuratorium, n.d.

Viktor Tourjansky

Arnold, Frank. "*Der Gouverneur.* Fahne und Ehre." In *Europa 1939. Filme aus zehn Ländern.* Ed. Hans Helmut Prinzler. Berlin: Stiftung Deutsche Kinemathek, 1989. Pp. 111–113.

Marci-Boehncke, Gudrun, and Wolfgang Gast. "Vexierbilder im Lichtspielhaus. Eine Analyse von Wirkungspotentialen am Beispiel des NS-Unterhaltungsfilms *Der Blaufuchs.*" *Augen-Blick* 15 (August 1993): 9–48.

Luis Trenker

Barbera, Alberto, Pietro Crivellaro, and Giovanni Spagnoletti, eds. *Il cinema di Luis Trenker.* Turin: Città di Torino/Goethe-Institut Turin, 1982.

Everson, William K. "Luis Trenker." *Films in Review* 33.5 (May 1984): 271–280.

——— "Trenker at 91 Still a Hit: Verbal Salvos re 'Art' Mark 10th Telluride." *Variety,* 14 September 1983.

Horak, Jan-Christopher. "Luis Trenker's *The Kaiser of California:* How the West Was Won, Nazi Style." *Historical Journal of Film, Radio and Television* 6.2 (1986): 181–188.

Koepnick, Lutz P. "Unsettling America: German Westerns and Modernity." *Modernism/Modernity* 2.3 (September 1995): 1–22. (on *Der Kaiser von Kalifornien*)

Kurowski, Ulrich. "Luis Trenker. 4.10.1892–13.4.1990." *epd Film* 7.6 (June 1990): 3–4.

——— "Luis Trenker/Zum neunzigsten Geburtstag." *epd Kirche und Film* 35.10 (October 1982): 16–18.

Leimgruber, Florian, ed. *Luis Trenker, Regisseur und Schriftsteller. Die Personalakte Trenker im Berlin Document Center.* Bozen: Frasnelli-Keitsch, 1994.

Luis Trenker 90 Jahre jung. Bozen: Kurverwaltung, 1982.

Seesslen, Georg. "Luis Trenker." In *CineGraph,* installment 22. Munich: edition text + kritik, 1993. Pp. E1–E5.

Zanotto, Piero, ed. *Luis Trenker. Lo schermo verticale.* Calliano (Trento): Manfrini, 1982. Parallel German edition: *Die weiße Leinwand.*

Gustav Ucicky

Angler, Dietmar H. "Das nationalistische Leitbild. Einige Bemerkungen—unter besonderer Berücksichtigung der Ucicky-Filme *Das Flötenkonzert von Sanssouci* und *Der Choral von Leuthen.*" *Filmwissenschaftliche Mitteilungen,* Sonderheft 1 (1965): 277–287.

Arnold, Frank. "*Aufruhr in Damaskus.* Sand und Sehnsucht." In *Europa 1939. Filme aus zehn Ländern.* Ed. Hans Helmut Prinzler. Berlin: Stiftung Deutsche Kinemathek, 1989. Pp. 103–105.

Dörfler, Goswin. "Gustav Ucicky." In *Anthologie du cinéma,* no. 11. Paris: L'Avant-Scène, 1984.

——— "Gustav Ucicky." In *CineGraph,* installment 5. Munich: edition text + kritik, 1985. Pp. E1–E5.

Hampicke, Evelyn. "Auf Feindfahrt. *Morgenrot* von Gustav Ucicky." In *Das Ufa-Buch.* Ed. Hans-Michael Bock and Michael Töteberg. Frankfurt am Main: Zweitausendeins, 1992. Pp. 320–323.

Kreimeier, Klaus. " 'Kerls, wollt ihr denn ewig leben?' Zur Wiederaufführung des Films *Der Choral von Leuthen.*" *epd Kirche und Film* 18.3 (March 1965): 3–5.

Mayer, Hans. *Theaterraum—Filmraum. Figurenspiel und Kameraperspektive—dargestellt am Emil-Jannings-Film Der zerbrochene Krug nach dem Lustspiel Heinrich von Kleists.* Munich: Liliom, 1992.

Rother, Rainer. "Action national. Gustav Ucickys Arbeit bei der Ufa." In *Das Ufa-Buch.* Ed. Hans-Michael Bock and Michael Töteberg. Frankfurt am Main: Zweitausendeins, 1992. Pp. 324–327.

Silberman, Marc. "The Ideology of Re-Presenting the Classics: Filming *Der zerbrochene Krug* in the Third Reich." *German Quarterly* 57.4 (Fall 1984): 590–602.

Töteberg, Michael, and Klaus Kreimeier, eds. *Morgenrot* (*Ufa Magazin* no. 10). Berlin: Deutsches Historisches Museum, 1992.

Trimmel, Gerald. "*Heimkehr.* Strategien eines nationalsozialistischen Films." 2 vols. Diplomarbeit Univ. Wien, 1992.

Paul Wegener

Möller, Kai, ed. *Paul Wegener. Sein Leben und seine Rollen. Ein Buch von ihm und über ihn.* Hamburg: Rowohlt, 1954.

Alfred Weidenmann

Seubert, Rolf. " 'Freigegeben für Kinder ab 6 Jahren.' Wie das nationalsozialistische Filmerbe vermarktet wird." *Medium* 24.3 (July–September 1994): 33–36. (on *Junge Adler*)

——— "*Junge Adler.* Retrospektive auf einen nationalsozialistischen Jugendfilm." *Medium* 18.3 (July–September 1988): 31–37.

Helmut Weiss

Lowry, Stephen. "Politik und Unterhaltung. Zum Beispiel *Die Feuerzangenbowle.*" In *Medienlust und Mediennutz. Unterhaltung als öffentliche Kommunikation.* Ed. Louis Bosshart and Wolfgang Hoffmann-Riem. Munich: Schläger, 1994. Pp. 447–457.

Witte, Karsten. "Wie faschistisch ist *Die Feuerzangenbowle?* Bemerkungen zur Filmkomödie im Dritten Reich." *epd Kirche und Filme* 29.7 (July 1976): 1–4.

Fritz Wendhausen

Popova, Lilia, and Knut Brynhildsvoll. "Some Aspects of Cinematic Transformation: The 1934 German Version of *Peer Gynt.*" In *Contemporary Approaches to Ibsen.* Vol. 7. Ed. Bjørn Hemmer and Vigdis Ystad. Oslo: Norwegian University Press, 1991. Pp. 101–111.

Franz Wenzler

Hanlon, Lindley P. "Film Document and the Myth of Horst Wessel: A Sampler of Nazi Propaganda." *Film and History* 5.3 (1975): 16–18.

Loiperdinger, Martin, ed. *Hans Westmar. Einstellungsprotokoll.* Munich: filmland presse, 1980.

Willy Zielke

Loiperdinger, Martin. "Die Geschichte vom *Stahltier.* Willy Zielke und die Reichsbahn." *Filmwärts* 30 (June 1994): 50–55.

Related Film Historical Studies

Albrecht, Gerd, ed. *Die großen Filmerfolge.* Ebersberg: Edition 8½/Just, 1985.

Antel, Franz, and Christian F. Winkler. *Hollywood an der Donau. Geschichte der Wien-Film in Sievering.* Vienna: Edition S, 1991.

Bertin-Maghit, Jean-Pierre. *Le cinéma français sous l'Occupation.* Paris: Presses Universitaires de France, 1994.

Bock, Hans-Michael, ed. *CineGraph. Lexikon zum deutschsprachigen Film.* Munich: edition text + kritik, 1984–.

Bredow, Wilfried von, and Rolf Zurek, eds. *Film und Gesellschaft in Deutschland. Dokumente und Materialien.* Hamburg: Hoffmann und Campe, 1975.

Bucher, Felix, and Leonhard H. Gmür. *Screen Series: Germany.* London/New York: Zwemmer/Barnes, 1970.

Bulgakowa, Oksana, et al. *Bismarck, Preußen, Deutschland und Europa.* Berlin: Freunde der deutschen Kinemathek, 1990.

Bulgakowa, Oksana, and Dietmar Hochmuth, eds. *Der Krieg gegen die Sowjetunion im Spiegel von 36 Filmen.* Berlin: Freunde der Deutschen Kinemathek, 1991.

Custen, George F. *Bio/Pics: How Hollywood Constructed Public History.* New Brunswick, N.J.: Rutgers University Press, 1992.

Dalle Vacche, Angela. *The Body in the Mirror: Shapes of History in Italian Cinema.* Princeton: Princeton University Press, 1992.

De Grazia, Victoria. "Mass Culture and Sovereignty: The American Challenge to European Cinemas, 1920–1960." *Journal of Modern History* 61.1 (March 1989): 53–87.

Dick, Bernard F. *The Star-Spangled Screen: The American World War II Films.* Lexington: University of Kentucky Press, 1985.

Doane, Mary Ann. *The Desire to Desire: The Woman's Film of the 1940s.* Bloomington: Indiana University Press, 1987.

Doherty, Thomas. *Projections of War: Hollywood, American Culture, and World War II.* New York: Columbia University Press, 1993.

Ehrlich, Evelyn. *Cinema of Paradox: French Filmmaking under the German Occupation.* New York: Columbia University Press, 1985.

Ferro, Marc. *Cinema and History.* Trans. Naomi Greene. Detroit: Wayne State University Press, 1988.

Fischli, Bruno. *The Third Reich in Films of the Federal Republic of Germany.* Trans. Eileen Martin. Munich: Goethe-Institut, 1982.

Freyermuth, Gundolf S. *Reise in die Verlorengegangenheit. Auf den Spuren deutscher Emigranten (1933-1940).* Hamburg: Rasch und Röhring, 1990.

Fritz, Walter. *Geschichte des österreichischen Films.* Vienna: Bergland, 1969.

Fyne, Robert. *The Hollywood Propaganda of World War II.* Metuchen, N.J.: Scarecrow, 1994.

Geschichtswerkstatt Hannover, ed. "Film—Geschichte—Wirklichkeit." *Geschichtswerkstatt* 17 (April 1989).

Gesek, Ludwig. *Filmzauber aus Wien. Notizblätter zu einer Geschichte des österreichischen Films.* Vienna: Österreichische Gesellschaft für Filmwissenschaft, 1966.

Grob, Norbert, ed. *Das Jahr 1945 und das Kino.* Berlin: Berliner Festspiele/Stiftung Deutsche Kinemathek, 1995.

Hay, James. *Popular Film Culture in Fascist Italy: The Passing of the Rex.* Bloomington: Indiana University Press, 1987.

Holba, Herbert, Günter Knorr, and Peter Spiegel. *Reclams deutsches Filmlexikon.* Stuttgart: Reclam, 1984.

Hurd, Geoff, ed. *National Fictions: World War Two in British Films and Television.* London: British Film Institute, 1984.

Jacobs, Lewis. "World War II and the American Film." *Film Culture* 47 (Summer 1969): 28–42.

Jacobsen, Wolfgang, Anton Kaes, and Hans Helmut Prinzler, eds. *Geschichte des deutschen Films.* Stuttgart: Metzler, 1993.

Jeavons, Clyde. *A Pictorial History of War Films.* Secaucus, N.J.: Citadel, 1974.

Jones, Dorothy B. "The Hollywood War Film: 1942–1944." *Hollywood Quarterly* 1.1 (October 1945): 46–59.

Kaes, Anton. *From Hitler to Heimat: The Return of History as Film.* Cambridge, Mass.: Harvard University Press, 1989.

Karpf, Ernst, ed. *Filmmythos Volk. Zur Produktion kollektiver Identität im Film.* Frankfurt am Main: Gemeinschaftswerk der Evangelischen Publizistik, 1992.

Kaspar, Gabriele, and Lothar Erdmann, eds. *MDR-Retrospective. "Die 50 besten deutschen Filme."* Berlin: Vistas, 1995.

Koshofer, Gert. *Color. Die Farben des Films.* Berlin: Spiess, 1988.

Kramer, Thomas, ed. *Reclams Lexikon des deutschen Films.* Stuttgart: Reclam, 1995.

Kramer, Thomas, and Martin Prucha. *Film im Lauf der Zeit. 100 Jahre Kino in Deutschland, Österreich und der Schweiz.* Vienna: Ueberreuter, 1994.

Landy, Marcia. *Fascism in Film: The Italian Commercial Cinema, 1931–1943.* Princeton: Princeton University Press, 1986.

Lant, Antonia. *Blackout: Reinventing Women for Wartime British Cinema.* Princeton: Princeton University Press, 1991.

Loiperdinger, Martin, Rudolf Herz, and Ulrich Pohlmann, eds. *Führerbilder. Hitler, Mussolini, Roosevelt, Stalin in Fotografie und Film.* Munich: Piper, 1995.

Manvell, Roger. *Films and the Second World War.* New York: Dell, 1976.

Mariani, John. "Let's Not Be Beastly to the Nazis." *Film Comment* 15.1 (January–February 1979): 49–53.

Marsiske, Hans-Arthur, ed. *Zeitmaschine Kino. Darstellungen von Geschichte im Film.* Marburg: Hitzeroth, 1992.

McClure, Arthur F. "Hollywood at War: The American Motion Picture and World War Two, 1939–1945." *Journal of Popular Film* 1 (Spring 1972): 123–135.

Mommsen, Hans. *From Weimar to Hitler: A Documentary Film Program.* Trans. Peter Green. Munich: Goethe-Institut, 1981.

Murphy, Robert. *Realism and Tinsel: Cinema and Society in Britain 1939–1949.* London/New York: Routledge, 1992.

Oertel, Rudolf. *Macht und Magie des Films. Weltgeschichte einer Massensuggestion.* Vienna: Europa, 1959.

Ott, Frederick W. *The Great German Films.* Secaucus, N.J.: Citadel, 1986.

Paris, Michael. *From the Wright Brothers to Top Gun: Aviation, Nationalism and Popular Cinema.* Manchester: Manchester University Press, 1995.

Patalas, Enno. *Sozialgeschichte der Stars.* Hamburg: Schröder, 1963.

Pfister, Thomas. *Der Schweizer Film während des III. Reiches.* Berlin: Selbstverlag, 1982.

Prinzler, Hans Helmut. *Chronik des deutschen Films 1895–1994.* Stuttgart/Weimar: Metzler, 1995.

Pronay, Nicholas, and D. W. Spring, eds. *Propaganda, Politics and Film, 1918–45.* London: Macmillan, 1982.

Rosenstone, Robert A., ed. *Revisioning History: Film and the Construction of a New Past.* Princeton: Princeton University Press, 1995.

Roth, Wilhelm. "Dokumentarfilm Erinnerung Manipulation Verdrängung Zerstörung Propagandafilm." *Filmkritik* 16.7 (July 1972): 375–381.

Rother, Rainer, ed. *Bilder schreiben Geschichte. Der Historiker im Kino.* Berlin: Wagenbach, 1991.

Saunders, Thomas J. *Hollywood in Berlin: American Cinema and Weimar Germany.* Berkeley: University of California Press, 1994.
Short, K. R. M., ed. *Film & Radio Propaganda in World War II.* Knoxville: University of Tennessee Press, 1983.
Sorlin, Pierre. *European Cinemas, European Societies, 1939–1990.* London: Routledge, 1991.
Steele, Richard W. *Propaganda in an Open Society: The Roosevelt Administration and the Media, 1933–1941.* Westport, Conn.: Greenwood, 1985.
Töteberg, Michael, ed. *Metzlers Film Lexikon.* Stuttgart/Weimar: Metzler, 1995.
Wolff, Udo W. *Preußens Glanz und Gloria im Film.* Munich: Heyne, 1981.
Wollenberg, H. H. *Fifty Years of German Cinema.* London: Falcon, 1948.

Interdisciplinary and Theoretical Approaches

Ades, Dawn, et al., eds. *Art and Power: Europe under the Dictators 1930–45.* London: Hayward Gallery, 1995.
Adorno, Theodor. *In Search of Wagner.* Trans. Rodney Livingstone. London: Verso, 1984.
——— *The Jargon of Authenticity.* Trans. Knut Tarnowski and Frederic Will. Evanston: Northwestern University Press, 1973.
——— *Minima Moralia: Reflections from Damaged Life.* Trans. E. F. N. Jephcott. London: Verso, 1978.
——— *The Stars Down to Earth.* Trans. Stephen Crook. London: Routledge, 1994.
Alberts, Claudia, ed. *Deutsche Klassiker im Nationalsozialismus. Schiller. Kleist. Hölderlin.* Stuttgart: Metzler, 1994.
Anderson, Benedict. *Imagined Communities.* Rev. ed. London: Verso, 1994.
Arendt, Hannah. *The Origins of Totalitarianism.* New York: World, 1958.
Arntzen, Helmut, et al. *Der Ursprung der Gegenwart. Zur Bewußtseinsgeschichte der Dreißiger Jahre in Deutschland.* Weinheim: Beltz, 1995.
Ayass, Wolfgang. *"Asoziale" im Nationalsozialismus.* Stuttgart: Klett-Cotta, 1995.
Baird, Jay W. *The Mythical World of Nazi War Propaganda.* Minnesota: University of Minnesota Press, 1974.
——— *To Die for Germany: Heroes in the Nazi Pantheon.* Bloomington: Indiana University Press, 1990.
Balfour, Michael. *Propaganda in War, 1939–1945: Organisations, Policies and Publics in Britain and Germany.* London: Routledge & Kegan Paul, 1979.
Barbian, Jan-Peter. *Literaturpolitik im "Dritten Reich." Institutionen, Kompetenzen, Betätigungsfelder.* Frankfurt am Main: Buchhändler-Vereinigung, 1993.
Barron, Stephanie, ed. *"Degenerate Art": The Fate of the Avant-Garde in Nazi Germany.* Los Angeles: Los Angeles County Museum of Art, 1991.
Bärsch, Claus-E. "Das Erhabene und der Nationalsozialismus." *Merkur* 43.9–10 (September/October 1989): 777–790.

Bartetzko, Dieter. *Illusionen in Stein. Stimmungsarchitektur im deutschen Faschismus.* Reinbek bei Hamburg: Rowohlt, 1985.

——— *Zwischen Zucht und Ekstase. Zur Theatralik von NS-Architektur.* Berlin: Gebr. Mann, 1985.

Bartov, Omer. *Hitler's Army: Soldiers, Nazis, and War in the Third Reich.* New York/Oxford: Oxford University Press, 1992.

Bataille, Georges. *Die psychologische Struktur des Faschismus. Die Souveränität.* Trans. Rita Bischof et al. Munich: Matthes & Seitz, 1978.

Bauer, Gerhard. *Sprache und Sprachlosigkeit im "Dritten Reich."* Cologne: Bund, 1988.

Behnken, Klaus, and Wagner, Frank, eds. *Inszenierung der Macht. Ästhetische Faszination im Faschismus.* Berlin: NGBK/Nishen, 1987.

Benjamin, Walter. *Illuminations.* Ed. Hannah Arendt. Trans. Harry Zohn. New York: Schocken, 1969.

Beradt, Charlotte. *Das Dritte Reich des Traums.* Munich: Nymphenburger, 1966.

Bergschicker, Heinz. *Deutsche Chronik 1933–1945. Ein Zeitbild der faschistischen Diktatur.* Berlin: Verlag der Nation, 1981.

Berman, Russell A. "The Aestheticization of Politics: Walter Benjamin on Fascism and the Avant-Garde." In *Modern Culture and Critical Theory: Art, Politics, and the Legacy of the Frankfurt School.* Madison: University of Wisconsin Press, 1989. Pp. 27–41.

Bessel, Richard, ed. *Life in the Third Reich.* Oxford/New York: Oxford University Press, 1987.

Bleuel, Hans-Peter. *Das saubere Reich. Theorie und Praxis des sittlichen Lebens im Dritten Reich.* Bern: Scherz, 1972.

Bloch, Ernst. *Heritage of Our Times.* Trans. Neville Plaice and Stephen Plaice. Berkeley: University of California Press, 1991.

——— *Vom Hasard zur Katastrophe. Politische Aufsätze aus dem Jahren 1934–1939.* Frankfurt am Main: Suhrkamp, 1972.

Boelcke, Willi A., ed. *The Secret Conferences of Dr. Goebbels: The Nazi Propaganda War, 1939–43.* Trans. Ewald Osers. New York: Dutton, 1970.

Boeschenstein, Hermann. *The German Novel, 1939–1944.* Toronto: Toronto University Press, 1949.

Bohrer, Karl Heinz. *Die Ästhetik des Schreckens. Die pessimistische Romantik und Ernst Jüngers Frühwerk.* Frankfurt am Main: Ullstein, 1983.

Bracher, Karl Dietrich. *Die deutsche Diktatur.* Cologne: Kiepenheuer & Witsch, 1969.

Bramsted, Ernst K. *Goebbels and National Socialist Propaganda, 1925–1945.* East Lansing: Michigan State University Press, 1965.

Bridenthal, Renata, Atina Grossmann, and Marion Kaplan, eds. *When Biology Became Destiny: Women in Weimar and Nazi Germany.* New York: Monthly Review, 1984.

Brock, Bazon, and Achim Preiss, eds. *Kunst auf Befehl? Dreiunddreißig bis Fünfundvierzig.* Munich: Klinkhardt & Biermann, 1990.

Brückner, Peter. *Das Abseits als sicherer Ort. Kindheit und Jugend zwischen 1933 und 1945.* Berlin: Wagenbach, 1980.

Brückner, Peter, et al. "Perspectives on the Fascist Public Sphere." *New German Critique* 11 (Spring 1977): 94–132.

Burleigh, Michael, and Wolfgang Wippermann. *The Racial State: Germany, 1933–1945.* Cambridge: Cambridge University Press, 1991.

Buruma, Ian. *The Wages of Guilt: Memories of War in Germany and Japan.* New York: Farrar, Straus & Giroux, 1994.

Carter, Erica, and Chris Turner. "Political Somatics: Notes on Klaus Theweleit's *Male Fantasies.*" In *Formations of Fantasy.* Ed. Victor Burgin, James Donald, and Cora Kaplan. London/New York: Methuen, 1986. Pp. 200–213.

Crew, David F., ed. *Nazism and German Society, 1933–1945.* New York/London: Routledge, 1994.

Cuomo, Glenn R., ed. *National Socialist Cultural Policy.* New York: St. Martin's, 1995.

Daiber, Hans. *Schaufenster der Diktatur. Theater im Machtbereich Hitlers.* Stuttgart: Neske, 1995.

De Grazia, Victoria. *The Culture of Consent: Mass Organization of Leisure in Fascist Italy.* Cambridge: Cambridge University Press, 1981.

——— *How Fascism Ruled Women: Italy, 1922–1945.* Berkeley: University of California Press, 1992.

DeLillo, Don. *Americana.* Boston: Houghton Mifflin, 1971.

——— *Running Dog.* New York: Vintage, 1979.

——— *White Noise.* New York: Viking, 1985.

Denkler, Horst, and Eberhart Lämmert, eds. *"Das war ein Vorspiel nur . . ." Berliner Colloquium zur Literaturpolitik im "Dritten Reich."* Berlin: Akademie der Künste, 1985.

Denkler, Horst, and Karl Prümm, eds. *Die deutsche Literatur im Dritten Reich.* Stuttgart: Reclam, 1976.

Diller, Ansgar. *Rundfunkpolitik im Dritten Reich.* Munich: Deutscher Taschenbuch Verlag, 1980.

Diner, Dan, ed. *Ist der Nationalsozialismus Geschichte? Zu Historisierung und Historikerstreit.* Frankfurt am Main: Fischer, 1987.

Drechsler, Nanny. *Die Funktion der Musik im deutschen Rundfunk 1933–1945.* Pfaffenweiler: Centaurus, 1988.

Drewniak, Bogusław. *Das Theater im NS-Staat.* Düsseldorf: Droste, 1983.

Dröge, Franz. *Der zerredete Widerstand. Zur Soziologie und Publizistik des Gerüchts im 2. Weltkrieg.* Düsseldorf: Bertelsmann, 1970.

Dümling, Albrecht, ed. *Banned by the Nazis: Entartete Musik.* London: South Bank Centre, 1995.

Dussel, Konrad. "NS-Staat und moderne Kunst." *Universitas* 47.9 (1992): 841–854.

Eagleton, Terry. *Ideology: An Introduction.* London: Verso, 1991.

Eco, Umberto. "Ur-Fascism." *New York Review of Books,* 22 June 1995, pp. 12–15.

Eichberg, Henning, et al. *Massenspiele. NS-Thingspiel, Arbeiterweihespiel und olympisches Zeremoniell.* Stuttgart/Bad Cannstatt: Frommann-Holzboog, 1977.

Elliott, David. "The Battle for Art in the 1930s." *History Today* 45.11 (November 1995): 14–21.

Ellul, Jacques. *Propaganda: The Formation of Men's Attitudes.* Trans. Konrad Kellen and Jean Lerner. New York: Vintage, 1973.

Emmerich, Wolfgang. "'Massenfaschismus' und die Rolle des Ästhetischen. Faschismusanalysen bei Ernst Bloch, Walter Benjamin, Bertolt Brecht." In *Antifaschistische Literatur.* Ed. Lutz Winkler. Vol. 1. Kronberg: Scriptor, 1977. Pp. 223–290.

Erikson, Erik Homburger. "Hitler's Imagery and German Youth." *Psychiatry* 5 (1942): 475–493.

Faye, Jean Pierre. *Theorie der Erzählung. Einführung in die "totalitären Sprachen."* Trans. Jürgen Hoch. Frankfurt am Main: Suhrkamp, 1977.

Fest, Joachim C. *The Face of the Third Reich: Portraits of the Nazi Leadership.* Trans. Michael Bullock. New York: Pantheon, 1970.

——— *Hitler.* Trans. Richard and Clara Winston. New York: Random House, 1975.

Fischer, Klaus P. *Nazi Germany: A New History.* New York: Continuum, 1995.

Fischli, Bruno. *Die deutsche Dämmerung. Zur Genealogie des völkisch-faschistischen Dramas und Theaters (1897–1933).* Bonn: Bouvier, 1976.

Focke, Harald, and Uwe Reimer. *Alltag unterm Hakenkreuz. Wie die Nazis das Leben der Deutschen veränderten.* Reinbek bei Hamburg: Rowohlt, 1987.

Frankfurter Kunstverein, ed. *Kunst im 3. Reich. Dokumente der Unterwerfung.* Frankfurt am Main: Zweitausendeins, 1979.

Frei, Norbert. *Der Führerstaat. Nationalsozialistische Herrschaft 1933 bis 1945.* Munich: Deutscher Taschenbuch Verlag, 1987.

——— "Wie modern war der Nationalsozialismus?" *Geschichte und Gesellschaft* 19 (1993): 367–387.

Frei, Norbert, and Johannes Schmitz. *Journalismus im Dritten Reich.* Munich: Beck, 1989.

Friedländer, Saul, ed. *Probing the Limits of Representation: Nazism and the "Final Solution."* Cambridge, Mass.: Harvard University Press, 1992.

Fritzsche, Peter. *A Nation of Fliers: German Aviators and the Popular Imagination.* Cambridge, Mass.: Harvard University Press, 1992.

Fromm, Bella. *Blood and Banquets: A Berlin Diary, 1930–38.* New York: Simon & Schuster, 1990.

Fromm, Erich. *The Anatomy of Human Destructiveness.* New York: Francisco: Holt, Rinehart and Winston, 1973.

——— *Escape from Freedom.* New York: Avon, 1965.

Gamm, Hans-Jochen. *Der braune Kult. Das Dritte Reich und seine Ersatzreligion.* Hamburg: Rütten & Loening, 1962.

——— *Der Flüsterwitz im Dritten Reich.* Munich: List, 1963.

Geyer, Michael. "Resistance as Ongoing Project: Visions of Order, Obligations to

Strangers, Struggles for Civil Society." *Journal of Modern History* 64, Supplement (December 1992): S217–S241.

——— "The State in National Socialist Germany." In *Statemaking and Social Movements: Essays in History and Theory.* Ed. Charles Bright and Susan Harding. Ann Arbor: University of Michigan Press, 1984. Pp. 193–232

Gispen, Kees. "National Socialism and the Technological Culture of the Weimar Republic." *Central European History* 25.4 (1992): 387–406.

Golsan, Richard J., ed. *Fascism, Aesthetics, and Culture.* Hanover, N.H.: University Press of New England, 1992.

Golsan, Richard J., and Melanie Hawthorne, eds. *Gender, Fascism, and Popular Culture.* Hanover, N.H.: University Press of New England, 1996.

Gravenhorst, Lerke, and Carmen Tatschmurat, eds. *Töchter-Fragen: NS-Frauen-Geschichte.* Freiburg: Kore, 1990.

Grunberger, Richard. *The 12-Year Reich: A Social History of Nazi Germany, 1933–1945.* New York: Holt, Rinehart and Winston, 1971.

Guérin, Daniel. *The Brown Plague: Travels in Late Weimar and Early Nazi Germany.* Trans. Robert Schwartzwald. Durham, N.C.: Duke University Press, 1994.

Harand, Monika. *Die Aussteiger als Einsteiger. Zivilisationsflüchtige Helden in der völkischen Literatur (1931–1944).* Stuttgart: Heinz, 1988.

Hartley, John. *The Politics of Pictures: The Creation of the Public in the Age of Popular Media.* London: Routledge, 1992.

Hartung, Günter. *Literatur und Ästhetik des deutschen Faschismus. Drei Studien.* Cologne: Pahl-Rugenstein, 1984.

Hass, Ulrike. *Militante Pastorale. Zur Literatur der antimodernen Bewegung im frühen 20. Jahrhundert.* Munich: Fink, 1993.

Heiber, Beatrice, and Helmut Heiber, eds. *Die Rückseite des Hakenkreuzes. Absonderliches aus den Akten des Dritten Reiches.* Munich: Deutscher Taschenbuch Verlag, 1993.

Hennig, Eike. *Zum Historikerstreit. Was heißt und zu welchem Ende studiert man Faschismus?* Frankfurt am Main: Athenäum, 1988.

Herding, Klaus, and Hans-Ernst Mittig. *Kunst und Alltag im NS-System. Albert Speers Berliner Straßenlaternen.* Gießen: Anabas, 1975.

Herf, Jeffrey. *Reactionary Modernism: Technology, Culture, and Politics in Weimar and the Third Reich.* Cambridge: Cambridge University Press, 1984.

Hermand, Jost. *Old Dreams of a New Reich: Volkisch Utopias and National Socialism.* Trans. Paul Levesque and Stefan Soldovieri. Bloomington: Indiana University Press, 1992.

Herzstein, Robert Edwin. *The War That Hitler Won: The Most Infamous Propaganda Campaign in History.* New York: Putnam, 1978.

Hewitt, Andrew. *Fascist Modernism: Aesthetics, Politics, and the Avant-Garde.* Stanford: Stanford University Press, 1993.

Hickethier, Knut. "The Television Play in the Third Reich." *Historical Journal of Film, Radio and Television* 10.2 (1990): 163–186.

Hildebrand, K. *The Third Reich.* Trans. P. S. Falla. London: Allen & Unwin, 1984.

Hinkel, Hermann. *Zur Funktion des Bildes im deutschen Faschismus.* Giessen: Anabas, 1975.

Hinz, Berthold. *Art in the Third Reich.* Trans. Robert Kimber and Rita Kimber. New York: Pantheon, 1979.

———, ed. *Die Dekoration der Gewalt. Kunst und Medien im Faschismus.* Giessen: Anabas, 1979.

Hinz, Manfred. *Massenkult und Todessymbolik in der nationalsozialistischen Architektur.* Cologne: Brill, 1984.

"Historikerstreit." Die Dokumentation der Kontroverse um die Einzigartigkeit der nationalsozialistischen Judenvernichtung. Munich/Zürich: Piper, 1987.

Höhne, Heinz. *Die Zeit der Illusionen. Hitler und die Anfänge des Dritten Reiches 1933–1936.* Düsseldorf: Econ, 1991.

Horkheimer, Max, and Theodor W. Adorno. *Dialectic of Enlightenment.* Trans. John Cumming. New York: Seabury, 1972.

Huber, Karl-Heinz. *Jugend unterm Hakenkreuz.* Frankfurt am Main: Ullstein, 1986.

Jäckel, Eberhard. *Hitler's World View: A Blueprint for Power.* Trans. Herbert Arnold. Cambridge, Mass.: Harvard University Press, 1981.

Jameson, Fredric. *Fables of Aggression: Wyndham Lewis, the Modernist as Fascist.* Berkeley: University of California Press, 1979.

Jeffrey, Ian. *German Photographs of the 1930s.* London: South Bank Centre, 1995.

Kaplan, Alice Yaeger. *Reproductions of Banality: Fascism, Literature, and French Intellectual Life.* Minneapolis: University of Minnesota Press, 1986.

Kasher, Steven. "*Das Deutsche Lichtbild* and the Militarization of German Photography." *Afterimage* 18.7 (February 1991): 10–14.

Kater, Michael H. *Different Drummers: Jazz in the Culture of Nazi Germany.* Oxford: Oxford University Press, 1992.

——— "Forbidden Fruit? Jazz in the Third Reich." *American Historical Review* 94.1 (February 1989): 11–43.

Kershaw, Ian. *The Hitler Myth: Image and Reality in the Third Reich.* Oxford/New York: Oxford University Press, 1987.

——— *The Nazi Dictatorship: Problems and Perspectives of Interpretation.* 3rd ed. London/New York: Arnold, 1993.

Ketelsen, Uwe-Karsten. *Heroisches Theater. Untersuchungen zur Dramatheorie des Dritten Reiches.* Bonn: Bouvier, 1968.

——— *Literatur und Drittes Reich.* Schernfeld: SH-Verlag, 1992.

——— *Von Heroischem Sein und völkischem Tod. Zur Dramatik des Dritten Reiches.* Bonn: Bouvier, 1970.

Kirk, Tim. *The Longman Companion to Nazi Germany.* London: Longman, 1995.

Kirkpatrick, Clifford. *Nazi Germany: Its Women and Family Life.* New York: Bobbs-Merrill, 1938.

Klemperer, Victor. *"LTI." Die unbewältigte Sprache.* Stuttgart: Deutscher Taschenbuch Verlag, 1969.

Klinksiek, Dorothee. *Die Frau im NS-Staat. Stuttgart:* Deutsche Verlagsanstalt, 1982.

Klönne, Arno. "Jugendliche Subkulturen im Dritten Reich." In *Schock und Schöpfung—Jugendästhetik im 20. Jahrhundert.* Ed. Willi Bucher and Klaus Pohl. Darmstadt: Luchterhand, 1986. Pp. 308–313.

Koenigsberg, Richard A. "Culture and Unconscious Phantasy: Observations on Nazi Germany." *Psychoanalytic Review* 55.4 (1968–69): 681–696.

——— *Hitler's Ideology: A Study in Psychoanalytic Sociology.* New York: Library of Social Science, 1975.

Koonz, Claudia. "Beauty and the Beast: The Aesthetics of Nazi Bio-Politics." *Culturefront* 3.1 (Winter–Spring 1994): 97–99.

——— *Mothers in the Fatherland: Women, the Family, and Nazi Politics.* New York: St. Martin's, 1987.

Kracauer, Siegfried. *The Mass Ornament: Weimar Essays.* Trans. and ed. Thomas Y. Levin. Cambridge, Mass.: Harvard University Press, 1995.

Kühn, Volker, ed. *Deutschlands Erwachen. Kabarett unterm Hakenkreuz 1933–1945.* Weinheim/Berlin: Quadriga, 1989.

Labanyi, Peter. "Images of Fascism: Visualization and Aestheticization in the Third Reich." In *The Burden of German History, 1919–1945.* Ed. M. Laffan. London: Methuen, 1988. Pp. 151–177.

Lacoue-Labarthe, Philippe. *Heidegger, Art and Politics.* Trans. Chris Turner. Oxford: Blackwell, 1990.

Lacoue-Labarthe, Philippe, and Jean-Luc Nancy. "The Nazi Myth." Trans. Brian Holmes. *Critical Inquiry* 16.2 (Winter 1990): 291–312.

Lane, Barbara Miller. *Architecture and Politics in Germany, 1918–1945.* Cambridge, Mass.: Harvard University Press, 1985.

——— "Nazi Ideology: Some Unfinished Business." *Central European History* 7 (March 1974): 3–30.

Laugstien, Thomas. *Philosophieverhältnisse im Dritten Reich.* Berlin: Argument, 1990.

Lerg, Winfried. "Zur Entstehung des Fernsehens in Deutschland." *Rundfunk und Fernsehen* 4 (1967): 349–375.

Levi, Erik. *Music in the Third Reich.* New York: St. Martin's, 1994.

Lidtke, Vernon L. "Songs and Nazis: Political Music and Social Change in Twentieth-Century Germany." In *Essays on Culture and Society in Modern Germany.* Ed. Gary D. Stark and Bede Karl Lackner. College Station: Texas A & M University Press, 1982. Pp. 167–200.

Loewenberg, Peter. "The Psychohistorical Origins of the Nazi Youth Cohort." *American Historical Review* 76.5 (December 1971): 1457–1502.

Loewy, Ernst. *Literatur unterm Hakenkreuz. Das Dritte Reich und seine Dichtung.* Frankfurt am Main: Fischer, 1983.

Löwenthal, Leo. *Literature and the Image of Man.* New Brunswick, N.J./Oxford: Transaction, 1986.

Lutz, Andrea. "Der 'Neue Diskurs' und die Ästhetik des Nationalsozialismus." *Augen-Blick* 15 (August 1993): 65–79.

Maenz, Paul. *Art Déco 1920–1940. Formen zwischen zwei Kriegen.* Cologne: DuMont, 1974.

Maier, Charles S. *The Unmasterable Past: History, Holocaust, and German National Identity.* Cambridge, Mass.: Harvard University Press, 1988.

Mairgünther, Wilfred. *Morbus Hitler. Ein Essay.* Kiel: Neuer Malik, 1989.

Manning, Susan A. *Ecstasy and the Demon: Feminism and Nationalism in the Dances of Mary Wigman.* Berkeley: University of California Press, 1993.

Marcuse, Herbert. *Negations: Essays in Critical Theory.* Trans. Jeremy J. Shapiro. Boston: Beacon, 1968.

Mattenklott, Gert. *Der übersinnliche Leib. Beiträge zur Metaphysik des Körpers.* Reinbek bei Hamburg: Rowohlt, 1982.

Mehrtens, Herbert, and Steffen Richter, eds. *Naturwissenschaft, Technik und NS-Ideologie. Beiträge zur Wissenschaftsgeschichte des Dritten Reichs.* Frankfurt am Main: Suhrkamp, 1980.

Merker, Reinhard. *Die bildenden Kunste im Nationalsozialismus.* Cologne: DuMont, 1983.

Meyer, Michael. *The Politics of Music in the Third Reich.* New York: Lang, 1991.

Milfull, John, ed. *The Attractions of Fascism: Social Psychology and Aesthetics of the "Triumph of the Right."* New York: Berg, 1990.

Mosse, George L. *Masses and Man: Nationalist and Fascist Perceptions of Reality.* Detroit: Wayne State University Press, 1987.

——— *The Nationalization of the Masses.* Ithaca: Cornell University Press, 1975.

———, ed. *Nazi Culture: Intellectual, Cultural, and Social Life in the Third Reich.* New York: Schocken, 1981.

Nerdinger, Winfried, ed. *Bauhaus-Moderne im Nationalsozialismus. Zwischen Anbiederung und Verfolgung.* Munich: Prestel, 1993.

Neumann, Franz. *Behemoth: The Structure and Practice of National Socialism.* London: Oxford University Press, 1942.

Ogan, Bernd, and Wolfgang N. Weiss, eds. *Faszination und Gewalt. Zur politischen Ästhetik des Nationalsozialismus.* Nuremberg: Tümmels, 1992.

Otten, Karl. *Geplante Illusionen. Eine Analyse des Faschismus.* Frankfurt am Main: Luchterhand, 1989.

Owings, Alison. *Frauen: German Women Recall the Third Reich.* New Brunswick, N.J.: Rutgers University Press, 1993.

Payne, Stanley G. *Fascism: Comparison and Definition.* Madison: University of Wisconsin Press, 1980.

Peuckert, Detlev J. K. *Die Edelweißpiraten. Protestbewegungen jugendlicher Arbeiter im Dritten Reich. Eine Dokumentation.* 2nd rev. ed. Cologne: Bund, 1983.

——— *Inside Nazi Germany: Conformity, Opposition, and Racism in Everyday Life.* Trans. Richard Deveson. New Haven: Yale University Press, 1987.

Picard, Max. *Hitler in Our Selves.* Trans. Heinrich Hauser. Hinsdale, Ill.: Regnery, 1947.
Pini, Udo. *Leibeskult und Liebeskitsch. Erotik im Dritten Reich.* Munich: Klinkhardt & Biermann, 1992.
Pohle, Heinz. "Wollen und Wirklichkeit des deutschen Fernsehens bis 1943." *Rundfunk und Fernsehen* 1 (1956): 59–75.
Pois, Robert A. *National Socialism and the Religion of Nature.* New York: St. Martin's, 1986.
Polster, Bernd, ed. *"Swing Heil." Jazz im Nationalsozialismus.* Berlin: Transit, 1989.
Quinn, Malcolm. *The Swastika: Constructing the Symbol.* London: Routledge, 1994.
Rabinbach, Anson. "The Aesthetics of Production in the Third Reich." *Journal of Contemporary History* 11 (1976): 43–74.
——— "Evil in the Shape of Light: Some Reflections on Nazism and Art." *Culturefront* 3.1 (Winter–Spring 1994): 81–83, 92.
Rathkolb, Olivier. *Führertreu und gottbegnadet. Künstlereliten im Dritten Reich.* Vienna: ÖBV, 1991.
Raulet, Gérard. *Natur und Ornament. Zur Erzeugung von Heimat.* Darmstadt/Neuwied: Luchterhand, 1987.
Reich, Wilhelm. *The Mass Psychology of Fascism.* Trans. Vincent R. Carfagno. New York: Farrar, Straus & Giroux, 1970.
Reichel, Peter. *Der schöne Schein des Dritten Reiches. Faszination und Gewalt des Faschismus.* Munich/Vienna: Hanser, 1991.
Reichhardt, Hans J., and Wolfgang Schäche. *Von Berlin nach Germania. Über die Zerstörungen der Reichshauptstadt durch Albert Speers Neugestaltungsplanungen.* Berlin: Transit, 1990.
Reimann, Viktor. *Goebbels.* Trans. Stephen Wendt. Garden City, N.Y.: Doubleday, 1976.
Reiss, Erwin. *"Wir senden Frohsinn." Fernsehen unterm Faschismus.* Berlin: Elefanten, 1979.
Reuth, Ralf Georg. *Goebbels.* Munich/Zürich: Piper, 1992.
Richard, Lionel. *Le Nazisme et la culture.* Paris: Maspero, 1978.
——— *Nazisme et littérature.* Paris: Maspero, 1971.
Ritchie, James MacPherson. *German Literature under National Socialism.* Beckenham: Croom Helm, 1983.
Ritter, Franz, ed. *Heinrich Himmler und die Liebe zum Swing.* Leipzig: Reclam, 1994.
Roh, Franz. *"Entartete" Kunst. Kunstbarbarei im Dritten Reich.* Hannover: Fackelträger, 1962.
Rosenfeld, Alvin H. *Imagining Hitler.* Bloomington: Indiana University Press, 1985.
Rupp, Leila J. *Mobilizing Women for War: German and American Propaganda, 1939–1945.* Princeton: Princeton University Press, 1978.
Ruppelt, Georg. *Schiller im nationalsozialistischen Deutschland.* Stuttgart: Metzler, 1979.
Sahl, Hans. *"Und doch . . ." Essays und Kritiken aus zwei Kontinenten.* Ed. Klaus Blanc. Frankfurt am Main: Luchterhand, 1991.

Schäfer, Hans Dieter. "Amerikanismus im Dritten Reich." In *Nationalsozialismus und Modernisierung*. Ed. Michael Prinz and Rainer Zitelmann. Darmstadt: Wissenschaftliche Buchgesellschaft, 1991. Pp. 199–215.

——— *Das gespaltene Bewußtsein. Über Deutsche Kultur und Lebenswirklichkeit 1933–1945*. Frankfurt am Main: Ullstein, 1984.

———, ed. *Berlin im Zweiten Weltkrieg*. 2nd rev. ed. Munich/Zürich: Piper, 1991.

Schell, Ralf, ed. *Kunst und Kultur im deutschen Faschismus*. Stuttgart: Metzler/Poeschel, 1978.

Schmeer, Karlheinz. *Die Regie des öffentlichen Lebens im Dritten Reich*. Munich: Pohl, 1956.

Schmidt, Maruta, and Gabi Dietz, eds. *Frauen unterm Hakenkreuz*. Berlin: Elefanten, 1983.

Schnapp, Jeffrey T. "*18 BL:* Fascist Mass Spectacle." *Representations* 43 (Summer 1993): 89–125.

Schoenbaum, David. *Hitler's Social Revolution: Class and Status in Nazi Germany, 1933–1939*. Garden City, N.Y.: Doubleday, 1966.

Scholz, Robert. *Architektur und Bildende Kunst 1933–1945*. Preussisch Oldendorf: Schütz, 1977.

Schulte-Sasse, Linda. "Friedrich der Grosse und Hitler. Der Körper des Königs/Führers zwischen Schaustellung und Panoptismus." *KultuRRevolution* 24 (January 1991): 47–51.

Schuster, Peter-Klaus, ed. *Nationalsozialismus und "Entartete Kunst."* Munich: Prestel, 1987.

Schütz, Erhard. "Das 'Dritte Reich' als Mediendiktatur. Medienpolitik und Modernisierung in Deutschland 1933 bis 1945." *Monatshefte* 87.2 (Summer 1995): 129–150.

——— " 'Jene blaßgrauen Bänder.' Die Reichsautobahn in Literatur und anderen Medien des 'Dritten Reiches.' " *Internationales Archiv für Sozialgeschichte der Literatur* 18.1 (1993): 76–120.

——— "Zur Modernität des 'Dritten Reiches.' " *Internationales Archiv für Sozialgeschichte der Literatur* 20.1 (1995): 116–136.

Selle, Gert. *Kultur der Sinne und ästhetische Erziehung*. Cologne: DuMont, 1981.

Siegele-Wenschkewitz, Leonore, and Gerda Stuchlik, eds. *Frauen und Faschismus in Europa. Der faschistische Körper*. Pfaffenweiler: Centaurus, 1990.

Sloterdijk, Peter. *Critique of Cynical Reason*. Trans. Michael Eldred. Minneapolis: University of Minnesota Press, 1987.

Smith, T. "A State of Seeing, Unsighted: Notes on the Visual in Nazi War Culture." *Block* 12 (1986–87): 50–70.

Staeck, Klaus, ed. *Nazi-Kunst ins Museum?* Göttingen: Steidl, 1988.

Staudinger, Hans. *The Inner Nazi: A Critical Analysis of Mein Kampf.* Baton Rouge: Louisiana State University Press, 1981.

Steinert, Marlis G. *Hitlers Krieg und die Deutschen*. Düsseldorf/Vienna: Econ, 1970.

Steinweis, Alan E. *Art, Ideology, and Economics in Nazi Germany: The Reich Chambers of Music, Theater, and the Visual Arts.* Chapel Hill: University of North Carolina Press, 1993.

Stern, J. P. *Hitler: The Führer and the People.* Berkeley: University of California Press, 1975.

Stollmann, Rainer. *Ästhetisierung der Politik. Literaturstudien zum subjektiven Faschismus.* Stuttgart: Metzler, 1978.

Stommer, Rainer. *Die inszenierte Volksgemeinschaft. Die "Thing-Bewegung" im Dritten Reich.* Marburg: Jonas, 1985.

Stommer, Rainer, and Claudia Gabriele Philipp, eds. *Reichsautobahn. Pyramiden des Dritten Reiches.* Marburg: Jonas, 1982.

Sultano, Gloria. *Wie geistiges Kokain . . . Mode unterm Hakenkreuz.* Vienna: Verlag für Gesellschaftskritik, 1995.

Taylor, Brandon, and Wilfried van der Will, eds. *The Nazification of Art: Art, Design, Music, Architecture and Film in the Third Reich.* Winchester, U.K.: Winchester, 1990.

Thamer, Hans-Ulrich. *Verführung und Gewalt. Deutschland 1933–1945.* Berlin: Siedler, 1986.

Theweleit, Klaus. *Male Fantasies.* Vol. 1: *Women Floods Bodies History.* Trans. Stephen Conway, Erica Carter, and Chris Turner. Minneapolis: University of Minnesota Press, 1987.

——— *Male Fantasies.* Vol. 2: *Male Bodies: Psychoanalyzing the White Terror.* Trans. Erica Carter, Chris Turner, and Stephen Conway. Minneapolis: University of Minnesota Press, 1989.

Thomae, Otto. *Die Propaganda-Maschinerie. Bildende Kunst und Öffentlichkeitsarbeit im Dritten Reich.* Berlin: Gebr. Mann, 1978.

Thomas, Katherine. *Women in Nazi Germany.* London: Gollancz, 1943.

Thompson, Dorothy. "Culture under the Nazis." *Foreign Affairs* 14 (April 1936): 407–423.

Uricchio, William. "Television as History: Representations of German Television Broadcasting, 1935–1944." In *Framing the Past: The Historiography of German Cinema and Television.* Ed. Bruce A. Murray and Christopher J. Wickham. Carbondale: Southern Illinois University Press, 1992. Pp. 167–196.

———, ed. *Die Anfänge des deutschen Fernsehens. Kritische Annäherungen an die Entwicklung bis 1945.* Tübingen: Niemeyer, 1991.

Van der Will, Wilfried. "Culture and the Organization of National Socialist Ideology." In *German Cultural Studies: An Introduction.* Ed. Rob Burns. Oxford: Oxford University Press, 1995. Pp. 101–145.

Vondung, Klaus. *Magie und Manipulation. Ideologischer Kult und politische Religion des Nationalsozialismus.* Göttingen: Vandenhoeck & Ruprecht, 1971.

Wander, P. "Aesthetics of Fascism." *Journal of Communications* 33 (Spring 1983): 70–78.

Wardetzky, Jutta. *Theaterpolitik im faschistischen Deutschland. Studien und Dokumente.* Berlin: Henschel, 1983.

Weber, Otto. *Tausend ganz normale Jahre. Ein Fotoalbum des gewöhnlichen Faschismus.* Nördlingen: Greno, 1987.

Welch, David. *The Third Reich: Politics and Propaganda.* London: Routledge, 1993.

Wense, Jürgen von der. *Blumen blühen auf Befehl. Aus dem Poesiealbum eines zeitungslesenden Volksgenossen 1933–1944.* Munich: Matthes und Seitz, 1993.

Westenrieder, Norbert. *Deutsche Frauen und Mädchen. Vom Alltagsleben 1933–1945.* Düsseldorf: Droste, 1984.

Westphal, Uwe. *Werbung im Dritten Reich.* Berlin: Transit, 1989.

Wistrich, Robert S. *Weekend in Munich: Art, Propaganda and Terror in the Third Reich.* London: Pavilion, 1995.

——— *Who's Who in Nazi Germany.* London: Weidenfeld and Nicolson, 1982.

Wolbert, Klaus. *Die Nackten und die Toten des "Dritten Reiches." Folgen einer politischen Geschichte des Körpers in der Plastik des deutschen Faschismus.* Giessen: Anabas, 1982.

Wolffram, Knud. *Tanzdielen und Vergnügungspaläste. Berliner Nachtleben in den dreißiger und vierziger Jahren.* Berlin: Edition Hentrich, 1992.

Zeman, Z. A. B. *Nazi Propaganda.* London: Oxford University Press, 1964.

Zentner, Christian, and Friedemann Bedürftig, eds. *Das große Lexikon des Dritten Reiches.* Munich: Südwest, 1985.

Zeutschner, Heiko. *Die braune Mattscheibe. Fernsehen im Nationalsozialismus.* Hamburg: Rotbuch, 1995.

Zielinski, Siegfried. *Audiovisionen. Kino und Fernsehen als Zwischenspiele in der Geschichte.* Reinbek bei Hamburg: Rowohlt, 1989.

Zitelmann, Rainer. "Nationalsozialismus und Moderne. Eine Zwischenbilanz." In *Übergänge. Zeitgeschichte zwischen Utopie und Machbarkeit.* Ed. Werner Süss. Berlin: Duncker and Humblot, 1990. 195–204.

——— "Die totalitäre Seite der Moderne." In *Nationalsozialismus und Modernisierung.* Ed. Michael Prinz and Rainer Zitelmann. Darmstadt: Wissenschaftliche Buchgesellschaft, 1991. Pp. 1–20.

Zortman, Bruce. *Hitler's Theater: Ideological Drama in Nazi Germany.* El Paso: Firestein, 1984.

INDEX

Adenauer era, 14, 20, 93–94, 166, 215, 386n2
Adorno, T. W., 154, 381n60, 387n17; *Dialectic of Enlightenment*, 16, 44, 159, 164, 187, 190, 324n39, 328n70, 373n87; *Minima Moralia*, 388n18
Adventures of Baron Munchausen, The (Gilliam), 194, 375n12
After the Thin Man (Van Dyke), 109
Akrobat schö-ö-ö-n (Staudte), 218, 219
Albers, Hans, 4, 8, 9, 16, 76, 136, 192, 194, 196, 197–198, 203, 206, 377n27; as exemplar of masculinity, 198–200, 208, 375n14, 378nn31,32, 380n51, 383nn74,75
Albihn, Karen, 136, 353n53
Albrecht, Gerd, 7, 11, 302n27
Allotria (Forst), 106, 112
All That Heaven Allows (Sirk), 142
Alte und der junge König, Der. See Old and the Young King
America and Americanism, 22, 99, 101, 103, 107, 330n13, 338n78, 346n64, 388n19; as German object of desire in *The Prodigal Son*, 78–79; Trenker's representation of New York City, 87–89, 332nn26,28, 337nn71,73, 338n76, 340n93; Weimar debates about Americanism and German national identity, 90–91, 338n75; racism and anti-Americanism, 92; fascist Italy and American mass culture, 344n31, 348n83. *See also* Disney, Walt; Hollywood
Amphitryon (Schünzel), 18, 112, 344n23
Anderngast, Maria, 80
Anders als du und ich. See Different from You and Me
Andreas-Friedrich, Ruth, 193
Andreas Schlüter (Maisch), 177, 181, 182, 189
And the Sky above Us (von Baky), 197
Anna Karenina (Brown), 135
Annelie (von Baky), 197
Antonioni, Michelangelo, 153–154, 333n39, 358n24
April, April! (Sierck), 112
Arendt, Hannah, 22, 323n35, 358n23, 379n41
Arnheim, Rudolf, 338n74, 347n68, 378n32

Baarova, Lida, 126
Back Then (Hansen), 139–140
Baker, Josephine, 90
Baky, Josef von, 197, 376n21, 379n38
Balázs, Béla, 29, 31, 37, 46, 49, 51, 310n18, 314n52, 315nn66,72, 340n86
Balz, Bruno, 139
Barlach, Ernst, 57
Barthes, Roland, 143, 179, 369n51, 370n60
Bateson, Gregory, 59–60, 63–64, 326nn57,64
Batman Returns (Burton), 6, 301n21
Battleship Potemkin (Eisenstein), 110
Bäumler, Alfred, 53
Bavaria (film studio), 125, 172, 175, 176, 216
Bazin, André, 201, 382n66
Becce, Giuseppe, 80
Beckmann, Hans Fritz, 101
Benitz, Alfred, 80
Benjamin, Walter, 14, 59
Benkhoff, Fita, 8, 116
Benn, Gottfried, 57
Bergfilme. See Mountain films
Bergson, Henri, 113
Berkeley, Busby, 106
Berlin-Alexanderplatz (Jutzi), 61
Berlin Film Festival, 2, 117, 197, 200
Berlin Olympic Games of 1936, 21
Bicycle Thief, The (De Sica), 85
Billinger, Richard, 331n16, 340n92; *Rauhnacht*, 89–90, 92, 339n83; *Paracelsus*, 177, 372n84
Birgel, Willy, 113, 182, 200, 371n68
Bismarck (Liebeneiner), 181
Bitomsky, Hartmut, 21
Black Roses (Martin), 101, 344n23
Blaue Licht, Das. See Blue Light
Blaufuchs, Der. See Fox Fur Coat

Bleys, Jean Pierre, 128
Bloch, Ernst, 43, 74, 75, 76, 86, 144, 145, 177, 325n51, 333n34, 368n36, 369n47, 378n32
Blonder Traum, Ein. See Happily Ever After
Blood and Soil, 41, 42, 47, 73, 80, 86–87, 90, 331n20, 332n31, 337n66. *See also Heimat;* Homeland films
Blue Light, The (Riefenstahl), 53, 161, 310n18; importance for Riefenstahl's postwar rehabilitation, 29, 311n24; plot summary, 29–30; artistic impetus and intention, 30; production history and various releases, 31, 311n25, 312n38, 314n50, 315n72, 316nn76,79,81; artistic influences and borrowings, 32–38; similarities to *Nosferatu*, 37–38; debates about political significance, 38; original narrative frame, 42; relationship between romanticism and modernity, 42–44; and Riefenstahl's filmed self-image, 44, 48; reception history, 45–51, 316n74, 317n83; credits, 309n16. *See also* Blood and Soil; Fanck, Arnold; *Holy Mountain; Lowlands*
Blumenberg, Hans-Christoph, 197
Blut und Boden. See Blood and Soil
Boese, Carl, 7
Bolvary, Géza von, 376n21
Borgelt, Hans, 118
Borsody, Eduard von, 142
Braun, Eva, 82, 84
Brecht, Bertolt, 61, 127, 129, 198
Breker, Arno, 6, 21, 23, 309n14
Broadway Melody of 1936 (Del Ruth), 106, 109, 116
Broken Jug, The (Ucicky), 5, 300n16
Brooks, Louise, 175
Brooks, Peter, 168
Brückner, Peter, 326n53
Büchse der Pandora, Die. See Pandora's Box
Bullock, Alan, 172
Bürger, Gottfried August, 194

Cabinet des Dr. Caligari, Das. See Cabinet of Dr. Caligari
Cabinet of Dr. Caligari, The (Wiene), 62, 69
Cadars, Pierre, 12, 61, 304n45, 382n69
Capra, Frank, 114, 117, 119
Capriccio (Ritter), 217
Carl Peters (Selpin), 161, 181, 377n27, 383n75
Chaplin, Charlie, 28, 45
Chaste Lover, The (Tourjansky), 127
Children of No Importance (Lamprecht), 60
Cioran, E. M., 361n64
Cocteau, Jean, 28
Cohl, Emile, 194
Colbert, Claudette, 119
Conti, Leonardo, 180
Cooke, Alistair, 125
Correll, Ernst Hugo, 55–56, 353n48
Courtade, Francis, 12, 61, 304n45, 382n69
Custen, George F., 150–151, 371n69
Cziffra, Géza von, 348n85

Damals. See Back Then
Damned, The (Visconti), 6
Damn This America (Vogeler), 94
Dawn (Ucicky), 56, 131
Day of Freedom (Riefenstahl), 29, 307n87
DeLillo, Don, *Americana*, 215, 221–222, 387n16; *Running Dog*, 1; *White Noise*, 6
Deppe, Hans, 7
De Sica, Vittorio, 85
Desire (Borzage), 104
Diesel (Lamprecht), 182, 190, 371n68
Dieterle, William, 359n34
Dietrich, Marlene, 104, 107, 121, 135–136, 137, 139, 140, 354n70
Different from You and Me (Harlan), 166
Dinesen, Isak, 356n10
Disney, Walt, 28, 104, 105, 210; Mickey Mouse in Germany, 110–111, 117, 345n42, 347n68
Dissolves, 44, 69, 89; in *Jew Süss*, 159–163, 361n59
Dr. Mabuse, the Gambler (Lang), 156, 359n38, 361n62, 384n82
Dr. Mabuse, der Spieler. See Dr. Mabuse, the Gambler
Doherty, Thomas, 64
Don Quixote (Pabst), 175, 189
Doppelte Lottchen, Das. See Two Little Lottas
Doubles, 89, 159, 188, 189, 361n62; in *Jew Süss*, 163–165; in *Münchhausen*, 205, 210–211, 212, 384n80
Drei-Groschen-Oper, Die. See Threepenny Opera
Drewniak, Boguslaw, 11, 354n56, 365n11, 366n27
Dreyer, Carl, 167
Duday, Bruno, 132
Dyer, Richard, 139

Eckert, Gert, 19–20
Effi Briest (Gründgens), 143

Eggebrecht, Axel, 118, 150
Einstein, Albert, 30
Eisner, Lotte, 175, 325n47, 366n24
Elsaesser, Thomas, 23, 29, 363n81
Emo, E. W., 7
Emperor of California, The (Trenker), 84, 85, 105–106, 108, 331n21, 332n30, 335n54, 338n78
Enchanted Day, The (Pewas), 214, 218
Es leuchten die Sterne. See Stars Are Shining
Eternal Forest, The (Springer/von Sonjewski-Jamrowski), 160
Eternal Heart, The (Harlan), 168
Eternal Jew, The (Hippler), 5, 149, 153, 155, 156, 159–160, 163, 358n27, 359n39, 360n53, 361nn59,62
Eustache, Jean, 137
Everson, William K., 84, 85, 335n34, 336n59
Ewige Jude, Der. See Eternal Jew
Ewige Wald, Der. See Eternal Forest

Faded Melody (Tourjansky), 113
Fährmann Maria. See Ferry Boat Woman Maria
Fairbanks, Douglas, 28
Fall Molander, Der. See Molander Affair
Fanck, Arnold, 31, 34–37, 81, 221, 309n14, 310n18, 311n30, 313nn43,46,48, 314n49, 339n80
Far Away and Yet So Close (Wenders), 221
Fassbinder, Rainer Werner, 28, 164–165, 308n8, 350n16, 361n63
Faust (Murnau), 164
Feigenbauer, Richard, 194
Ferro, Marc, 159, 305n59
Ferry Boat Woman Maria (Wysbar), 108
Feuerteufel, Der. See Fire Devil
Feuerzangenbowle, Die. See Punch Bowl
Fiedler, Werner, 307n80
Film-Kurier, Der, 15, 20, 45, 46, 80, 88, 92, 101, 105, 130, 131, 132, 136, 379n38
Final Accord (Sierck), 130, 131, 141
Fire Devil, The (Trenker), 83, 333n40, 334n49, 336n62
Florentine Hat, The (Liebeneiner), 217
Florentiner Hut, Der. See Florentine Hat
Flüchtling aus Chicago, Der. See Fugitive from Chicago
Flüchtlinge. See Fugitives
Ford, John, 85
Forst, Willi, 4, 20, 106, 112, 127, 158, 176, 305n54, 347n78, 386n1
Förster vom Silberwald, Der. See Game Warden of the Silver Forest
Foster, Jodie, 6, 28
Foucault, Michel, 187
Fox Fur Coat, The (Tourjansky), 127, 307n80
Franco, Francisco, 132, 352n39
Frederick the Great, 75
Fresh Breeze from Canada (Kenter/Holder), 76
Freudlose Gasse, Die. See Joyless Street
Fridericus (Meyer), 181
Friedemann Bach (Müller), 181, 182, 189
Friedländer, Saul, 210, 301n20, 314n63, 384n77
Friedman, Mihal, 15, 162–163, 359n39, 360n51, 371n71
Friedrich, Caspar David, 32–34, 311n27, 312nn33–36
Friedrich Schiller (Maisch), 177, 181, 189
Friesennot. See Frisians in Peril
Frischer Wind aus Kanada. See Fresh Breeze from Canada
Frisians in Peril (Hagen), 76, 108
Fritsch, Willy, 17, 98, 101, 102, 116, 117, 118, 347n78, 348n85, 386n1
Froelich, Carl, 112, 142, 176, 221, 353n50, 355nn75,77
Fugitive from Chicago, The (Meyer), 75
Fugitives (Ucicky), 17, 20, 56, 76–77, 132, 330nn9,11, 377n27, 378n32, 383n74

Gable, Clark, 105, 117, 119
Game Warden of the Silver Forest, The (Stummer), 94
Garbo, Greta, 125, 130, 135, 139, 140, 175, 354n70
Gardner, Robert, 50
Garland, Judy, 139
Gasparone (Jacoby), 106
Geheimnisse einer Seele. See Secrets of a Soul
George, Heinrich, 182, 200, 324n45
Germanin (Kimmich), 333n40
German Wants to Go Home, A (Wegener), 20, 75–76, 378n33
Girl from the Marsh Croft, The (Sierck), 131, 141
Gladitz, Nina, 310n19
Glückskinder. See Lucky Kids
Goebbels, Joseph, 1, 2, 9, 11, 13, 16, 18–19, 20, 21, 23, 53, 66, 74, 81, 83, 84, 104, 106, 107, 114, 118, 125, 127, 141, 144, 149, 150, 157, 171, 172, 174, 194, 196, 197, 201, 202, 211,

Goebbels, Joseph (*continued*) 220, 222, 223, 330n40, 348n84, 361n64; early film policies, 54–55, 61, 67–68, 333nn34,35, 341n97, 343n17, 345n40, 367n32; appreciation of American films, 108–109, 121–122, 345n36; and Leander, 128, 135, 353n50; disdain of intellectual filmmaking, 130, 351n31; reaction to Roosevelt's "quarantine" speech, 133; in Harlan's memoirs, 165–166; "total war" speech, 193, 212; wartime film policies, 203; desire to create a dominant cinema, 215–216, 217, 218; and Riefenstahl, 312n31, 316n75, 317n89; and Sierck, 353n48

Goetz, Curt, 101, 115, 118, 347nn73,75

Gold, Käthe, 17

Golden City, The (Harlan), 144, 168, 331n16

Goldene Stadt, Die. See Golden City

Gold in New Frisco (Verhoeven), 106

Goll, Yvan, 90

Gone with the Wind (Fleming), 379n43

Good Seventh Wife, The (Liebeneiner), 218

Göring, Hermann, 55

Grafe, Frieda, 37, 307n85

Grass, Günter, 323n34

Great Freedom No. 7 (Käutner), 218

Great King, The (Harlan), 167, 168, 363n6

Great Love, The (Hansen), 140

Great Sacrifice, The (Harlan), 143–144, 167

Green Is the Heather (Deppe), 94

Gressieker, Hermann, 106–107, 109, 130, 133

Grob, Norbert, 167–169, 197, 362nn78,80

Große Freiheit Nr. 7. See Great Freedom No. 7

Große König, Der. See Great King

Große Liebe, Die. See Great Love

Großstadtmelodie. See Melody of a Big City

Grunberger, Richard, 9, 136

Gründgens, Gustaf, 136, 143, 176, 351n31

Grün ist die Heide. See Green Is the Heather

Gülstorff, Otto, 197

Gute Sieben, Die. See Good Seventh Wife

Hallo Janine (Boese), 342n2

Hamsun, Knut, 87

Hans Westmar (Wenzler), 56, 64, 81, 152, 338n78

Happily Ever After (Martin), 101, 347n78

Harbou, Thea von, 49, 320n4

Harlan, Veit, 4, 5, 10, 12, 113, 143, 149, 150, 155, 158, 159, 176, 217, 306n71, 360nn45,46, 361n64; memoirs, 165–166, 362n69; object of postwar controversy, 165–167; recent German defenses of work, 167–169

Hartl, Karl, 176

Harvey, Lilian, 20, 98, 99, 101, 102, 116, 117, 118, 120, 121, 122, 342n6, 347n78, 348n85, 386n1

Hasler, Emil, 197

Hay, James, 344n31, 348n83

Hecht, Ben, 115, 116, 347nn65,66

Heilige Berg, Der. See Holy Mountain

Heimat, 73, 86, 88, 96, 132, 211; defined, 74, 94, 329n1. *See also* Blood and Soil

Heimat (Froelich), 142, 143, 221, 355nn75,77

Heimat (Reitz), 94, 142–143, 221

Heimatfilme. See Homeland films

Heimkehr. See Homecoming

Herf, Jeffrey, 43–44, 349n3, 362n65, 385n85

Herrin von Atlantis, Die. See Mistress of Atlantis

Herrscher, Der. See Leader

Herzog, Werner, 221

Hess, Rudolf, 55

Heuser, Kurt, 176, 180, 189, 331n18, 368n33, 369nn44,45, 370nn54,55, 371n75

Hinkel, Hans, 335n51

Hinz, Werner, 113

Hippler, Fritz, 16, 138, 149, 155, 156, 159–160, 171, 176, 177, 199, 202, 306n64, 368n41, 370n59, 376n23

His Best Friend (Trenker), 82

History, representations of, 152, 177–178, 180–181, 371n70; genius films, 181–183. *See also Jew Süss*; *Paracelsus*

Hitler, Adolf, 1, 2, 5, 6, 8, 9, 21, 23, 28, 39, 45, 46, 48, 49, 55, 69, 74, 81, 83, 86, 107, 110, 112, 114, 118, 122, 127, 128, 129, 141, 157, 168, 174, 196, 202, 203, 210, 218, 221, 222, 223, 318n90, 384n78; *Mein Kampf*, 29, 150, 163; and Leander, 128; resemblance of life to narrative of *Jew Süss*, 163–164, 165; filmic image, 171–172, 180, 182–183, 188, 190, 363n4, 371n72; on function of history, 171, 176–177; favorite films, 300n16

Hitlerjunge Quex. See Hitler Youth Quex

Hitler's Children (Dmytryk), 325n52

Hitler Youth Quex (Steinhoff), 7, 63–66, 74, 152, 160, 321n18, 326n64, 327n65; as Nazi master narrative, 53–54; source and other adaptations, 55–56, 320nn12,13, 321n14; and other "martyr" films, 56; plot summary, 56–57; as object lesson for German youth, 57–60, 328n79; fam-

ily and class relations, 58–59; conscious recourse to Weimar cinema, 60–62; as overt propaganda, 64, 326n61; as example of early Nazi film aesthetics, 68–69, credits, 319n1
Hoberman, J., 6, 317nn84,88, 340n90, 388n19
Hochbaum, Werner, 136, 218
Hoffmann, Hilmar, 328n78
Hollstein, Dorothea, 152, 358n21, 361n56
Hollywood vis-à-vis Nazi Germany, 6, 13, 23, 88, 103–112, 216–217, 305nn54,61, 307n87, 342nn12,13, 343n21, 345n35, 348n82; Nuremberg rally as musical, 14; attempts to emulate American cinema, 14, 19, 99, 114–117, 121, 122, 126, 133, 198, 211–212, 346n51; relation of *Jew Süss* to biopics, 150–151; genius films and Nazi biopics, 181–182, 371n69; and Nazi war effort, 203, 215–216, 343n22. *See also* America and Americanism; Disney, Walt; *It Happened One Night*
Holocaust, 149, 150, 165, 210, 218, 223
Holocaust (American television series), 6
Holy Mountain, The (Fanck), 35–36, 40, 311n30, 313n46, 333n38
Homecoming (Ucicky), 132
Homeland films, 93–94. *See also* Blood and Soil; *Heimat*
Homoeroticism, 65, 208, 327n68, 383n74. *See also* Masculinity
Hoppe, Marianne, 142, 143
Hörbiger, Paul, 8
Horkheimer, Max, 16, 159, 164, 187, 190, 324n39, 328n70, 373n87
Horney, Brigitte, 113, 127, 200, 366n25, 375n14, 378n33
Horrigan, William, 128, 351n18
Hull, David Stewart, 9, 12, 127, 150, 176, 196, 302n34, 304n46, 338n78, 339n79, 369n43, 375n15, 379n43, 382n69
Huxley, Aldous, *Brave New World*, 12, 121

I Accuse (Liebeneiner), 13, 180
Ich klage an. See I Accuse
Ich liebe Dich. See I Love You
If We All Were Angels (Froelich), 112
Illusion (Tourjansky), 127, 218
I Love You (Selpin), 383n73
Imitation of Life (Sirk), 142
Immensee (Harlan), 168
In weiter Ferne so nah! See Far Away and Yet So Close
Irmin-Tschet, Konstantin, 61, 65–66, 101, 378n33
It Happened One Night (Capra), 99, 101, 117, 342n4; reception in Nazi Germany, 114, 119, 122

Jacoby, Georg, 7, 348n82
Jaeger, Ernst, 104, 308n4, 343n15
Jagger, Bianca, 28
Jagger, Mick, 6, 28
Jannings, Emil, 136, 182, 200, 369n50
Jews and Nazi Germany, 111, 121, 149, 202, 212, 358n23, 361n64, 385n85; anti-Semitism in prewar films, 152–153; anti-Semitic comedies, 153; anti-Semitic films of 1940, 153–154; Jews as alleged manipulators of images, 154–158; visual shapes of Nazi anti-Semitism, 159–164, 165–166, 205, 358n21, 361n56; Jews as German projections, 164–165, 210–211; anti-Semitism and innuendo, 381n60. *See also* Dissolves; Doubles; Holocaust; *Jew Süss*
Jew Süss (Harlan), 5, 7, 10, 13, 21, 145, 173, 205, 221, 356nn9,10, 370n54, 381n59; as infamous film, 149–150, 167; and Hollywood biopics, 150–151; plot summary, 151–152; as vehicle to bolster German identity, 153–154; reworks Weimar cinema, 155–158; dissolves and doubling, 158–164; Süss as secularized Nazi devil, 164; postwar reception, 165, 168, 169; as object of postwar court proceedings, 166; credits, 355n1; as adaptation, 357n13
Joyless Street, The (Pabst), 175
Jud Süß. See Jew Süss
Jugend. See Youth
Jung, C. G., 177, 181, 364n8, 370n64
Junge Adler. See Young Eagles
Jünger, Ernst, 57–58, 322n25
Jutzi, Phil, 194, 325n46, 380n56

Kaiser, Georg, 57
Kaiser von Kalifornien, Der. See The Emperor of California
Kalbus, Oskar, 41, 76, 200, 330n11
Kameradschaft (Pabst), 175, 176, 189
Kant, Immanuel, 34
Kaplan, Alice Yaeger, 158, 161, 325n48, 361n58, 382n69
Kardorff, Ursula von, 385n89

Kästner, Erich: as scriptwriter for *Münchhausen*, 197–198, 203–204, 206, 208, 209, 376nn20,23, 377n28, 381n61, 382n67, 383n71; *Fabian*, 204, 208, 211, 380nn53,55
Kater, Michael H., 107
Käutner, Helmut, 12, 143, 218, 220
Kemp, Paul, 8, 101, 116
Kettelhut, Erich, 101, 106
Keusche Geliebte, Die. See Chaste Lover
Kitsch, 40, 210, 314n63, 315n64, 384n77. *See also* Friedländer, Saul
Kleist, Heinrich von, 327n69
Klitzsch, Ludwig, 202
Knock out (Lamac/Zerlett), 116
Koch, Gertrud, 361n63
Kohner, Paul, 83, 331n24, 333n38, 334n47; and Trenker, 80, 84–85, 335nn55,56, 340n97
Kolbenheyer, Erwin Guido, 125, 177, 367n32, 369n49
Kolberg (Harlan), 5, 7, 13, 166, 167, 168, 169, 203
Komödianten. See Traveling Players
Kongo-Express (von Borsody), 142
Koonz, Claudia, 318n94
Kracauer, Siegfried, 93, 115, 189, 304n50, 313n46, 326n64; "The Mass Ornament," 14, 337n71; *From Caligari to Hitler*, 38–39, 42, 82, 303n41, 310n20, 313n44, 361n62, 373n89, 378n32; "Cult of Distraction," 109
Krach um Jolanthe. See Trouble with Jolanthe
Krauss, Werner, 90, 157–158, 161, 162, 170, 173, 178, 179, 184, 185, 339n83, 359n43, 360nn44,46, 369n47, 373n90, 376n20
Kreimeier, Klaus, 9, 11, 127
Kreuder, Peter, 101
Kreutzberg, Harald, 176, 185, 372n85
Kreutzersonate, Die (Harlan), 167
Kriegk, Otto, 1
Kuhle Wampe (Dudow/Brecht), 61, 62, 216
Kulturfilme, 20, 21
Kuntze, Reimar, 80
Kurowski, Ulrich, 330n14, 337n67, 350n16

Lacan, Jacques, 27, 320n5
Lacoue-Labarthe, Philippe, 21, 68, 193, 210, 211, 312n36
La Habanera (Sierck), 124, 139, 157, 220; plot summary, 125–126; compared to *The Prodigal Son*, 126, 145; initial reception, 129–131; contrasts North and South, 132–133; location shooting during Spanish Civil War, 132; fever and quarantine motif, 133–135; female desire, 140–141, 143; final sequence, 141–142, 145; credits, 349n4
La Jana, 140
Lamac, Carl, 116
Lamprecht, Gerhard, 60
Lang, Fritz, 61, 62, 156, 335n55, 384n78
Last Act, The (Pabst), 189
Last Illusion, The (von Baky), 197
Leader, The (Harlan), 167, 306n71
Leander, Zarah, 4, 126, 128–129, 131, 132, 159, 307n80, 353n50, 355n75; compared to Garbo, 129; as Nazi star sign, 135–145, 354nn64,65; compared to Rökk, 140, 354n69
Lehnich, Oswald, 130
Leinen aus Irland. See Linen from Ireland
Leiser, Erwin, 8, 10–11, 165, 182, 302n29, 370n58
Lessing, Theodor, 90
Letzte Akt, Der. See Last Act
Lichtbild-Bühne, 15, 56, 80, 103
Liebelei (Ophüls), 218
Liebeneiner, Wolfgang, 1, 10, 112, 126–127, 130, 172, 180, 305n54, 352n33
Liebesbriefe aus dem Engadin. See Love Letters from the Engadine Valley
Lied der Wüste, Das. See Song of the Desert
Life of Emile Zola, The (Dieterle), 150
Lightning around Maria (Trenker), 82, 341n95
Linen from Ireland (Helbig), 153, 361n56
Lingen, Theo, 8
Lives of a Bengal Lancer (Hathaway), 105
Lost Traces (Harlan), 168
Loved by the Gods (Hartl), 182
Love Letters from the Engadine Valley (Trenker), 337n70, 338n78, 339n80
Löwenthal, Leo, 87
Lowlands (Riefenstahl), 48–49, 221, 310n19, 315n66, 317n88
Lowry, Stephen, 15
Lubitsch, Ernst, 104, 386n1
Lucas, George, 28; *Star Wars*, 6
Lucky Kids (Martin), 143, 347n78; compared to *The Prodigal Son*, 99, 126; plot summary, 100–101; initial reception, 103, 349n88; as competitor with Hollywood films, 111–112, 114–117, 342n4, 346n64; postwar reception,

117–118, 220; sex and gender roles, 119–121, 348nn79,81; credits, 341n1

M (Lang), 61, 361n62
Macht der Bilder, Die. See Wonderful Horrible Life of Leni Riefenstahl
Madame Bovary (Flaubert), 143
Madame Bovary (Lamprecht), 143, 353n43
Mädchen in Uniform (Sagan), 344n23
Mädchen Johanna, Das. See Young Joan of Arc
Mädchen vom Moorhof, Das. See Girl from the Marsh Croft
Madonna, 6, 27
Maisch, Herbert, 177
Makavejev, Dusan, 28
Mann will nach Deutschland, Ein. See German Wants to Go Home
Marcorelles, Louis, 304n44, 365n16
Marcuse, Herbert, 86–87, 321n19, 322n26
Marian, Ferdinand, 148, 157, 158, 205, 206, 353n43, 359n42, 360n50, 366n25, 381n59
Marie Antoinette (Van Dyke), 150
Markus, Winnie, 214
Martin, Paul, 99, 101, 103, 118, 121, 342n6, 347n78
Masculinity, 49, 60, 198–200, 208, 219, 378n31. *See also* Albers, Hans; Homoeroticism; Sexuality; Theweleit, Klaus; Women and National Socialism
Maske in Blau. See Mask in Blue
Maskerade. See Masquerade
Mask in Blue (Martin), 101, 342n5
Masquerade (Forst), 20
Mass ornaments, 6, 14, 22, 62, 75, 100, 337n71
Mayer, Carl, 31, 310n18, 315n72
Mayer, Hans, 354n70
Mein Kampf (Hitler), 29, 150, 163
Méliès, Georges, 194, 201
Melody of a Big City (Liebeneiner), 172
Menschen vom Varieté. See People from the Variety
Menzel, Gerhard, 130, 131–133, 144, 330n9, 352nn36,38
Metropolis (Lang), 315n71, 330n4, 338n76
Meyer, Andreas, 99, 117, 118
Meyer, Hermann, 113
Meyer, Johannes, 75
Mistress of Atlantis, The (Pabst), 175, 189
Mitscherlich, Margarete, 49
Model Husband, The (Liebeneiner), 112
Molander Affair, The (Pabst), 175
Möller, Eberhard Wolfgang, 157, 357n20
Morgenrot. See Dawn
Moser, Hans, 8, 10, 221
Mosse, George, 177
Mother Krause's Trip to Happiness (Jutzi), 61, 216, 325n46
Mountain films, 34–37, 47, 81, 221, 313nn43,46,48, 339n80, 386n1; postwar assessments, 38–39. *See also Blue Light*; Fanck, Arnold; *Holy Mountain*; Riefenstahl, Leni; Trenker, Luis
Müller, Ray, 27, 29
Müller, Traugott, 182
Münch, Karl, 99
Münchhausen (von Baky), 5, 192, 218, 384n79, 385nn84,88; as centerpiece for Ufa's twenty-fifth anniversary celebration, 194, 376n20; history of Münchhausen adaptations, 194, 374n9, 375n10; plot summary, 195; historical reputation, 196–201, 213, 220, 375nn14–16, 379n43; cinema and war, 202–203; Kästner's script, 203–204, 377n28, 382nn67,68; as self-reflexive film, 204–205; Cagliostro, 205–206, 222, 381nn59,61, 382n62, 384n80; as Nazi war fantasy, 207–213, 375n13; credits, 374n6; different versions, 375n18; compared to other wartime films, 385n90
Münchhausen's Last Adventure (Jutzi), 194, 380n56
Münchhausens letztes Abenteuer. See Münchhausen's Last Adventure
Murnau, F. W., 37, 156, 164
Mussolini, Benito, 82, 107
Mustergatte, Der. See Model Husband
Mutter Krausens Fahrt ins Glück. See Mother Krause's Trip to Happiness

Nacht der Regisseure, Die. See Night of the Directors
Nagy, Käthe von, 16, 126
Nancy, Jean-Luc, 68, 193, 210, 211, 312n36
Nazi aesthetics, 13–14, 307nn85,86, 314n63, 328n78; the *Gesamtkunstwerk*, 21, 131, 307n87, 337n67; and mass culture, 21–22; official Nazi art, 23; Riefenstahl's films as exemplars, 28–29, 30; reactionary modernism, 43–44; role of beauty, 51, 318n98; body language, 65; early film aesthetics, 67–68; Nazi self-fashioning, 209–210. *See also* Dissolves;

Nazi aesthetics (*continued*) Kaplan, Alice Yaeger; Kitsch; Mass ornaments; Orchestra principle; Propaganda; Sontag, Susan; Witte, Karsten
Negri, Paula, 4, 126, 143
Neher, Carola, 175
New German Cinema, 28, 94, 215, 220–221, 308n8, 336n58. *See also* Fassbinder, Rainer Werner; Herzog, Werner; Reitz, Edgar; Sanders-Brahms, Helma; Wenders, Wim
Newton, Helmut, 27
Nibelungen, Die (Lang), 384n78
Nielsen, Asta, 138
Night of the Directors, The (Reitz), 221
Night Porter, The (Cavani), 6
Norkus, Herbert, 55, 57
Nosferatu (Murnau), 37–38, 314nn52,54,56, 359n39, 372n80; reworked in *Jew Süss*, 156–157, 361n62

Ohlsen, Jürgen, 322n21, 327n68, 328n77
Ohm Krüger (Steinhoff et al.), 115, 182, 190
Old and the Young King, The (Steinhoff), 75, 80, 108, 330nn4,5, 377n29
Olympia (Riefenstahl), 6, 22, 29, 31, 45, 161, 310n17
Ondra, Anny, 347n68
Opfer der Vergangenheit. See Victims of the Past
Opfergang. See Great Sacrifice
Ophüls, Max, 127
Orchestra principle, 20, 152–153, 306n76
Orient Express (Martin), 101
Orwell, George, 12
Our Daily Bread (Vidor), 104
Overcome by Love (Trenker), 82

Pabst, G. W., 62, 160, 172, 181, 182, 183, 188, 365nn11,12, 366n25, 367n26, 369n46; controversies about wartime activities, 174–176, 189–190, 365nn13,14,16, 366nn21,23
Pachter, Henry, 180, 183, 368n38
Pandora's Box (Pabst), 175
Panitz, Hans-Jürgen, *Fast ein Jahrhundert (Almost a Century)*, 79, 96
Paracelsus, 173, 368nn36,38, 369n47; role in Nazi propaganda, 176–177, 180–181, 367n30; 450th birthday, 177, 372n84; as nonsynchronous figure, 180; as volatile and self-destructive personage, 181–182; radical solipsism, 183. *See also* Kolbenheyer, Erwin Guido
Paracelsus (Pabst), 170, 172–173, 177, 364n9, 365n10, 369n52, 371n71; plot summary, 173–174; ideological provenance, 174–175, 365n16, 369n43, 372n77; continuities with other Pabst films, 175; as historical film, 177–178, 180–181, 369n44, 370n54; delayed appearance of hero, 178–180; as genius film, 181–184; fixation on main figure, 183–184, 186–188; as pathology, 187–188; representation of death, 188–189, 373n90; credits, 364n7; box-office failure, 367n27; sources, 367n32, 368n33, 373n88; compared to Schnitzler's play, 370n61
Patalas, Enno, 15, 153, 378n33
People from the Variety (von Baky), 197
Peter Ibbetson (Hathaway), 104
Peternell, Pert, 177
Petley, Julian, 15, 183, 302n34, 343n18, 365n10
Petterson & Bendel (Brauner), 152, 353n53, 357n16
Peuckert, Detlev, 106–107, 326n53
Pewas, Peter, 214, 218
Picard, Max, 69, 190
Piel, Harry, 386n1
Pillars of Society (Sierck), 76, 130
Pommer, Erich, 85, 335n56
Postmaster, The (Ucicky), 144
Postmeister, Der. See Postmaster
Poulantzas, Nicos, 217
Powell, Eleanor, 106
Praunheim, Rosa von, 351n24
Preußische Liebesgeschichte. See Prussian Love Story
Prodigal Son, The (Trenker), 160, 330n14, 331n15, 339n83; as national epic, 74; as exemplar of "Heim ins Reich" cycle, 76, 78; plot summary, 78; positive reception in Nazi Germany, 79–81, 332n30; postwar reputation, 85–86, 336n61; as example of blood-and-soil discourse, 86–89; representation of New York City and Great Depression, 87–88, 339n79; function of *Rauhnacht* sequence, 89–90; role of blacks, 91–92; relation to postwar *Heimatfilme*, 93–94; as cornerstone of Trenker's reputation, 96; compared to *Lucky Kids*, 99, 126; compared to *La Habanera*, 126, 145; credits, 329n3. *See also Heimat*; Kohner, Paul; Mountain films
Propaganda, 11, 65, 117, 154, 166, 180–181, 217, 299n5, 302n28, 303nn36,43, 319n3, 324n39,

326n60, 333n34, 345n40, 387n17, 388n18; Anglo-American wartime reactions, 64; and anti-Semitism, 149–150, 153. *See also* Goebbels, Joseph; Nazi aesthetics; Orchestra principle
Prozeß, Der. See Trial
Prussian Love Story (Martin), 101
Puig, Manuel, *Kiss of the Spider Woman*, 124, 329n2
Punch Bowl, The (Weiss), 5, 160, 385n90
Punks Comes from America (Martin), 76, 330n13
Punks kommt aus Amerika. See Punks Comes from America

Querelle (Fassbinder), 28

Rabenalt, Arthur Maria, 12, 127, 350nn5,8, 366n25
Raddatz, Carl, 200
Raspe, Rudolf Erich, 194, 375n10
Rebel, The (Trenker), 67, 81, 83, 108, 330n14, 331n21, 333n35, 338n74, 339n83
Rebell, Der. See Rebel
Reception of Nazi films: film festival programs, 2; museum exhibits, 2–3; matinees for senior citizens, 3–4; memoirs of stars, 4; television screenings and talk shows, 4; commercial distribution of videocassettes in Germany and U.S., 4–5; university courses and scholarly discussions, 5; public screenings and celebrations, 5; appropriations by American mass culture, 6–7; critical and negative approaches, 8–11, 299n5, 321n18; redemptive and revisionist approaches, 9–12, 129, 302n26; stress on overt messages and themes, 11; postmodern relation to Nazi images, 23–24, 220, 301nn18,20; debates about Riefenstahl, 28–29, 299n5, 309n10, 314nn59,60, 316n74, 317n83; auteurist appreciation of Riefenstahl, 39, 46–47, 317n83; Trenker at Telluride, 336n58; appreciations of Harvey and *Lucky Kids*, 117–118; Leander as idol, 129; debates about Harlan, 166–169; right-wing radical and neofascist responses, 221; cineastes and Sirk, 350n16, 351n18
Reich, Wilhelm, 58, 323n33
Reinhold, Annelies, 175, 184
Reise nach Tilsit, Die. See Trip to Tilsit
Reitz, Edgar, 94, 221
Rembrandt (Steinhoff), 181, 190
Renker, Gustav, 32, 311n30
Request Concert (von Borsody), 10, 21, 172
Resistance, 218; film industry as alleged site of opposition, 9, 11–12, 99, 117–118, 121, 129; film world as safe haven, 127, 350n12; ideology and aesthetic resistance, 144, 203, 372n77
Rich, B. Ruby, 305n61, 318n95
Richter, Hans, 194
Rider on the White Steed, The (Oertel/Deppe), 108
Riefenstahl, Leni, 5, 6, 10, 12, 13, 14, 20, 21, 22, 23, 80, 100, 110, 161, 172, 216, 217, 307n87, 309n14, 318n92; postwar reception and controversial status, 27–29, 31, 149, 221, 299n5, 309n10, 310n19, 317n83; postwar attempts at rehabilitation, 30–31; film debut in *The Holy Mountain*, 36; combines romanticism and technology, 37; ethnographic intensity, 41; racism and anti-Semitism, 46, 316nn75,77, 340n86; attempts to cast self as victim, 48–49, 51; and Hitler and National Socialism, 49, 51, 318n90; and Trenker, 81–82, 333nn38,40, 334n45; and Fassbinder, 308n8; and Goebbels, 312n31, 316n75, 317n89; and Pabst, 366n25
Riess, Curt, 194, 324n45, 376n20
Ritter, Karl, 12, 55, 61, 352n39
Rivel, Charlie, 219
Robert Koch, der Bekämpfer des Todes. See Robert Koch, the Enemy of Death
Robert Koch, the Enemy of Death (Steinhoff), 182, 189, 369n50
Robert und Bertram (Zerlett), 153
Rogers, Ginger, 99
Rökk, Marika, 8, 106, 126, 140, 338n78, 348n82, 354n69
Romance in a Minor Key (Käutner), 143, 218
Romanze in Moll. See Romance in a Minor Key
Roosevelt, Franklin Delano, 133, 135
Rosenberg, Alfred, 145, 301n18
Rosenfeld, Alvin, 24
Rothschilds, Die (Waschneck), 153
Ruf, Der. See Last Illusion
Rühle, Günther, 128
Rühmann, Heinz, 4, 8, 10, 176, 221
Rust, Bernhard, 58
Ruttmann, Walter, 216, 330n14, 332n31, 386n1

SA-Mann Brand (Seitz), 56, 64, 81
Sanders-Brahms, Helma, 48, 128, 139, 221, 381n59

San Francisco (Van Dyke), 104, 106, 345n35
Sarris, Andrew, 39, 314n60
Schäfer, Hans Dieter, 107–108, 121
Schatten der Vergangenheit. See Shadows of the Past
Schelling, Friedrich Wilhelm Joseph von, 36–37
Schenzinger, Karl Aloys, *Der Hitlerjunge Quex*, 51, 55, 62, 67, 322n22
Schiller, Johann Christoph Friedrich von, 177, 368n40
Schilling, Niklaus, 221
Schimmelreiter, Der. See Rider on the White Steed
Schirach, Baldur von, 54
Schlesinger, Klaus, 300n14
Schlußakkord. See Final Accord
Schmeer, Karlheinz, 328n76
Schmeling, Max, 80, 340n89
Schneeberger, Hans, 31
Schreck, Max, 157
Schritt vom Wege, Der. See Effi Briest
Schüchterne Casanova, Der. See Timid Casanova
Schulte-Sasse, Linda, 150, 327n64, 356n9, 363n81, 371n65
Schünzel, Reinhold, 12, 112
Schwark, Günther, 130
Schwarze Rosen. See Black Roses
Secrets of a Soul (Pabst), 189, 369n48
Seiler, Paul, 129
Sein bester Freund. See His Best Friend
Sergeant Berry (Selpin), 106
Seven Slaps (Martin), 118
Sexuality, 15, 39–40, 119–121, 128, 198, 200, 204, 205–206, 207, 217. *See also* Masculinity; Theweleit, Klaus; Women and National Socialism
Shadows of the Past (Hochbaum), 136
Shanghai Express (von Sternberg), 107
Sieben Ohrfeigen. See Seven Slaps
Sieg des Glaubens. See Victory of Faith
Siegfried and Roy, 28
Siemsen, Hans, 327n68
Sierck, Detlef (aka Douglas Sirk), 5, 76, 112, 126, 167, 350n12; as exception to Nazi rule, 127, 350n14, 351n18; self-conscious and subversive style, 128–129; as director of *La Habanera*, 130, 133, 141–142; reputation in Nazi Germany, 130–131, 136, 144, 351n28; and Gerhard Menzel, 131–132; and Goebbels, 135, 353n48; film treatment of women, 141–142, 144–145; postwar reception, 350n16
Sima, Oskar, 101, 116
Siodmak, Robert, 61
Sirk, Douglas. *See* Sierck, Detlef
Sloterdijk, Peter, 158, 211, 380n53, 384n82
Slums of Berlin (Lamprecht), 60
Snow White and the Seven Dwarfs (Disney production), 110–111, 117, 212, 379n43
Söderbaum, Kristina, 113, 126, 128, 159
Sokal, Harry, 31, 46, 315n72, 316nn75,79
Song of the Desert, The (Martin), 101
Sontag, Susan, 308n1; "Fascinating Fascism," 13–14, 15, 22, 28–29, 38–40, 304n49, 314nn59,60. *See also* Nazi aesthetics
Speer, Albert, 6, 23, 299n2
Spengler, Oswald, 73
Spielhofer, Hans, 19
Staal, Viktor, 200
Stahl, John M., 167
Stalingrad, Battle of, 171–172, 193, 212
Star of Rio (Anton), 140
Stars Are Shining, The (Zerlett), 140, 194, 218
Staudte, Wolfgang, 12, 218, 219
Stauffer, Teddy, 107
Steinhoff, Hans, 12, 75, 80, 100, 324nn41,43, 369n50, 377n29; as director of *Hitler Youth Quex*, 55, 61, 66
Stern, J. P., 170
Sternberg, Josef von, 28, 127, 167
Stern von Rio. See Star of Rio
Strasser, Gregor, 58
Strauss, Franz Joseph, 168
Streicher, Julius, 27, 46
Stroheim, Erich von, 167
Stützen der Gesellschaft. See Pillars of Society
Syberberg, Hans Jürgen, 1, 221

Tag der Freiheit!—Unsere Wehrmacht. See Day of Freedom
Taming of the Shrew, The (Shakespeare), 143
Telluride Film Festival, 85, 336n58
Terra (film studio), 175, 216
Testament des Dr. Mabuse, Das (Lang), 218, 386n1
Test Pilot (Fleming), 105
Theweleit, Klaus, 58, 63, 65, 204, 315n71, 323nn30,31, 373n86, 383n72
Thief of Bagdad, The (Berger/Whelan/Powell), 212, 379n43

Thiele, Herta, 61
Thiele, Wilhelm, 61
Thorak, Josef, 23, 83, 309n14, 335n51
Threepenny Opera, The (Pabst), 61, 175, 176, 324n42, 365n11
Tiefland. See Lowlands
Timid Casanova, The (Lamac), 116
Titanic (Selpin/Klingler), 218
Tobis (film studio), 125, 216
Togger (von Alten), 115
Toller, Ernst, 57
To New Shores (Sierck), 130, 136, 141, 355n72
Tourjansky, Viktor, 113, 127, 218, 386n1
Traumulus (Froelich), 108
Traveling Players (Pabst), 160, 175, 182–183, 189, 365n12
Trenker, Luis, 5, 12, 28, 67, 72, 76, 99, 110, 160, 330n14, 333n39, 335n55; and *Heimat*, 73–74; self-avowed champion of German homeland, 79, 331n20; debut in mountain films, 81; and Riefenstahl, 81–82, 333n38; postwar celebrity, 82, 337n67, 340n91; wartime activities and allegiance to Hitler, 83–84; claims to be oppositional figure, 84; shifting relationship to homeland, 94, 96, 331n24, 340n93; as icon, 95–96, 331n19, 336n62; and Goebbels, 333n40, 341n97; as lady's man, 334n46, 337n70
Trial, The (Pabst), 175
Trip to Tilsit, The (Harlan), 168, 359n35
Triumph of the Will (Riefenstahl), 1, 6, 7, 13, 14, 28–29, 80, 201, 312n31, 315n73, 318n93, 348n84, 371n72
Trouble with Jolanthe, The (Froelich), 20
Truxa (Zerlett), 218
Tschechowa, Olga, 126
Two Little Lottas, The (von Baky), 197

Ucicky, Gustav, 56, 176, 305n54
Ufa, 20, 76, 77, 101, 108, 112, 117, 118, 122, 125, 127, 128, 129, 130, 132, 135, 139, 140, 142, 211, 216, 220, 221; seventy-fifth anniversary in 1992, 2–3, 213, 299n8; importance in post-1989 Germany, 3; and *Hitler Youth Quex*, 55–56; twenty-fifth anniversary in 1943, 194, 197, 202, 203, 374n7
Ullrich, Luise, 136, 197, 339n83
Under the Bridges (Käutner), 218, 220
. . . und über uns der Himmel. See And the Sky above Us
Unehelichen, Die. See Children of No Importance
Unsterbliche Herz, Das. See Eternal Heart
Unter der Brücken. See Under the Bridges

Verflucht, dies Amerika. See Damn This America
Verklungene Melodie. See Faded Melody
Verlorene Sohn, Der. See Prodigal Son
Verrufenen, Die. See Slums of Berlin
Verwehte Spuren. See Lost Traces
Verzauberte Tag, Der. See Enchanted Day
Via Mala (von Baky), 197, 218
Victims of the Past (Bock-Stieber), 51
Victory of Faith (Riefenstahl), 29
Virilio, Paul, 192, 203, 380n48
Von der Liebe besiegt. See Overcome by Love

Warhol, Andy, 6
Waschneck, Erich, 7, 153
Wasser für Canitoga. See Water for Canitoga
Water for Canitoga (Selpin), 106, 200, 383n74
Wayne, John, 85
Weber, Fritz, 333n44
Wegener, Elsa, 49
Wegener, Paul, 75
Weidenmann, Alfred, 328n79
Weihmayr, Franz, 133
Weill, Kurt, 127
Weimar cinema, 13, 14, 200, 201, 205, 215, 216, 325n47, 365n10, 386n1; framed narratives, 34, 198, 313n42; negative Nazi reactions, 60–62, 69, 320n8, 324n44; alleged Jewish domination, 155–156, 211–212, 324n42, 385n86. *See also Dr. Mabuse, the Gambler*; Doubles; Fanck, Arnold; Lang, Fritz; Mountain films; Murnau, F. W.; *Nosferatu*; Pabst, G. W.
Weiser, Grete, 8
Welch, David, 11, 64, 182, 303n43, 304n44, 326n60
Wenders, Wim, 2, 3, 220–221
Wen die Götter lieben. See Loved by the Gods
Wendtland, Karlheinz, 12, 150
Wenn wir alle Engel wären. See If We All Were Angels
Werder, Peter von, 73
We're Dancing around the World (Anton), 14
Werner, Ilse, 8, 213
Wessel, Horst, 202
Wessely, Paula, 4
Westfront 1918 (Pabst), 175

Wetterleuchten um Maria. See Lightning around Maria
Wieck, Dorothea, 348n82
Wieman, Mathias, 44, 99, 312n37, 315n65, 345n35
Wir tanzen um die Welt. See We're Dancing around the World
Witte, Karsten, 14, 15, 29, 106, 160, 167, 198, 207, 305n52, 321n20, 327n65, 330n12, 338n74, 342n4, 369n46
Wizard of Oz, The (Fleming), 190, 201
Women and National Socialism, 15, 40, 49, 125, 144–145, 179, 189, 200, 209, 305n58, 318nn94,95, 348nn79,81, 353n50, 354n70, 378n34, 382nn63,64,67,68, 383nn71–73; Weimar mountain films, 36, 40, 206–207; Leander as female role model, 128, 136, 139–140; representations of female beauty, 138, 355n72; in melodramas, 141–144, 220; female spectatorship, 142–143, 373n87. *See also* Masculinity; Riefenstahl, Leni; Rökk, Marika; Sexuality; Theweleit, Klaus
Wonderful Horrible Life of Leni Riefenstahl, The (Müller), 27, 29, 48, 317n84
Wood, Robin, 37, 314nn54,55
Wunschkonzert. See Request Concert
Wysocki, Gisela von, 49, 192

Young Eagles (Weidenmann), 328n79
Young Joan of Arc (Ucicky), 132
Youth (Harlan), 113, 167–168

Zeman, Karel, 194
Zerbrochene Krug, Der. See Broken Jug
Zerlett, Hans H., 7, 106, 116, 153, 340n89
Zielinski, Siegfried, 166
Zielke, Willy, 216
Zu neuen Ufern. See To New Shores